Lily Briscoe's Chinese Eyes

Lily Briscoe's Chinese Eyes

BLOOMSBURY, MODERNISM, AND CHINA

Patricia Laurence

The University of South Carolina Press

© 2003 Patricia Laurence

Cloth edition published by the University of South Carolina Press, 2003
Paperback and ebook editions published in Columbia, South Carolina,
by the University of South Carolina Press, 2013

www.sc.edu/uscpress

Manufactured in the United States of America

22 21 20 19 18 17 16 15 14 13   10 9 8 7 6 5 4 3 2 1

The Library of Congress has cataloged the cloth edition as follows:

Laurence, Patricia Ondek, 1942–
  Lily Briscoe's Chinese eyes : Bloomsbury, modernism, and China / Patricia Laurence.
    p. cm.
  Includes bibliographical references (p.) and index.
  ISBN 1-57003-505-9 (alk. paper)
  1. English literature—20th century—History and criticism. 2. Bloomsbury group. 3. Chinese literature—20th century—History and criticism. 4. Literature, Comparative—English and Chinese. 5. Literature, Comparative—Chinese and English. 6. English literature—Chinese influences. 7. Chinese literature—English influences. 8. Modernism (Literature)—Great Britain. 9. Modernism (Literature)—China. 10. Xin yue she. I. Title.

PR478.B46L38 2003
820.9'00912—dc21   2003008688

ISBN 978-1-61117-148-8 (pbk)
ISBN 978-1-61117-176-1 (ebook)

To my mother, Ann Ondek, who first read to me the nursery rhyme "Did You Ever Dig to China in Your Own Backyard?" from the worn, red Childcraft volume. Little did she know that one day, I would.

Contents

List of Illustrations / xi
Foreword, by Jeffrey C. Kinkley / xv
Acknowledgments / xix
Abbreviations / xxiii
Historical Time Line / xxv

Introduction / 1
   Images on a Scroll / 5
   Maps of Seeing / 9
   The Historical Moment / 12
   The Formation of Literary Communities and Conversations in China and England / 15
   The Uses of Letters / 22
   Empiricizing the Theoretical / 29
   Evolving Modernisms / 34

CHAPTER ONE
Julian Bell Performing "Englishness" / 37
   The Sentimental and the Modern: Pei Ju-Lian (Bell, Julian) Teaching in China / 37
   The Provincial Turns Political / 58
   From Fairy Stories to Letter Quarrels: Julian Bell and Ling Shuhua / 63
   Translating Together: Julian Bell and Ling Shuhua / 82

CHAPTER TWO
Literary Communities in England and China: Politics and Art / 100
   Imagining Other Communities: The Crescent Moon Group / 100
   Politics and Art / 112
   A Parallel Community: Bloomsbury / 118

Chapter Three
East-West Literary Conversations: Exploring Civilization and Subjectivity—
G. L. Dickinson and Xu Zhimo / 126
  Terms That Fold and Unfold Meaning: Civilization and Subjectivity / 126
  Xu Zhimo: "The Great Link with Bloomsbury" / 129
  An English Don in a Chinese Cap: G. L. Dickinson / 135
  The Cultivation of the Romantic Self: Xu Zhimo / 137
  Feeling as a Transgressive Act: The Narration of "Self" in Developing
    Chinese Modernism / 155
  Redefinitions of British "Civilization": G. L. Dickinson / 160
  The Unwritten *Passage to China*: E. M. Forster and Xiao Qian / 176
  "The Unpopular Normal": E. M. Forster's Expanding Notions of
    Transnational Sexuality, Culture, and the British Novel / 184
  Swallowing and Being Swallowed: Poverty in China and the British
    Novel / 198
  British Modernism through Chinese Eyes: Katherine Mansfield,
    D. H. Lawrence, James Joyce, T. S. Eliot, and Virginia Woolf / 202
  Interrupted Modernism / 216

Chapter Four
Chinese Landscapes through British Eyes / 222
  The Naturalist Landscape: Julian Bell / 227
  The Painter's Eye: Vanessa Bell and Ling Shuhua / 234
  Constructing the "Narrow Bridge of Art": Virginia Woolf and Ling
    Shuhua / 246
  China on a Willow Pattern Plate: Charles Lamb, George Meredith, and
    Arthur Waley / 296
  Expanding "Englishness": *Le Jardin Anglo-Chinois* and the Kew
    Gardens Pagoda / 313

Chapter Five
Developing Modernisms / 326
  Incorporating "Chinese" Eyes / 326
  Chinoiserie and the International Chinese Exhibition / 335
  "The Liquidation of Reference" / 341
  The Aesthetic Gaze / 346
  The Epistemology of Boundaries: Subject and Object / 351
  The Crisis in Representation: Aesthetic Reciprocity / 358

Leaving Things Out: The Line / 367
Flatness and Plasticity / 375
The Literary Effect of Visual Aesthetics / 378

Postscript / 388

APPENDIX A
Index of Chinese and British Figures / 395

APPENDIX B
Selection from Ling Shuhua's Story "Writing a Letter" with Julian Bell's Annotations / 403

APPENDIX C
Table of Contents, *Selections of Modernist Literature from Abroad,* eds. Yuan Kejia, Dong Xengxun, Zheng Kelu, 1981 / 409

Notes / 411
Bibliography / 419
Index / 445

Illustrations

BLACK-AND-WHITE ILLUSTRATIONS

Map of China / xxix
Ling Shuhua in modern dress / 3
Julian Bell (Mr. Pei Ju-Lian), professor of English, Wuhan University, 1935 / 6
Lake at Peking University, Peking, China, ca. 1936 / 7
Chen Yuan (Xiying), dean of humanities, Wuhan University, 1935 / 8
Professor Fang Zhong, dean of foreign languages, Wuhan University, 1935 / 9
Margery Fry by Roger Fry / 16
Still Life with Tang Horse by Roger Fry / 17
Chinese translations of Virginia Woolf's novels / 43
English speaking contest, organized by Julian Bell / 45
Julian Bell's English literature students, 1936 / 45
Ye Junjian, Julian Bell's favorite student at Wuhan University / 47
The triangle: Julian Bell; Chen Yuan, Ling's husband; and Ling Shuhua / 61
Julian Bell, 1936 / 67
Ling Shuhua, 1936 / 69
Lin Huiyin, Rabindranath Tagore, and Xu Zhimo in India, 1928 / 71
Liao Hong Ying, confidante of Julian Bell and Innes Jackson Herdan / 75
Ling Peng Fu, grandfather of Ling Shuhua, in western attire / 76
Ling Shuhua and her four sisters, ca. 1910–15 / 77
Hsiao-ying Chen, daughter of Ling Shuhua, ca. 1936–37 / 79
Julian Bell with Hsiao-ying Chen, ca. 1936–37 / 80
Ling Shuhua with her daughter, Hsaio-ying Chen, ca. 1936–37 / 81
Illustrations from Ling Shuhua's autobiography, *Ancient Melodies* / 85–87
Rabindranath Tagore, Indian poet / 102

Symbol of the Crescent Moon group / 103
Qu Qiubai and Lu Xun of the Chinese League of Left-Wing Writers / 105
I. A. Richards and Dorothy Richards at a university luncheon in China / 124
Dadie Rylands and Virginia Woolf / 130
G. L. Dickinson, Cambridge don, in Chinese cap / 135
Leonard Elmhirst, Xu Zhimo, and Rabindranath Tagore at Dartington Hall, 1928 / 146
Chinese and British intellectuals / 151
Sidney Webb / 161
Beatrice Webb / 161
Cover of G. L. Dickinson's *Letters from John Chinaman* (1901) / 165
Lytton Strachey and Virginia Woolf / 172
E. M. Forster by Dora Carrington / 177
Cover of Julian Bell's *Work for the Winter* (1936) / 189
Mei Lanfang, famous female impersonator in the Beijing Opera / 191
Xiao Qian in knickers, 1930s / 212
Wen Jieruo, translator, holding Joyce's *Ulysses* and Chinese translation / 213
Yuruo and Jin Di / 214
Xiao Qian / 215
Qu Shijing and Quentin Bell / 217
John Maynard Keynes by Gwendolyn Raverat / 226
The Western Hills, near Beijing / 230
Julian Bell and guide hunting in Tibet, 1936 / 232
Vanessa Bell, 1932 / 236
Ling Shuhua, ca. 1930s / 236
Invitations to Ling Shuhua gallery openings / 245
Virginia Woolf by Man Ray / 248
The "three talents of Luojia": Su Xuelin, Ling Shuhua, Yuan Changying / 266
Xiao Qian and his wife, Wen Jieruo / 296
Still Life, the Sharuku Scarf by Duncan Grant / 304
Lopokova Dancing by Duncan Grant / 307
Dartington Hall, Totnes, England / 310
Illustration from Wu Cheng'en's *Monkey* by Duncan Grant / 311
The Chinese pagoda, Kew Gardens, London / 318
Liberty catalog cover, "Eastern Antiquities" (1877–1900) / 330
The pagoda dress / 335

COLOR PLATES

following page 226

1–8. Ling Shuhua's Friendship Scroll, compiled 1925–58
  1. *Landscape* (ink wash) by Roger Fry
  2. *Two Horses Galloping through Long Grass* (ink) by Xu Beihong
  3. Dora Russell inscription and *Gentleman under a Pine Tree* by Zhang Daqian.
  4. *Impression of Two Westerners* (ink) by Lin Fengmian
  5. *Gentleman in a Boat among the Reeds* (ink) by Chen Xiaonan
  6. *Tolstoy* (ink) by Wen Yidou
  7. *Child with Ball* (ink) by Wang Daizhi and inscription by Xie Bingxin
  8. *Two Children Walking Away* by Feng Zikai
9–10. Floral watercolors by Duncan Grant
  11. Bookmarks by Duncan Grant
  12. Silk fan and two boxes painted by Duncan Grant
13–16. Calendars by Vanessa Bell
  17. *From Geneva to Montreux, Switzerland,* painting on silk scroll, by Ling Shuhua
  18. Scroll of Sissinghurst by Ling Shuhua
  19. Blue willow plate, adaptation of Chinese design
  20. *Daughters of Revolution* by Grant Wood
  21. Cover of Ling Shuhua's autobiography, *Ancient Melodies* (1953)
  22. Duncan Grant cover for Wu Cheng'en's *Monkey*
  23. Portrait of Julian Bell as an infant by Vanessa Bell (1908)
  24. Sketch of Julian Bell by Vanessa Bell
  25. Julian Bell and Roger Fry playing chess by Vanessa Bell

Foreword

Modernism seems more than ever a genuinely international movement in this intriguing and path-breaking book. Examining the Bloomsbury and Crescent Moon groups at home and abroad, in England and China, Patricia Laurence asks us to see Chinese arts through the lens of British modernism, and the modern British legacy through contemporary Chinese eyes. We vicariously enter an educated and privileged circle that wrote, painted, and traveled. In China, these visionary avocations tended to merge and support each other. What was new in the twentieth century was the public embodiment of such pastimes in women, including Ling Shuhua—writer, artist, and finally, expatriate. Meantime, Bloomsbury "performed" the ancient Chinese literati's "amateur ideal." In Bloomsbury, women were not just present but preeminent.

The artists here reveal themselves not just through their works, but also in private letters, many of which were mostly overlooked until Professor Laurence sought them out on her own pilgrimage of interviewing and artistic self-discovery in Britain and China. Hers is the first full account in English of the romance between Ling Shuhua and Julian Bell. Bloomsbury's fabled eccentricities and self-absorption are on display, and so are occasional lapses into racism (directed mostly at peoples of darker skin color than the Chinese), but there is little of the insularity and snobbishness often attributed to Bloomsbury, far less any imperialist sympathies. By the time we see Julian Bell, his mother, Vanessa, his aunt, Virginia Woolf, her husband, Leonard, Marjorie Strachey, Vita Sackville-West, and Harold Acton play their respective larger and smaller roles in encouraging, polishing, publishing, and promoting Ling Shuhua's memoirs in English, we come around to Professor Laurence's view of Ling Shuhua as a Chinese member of Bloomsbury.

The Chinese writers, scholars, and painters—Xu Zhimo, Xiao Qian, Ling Shuhua, and her husband, Chen Yuan, even Ye Junjian, the leftist—likewise appear far more open and experimental than their class-conscious, anti-imperialist, and notably anti-British colleagues. Recent studies by Yan Jiayan in Chinese and by Leo Ou-fan Lee and others in English have detailed the rise of a 1930s Shanghai modernism in fiction and film. David Der-wei Wang finds commercial and popular antecedents for the tendency even before the 1911 republic. Professor Laurence's work reminds us that there was also a separate, more academic modernism from the Beijing culture. In quest of new kinds of consciousness and fresh techniques for conveying them, it avoided Shanghai's fascination with urban glitz and material progress, instead delving inward to the soul itself. The major figures were, ironically, southern provincials who before and after the May Fourth incident of 1919 overthrew the classical language in favor of a modern literary Beijing vernacular. Though scattered to the four winds by war and revolution, they tried to re-establish themselves as a new Beijing-style mandarinate, the better to remake the sensibility of the Chinese people. In fiction, the experimentalists include Feng Wenbing (of Hubei), the Crescentist Shen Congwen (of Hunan) and his protégés, and Lu Xun (of Zhejiang), if only by dint of his prose poems. Ling Shuhua and Shen Congwen's protégé Xiao Qian, author of the modernist novel *Valley of Dream*, are the "native Beijingers" who went to the provinces—and to Britain.

China's modernist works, mostly forgotten or even banned after 1949, were revived and celebrated after the death of Mao Zedong in 1976. Yet, in 1983 the whole tendency came under attack again. International modernism is still prejudicially rendered in Mandarin not as "modern-ism," but as "the modern *school*," or "clique," as if it were by nature a decadent, bourgeois, political bloc in the service of foreigners. North America since the 1990s has published a good many sympathetic books about the Chinese "modern" and "modernity," but the idea of "modern*ism*" seems to have got lost. This may reflect taboos from mainland Chinese politics and postcolonial criticism, and also the burgeoning nationalism of the mainland and Taiwan, buttressed by Hegelian views of history and pride in Chinese modernization. Professor Laurence's work is an internationalist antidote for determinist perspectives that would negate the role of the individual.

Beijing modernism was based on a linguistic revolution at the turn of the 1920s, but its prose and poetry technique, and Shanghai's, too, entered real modernist territory only in the 1930s and 1940s. Hu Shi and Xu Zhimo drew inspiration from imagism well before that, but Hu Shi was not a major poet, and Xu Zhimo's own poems are romantic. Some might say that the Chinese writers contributed modernist works to the international movement when it was on the wane, if not already over. But not if we see the larger movement as a crisscrossing of experiments from the variant sequential experiences of many nations and languages, until those experiments achieved, in Malcolm Bradbury and James McFarlane's famous words from the preface of their book, *Modernism,* not a linear progression, but a "compounding": an "interpenetration," "reconciliation," "coalescence," and "fusion." Although his Aunt Virginia had quipped that human character changed "on or about December 1910," Julian Bell, like academics today, conceptualized "the Moderns" in two broad periods: 1890 to 1914, and 1914 to 1936. Nineteen thirty-six was the year in which he taught this history of modernism to his Chinese students in Wuhan. He did not mean to imply that modernism, or Bloomsbury, was dead.

When Virginia Woolf wrote *To the Lighthouse,* she gave her painter character Lily Briscoe "Chinese eyes" with which to see British landscapes and people. The novel calls those eyes the source of her "charm," but also the reason why she may find it difficult to marry. The implications of Patricia Laurence's book named after Lily's eyes lead us into just as many kinds of "ambiguities," to borrow a figure from William Empson, whose bridging of Chinese and English sensibilities also appears in this book. Should modernism be historicized at all? If not, one might see not just a Chinese but a Chinese "modernist" influence on Bloomsbury's art, by way of "abstractionism" in landscape paintings a thousand years old. However, literary historians in China "always historicized." Meanwhile, Chinese modernist artists embraced the international movement partly for its anti-mimeticism, which they thought stood against China's "realism" or "classicism," according to borrowed presumptions from Western literary evolutionism. In the early 1920s, Shen Yanbing (Mao Dun) also loved modernism (which he thought of as symbolism or neo-romanticism), in private. But he preferred for *China's* writers to perfect a stage of Chinese "realism" first. Most Chinese writers and critics followed him. Whether we see modernism with "Chinese" or "Western" eyes, twentieth-century or twenty-first, Patricia Laurence has opened them much wider.

JEFFREY C. KINKLEY
Bernardsville, New Jersey

Acknowledgments

This book, a journey, was supported by a caravan of friends, colleagues, experts, libraries, and institutions in America, England, and China. First, I acknowledge the libraries that furnished the letters, writings, and photographs that are central to this book. I consulted several major collections: The Berg Collection of the New York Public Library for the letters, papers and art of Ling Shuhua, Julian Bell, Vanessa Bell, and Duncan Grant; The Modern Archives, King's College, Cambridge University, Cambridge, England, for the correspondence of Julian Bell, Vanessa Bell, G. L. Dickinson, Maynard Keynes, Archibald Rose, Helen Morris (née Soutar), and Lettice Ramsay; the Tate Gallery Archives in London for the correspondence between Julian Bell and Vanessa Bell; University of Sussex, Brighton, England, for the letters of Virginia Woolf, Julian Bell, and Leonard Woolf; Dartington Hall Library, Totnes, England, for letters and photographs of Xu Zhimo, Ling Shuhua, and Rabindranath Tagore; the Columbia University Library; the Cornell University Library, the City College of New York Library; the Wuhan University Archives, Hankou, China, for writings and photographs of Julian Bell; the Shanghai Public Library for the writings of Bertrand Russell, Maynard Keynes, and Ling Shuhua; and the Beijing University Library for background materials.

I also gratefully acknowledge the assistance of many dedicated librarians along the way: first, Ms. Jacqueline Cox, formerly chief archivist of the Modern Archives, King's College, always hospitable and helpful in guiding me through the archives during my trips to the collection, as well as Ms. Ros Moad, archivist; Ms. Beth Inglis, Modern Archives, University of Sussex, for her lively and speedy assistance with the Monk's House Collection; Mr. Steve Crook and Phillip Milito of the Berg Collection, New York Public Library; Ms. Jennifer Booth, archivist, Tate Gallery Archive; Mr. Xu Zhengbang, chief archivist, Wuhan University Library, Wuhan, China; Mr. Richard Uttich, chief reference librarian at the City College of New York; Ms. Nancy McKechnie, archivist, Vassar College; and to Karen V. Kukil, associate curator, Mortimer Rare Book Room, Smith College, Northampton. I also acknowledge The Society of Authors as the Literary Representative of the Estate of Virginia Woolf. In addition, thanks to the translators who assisted me in my travels and in translating Chinese works: Ms. Yiming Ren, assistant professor, Shanghai Academy of Social Sciences; Ms. Guo Liang, liaison at Wuhan University; Ms. Xu, graduate student at Wuhan University; Ms. Ming Chun-Ho, a faithful and hard-working assistant; and Mr. Wai-chi Lau, knowledgeable about Chinese culture. Funding for travel to libraries was generously provided by PSC-CUNY Travel Grants in 1995 and 2000.

My perspectives in this study were enriched by participation in the Modern China Seminar, Columbia University, that graciously accepted me, a fledgling, into its historical fold, particularly Professors Jeff Kinkley, Frank Kehl and Don Watkins, who provided me with a steady stream of China clippings; and the Women Writing Women's Lives Seminar that contributed to my thinking about the letters and lives represented in this book. I also express appreciation to the university seminars at Columbia University for their help in publication. I also thank my CUNY colleagues for supportive conversations over the years: Professors Kathy Chamberlain, Vicki Chuckrow, Sid Feshbach, Barbara Fisher, Joyce Gelb, Roberta Matthews, Liz Mazzola, Marylea Meyersohn, Geraldine Murphy, Ellen Tremper, and Barry Wallenstein. My friends in China were invaluable to my navigation of foreign waters: Professors Qu Shijing, He Shu, Yiming Ren, and Tao Jie. And for sharing memories of China, I thank Jin Di, Xiao Qian (d. 1999), Wen Jieruo, Yuan Kejia, Zhao Luorin, Wang Xin Di, C. T. Hsia, and Ye Junjian (d. 1999).

I thank friends and colleagues, particularly Professor Jeffrey Kinkley, St. John's University, who has graciously written the foreword to this book as well as reading and commenting generously, throughout this project; Professor Mary Ann Caws, Graduate Center, CUNY, adviser and friend, whose "maybe's" and "perhaps's" have more direction than most "yes's" and "no's"; Professor Diane Gillespie, Washington State, for her encouragement and her critical acumen, which has improved this book; and Professor Irv Malin, CUNY, for support in the last phase of this project. Others who read parts of the manuscript are Professors Yuan Kejia and Jin Di, always wise, helpful, and supportive in my China explorations and arrangements; Professors Ann Berthoff, Tao Jie, Mary Lea Meyersohn, and Peter Stansky. Special thanks to Professors Yiming Ren, Shanghai Academy of Social Sciences, and Timothy Tung, CUNY, for providing helpful assistance with Pinyan spelling. I was also fortunate during the writing of this book to be in conversation with Hsaio-ying Chinnery, the daughter of Ling Shuhua and Chen Yuan, in London. Her generosity in talking to me of her mother and father, and her kindness in showing me some of her paintings from her big trunk, providing a small painting for reproduction, and giving permissions for quotation are greatly appreciated. In addition, the Bell family has been generous in providing information and permissions for this study: the late Quentin Bell, Ann Olivier Bell, Angelica Bell, and Henrietta Garnett.

For friendship during the years of writing: Nili and Alberto Baider, Daniella Daniele, Beth Daugherty, Betty Eisler, Nancy Newman Elghanyan, Diane Gillespie, Terry and Mike Goldman, Allen and Paula Goldstein, Bella Halsted, Florence Jonas, Trudi Kearl, Leslie Hankins, Roberta Matthews, Marylea Meyersohn, Martha and Richard Nochimson, Sandy and Jim Rosenberg, Allen Tobias, Sarah Bird Wright, Carol Zicklin, and the late Bob Zicklin. Gratitude also to my sister, Terry, and her husband, Jeffrey, for their generosity of spirit. A special thanks for generous hospitality and good talk and roasts during my stays in London to Jean Moorcroft Wilson and Cecil Woolf. I also thank Professor George Simson, the Center for Biographical Research, University of Hawaii, and Dr. Frances Wood, Center for Chinese Studies, SOAS. For permission to use slides of Ling Shuhua's friendship scroll in this book, I gratefully acknowledge Michael Sullivan, the eminent critic of Chinese art.

Virginia Woolf says that "books are built upon books" (*A Room of One's Own*, 130). This one is no exception and it rests upon the groundbreaking work of Pete Stansky and William Abrahams, *Journey to the Frontier* (1966) on the life of Julian Bell and his participation in the Spanish Civil War. I am also grateful to the Asian specialists mentioned in this book, whose work enlarged mine. Special thanks also to my agent, Jeanne Fredericks, for her patience and support; and to Laura Moss Gottlieb for her excellent index. To Barry Blose, my learned, thoughtful editor at the University of South Carolina Press, I express a heartfelt, *sie sie*, for seeing it through.

To my children, Ilana and Jonathan, *merci* and *gratzie*, for taking me into their wide, wide worlds of travel and learning in Europe; to my son-in-law,

Regis Zalman, for his help with graphics, and taking me into the worlds of art and cyberspace; and to my new grandson, Noah, for joy. Last, but not least, my husband, Stuart, for his good humor during my periods of intense writing, and his skills of persuasion and reasoning that have surely honed mine.

The reader will note that the Pinyin romanization system, the official romanization of the People's Republic of China (PRC), has been used for the spelling of Chinese names and words throughout this book. To clarify people, places, and events, a historical time line is included in the front of the book. A brief description of the major Chinese and English figures who appear in this book can be found in the appendices, and a map of China noting cities referred to in this study is included on page xxix. Original spellings in the letters cited in this book have been preserved.

My final note is that, though this book is a double-venture into the worlds of China and England, I am by training and profession a British modernist and a Virginia Woolf specialist. This may help explain the emphasis of the book and the choice of texts. It may also explain my method, which moves from biographical to cultural and literary criticism, perhaps still on the margins of a new direction in criticism.

Abbreviations

Berg	Berg Collection, New York Public Library
CHAO	Charleston Papers, Modern Archives, King's College, Cambridge
EMF	E.M. Forster Papers, Modern Archives, King's College, Cambridge
Hu Shih	Hu Shih Papers, Cornell University, Ithaca
IAR	I. A. Richards Collection, Magdalene College, Cambridge
JHB	Julian Bell Papers, Modern Archives, King's College, Cambridge
LKE	Lemand K. Elmhirst Overseas Collection, Dartington Hall, Totnes
REF	Roger Fry Papers, Modern Archives, King's College, Cambridge
MHP	Monk's House Papers, University of Sussex, Brighton
Tate	Tate Gallery Archives, London
Wuhan	Wuhan University Archives, Wuhan

Historical Time Line

England

China

1600

1644–1911 Manchu, or Qing Dynasty

1700

1800

1837–1901 Queen Victoria reigns

1839–42 First Opium War between England and China
1856–60 Second Opium War

1862 G. L. Dickinson, don and writer, born
1866 Roger Fry, artist and critic, born
1879 Vanessa Bell, painter, born
1882 Virginia Woolf, novelist, born

1895 Xu Zhimo, poet, born

1900 *1899–1900* Boxer Rebellion (nationalist response to foreign intrusion)
1900 Ling Shuhua, writer and artist, born

1908 Julian Bell, poet and activist, born

1910 Xiao Qian, journalist and writer, born

England

1914 Outbreak of World War I

1918 World War I ends

1919 Woodrow Wilson initiates League of Nations

1920 Women in U.S. get right to vote

1928 Women gained the right to vote

1936–39 Spanish Civil War

1939 England enters World War II

1945 World War II ends

1950–53 Korean War

China

1911 Revolution against the Manchu Dynasty; establishment of the Chinese Republic; Sun Yat Sen founds Guomindang (Nationalist Party)

1916–28 Warlord Era feuding warlords

1919 May Fourth literary movement begins in Beijing

1926–27 Chiang Kai-shek's Northern Expedition

1931 Japanese occupy Manchuria

1934–35 Red Army's Long March

1937–45 Sino-Japanese War fought in China

1945 China emerges as one of "Big Five"

1949 Mao Zedong founds People's Republic of China; Chiang Kai-shek removes Nationalist government to Taiwan

1958–60 Great Leap Forward

1966–76 The Cultural Revolution

Lily Briscoe's Chinese Eyes

Map of China. By permission of Lois Snow.

INTRODUCTION

I first came upon Chinese and English landscapes in my modernist daily life in encountering the romance of Julian Bell and Ling Shuhua in a cache of Bloomsbury letters and papers at a Sotheby's auction in London in 1991. Perusing the catalog for the sale, I noticed an entry:

> 363. Woolf (Virginia) and the Bloomsbury Group. Collection of Papers of the Artist Su Hua Ling Chen [Ling Shuhua], including series of letters to her by Julian Bell, Virginia Woolf, Vanessa Bell, Vita Sackville-West and others. The Chinese artist Su Hua Ling Chen (1900–90), who was daughter of a Mayor of Peking [Beijing] and attended the wedding in 1922 of Pu Yi (the "last Emperor"), gained entrance to the Bloomsbury Group through her relationship with Julian Bell, who in 1935 was Professor of English in Hankow [Hankou, one of the three districts in Wuhan city] and with whom, as the present letters reveal, she had a love affair before he went off to his death in the Spanish Civil War in 1937. ("English Literature and History Sale," Sotheby's Catalog, July 18, 1991)

Intrigued by a new figure in the Bloomsbury constellation, Shu-Hua Ling Chen (Ling Shuhua), I approached the odd packet of materials containing letters by Virginia Woolf, Ling Shuhua, Julian Bell, Vanessa Bell, Vita Sackville-West, Leonard Woolf, and others. Permitted a few days to read through the packet before the auction, I found letters that revealed the intrigue of a mercurial, cross-cultural love affair between Julian Bell, the son of Vanessa Bell and nephew of Virginia Woolf, and Ling Shuhua, a married Chinese painter and writer. Their friendship began during the period that he taught at National Wuhan University in Hubei (Hupeh) Province in China, 1935–37. In addition, there were photographs, and small bookmarks and calendars painted by

Vanessa Bell and Duncan Grant. Taking my cue from Maud Bailey of A. S. Byatt's *Possession,* I let myself into the mysteries of a relationship that I had never heard of in my ten years as a Woolf scholar. The subject has been muted in both China and Bloomsbury, though the scholars Peter Stansky and William Abrahams did reveal that Julian Bell had a "friend" in China, referred to as "K" in their excellent 1966 study of Julian Bell and John Cornford, *Journey to the Frontier.* In her 1983 biography of Vanessa Bell, Francis Spalding acknowledges that Shuhua was an "invaluable friend" to Julian in China. But Spalding notes in a letter to Ling Shuhua that she has "altered the passages" in the biography that she wished her to change (Frances Spalding to LSH, 4 October 1982, NYPL). In China, the relationship has also been discreetly avoided. In a conversation with Ye Junjian, Julian's student and confidante in 1994, he wryly observed that Julian's relationship with Ling Shuhua "was a personal sort of thing." In another conversation in the same year with Xiao Qian—journalist, writer, and translator living in Beijing—he more openly related his belief that "Ling was a lover of Virginia's nephew, Julian Bell." Mr. Xu Zhengbang, archivist at Wuhan University and friend of Professor Fang Zhong (now deceased), Julian Bell's colleague and friend at Wuhan, 1935–37, said that he knew nothing of the affair. (Fang Zhong, according to Mr. Xu, was the person best informed about Julian's situation in Wuhan.) Discretion and politics then has dictated relative silence in both countries.

On the day of the Sotheby's auction, I sat in the first row with a friend and turned squarely toward the audience to see who would purchase the coveted collection of letters. British bidders, I discovered, signal the auctioneer with the flick of a discreet eyelash. Before I could identify the buyer, the auctioneer caroled, "sold." Abiding by the auction house's rules of privacy, I wrote a letter to the manager to be passed on to the buyer, requesting to read the packet of letters as part of a scholarly project. I trusted my request to the fates: a private buyer has no obligation to respond to such a letter. Three months later, I received a phone call from the Bloomsbury collection's purchaser, who, to my delight, was the library in my hometown, the Berg Collection of the New York Public Library. I raced down to be greeted by Steve Crook, head archivist of the Berg collection, who amiably allowed me to read through the uncatalogued collection of papers. As I read further, I discovered that both Julian Bell and Ling Shuhua were, importantly, part of a web of relationships between two literary and intellectual communities: Bloomsbury, a literary community in England initiated about 1905 that had considerable cultural influence by the late 1920s and was a force in the making of modernism; and the Crescent Moon group, a cosmopolitan Beijing literary clique of repute in China that identified with English liberalism and literature and thrived around 1925–33. I read through hundreds of letters in the Berg Collection in the New York Public Library, the Tate Gallery Archives in London, the King's College Archives in Cambridge, the Dartington Library in Totnes, and the Wuhan University Archives in Wuhan, China. Along the way, I have, when possible, interviewed Chinese intellectuals, critics, and writers on my trips to China. The cameo that inspired this work—the relationship between Julian Bell and Ling Shuhua—developed into a cultural and literary study. But it begins with the life of Julian Bell who was a poet, essayist and activist of the second generation of Bloomsbury; and Ling Shuhua, painter, calligrapher, writer and collector who was the wife of Chen Yuan. Both Ling and Chen were connected

Ling Shuhua in modern dress. By permission of the Henry W. and Albert A. Berg Collection of English and American Literature, The New York Public Library, Astor, Lenox and Tilden Foundations.

to the Crescent Moon literary group, often labeled the "Chinese Bloomsbury." They were part of a more academic modernist movement in Beijing different from the glitter of the cosmopolitan trends in Shanghai.

Behind this critical work then is the specter of my own journey out of American literary circles and British modernism into the fascinating literary, cultural, and political world of Republican China, a period bracketed by two movements—China in the establishment of the Republic of 1912 and the People's Republic of 1949. It not only prompted me to move out of the sometimes claustrophobic Bloomsbury and to take a brick out of the linguistic wall of China in studying Mandarin for two years, but also to compare my imagined China to contemporary actualities. It led me to travel to difficult and beautiful places to explore the possibilities of research in a different cultural and political space in order to register in my own experience the postmodern and postcolonial debates on identity, culture, and nation. It has made me less glib.

When I reflect on this rather wild journey, I realize that it was partly an escape from my growing discomfort in postmodern studies in which I had been immersed during graduate school and in my first book, *The Reading of Silence: Virginia Woolf in the English Tradition* (Stanford University Press, 1991). My criticism then was removed, as much of postmodern and some postcolonial criticism is, to a critical space in which one is suspended without "origin" or "place." This book marks a decision to practice what I had theorized in *The Reading of Silence:* to suspend myself in an unknown landscape such as one of the surrealist women figured in Max Ernst's *Une Semaine de Bonté.* Remembering a twilight walk across a narrow part of the Yangtze River in Chungking, China—a walk across a narrow "floating bridge" suspended on barrels with no handrails—I realize now what a brave venture this has been. In this book, I arrive to ponder "place," as Eudora Welty, one of my favorite writers, urges, but an unknown place. In this place, China, I discovered not only new, strange, confusing, and beautiful landscapes and people, but answered, for myself, Stuart Hall's question of what changes and what stays the same when you travel. For years I had loved old China: I read Arthur Waley's translations of Chinese poems, looked at dizzying landscapes and mute Chinese calligraphic scrolls, gazed at the Benjamin Altman Collection of Chinese Porcelains at the Metropolitan Museum of Art, and admired the bronze vessels of the Zhou period in the wonderful reconstructed Shanghai Museum, as well as the simple wooden figures of the Eastern Han period.

Impatient with theorizing that seemed suddenly like quicksand, I jumped across an ocean and part of a century to walk across a floating bridge on the Yangtze River. I discovered in travel and in the act of writing why I sought a new proving ground. A Place. As Eudora Welty says of "Place" in fiction, I say of criticism:

> Place . . . is the named, identified, concrete, exact, and exacting, and therefore credible, gathering spot of all that's been felt. . . . Location pertains to feeling, feeling profoundly pertains to Place; Place in history partakes of feeling, as feeling about History partakes of Place. ("Place in Fiction," 6)

I have traveled to China three times in the past decade, entered into its history, given lectures on literature, and have identified with Julian Bell's teaching of English literature (Shakespeare, the moderns, and English composition) at Wuhan University, 1935–37. In Wuhan, I too saw the concrete blocks of buildings with the lovely, horned Ming-styled painted roofs erected in the early part of the century; the classrooms with concrete floors, and long mahogany desks and benches; windows inviting a leafy landscape into the rooms in which Julian taught; and amid the hills, the beautiful, clear East Lake on which Julian sailed. Walking behind the two-story building that Julian Bell resided in during his stay at Wuhan, I too climbed the steep wooded and rocky Luojia Hill to Ling Shuhua and Chen Yuan's well-built Republican style house.

IMAGES ON A SCROLL

From this place, I moved into the personal relationships and then the art of the British and Chinese communities. The filaments of this cultural web extend from the personal relationship of Ling Shuhua and Julian Bell captured in letters, Julian Bell's China photo album, Ling Shuhua's friendship scroll, and the manuscripts of Ling Shuhua's stories. The photographs in Julian Bell's China photo album dissolve into a cultural and aesthetic conversation that is revealed on another document, the friendship scroll of Ling Shuhua, now in the possession of the eminent art critic, Michael Sullivan. The other documents that link Bloomsbury and the Crescent Moon group are the letters between Ling and Bell, and Ling Shuhua's stories edited by Julian Bell, to be discussed in the opening chapter. The discovery of Julian Bell's photo album of his days in China, 1935–37, on my trip to China in March 2000 and then the friendship scroll and manuscripts of Ling Shuhua's stories animated the figures in this study. In the album that Julian made, he included snapshots of himself, tall and handsome in a Chinese robe; his favorite photograph of beautiful Ling Shuhua in a fur hat posed between two stone Buddhas; Ling's scholarly looking husband, Chen Yuan; a portrait of the "triangle," Julian kneeling next to Ling Shuhua and Chen Yuan; the "three talents of Luo Jia," Su Xuelin, Ling Shuhua, and Yuan Changying; Ling Shuhua's charming daughter, Ying; as well as friends at Wuhan University; and the beautiful landscapes that he explored in Tibet with his student, Ye Junjian.

Ling Shuhua's friendship scroll links Bloomsbury and the Crescent Moon group as it contains the inscriptions and sketches of leading figures in both communities and was carried from China by the well-known poet Xu Zhimo. The discovery of artifacts, the China photo album and the friendship scroll, as well as the manuscripts of Ling Shuhua's stories, drew a tangible connection to the romantic and literary crossings, and spurred me on. They are historical and aesthetic traces of the romance and cultural and literary exchange, and two places—Cambridge, England, and Wuhan, China—inscribed in this book. Xu Zhimo carried the small hand scroll, compiled between 1925–28 by Ling Shuhua and her friends, to England when he visited Cambridge University in 1922–23. The scroll limns the relationship between British and Chinese intellectuals and artists, many of them members of the Bloomsbury circle in England and the Crescent Moon group in China. Such a scroll, Michael Sullivan

Julian Bell (Mr. Pei Ju-Lian), professor of English, School of Humanities, Wuhan University, China, 1935. By permission of the chief archivist, Wuhan University, China.

Lake at Peking University, Peking, China, ca. 1936; "Skating in Chinese Robes, a very dignified accomplishment." Julian Bell, photographer. By permission of the chief archivist, Wuhan University Library, China.

describes as both an album in which friends of the owner sketch drawings, poems, and calligraphy, and a symbol of the friendship of the people who inscribe it. The twenty-two items on the scroll, which link Bloomsbury to China, include Dora Russell's (wife of Bertrand) handwritten quotation from Hypatia; Xu Beihong's (a well-known painter who studied art in Paris) sketch of a horse galloping through tall grass; Wen Yiduo's (a leading poet of the Crescent Moon group) sketch of Tolstoy; Rabindranath Tagore's (Indian poet and philosopher) Sanskrit poem; and Bing Xin's (May Fourth writer) inscription.

Julian Bell entered into this Chinese history when he decided to teach English literature at National Wuhan University, 1935–37. Like many Americans and English who venture to teach in China today, he traveled with a cultural combination of curiosity, ignorance, enthusiasm, stereotypes, and sympathy.[1] Introduced to a group of friends by Margery Fry—the sister of Roger Fry who had visited China in 1933, supported by Boxer Indemnity Funds[2]—he met Ling Shuhua. Xiao Qian related in a 1995 interview that Margery Fry was "very motherly, a social worker." In the thirties, many British and Americans went to China, sometimes to influence cultural and educational developments and to ward off Japanese influence. Julian was charmed and guided through Chinese culture by Ling Shuhua; later, he would support the talented painter in her literary ambitions and help her translate her short stories into English. But the relationship did not remain platonic. He wrote to Marie Mauron in France soon after his arrival in China:

> Really, I am falling a bit in love with China—also, platonically, yes, I assure you (for particular reasons, social and so on) with a Chinese woman. She is charming—the wife of the dean of the Faculty of Letters, a highly intelligent and amiable man, one of Goldie's students. She's the daughter of a mandarin, a painter and short story writer, one of the most famous in China. She's sensitive and delicate, intelligent, cultivated, a little malicious, loving those gossipy stories, etc., that are true about everyone, very gay—in short, one of the nicest and most remarkable women I know.

Julian's friendship with Ling Shuhua described here fully for the first time in an English publication, importantly adds another figure to the Bloomsbury constellation and reconfigures, among other events, Bloomsbury's relation to China, readjusting some criticism, perhaps, of imperialist sympathies, given that they developed "contrapuntal perspectives" (Edward Said, *Culture and Imperialism*, 32) to mainstream British society.

I, a traveler too, enter into this past cultural moment, identifying with Julian Bell as he tried to learn Chinese and understand the culture with little linguistic or cultural preparation. Archibald Rose, the economist with connections in China, noted upon Julian's departure in 1935 that he had "rarely met

Chen Yuan (Xiying), dean of humanities, husband of Ling Shuhua, Wuhan University, China, 1935. By permission of the chief archivist, Wuhan University Library, China.

INTRODUCTION / 9

Professor Fang Zhong, dean of foreign languages, Wuhan University, China, 1935. By permission of the Chief Archivist, Wuhan University Library, China.

anyone going out to China before with so little guidance," (Letter to Eddy Playfair, 12 November 1935). Despite his lack of preparation, Julian learned some Chinese, appreciated the landscapes and cities of China, and entered into the challenge of outdoors physical life as he did in England. He sailed the boat made for him in China across the beautiful lake near the Wuhan campus, and enjoyed shooting in the wilds of Tibet. These sporting activities might conjure images of the "imperialist predator" ranging freely in another's space; however, Julian, like others—for example, I. A. Richards and his wife—loved the landscapes of China. During this period, he traveled to Tibet with one of his favorite students, the translator and writer Ye Junjian, who eventually made his way to England, and Derek Bryan and Hansen Lowe. Xu Zhimo also traveled to England and became a student of G. L. Dickinson. I travel then, as many critics practicing a new kind of "global criticism" intertwined with travel, tracing these conversations, casting my eyes, like Lily Briscoe, the English artist in Virginia Woolf's novel *To the Lighthouse,* across oceans.

MAPS OF SEEING

Virginia Woolf glancingly relates to my travel as she confers upon Lily Briscoe "Chinese eyes . . . aslant in her white, puckered little face." She presents in this novel an artist enriched by the "foreign," or, more specifically, Chinese discernment. Lily's "Chinese eyes" suggest not the Empire's foraging glance toward the distant lands of China and India for trade and gain, but the new aesthetic voyaging in the East during the modernist period. A new space unfolds before Lily, the English artist with postmodern yearnings for "a hundred pairs of eyes to see with." Her eyes map the East that Julian Bell and other English travelers and writers would explore and value in the next century just as the materials and perspectives of African art inspired the cubists in France. As the modernists in England looked to the East, a vast mass of new cultural, philosophical, aesthetic experiences and perceptions emerged at the beginning of the twentieth century and would challenge British perceptions. Lily's embodiment of "Chinese eyes"—Woolf's brilliant cultural, political, and aesthetic stroke—suggests then not only the incorporation of the Chinese aesthetic into the "English" artist, but also European modernism's and, now, our own questioning of our cultural and aesthetic place or "universality." Chinese spaces are then mapped onto British modernism to enlarge the Eurocentric discourse that presently surrounds this movement.

The British looked to China at the beginning of the twentieth century as did Lily Briscoe, and, now, we, to create new mappings, not only in economic markets but in cultural, political, and aesthetic space. It was a period, 1912–49, in which China became increasingly international, in spite of the self-contained character of China and the difficulty of communication and travel in the early part of the century. At the same time, Chinese writers and intellectuals reached out—part of China's developing autonomy and engagement in foreign relations—to explore the West and absorbed its humanism and liberalism through its literature. This occurred particularly during the May Fourth 1919 literary movement, when many Chinese writers looked outward, traveled abroad, and brought home new ideas of the avant-garde to contribute to the shaping of Chinese literature. Those in the Crescent Moon group were a part of this 1919 movement. Today's reworking of the "global" critical terrain that includes the economic, political, and cultural repositioning of China (Mainland, Taiwan, and Hong Kong) since 1976 is an extension of the kind of early conversation and literary crossings presented in this study. In exploring the "space of art" that contributes to the space of nation—or the "cultural roots of nationalism" as advised by the prescient Benedict Anderson (*Imagined Communities*, 7)—this study counters restrictively ideological notions that do not admit both the pluralism and ambivalence in the discourse of any nation often reflected in various kinds of writing. This is to be found in the ambiguities and complexities of letters, journals, autobiography, biography, and fiction rather than official literary or historical accounts. The cultural and literary formations that emerge from these more personal, individualized narratives anticipate the discourses, contradictions, antagonisms, and stereotypes that later formed English and Chinese modernity, modernism, and nationalism.

Broadly, my study and my own travel follow Julian Bell and a figurative Lily Briscoe, an English artist, as I attempt to trace the movements, conversation, and connections between two literary communities in England and China, Bloomsbury and the Crescent Moon group. These groups were not formal and never issued a manifesto in the style of the dada or surrealist movements; initially, each was just a group of friends who shared intellectual and aesthetic interests. Their writings, however, illuminate what Partha Chatterjee calls "the inner spaces of community ... the sphere of the intimate," a narrative that was increasingly displaced by the imperialism in England and nationalism in China. These "practices," reflected in unpublished letters, diaries, interviews, journalism, criticism, essays, short stories, novels, and visual art, reveal the "fissures" and "discontinuities" in the concept of "nation." In emphasizing these "local" communities, the dichotomies of East and West and England and China are deconstructed. The monolithic terms "nation" and "modernism" are presented in ways that dramatize differences; personal, cultural, and aesthetic conversations demonstrate the complexity and multiplicity within these categories that are frozen in our language.

The writings are arranged here in a continuum from the biographical to the literary, the cultural, the national, and the aesthetic, to restore the "nonsequential energy of lived historical memory and subjectivity ... [that] tell other stories than the official sequential or ideological ones produced by institutional power" (Edward Said, "Opponents, Audiences ..."). Why and how England began to value the artistry of China as a novelty, and, the Chinese, the modernism of England, is a question that motivates this book. What is found in the literature and the art of the Edwardian and Republican periods are new forms of consciousness and expression that break with older forms of belief. Edwardian writers began to limn the subject and subjectivity in literature in new ways, aiming to put the mind on the page; May Fourth writers in China began to construe a different kind of self in relation to the story of nationhood. This new narrative of self began to challenge official stories during a period of national crisis in both countries—during the Sino-Japanese War in China and under the threat of World War II in England. Just as the centrifugal forces of nationhood developed, the centripetal forces of individual voice and subjectivity emerged.

New kinds of hybrid formations in culture and aesthetics emerge. As described by Homi Bhabha, "the point of intervention" in such a study shifts "from the identification of images as positive or negative to an understanding of the process . . . made possible by the stereotypical discourse" ("The Other Question," 18). In using recent theories of nationalism, postcolonialism, postmodernism, anthropology, and literary criticism, my vocabulary too is admittedly *hybrid*, due to this study's attempt to define a new space *between* the fields of nationalism and culture. These new formations emerge from what James Clifford has described as "traveling cultures" (*Ethnography of Travel*, 173), the "understudied elements" of a culture that reflect how cultures are constantly changing in the borderlands in relation to one another as in these two intellectual and literary communities. In these cultural borderlands, I realized that many of my previous assumptions about the patterns, place, and uses of literature in a culture that I considered normal were, in fact, conditional. My study then works "with a notion of comparative knowledge produced through an *itinerary*" (Clifford, *Travelling Cultures*, 105), both mine and others, and contributes to the kind of "geopolitical thinking" encouraged by Susan Stanford Friedman in her recent book, *Mappings*.

THE HISTORICAL MOMENT

Fredric Jameson reminds literary critics to "historicize" and, following this advice, my study connects national and fictional discourse. The Chinese writers and artists in this study formed cultural attachments to England amid the vortex of revolutionary and national forces that was Republican China in the early part of the century. From the twenties through the forties, there was high patriotic feeling that developed in resistance to Japan's brutal incursions in China, and yet the taste for English, American, and Russian literature developed at the same time. As noted by Perry Link, among those Chinese who had traveled abroad during this period, the taste for Western literature was greater than in any generation before or since. Xu Zhimo, Lu Xun, Chen Yuan, Shen Congwen, Ling Shuhua, Hu Shi, Wen Yiduo, and Xiao Qian traveled to or imagined England, America, and the West. In reading some of these Chinese and British writers in juxtaposition, Chinese writers are brought into the modernist order and discussion in Anglo-American scholarship. In reading them as incipient modernists initiating new subjects and styles of writing in China, their contributions are acknowledged, relieving them of the ennui of the socialist realist tradition or the postmodern fashioning of contemporary critics in China. Nevertheless, national and historical currents coursing through these literary communities are observed.

In presenting the "sphere of the intimate" in the letters, journals, and writings of artists and intellectuals within specific historical and national discourses, I challenge postcolonial theories that ignore time and space, those that emphasize either the universality in the human condition, like Naipaul, or linguistic nationalism, as in the work of Ngũgĩ wa Thiong'o. Japanese and Indian critics, among others since the early eighties, have begun to map this specificity. This study enters this strand of criticism and traces aesthetic lines in early twentieth-century Chinese culture during a period of openness between China and England. Though anti-imperialist discourse was strong in the Republican Period of China, 1911–49, these cultures met and imagined one other, in what is now fashionably termed a global encounter. In mapping a new cultural and aesthetic space alongside economic expansion, we observe how China is imagined into existence—how it acquires shape in the British imagination, daily life, institutions, and arts. We see how aesthetic communities in England began to feel connected to faraway places in China, though this nation was, in Benedict Anderson's sense, largely "imagined," but powerful in terms of literary and cultural communication and influence. A personal sense of the meaning of "my country" is conveyed through the eyes of writers and artists at a particular historical moment, at a juncture of waning nationalism in England and waxing nationalism in China. It was a period in which China was emerging as a national power after a century of being the "sick man of Asia." The conversation begun on the aforementioned friendship scroll continued as writers and artists traveled before the Sino-Japanese conflict heightened in the mid–1930s, and continues today, after the cultural gap of the Maoist period. It was a historical period that permitted literary and aesthetic interplay. This was part of the fallout of a century and a half of British trade, exploitation, and relationship with China.[3]

China was viewed by the British among other nations (France, Russia, Germany, and Japan) not only as a semi-colonial space, but also, as Lisa Lowe observes in the French context, "a desired position outside Western politics and signification" (*Critical Terrains,* 160). The attraction to the other, Marianna Torgovnick confirms, is often "conditioned by a sense of disgust or frustration with Western values" (*Gone Primitive,* 153), a theme to be developed in the discussion of Goldsworthy Lowes Dickinson in chapter 3. China was a faraway place but often functioned symbolically, responding to English needs, "becoming the faithful or distorted mirror of the Western self" (Torgovnick, *Gone Primitive,* 153).

Both the Chinese and the English cultures were in a period of political and historical upheaval in the first half of the twentieth century. At the same time that the Chinese lived through the brutal period of the Sino-Japanese War and the confusions of the civil war, the British lived through the domestically conflicted World War I and the bombardments of World War II. The violent cultural contact and reflection about the 1900 Boxer Rebellion against foreign missionaries in China served as a defining moment in its cultural and political relationship. The indemnity leveled against the Chinese after the Boxer Rebellion provoked not only moral outrage and political salvos among the British themselves, but also some of the first historically and politically engaged literary works in England. Both G. L. Dickinson, the Cambridge don, historian and participant in the creation of the League of Nations, and Lytton Strachey, the well-known biographer of Queen Victoria, were to memorialize this event in their writing. Dickinson wrote a satiric, anonymous series of letters critical of English violence against the Chinese rebelling against British missionary activity, "Letters from a Chinaman," in the *Saturday Review* (later published as a book, *Letters from John Chinaman,* in 1903); Lytton Strachey wrote a satirical melodrama on the vicious and dramatic Empress Cixi and the Emperor, *A Son of Heaven,* produced in 1928. The interest was returned when Strachey's *Queen Victoria* appeared in China in 1940, translated by Bian Zhilin. The May Fourth 1919 literary movement in China marked England's further turn toward literary interest and translation. Arthur Waley's first translations of Chinese poetry appeared in 1918–19, and Duncan Grant's illustrated edition of Waley's translation of Wu Cheng'en's *Monkey* (*Xi You Ji*) followed. In 1933–34, Roger Fry, (according to Kenneth Clark) one of the most important British art critics of the twentieth century, delivered the Slade Lectures on Chinese Art at Cambridge, having already challenged the English art world in 1910 and 1912 with his two Post-Impressionist Exhibits that presented

French and other avant-garde European art to a conservative British audience. At the same time he mounted these exhibits, he began to note the influence of the East in his 1910 reviews of the art of China, India, Java, and Ceylon. Fry was remarkably free of cultural prejudice and aesthetically open to China and the art of the East at this time, and not the "arrogant" critic that Marianna Torgnovnick portrays in relation to African art (87ff).

The art of China—its ceramics, paintings, calligraphic scrolls, fashions, objets d'art—had been circulating in British homes and culture for centuries, most noticeably in the blue and white willow patterns of Spode-Staffordshire, Wedgwood, and Adams and Davenport. To the Chinese, these objects were viewed as handicrafts but became "art" because of Western appreciation. In addition, Liberty Department Store as a quasi-museum presented the art of China at the turn of the century, as did the International Chinese Art Exhibition in 1935–36 at Burlington House, London. During this period, G. L. Dickinson, I. A. Richards, Beatrice and Sidney Webb, Harold Acton, and Julian Bell also traveled to China, made possible by the new two- to three-month ship voyages. Intellectuals and artists were curious about this faraway place that they had experienced not only through the discourse of imperialism, commercial trade, and missionary activity, but also through its art—not only the domestic art of chinoiserie incorporated into British life since the eighteenth century but also its poetry and refined landscape paintings on scrolls and on glorious ceramics. This group would initiate another kind of discourse that would go beyond the imperial discourse surrounding them that mainly focused on the political. They would develop another kind of narrative, more sensitive to the ambiguities and complexities of the aesthetics and history between England and China. They would create cultural and literary texts with a new focus on the aesthetic crossings.

THE FORMATION OF LITERARY COMMUNITIES AND CONVERSATIONS IN CHINA AND ENGLAND

We discover through letters that Margery Fry, the sister of art critic and painter Roger Fry, was the first of the British group to travel to China with Mary Michaelis in 1933. She was part of the Universities China Mission, endowed from the indemnity paid by China to England after the 1900 Boxer Rebellion against European missionary presence in northern China. While on a lecture tour of the country, Marjorie Fry met Ling Shuhua, about whom she

Margery Fry *by Roger Fry.* By the kind permission of Annabel Cole.

Still Life with Tang Horse *by Roger Fry.* © *Tate, London 2002. By the kind permission of Annabel Cole.*

raved in letters, and Ling Shuhua's husband, Chen Yuan, dean of the School of Arts and Letters at National Wuhan University. Both became part of the Crescent Moon group, a literary community founded by poet Xu Zhimo in 1925–26. Marjorie Fry's connections, as well as Liao Hong Ying, a Chinese exchange student, and Boxer Indemnity Funds enabled Julian Bell to also travel to China to teach English literature at National Wuhan University (Vanessa Bell to Julian Bell, 7 December 1935).

Margery Fry developed a lifelong sympathy for the culture of China, as did her brother, Roger Fry. Ling Shuhua wrote to Margery Fry after her trip that she was delighted to receive two lithographs of Roger Fry's—one to be placed in the Girls' Hostel; the other to be given to the president of National Wuhan University, Mr. Wang. Shuhua referred in the same letter to Roger Fry's landscape drawn on the friendship scroll that Xu Zhimo brought back to Ling Shuhua from England. Shuhua treasured her scroll in China; Marjorie Fry valued the Tang horses and figures that she brought back from China to England (plate 1). Julian Bell sent back a jade ring that Vanessa Bell always wore, according to her granddaughter Henrietta Garnett; two jade lions remain in the dining room at Charleston; and a jade fish sent to Leonard Woolf can still be seen in Monk's House. Personal connections and tastes then flowered into formal aesthetic interest in England.

The phenomenon of "community," illustrated above, and as defined by Benedict Anderson and Partha Chatterjee, and "conversation" or "dialogue" as elucidated by Mikhail Bakhtin shape this study. In light of the conversations of British and Chinese intellectuals and writers delicately traced on Ling Shuhua's scroll and pictured in Julian Bell's China photo album, "dialogue" and "community" become the main metaphors and theoretical concepts that structure the argument of this study. The communities focused upon are, first, actual groups of friends in literary and intellectual circles in which the members know one another and share a sense of kinship and comradeship within their own nations—one definition of community offered by Benedict Anderson. Yet influences are varied and numerous, and these communities, it must be remembered, exist in nations. Anderson notes that theorists of nationalism have often been perplexed by "the objective modernity of nations to the historian's eye vs. their subjective antiquity in the eyes of nationalists" as well as "the political power of nationalisms vs. their philosophical poverty and even incoherence" (*Imagined Communities*, 5). In this study, China's "antiquity," stability, and landscapes become preeminent in the eyes of the British Edwardians and modernists at the same time that China endures the wrenching Sino-Japanese War and civil war that bring destruction and threaten incoherence. The romanticism, humanism, and freedoms to be found in British society and literature were a magnet to the Chinese intellectuals and writers at a time when England was whirling from the effects of World War I and questioning its "civilization" and "empire." This leads us to Anderson's concept of "imagined communities," in which he posits that the members of nations never really know their fellow members, "yet in the minds of each lives the image of their communion" (6). He goes on to elucidate the way nations are "imagined" or "invented" by other nations that never have face-to-face encounters. Nations imagine themselves and other nations and present more coherence than actually exists. What then are the cultural roots of these mutual imaginings of nation? The intellectuals, artists, and writers in this study construct their notions of their own nations as well as the other in the usual way that we imagine and create each other, from within their own ideologies: visual images afloat in the culture, the information in textbooks, the representations on maps, the classifications and art in museums, the generalized information gathered through travel, the consciousness and language in literature, and government propaganda. "Contrapuntal perspectives," described by Edward Said, emerge from these cultural and literary encounters that are sometimes parallel or discrepant, sympathetic or oppositional. In allowing these two groups to play off each other in literary relief, this study dramatizes literary and cultural perspectives that might not be visible if studied in isolation or perspectives that would be suppressed or closed off because of politics.

The communities of Bloomsbury—a group of writers and artists that influenced literary and artistic tastes and development in England—and the Crescent Moon group—similarly, a respected literary group, some of whose members knew English or who traveled to, studied in, or were imaginatively drawn to English literature and art—are the cases in point. Xiao Qian, one of China's leading journalists and writers who traveled to England as a war reporter in the 1940s, noted in a personal letter that the Crescent Moon group in China "was known as the Bloomsbury of China because they believed in art-for-art's-sake and not in writing propaganda." He also noted that they were mostly influenced by British writers of the 1920s and 1930s (Xiao Qian to the author, June 1994). According to the political scruples of the day, the group was considered "decadent" in China because of its apolitical, liberal, democratic, individualist, pro-aesthetic and antiutilitarian views of literature and life. The literary societies of the time expected the "so-called Crescent Moon group," as Leo Ou-fan Lee describes it (to mitigate a politicized identity), to enter into the polemics of the time. China was then whirling from the effects of the Sino-Japanese War and the civil war. The mission of literature and art, wielded as "weapons to educate the people," implied, according to Mao in his talks on literature at Ye'nan, social responsibility and political alignment. Writers coped in various ways: Shen Congwen took up the study of Chinese costume and was silent; Ling Shuhua aligned herself with British writers and was criticized; Ding Ling shifted from one political side to another and suffered critical attack and arrest. Other authors were forced to join the ranks of literary officials to remind other authors of their social responsibilities.

Despite these cultural differences and the political climate, both literary communities, Bloomsbury and the Crescent Moon group, shared an aesthetic "paradigm," a "constellation of beliefs, values and techniques" (Kuhn, *Structure of a Scientific Revolution,* 175). Both communities during a time of war struck a pose—pacifism in Bloomsbury during World War I and detachment from the polemics of the communists in the Crescent Moon group—to focus on the expression of individual belief, voice, and art. Their stances were read as political statements, and as Perry Link observes in his challenging book *The Uses of Literature,* "In a highly politicized atmosphere, the purposeful demonstration of an apolitical alternative for art could itself be read as a political statement" (321). This "apolitical" stance of the Bloomsbury group in England and the Crescent Moon group in China was maligned in its day and after. But what is important about these visionary groups of artists is that they came through the Edwardian, modernist, and May Fourth eras with their cosmopolitan sensibilities and modernist principles intact. Their commitment to a cross-cultural modernism with a foreshadowing of postmodernism reverberates today in the legacy of Virginia Woolf's experimental writing and feminism; in Leonard Woolf's political and cultural prescience, in E. M. Forster's postcolonial consciousness and novels, and in the cosmopolitan stance and modernist tendencies of the Crescent Moon group, which was criticized in its day and banned under Mao, but now is increasingly appreciated in China.

The second concept that structures this book is "conversation," or "dialogue," as elaborated by Bakhtin in "Dostoevsky's Polyphonic Novel," among other works.

The "socio-ideological language consciousness as it becomes creative . . . becomes active as literature" (*Dialogic Imagination,* 295). It reveals the many voices, the "heteroglossia," in both the Chinese and English texts and notions of nation surveyed in this study. A constellation of personal, literary, aesthetic, and national dialogues or conversations are presented in this book through the fields of vision in letters, journals, autobiography, visual arts, and literature. They illustrate Bakhtin's observation on the "polyphonic" novel, for example with the novelist Dostoevsky's "gift for hearing and understanding all voices immediately and simultaneously" where others hear a single thought or voice. In listening for a multivoiced China and England in the Republican and modernist periods, I capture some of the "polyphony" of the cross-cultural conversation of the world that Bakhtin describes as:

> . . . complex and multi-structured. In every voice . . . [we can] hear two contending voices, in every expression a crack, and the readiness to go over immediately to another contradictory expression; in every gesture . . . [a]

confidence and lack of confidence simultaneously; . . . [we] perceive the profound ambiguity, even multiple ambiguity, of every phenomenon. (*Problems*, 30)

In hearing these many voices, this study acknowledges the association of modernism with imperialism, which has been supported by considerable Marxist analysis—V. G. Kiernans's *The Lords of Human Kind: Black Man, Yellow Man, and White Man in an Age of Empire* and Benita Parry's *Conrad and Imperialism*, for example—but goes beyond this well-documented perspective. It finds voices other than the "imperialist" or "colonialist" in the British community, and asserts that there are other structures of power and oppression in Chinese Marxism and nationalism also. It listens, as Partha Chatterjee urges, to a "narrative of self" that is sometimes "suppressed under a narrative of changing times" (*The Nation and Its Fragment*, 138) in a nation. This individual voice to be found in letters, journals, autobiography, and fiction may be muffled in certain countries and periods of history. This book advances the notion that these voices, multiple, varied and oppositional, emerge from "the inner spaces of community." These individuals could present their lives only by "inscribing it in the narrative of nation" (138), an evolving nation, a nation of the future.

Witnessing the dissolution of the "the master narrative" described by Edward Said, as well as the "totalizing claims of a nationalist historiography," we move on to describe marginal, fragmented, unofficial, and unacknowledged discourses as represented in various kinds of writing, and the conditions that made them possible. Now that the domains, East and West, have been theorized, we can "trace their mutually conditioned histories [and] . . . numerous fragmented resistances" (Chatterjee, *The Nation and Its Fragment*, 13). This movement advances this field of discourse "as one of contention, peopled by several subjects, several consciousnesses" (137), including, importantly, women.

"Conversation" and "dialogue" then should be understood by the reader to operate on several levels throughout this book: personal "conversations" in which individual artists write or speak and answer the needs of another; cultural conversations in which certain literary and artistic groups assume importance as the embodiment of a changed consciousness; aesthetic conversations that incorporate mutual reflection and parallel interest in an evolving international modernism; and political conversation in which individual voices are "inscribed in the narrative of nation." Rey Chow's warning about "imprisoning other cultures" (1988) within conventional thinking and categories of the West or within a "single-voiced" narrative, as described by Bakhtin, is thus heeded through the presentation of many voices in many kinds of writing.

THE USES OF LETTERS

Following Virginia Woolf's advice, "Write biography. Write criticism. Find a new form for both," my writing has a new critical form for postmodern and postcolonial criticism. It is grounded not only in the many voices to be found in biography and history as recorded in unpublished letters, diaries, historical documents, interviews, and journalism, but it incorporates visual arts and literary study also. This book was begun in the belief that present literary theory in America and China is quicksand unless grounded in specific lives, and historical and literary conversations and communities. The introduction of previously unpublished letters of various members of Bloomsbury in England and the Crescent Moon group in China mark this study. When reading these letters, we become aware of two points of reading. First, we enter, to a degree, the time in which they were written: we become alert to the way in which individuals in families and communities imagine and create, articulate and silence one another, personally and culturally. We read them reading themselves into history. For example, when Julian Bell is in China, he writes to Vanessa Bell, his mother, in a paternalistic way about his sister, Angelica, and her virginity:

> Well, this would have seemed a most improbable letter fifty years ago wouldn't it? Even now, I suppose 99 out of a hundred people, or more, would consider it appalling a son should write like this to a mother about a sister. I like to imagine us all being very famous, and then in some new Victorian age, our letters being publicized. The embarrassed moments of editors. The protests that this is a forgery. The damnation's of the Sir Leslie's [Sir Leslie Stephen, Virginia Woolf's father]. I won't get much fun out of shocking the bourgeois, but I should with this—if one could see. (25 December 1935)

"If one could see" what we in the present day think, as Julian remarked from his vantage point in 1935, one would see that we do experience the "embarrassed moments of editors," the "protests" of the family, and that the temper of our times continues, in various ways, to prevent certain revelations.

Letters can also be misleading because of "the way one reads them all together, when in reality they, of course, are spread over time" (VB to JB, 8

November 1935). And when they are spread over time, it is sometimes difficult to locate them because of the vagaries of personal lives and historical events. The story of this period is not presented seamlessly, but with the gaps and silences of political and cultural upheavals in China. At times, large-scale migrations of the Chinese population during war or political turmoil affected my pursuit of letters as intellectuals and writers were often in flight. One reads of "lost letters," lost because Hankou or Canton (Guanzhou) had fallen or lost because they were diverted to post offices in now "captured towns." The Chinese fled the Japanese invasion and war on their soil from July 1937 to 1945, and personal property was lost during the migration of the nationalists to Taiwan in 1949. In addition, the Cultural Revolution, 1966–76, coerced the movement of urban intellectuals and their property from the cities to rural areas, as well as, sometimes, the destruction of the four "old things" (letters, books, scroll paintings, and furniture) by the Red Guards. Letters have also been repressed in China and England for personal reasons or were lost, and it has led to gaps and silences in this study as eloquent as the letters themselves. For example, the letters and other accounts of both Xu Zhimo and Ling Shuhua were lost during both the Cultural Revolution and Shuhua's emigration to England.

As I was unable to find the cache of letters Ling Shuhua sent to Julian after he left China or her account of their affair that she alludes to in a letter, or letters between Xu Zhimo and Shuhua or Roger Fry and Xu Zhimo, Ling Shuhua is created largely from the biographical accounts of others, her published writings, and a few of her letters. She becomes in this book, nevertheless, a new voice in the Bloomsbury constellation. Other letters of principal figures were destroyed or locked in secrecy in British and American libraries because of the fear of potential harm to Western-identified Chinese intellectuals or artists who had returned to China after 1949. What is presented then is created from the "scraps, orts and fragments" (Woolf, *Between the Acts,* 188).

Another epistolary issue is that reading a batch of letters of one writer without corresponding replies can be misleading, given our practice of reading letters in collections in different libraries with differing intervals, and given other occupations. For example, Julian Bell's China letters are in King's College, Modern Archives, while Vanessa Bell's China letters are in the Tate Library. One reads only one side of the conversation, imagining the other until one can read the actual responses. Sometimes the reading is delayed because of teaching obligations, funds, or the letters are not deposited in libraries by the families as they, understandably, protect privacy and reputations. Batches of letters are then read from one perspective only; conditions make it impossible to read letters in dialogue, as they were written. Consequently, this study emerges out of what I call constellations of letters and the interweaving of perspectives spread over time. The letters provide the basis for the reconstruction of cultural and literary perspectives of Bloomsbury and, to some extent, China. Adding new Chinese voices through letters and other writings to the discussion of Bloomsbury and modernism enables an American critic to develop literary-critical eyes the way Lily Briscoe did with painting. Importantly, the letters and diaries gave me a sense of the literary and cultural issues within a literary community, and these empirical findings helped create the theoretical underpinnings of this book.

Letters are also fragmentary and incomplete in their development of thoughts, ideas, and feelings. What we take from them are the insights of a day, a kind of shadow thinking about the cultural, aesthetic, literary, and political thoughts of two leading communities in China and England that helped to create the taste of their day. However, since some of the members of these groups were leading intellectuals and writers, what they think is significant, and when read together, certain salient issues emerge.

The inclusion of letters among a variety of genres in this study is an extension of Ferdinand de Saussure's theory of networks of meaning. Different kinds of narration and discourses about China and England reveal that there are many ways of being Chinese in England and China; there are similarly many ways of being English in China and in England. Rather than expanding Englishness, this book acknowledges the variety of ways of being English that have always existed, but until now have been unnamed. If we are to represent the many Chinas, the many ways to be Chinese in England and China (as well as English in China), then the examined documents and genres should also express a wide range of genres, narration, and notions of objectivity and subjectivity. This study then employs nonfiction letters, diaries, newspapers, government reports, and fiction written, approximately, during the period of 1910–49: fiction written about the Chinese by the British, fiction written about the Chinese inside China, English fiction about overseas Chinese, Chinese fiction that focuses on traveling scholars overseas, fiction that uses China for what Marianna Torgovnick terms the "primitive" slot in her provocative book, *Gone Primitive,* and fiction that uses China to politically polarize positions (Spence, "Chinese Fictions," 100–101).

This study will focus on the themes of Westerners living within China (Julian Bell, I. A. Richards, William Empson), overseas Chinese in England and America (Xu Zhimo, Hu Shi, Xiao Qian, Ling Shuhua), and, most importantly, the fictions of "internal Chinas" in which China becomes a trope or a discourse among the British, as the British or Westerners become a trope in China. A China-of-the-mind is created through the British discourse about Chinese intellectuals, artists, art, exports, and politics. Another category, British travelers in China, is also presented: G. L. Dickinson, Harold Acton, Beatrice and Sidney Webb, and Bertrand Russell. As we read, we find among the many British discourses emerging during this period "how serious a matter it is when the tools of one generation are useless to the next" (Woolf, "Mr. Bennett & Mrs. Brown," 331).

This study departs from great-men or great-women theories of biography, and presents English and Chinese figures as part of a larger, pulsing, social and literary network expanding upon notions like Bonnie Kime Scott's modernist network. Those who were loosely aligned with Bloomsbury or who expressed interest in China might be grouped in several ways: writers and critics, Virginia Woolf, E. M. Forster, Lytton Strachey, Vita Sackville-West, Roger Fry, W. H. Auden, Christopher Isherwood; artists, Vanessa Bell, Duncan Grant, Dora Carrington; translators, Harold Acton, Arthur Waley; travelers: W. H. Auden, Christopher Isherwood, Margery Fry; teachers, I. A. Richards, William Empson, Julian Bell, Innes Jackson, Lettice Ramsay; socialists and philosophers, Bertrand Russell, G. L. Dickinson, Sidney and Beatrice Webb; and economic and political thinkers, J. M. (Maynard) Keynes, Archibald Rose, Leonard Woolf. The first generation, mainly G. L. Dickinson and Roger Fry, stimulated the curiosity of Julian Bell, W. H. Auden, Christopher Isherwood, I. A. Richards, and Harold Acton to visit or live in China. These individuals were not official ambassadors to China and no claims are made that all were necessarily the most important figures of the day, but some are among England's leading modernist intellectuals and writers.

The parallel community of intellectuals, writers, and painters in China—many of whom were English-speaking, or who traveled to England or America or imagined these places and literary communities in their writings—provides the tension of another culture to be read in dialogue with and sometimes in resistance to the British community. Immediately, differences in literary, cultural, and political labeling in China and England emerge in this attempt at comparative analysis. While the writers in England are encompassed by the literary and cultural designation of modernism, the Chinese writers emerge from the Republican Period, 1911–49, a political and historical designation. Xu Zhimo, Ling Shuhua, Chen Yuan, Lu Xun, Hu Shi, Guo Moruo, Bing Xin, and Yu Dafu, who are focused upon or mentioned in the course of this study, are associated with the May Fourth literary movement[4]; Lao She, Ding Ling, Wen Yiduo, Shen Congwen, Ye Junjian, Cao Yu, and Xiao Qian's literary writing emerged more fully in the 1930s during the early period of the Sino-Japanese War and the civil war strife; and Zhang Ai Ling's stories and Xiao Qian's journalistic writing are associated with writing in the 1940s just before the establishment of the People's Republic of China. Importantly, the actual and imagined dialogue between these writers before the founding of the PRC created a new aesthetic space between the cultures. As I recovered some of the conversation through my work in libraries in England, America, and China, an internal critique of both England and China emerged that would not be as visible without this research. Though these authors, with the exception of Lu Xun and Ding Ling, are probably unknown to most European modernists, all contributed to cultural invention, understanding, and literary engagement with the West, even though they may not all be considered influential from the perspective of Asian scholarship. Chinese literary critics in China and America in the generation after these writers—Yuan Kejia, Jin Di, Qu Shijing, C. T. Hsia, Leo Ou-fan Lee—are also mapping a new aesthetic space based on the writings of the Chinese and modernist authors. It should be noted, however, that given my background, the emphasis is on the British discourse about China. In modestly mapping this new aesthetic and cultural space, I hope that other writers and critics with other linguistic, cultural, and scholarly talents will continue its development. My inquiry may be questioned by some—those who wish to essentialize the critical discussion—threatening at times "to demolish the only premises on which I can speak" (Rey Chow, *Violence,* 90)—as a modernist and literary theorist with wide reading (in translation) in the area of early twentieth-century China.

This study highlights the postmodern position that there are many points of reception of a work, in time as well as place. Yuri Tynyanov, the Russian formalist, reminds us that there is a difference between how a figure or literary phenomenon appears to his contemporaries or in his own culture, and what effects he may have "in enabling future developments in art" or criticism in his own or other countries ("On Literary Evolution," 729). The art and writings presented here can "mean" what Chinese critics of the 1930s, as well as what contemporary Chinese critics assert; in addition, the works can also enter into my Anglo-American critical discourse—part of the goal of this book—and be interpreted variously, or, at times, with limited understanding from another cultural place. The misperceptions and negotiations of meaning are part of the opening of dialogue where linguistic and cultural walls have been, until recently, more difficult to transcend than even the Great Wall of China. For example, Lu Xun and Xu Zhimo are now considered very important writers and reformers in China, though their reputations have waxed and waned depending on the politics of the day; Hu Shi, who helped to theorize the May Fourth literary movement is now considered an important cultural reformer in America and Europe, but was once criticized in China for his associations with the West. Ling Shuhua, writer and painter, and Chen Yuan, historian and well-known literary editor and critic, were vilified during the Republican Period because of their alignment with the Crescent Moon group, English tastes, and the Nationalist Party. Now they are appreciated as leading intellectuals and writers of their day by a new generation in mainland China as revealed in recent articles, reviews, and translations, for example, the first Chinese translation of Ling Shuhua's *Ancient Melodies* (published in English in England in 1953) in 1994. What becomes a literary phenomenon in this book from an American or British perspective in the new millennium may have once been dismissed as "bourgeois" or "decadent" in the Chinese context; writings valued now may once have been repressed in China; texts without influence in China in the 1920s and 1930s may now have an effect in England; texts considered slight in literary England may now have more of an effect in China; and Chinese works recently translated in America or England may fast become part of Anglo-American speculation and criticism. We find then that the works of these writers and artists are more complex and varied in sensibility, style, and content than has been proposed by some critics who engage in various kinds of labeling, naming, and name-calling. Whenever access was possible, I tried to gather a modest amount of criticism published in China surrounding the major figures in this study at two points in time: criticism written during the period they wrote, 1920s through 1940s, and, now, in contemporary times. I have also read the Chinese debates of the 1980s about the movement of "modernism," as manifested in China, as well as works on modernism by Chinese and Chinese-American critics, and brought them into the conversation of this book.

In addition to translation, a generally underrated and underfunded aspect of cultural and literary communication, particularly in China, there has been travel. Writers and literary critics in China who lived through the Sino-Japanese War, the civil war or the Cultural Revolution, sometimes left China, traveled back and forth for study or journalism, sometimes to America, to England, and then back again to China. Other critics and writers in England and America traveled to China or maintained it as a place in the mind. Similarly, some Bloomsbury writers, artists, and intellectuals were culturally bashed within England but were influential abroad.[5] At the same time, Anglophone Chinese writers in the Crescent Moon group were attacked for their "art-for-art's-sake" philosophy and vilified for "class" associations at home in China, but they were lauded for this position when visiting the writers or intellectuals of Bloomsbury. Each group when traveling to Europe or to China, physically or imaginatively, was "valued" differently because they became something new in the country they visited; sometimes, they enabled or reinforced thinking and writing about subjects that might not have been encouraged or have been possible to write about at home. Some of the Chinese writers visited England, particularly King's College, Cambridge University, expressing curiosity about the West; subsequently, they not only theorized anew about Chinese literature when they returned home but also wrote about English and American modernist literature and culture, and met or corresponded with the English literary and intellectual circle. Their ideas about literature when they returned to China were conditioned by their visits to England. This phenomenon is perhaps another example of the intermingling of cultures and the interest in the West that was expressed after the Han Period, 2–7 A.D., when monks and traders brought new ideas of trade and salvation as they traveled the Silk Road, a network of routes in northeast China. I too join the Silk Road critical circuit as a traveler to China, introducing modern Chinese figures and literature into my modernist discussion. Therefore, as Tynyanov asserts, "the value of a given literary phenomenon must be considered as having an evolutionary significance and character" over a period of time in different countries (728).

I study the authors, works, letters, and interviews, with all their variety and richness, in relationship with each other and not as isolated figures. Intellectuals and authors are not just single figures or artistic flashes and anomalies in the culture or fixed political or literary ideologies, but are also part of a cultural and aesthetic network. Literature here is not read solely in response to material conditions and the political or social context of the time as represented in traditional Marxist criticism. In the increasingly global domain of literary criticism, I follow Roland Barthes, who asserts that there is no one "reading" of a text but many "readings"—in different cultures, at different historical periods, at different generic distances, and historical and theoretical points of reception. Reading is evolutionary. Like Virginia Woolf's lighthouse or Ling Shuhua's scroll, when viewed from faraway, we see one thing; when we approach closely with a particular cultural, historical, critical, or political frame, we observe something else. In Virginia Woolf's *To the Lighthouse*, James approaches the lighthouse on a boat with his father, Mr. Ramsay, and his sister, Cam, after viewing it for years from afar on the shore of his childhood. He reflects, "So that was the Lighthouse, was it? No, the other was also the Lighthouse. For nothing was simply one thing. The other lighthouse was true too" (277).

EMPIRICIZING THE THEORETICAL

The starting point of this book is empirical as I examine the "intimate spheres" of literature in both cultures. In juxtaposing a group of English writers (loosely, Bloomsbury) with a group of Chinese writers, in "a network of differences," as Ferdinand de Saussure advances, both groups are theoretically, culturally, and politically removed from their overworked positions. Bloomsbury, for example, is removed from the postmodern position of representing an elite British class or colonial "empire." Through these letters, we learn that Bloomsbury was not as insular or xenophobic as critics claim, but sympathetic to Chinese civilization and receptive to forms of art that opened up foreign texts and contexts. Similarly, the Crescent Moon group is relieved of the Socialist critique of its "decadent" and "Western-identified" position. Both communities are decentered and are instead theoretically, structurally, and, culturally placed in "a system of interdependency" that Ferdinand de Saussure has brilliantly posited about general principles of "meaning" in his *Course*. What is of linguistic, cultural, or literary "value," according to de Saussure "results solely from the simultaneous presence of others . . . its content is really fixed only by the concurrence of everything that exists outside it" (114–15). The value then of an individual writer or thinker or literary community is determined by critically viewing his relationship and interdependency. Critics are, whether wittingly or unwittingly, creating an international map of modernism that fills in sections of the aesthetic canvas, eschewing Anglo- and Eurocentric contributions alone. Derived from de Saussure, the model could be described as a three-dimensional grid composed of moving layers of meaning composed of various discourses: personal, gendered, religious, literary, generic, aesthetic, national, imperial, political, and economic. What one sees from above/below or side perspectives of these overlapping layers of moving meaning, depends upon the angle of the view, what is salient from a particular personal, political, or theoretical position.

Thus, this study of particular literary communities in England and China uses critical tools and theory that suit a new international generation. We create a new map of modernism because we travel to actual and imagined places and through geographical and cyberspace more freely. The many Englands presented here reveal that there were intellectuals and writers in England who, unfazed by the turbulent Chinese politics of the day, or whispers of "socialism," "communism," or cultural "strangeness," were philosophically, culturally, and aesthetically drawn to China and its culture, art, and literature; similarly, different Chinese intellectuals and writers were drawn to the literature and humanism of England. This book isolates a time and place where this relationship lived, approximately 1900–49.

A new way of recording this relationship emerged in 1978 when Edward Said's groundbreaking work, *Orientalism*, established the Orient as "one of the [West's] deepest and most-recurring images of the Other" (1). Though Said's Orient is mainly the Middle East and India, and "mainly, though not exclusively, a British and French cultural enterprise" (4), he focuses our attention on the "discourse" of Orientalism. This is defined as "the style, figures of speech, setting, narrative devices, historical and social circumstances, not the correctness of the representation nor its fidelity to some great original" (21). This discourse is woven, he asserts, from colonial designs, institutions, scholarship, novels, imagery, vocabulary, and bureaucracies (8). Cliches about England and China may be drawn like iron filings about these predictable poles of "imperialist" England and "subjugated" India, Africa, or China, but the field takes a turn when Said, in his 1995 study, *Culture and Imperialism*, records Third World response to Western dominance: "there are always resistances" to domination (186), he asserts, as represented in this book.[6]

Aijaz Ahmad develops this notion of "resistant" and "alternative discourses" while, at the same time, disputing "the undifferentiated discourses" set up by

Edward Said. Ahmad writes, "It is rather remarkable how constantly and comfortably Said speaks . . . of a Europe, or the West, as a self-identical, fixed being which has always had an essence and a project and a will" (183). Countering this "essentializing" of the West—there are many Wests and many Easts—literary groups in this study are removed from formulaic "oppressor" and "oppressed," "master" and "servant," and "colonized" and "colonizer" positions, and are presented as more nuanced and complicated resisters and subverters of the cultural and political currents of their respective cultures. This book complicates the oft-presented geographical, cultural, and political binaries, East and West, and interlaces other categories of experience and analysis that focus upon nationalism, imperialism, capitalism, Marxism, feminism, cultural study, and aesthetics. The metaphors and practices advanced here emerge from the critical domain of international critics Aijaz Ahmad, Benedict Anderson, Homi Bhabha, Mikhail Bakhtin, Partha Chatterjee, Rey Chow, James Clifford, Michel Foucault, Susan Stanford Friedman, Lydia Liu, Leo Ou-fan Lee, Edward Said, Ferdinand de Saussure, Haun Saussy, Gayatri Spivak, and Yip Wai-lim, who illustrate the many communities, discourses, and layers in the archaeology of binaries such as East and West. They establish a new kind of geography of literary study on a global canvas. But reasoning across cultural, literary, and political systems and finding "the transnational condition that informs any local cultural formations" (Friedman, *Mappings,* 111) is difficult.

Bloomsbury and the Crescent Moon group distinguished themselves from the official thinking about each other's culture: each was beleaguered in its own country. This approach allows the shared strategies of agency and resistances under both imperialist and socialist structures of power to surface. While writing this book, however, I encountered readers and reviewers who were reluctant to read these English and Chinese writers in juxtaposition in order to bring the Chinese writers into the modernist ken. Some readers shut out the comparative view, describing Bloomsbury or the Crescent Moon group as "decadent," "snobbish," "elitist," "racist," "capitalist," "Western," "pro-Western," "nationalist," "contradictory," "socialist," "communist," or dangerously "hybrid"; others were put off by foreign-sounding Chinese names, the politics of the PRC, or the tensions between PRC and Taiwan authors and political cultures. Some resisted what one critic termed a "positive transnationalism," preferring to document again the historical and cultural crimes committed against China. There were other critics who insisted that modernism could only be a tainted movement, an outgrowth of imperialism. In the interest of maintaining "difference," victimhood, or some essentialist notion of national identity, I was reminded how the personal identity of critics and the nations into which they are born or to which they travel are always in formation, including my own as I travel to China geographically and imaginatively, and as America and the international community re-forms after the 9/11 terrorism. As critics learning other cultures and languages, we are in a position of vulnerability—of personal and critical flux—as we move to different countries in place and mind. And yet these cross-cultural voyages must be bravely taken. Virginia Woolf reminds us, "Literature is no one's private ground; literature is common ground. It is not cut up into nations; there are no wars there. Let us trespass freely and fearlessly find our own way for ourselves" (*The Moment*, 154). Cultural understanding in the world may now be at a low point, but "it's through art that one country can nearly always speak reliably to another, if the other can hear at all. Art, though, is never the voice of a country; it is an even more precious thing, the voice of the individual, doing its best to speak, not comfort of any sort, indeed but truth" (Welty, *Place*, 2).

Broadly, this study then has two goals: first, to reveal multiple discourses and forms of modernism in China located through extensive research in letters, diaries, and fiction during the Republican period; second, to include China and the Chinese aesthetic in a network of interdependency and to reconfigure international modernism. This study will thus enable readers and critics to see the cultural and aesthetic relations between England and China in evolution, playing down earlier reductionist critical positions that present the British solely as "demonic" agents of "influence," "imperialism," and "cultural thievery," and the Chinese as "oppressed" or "humiliated" victims.

The chapters of this book are empirical and theoretical. The study begins with a description of Julian Bell's China days and *Diary* framed by James Clifford's theory of the ethnography of travel. Chapter 1, "Julian Bell Performing 'Englishness,'" sketches both Julian's voyage to Wuhan University in China in 1935 to teach English literature and to observe Chinese socialism, and his relationship with the talented Chinese writer and painter Ling Shuhua. Described as a "Chinese Bloomsburian," her links to the Crescent Moon literary group in China as well as Bloomsbury are established here.

This leads to chapter 2, "Literary Communities in England and China: Politics and Art," which describes the history and aesthetic stances of the British circle of Bloomsbury and the Crescent Moon group in China, both of which thrived in the 1920s and early 1930s and were imaginatively connected. In establishing the historical and political context in each country that created their similar tendency toward "art" that ignores politics, the philosophical and aesthetic tensions between politics and art during a time of war—the Sino-Japanese War in China and the beginnings of World War II in England—are unraveled.

Chapter 3, "East-West Literary Conversations," compares the British preoccupation with the idea of "civilization" to the movement toward "subjectivity" of some Chinese writers during the Republican period. These terms oscillate in the discourse presented in this chapter between G. L. Dickinson, the Cambridge don and historian, and Xu Zhimo, the well-known and flamboyant Chinese poet. The second part of this chapter extends the exploration of subjectivity in conversations between E. M. Forster, the eminent novelist, and Xiao Qian, a Chinese journalist and writer of repute, evolving into exploration of the themes of homosexuality, modernism, and nationalism in the British novel.

Chapter 4, "Chinese Landscapes through British Eyes," presents, first, snapshots backdrop of eighteenth-, nineteenth-, and twentieth-century landscapes of China, through the eyes of William Anderson, an artist on Lord Macartney's trade expedition to China, 1792–94; Felix Beato, a photographer, observing the destruction of Beijing and the Old Summer Palace at Wanshoushan after the Second Opium War, 1856–60; and a twentieth-century economist, J. M. Keynes, projecting railway lines to carry British products into the Chinese landscape. Shaped by the demands of British imperialism, they are our earliest glimpses into China and serve as valuable background to the later landscapes presented in this chapter through the eyes of artists: painters and writers. The views of China of naturalist Julian Bell and painters and writers Vanessa Bell, Ling Shuhua, and Virginia Woolf are illuminated here. The newly interpreted correspondence between Virginia Woolf and Ling Shuhua presents their thoughts about the personal writing of women during a time of war, the beginning of the Sino-Japanese War and World War II, as well as a cross-cultural discussion of the genre of autobiography. Next, the cultural tropes of landscape emerge on the popular blue and white willow plate and in *anglo-chinois* gardens, images that circulated in British culture and contributed to the development of the "Chinese eyes" of the British modernist.

This then leads to chapter 5, "Developing Modernisms," which traces the aesthetic and literary consequences of cultural and economic contact between England and China that contributes to a developing international modernism, 1900–49. The fusion of British and Chinese aesthetics in the development of "chinoiserie" is described as well as the aesthetic reciprocity in the evolution of modernist concepts such as "subject and object," "rhythm," "line," "plasticity," and "flatness" in British and Chinese art.

The place of China in developing modernism is not only literary: as postmodernism has taught us many "texts" are to be found in the establishment of railway lines and in student rebellions as well as in painting, calligraphy, architecture, gardens, fashion, porcelain, and consumer products. Since painting and writing in Chinese art are only a blink away, this study, in adopting "Chinese eyes," is "literary." The space of this book then is linguistically, culturally, and aesthetically "between" China and England, many of the Chinese writings written by those in the Crescent Moon group in English, or read in translation.

EVOLVING MODERNISMS

This study joins others that highlight the contributions of China, Japan, and India to a global modernism, a movement away from Anglo-Euro-American models. Though the "Orient" has been largely defined as the Middle East and Africa in the works of Edward Said, and as India in the criticism of Partha Chatterjee and Homi Bhabha, this study expands the notion. It expands the modernist archive including reportage, letters, diaries, essays, autobiography, poetry, short stories, novels, and other modes of communication and travel. Much of the evolving exploration of British and American modernism by Asian specialists has focused on poetry, such as Zhaoming Qian's *Orientalism and Modernism*, which demonstrates how the Anglo-American poetic revolution of the 1910s and 1920s, and more specifically Ezra Pound and William Carlos Williams, were inspired by the poetry of the Far East. Similarly, there is scholarship on Wallace Stevens's poetic landscapes in which one catches glimpses of Chinese or Japanese landscape painting or the poetic lyrics of Li Bo, Wang Wei, or Bo Zhuyi. There are studies of the influence of Ezra Pound's translations from the Chinese in *Cathay* on the early imagists as well as Yeats, Eliot, and William Carlos Williams.[7] In reframing British or European modernism to include more Chinese literature and communities such as those represented in this study, modernism is configured as a "system" in which it is acknowledged that literary people and communities in different parts of the world are interdependent. Modernism, a marker of literary concentration in this study, is not a fixed boundary and roughly covers the modernist period in England, 1910–41, and the Republican period in China, 1911–49, spanning what most British and Chinese literary historians would consider important events in international modernism's history. Looking at this period from our point of reception in the present day, we see a global canvas because of the new cultural and political visibility of China encouraged by a new openness to the West that began in the early eighties, to the present membership in the World Trade Organization and developing political and economic interdependency, and the projected Beijing Olympics, 2008. Now, there is more information about Chinese culture in America, and there is more translation of Chinese literature than ever before. Culture follows economics. This study, then, traces the developing movement of international modernism as it went its own way, picking up the force of French postimpressionism, German expressionism, Italian futurism, American imagism, Russian avant-gardism, suprematism, Orphism, and, as this book contends, Chinese and Japanese aesthetics. It places China in the network of differences, as its aesthetic and cultural presence will change the "value" of any particular modernism that sits at the table of international modernism.

What is revealed in the letters presented in this study is that each of the Bloomsbury writers, artists, and intellectuals—or those in a circle resistant to Bloomsbury—interpreted or created his or her own "China." For example, G. L. Dickinson found cultural grandeur in his visit to China in 1911, while Beatrice and Sidney Webb found dirt, social decay, and disintegration. For Dickinson, the philosophy and aesthetic of the past was foremost; for the Webbs, current social reform; for Roger Fry, Vanessa Bell, and Duncan Grant, "the vast mass of new aesthetic experience" (Fry, "Oriental Art," 793).

Many Chinas and many Englands will be presented in this book, a critical turn advocated by critics Lydia Liu, Shi Shumei, and Haun Saussy. All become part of a dialogue about the concepts of fixed English and Chinese identities in a moving world of culture, politics, and aesthetics. Some of the questions I pose about personal, literary, cultural, and national identities are: What changed the Chinese writers and intellectuals who traveled to England to encounter different literary, cultural and political assumptions from the twenties through the forties? What stays the same and what changes, as Stuart Hall says, when writers and artists travel? Were their literary and cultural subjectivities changed when the political and cultural vocabulary through which they were constituted was being torn apart because of political and cultural events at home as well as their encounters with a new culture? What does it mean to be "Chinese" in England or "English" in China during the Republican period? Can fixed national or political labels address the ambiguities of experience—personal, cultural, and literary—that these intellectuals and writers express in letters, diaries, and literature? How do personal, political, cultural, and aesthetic encounters such as those represented in this study mobilize the ideology, prejudice, aesthetics, and politics of each culture, as Yip Wai-lim poses in his fine study, *Diffusion of Distances?* What understandings and misunderstandings are revealed? How was English modernism represented in China, and the Chinese aesthetic in England, in the early twentieth century? What happens when fixed labels such as "period," "dynasty," "modernism," or "*modeng*" are unable adequately to describe and account for the movements that are emerging in different places in the world? How do different intellectual communities with different cultural, historical, and aesthetic grounding represent themselves to themselves and to others? And to turn the gaze on myself, by training and profession a modernist, how will I, an American critic in the new millennium "represent" this community? How will Asian specialists in America, Mainland China, and Taiwan represent English authors? As I. A. Richards wisely noted about comparative studies of this kind, "What is needed, in brief, is a greater imaginative resource in a double venture—in imagining other purposes than our own and other structures for the thought that serves them" (*Rhetoric,* 41). My book then is an attempt to open up a cultural and literary space between American, British, and Chinese critics where we can develop a stance and a vocabulary that describe the complexities of our literary and cultural relations during the modernist and Republican periods.

Chapter One

Julian Bell Performing "Englishness"

THE SENTIMENTAL AND THE MODERN: PEI JU-LIAN (BELL, JULIAN) TEACHING IN CHINA

Julian Bell was restless. When he graduated from Cambridge University in 1930, he, a poet and activist, wanted to be on the move. Before attending Cambridge, he traveled to France; in 1935, he traveled to China to teach; and in 1937, he became an ambulance driver in the Spanish Civil War. His developing identity as a young man was formed through travel. His "location," as James Clifford observes about such experiences, was "an itinerary rather than a bounded site—a series of encounters and translation" (11) in England, France, China, and Spain. This chapter then traces his restlessness, his inward travel as a boy, and then his actual dwelling in China as a man. It argues that his journey to China was a site not only for his developing political identity, but also a backdrop for an evolving cultural and aesthetic movement, modernism.

"Literal travel," as James Clifford states, "is not a prerequisite for irony, critique or distance from one's home culture" (*Routes,* 4). Julian, not as inward or pacifist or, perhaps, as talented as some in the Bloomsbury circle he emerged from, had been traveling away from home and into battle and history in various countries since the time he was a boy at Leighton and Owens Schools. And yet he was also fixed on home. When he wrote to his mother, Vanessa Bell, of his decision to go to China, we hear the familiar refrain: "I hope this letter won't be upsetting to you." He had an unusually close, honest, some might say, cloying relationship with his mother:

Hogarth Press colophon

I don't want to spend my life away from you, I'm appalled at the thought of leaving you all for three years—it seems a terrific slice out of life. I shall be thirty then—1938. . . . It's the most drastic step I've ever taken I think, after getting born. (16 July 1935)

As Charles Mauron would observe at Julian's memorial, after his death as an ambulance driver in the British Medical Unit in the Spanish Civil War at twenty-nine, he needed elbow room as he moved away from his sometimes stifling home in Bloomsbury to become a "man of action" in China and then Spain.

Kathleen Raine says of their generation, "Just before the outbreak of the second world war, the unreality upon which we were treading rose like a mounting tidal wave; we seemed, straws and corks and drifting fragments that we were, to be soaring to the crest of some strange realization . . . when the wave broke and crashed us all down" (*The Land Unknown,* 86). Julian's temperament and the times led him to select from his environment that which would psychologically bolster his generation: activism. As Woolf describes this generation in "The Leaning Tower":

> In 1930 it was impossible—if you were young, sensitive, imaginative—not to be interested in politics; not to find public causes of much more pressing interest than philosophy. In 1930 young men at college were forced to be aware of what was happening in Russia; in Germany; in Italy; in Spain. They could not go on discussing esthetic emotions and personal relations. They could not confine their reading to the poets; they had to read the politicians. They read Marx. They became communists; they became antifascists. (142)

Julian Bell was no exception. In 1937, Raine wrote to Julian, observing his political commitment and his "constitutional honesty": "I never wrote to you in China then they told me you were in Spain driving an ambulance. More than ever like War and Peace. . . . I suppose medical aid is possibly less dangerous than fighting but I am sorry you are there" (February 1941).

War and hunting had been Julian Bell's hobbies since the time he was a boy—hawks, birds of prey, his favorite. Images of Julian roaming freely on the grounds of Charleston or Wissett as a child appear in Virginia Woolf's *Diary,* his untamed side implicit in her descriptions: "peppery," "undisciplined," "uncouth rather, yet honest," and "old ruffian." Brought up permissively, he apparently ran wild and was often up to tricks and mischief. His mother,

Vanessa Bell, notes in her 1937 *Diary,* "when he was 6 [1914,] Asheham—the war . . . soldiers marching past along the road at the bottom—London air raids—I believe he was cross at not being taken out to see them" (8). He read books at Owens like "Famous Land Fights" and played war in the shadows of pacifist Bloomsbury; he had dreams of mapping and numerous sketches of strategies for battles and war can be found in his papers at King's College. The pacifist stance of his family of conscientious objectors, isolated from mainstream sentiments in England during World War I, was undeniably difficult and isolating for Julian. The message sent was that certain kinds of "action" were "bad." As examples of correct behavior, Duncan Grant and Bunny Garnett had taken up fruit farming as conscientious objectors at a farm near Charleston in 1916, the same classification as Clive Bell and Adrian Stephen; and Leonard Woolf was also exempted from the war because of his "permanent tremor" and Virginia Woolf's precarious mental health (Virginia Woolf to Vanessa Bell, 14 May 1916, *Letters,* 2:95). Yet Julian "traveled" and made "war," first in his drawings for strategic battle and war in Greece and Ireland, and then actual travel to China and Spain, places that would be crucial to his developing identity. Actual wars—not sketches of war strategies—surrounded him in both the turbulent Sino-Japanese War and growing civil war in China. "The making and unmaking of identities," according to Clifford, "takes place in contact zones, along the policed and transgressive intercultural frontiers" (*Routes,* 7). As we trace Julian's military interests in childhood and his encounters in China, we might speculate about the conflicts between the pacifist forces in his home and the unruly forces in England that "variously empowered and compelled him" to travel away to wars in China and then Spain. This is vividly described in Peter Stansky and William Abrahams' book about Julian Bell and John Cornford, *Journey to the Frontier.*[1] Going to China was an escape from Bloomsbury, "a genteel form of suicide" (250).

In 1937, Julian Bell penned some notes for a memoir, sometimes called his *China Diary.*[2] Just shy of twenty-nine, he wrote in his *Diary* after his sixteen-month stay at National Wuhan University, Hankou [Hankow], China, September 1935–January 1937, that he had "ceased to be a young man in any serious sense." Yet, he said, he still sometimes had the "feeling of not being perfectly grown up" (1). These ambivalent feelings about maturity, reflected in the writing, adventures, passions, and tensions of his short life are expressed as he leaves China and plans to join the Spanish Civil War with thousands of idealists from all over the world—just as Picasso finishes his painting of the horrors of war in *Guernica*. Feeling perhaps that his life might be in danger because of what he, with exaggeration, termed his "revolutionary activities" in China, he is impelled, he says, by "natural sentiment and vanity" to "leave a monument," his *China Diary,* a rather loose assortment of descriptions and observations of about fifty notebook pages.

When Julian wrote, it was a defining moment of his generation that lived under the threat of war. Revolution was in the air and not even T. S. Eliot's insistence on tradition, as Kathleen Raine would write, "could arrest the progressive dismantling of civilization (which indeed he [Eliot] himself saw) from the Impressionists to the Cubists, from the Surrealists to the Existentialists" (*The Land Unknown,* 150). Virginia Woolf observed at this time, "everywhere change, everywhere revolution. In Germany, in Russia, in Italy, in Spain, all the old hedges were being rooted up, all the old towers were being thrown down" ("Leaning Tower," 147). Observing only revolutions in Europe, Julian would expand Woolf's sites to the revolutions in Spain and China.

It is not irrelevant then, as Maynard Keynes would state in a testimonial for Julian after his early death, that he grew up in a circle of British life that would "prove of some real importance in his ability to convey to Chinese pupils the current thought and feelings of the English" (Julian Bell, *Testimonials in Support of Application*). Growing up in Bloomsbury, said Keynes, also gave Julian the opportunity to know intimately those who did much "to mold the direction of taste and accomplishments in both literature and art." Julian, however, would not only convey Bloomsbury tastes in China, but also the political commitments and partisanship of a new generation in England.

When Julian arrived in China, he discovered like many of us that he liked the people, the country, and teaching. He wrote home, "My neighbors, the Chens, are angels of light. And ultra-Bloomsbury-Cambridge culture. He's a friend of Goldies [Goldsworthy Lowes Dickinson]. Both know Shu [Xu Zhimo], the great link with Bloomsbury. The whole social ambiance incredibly like home" (Letter to Eddy Playfair, September 1935). Stuart Hall asks, "What stays the same when you travel?" (Clifford, *Routes,* 44). In Julian's experience, what remained the same was the desire for the intimacy, friendship, and intellectual conversation that he had experienced in his home among Bloomsbury friends. It is what he found and maintained in China through the Chens. What transformed was his maturity and sense of self, as he was entangled in a mercurial affair with a married woman from another culture that did not welcome such public "intimacies": his Armageddon.

Though apprehensive relatives and friends warned of his lack of cultural and linguistic preparation for travel to China, Julian fared well because he was open, curious, physically fit, not concerned about amenities, and, importantly, was immediately drawn into the intellectual community of the Chens. Innes Jackson Herdan, at Wuhan at the same time, described him as "impulsive" and "kind." He charmed Chen Ling Shuhua, the wife of the dean who hired him, and she became his linguistic and cultural guide from the start. He also maintained a certain cultural "fixity" (Clifford, *Routes,* 42) about the landscape of China, relating in a 1936 Wuhan essay that elements of the Mediterranean were present in Wuhan's outdoor life. On the streets, he observed people quarreling and bargaining as in Marseilles and Dijon, and he saw something of England in "the grey subtleties of rain and the brown and green landscape." Yet he was also alive to the "foreign," the astonishing sight of the foreign junks on the river. He later remarked in the same essay that he was surprised by and drawn to the respect for art and literature that he found in Chinese culture, another aspect that made him feel at home ("The Road to Wuchang").

Julian's generation would eventually *act* in the world. The favored Cambridge word, "detachment," as Kathleen Raine, Julian's contemporary at Cambridge would say, was "no longer used: now we were 'observers,' God's spies seeing far beneath us the human scene, as if we were ourselves at once spectators and authors of that play but not its enactors" (*The Land Unknown,* 86). Julian searched for a job after a year's sojourn in Paris, 1927–28, and graduation from Cambridge University in 1930. After odd writing jobs in London, he talked of going to Spain but was discouraged by his family. Consequently, he decided to go China, and acquired his teaching post through Margery Fry's contact with the Chens, when she visited China in 1933 as well as through Liao Hong Ying, a visiting scholar from China at Oxford. Both Margery Fry and Mary Michaelis who traveled with Liao were part of the Universities China Mission endowed by the Boxer Indemnity. Beginning in 1934, Indemnity Funds were set aside to enable educational exchange, and this was enormously important for the development of National Wuhan University as well as many cultural projects and relationships described in this book.

These funds enabled Margery Fry, a social reformer who helped to found the Howard League for prisoners, to make a lecture tour of Chinese universities and to visit prisons and factories. During this tour, she observed children laboring in the silk factories of Shanghai. She wrote of the

> wretched little girls standing shaking with fatigue, stirring cocoons in boiling water, their hands and faces sodden with steam, small boys handling red hot metal in a wretched roofed space in between two buildings, the only place they have to live and sleep and work (probably to die in). (Jones, *Margery Fry*, 196)

China and its hard-working people made a big impression, and upon her return, she gave talks all over England. She spoke of her observations of Chinese prisons, and an eighth-century poem, "On Finding a Painting of Buddha on the Wall of His Prison Cell" appeared in the *Howard Journal*. The desperate living conditions she saw propelled her to work for the China Campaign Committee (as did Dora Russell and Dorothy Woodman, wife of Kingsley Martin) that sent humanitarian aid and medical supplies to China in the 1940s under the auspices of madame Chiang Kai-shek. They tried to keep China and its problems in the news.

Not only did Margery Fry travel to China to lecture and observe the culture, but she also met the Chens. She first introduced Bloomsbury through presenting a painting by her brother, Roger Fry, to Professor S. K. Wang, the president of the University. After meeting Margery Fry, Liao Hong Ying, a student, traveled from Wuhan, China, to Oxford University in England in 1935 as a Boxer Indemnity scholar to study agronomy. After becoming acquainted with some in Bloomsbury, it was she who recommended Julian Bell for the job in English, following Magnus Irvine at Wuhan. Julian's professorship in Wuhan would also be partially supported by Boxer Indemnity Funds.

Julian's letters and *China Diary* reveal his engagement with teaching at Wuhan National University, which he compared favorably to Cambridge. In the contract of appointment between the Sino-British Cultural Association and National Wuhan University, he was appointed to be a professor of English and English literature for two years. For various reasons, Julian arrived at National Wuhan University late, after the term began and several cables to Dean Chen indicate that he had "difficulties" that prevented earlier arrival (perhaps his illness, see note 7 and Sino-British Cultural Association, Appointment Process Letter). The appointment, dating from 1 October 1935, contained a one-year probation. The teaching periods were from nine to twelve hours per week and the salary 700 pounds per year, 300–400 pounds from the university and the balance from the Board of Trustees for the Administration of Boxer Indemnity Funds, remitted by the British government for the establishment of the professorship. Julian was also to be provided "living accommodations . . . at moderate rates" by the university, and after the expiration of the contract, or after the first year in case either party wished to terminate, 110 pounds for passage to England. After the first probationary year, Julian was appointed for a second year in a University document that indicated that he filled the vacant chair "to the great benefit of the students [and] the latter did admirably well with his indefatigable zeal during his period of teaching in 1935–36." His contract was signed by S. K. Wang, president of the University and Shi Ying, dean of technology, a representative of the Sino-British Association, who was later politically associated with the nationalists. His academic

Chinese translations of Virginia Woolf's novels. Courtesy of the author.

dean was Chen Yuan, Shuhua's husband; his chair, Professor Fang Zhong. These details became important when Julian had to terminate his contract because of the scandal of his affair with Ling Shuhua approximately sixteen months later.

He was known to most at the university as a "poet" and described in the National Wuhan University List of Faculty, 1935–38, as "M.A. Cambridge. Writer research student." He taught three courses at National Wuhan University: English composition and Shakespeare (about ten pupils in each class), and gave a public lecture once a week on the English modernists, totaling about sixteen hours of lecture and supervision. Julian complained to Playfair that he was overworked because he had to spend so much time preparing. He also wrote to his mother that he had difficulty with the modern literature course and wondered "why I thought myself fit to lecture to anyone on English literature" (16 October 1935, CHAO).

Eddy Playfair marveled at his covering French literature, ethics, military history, politics, and "almost anything but English literature" in his courses (29 March 1936). He sarcastically urged him to publish his lecture notes as his own *Letters from John Chinaman*,[3] playing upon G. L. Dickinson's satire on the English stance on the Boxer Rebellion. Playfair queried, "Are you resolved to overthrow Confucianism and the civilisation of millennia before you leave China, and to substitute that of Cambridge and Bloomsbury? It sounds like it" (17 April 1936).

Julian's academic stance in China suggests James Clifford's notion of "traveling culture." He brought Bloomsbury ethics, British modernism and literary criticism to Wuhan. His teaching of "Bloomsbury" in China is confirmed in a letter to his aunt, Virginia Woolf:

> It's lovely country and the Chinese are charming; lecturing on the moderns, 1890–1914; 1914–36. I have to read the writers; what is one to do: we all write too much; I shall make the Lighthouse I think, a set book. (undated, ca. fall 1935)

In his official 1936 course description, he added, "The course mainly teaches modern British literature, also introducing other European countries. . . . Important writers and their works of each period are studied together with the literary trend and the historical background. Students must read several required readings" (National Wuhan University Course Descriptions). When Julian introduced *To the Lighthouse* in English to his Chinese students, translations,

English speaking contest, organized by Julian Bell for his literature students, Wuhan University Library steps, including Ye Junjian, far left. By permission of the chief archivist, Wuhan University Library, China.

Julian Bell's English literature students from the department of Chinese literature, 1936. By permission of the chief archivist, Wuhan University Library, China.

another form of travel, already existed in Chinese. In the 1930s, in fact, there were already translations of *A Room of One's Own* and *Flush*. During the same term, he was also teaching "Literary Criticism," a discourse undeveloped in China at the time. His description: "The course studies literary theories of Western literature and the development of different literary schools from the historical point of view. It covers from the Greek, Roman period to the Renaissance to recent times. The course also includes speaking and reading classics." During the same semester, Dean Chen was teaching "European Novels" from Russia, France, and Germany. The influence of this humanist tradition on Chinese thinking from the May Fourth movement through the period that Julian Bell was in Wuhan cannot be underestimated. We note, then, that the Boxer Indemnity Fund, at one time administered by Bertrand Russell in England, enabled intellectual contacts all over China, particularly in Beijing, Shanghai, Tianjin, and Wuhan. Through the teaching of Julian Bell, I. A. Richards, William Empson, and others in the thirties, Chinese students learned of modern British literature. This "way into" the culture—through travel, translation, and teaching—encouraged later literary experiments in China to be described in chapter 3, "East-West Literary Conversations." What happens in travel is that "one group's core is another's periphery" (Clifford, *Routes*, 25): modern British literature became a periphery in China during parts of the Republican period.

Upon arrival in China, Julian was given a Chinese name, "Pei Ju-Lian," (Bell Ju-lian, a phonetic rendering of his name, *p*s now changed to *b*s in pinyin, a modern Romanization of Chinese), which later led to humorous banter from Eddy Playfair. He wrote there's "a pleasantly puritan tang about it-Hope-to-keep chaste Bell, or Extreme-integrity Bell, or even Very-cheap-auction Bell" (Letter to Julian Bell, 26 November 1935). Later, Archibald Rose informed him that the most suitable meaning for Pei Ju-Lian would be, "Peace of mind founded upon ancient tradition" (6 January 1936).

In the end, though, China did not bring peace of mind to Julian. He brought the Bloomsbury ethic of personal relations to China. He wrote to Virginia Woolf, "China's leading woman writer, my Dean's wife with whom I'm platonically in love . . . is a passionate admirer of your work" (undated, probably fall 1936, Monks House Papers). Shuhua was "like" Virginia, and focused upon her developing career as a short-story writer.

Julian was quite engaged with his students and described them to Marie Mauron in France soon after his arrival: "I have ten advanced students, rather shy but very gifted, rather intelligent, three or four of them with talent as writers, I think. Like all Chinese, they are charming" (24 November 1936). The word "charming" used to describe the Chinese will appear again in other's letters. He noted his students' reading, their appearance, and evaluated their progress in the *China Diary*, keeping a journal like many teachers who have since traveled to China:

> Zhong [Chung], C. C. has Aristotle, Ibsen, classics, Greek. All the whole plays. Corneille. Reads from Moliere. Long crooked face. Khaki dress. Good fluent English. Talkative. Well read.
>
> Yuan, E. K. is very honest.
>
> Wu Bin is honest tho' not brilliant. good vivid writing and very charming.
>
> Zhang [Chang] En-Shou is very bright, a born moralist, and doesn't seem to me to copy from the authorities.

Ye Junjian, Julian Bell's favorite student at Wuhan University. Julian Bell; photographer. By permission of the chief archivist, Wuhan University Library, China.

Zhou [Chuo] Shihmei rather elementary.

Tong, also, elementary. small. black double-teeth. [Missionary?] not much doing. On the whole a decent standard of intelligence.

Shao, Penjian. Othello. As You Like It. very good continental list. reads French. Pearl Buck. Chinese dress, round face able to talk.

Nieh, Fujian. very talkative and intelligent.

One of Julian's students, Ye Junjian, with whom he would develop a close friendship, is described as well read, very intelligent and charming:

Yeh, C. C. (Ye Junjian) is also intelligent and independent. Macbeth. Another mention of Dostoevsky. The paragraph uses: not so good. Supervision: G. Eliot, Balzac, M. Bovary, Maupassant, G. Sand, A. France (little), Zola, Wells, Wilde, Shaw, Dostoevsky, Turgenev, Chekoff, Gogol, Pushkin, Gorki, Ivanoff, Lybedev, [Dischenko]. Handsome, open face, khaki, very intelligent indeed. Charming. Read a Conrad.

Evidence that Ye Junjian is a favorite is confirmed in correspondence. Julian wrote to Vanessa, "Yeh [Ye] paid me a visit this morning: I think he likes me a good deal: he's a most promising writer and very handsome" (10 January 1936). He referred often to Ye's charm, intelligence and popularity, and to a 1936 summer journey to Chengdu where he was "a perfect traveler." Also on this one-month venture into Tibet was Derek Bryan, Vice-Counsel in Chunking, Foreign Services, and Hansen Lowe, a geologist. In an interview, Derek Bryan described Julian as "very fit," as he frequently engaged in shooting and boating. In a later letter to Eddy Playfair, Julian noted that "his favorite pupil," now a teacher at National Wuhan University, had insomnia and was about to have a nervous breakdown because he was being overworked by the university (13 April 1936, JB). Christopher Isherwood and W. H. Auden, who also met Ye in China, commented on his "charm"; E. M. Forster observed the same when Ye visited England.

In my interview with Ye Junjian in China in August 1995, he acknowledged that Julian Bell was his teacher in British studies at National Wuhan University the year before he graduated and went to Japan in 1936. But Julian, more importantly, he said, was "my friend":

We were together. We were very good friends . . . yes, only the last year. Of course, not much study of literature; rather we had private conversation. . . . yes, friendship. Of course, he was not a typical British intellectual.[4]

This intimacy is confirmed in a letter from Ye to Julian as he made his way to Nagasaki in 1936. Ye spoke personally of women, suggesting that Julian had become his teacher in more ways than one. Having met a friendly German woman traveling alone without her husband, he fantasized about her departing words, " 'If [only] you could travel with me!' . . . Believe me, my teacher, this is a real romantic fact I ever experienced in my life; it is not a lie." Later he described Japanese girls who are "particularly lovely," and said that he was "almost fascinated by the girl-boys!" (YJ to JB, 14 February 1936).

Ye, armed with an introduction from Julian Bell, made contact with the editor of *Tian Xia Monthly*, and worried about his English being good enough to do a translation. Waxing expansively, he wrote what he later dismissed as "nonsense," his liking of Europeans, particularly females, and he noted that he became "even religious" when he thought "the world is full of so much nice and lovable people" (14 February 1936). He advised Julian to return home via Russia, a country he himself longed to visit, rather than Burma because of the danger of bandits. But Julian died while Ye was in Japan.

In Japan in 1936–37, Ye was in a culturally compromised position, "a paradoxical situation," he related in his interview. On the one hand, the Chinese were fighting a brutal war with Japan on Chinese soil; on the other, Japan itself was still a relatively stable country (while China was in chaos) that offered young, talented Chinese career opportunities in translation. Here again, travel to Japan offered an "identity" not available in China at the time, as England would offer cultural and aesthetic detours for other Chinese intellectuals and writers, at other times, when nationalism was oppressive at home. Ye was a Marxist sympathizer and a progressive writer who identified with Lu Xun. Xu Zhengbang, the archivist at Wuhan University, noted in a conversation that Ye Junjian was introduced to be a teacher and translator in Japan by Chinese progressives. The relationships Ye had in Japan with "another generation" of Japanese were not, as he related in an interview, characterized by the "brutality" that the Chinese experienced at the hands of the Japanese just before the official breakout of the war in 1937. Here again, travel made a difference. The change in place of encounter transformed a young Chinese translator's "Chinese" identity and relation with the Japanese, reminding us again of "identity [Ye's Chinese identity] as a politics rather than an inheritance" (Clifford, *Routes*, 46). Had Ye been on Chinese soil, he might have been one of the thousands killed in the Japanese rape of Nanjing; instead, he reported that he was treated with respect—though Chinese—in his professional role in Japan.

Julian clearly admired him, noting to Playfair that Ye had written a novel in Esperanto and "he keeps himself at the university by journalism and translations, and comes of a poor landowners family in the depths of the country. Ten times as alive, awake and conversational as any of the others" (4 May 1937). It is this background that led to Ye to association with communist leftist factions, as well as travel to Russia. He and Julian shared an interest in politics, and he asserted, "Of course Julian Bell came to China not for [laugh] the sake of teaching or for liberty's sake. He was interested in the situation in China . . . He was in touch with most of the progressive intellectuals." Nevertheless, Ye described Julian as a "poet" not a "politician" when he arrived, and, indeed, though Julian was giving up on poetry, this reputation preceded him in China. But sixteen months after his arrival, when Julian quit his job to join the Spanish Civil War, Ye notes his political transformation. "At that time the situation was very acute, the fight between fascism and democracy in Spain. A lot of young men went there to fight in the name of democracy . . . a lot of Americans went there, still more Europeans, most of them were accomplished . . . writers . . . a lot of young celebrities" (interview by the author). While England, France, and the United States cultivated a neutrality about the war, the Soviets developed strategies for controlling the Spanish Republican Army and the government, and young men like Julian fell.

Ye continued to write to Julian after his departure from China. Leo Harvey, another Englishman from Oxford, would replace Julian in October 1937 and stay only six months until March 1938. Ye, because of his fine English skills, became an important translator in China during the Sino-Japanese War for English writers like W. H. Auden, whom Ye described as personally "careless" in his homosexual relations in China, and Christopher Isherwood, whom Ye observed was "sensible." Agnes Smedley, for whom he also worked as a translator, was someone he liked but whom he described as "temperamental." She reacted, he said, in a "fit of anger" over his being reassigned by the Chinese government to work as a translator for someone else in the Communist Party instead of her. He also worked for Mao Zedong. Upon Julian's death, he wrote to Vanessa Bell, visited England, 1944–49, and studied at King's College with Dadie Rylands in the footsteps of Xu Zhimo. He assessed this "the best period" of his life. When he was in China during the war before the surrender of the Japanese, he worked very hard as a translator, but when he went to Cambridge, he wrote, "I was deeply involved in my personal writing. I did some writing because I didn't have time in China. It was I think the best period in my life in Cambridge because I was far away from these conflicts" (Ye, Interview by the author). Travel to England empowered him as a writer, creating conditions not available to him as a working translator in China; it brought an identity and peace of mind not available in China. This, too, is a benefit of travel. In the 1950s, he again visited England and was escorted around London and Cambridge by Bloomsbury friends.

Julian adopted a "crusading spirit" while teaching in China and often spoke of "shaking up" the "timid" students, particularly about sex and the expression of sentiment, as he had with Ye Junjian. He lectured on the "indecencies of the moderns" and he criticized the students' "sentimentality." He was "puzzled" by the unfamiliarity of forms that his students favored: "I find that students prefer to write sketches, descriptions, prose poems, rather than essays of the type I am familiar with." Believing that this intellectual stance was encouraged by the teaching methods, he complained about conventional letter-writing exercises: "Really what I am reading here is English manners . . . who teaches them to do such silly things?" He criticized the method in a note to Shuhua, observing that the students during a composition class "invent means by which an idiot foreigner can be conveyed from Hankou [Hankow] to Wuchang, and write a letter explaining how useful too" (undated). Correcting the business letters of students, Julian objected to the pedagogic approach, used more frequently for girls, Shuhua reported in her autobiography, *Ancient Melodies*. In reflecting upon Samuel Richardson and the epistolary origins of the English novel, we note that letter writing does cultivate the personal voice that informs the genre of the English novel. It is perhaps this cultivation of the personal voice and letter-writing experience that propelled women writers such as Bing Xin and Ling Shuhua into the writing of children's stories and then short stories in China.

In an early essay that Julian wrote for a National Wuhan University publication in 1936, he notes, however, that there is "a general—and to an Englishman astonishing—respect and taste for the arts and literature. . . . But what is curious to the foreigner is to find that the arts are pursued above all by the cultivation of sensibility, of taste, of intuition." With his respect for the "application of intelligence to the world of emotions"—his anti-sentimentalism campaign described above—and to the analysis and discussion of art, he is surprised to find, in the end, that the Chinese painters and poets who cultivated "sensibility" and "intuition" are "at least as successful, judging by results as those of pure intelligence" (*The Road to Wuchang*). With a strong shift to appreciation of the Chinese culture, he yields his predisposition to eighteenth-century "rationalism" and English "intelligence" to Chinese "sensibility." He acknowledged, at one point, that what seemed to him to be the "natural attitude" was not so to the Chinese people that he met.

As part of his campaign against "sentimentality," Julian gave the students specimens of I. A. Richards's literary passages from *Principles of Literary Criticism* (JB to EP, 16 May 1936), attempting to hone the students' criteria for literary judgment and to nurture the "theorizing" skills he found lacking. Bell had rejected both I. A. Richards and T. S. Eliot in his Cambridge days. He felt that they among the moderns believed themselves to be in reaction against the romantics, but were themselves "inverted romantics." Writing in the *Cambridge Review,* five years before his voyage to China, he historicized romanticism as nearly everything in England after 1798 and France after 1820. He distinguished "romantics" (and particularly romantic poetry) by "their metrical licentiousness . . . their constant appeal to the emotions . . . their confused thinking . . . and their ability to use vague suggestions to produce aesthetic effects by religious overtones of language." He was quite vehement in his rejection of T. S. Eliot's religious and moral overtones and politics and allied Eliot with other nationalist and reactionary politicians including Herr Hitler and Signor Mussolini in an essay he wrote at Cambridge, "Politics and the Good Life." He attacked Eliot's "Commentaries" that appeared in the January and April 1931 *Criterion,* particularly what he labeled the "fascism" of forcing tastes upon others in the name of "Values and the Good Life." He particularly resisted Eliot's assertion, "Asceticism must first, certainly, be practised by the few, and it must be definite enough to be explained to, and ultimately imposed upon, the many; imposed in the name of something in which they must be made to believe" ("Ecrasez L'Infame"). Julian, a socialist, accepted Bentham's utilitarian formula that "poetry is as good as pushpin," and was insistent on the equal value "of a Vendean peasant's state of mind listening to M. le Cure's sermon to a garage hand's at the cinema" (*Politics,* 7). Fearing Eliot's authoritarianism, he was alarmed by "a marked similarity" between Eliot and his friends' "judgments of value and the programs of Nazis and Fascists" (*Politics,* 2). The authoritarian tendency in Eliot identified by Julian (and developed in Frank Kermode's *The Sense of an Ending*) is prescient given recent criticism on Eliot and anti-Semitism.[6] Interestingly, Julian did not comment on the totalitarian, the authoritarian aspects of Chinese culture or the "moral" or didactic use of literature in China at the time.

This literary-critical evolution is revealed in his *China Diary*. First, he was a disciple, like everyone in Cambridge, of G. E. Moore's *Principia Ethica* valuing pleasure in literature. At Cambridge, he became more "consciously and unconsciously literary." He noted that he "read . . . Eliot and Richards and . . . Wyndham Lewis, and after a first stage of self-conscious virgin naturalism set about becoming a thoroughgoing classicist reactionary—a phase that led into . . . dealings with [Alexander] Pope" (*China Diary*). In an essay, "Ecrasez L'Infame," he attacked Eliot, who, he observed, set himself up as a moralist, even a "messiah." He attacked the kind of community that Eliot envisioned as realizing "the good life": "The population should be homogeneous. What is still more important is unity of religious background . . . And a spirit of excessive tolerance is to be deprecated." Identifying Eliot with the Catholic political ideal of a G. K. Chesterton or Engelbert Dollfuss, Julian rejected the messianic stance as he rejected "the prophet" in D. H. Lawrence.

Julian's stance toward Eliot differed from other poets of his generation at Cambridge. Kathleen Raine, for example, noted that "The Waste Land" had given her generation's spiritual state "its enduring expression":

> It was a shock to many of us, who in his "Waste Land" recognized our own world, when it presently began to be whispered that T. S. Eliot was a Christian; what to us was mere reality was to him the hell of Dante, the state and place of those cut off from God. We disregarded his theology; yet a generation saturated in Atheism, Freudianism and Marxism inhabited, as we inhabited no other poem, Eliot's "The Waste Land." (39)

Julian, too acknowledged that "Eliot and Huxley were Cambridge, Joyce never."

As I read Julian Bell's letters and writings along with the Chinese critic He Li (probably a pen name), the tensions and confusions in the term "modernism" mounted. In He Li's discussion of "Modernism and China," summarized from the important *People's Daily* 1983 debate, I was confirmed in my view that modernism was more than literary techniques. It was a cultural and political issue. Julian Bell criticized the Chinese "sentimental" literary taste and longed for the application of hard "masculine" intelligence to the arts and the introduction of British modernism (or, at least, Bloomsbury) into China, but he was discussing culture and politics. This sentimental strain would later develop into Butterfly literature in China (Yuan Yang Hu Die). In reading the criticism of He Li, I discovered that the stream-of-consciousness style, or the stream of personal feeling, was perceived as "western," "narcissistic," "bourgeois," and "weak." The didactic tendencies apparent in socialist-realist writing, and later reinforced by the Communist Party's uniform views of literature, are asserted by He Li—though Julian Bell failed to remark upon these distinctions in his writing.

Lecturing on the moderns at National Wuhan University, Julian writes to Virginia Woolf explaining that he will divide the course into two parts, 1890–1914 and 1914–36, and that he will "make the Lighthouse, I think, a set book." Julian, a classicist, was drawn to the eighteenth century and wrote his King's College thesis on Pope. He praised the moderns for freeing literature of cant and praised their economy and use of concrete and exact words and images. In his Hogarth Letter on Roger Fry, he writes of being ashamed of "feelings" and "sentimentality"—perhaps a quality nurtured in British boarding schools. Despite his great affection for Roger Fry, who may have influenced him more than anyone except his mother, he writes:

> I have always found it very difficult to write about serious, extensive, publishable emotions. They inhibit my powers of writing verse completely, and even in prose I become ashamed at my sentimentality. I have the highest admiration for those who can turn their private emotions into the impersonal parallel constructions of deliberate art; for my own part, I can only escape sentiment by frigidity. (*Memorial Volume*, 258)

Frigidity: blurring sentimentalism, romanticism, and private emotions, he turns away from the "worn-out uselessness of the romantic tradition." His temperamental affinity, then, is for the rationalism of the eighteenth century. But it is not only the subject matter of the romantics but the style, the subjectivity and vagueness, and Julian's desire as a poet for "a return to simpler, firmer more exact forms."

Roger Fry, art critic and mentor to Julian, is praised in Julian's frustrated Hogarth Letter because of his rationalism and scientific spirit, so subtle that he "could cope with and enjoy chaos itself" (*Memorial Volume*, 261). Admiring the way Fry uses "his sensibility as a piece of apparatus, taking readings and giving one results," Julian rejects people who gush or go into raptures over scenery and sunsets partly because of "the vulgarity of showing emotion" (Hogarth Letter, 18) — a reaction, undoubtedly, to Victorian sentimentality, and the policy of repression of feeling in the boarding schools that he and other young British men such as George Orwell attended and suffered. Julian, however, was unaware that the expression of emotion and feeling meant something different in China at this time. To express private emotion was culturally unfamiliar in Chinese literature and was even then a transgressive act.

China at this stage — politics and literature being more overtly intertwined — indulged in the old sentimentalities in Butterfly literature, popular in 1910–20, as well as certain periods of British literature, particularly romanticism. The Chinese were drawn to romanticism probably because they had a predilection for subjects in which man did not generally appear: the landscapes described in romantic poetry or in painting. They also were drawn to the expressions of self, of subjectivity, and the confessional nature of the poetry. Yet though they preferred these aspects of British romanticism, they neglected one of the important dimensions of the movement, the transformative power of the imagination. They absorbed rather the popular notions of the Byronic romantic hero bent on the dramatic expression of self and personality. This aspect appealed to some Chinese writers, as did Butterfly literature, because it allowed for more overt expression of the emotional life not contained in the traditional Chinese lyric of restraint. This expression of the emotional in literature also may have been a response to a national agenda that had often subsumed the discourse of the individual voice into that of nationalism and patriotism. Mao Zedong theorized "class revolution" in his Yan'an Talks on literature in 1942, but omitted "feeling," "consciousness," and "subjectivity," terms that emerge in the discussion of romanticism between G. L. Dickinson and Xu Zhimo. Chinese writers and intellectuals such as Xu Zhimo and Hu Shi of the May Fourth literary movement in China proposed a new expression of the fullness of individual feeling. They were drawn to what Julian Bell and other British labeled "sentimentalism" or exaggerated feeling, perhaps best represented by Shelley's gesture "I fall upon the thorns of life, I bleed." In general, in the China of the time, the cultivation of such states of mind would be considered an indulgence and did not serve national needs.

I. A. Richards, himself a teacher and reformer in China during the 1920s and 1930s, and his practical criticism proved useful to Julian in his campaign against "sentimentalism" in China, though Julian had reservations about

Richards's critical stances. Richards observes, among politer terms of abuse, few are as effective as "sentimental" or "sentimental rubbish," which is almost the equivalent of "silly" in England. Since the term is an attack on "feeling" rather than "thought," it hints at some kind of weakness of "sensibility" that is hard to rebut. Richards notes that the word "is sometimes not so much the instrument of a statement as an expression of contempt" (*Practical Criticism*, 255), and in his students' responses to his poetry protocols, he finds that the word wavers between foggy description and abuse. Perceptively, he states that "we often use it to say only that there is something wrong in the feelings involved by the thing, whatever it is, which we call sentimental. And we do not attempt to specify what is wrong" (256).

Julian expressed this contempt described by Richards as he bewailed the Chinese love of A. E. Housman. He continued his attack on the discourse of Chinese "sentimentalism" by associating it with the "primitive" in a letter to his mother. The connection between the Chinese and "negroes," as well as earlier mention of women, is revealing. It propels the word "sentimental" into networks of meaning that relate to both racism (primitive, barbarian, cannibal, uncivilized) and sexism (women, feminine feeling) that Marianna Torgovnick writes of in *Gone Primitive*. Julian writes:

> I'm conducting an anti-sentiment campaign—Chinese can't make much of "the moderns," lap down worst products of romanticism like negroes debauched with trade gin. That's what comes of living by sensibility alone.
> (JB to VB, undated, probably 1936)

The racial prejudice in the simile "negroes debauched with trade gin" diminishes both "negroes" and the "sentimental" Chinese taste in one stroke. Julian's description is a political and cultural insult contained in the modernist association between race (the "primitive" Chinese, Indians, negroes), gender (women's expression of emotion and feeling), and styles of literary expression pejoratively described as "sentimental."

Vanessa similarly responded to Julian's remarks, "How odd in a way desperate your students sound with their sentimental romanticism" (VB to JB, 5 July 1936). Again, later, she remarked, "Your view of the Chinese is very interesting and I'm inclined to think you must be right—otherwise surely they couldn't have remained aloof from the world. Nothing but this kind of exquisite dallying with emotion could prevent them from getting involved in practical life and I quite see that it must be termed sentimental" (22 September 1936). Given the "practical life" of the Chinese students at the time, coping with the brutal incursions of the Japanese into China, Vanessa's remark is uninformed. It is difficult, however, to specify the meaning of the term "sentimental," a response that would generally imply an overreaction to the occasion, without knowing the authors or the cultural occasions that elicited this remark from Julian Bell. What is clear is that there is a cultural predisposition toward certain styles of expression and description in literature and cultures, another aspect of "translation" from one language, literature, and culture to another.

It should be noted here that women are also described or criticized as being "sentimental" in English novels, the criticism being that their feelings are too easily stirred or expressed in ways deemed to be excessive like the "primitive" Chinese that Julian described. The word "sentimentalism" is bandied about in the letters, and the term gains its cultural charge not only from the reaction against Victorian sentimentalities of family and nation, but also from its associations with "feelings," the "feminine," and the "romantic." British modernism was defining itself in opposition to these qualities.

Even to the Chinese, the words "sentimental" and "romantic" meant a kind of indulgence in the inner life and feeling during a period of heightened nationalism and utilitarianism in the late 1920s through 1930s. It was applied often to writers in the Crescent Moon group considered to be too interested in the individual, the personal, the psychological of British modernism, and too little interested in the "realism" of Soviet Union and Japanese socialist circles—a stance that can be found, for example, in early forms in Mao Zedong's Talks at Yan'an. This tendency develops in Marxist criticism, and we note the strains in the Russian formalist critic Mikhail Bakhtin, who praises Dostoevsky's "socially" wrought novels while lambasting, in contrast, "the degenerate decadent psychologism of Proust and Joyce, signaling the decline and fall of bourgeois literature" (*Problems*, 37). The modernist stream of consciousness or indirect discourse that sought to represent the inner life of thought and feeling (such as in Mansfield's work) would often be viewed as a "sentimental" fantasy in China in the late 1920s. Here, the critic, Qu Qiubai, also uses "sentimental" to criticize the literary taste of Xu Zhimo and his literary society, who were drawn to expressive, Western literature at a historical moment when the Marxist Literary Research Society announced its "realism." The caustic response of the realists to the Crescent Moon group was based then on the Crescent

Moon's embrace of "romantic" or "fantasist" literature as well as their Western-oriented values.

What Xu Zhimo and other Chinese writers reveal in their so-called "sentimental" responses to certain kinds of Western literature is that literature was a safe space to express feeling and interest in psychology and other forms of individualism and expression snuffed out in Chinese culture by the authoritarian, socialist government and the desperation of daily life in a time of war. The term "sentimental," malleable in its use in different cultures, will help to organize a later dialogue between E. M. Forster and Xiao Qian in chapter 3, "East-West Conversations." Their conversation, the specificity of which wards off current postcolonial cliche, grounds an aspect of early aesthetic and intellectual encounter that prepares the way for later modernist aesthetics.

THE PROVINCIAL TURNS POLITICAL

When Julian first arrived at National Wuhan University on a two-year teaching contract, he described it to Virginia Woolf as "a provincial affair," a university with a staff of about one hundred. National Wuhan University was 400 miles up the Yangtze River from Nanjing, a university outside the town on a hill overlooking beautiful East Lake. Established in 1928, Wang Shijie was designated as the president of the university, and he set about persuading many Beijing University faculty to join him, among them Chen Yuan, who became dean of humanities. Wang sought to make Wuhan the best university in central China, to rank, as Su Xuelin reports with "Cambridge University, Columbia University, the University of Berlin and the University of Paris." Wuhan achieved a fine reputation in a short time, though the anti-Japanese and civil wars disrupted its growth.

Many of the faculty that Julian met in the 1930s had been to Europe and were, according to Mr. Xu Zhengbang, "open" and "liberated." Instead of a settled or "antique" place, Julian was surrounded by people with complex histories of travel and movement. Julian, with his limited language skills and access to the Chinese culture, nevertheless, passed judgment: it was "provincial" and he wished he were in Sichuan or Peiping (Beijing). Woolf responded to his complaint, commenting on "the mitigated culture" of Wuhan, comparing her own poignant and tragic youthful experiences to his:

> I hope now you are not dismal; still it's a curse, your being so far away and then expect the mitigated culture of your university is rather like skimmed

milk. That's what some of the other English professors felt, I know. I expect it will be much better when you ride off into the wilds with your charming student [Ye Junjian]. And I expect in after years the reality will seem much more exciting than it does now. It will make a background. In fact I think you are much to be envied. I wish I had spent three years in China at your age—the difference was, though, at your age, what with all the family deaths and extreme intensities—father, mother, Stella, Thoby, George, Jack—I felt I had lived through all the emotions and only wanted peace and loneliness. All the horrors of life had been pressed in to our eyes so very crude and raw. (21 May 1936).

Woolf envied his youthful explorations given the deaths and "extreme intensities" in her family. He complained, nevertheless, that one could not get the full force of China in Wuhan as one might, for instance, in Sichuan:

there's no real culture—even faintly foreign society. And the Chinese are, I feel very different, if one wants intimacy of intellectual conversation. At least these rather stiff and provincial academics are. Peiping [Beijing] is utterly different; there are genuine flexible Chinese, some intelligent foreigners mix with them. (Letter to EP, February 1936)

Julian here equates "real" culture with the presence of "foreign" or Western culture in China rather than the indigenous culture. His desire for social and intellectual intimacy and his need to find English-speaking foreigners reveal not only his preference for certain cultural styles of discourse but also cultural arrogance and limited understanding of Chinese intellectual circles.

This sense of the "provincial," however, did not last. Julian soon discovered that Wuhan was in a state of political turmoil because of the North China imbroglio. This excited his political interests. Because of its central location in China on the Yangtze River, opposite the more commercial city of Hankow, Wuhan was a strategic city, often in the center of political crosscurrents. The Japanese were advancing in northern China, and as the Japanese forces neared, Julian observed that there was great tension among his colleagues, who talked of death "to keep their courage up, and generally rather Rupert Brooke on the pontoon feeling and the Reichstag fire" (JB to EP, 1 November 1935). He observed that all the Chinese seemed to want war with the Japanese, though most expected defeat. Always thinking about strategy as he had from his days at Cambridge—here he is in the middle of a "real" war—Julian thought it would be wise for the Chinese to wait. At the same time, the revolution within the country continued, and Julian wrote to Playfair that there was no question that Chiang Kai-shek [Jiang Jieshi] had beaten the communists, causing them to withdraw into the mountains for the winter. A year later, in December 1936, Julian would learn that the communists had besieged Jiang Jieshi [Chiang Kai-shek] and virtually imprisoned him in Xi'an in order to create a unified Chinese front to the Japanese. Hu Shi, ambassador to the United States in 1937–38, reflecting on the situation that Julian observed, stated, "If I were asked to sum up the present condition in my country, I would not hesitate to say that China is literally bleeding to death" ("Biography").

Julian took sides against the Japanese during the Sino-Japanese War (1937–45), and admitted to Playfair that he was so "very pro-chinese in the political situation—and so unpatriotic. Terrible currying favor like this, no doubt, but I can't help thinking it really gives them a juster image of England if I slay Mr. Kipling and Sir John Sims" (12 October 1935). One senses here that Julian is "performing" being English, in the sense that Judith Butler writes about "performing" gender, humorously pretending to slay the imperial notions of a Rudyard Kipling in India in China, not an attractive stance given the suffering of China during this war. The students at Wuhan, sensitive to China's "weak" stance internationally, attacked the faculty for its passivity and politics while the civil struggle between the nationalists [Guomindang] and the communists raged, and the Japanese advanced. In early 1937, the antiresistance movement against Japan developed on the campus just as Julian was about to leave. The Communist Party stance was more aggressive than the nationalist's, and many of the faculty, according to Julian, were "timid." Students went off to fight to be a part of the war.

What Julian's politics were in China at this moment remain unclear: both the British and the Chinese interestingly make different claims. Quentin Bell in *Bloomsbury Recalled,* the memoir that he completed just before his death, claimed that Julian was "never" procommunist. Given Julian's sympathy with the students who wanted to fight the Japanese and his criticism of the "timid" faculty, it is a fair assumption that he identified with the more aggressive communist stance at this time. When I visited China in March 2000 and discussed Julian's political views with the informed Mr. Xu Zhengbang at Wuhan, he said that the Chinese felt that Julian was procommunist, "and that's why I like him," he added. However, when Julian wrote to Ling Shuhua from London in 1937, he spoke of arguing "acrimoniously" with Vanessa and his friends "who are all drifting toward communism" (30 March 1937). But having seen the force of "the reds" in China, he allied himself with socialism, but not communism, at home.

W. H. Auden and Christopher Isherwood also journeyed to Wuhan University to be near the front lines of the Sino-Japanese War, January to July 1938, to write "a travel book." About six months after Julian's death in the Spanish Civil War, they arrived in Wuhan. They described the campus:

> The university buildings are quite new: they were started in 1931. Their neo-Chinese style of architecture brilliantly combines the old horned roofs with the massive brutality of blank concrete. From the distance, the huge central block, with its rows of little windows, standing magnificently in a

The triangle: Julian Bell; Chen Yuan, Ling's husband; and Ling Shuhua. Julian Bell, photographer. By permission of the chief archivist, Wuhan University Library, China.

wild hilly park beside a big lake, reminds you of pictures of Lhasa. . . . The interior is disappointing, chiefly, no doubt, because the war has cut short the work of decoration. (*Journey to a War,* 159–60)

The university was founded in 1927 but the buildings and dormitories were not completed until about 1931: further work was delayed by the war. The funds were half from Boxer Indemnity Funds, half from the Provincial Chinese government, and the design, interestingly, came from an American architect, F. H. Kalles. Recently, I was told Yale University architecture students traveled to Wuhan to study this architectural style. Auden and Isherwood noted that there were few students at Wuhan when they arrived, mostly postgraduates, and that education was inexpensive. A student needed about 200 Chinese dollars a year for his fees, and family sentiment in China was so strong "that the most distant relatives feel themselves bound in honor to subscribe something towards the education of a really promising scholar" (160).

In Wuhan, the strategic center of the Sino-Japanese War, Julian's theoretical interest in war strategy and politics became engaged on the battlefield of China. Though known as "a poet" when he arrived, he left with a political purpose and imagined writing polemics as he made his way to the Spanish Civil War. Ironically, in 1938, after his death, the theater of the Sino-Japanese War came to Wuhan, and the Japanese took over Canton and Hankow, and Wuhan University moved to West China. Julian Bell not only had the historical impulse to see things as they were in China during his stay, but he also developed a political purpose to urge the world in a certain direction and to fight fascism on its newest front in Spain. He had been preoccupied with the Spanish cause even when in England, and he seemed to finally abandon his aesthetic gaze in China, at least as a profession. Of the second generation of Bloomsbury, he was committed to politics not only because war seemed to be his hobby since the time he was a boy, but also because his generation was drawn into it by the wars in Europe. He decided, after a certain stage, to leave the practice of poetry and painting behind (not particularly encouraged by his family) and to become a good man of action. This was revealed not only by his participation in the politics of China and Spain, but also in his expressed desire "for a violent finish in hot blood" (Julian Bell to Vanessa Bell, 18 January 1937). Had he lived, perhaps he would have become a journalist as Virginia Woolf predicted, emulating Peter Fleming whose life and work he envied, with his years in China and Spain as the backdrop.

FROM FAIRY STORIES TO LETTER QUARRELS: JULIAN BELL AND LING SHUHUA

When Julian arrived in China, he wrote to Eddy Playfair that he was getting into a delicate situation "with the nicest woman I've ever met, Shuhua, my dean's wife. She's as sensitive as Virginia is, intelligent, as nice or nicer than anyone I know is, not pretty but attracts me; a Chinese Bloomsburian" (1 November 1935). Innes Jackson Herdan in her book also described Ling Shuhua as "a great charmer!" Shuhua's friend and fellow writer, Su Xuelin, described her first meeting with Shuhua: "She arrived at Yuan's home with her newly-wed groom, Chen Yuan. She was really beautiful and elegant, like her literary style" (*Luo Jia*, 1990).

Julian, Herdan reported, was "rather apart from the academic circle" there, but she spoke of the lively evenings "spent with him at his house on Luojia Shan, agreeably furnished in the Chinese style and decorated with paintings by his family" (*Liao Hongying*, 81). Julian stayed in Wuhan only sixteen months—from October 1935 to January 1937—leaving a whiff of scandal over his love affair with Ling Shuhua. She was a calligraphist, painter, poet, and short-story writer with a modest reputation in China at that time, and wife of the dean of humanities who hired him. Of his relationship with the talented and temperamental poet and painter, eight years his senior, he later wrote to Virginia Woolf that his "vie amoureuse . . . had reached a point of sheer fantasy that you wouldn't swallow in a restoration play . . . and which has forced me to resign" (5 December 1936). National Wuhan University was provincial, and the Chinese, according to Julian, far too moral. It is not surprising then that early in the *China Diary*, Julian wrote that "one part of a memoir of my life which should go on record is my peculiar adventure in China, but this would be indiscreet to put on paper." It is also considered "indiscreet" to speak of Julian Bell and Ling Shuhua's relationship in China today.

Teaching, translating, learning Chinese, practicing calligraphy, shooting ducks and boar, sailing, and being guided through the culture, politics, food and art of China by Ling Shuhua, Julian's relationship began like a Chinese fairy story. The beautiful and talented Chinese mandarin fell in love with the "ruffian" of British Bloomsbury. But she was already married, Julian, by his own admission, "polygamous by nature," and the relationship ended in a storm. His cultural encounter in China was constantly being remade, as he developed "transgressive" relationships. As noted earlier, Ling Shuhua, a mercurial painter and poet, welcomed Julian to Wuhan with her husband, Dean Chen Yuan. Having been introduced to the Chens by Margery Fry, Julian wrote early of cultural differences relating to "intimacy" in Bloomsbury and China:

> The Chens grow nicer and nicer the more I see of them—friendly, sensitive, intelligent—the sort of people we should all be devoted to. So far, we've not been able to get an English intimacy, because of our background differences and the fact—we have only known each other for so short a time: we can hardly talk sex or politics, and I find myself doing an unfairly large share of the talking, because they can't speak English—naturally—as fluently as I can: I hope to start Chinese before the month is out. (JB to VB, 16 October 1935)

Such views reveal his cultural and linguistic myopia. Yet the issue of finding the kind of open and intellectually lively cosmopolitan conversation in English that he was used to in Bloomsbury was an issue.

Dividing his life in the *China Diary* into sensations, ideas, and love affairs, Julian acknowledged that "a leading motif" in his life was his love affairs. Many in Cambridge were aware of his amorous propensities and viewed him as a Lothario, though it is clear from his writing and his friends, as will be developed later, that love was but part of the puzzle of Julian's identity. Eddy Playfair, relishing Julian's amorous adventures, responded in letters to his early descriptions of Shuhua, and asked "to hear the whole story, without reticences, of your relations with her . . . what age is she, by the way." Playfair assured Julian of his "complete secrecy; no one shall hear a word about her . . . get out your little camera, take a photograph of her . . . It sounds most exciting—but don't get in trouble with your dean" (26 November 1935). Julian responded, describing Shuhua:

> She's very shy, verbally and physically. . . . It's my oddest affair to date. She's as intense and passionate as your old enemy Helen [Soutar] is also a self-torturer and pessimist asking reassurance. And both jealous and not wanting to lose face. On the other hand, intelligent, charming, sensitive, passionate and a malicious storyteller. And a perfect adviser on social situations: she's saved me gaffes innumerable. (27 December 1935)

It began as a "purely platonic affair," but Eddy, knowing Julian, asked if it would remain so when his venereal "cure"[7] was completed. Nothing remained secret in Bloomsbury—gossip being a glittering value—and Julian was wildly indiscreet in his letters home. This led Anthony Burgess to speak of Julian being in "hot water" early in November 1935 (Anthony Burgess to Eddy Playfair, 18 November 1935), only three months after he arrived in China. And Marie Mauron reported that at Margery Fry's party, "Julian demandait a tous les Chinois, avec discretion mais d'un facon pressante, quelles etait les possibilites de concubinage" (EP to JB, 18 January 1936). (Julian asked all the Chinese in a discreet but insistent manner, what were the possibilities of concubinage). Julian wrote to everyone about Shuhua with little thought of her reputation or his position: Eddy warned him, as did Vanessa that it was "horribly dangerous" (EP to JB, 1 January 1936). He reminded Julian that he could always come home, but warned that "poor Sue" (her name now anglicized by Julian and friends) would bear the personal and cultural brunt of his escapade, and that the issue of Dean Chen "losing face" was more of an issue in China than it would be in England. Vanessa, Eddy, and Quentin from afar anticipated the consequences of Julian's doing what he always did—philandering—but this time in a different cultural space with consequences. Julian seemed culturally naïve, and certainly insensitive to Dean Chen's "loss of face" in the college culture, given that he was a dean, were the relations to become known. Julian thought of himself as "more mature" than the Chens when the affair was discovered, but, in fact, it was he who was culturally naive and displaced in the Chinese context. Julian was not in Bloomsbury but he carried it like a chalice within.

Though Eddy feared sermonizing, he expressed his anxiety in his letters, sounding like a wiser, older brother to a somewhat frisky adolescent. He advised Julian to stop gossiping and to let the affair disappear into silence: "The dean's wife is rapidly becoming, in the public eye, one of the better myths of the Julian cycle" (15 March 1936). Julian, however, enjoyed the "Julian legend," and sounded quite the exhibitionist, joking that his reputation at home would be enhanced; Playfair, however, was determined to "scotch" his indiscretions. Playfair, more mature, working as a private secretary to a politician at the Treasury, was aware, as Julian was not, that he was wrecking his career for love, Julian having not yet achieved a delicate balance between the two. At the beginning of Julian's relationship, however, Playfair, had relished Julian's amorous adventures: "I've seen her photo; she's not my type, but she looks very sweet. But Quentin and I have both lost our hearts to the Dean of the Women, who is absolutely lovely. Tell me more about her" (1 January 1936).

Ye Junjian, Julian's student, when interviewed in China in 1995, a year before his death, said that Ling Shuhua "was not beautiful but cultured." He discreetly described Julian's association with her as "a personal sort of thing. I don't think they talked much about politics. Or about literary kind of purpose. They enjoy the kind of talk (laughter) as the British do over tea." Xiao Qian, the journalist and writer, also merrily revealed in another interview in 1995 that his wife did not want him to be alone with Ling Shuhua when she visited them in the 1930s, as she was known as a "liberated woman."

With many British stereotypes of China on his screen—from the image of a calm civilization (China was anything but at the time) to Confucius to tea to pigtails—Eddy praised Shuhua:

> Sue seems, from your description, to be everything one expects the Chinese not to be; one thinks of them as calm, infinitely experienced, reliable, rather literary in their emotions; but Sue sounds as if she wouldn't be at all out of place in the love-life of Cambridge—thousands of years of calm civilisation all gone for nothing. However, I recognise that, however great Confucius may be as a sage, one could imagine better mistresses than those shaped in his likeness; he would hardly be your cup of tea. Nor I suppose on reflection, that of the contemporary Chinese. But at this distance, it's so hard not to put pigtails on them. (25 January 1936)

Playfair went on to remark that Shuhua, in the photographs, was far prettier without her spectacles, and noted that she had a "very individual, intelligent and sensitive face, I thought, and rather surprisingly occidental in expression." One wonders what an "occidental" expression is, as he goes on to add, "isn't her nose rather more Western than most of them?" (25 January 1936). Epithets such as "Chinks" and the stereotypes of "pigtails" and "noses" and "occidental" expressions and of people being "fundamentally different" are intermittent themes in Julian and Playfair's "oriental" letters revealing their prejudices and essentialist notions of race.

In general, however, Julian Bell, like many other British intellectuals of the time, described the Chinese as more "charming" than the Indians and the Japanese. When he arrived at Wuhan, he noted that "some of the Japanese are agreeable, but not really as charming at the Chinese. I feel they've none of the Chinese good sense and good feeling: it's all . . . brittle, artificial, diluted: too much unintellectual grace. I hope the Chinese won't disappoint my expectation too completely" (JB to EP, 12 September 1935). In another letter, he expressed virulent prejudice about the Indians while reading E. M. Forster's *A Passage to India,* England's colonization of India generating intense feelings of Indian "inferiority."

Hostility toward the Indians, and Julian's prejudice and racist associations are representative of a certain English class:

> How glad I am to be among human beings [Chinese], not his [Forster's] revolting blacks [Indians]. What India needs is strong government—whips and firing squads—by a really fanatical group of English communists. If one could rout out their religion and philiprogenitiveness [i.e., large families] . . . China suffers too from this disease. (JB to EP, 3 February 1936)

China, on the other hand, distant, in semi-colonial relationship with the British, never occupied the same psychological space of subject nation, subject people, as India. The relationship did, however, include the shameful Opium

Julian Bell, 1936. "How grand you are in your Chinese robe" (Eddy Playfair). By permission of chief archivist, Wuhan University Library, China.

Wars in the middle of the nineteenth century when the British forced the export of the drug to China while the Chinese, loathing its effect on their population, attempted to dump it in the harbor. The British and French retribution for Chinese rebellion included the burning and looting of the beautiful Old Summer Palace at Wanshoushan photographed by Felix Beato in the late 1850s.

Later, however, Julian expressed his disappointments, also stereotyping the Chinese, accusing them as a people of having a "factual" or "practical" "Chinese mind" (JB to EP, 11 March 1936) and referred to his students as being of a "shy and inarticulate race" (JB to EP, 20 March 1936). In other moments of irritation, Julian stated that "the Chinese are an inferior race—anyway, Chinese men. The women one's prepared to find an inferior race here as elsewhere and they really do it rather the better for being Chinese." Here he hid a sly compliment to Chinese women in his sexism. He blurted out a shameful eugenics stating that "an intelligent Tamerlane would introduce mass castration into this country and cross the women with nordic and aryan stocks—you might get something rather good. Certainly there's a much higher average of looks than the Western women" (21 October 1936). Given the egalitarianism in Bloomsbury and the talented women who surrounded Julian in his youth, Vanessa Bell and Virginia Woolf among others, it is shocking to read his overtly sexist and racist observations. It reveals, perhaps, that the cultural force of male society in British boarding schools and Oxbridge can triumph over actual egalitarian experiences within the family.

Establishing his niche in Anglo-China, Julian adopted some of its culturally insensitive attitudes, but, nevertheless, sought to know more of Chinese-China through which Ling Shuhua guided him. Always social, Julian was a part of both Anglo-Chinese and Chinese society during his stay, and Playfair wrote that he heard that Julian was popular in Wuhan and everyone talked about him (25 July 1936). Julian found after the first three months that he was out every night with the Chinese, the missionaries, the wives: "It's all fun. I go on admiring the people, being thrilled by the beauty of the place, and fascinated by the life" (JB to VB, 11 December 1935). We see him in his description in his "lovely warm Chinese gown," given to him by Ling Shuhua, feeling "absurdly English and self conscious," but enchanted by China, nevertheless. Loving wicked gossip, he commented on the Wesleyan chancellor's adulterous affairs; the "buggery" of John Lehmann, best known as an editor and publisher who founded Penguin New Writing; Harold Acton, the poet, acting "very

Ling Shuhua, 1936, Julian Bell's favorite photograph; Julian Bell, photographer. By permission of the chief archivist, Wuhan University Library, China.

chi-chi and homo, but high culture to the hilt" (JB to EP, 22 January 1936). Though socially engaged with Anglo-China, he does not forget to inquire about his sister, Angelica, and her virginity and he reports in intimate detail on the progress of his affair with Shuhua to his mother—a kind of cloying family intimacy.

Over the course of his stay, Ling Shuhua was drawn to him as a companion, or as he phrased it early in their relationship, "my Chinese secretary-interpreter" (JB to VB, 7 January 1936). The ups and downs of his yearlong affair with Ling Shuhua (probably January 1936 until his departure January 1937) were recorded in his letters to Vanessa Bell, Eddy Playfair, and John Lehmann, but references also appeared in his correspondence with Virginia Woolf, Harold Barger, Quentin Bell, among others. "Take care not to be sacked," wrote Harold Barger to Julian Bell in China, echoing many who wrote to him about his "reckless" love affair in China. Barger (nicknamed "Seacoal"), a fellow Apostle from his Cambridge days, corresponded with Julian not only about the approaching war in England but the international situation and Julian's "vie amoureuse." Julian announced his interest in Ling Shuhua to Vanessa at the end of November 1935, three months after his arrival:

> Oh Nessa dear, you will have to meet her one of these days. She's the most charming creature I've ever met, and the only woman I know who would be a possible daughter-in-law to you (she isn't, being married with a charming child and ten years too old) that she is really in our world and one of the most gifted, the nicest, most sensitive and intelligent people in it. I don't know what will happen. I think when I'm cured I shall probably get her involved: at present I'm not physically disturbed—less by her than others—but I know myself well enough to know that the parade follows the flag, etc. (22 November 1935)

"She is really in our world" is a sentiment that Julian repeated. In another letter, Virginia Woolf wrote to Julian, "I feel the Orientals have been baked out of the same blood that we have; all so quiet and stealthy and demure" (VW to JB, December 1936). A Chinese artist would fit into Bloomsbury. But "Sue's" character was complex, emotional:

> She's a desperately serious person, with great reserves of unhappiness: she says she's lost faith in everything, and is now working to find love, something to believe in. She's subtle, sensitive, very complicated—also torn between an introspective—analytic part and a very fragile easily-damaged sensibility. And sensible and intelligent. And also very romantic at heart. And, I should imagine, nervously and ecstatically passionate. She wouldn't let me make love to her to any extent at all last night. And she looks lovely—above all when I can get her to take off her spectacles—and is at once self-possessed, sure of her world, and devilish. And inexperienced in love. . . . (JB to VB, 18 December 1935)

Julian mentioned Ling Shuhua's having been passionately in love with Xu Zhimo (to be discussed in chapter 3, "East-West Conversations"), and Ying Chinnery, Shuhua's daughter, also noted in an interview that her mother "was chasing after Xu." She observes:

> But I think Xu only regarded her as a confidante. He left a lot of letters and diaries with her when he went abroad [1923–24]. It was still with her when he died [1931]. I think there were a lot of upsets when Xu's widow [second

wife] tried to retrieve the letters. Xu was also in love with Lin Huiyin who also wrote letters to Xu. I don't understand why there isn't one scrap of letter or poem by Xu in my mother's place. My guess it is that she was jealous of Xu's friends and might have become a secret enemy of Xu. My father was his best friend. I think my father was introduced by Xu to my mother. (communication to the author, 1 February 1998).

A recent book by Heng-wen Gao, *Xu Zhimo and the Women in His Life* is coauthored by Gao Heng-wen and Sang Nong (in Chinese), corroborates this view, detailing how a treasure chest of diaries and letters that Xu Zhimo had written, perhaps to Lin Huiyin, the rather young daughter of Xu's admired mentor, Lin Changmin, then in Middle School in Cambridge, 1922–24, and other letters, perhaps to Ling Shuhua. According to a summary I received of this work, however, Xu Zhimo entrusted the chest of letters to Ling Shuhua. When the chest was requested by Hu Shi, a close friend of Xu's after his death, it is said that Hu Shi found that some of the pages of a diary and some letters were missing. These selective letters and diary were then turned over to Xu's second wife, Lu Xiaoman. Much remains speculation, as the diaries and letters

Lin Huiyin, Rabindranath Tagore (Indian poet), Xu Zhimo, on tour in India, 1928. By permission of the Dartington Hall Trust Archive, Totnes, England.

cannot be located now.[8] But sources hint at Xu's affair with Lin Huiyin, and Shuhua's with Xu Xhimo. Nevertheless, Shuhua remained Xu Zhimo's intimate friend and married Chen Yuan, according to Julian Bell, out of "kindness, duty, wanting to be married."

Throughout December 1935, Julian intensified his plan "to invent some way of going to bed" with Shuhua, though there were some indelicacies because of his venereal disease. He wrote more often (ten letters) during this period of December and January to his mother:

> I had started another letter to you yesterday but Sue came in and read it and took frantic offense at a passage about her, so that she now threatens to break off our affair—not, thank God, our friendship. We've been having an exhausting scene earlier this evening. But I think I can in the end bring her round—I'm by now very heavily involved, and shall be desperate if I can't. She's definitely the most serious, important, and adult person I have ever been in love with—also the most complicated and serious. And one of the nicest and most charming. So as I prophecied, a period of storm has set in. (6 December 1935, CHAO)

But a month later, Julian wrote with Bloomsbury candor of his Chinese mistress:

> I'm enjoying life as I haven't done for years: Peking [Beijing] is one of the great capitals of the world—oddly like Paris, at times. Could you imagine anything more perfect than coming to Paris with a mistress who really knows the town, is devoted to one, is perfectly charming, has an impeccable taste in food—it's the dream of a romantic-man-of-the-world: the sort of thing Clive ought to do. Also, I am meeting Chinese intellectuals, and English, going to the theater, skating (badly on bad ice), and making love. (18 December 1936).

Clive Bell's modeling of Julian's notions of romance is an interesting detail here, and it is his influence on Julian's attitudes toward women and social life that seemed to have more sway in his short life than his talented mother and aunt. The romantic storm continued intermittently throughout the year, and the letters reveal the traces of British culture on China and China on England. It is this overlay that interests us sixty years later as Julian declared to Shuhua: "I don't think many people have had as much of China in so short a time" (7 December 1937). Though the first part of the relationship might be traced through Playfair and Vanessa's correspondence, the latter "letter quarrels" reveal the personal and cultural tensions between them after Julian leaves China under the cloud of scandal. Having found only four of Shuhua's letters, in spite of inquiries all over the world, I can only infer from Playfair and Vanessa's letters the kind of risks that Julian was taking. He planned to go to Beijing with Shuhua for three weeks in January 1936 "and there to bed together." He outlined to his mother (oddly enough) practical strategies for their affair:

1. keep secret and occasionally go to a hotel in Hankow [Hankou];
2. divorce by consent from her husband;
3. she'd live near and I'd go and see her;
4. I'd engineer a transfer to some other university and she could come. If this happened, I might marry her (I hope under Chinese law which makes a divorce by mutual consent a mere matter of public declaration). (10 January 1936)

Julian is further impressed with Shuhua in Beijing, where released from the strictures of the New Life movement,[9] she waved her hair, put on makeup, discarded her spectacles and dressed up. He described her as an "admirable mistress" but "on the whole I shouldn't put her very high in bed: on the other hand she's so charming out of it that I don't mind" (JB to EP, 22 January 1936). Julian, motivated by self-interest, kept his head about him, not desiring to marry Shuhua, but rather to live with her in China, and, perhaps, take her back to England for a year. He would still reflect upon his relationship with Toni Piri in letters, and confessed to his mother that he had "not really forsworn polygamy" (10 January 1936, CHAO). We read between the lines, for example, in the letters of Liao Hong Ying—a woman who was an agronomist at Wuhan and was an exchange scholar at Oxford in 1935—that he was having an affair with Innes Jackson while pursuing Ling Shuhua. Jackson, like Shuhua, would become "too serious" and drive Julian into emotional turmoil in China.

Throughout the letters, it is clear that Vanessa was "upset and miserable," feared scandal and even danger to Julian's life. Consequently, many of Julian's letters to Vanessa begin "be tranquil" and offer reassurance. He answered her concern point by point:

1. neither Sue nor I intend scandal;
2. in event of accident I shall do my best to prevent scandal;

3. Sue is economically independent and could also come to live in Beijing where she has great many friends;
4. it's been made pretty clear between us that there's no question of marriage. (26 January 1936)

Julian believed that Chen Yuan's "desire to save face" would help in a crisis. He nevertheless wrote that Vanessa should

> be prepared for a cable saying, "all is discovered" and a demand (or money to pay my passage home, or news that I've married her and found some other job in the country. Or that she has committed suicide as she fairly often threatens) . . . it's all a bit unreal. (Letter to VB, 17 January 1936, CHAO)

Though "unreal" to Julian, suicide over love was a part of the tradition of love as expressed in classical Chinese literature. In Tsao-Hsueh-Chin's work *Dream of the Red Chamber*, there is jealousy among the wives and husbands in the feudal model of concubinage. It is not unusual to read, for example, the story of Golden Bracelet who displeased her husband because of a minor flirtation:

> For some reason or other, Tai-tai was displeased with her and sent her back to her own family. She cried most of the time after she got home. But no one paid much attention to her. Then yesterday she disappeared, and the next thing you know, someone discovered a corpse in the well. (162)

Ling Shuhua, despondent, threatened the same: "What a life I am carrying on! For whom I am doing this sort of torture" (Letter to Julian Bell, probably December 1937). But in the final stages of her relationship with Julian, their intimacy was revealed to Chen Yuan (sometimes referred to as "T. P." or "Tunpo" or "Tongbo") by Liao Hong Ying, who was also friends with Julian and Ling Shuhua. Though Liao followed her conscience in reporting Julian's affair, Julian considered this a betrayal and noted in a letter to Shuhua that Liao Hong Yin was always jealous and, he charged, "rather a lesbian" (JB to LSH, ca. 1937). After the revelation of the affair, Julian resigned from Wuhan, though he wrote to Shuhua that both presidents of the university urged him not to withdraw. The Richardses, Ivor and Dorothy, were in Beijing at the time, and an entry in Dorothy Richards's *Diary 1936* suggests that they did not know the rumors about Julian's love life, though everyone in London did. Dorothy writes, "Miss Liao came in at 9:30 and confirmed Julian Bell's resignation of Wuhan—*In*comprehensible." Julian had been invited to dinner at the Richards's home in Beijing on 8 September 1936; yet, seemingly, they knew little. The Richardses were considered "most charming people" and Liao Hong Ying, after being given an introduction by Julian, had written that Mrs. Richards "is beautiful and oh, her taste in dresses. It is a delight to look at her" (Letter to Julian Bell, 25 November 1935).

Liao Hong Ying, a talented mathematician and agricultural chemist, had been a Boxer Indemnity scholar in England in the early thirties at Somerville College, Oxford, where Marjorie Fry was principal. Here she, importantly, met Innes Jackson (Herdan), another student at Somerville, who would travel back to Wuhan with her to study poetry and calligraphy during the time when Julian Bell was there. They remained lifelong friends, of which Innes Herdan wrote a testament in her 1996 biography. Julian Bell had an affair with Innes Jackson Herdan after his breakup with Ling Shuhua. Ying suggests this in a letter written after his departure: "Innes knows the value of experience and she loves you without forcing you to marry her." Innes sailed away from China with Julian and when Shuhua met Innes at the boat, "Julian carried it off" (to Julian Bell, 31 March 1937).

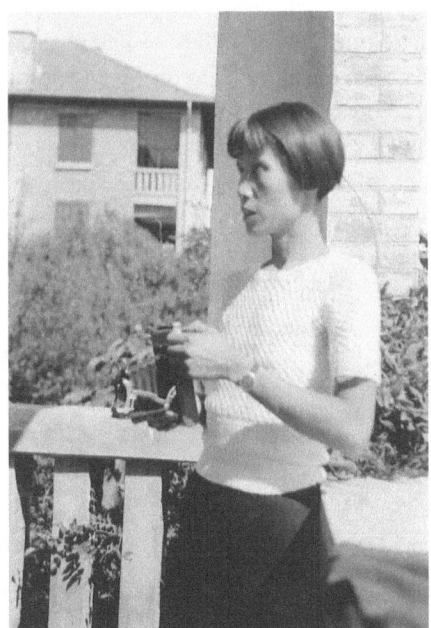

Liao Hong Ying, mathematician and chemist, confidante of Julian Bell and Innes Jackson Herdan. By permission of Derek Bryan.

Ling Peng Fu, maternal grandfather of Ling Shuhua, in western attire. By permission of the Henry W. and Albert A. Berg Collection of English and American Literature, The New York Public Library, Astor, Lenox and Tilden Foundations.

Letter quarrels erupted in Julian and Ling Shuhua's letters as he prepared to leave China because of the scandal and to finally go off to the Spanish Civil War. The letters reveal that Julian, as he said, was "not by nature monogamous." He remarked in a letter to Vanessa that "it's a bore when doing the romantic thing involves one in prosaic consequences. Like marrying Lydia [Maynard Keynes marrying Lydia Lopokova]—or, for that matter, marrying Sue" (18 January 1936). Being clearheaded about her future and the probability of a divorce from Chen Yuan, Julian encouraged Ling Shuhua to establish her economic independence by straightening out her inheritance of property in Beijing. Julian wrote to Playfair that she "is lucky enough . . . to both own a good deal of property, and to be easily able to earn her living by writing and painting" (3 February 1936). Shuhua's father had been the mayor of Beijing and governor of Hebei Province and held extensive land in the middle of the city that was never equitably divided among his ten children. As he departed China, Julian feared what might happen to Shuhua from her "wicked sister" (JB to Ling Shuhua, 8 February 1937), who supposedly tried to manipulate her out of her portion of the land. Shuhua closes a letter with the image

"It is winter here and my mind is winter too" (3 March 1937). Julian was philosophical about his sexuality and life choices and, as he sailed home, he wrote to Shuhua, "I love you as much as I can anyone" (9 March 1937). Earlier, though, he had written that he was sorry: "it's very bad luck to love and be loved by a barbarian. I think you're more civilized than I am—better—really better—just as I think Nessa is" (24 December 1936). To Eddy Playfair, though, he wrote more cynically: "And much more troublesome, I'm getting pretty bored with f—, but cant give it up, and that people like Innes and even Shuhua—people who have to be taken seriously, emotionally, and looked after and attended to—are ceasing to be my cup of tea" (14 December 1936).

There is another refrain in the letters: Shuhua's suicide threats and Vanessa's unhappiness about his decision to go to Spain. Julian wrote honestly to Playfair of his Scylla and Charybdis—Vanessa and Ling Shuhua—as he left China: "I can't face a continuous argument on what's essentially a matter of my saving my soul and Nessa's feelings. Of course I don't care about privacy. I take it it's like S. H. everyone knows" (1937). He continued, "I'm feeling simply bloody, both about it and S. H. The plan I made was really too precarious, it

Ling Shuhua, first on left, and her four sisters, ca. 1910–15. By permission of the Henry W. and Albert A. Berg Collection of English and American Literature, The New York Public Library, Astor, Lenox and Tilden Foundations.

hasn't worked, and all's discovered. I seriously expect to learn of her suicide, about 50/50 chances I should say" (1937). He often urged Shuhua, "And don't, oh don't get suicidal again." He made passing references to Shuhua's desperate, jealous, and melodramatic scenes, her "suicidal passion" for Mongolian knives (Letter to VB, 22 January 1936), and her "carrying about a small phial of Japanese rat poison" (Letter to EP, 4 September 1936). Her extremity led Julian to monogamy—he sleeps with no one but Shuhua during this period—for as he says to Eddy, "I do not want Sue hanging herself in my house . . . I see from your reactions I'm making Sue look a gorgon. Well, she's not—only a woman in love" (25 September 1936). In a series of what appears to be letter quarrels, judging mainly from Julian's letters, he declared to Shuhua, "I can't live by emotion. You can" (17 March 1937).

Though Chen Yuan had forbidden him to write or see Shuhua after they were discovered, Julian, nevertheless, took the risk of inviting her to join him in Beijing and then to wend their way down to Canton [Guangzhou] for the Western new year, January 1937. He feared that Chen Yuan would hear that he had gone and "will guess that we met . . . no need to feel he was losing face" (December 1936). When Eddy Playfair wrote asking what Chen Yuan was like, Julian responded:

> . . . very good, limited intelligence, a very abrupt, reserved manner (this is universally remarked). A dry humour, a genuine taste—of a dry, narrow kind for literature, and immense scholarship. Fond of his daughter—a complete charmer. Also was & perhaps is in love with his wife. Not actually impotent, but seriously very cold and incompetent . . . a stiff man: a frightening opponent as least in intelligence and cunning. (2 February 1936)

Chen Yuan was formidable to many people. Mr. Xu Zhengbang, curator of the Archives at Wuhan University, reinforces this, describing the Dean as "very serious . . . strong-minded, even stubborn and rigid . . . not romantic" (interview by the author). Su Xuelin also remarked that "he was indeed a person of cold appearance and warm heart. Thanks to his poor eloquence [other sources also acknowledged that he stuttered], he was not good at expressing emotions, yet he liked to make wisecracks and dampen one's enthusiasm. Many people misunderstood him and even hated him" (*Luo Jia,* 1970). Mr. Xu Zhenbang also suggests that Chen's "ironic" and "rigid" manner were traits that may, at times, have led him into difficulty with his faculty and staff in the humanities. At these times, he said, Ling Shuhua would enter the situation and try to resolve the issues. Nevertheless, his "liberated teaching style" influenced by the years he spent in England was admired (interview with Zhengbang).

What is also startling about Julian's description of Chen is that this is one of the few instances in which the Chens' "charming" daughter is mentioned. During the period of Julian's stay, Ying seems not to have figured significantly in her mother's daily life, at least as revealed in this correspondence.[10] Julian, however, described her as a "charmer" in his letters and included photographs of her in his China photo album.

Julian wrote to Shuhua with bravado, though he often remarked that Vanessa was distressed because he was running risks. He wrote:

> I simply can't make out what all the fuss is about and why you should think it necessary to try and wound my feelings in the way you do—particularly by some of your sillier remarks about Chinese and "white men." What in the world that sort of nonsense has to do with the present situation I can't for the life of me understand. . . . Will you say I want you to commit suicide if

Hsiao-ying Chen, daughter of Ling Shuhua, ca. 1936–37; Julian Bell, photographer. By permission of the chief archivist, Wuhan University Library, China.

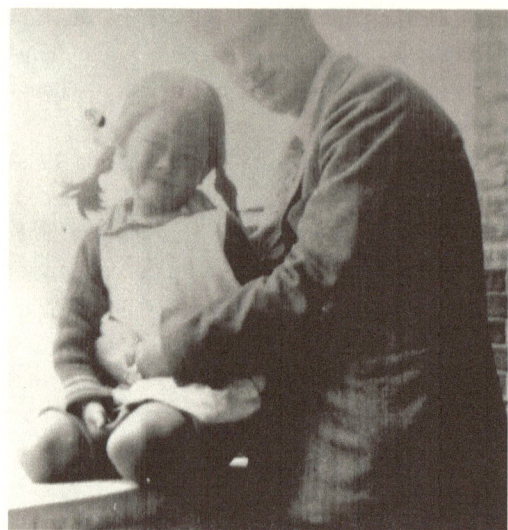

Julian Bell with Hsiao-ying Chen, daughter of Ling Shuhua, ca. 1936–37. "Sian Yung. The Chen's daughter: a great charmer, with whom I'm on the best of terms" (JB). By permission of the chief archivist, Wuhan University Library, China.

I say that you would do well to stop cultivating sensitiveness for a little and take a more realistic view of the situation. (17 December 1936)

The choice of words, "white men," as well as earlier references to Julian being a "barbarian," and it being "bad luck to be loved by a barbarian" (LS to JB, 17 December 1936) suggest the cultural tensions in their cross-cultural romance, submerged to the end when they surface in quarrels. A "barbarian" was anyone who was not Chinese. Though the emancipation of women was a theme in the May Fourth literary movement, and Henrik Ibsen's *A Doll's House* had been translated quite early in China, Shuhua was a perplexed Nora in a cultural world unready for her. There is also a letter from Julian to Shuhua in which he responded, apparently, to her charge that he was treating her as a "child" and not a "modern" woman, with all the sexual connotations that this word bore in China. Julian wrote:

> And I think that you are simply silly about saying I treat you as a child and a person who has to be looked after. You know perfectly well that I have always taken you extremely seriously, and that I have often taken your judgment against my own, that I have accepted your advice about people and the university, and that I allowed you to run all the practical side of our affair.

Ling Shuhua with her daughter, Hsiao-ying Chen ca. 1936–37. By permission of the chief archivist, Wuhan University Library, China.

Julian is defensive and added,

> Well, you have shown that you're not very good at running secret affairs and deceiving people, and that your judgment can be mistaken. . . . Why should you mind if I know more about the psychology of situations like ours than you do? Why do you think that means I don't treat you as a modern woman. Do you think its disrespectful of me to think that I have more knowledge than you do about economics or strategy? And do you think you are superior to me when you show that you know more about the arts than I do, and are a great writer, while I am not? Surely, the first thing about friendship is that one is ready to admit that ones friends may know more than one does oneself about certain matters, and one is ready to be guided by them. (12 December 1936)

He ended, nevertheless, that her hurtful letters "will not stop me from loving you," lending hope that they would meet in England.

> But so many things would be nice. The nicest would be if we beat the Fascists and you beat the Japanese and next autumn you come to Charleston and we will walk down the garden paths and admire Nessa's flowers and the goldfish in the pond and the trees and fruit, and be reminded of Pekin and

the parks and you shall write chinese poems and paint chinese pictures about English scenery, and we shall never have to worry about respectability and conventions and gossip and live happily ever after. (To Ling Shuhua, 18 December 1936, Berg)

He held out romance to her, not having "forsworn polygamy" or his venture in the Spanish Civil War, as he sailed away. But he also offered a corrective philosophy: "Life's a bad business, but not a tragic one; no doubt we shall suffer pain, but there's no need to suffer unendurably, and no need to make suffering rule our lives. Theres always something to do and something to happen" (Letter to LS, 12 January 1936). He might well have been paraphrasing Bloom in Joyce's *Ulysses:* "Plenty to see and feel and do yet."

In later letters, he plotted for her to receive his letters at the post office in the name of "Lucy Chin" and warned her, Bloomsbury style, not to give in to Chen Yuan or "conventional people," informing her, "you're not really by nature a wife or housekeeper, you ought to live more fully without entanglements" (30 March 1937). In spite of his despair about a future together, he urged her to "make an amiable arrangement with TP for a separation. If you can't go to bed with him, then clearly a separation is necessary" (23 March 1937).

Julian was evolving into a polemical writer in China. He wrote to Shuhua, "I feel I've a certain amount to say to my contemporaries in England and Europe generally. They've gone so hopelessly off the track with their silly hatreds and enthusiasm: I should like to make them see what nonsense it is to hate your enemies" (undated). He also wrote that he might go to Burma because "it would make something to write. What I want now is to do a piece of self-advertisement (that's one reason, tho a minor one, for Spain)," reflecting Virginia Woolf's opinion that he would have a basis for a career in journalism after his trip to the East. Due to his early death, though, Julian never became this voice of a new, more overtly politically-engaged Bloomsbury.

TRANSLATING TOGETHER: JULIAN BELL AND LING SHUHUA

The relationship between Julian and Shuhua activated Julian's literary sensibilities as he collaborated with her on translating some of her short stories into English for the British market. Julian wrote to Vanessa in December 1935, three months after he arrived, that he was helping translate some stories and added that he would "inflict a batch of translations on Bunny [David Garnett] and Virginia before long. I should like to get Sue read in England: she might be a success" (17 December 1935, CHAO). A year later he added, "They're extraordinarily good. I wonder if Virginia would allow the existence of a woman writer in Chinese" (18 December 1936, CHAO). Virginia not only allowed but encouraged Shuhua to write her autobiography after Julian's death in the Spanish Civil War, July 1937, as discussed in chapter four. In February, he sent a translation of a classical poem that Shuhua had translated along with a short story "with some corrections and help":

> On the dress dust of travel
> winestains:
> Wandering anywhere, one
> might lose one's
> heart.
> In my last life I must
> have been a
> minor poet
> Riding a donkey in the
> rain through
> Che Men. (JB to EP, 12 February 1936)

In March 1936, Eddy Playfair thanked him for sending Sue's translation but asked, "I should like to know how much was yours and how much hers" (15 March 1936). Julian wrote that they worked together every morning from ten to twelve, and described their process:

> I call it translating but it's a queer business really only possible given our very peculiar conditions. She turns her own Chinese into English—a quite comprehensible very grammatical language. Then I cross-examine her on the exact shade of meaning she wants, which usually involves some literal character translation. . . . Having got the exact ["general" crossed out] idea of the meaning, I proceed to invent an English sentence and type it, putting in a good deal, particularly tenses, after expanding compressed words into images and supplying roughly parallel English idioms and conventions etc. The result is to me very exciting: I hope it is to other people. (Letter to EP, 20 March 1936)

The translation method described here—writing first in Chinese and then translating into English—is one through which Ling Shuhua felt she found more "freedom" in her style and yet could "keep more Chinese flavor in expression" (LS to Leonard Woolf, 6 July 1952). Julian's engagement with translating Shuhua's writing was another flowering of his early poetic interests. His interest in translation (Virginia and Leonard Woolf also engaged in similar projects with Russian writers) was a literary activity that, at the time, was neglected by critics. During the period that Julian was in China, he not only encouraged Ling Shuhua to write short stories but also her autobiography, attesting to her superior writing style compared to, for example, Josephine Tey-Heat and Pearl Buck. When he was off on a journey to the Yangtze gorges, he wrote, "I hope you're writing your biography hard. If you haven't done so ... look at Hudson's 'Far Away and Long Ago.' I saw it among your books last winter" (5 August 1936). Aggrandizing her talents in the flush of love, he wrote to Eddy Playfair that her stories were comparable to Chekhov's. In 1953, Ling Shuhua wrote to Leonard Woolf of Julian's aspirations for her: "Julian always said to me that my stories and style reminded him of the Russian novels, which he was fond very much during his student day. I had in mind to write a book something like Tolstoy's War and Peace" (3 June 1953). Ling Shuhua, like Julian Bell, overestimated her talents. But she continued to write after Julian left China and wrote of trying to get assistance with her English style from the eccentric Ms. Romola Sykes, but complained that Sykes had little "patience to do correcting and interpreting." By 1955, with very little writing to her credit since China, Shuhua wrote, "Every day life now is a bore. Talent has been dimmed by time I suppose. Yet I want to try" (Letter to LW, 28 November 1955).

Shuhua began to write her autobiography after Julian's death, and was nurtured in this project by Virginia Woolf, Vanessa Bell, Vita Sackville-West, and Leonard Woolf (who published her autobiography, *Ancient Melodies,* in 1953 at the Hogarth Press). Julian compared Shuhua to his friend F. L. Lucas in a letter—the same sentimentality, romanticism, melancholy—yet admired what Bloomsbury almost required in a member of the set, a sharp tongue. But what drew Julian to Ling Shuhua was her passion about things aesthetic—literature, painting—and the poetry of her life. He found with her the intellectual intimacy that was hard for him to come by in China. Julian sought to be a man of action, having failed to find a profession in England and his interest in poetry having lapsed. He no longer sought to cultivate his own poetic gifts, and so nurtured her literary talent. He ironically announced to Eddy Playfair, "so I

Every morning after breakfast Ma Tao would come to take me out

Illustrations (a–f) from Ling Shuhua's autobiography, Ancient Melodies: Life in Peking as a Child. *By kind permission of Hsiao-ying Chen Chinnery.*

a.

Our house in Peking

b.

c.

d.

Tutor Ben and I

e.

Lao Chou took me to Lung-Fu-Shieh Temple

f.

shall get my place in literary history, after all, as an important formative influence of the third period of her works—that is, if I don't get it as the cause of her suicide" (1 March 1936).

It is not unusual for couples to collaborate on literary works, but the authorship of the resulting texts is unclear, the responsibility and credit for writing depending upon whom takes up the pen.[11] We have the examples of romantic couples Elizabeth and Robert Barrett Browning, George Eliot and G. H. Lewes, Simone de Beauvoir and Sartre, Colette and Henry Gautheir-Villars, Sylvia Plath and Ted Hughes; brothers and sisters, Christina and Dante Gabriel Rossetti, Charlotte Bronte and Patrick Branwell, and William and Dorothy Wordsworth. Julian and Ling Shuhua's translation collaboration is interesting, not only because it is a heightened romantic and literary moment, but because the manuscripts of the texts reveal cross-cultural tracings. There are not only the usual issues of attribution in these kinds of collaboration, but the added dimension of cultural and linguistic misunderstanding, given that Julian had a minimal amount of Chinese and taught his classes and spoke to Ling Shuhua in English. Ling Shuhua was more proficient in English than he in Chinese.

The manuscripts of three of Shuhua's stories with some of Julian's emendations are compared in the next section to the published versions of the stories in *Tien Xia Monthly*, published in English in China in 1937 (see appendix B). One, of course, can never answer Playfair's question about where Shuhua ends and Julian begins in these translation efforts, but judging from some of the final handwritten emendations, we can observe editing choices, particularly of vocabulary and style. In this narrative detail, and in his encouragement of certain sexual themes in his letters, Julian encouraged the subject of sexuality, which was traditionally unspoken in Chinese women's writing. Despite centuries of traditional female modesty, Julian attempted to export Bloomsbury to China. He boldly (and naively) advised Shuhua:

> Apart from the question of decency and publication, could one even describe the process of going to bed with someone quite clearly and accurately and truthfully; not excited or mystical or metaphorical, but calling everything by its right name and giving, accordingly, all the sensations involved. I wonder if you'll ever do anything of the kind. Certainly you must write stories in which people do go to bed together . . . really truthfully without sentimentality, pornography, mysticism, the predominant qualities in the experience as experience. (24 November 1936)

As with the arts, Julian's generation saw the conventions of morality, not as rules to be learned but to be broken. As Kathleen Raine wrote, "in the conventions of morality we saw only a refusal to confront truthfully the issues of life; in life, as in art, we must find the answers for ourselves" (*The Land Unknown*, 150). Julian had lived his life this way beginning in his Cambridge years when he wrote home to his mother about Angelica's virginity or that he was having his infatuation and first love affair, a homosexual one, with Anthony Blunt (*Diary*, Vanessa Bell, 37). Attempting to dissolve Ling Shuhua's cultural taboos, Julian boldly crossed boundaries. Who else but a Bloomsberry used to challenging Victorian repression would take on the tradition of repression of love and sex in Chinese literature? Ling Shuhua never did write of these experiences in the way that Julian desired. Though critics today speak of the "censorship" that sometimes occurs in male-female literary "collaborations," in this particular cross-cultural relationship, Julian attempted to open modernist perspectives on women's constraints and sexuality, as a theme, to Ling Shuhua.

This new psychological and cultural space threw into relief recessed aspects of Chinese culture, enabling the creation of new cultural and aesthetic maps. In Ling Shuhua's case, repressed sexuality, dissatisfactions in relations between men and women and in traditional families emerged as themes in her writing. She could write with an imaginary English audience in mind, and say what could not yet be said in China. This notion of a shadow audience is as true today when contemporary Turkish writers may write more freely in Germany or Algerian writers, in Paris. Various kinds of geographical or psychological displacement—diasporas—free writers of their own cultural and political constrictions. This displacement is not "poetic"; the geographical shift and refugee state caused by war or political conditions are often psychologically and physically brutal. But what displacement makes possible is "connection" as migration is the major theme of the new millennium. Through this movement and displacement, we all become in one way or another "strangers" or "other," and that leads to new understandings and connection.

Julian and Shuhua translated and edited at least three of her short stories together: "Writing a Letter," "A Poet Goes Mad," and "What's the Point of It." These were stories that Shuhua wrote while Julian was in China, and one discovers in the letters that he encouraged their publication in England through his literary network. In reviewing these stories in manuscript form circulated in England, but never published, one finds Julian's handwritten editing on Shuhua's typed pages (appendix B). Though it is impossible to ascertain the extent of his involvement in the translation of the stories in earlier stages, the available manuscript of the last draft of three stories was sent by Julian first to David Garnett, who sent them to R. A. Scott-James, the editor of *The London Mercury*, who rejected them August, 1936. These manuscripts embody, as no other artifacts discovered in the course of this study, a relationship between Julian and Shuhua. The tracings of his editing on her writing conveys a sense of their literary intimacy that all the lost conversations and lost letters of Shuhua cannot.

In Shuhua's story "Writing a Letter," an illiterate woman, Mrs. Chang [Zhang], visits the educated Miss Wu, who is preparing for her Imperial Examinations,[12] an exam at that time reserved for men. Mrs. Chang asks her to write a letter to her husband, an army official away in Hunan. It is a poignant story because Mrs. Chang [Zhang], though acutely aware of her lack of education and the differences between her and Miss Wu, nevertheless pours out the sadness of her life to another woman in a long monologue that she previously couldn't relate to an elderly male letter writer who told her "that writing a letter isn't like talking, there are all sorts of words you can't write down." Shuhua relates the complaints and ambivalence of a married woman with children in the China of the time. Questioning women's traditional roles, Shuhua, through this story, introduced new subject matter about women and children encouraged by the May Fourth movement to be described in chapter 2, "Literary Communities in England and China." In addition, the epistolary device highlights the representation of the voice of an illiterate woman through the pen of an educated one. Virginia Woolf in her Introductory Letter to Margaret Llewelyn Davies's collection of factory women's writing, *Life as We Have Known It,* by Co-operative Working Women, reveals the same sympathy with the hardships in the lives of obscure women.

The themes of the story relate first, as seen through Mrs. Chang's [Zhang's] illiteracy, the inequalities of class as well as sexism in the culture: "You don't know what it's like," she says to the educated Miss Wu, "to be blind with your eyes open. How nice it must be for you, being able to write down everything you think of . . . able to write as quick and clear as a book." She notes that her husband favors her son and that her daughters are bashful around him, which makes him angry with them. Then she represents what is unrepresented until the 1920s in China as she relates the quarrels in her domestic life with her husband. She aggressively introduces the notion of getting a job, saying to her husband, "Don't think I'll stick with your family for ever. Look here, tomorrow I'll get a job for myself: I don't care about losing face like this." Proclaiming "I am not your slave" and that getting a job is "better than leading a dog's life with you," Shuhua's female characters say things that can be found in few other stories of the time, challenging the tradition of female subordination and the value of "saving face." It is no wonder, then, that Shuhua's stories were rejected by the Marxist critics of the time, such as Qian Xingcun, who charges her heroines with "buffoonery, weakness in their dull dry souls." Shuhua is referred to as "a progressive bourgeois intellectual" describing "bourgeois females," and her female characters are viewed as "degenerate." The intention of the author, says Qian Xingcun, is "to show the real life of rich ladies" (*Flowers in the Temple,* introduction).

Mrs. Chang [Zhang] topples the Confucian verities of Chinese family life with frank language (as Virginia Woolf will expose Victorian shibboleths in *To the Lighthouse*) in complaining about motherhood and her children:

> I've never slept at night. As soon as I've closed my eyes this boy wants to go piss or that girl starts crying with a stomachache, or the baby screams because it's hungry.

Despite being quite "modern" in her complaints, she nevertheless fears, as many female characters in 1920s Chinese fiction do, becoming one of those "modern girls" who, as her mother says, "run away with some wild man." This theme of "modern" girls studying in the university, becoming "westernized," and becoming a sexual threat to other women is a common one. These women are repudiated and labeled "whores" and "prostitutes" because of their perceived sexual liberalism. In fact, Mrs. Chang [Zhang] is writing the letter to her husband to stir him up because she suspects that he is involved with one of these "modern" girls. However, it is important to note that later such westernized "modern" girls become "the object of desire," as observed by Shi Shumei in the stories of cosmopolitan Shanghai writers like Liu Na'ou:

> Departing from the representation of Westernized women in the nationalist imaginary, the modern girls' sexual promiscuity, rather than condemned on moral grounds, becomes the mark of her free will to pursue her own desires ... she embodies the speed of modernity that demands pursuit. (Shi Shumei, "Gender, Race, and Semicolonialism," 952)

Such educated women are suspect; the society that Shuhua captures is in flux. Observing that the differences between boys and girls are disappearing, Mrs. Chang [Zhang] admires a neighbor, Miss Hwang [Huang], who "works much better than a boy," earning one hundred dollars (£6) a month, and is able to afford nice dresses. Ambivalent about the value of Miss Hwang's [Huang's] single, productive life, she asserts that she "looks like a sack of potatoes" in her pretty dresses, and then cites the proverb, "Dressed by her father, she looks pretty, dressed by her husband, looks lovely, dressed by herself, what's the good of it?" But then she confesses that she, a married woman, is not dressed by her husband. She expresses jealousy of her mother-in-law, who receives material for a fine dress from her husband, though he hasn't bothered to buy his own wife a dress in twelve years. She goes on to speculate that her unkind husband is not successful because of his "foul mouth."

This theme of an abusive husband, startling for the China of the time, is introduced in a conventional "innocent" frame of an illiterate woman dictating the story of her life to a woman who can write. Shuhua has framed an opportunity for one woman to talk to another about the sadness in her marital life to reveal her inner life in the absence of men. She says "writing a letter isn't like talking," And though she says she has "a great deal" to say, in the end, none of the talk in the story appears in the official letter to the husband: "Please say the letter got to me, and that everyone's well at home. If it's convenient, will he send another piece of dress material to me. Have you written that? I think perhaps it's better not to write . . . two sentences are quite enough."

If we read this story as a letter on the cultural margins, or perhaps a letter lost in cultural space, we note that though the women of China may have a great deal to say, it never gets into "official letters." Personal letters, the genre in which Chinese women were encouraged to write in school, sometimes transformed into the discourse of their short stories, as this one by Ling Shuhua, or memoirs like Lu Jingqing's *Wanderings* (1932). Because the 1930s were a time of increasing Party control of literature (and Mao would advance socialist realism in 1942) as well as nationalist censorship, there were few female authors who continued like Shuhua to write stories that questioned women's roles into 1936–37. Though there was a flourish of stories about the "new woman" after the May Fourth literary movement, even Ding Ling, for example, who wrote of adventurous "modern" women in China in the 1920s, wrote more doctrinaire stories in the 1930s after her companion, Hu Yepin, was killed because of his Communist Party activities. Two levels of a woman's voice are then captured in Shuhua's story—private and public—through the device of "telling" another woman the story of her life while repressing this story from being "written" in the public letter. The frame of both stories is maintained with references first to Mrs. Chang [Zhang] as the talker, Miss Wu as the silent listener: "What do I want to say," "Don't you think I'm right Miss?" The structure, in fact, is something like Strindberg's play "The Stronger," which has considerably more tension but the same structure of one woman talking, the other listening. Secondly, we begin to access a deeper level of the woman's being with Mrs. Chang's [Zhang's] narrative phrases "I say to myself" or "Why even when I've thought it out in my mind." Consequently, we do not just know what Mrs. Chang [Zhang] "does" as part of her familial duties in the Confucian tradition, but Ling Shuhua begins to admit what she "thinks" and "feels" into the narration, part of modernist inward turnings. Shuhua (like Virginia Woolf, and Emily Brontë, before her) sought to "free life from its dependence on facts" (*Room of One's Own,* 19) in her stories, in opposition to a materialist Marxist stance.

What is interesting about these phrases of consciousness ("thinks," "feels") spoken by Mrs. Chang [Zhang] is that it is Julian Bell who has refined the phrases in his editing of the stories. Looking at the way in which his literary and cultural sensibility might be traced in emendations on Shuhua's stories, we see that he refined Shuhua's "thinking" words [see appendix B]. For example, when Ling Shuhua wrote "think," he replaced it with "say to myself"; when she wrote, "even when I'm thinking," he crossed it out and wrote "I've thought it out in my mind." Another significant kind of emendation is Julian's decision to cross out many of the poetic proverbs or metaphors that Shuhua uses to somehow cap descriptions of people, a style of writing that she also employs in her autobiography, *Ancient Melodies.* Noting that he either crossed out a proverb completely or suggested that it be footnoted, we observe what is under cultural erasure with an English reader and Chinese writer. He resisted the unfamiliarity of the cultural formula or the visualization, so much a part of Shuhua's painterly writing style. For example, he chose to footnote an image of a writer portrayed as a painter holding a brush: "Look at that Miss Wu, how well she gets on, able to write as quick and clear as a book." Julian had crossed out the more poetic and visual, "She can hold her brush for a thousand words."

He crossed out an image of "grown-up people" that Ling Shuhua visualized metaphorically as "withered flowers and bare trees":

And whenever this father comes back, he always grumbles that there's no savings left for him at home. I often say the grown-up people don't need to go about dressed up [Julian crossed out "are like withered flowers and bare trees"] while a child ought to look nice [Julian crossed out "is like a flower"]. (4)

He crossed out a proverb describing the mother-in-law's attractive dress and look:

And everyone who saw her said the older she gets, the finer she dresses, she's certainly improved by age. [Julian writes, "omit" next to "like the *Lao Lai Qiao,*" meaning "becomes charming with age, grass that turns red in autumn"]. (6)

He relegated a description of the officers who go out with girl-students in the text to a footnote: "If you haven't a girl to walk out with they'll call you a poor fish, and say you don't know what the thing [Literally 'say you are not civilized']." Perhaps Julian felt these particular metaphors or proverbs didn't translate well or were too "wordy," "poetic," or revealed the sentimental "Chinese" qualities that he complained about in his students' writing. Julian's emendations reduced the richness of her style: he omitted visual metaphors—the contribution of Chinese poetry and art to British modernism in the thesis of this book—to the cultural margins of Shuhua's modern short story. Such are the issues of cross-cultural editing; nevertheless, we know from a letter to his mother that he was entranced by Shuhua's stories and he wrote of an old woman's conversation in one of the stories as like "Miss Bates [of Jane Austen's *Pride and Prejudice*], only the mentality of Lottie or Mrs. Stephen's. Very amusing, at least, I think so" (17 December 1935).[13]

Scrutinizing his choices now in the present day with a different set of literary and cultural criteria, I observe that Julian Bell denied some of the poetic and visual qualities of her writing, "the Chinese flavor" that Virginia Woolf urged her to keep. In addition, he did not see the proverbs in her writing as part of her method of character building or the importance of proverbs in Chinese culture and writing. A moral saying that might seem empty to a British reader like Julian would carry cultural weight, particularly in the formation of the qualities of an elderly character of a certain generation, for a Chinese reader. When Shuhua wrote to Leonard Woolf in 1952, she asserted that her autobiography was about ordinary Chinese people whose "thoughts are controlled by old sayings and proverbs that are handed down from generation to generation after generation. They don't know what is moral but they know what is human" (11 July 1952). With this in mind, we note that Julian suggested that many of her proverbs be footnoted or left out, changing the texture and Chinese flavor that Woolf urged her to keep. We also note that when this translated story was published in *Tien Xia Monthly* in 1937, some of the proverbs that Julian suggested be footnoted were left out by the editor, her husband, in the final version. Julian denied the easy reciprocity between Shuhua's visual and verbal, painterly and poetic imagination. Either he was not socialized into this as a British reader, or perhaps he found too much "naturalist" description—something that he was trying to excise from his own poetry at Cambridge. Shuhua and Julian, nevertheless, translated her work together, their misunderstandings as important to this literary and cultural study as their understandings.

This exchange between the poetic and the painterly eye is evident in another story of Shuhua's, "A Poet Goes Mad." In this story, the temperamental Shuhua, who, like Virginia Woolf, had her suicidal moments, writes of the modern topic of "madness" and a poet's state of mind. When published in *Tien Xia Monthly,* this story included the note that it was "translated by the author and Julian Bell," giving Julian credit for involvement in this story, though he was not credited for the earlier one. The story tells of a young married woman, Song Ch'en [Song Chen] who goes mad, and is then joined in this state by her poet-husband, Che Hsing [Zhe Xing]. This is a story that wanders, not only in its theme of the meandering of the mad wife, but also in the aimless travel of the husband, and, indeed, the plot. The terrain of the story is quite different from most Chinese fiction of the period. Not focused on "talk" as in "Writing a Letter," it contains exquisite metaphors and passages of landscape that soar with beauty, sometimes as an objective correlative to a state of mind. For example, the young woman's illness is described with telling details: her fascination with the chrysanthemum pattern made on her dress by a dog's paws (reminiscent of Charlotte Perkins Gilman's "The Yellow Wallpaper"), her involvement with caterpillars in a box who "haven't slept long enough." Like a young child, Song Ch'en [Song Chen] plays with two dogs named Huaer and Hei-er. A footnote indicates that the names can be translated as Flower-one, Black-one, or more positively, Spotty-dog, Black-dog. Such translations reveal to us the amount of visualization inherent in the Chinese language that is lost to us in translation.

Though still representing Song Ch'eng's [Song Zhen] character and depression through description rather than through the "interiority" that Virginia Woolf speaks of "Mr. Bennett and Mrs. Brown," one can see that Shuhua is interested in states of mind. She hints at a technique that will go beneath the surface, beyond observation.

> Che Hsing [Zhe Xing] turned and looked at the winding path among the old trees with their fresh green leaves and the name of Hsiang Che [Xiang Zhe] temple reminded him of the magnolia scent, and hence of his wife; sadness fell over his heart like a descending fishing net [footnote: The circular casting net, which is thrown so as to spread out on the surface and fall above the fish].
>
> In the early spring morning the silver threads of rain drifted before the gusts of cold wind, looking like the fine silk in a weaving shuttle, covered T'ien T'ai Shan [Tian Tai Shan] and the winding mountain path.

The visual images are startling and summon landscapes from all the Chinese scrolls that we have seen and the Tang poetry that we have read, one merging into another. In Western art, we perhaps only experience this merging in the visual and poetic forms captured in the innovative uses of typography during the futurist and dada periods. Shuhua, it should be noted, also wrote an article on Chinese painting, which Julian attempted to but never did get published in England. Julian writes in a letter to Vanessa "that criticism was not her [Shuhua] strong point—it never is, in China—but she's certainly far more learned than most of the critics in England or even in China: apparently painting has been neglected recently" (22 December 1935). Her strength, rather, in these stories, as in her autobiography, is in the poetic flashes, verbal and visual:

> Turning a shoulder of the mountain . . . the pine needles of early spring were a green as beautiful as that of rice in the south Chinese April. . . . In front of him was the unbroken ridge of Chu Lung Shan [Zhu Long Shan]. The rain had stopped, and the clouds were flowing across the mountains in a broad tide. At one place a group of white clouds hid the shoulders, in others the watery grey mists covered them, making mountains and sky of the same colour. Their skirts could not be seen. A million mountain folds: cloud: Sky and earth confused, undistinguished. He sat lightly on the rock, chanting the lines, forgetting about his own unhappiness. "I have been very lucky today," he said to himself. "I have seen the inspiration of Wang Wei, and the motif of Mi's clouds and mountains."

Wang Wei is a renowned Tang poet, and the Mis Mi Fu and Mi Youren, father and son, are Song painters famous for their landscapes. This mixture of poetry and painting interweaves thematically and stylistically in a way unique to the Chinese. It is hard to believe that a Chinese critic of the time, Qian Xingcun, would diminish Shuhua's efforts by slapping the label "progressive bourgeois intellectual" with little appreciation of the heightened visual descriptions and subjectivity that earned her the critical epithet of the "Chinese Katherine Mansfield":

> Che Hsing [Zhe Xing] wondered what the scent was . . . There he met a stronger gust of the scent, which now seemed to him to be a mixture of lotus flower and cassia. "Oh, it's magnolia" he said, stopping before a tree some twenty feet high, the branches covered with white flowers. The magnolia is beautiful, and yet it smells delicious too: the flowers grow straight from the ends of the twigs, stiff and angular, without the sinuous grace one might expect. The petals are white and creamy, with the powdery appearance of so many flowers, and on the leafless boughs stand out detached with something of the cold air of winter plum blossom. He walked round the flowers once or twice: there was no shadow of a human being in the monks cells, and the lamp in front of the buddha only cast a feeble light through the hanging banners. Two magpies, that had been prancing on the threshold hopped into the pavilion, jerking their heads and looking about them.

And in another passage appear the oft-referred-to scents of the Chinese magnolias, and moths, perhaps reminding us of Virginia Woolf (but her moths appear at night):

> In front of him grew a group of old cedar trees, thirty or fourty feet high, the trunks rising very straight, the needles a deep green, and the upper branches gnarled and angular, like the brushwork of the Song and Yuan painters. Through the cedar grove one could see here and there the line of a dark red wall. Over the wall, a yellow tiled pagoda, and beside it a number of white blossoming trees. Small yellow moths were fluttering through the trees and rising across the temple wall. A gust of wind brought the mixed scent of cedars and what seemed to be scented narcissus [lan-hua, epidendrum]. . . . There he met a stronger scent, which now seemed to him to be a mixture of lotus flower and cassia. "Oh, it's mu-pi hua [a scented species of early-flowering Chinese magnolia]," he said, stopping before a tree some twenty feet high, the branches covered with small white flowers.

We "see" and "smell" this poetry-prose: nature intertwined with art and psychology. Yet the "dark places of psychology" remain unexplored in this story, as the vocabulary of psychology or "madness" was less developed in China in 1936 than in England. Words were needed to enrich the terms "ennui" and "coldness" from Flaubert, from Freud to describe the wife's state.

Residing still in descriptions of predictable family cliches, the Chinese writer rarely explored, at this time, the state of mind of a character or the complexity of a relationship. Such a writer was usually propelled more by description of kinship or citation of proverbs, a tradition in China, than exploration of psychology. Little explanation, for example, is offered for the young woman's state of mind except the unconvincing reflection of the mother-in-law—a type whose insensitivity is legion in Chinese literature—that perhaps she erred when she urged the young woman to marry her son when she was still in mourning for her mother and brother, the young woman having always been a model of obedience and goodness. Again, Ling Shuhua reveals the psychological and emotional "cost" of Confucian domestic "virtue" in Chinese women. The son, stymied also, is, nevertheless, enchanted by his young wife even in madness but puzzled when his foot knocks against "modern books lying in a heap of bright silk embroidered shoes" near her bed—"his books." The grandmother reports that she saw her with the books in her hand, asleep. This red herring or perhaps "message" about the influence of "modern" books, plus the Ophelia-like descriptions of Song Ch'eng's [Song Zhen's] state, perhaps strike the wrong note.

Like Virginia Woolf, Shuhua attempts to describe the wife's illness. Unlike Woolf and other modernists, Shuhua is not as successful as she attempts to achieve with description what they do through the narration of interiority. Not surrounded by women writers experimenting with new styles and narrative techniques to capture the mind on the page, she cannot represent what Woolf does, for example, in the dreaming Rhoda of *The Waves*:

> Now I cannot sink; cannot altogether fall through the thin sheet now. Now I spread my body on this frail mattress and hang suspended. I am above the earth now. I am no longer upright to be knocked against and damaged. All is soft, and bending. . . . Out of me now my mind can pour. . . . Oh, but I sink, I fall! (*Waves*, 27)

Nevertheless, Ling Shuhua explores the theme of mental illness, modern even for Woolf (see "On Being Ill") in a woman and a poet-husband, though the theme is embodied in impressionistic description or gestures: "two shadows sauntered down the paths together, and the two voices were heard." In "Writing a Letter," Ling Shuhua moves forward in her technique, using the device of dictating a letter to hint at the interior life of a woman through her "talking" to another woman. In "A Poet Goes Mad," she uses brilliant poetic and visual descriptions of nature as the objective correlative of a little-explored state of mind in Chinese fiction—madness. In "What's the Point of It?" Ling Shuhua explores the mind of an educated woman, a translator, as she goes through her day translating, talking with neighborhood women, shopping—perhaps a Chinese Mrs. Dalloway. Ling Shuhua's writing banned under Mao but brought back in China's post-Cultural Revolution revival, reveals the growing interest in the interior life and individual state of mind of characters, a magnet that drew the Crescent Moon group to Bloomsbury writers in 1920s and 1930s.

Chapter Two

LITERARY COMMUNITIES IN ENGLAND AND CHINA

Politics and Art

IMAGINING OTHER COMMUNITIES: THE CRESCENT MOON GROUP

In 1936, Julian Bell described Ling Shuhua as "a Chinese Bloomsburian." That expression aptly describes a quality of openness and a view of art shared by Chen Yuan, her husband, and many of the Chinese scholars who returned to Beijing from sojourns in England around 1925. Resisting the "obsession with China" that C. T. Hsia criticizes in modern writers, this group was "international in mind and spirit, at a time when China was not. The scholars and writers shared national affinities" (Link 107), participated in the May Fourth literary movement, and taught at Beijing University in a spirit of humanism and liberalism. They returned to a China that was going through a period of political turmoil, but as Su Xuelin, writer, critic, and friend of the Chens, remarked, "a New China was already born . . . how could those returned scholars not contribute their due. Beijing University was a venue where, at this time, two different cultures of the seventeenth and twentieth centuries were about to converge. How could talented people not be there to attend?" (*Luo Jia*, 1).

This study is grounded then in the history of this group of literary friends in Beijing as well as a broadly defined circle of intellectuals and artists in Bloomsbury in England. With its emphasis on specific writers in definable literary communities and nations at a particular outward-looking historical moment—

 *Crescent Moon group symbol*

rather than a polarized sweep of "East" and "West"—it leads to a closer reading of individuals such as Chen Yuan, Xu Zhimo, and Ling Shuhua. It posits an "interrupted modernism" (*modeng* or *xiandai*) that began in China on or about 1919, just as modernism in England happened "on or about 1910," as announced by Virginia Woolf in her essay "Modern Fiction." This study values analysis over postmodern cliches often ungrounded in the experience and texts of specific artists, times, and places. In focusing on the thinking, writing, and travel of both the Crescent Moon group during the Republican period and Bloomsbury during the modernist period, my study illuminates the dream work of the "imagined community" of nation of which Benedict Anderson writes. These groups share a likeness because they were considered "elites," or intellectuals of an "orchid class" who viewed their societies from a certain cultural vantage point during a time of change and turmoil. "Civilization," as defined in earlier periods, was crumbling in both cultures: this gives their works a certain likeness.

These two communities grappled with the relationship between art and politics during the Republican and modernist periods, and this has relevance to contemporary critical and theoretical concerns. Like Lu Xun, the well-known Chinese writer and political reformer who gave up the study of medicine to follow a literary calling that would help shape the national spirit, the Chinese writers to be discussed were exploring a wide spectrum of personal, cultural, and national issues through letters and literature. This literature will be viewed as "intimate expression" in the context of nation, a stance suggested by the critic, Partha Chatterjee.

Chen Yuan, a key figure in the Crescent Moon group, was a leading historian, literary critic, and intellectual in China. In 1924, while at Beijing, Chen Yuan established an important magazine, the *Contemporary Review*, 1924–28, the title perhaps taken from the British publication. Though the *Review* was mainly a forum for political criticism, literary works were included, and Shen Congwen, Hu Yepin (the lover of the well-known female writer, Ding Ling), and Ling Shuhua gained status in literary circles because of their publication in the *Review*. In addition, Shen Congwen, the most talented of the literary group, was supported by both Chen Yuan and Xu Zhimo in this magazine in the 1920s and 1930s, and after years of political turmoil was recognized as a gifted storyteller of rural China. The *Contemporary Review*, though only a weekly of about ten pages, was considered a "main newspaper," and according

Rabindranath Tagore, Indian poet. People's Publishing Company, China.

 Symbol of the Crescent
Moon group

to Su Xuelin "was well-known for its just attitude, penetrating discussion and was known as a truthful, outstanding magazine among its contemporaries at that time" (*Luo Jia*). It was popular on the newsstands, and it seems that the first article that readers turned to was Chen's column, "Xiying's Small Talk." It was in this column that he courted fame as well as disaster in attacking Lu Xun, the popular writer and political organizer, ostensibly over an upheaval at Women's Normal University.

The Crescent Moon group, taking its name from a collection of poems of the Indian poet Rabindranath Tagore, sought to collapse the struggle between East (China) and West (England, America) by adopting the imagery of a third nation (India) in the image of a "Crescent Moon" [Xin Yue Pai].[1] This was an early and brave act of deconstruction of the behemoth polarities of East and West by a Chinese literary group, a trend that continues in the work of contemporary critics Tani Barlow, Xiaomei Chen, Lydia Liu, Shi Shumei, and in this study. Chen Yuan was also one of the founding members of the Crescent Moon group, loosely assembled around 1925, and the magazine *The Crescent Moon Monthly* in 1928, after the demise of the prestigious *Contemporary Review*. He was familiar with and sympathetic to British culture, history, and literature, having studied in England, 1917–25, at the London School of Economics, where he earned a doctorate. He returned to China in 1925 to teach at Beijing University. In the thirties, he served as dean of humanities at National Wuhan University, as president of Fu-jen University, and then president of Beijing Normal University in 1952 when it absorbed Fu-jen.

The 1920s in Beijing were perilous times, as the university was under military control, and, according to Su Xuelin, it "exploited the masses to nurse its military strength." Salaries for professors were meager and were paid late, if at all. "There were many teachers in Peking [Beijing] who taught by day and pulled a rickshaw by night. Ask yourself if you have the muscle to pull a rickshaw, if you have, then you can teach. If not please think twice" (*Luo Jia*, 3). Nevertheless, the ambitions of overseas students like Chen Yuan, who had worked with H. G. Wells in London, were high, and Chen returned to teach in the ancient capital of culture. He joined other important figures, Hu Shizhi, the leader of the New Culture movement, and Gu Zhegang, leader of the Ancient History debate, along with scholars such as Gu Hongming, Wang Guowei, Liang Qichao, and, most importantly, literary figures Lu Xun (author of *The True Story of Ah Q*), Zhou Zuoren (publisher of *Yu Si*), and poets Guo Moruo, Wen Yiduo, and Xu Zhimo. Xu Zhimo was well known for his attractive and flamboyant personality. His presence alone, according to Su Xuelin, was enough to draw Chen Yuan to Beijing.

Chen Yuan's career was intertwined with Lu Xun, famous author of *The True Story of Ah Q,* the satirical story of a destitute peasant. Su Xuelin described their feud in an article in 1970 written after Chen's death. Chen Yuan, according to Su, advocated "so-called pure literature, free from political slogan," a stance that Lu Xun attacked: "at a time of national crisis . . . you [dare to] preach this kind of detachment in literature" (*Luo Jia*). Chen, according to Ye Junjian, a leftist and former student of Julian Bell's, "was leading the young people. That's why they attacked him . . . that's why he had to explain" his detachment (interview with Ye Junjian by the author, 1995). Su Xuelin added that it was a bitter literary fight that was fueled by Lu Xun's becoming "green with jealousy" over Chen's success with the *Contemporary Review,* displacing Lu Xun and his brother's literary position in Beijing literary circles. Rabindranath Tagore observed that Chen and his *Contemporary Review* colleagues were viewed as having a "dilettante attitude" toward writing, and Lu Xun wanted to "clip the wings of future bureaucratic scholars" ("Literary Debates," 20). Xu Zhimo, editor of the Crescent Moon magazine, also entered the fray in defense of the much-attacked colleague, and apologized for the personal nature of the "war of the pen." Though he did not approve of the character of Lu Xun, he admitted to admiring his writings as the "Nietzsche of China." Many of the Crescent Moon labels for Chinese leaders, like this one, were openly Eurocentric, an expression of their desire to connect with and, at times, to use the West as a standard of comparison. The Crescent Moon group under the leadership of Xu Zhimo was attacked for its tempestuous expressiveness and so-called "Western identification" as well as its resistence to social realist writing of the sort that Lu Xun advocated. It was one more feud in a Beijing filled with hundreds of literary societies that vied with one another.

Qu Qiubai and Lu Xun, *founders of the Chinese League of Left-Wing Writers.*
People's Publishing Company, China.

Lu Xun was active in this contest, though the Crescent Moon largely ignored it, and he consolidated members of the Creation Society and, with other left-wing groups, formed the Chinese League of Left-Wing Writers (1930–36). He and Qu Qiubai, a Communist Party member, became spokesmen for this group. Though Lu Xun still claimed to believe in art and words as weapons, he increasingly turned toward revolutionary activity, and, in 1930, warned the members of the League of the dangers of "simply shut[ting] yourself up behind the windows of your study":

> In my view, it is very easy for "left-wing" writers today to turn into "right-wing" writers. First of all, if you simply shut yourself up behind the windows of your study instead of keeping in touch with actual social conflicts, it is easy for you to be extremely radical, or "left." But the moment you come up against reality all your ideas are shattered. . . . This is what is meant in the West by "salon socialists." . . . It is easy to become "right wing" if you do not understand the actual nature of revolution. Revolution is a bitter thing, mixed with filth and blood, not so lovely as the poets think. (Spence, *The Gate of Heavenly Peace*, 277)

Chen Yuan and the Crescent Moon group took a different literary stance. The confluence of writers and scholars at Beijing University, the New Culture movement, and the establishment of the *Contemporary Review* led to their sponsorship of poetry readings about 1925–26, and then this turned into a somewhat more formal association about 1928–33. The group, composed of highly educated individuals, most of whom had studied abroad in England and America, evolved from friendships among intellectuals and artists of two generations (Kinkley, *Odyssey*, 82–83). Many of the younger generation, students during the 1920s, graduated from Qing Hua School, which became Qinghua University; and the older, more established group, were associated with Beijing University, including Hu Shi, Xu Zhimo, Chen Yuan, Wen Yiduo, Roao Mangkan, among others (Tung, "The Search for Order and Form," 32). This Beijing group was more academic and intellectual than modernist literary counterparts in Shanghai, drawn to the cosmopolitan glitter of that city.

The magnetic Xu Zhimo organized the Crescent Moon group. Wilma Fairbank in her book about Lin Huiyin, the architect, and Liang Shicheng, son of the renowned philosopher Liang Qichao, writes of Xu's gift as "his uncanny ability to find and gather kindred spirits and to ignite in those who surrounded him new concepts, new aspirations, and, not least, new friendships" (*Liang and Lin*, 12). Xu, a flamboyant personality and writer, had also traveled to Russia in 1920 and was not impressed; he also traveled to England in 1922–23, and to India with Tagore and Leonard Elmhirst in 1928. The main representatives of the group then were the warm-hearted and talented Xu Zhimo, one of China's leading poets on the faculty of Beijing University; Chen Yuan, editor of *Contemporary Review*, forerunner of the *Crescent Moon Monthly*; and the talented writer Shen Congwen. There was much literary and political contention surrounding this group during its short life. Classified as a political clique, the Crescent Moon group was attacked at times for being detached from the political fray and at other times for association with the nationalists. They were viewed as a group of elitist "gentlemen" (a term of scorn) associated with English culture and literature and with the "art-for-art's-sake" philosophy. This is reflected in a statement by Ding Yi:

> Before the Northern Expedition campaign (1926–27) . . . [the Crescent Moon group] repudiated Communism by relying upon the imperialists and by fawning upon the warlords of northern China. After the Northern Expedition campaign, they gave themselves to their new master—the reactionary government of Chiang Kai-shek [Jiang Jieshi]—and opposed revolutionary literature. (Tung, "The Search for Order and Form," 1)

We observe in Ding Yi's commentary the intertwining of political and literary assessments in China in the late 1920s and early 1930s. The Crescent Moon group came to be considered a sinister force—the "enemy"—by the prevailing socialist ideology in the 1930s. Drawn to the ideas and art of the West, they were labeled, at various times, "Anglo-American identified," "Western," "capitalist," "bourgeois," "rightist," "nationalist," "anticommunist," "anti-soviet," and "anti-revolutionary." Xiao Qian, in a 1995 conversation, reported that they were described as "the Bloomsbury of China," because they were perceived as being in an "ivory pagoda." They were viewed as sharing the same "detachment" from politics and social responsibilities that some believed was exhibited by Bloomsbury. The group itself never identified a political affiliation, but by its silence implied one. Their main struggle was to make art independent of politics and this was a dangerous stance in China where literature was theorized as serving the nation. All around them was political turmoil and propaganda in the late 1920s; yet they strove to write poetry and fiction unmoored from the loyalty to "event" and "truth" that propelled the writing of "history," from writing that served the nation, and from loyalty to socialist formulations of "art."

Bonnie McDougall confirms this stance of the Crescent Moon group in stating that they emphasized romanticism without Marxism in her thorough study, *The Introduction of Western Literary Theories into Modern China 1919–25*. It is important to note that romanticism took on Chinese characteristics at this time: it was not understood in terms of nineteenth-century British romanticism, except as one point of reference in a modernist web. Those Chinese intellectuals and writers who were influenced by the personalities, lives, and poetry of the British romantics after studying in England, and who carried this spirit and philosophy back to China, did so in a romantic spirit of clashing systems of thought and expression of personality during a period of swift change in the Chinese culture, in a spirit of revolution. The British romantic preoccupation with the transforming power of the imagination did not inspire the Chinese, but rather a personalized romanticism of individuality and rebellion. Whatever partial adoption of British romanticism was vaunted by the Crescent Moon group, this attachment was, nevertheless, the "only serious check on the trend toward socialist realism and proletarian literature" in China, according to Tagore, India's well-known poet (Tung, "The Search for Order and Form," 167). This is yet another illustration of the way in which the Chinese writers imagined the English, taking from the culture what fulfilled their own literary or cultural needs.

The group was drawn to English literature in the late twenties and early thirties, a time when such a stance was, at the least, "politically incorrect," and, later, "criminal." Indeed, the first issue of the *Crescent Moon Monthly* was modeled after the Victorian *Yellow Book,* as the *Contemporary Review* had earlier been modeled on the British publication of the same name. More than other literary groups in China at this time, Crescent Moon's writings appeared in or were translated into English. Three of its associates—Ling Shuhua, Chen Yuan, and Xu Zhimo—came from banking or ruling or landowning families that would have been labeled "gentry" or "court writers" or "capitalists" during the period after 1928 when, Tung states, "there was a conscious movement to subserviate literature to a definite political goal and ideology" ("The Search for Order and Form," 11). There was a political reaction to the Crescent Moon group, associated in the popular mind with "elite" landowners and capitalists, though they did not, according to the writer Ye Junjian, "do anything for Chiang Kai-shek [Jiang Jieshi]" (Interview by the author), or, according to the sinologist Jeff Kinkley, "associate with Chiang and his Nanjing government and Nanjing journals" (personal communication with the author). Their literary opinions and stances were vilified as a consequence of their class position and association with study, travel, or interest in the West.

Despite this harsh contemporary assessment, several writers who were founders or associated with the society—Shen Congwen, Xu Zhimo, Ling Shuhua, and Chen Yuan, for example—have now become important to a new generation of readers in contemporary China and America for their literary perspectives and style.[2] In the new *Columbia Anthology of Chinese Women Writers,* for example, the editors, Amy D. Dooling and Kristina M. Torgeson, now speak of Ling Shuhua as "one of China's most highly regarded writers" (*Writing Women in Modern China,* 175), though she was once vilified for being "decadent," "bourgeoisie" and "imperialist." During their period, they were regarded as anathema because of their complicated cultural and political positions. But, as Benedict Anderson has noted, "All profound changes in consciousness, by their very nature, bring with them characteristic amnesias. Out of such oblivions, in specific historical circumstances, spring narratives" (*Imagined Communities,* 204).

What is now emerging from China is a new narrative about the writers focused upon in my study. Despite the waxing and waning of their reputations, both literary groups contributed to a developing modernism then in formation in different parts of the world. "Art," as Virginia Woolf said, "is the first luxury to be discarded in a time of stress" ("The Artist and Politics," 227). We sense in the dialogues to be presented in chapter 3 between Chinese and British intellectuals—the effect of the Sino-Japanese War and civil war in China and World War II in England on art—art in a time of war. It was a time when, despite the popularity of Bloomsbury and the Crescent Moon group, politics and art were in tension. It was a time when "a feeling for the passions and needs of mankind in the mass" ("The Artist and Politics," 227) was bred in artists of both communities.

Though Ling Shuhua was not described as a "member" of the Crescent Moon group (it is doubtful whether any women were), she was the wife of a leading member, Chen Yuan. Through Chen's editorship of *Contemporary Review,* he met, published, and later married Ling Shuhua, who was then a student at the university. Su Xuelin cryptically described this marriage in her personal anecdotes on Chen: "Moving a distant smiling hibiscus into the empty house, Chen had the best harvest though it was hard to be a poor Professor in Peking [Beijing]" (*Luo Jia*, 2). In a 1995 interview, Julian Bell's student Ye Junjian said that Shuhua "was attached emotionally [to the group]. They were all good friends and some very accomplished." Ye identified more with the "left," and described the Crescent Moon group as "court writers" who were "removed from the national crisis . . . detached . . . though they didn't do anything for Chiang Kai-shek" (Interview by the author). Their philosophy was "not to indulge in so-called political struggle," a kind of detachment that was considered by some of the other literary groups as criminal during a period of national crisis. Ye Junjian later identified with the Society of Literary Studies. "We were not opposed to Shakespeare or British culture," he said. "Of course, I was very young then you see. But emotionally there was a national crisis. It was no time to retreat." He added, however, that he "was too young to be of any use" in political and literary struggles at the time.

 The first issue of the *Crescent Monthly* appeared just as Beijing students protested against yet another Japanese ultimatum against China. Tired of the humiliations and concessions of the Chinese government to foreign powers, students and intellectuals joined to protest the country's weak political stance. Many students were massacred in March 1926 at the Gate of Heavenly Peace, prescient of the violence in Tiananmen Square in 1989. Wen Yiduo in the first issue of the *Crescent Moon Monthly* commemorated them. Ding Yi described the first issue of the magazine's periodical, the *Crescent Moon Monthly*, as containing its philosophy, "The Attitude of the Crescent Moon," in which Xu Zhimo, in conjunction with the other editors, announced his distress about the "chaos" in China, the disappearance of "standards of value," and the importance of using "reason" to discipline "passion." Articles on Thomas Hardy, translations of Elizabeth Barrett Browning's poetry, an article on realist fiction, and a political satire by Shen Congwen, "Alice in China," also appeared, suggesting its literary content but serious social preoccupations as well. Though interested in the study of English writers and developing notions of interiority in Chinese literature, the Crescent Moon group also wanted to rectify certain aspects of Chinese society as stated in Hu Shi's 1929 preface: sentimentalism, decadence, aestheticism, utilitarianism, didacticism, attack-ism, radicalism, refine-ism, pornography, fanaticism, commercialism, sloganism and "-ism" (Tung, "The Search for Order and Form," 72–73). It is apparent then that different literary and political passions arose from the prevailing literary groups—the Creation Society, the Literary Studies Society (later, League of Left-Wing Writers), and the Crescent Moon group. The discourse surrounding them was and remains confusing.

In capturing this evanescent dialogue within and between literary communities, we discover that the ideology, prejudice, and the political and aesthetic grounding of each culture are mobilized in conversation. "The mutual reflection and limitation" of each culture, as Yip Wai-lim refers to it, is revealed in specific encounters observed in this study. The literary debates presented in this chapter through letters and other writings contribute not only to a developing epistemology of modernism in England and China in the 1920s and 1930s, but also to contemporary debates about the British postcolonial stance toward other cultures and literatures, and contemporary debates about "realism," "romanticism," "sentimentalism," and "subjectivity" in China.

As the debates emerge, it seems, at times, as if the "names" of schools or movements contend with one another. He Li, a Chinese critic who was part of an important symposium on modernism, wrote a series of articles on "Modernism and China" in the *People's Daily* in 1983 that focused on the debate. Writing during the period of the "anti-spiritual pollution" campaign, October–December 1983, that coordinated an attack on modernism and existentialism, he expressed his concern about "certain disturbing tendencies [that] have become evident" (46) in literature that he was anxious to counteract. He opposed those Chinese writers who "expressed an unprincipled and open admiration for" modernism (47), which is associated throughout his article with the decline of Chinese classical literature, and the growing influence of British modernism, which, in turn, is equated with the demonic West. What Li ironically neglects—in what I label a false debate—is the richness of the influence of Chinese and Japanese aesthetics, as well as other European and American movements, on the development of British modernism, as well as a growing international modernism. So obsessed is he with the "foreign" (which equals "England") that he frames the debate with the tired polarities of an earlier cultural and historical period, ignoring the actual interanimation of Chinese aesthetics with British modernism itself during the period of this study. British modernism becomes a red flag to critics with a "xenophobic obsession" with national purity, as Geremie Barmé remarks (He Li, 41). Mainland Chinese critics joined at various periods to staunch the flow of modernism as represented by Bloomsbury or the Crescent Moon group into China. Nevertheless, the Crescent Moon group thrived in China from 1928–33, when Bloomsbury was already an influential cultural force in England. After the death of Xu Zhimo and the closing of the *Crescent Moon Monthly* in 1933, this liberal literary society with its international vision bowed out of the Chinese literary arena. The League of Left-Wing Writers then assumed center stage.

POLITICS AND ART

The Crescent Moon group was attacked for being "detached" from the desperate politics of the day; Bloomsbury was accused of "escaping to the inner life," as it fashioned its art under the banner of pacifism during World War I. Writing that seemingly ignores politics is often seen as dangerous during times of national distress and national unification. This attitude prevailed, for example, during the Sino-Japanese War in China, during World War I in England, and even today in the aftermath of the terrorist attacks on the World Trade Center and the Pentagon in America. Yet the artists and intellectuals of Bloomsbury and the Crescent Moon group experienced the facts of history even when seeming to ignore them, and, at times, transformed the facts and feelings into art. In a letter to Julian Bell in China in 1936, Virginia Woolf describes Vanessa Bell and Duncan Grant's "escape" into art as "Europe blazes"; yet she limns the tension between politics and art that she experienced. She tells of a visit to Charleston:

> We had tea at Charleston, on Sunday, and found them all very well, and I think once more hopped out of the frying pan on the cool green pastures of painters art. How I envy them [Vanessa and Duncan]. There they sit, looking at pinks and yellows, and when Europe blazes all they can do is screw their eyes up and complain of a temporary glare in the foreground. Unfortunately, politics gets between me and fiction. (21 May 1936)

Woolf would claim that she was "not a politician: obviously. Can only rethink politics very slowly into . . . my own tongue" (Woolf, *Diary*, vol. 5, 12 October 1937, 114). But *Three Guineas* demonstrates that she could rethink it, while the above image of Vanessa and Duncan "looking at the pinks and yellows when all Europe blazes" crystallizes another aesthetic stance. Vanessa and Duncan and some others in Bloomsbury shaped by their pacifism in World War I were not much interested in politics. Seen in the context of writers like Vera Brittain or Winifred Holtby, their words seem "empty." Yet even they were drawn into events. As Julian Bell humorously notes in a letter from Wuhan, he "was really frightened when Nessa started writing about politics . . . a really appalling situation if Nessa noticed it." (Letter to Virginia Woolf, undated). Yet Vanessa's "detachment" is, perhaps, belied in letters, as she reveals "a habit of mind, a structure of feeling" (Hanley, *Writing War,* 7) on the home front. When she wrote to Ling Shuhua in 1940, she stated that she felt "dead and cut off from the outside world" during the war (14 February 1939, Berg). She reported the air raids in London, her anxieties and the fear that people would be killed; in addition, she painted "Triple Alliance" with war as her subject.

The question of the relationship between politics and art was being thrashed out in both China and England in both literary communities, always an uneasy relationship, but one thrown into crisis during a time of war. The larger questions are thus raised about the uses of literature and "what is real and to whom." Woolf stated in her 1940 essay, "The Leaning Tower," that "the poet in the thirties was forced to be a politician. That explains why the artist in the thirties was forced to be a scapegoat." If poets like Auden and his school incorporated politics that were "real," then other artists who did not follow suit remaining in the ivory tower escaping from "reality," deserved, in the popular imagination, to be attacked.

British artists questioned the uses of public language during this time of national distress, and announced that there was a crisis. The BBC presented Virginia Woolf's talk "How Words Fail" and George Orwell's public debate on words, and formed the BBC "Advisory Committee for Spoken English." Woolf delivered "How Words Fail," which later became her essay "Craftsmanship," on 20 April 1937, at the same time that Orwell sponsored BBC broadcasts on the crisis in public language, some of which were later incorporated into his essay "Politics and the English Language" (1946). Her broadcast joined a dialogue between Roger Fry and I. A. Richards, a debate on aesthetics, science, and politics within Cambridge circles. It was a time when there was much discussion of the public use of words by the media—journalists, magazine writers and radio commentators. They questioned how words—in literature, journalism, and popular texts—relate to various definitions of what is "real," how words "mean" during a time of war? Orwell's sense that much written English was "ugly and inaccurate" (113) and full of bad habits led to his more fully developed notion, "Thought corrupts language, language corrupts thought." "The great enemy of clear language," he says, "is insincerity" (173). Public thought and language that was fuzzy could lead people into totalitarianism or fascism without their knowing it.

Similarly, the work of the newly formed BBC Advisory Committee on Spoken English, sometimes called the Society for Pure English (founded in 1933 and reconstituted 1934–35), also sought "clarity" and "correctness," but in pronunciation by "ascertaining the views of authoritative English speaking persons throughout the Empire and America" (BBC Advisory Committee, minutes, 30 November 1933). Robert Bridges was the first president of this committee, and, after his death, Richard Lloyd Jones, university reader in phonetics at the School of Oriental and African Studies in London, took over. I. A. Richards was a member of the committee, along with George Bernard Shaw. A little-known fact, recorded in the minutes of the society, is that a Miss Virginia Woolf was asked to be a member when they were seeking new members drawn from a younger generation who might represent modern linguistic trends to the committee (BBC Advisory Committee on Spoken English, minutes, 30 November 1933). Virginia Woolf wrote to Logan Pearsall Smith on December 5, 1933, that she was honored to be asked to be on the "Pronounciating [sic] Committee" but draws his attention to the fact that her "education was extremely defective, I have no special knowledge of words or their pronounciation [sic], and frequently find myself at fault in pronouncing Biblical or classical names" (*Letters,* 5:256); in March 1934, she asked him to withdraw the invitation "as she has never sat on a Committee in her life," and in May she again asserted she would be of "no use." The committee met without her and among the list of newly minted words being considered for pronunciation on the radio were some relating to the threat of war and conditions in the world. For example,

Swastika	SWOSTIKKA
Pogrom	POGROM
Asiatic	AYSHIATIC
Canton	geog. CANTON
	heraldic CANTON
English	ING-GLISH

Given this context, we might consider Woolf's essay "Craftsmanship" in dialogue with George Orwell, I. A. Richards, and the Advisory Committee.

Aware of Orwell's concern with the collapse of public language, Woolf's essay also hints at this dissolution on the eve of World War II. Orwell later formulated his criticisms in his essay "Politics and the English Language": staleness of imagery, lack of precision, dying metaphors, verbal falselimbs, pretentious diction, and meaningless words. Orwell and Woolf pit themselves against the pragmatists of the day—the politicians, the journalists, the Society for Pure English, and politicians who would attempt to fix the meanings of words. Woolf notes that "when words are pinned down they fold their wings and die" ("Craftsmanship," 206).

Using a different vocabulary, Woolf, like a good deconstructionist, asserts that any word "intended" to have a particular meaning and "intended" to be useful may still escape into many meanings and uses in society. What Woolf calls "suggestiveness," Derrida labels "traces." Importantly, it is this various aspect of words, language, and mind that will be denied by some politicians in England, and embraced by Fascists during the war. Determined to preserve the "privacy," the suggestiveness, and the "traces" of words for writers like herself, Woolf is intent in "Craftsmanship" on preserving their "freedom" and aesthetic use. Helpless before journalists, she tries to stem the "public" trammeling of words. She mourns the loss of distinction between the private and the public in the practice of journalists, a distinction that is further blurred during the war (see Laurence, *The Facts and Fugue of War*). In 1937, she writes in her *Diary* of the presence of a "bug" who has stolen into her house to take notes on her life. Her distaste for this journalist enters into a poem, "Just as the bug's body bleeds in pale ink recording his impressions of a private house in the newspapers for cash" (Quentin Bell, 2:254). She suggests that "in time to come writers will have two languages at their service; one for fact, one for fiction" ("Craftsmanship," 200) and "signs" will be the useful language of fact. But she is as alarmed as Orwell with the separation of thought, feeling, and language, for words "seem to like people to think and to feel before they use them" (205).

Woolf's views here are also in tune with I. A. Richards, who asserts in his writings about the same time that words are not "rigid crystals." He presents his concept of the "interanimation" of words—the rich association in words—that Ann Berthoff has so eloquently discussed in her book *Richards on Rhetoric*. If we accept that the meanings of words evolve from both the popular rhetoric of journalism as well as literary writing, then this moment represents the struggle between the political and aesthetic uses of language. One use of language and literature is for political ends and propaganda, a literature that serves national goals as advocated by Mao Zedong in China, or practiced during periods of fascism. During such times, the aesthetic dimension of words and literature shrinks before the mission of the nation.

Examining Woolf's essay, we note the assertion that "words never make anything that is useful" ("Craftsmanship," 198) as a parry to the utilitarian stance developing in the Society for Pure English and Basic English, led by Jeremy Bentham, C. K. Ogden, and I. A. Richards. Woolf, however, was not a teacher of English as a foreign language as were I. A. Richards, William Empson, and Julian Bell in China, and so the pragmatic aspects of language were not salient in her philosophy. What she and others feared at this time was propaganda or centralized control of language leading to fascism, an idea that she develops more fully in her polemic *Three Guineas*. In "Craftsmanship," however, she brilliantly illustrates the way the mind "plays" with words as she ruminates on the train. Woolf's stance that the "power of suggestion is one of the most mysterious properties of words" (203) is political in the context of this discussion. We see in this essay, written about the same time as *Three Guineas*, that she does indeed "fight with words." Words, she says, "do not like to have their purity or impurity discussed. If you start a Society for Pure English, they will show their resentment by starting another for impure English—hence the unnatural violence of much modern speech" (206). At the end of her essay then, Woolf sends up a tirade against the modern use of words, stating that one reason why there is not a great poet, novelist, or critic in England at that time is because words are not free. She is responding, perhaps, to the strictures of the Society for Pure English, as well as the broader cultural attempt to neutralize the multiple meanings of words during the war effort. During the same period in China, writers were sometimes only able to write and publish literature for social use, for the "edification" of the people, another way of limiting the freedom of a writer. Words, Woolf says, "are highly democratic . . . they hate anything that stamps them with one meaning or confines them to one attitude, for it is their nature to change" (206). Language and writing, as Jacques Derrida will articulate half a century later, is a "trace," a moment in the discourse of experience and life, and is always, "sous-rature" (under erasure).

Here Woolf prepares for those like F. R. Leavis who will develop the "moral" and utilitarian purposes of literature. This notion of the morality to be conveyed by literature—that people's behavior has much to do with the literature they read—is also a belief with deep roots in China. Woolf, the writer, however, separates the "aesthetic" from the "useful," a distinction contained, for example, in Richards's and Ogden's Basic English philosophy of reducing the vocabulary of English to 850 words so that it can be "useful" and easily learned by speakers of foreign languages. She asserts simply that "it is their nature not to express one simple statement but a thousand possibilities" (200), knowing from her experience the instability of language that later deconstructionist and postmodern critics will theorize. She admits that words can be caught, sorted, and placed in alphabetical order in dictionaries, "but words do not live in dictionaries; they live in the mind" (204). She observes the instability and historical and personal "traces" in words, and, surprisingly, introduces "semiotics," or the language of signs, in this essay. She notes that because in 1937 people have acknowledged the multiple meanings of words, another language is being invented, the language of signs. There is, she says

> one great living master of this language to whom we are all indebted, that anonymous writer—whether man, woman or disembodied spirit nobody knows—who describes hotels in the Michelin Guide. He wants to tell us that one hotel is moderate, another good, and a third the best in the place. How does he do it? Not with words; words would at once bring into being shrubberies and billiard tables, men and women, the moon rising and the long splash of the summer sea. He sticks to signs. (200)

This is somewhat similar to Richards's reduced model of language, Basic English, that he taught in China for general communication. Though we no longer share Woolf's faith that words "tell the truth" and "survive the chops and changes of time longer than any other substance" (201)—indeed words and ideas mutate in different historical times and places as this book attests—she articulates the flickering nature of words.

What is finally interesting in this discussion of the relationship between politics, language, and art—words for propaganda and words for art—is that it connects with literary discussions in China. A discussion of words conceals an ideology. When Woolf develops the image of words "marrying" and collapsing the boundaries of class and race, she is revealing British ideology of class and commoners:

> And how do [words] . . . live in the mind? Variously and strangely, much as human beings live, by ranging hither and thither, by falling in love, and

mating together. It is true that they are much less bound by ceremony and convention than we are. Royal words mate with commoners. English words marry French words, German words, Indian words, Negro words, if they have a fancy. Indeed, the less we enquire into the past of our dear Mother English the better it will be for that lady's reputation. (205)

Intertwining class thinking, good manners, and the chastity of "mother English" in the imagery and the argument, Woolf importantly suggests here the culturally "promiscuous" and "democratic" nature of the developing modernist movement and vocabulary that will reach out to many cultures—European and Asian—for its enrichment. Importantly, the intellectual and artistic circle of Bloomsbury was a part of this modernist movement.

A PARALLEL COMMUNITY: BLOOMSBURY

The British community "Bloomsbury," formed in Edwardian London about 1904 in the neighborhood known as Bloomsbury, parallels the Crescent Moon group in its oppositional aesthetic stance during a time of rising nationalism. Over the past thirty years, there has been a resurgence of interest in this circle, just as there has been renewed interest in the Crescent Moon group in the past decade in China. The artists and intellectuals in Bloomsbury came from the worlds of literature, painting, law, economics, politics, and colonial administration. Though the "unconscious inheritors of a tradition," as Virginia Woolf would say, they, nevertheless rebelled against certain Victorian cultural conventions and sexual standards. This group, like the Crescent Moon group in China, was described in many ways: by those who were part of it, those on the fringes, those who were fascinated by it, those who condemned it, and those who were repelled by its sexual views, culture, and politics. Contemporaries sketched it and present day critics continue to limn its outlines.[3] Perhaps it is most accurate to say that during the time it flourished, about 1904–32, Bloomsbury was a group of friends, public intellectuals, and artists—just like the Crescent Moon group in China—and not only did their conversations come to be perceived as representative of English intellectual and artistic life, but their work became acknowledged among its most celebrated contributions. In retrospect, it was labeled a "movement," though it never presented a formal manifesto or statement of purpose. It is the best known of many aesthetic groups in England: the Evangelical, the Gothic Revival, the Oxford, the Tractarian, the pre-Raphaelite, and the Arts and Crafts movements. E. M. Forster, a so-called member, considered Bloomsbury "the only genuine movement in English civilization" (Rosenbaum, *The Bloomsbury Group*, 25). Sir Leslie Shane, less sanguine, thinks:

> [Bloomsbury] would include all the flowers of the modern Cambridge Humanism based on G. E. Moore's philosophy. They sought to bring art into life. They scorned British materialism and conventional religion. They promoted individualism. They upheld the standards of truth and beauty. They called for tolerance and integrity. They wrote novels and criticisms. They surveyed and even painted pictures. They gave their message in print rather than with the voice. They scribbled, they lived, they argued, they enjoyed a certain existence of self-esteem, they were given a respectful hearing, and, with the exception of a few fine flashes they have passed into nothingness. (365)

The "fine flashes" were more significant than Leslie Shane admits. But the "war between the high-brows and the low-brows," as Aileen Pippett referred to it in 1955, continues in England today with Bloomsbury bashing by the likes of John Carey, Roger Poole, and Tom Paulin. Much critical evidence, however, has been brought to bear, illuminating Leonard Woolf, Virginia Woolf, Maynard Keynes, G. L. Dickinson, Roger Fry, and E. M. Forster's engagement with the history of their times to counteract the charge that this community was monolithically apolitical, imperialist, colonialist, snobbish, and detached from contact with the "real" world.

One might begin a sketch of the individuals and generations summoned to this study by their connections with China by expanding on Clive Bell's 1913 Bloomsbury diagram:

1ST GENERATION

G. L. Dickinson (1862–1932): political philosopher and don
Bertrand Russell (1872–1970): philosopher and mathematician
Roger Fry (1866–1934): art critic
E. M. Forster (1879–1970): novelist
Virginia Woolf (1882–1941): writer
John Maynard Keynes (1883–1946): economist
Vanessa Bell (1879–1961): painter
Duncan Grant (1885–1978): painter
Clive Bell (1881–1964): art critic

Leonard Woolf (1880–1969): political theorist, writer
Lytton Strachey (1880–1932): biographer
Arthur Waley (1889–1966): translator
George Rylands (Dadie) (1902–98): poet, actor, don

2ND GENERATION
Julian Bell (1908–37): poet, political activist
Quentin Bell (1910–97): writer, artist, art historian
Angelica Bell Garnett (1918–): writer

Those who were loosely aligned with Bloomsbury, or in antagonism with it, with an expressed interest in China might be loosely categorized as the Aesthetes (Arthur Waley, Roger Fry, Harold Acton); the Pragmatists (I. A. Richards, William Empson, John Dewey, Bertrand Russell); the Travelers (Christopher Isherwood, W. H. Auden); the Quakers (Margery Fry, Helen Woodman, Mary Michaelis); the Romantics (G. L. Dickinson); the Teachers (Julian Bell, Lettice Ramsay, I. A. Richards, William Empson); and the Socialists (Sidney and Beatrice Webb, Bertrand and Dora Russell).

As in the discussion in the earlier part of this chapter of the splintered literary groups in China, there were differences in literary and aesthetic stances in Bloomsbury. However, it was the force of science and scientific thinking more than politics that molded the critical temperament of the time. When English intellectuals influenced by scientific principles were trying to systematize literary criticism in the 1930s, Chinese literary groups were in a state of political tension about the relationship between politics and art because of the split between the nationalists and the communists and the desperation of the impending Sino-Japanese War. The lives and aesthetic stances of Roger Fry and I. A. Richards perhaps best represent some of the issues. After Roger Fry's death in 1934, Julian Bell, on his way to China, wrote a draft of an essay on Fry's life for Virginia and Leonard Woolf's Hogarth Press letter series. It was to be, Julian Bell said in his Cambridge notes, "a letter from a poet to a scientist, both sharing a good deal in their way of looking at life; a letter that will try to give an account of one of the few men of genius who have ever made a real synthesis of the attitudes of the artist and the scientist."

The question that Fry most commonly asked as an art critic is "why does this work of art produce an emotion in me?" This question grew organically from G. E. Moore's philosophy, popular with Cambridge undergraduates and Bloomsbury, which simply put forth the "value" of the appreciation of art and beauty (as well as friendship). All of Cambridge was moving beyond "value," and asking "why" works of art affected them, initiating the next stage of literary criticism which asked "how" the aesthetic emotion is produced. To Fry's question of "why," Richards added a generation later, "*how* does this work of art produce an emotion in me and other readers?" This question of process, the "how," and the inclusion of other readers in the evaluation of response to literature was a new one in Cambridge. It was a product of the developing scientific spirit entering art criticism through the new field of psychology, and would evolve into practical criticism and then New Criticism in the 1930s. Julian Bell, representative of the second generation of Bloomsbury, articulates this stance in a letter to Helen Soutar while a student at King's College in 1930:

> As for criticism . . . you must choose between making moral judgments on writer's ideas or being a psychologist studying the causes and nature of certain mental phenomena. . . . For my own part . . . the critic is a scientist, and a psychologist, and that his business is, by studying on the one hand technique, on the other human minds, to discover the truth about society. Anyway, I think myself that unchecked, bare speculation, is, with two exceptions, the most exciting of human activities and aesthetics one of the best. (29 March 1930)

I. A. Richards goes further in his works *Practical Criticism* (1929) and *The Foundation of Aesthetics* to explain how readers arrive at judgments, both mistaken and sound, in literature. Fry's theories and observations, on the other hand, contain only the authority that another observer is willing to concede to it because the opinion comes from Roger Fry, one art critic. Fry asked "why"; Richards asked "how." Fry observed himself, "the knowing self"; Richards observed the response of "others," not only his Cambridge undergraduates but Chinese students as well in his sojourns in China. While Fry, of a different generation and aesthetic, asked what art does to the "soul," Richards asked what does it do to the "mind." What develops is the field of aesthetics and psychology and the groundwork for New Criticism.

In Richards's own ingenious and well-known "experiment" with his Cambridge students, reported in *Practical Criticism,* he issued sheets of poems ranging from Shakespeare to lesser-known poets such as Ella Wheeler Wilcox, concealing the authorship of the poems. Students were asked to comment freely in writing about the quality of diverse poems over the period of a week.

The results reveal what every teacher knows—the misconceptions and misperceptions in literary value judgments. After studying the student responses or "protocols," Richards would lecture the following week about the understanding and misunderstanding embodied in student "opinion" of what was good poetry and what was bad. He called this experiment "a record of a piece of field-work in comparative ideology," its aim being to improve communication about literature.

> When we have solved, completely, the communication problems, when we have got, perfectly, the experience, the mental condition relevant to the poem, we have still to judge it, still to decide upon its worth. (*Practical Criticism*, 11)

Richards attempted to keep objectivity and "science" in balance in the psychology of aesthetic response. Nevertheless, Terry Eagleton, a contemporary Marxist literary critic, is critical of Richards's "experiment":

> Reading Richards' undergraduates' accounts of literary works, one is struck by the habits of perception and interpretation which they spontaneously share—what they expect literature to be, what assumptions they bring to a poem. . . . None of this is really surprising: for all the participants in this experiment were, presumably, young, white, upper- or upper middle class, privately educated English people of the 1920s. (15)

Eagleton's ignorance of Richards's comparative venture and lifelong passion to find a way to teach English to the masses in China as well as England is glaring. He neglects to mention Richards's later comparative educational work conducting protocols with Chinese students reading, among other things, Thomas Hardy's *Tess of the D'Urbervilles,* reported in *So Much Nearer.* Here Richards observes the Chinese students' reaction to Tess's death at the end of the novel. Listening intently to Richards's reading of the last scene of the novel, Tess's suicide, a big cheer goes up in the classroom. Richards, puzzled by this response to the tragic moment, discovers that the students cheer because Tess has gotten her just desserts for disobeying her father at the beginning of the novel. Chinese students respond to the novel, says Richards, according to *their* patriarchal and Confucian family value of obedience to parents. The tragic Greek framing of Hardy is not experienced. More recent readings of Hardy's *Tess* that I discovered in discussions with Ren Jinsheng, formerly deputy editor of the People's Literature Press in Beijing, is that Tess is not as likable a character as Jane Eyre to Chinese women readers. She noted that Tess is considered to be of "weak" character because she follows the "fates," becoming a "victim" of two men, instead of asserting her independence and agency as the admirable Jane Eyre.

This organized study of art and literature, the developing British fields of literary criticism and aesthetics, attracted Xu Zhimo while he was visiting Cambridge, as well as other Chinese writers and critics. Xu's calligraphy on the frontispiece to C. K. Ogden, James Wood, and I. A. Richards, *Foundations of Aesthetics* (1921), attests to his Cambridge conversation about "criticism" with members of the Heretics Club, of which Richards was a member. The two characters, zhongjian (zhong-yong) meaning "the golden mean" represent the Chinese philosophy of balance and calm. Yuan Kejia, a Chinese poet and literary critic, reported that he was influenced in an early stage of writing by Xu Zhimo's poetry and that in the 1930s and especially in the 1940s, the South-West Associated University—the wartime combination of Beijing University, Qinghua, and Nankai Universities—"was then the lively center of literary modernism" (Interview by the author). Poets, novelists, critics, and translators gathered at these universities, read Xu Zhimo, T. S. Eliot's "Tradition and the Individual Talent," translated in the 1930s, and loved living in old Beijing. In 1938, a student of Richards's at Harvard and an advocate of New Criticism, William Empson, according to Yuan Kejia, "taught at Lianda, and had exerted direct influence on his students" (Interview by the author). He taught English poetry in the same year that Auden traveled to the Chinese battlefronts with Christopher Isherwood. Bian Zhilin and Cao Baohua along with I. A. Richards and William Empson (on their important visits in the 1920s and early 1930s) introduced *Practical Criticism* into China. In the 1940s, critics like Yuan Kejia used *Practical Criticism* to refute Marxist critics just as British romanticism was used by Xu Zhimo and the Crescent Moon group to oppose political trends in the decade before. The rich intellectual dialogue engendered by these visits of British and American professors, intellectuals, and writers cannot be underestimated in the developing terrain of literary criticism, cultural relations, and international modernism. The foreign culture of British literary circles bolstered dissident literary views within China.

Generation, temperament, and linguistic style aside, Fry and Richards did agree on one thing: they both admired the culture of China. Both were drawn

I. A. Richards and Dorothy Richards. "University luncheon. Note the bottles on the little table among which I had been long at work. I certainly look the only person present who is enjoying himself" (I. A. Richards). By permission of the Master & Fellows, Magdalene College, Cambridge University, England.

to the "foreign," particularly the East: Fry, aesthetically; Richards, culturally and pedagogically. Richards traveled to China five times (1927, 1929–30, 1936–38, 1950, 1979), and one of his stays overlapped with Julian Bell's. Julian writes to Shuhua, 4 September 1936, asking whether "Richards is back." While in China, Richards struggled to establish a nationwide experiment in Basic English in China (modelled after a Chinese teacher, Yen)—only to have his best effort in 1937 destroyed by the Sino-Japanese War. Richards wrote that "the Nanking government had set up with the minister of education a committee to put my recommendations on Basic into action wherever the authority of the government could be enforced." Richards was at Yenching [Yanjing] University and Beijing University Medical Center when it was taken over by the Japanese puppet regime around 1938, forcing him to abandon his Basic English project. He then became part of the university in exile in Wuhan, arriving there about six months after Julian Bell left.

During these visits to China, Richards and his wife, Dorothy, both physically vigorous, scaled the mountains of China, appreciating the incredible beauty of the actual landscape in ways that few English did at that time. Fry, in the meantime, studied and lectured about early Chinese ceramics during the Qin and Han Dynasties in Cambridge's prestigious Slade series in 1933–34, incorporating aspects of Chinese aesthetic principles into his own ceramics produced in the Omega Workshop. Richards was drawn to comparative cultural and linguistic study as well as engaged by practical teaching methodology as revealed in *Mencius on Mind*. Though one focuses more squarely on the aesthetic, and, the other, on the pragmatics of teaching and translating, new aesthetic and pedagogical worlds opened for them in Asian culture. Both believed that English culture should begin to take account of this.

Chapter Three

EAST-WEST LITERARY CONVERSATIONS

*Exploring Civilization and Subjectivity—
G. L. Dickinson and Xu Zhimo*

TERMS THAT FOLD AND UNFOLD MEANING: CIVILIZATION AND SUBJECTIVITY

Both G. L. Dickinson (1862–1932) and Xu Zhimo (1896–1931) engage in self-fashioning in their writing. They "perform," as Judith Butler might say, East and West. Traces of China linger in the Chinese cap worn by G. L. Dickinson, a don at Cambridge University who emoted about the contemplative wonders of the ancient civilization of China to his students; and the image of an English gentleman is projected in the trousers worn by Xu Zhimo, a leading Chinese poet and critic of repute who studied at Cambridge and urged, upon his return to China, the expression of "true personality" and emotions embodied in the British romantic poets. These cultural badges—the Chinese cap and the British trousers—reflect identification, the way a T-shirt, an ethnic pocketbook, a flash of foreign tapestry, does today. The adoption of a fashion not only is a "familiarization" of the "foreign" but sometimes also expresses sympathy with another culture. In my own travels to China, the Mandarin-style jackets that I purchased and wore at home in the streets of New York City reminded me always that there was another place that had oases of beauty and a culture that challenged my thinking. After travel to or reading about another place, a trace of clothing may become part of a costume that signals "a change of

Peking University stamp

heart"—cultural heart—a phrase often used by both G. L. Dickinson and Xu Zhimo, who was mentored by both Dickinson and Dadie Rylands at Cambridge University. It may also embed criticism of one's own culture. Xu Zhimo's participation in the May Fourth 1919 movement revealed his criticism of his own culture and led him to found the Crescent Moon group described earlier. This chapter provides the biographical and historical background to his aesthetic stance.

Cultural Attraction

Despite the horrors of World Wars I and II, England maintained a relatively stable cultural and aesthetic environment at home because the greater part of these wars were fought in other places; in China, on the other hand, the Sino-Japanese War and the civil war displaced large portions of the population, ravaged the land and put Chinese culture under arrest. G. L. Dickinson largely ignored this cultural and political chaos, and held a cameo of an ancient and idealized, meditative culture of China and its arts. The British, in general, had only a limited response to the political upheaval and remained a presence along with other foreign concessions in the coastal city of Shanghai, which in 1927 was the most cosmopolitan and crime-ravaged city in China. More attuned to the stereotypes of the sedate, inward-looking temperament of the Chinese, and their idealized, antique past reaching back to the wonderful Zhou bronze art of 2000 B.C., the British neglected China's desperate and turbulent contemporary political situation. Letters, diaries, and other unpublished documents reveal the terms applied to the country by the British in the 1920s: exotic, strange, mysterious, antique, traditional, foreign, ritualistic. The people were described as tactful, reticent, subdued, polite, well-mannered, subtle, traditional, decorous, charming, suspicious. The word "antique," often applied to China by the British, contains its own archaeology in two different cultures. "Antiquity," centuries of tradition and history, is something the Chinese treasured in their own culture during this period of political, cultural, and literary upheaval that began with certain kinds of "modernizations" after 1911 when China became a Republic. At the same time, why and how, as Benedict Anderson has observed, a certain nation, England, at a certain historical moment, begins to value the "antiquity" of a China as a "novelty" (xiv) during its own period of political ferment is a question that motivates this book. What is found in the narratives, for example, of G. L. Dickinson and Xu Zhimo are new forms of consciousness in artistic communities that begin to break with older forms of belief and feeling and memory. This itself creates its own narrative in a time of flux.

The artists studied here separated themselves from the general cultural and political stream, and articulated their sympathy and desire to connect with other artists in China. China became the object of English fascination and imagination, much as Africa intrigued the French, and political and cultural realities were muted in the quest. As China's imperial power declined and its nationalism split at the beginning of the twentieth century, the British, caught in an aesthetic time lapse, focused upon its "antiquity." We note the ironies, just as the traveler Julian Bell discovered, of such encounters as the envisioned ancient and settled place explodes into a complex and troubled history in the first half of the twentieth century. From a postcolonial stance, romanticized views or ideologies that inform the aesthetic representations of China also cloak its poverty, famine, floods, and war. Cultures, however, take from one another what they need. China was far away: information traveled slowly—it was a three-month voyage by ship—and it was linguistically detached with a system of characters that puzzled the English. The linguistic and geographical walls were perhaps too high to traverse at the time (that we now bound with the Internet), and therefore antique or historical China was useful in British literature and art. *Mis en abime*—the flash of a fan, a screen, a Chinese fashion, blue and white porcelain—conjured the feeling of a place, the sense of the foreign, in a painting or a home. This work, however, focuses not only on what the English or Chinese artists and writers "see" once they "incorporate" other views (with all the connotations of the root of the word, "corpus"—body—"embody"); it also attempts to understand what cultural needs and tensions are concealed in the mutual aesthetic receptivity of England and China in the early part of the twentieth century.[1]

G. L. Dickinson and Xu Zhimo constructed their respective China and England from imagination, reading, and visits. G. L. Dickinson, aware of the long and devastating history of English economic exploitation and a founder of the League of Nations before the Great War, longed for a temperate and moderate civilization like ancient China without aggression and war; Xu Zhimo, a romantic personality and poet, desired to unleash into Chinese life and literature the passions of the body and the personality, the drama and expression of the individual that he had observed in British romantic poetry and England of the time. Though this British don and Chinese writer were separated by cultural difference, both believed in national change through a "spiritual revolution" in their respective countries. History structured, to some degree, the literary and cultural subtext of Dickinson and Xu's conversation, and, as representative thinkers and writers, their conversations and their lives are "inscribed in the narrative of nation" (Chatterjee, *The Nation and Its Fragments*, 138). The imperialism of the British, the nationalism of the Chinese and the developing discourse on "self," "sentimentalism," "feeling," "modernity," and "modernism" settled into the imperceptible spaces of their talk and writing. The English, having just emerged from the Great War, were preoccupied at the beginning of the twentieth century with "the forces that make and unmake civilization" (*Three Guineas*); on the other hand, the Chinese intellectuals presented in this book were concerned with national consciousness and individual self-expression in a nation that sometimes subsumed their individual voices. The British, on the cusp of modernism, were bored by the kind of soulful language brandished by poets like Xu Zhimo, expression that they considered a throwback to the worst aspects of British romanticism. It was an age that craved economy of expression.

XU ZHIMO: "THE GREAT LINK WITH BLOOMSBURY"

A photograph of Xu Zhimo taken upon his return to China from Cambridge in 1923 reveals British trousers peeping beneath his Chinese gown. Though Chinese were shot for wearing Western trousers during the Boxer Rebellion in 1900, Xu, like many returning from study in the West, adopted the dress and manners of "British gentleman of repute" upon his return to Beijing. Later in China, the term "gentleman" would become a term of contempt when applied by the leftists to the "decadent bourgeois" (gentry = *shenshi*) or those who were drawn to the study of English literature. During his first trip to Cambridge (September 1921–October 1922), however, Xu wrote of spending his time studying with gentlemen and sauntering on the banks of the Cam, studying his soul mates, the British romantic poets. Arriving at King's College as a special student in 1921, he became, according to Gaylord Leung in "English Friends," a lifelong friend of G. L. Dickinson, Dadie Rylands, H. G. Wells, Roger Fry, and Bertrand Russell, and was introduced to Arthur Waley and Laurence Binyon. Xu was drawn, as his British mentors were, to the intellectual and aesthetic possibilities of a different culture.

Dadie Rylands and Virginia Woolf. By permission of the Provost and Scholars of King's College, Cambridge University Library, England.

Shortly after Xu arrived at Cambridge in 1920, he wrote to his family that he enjoyed "communicating with celebrated English scholars" (Leung, *English Friends,* 23). Cambridge was a welcome escape from the historical maelstrom that was then China. Initially, Xu had traveled to Clark University, lured from Shanghai along with many other Chinese students in 1918–19 to study banking, the family business. He was the son of Xu Shenru, a banker in Zhejiang Province. Xu wrote, "I have checked my family record. Since the Yung-lo reign [of the Ming dynasty] no single poetical line worth reciting had been written in this household" (Leo Ou-fan Lee, 125). Having been a favorite student of Liang Qichao's (1873–1929), a famous scholar in China, he was well trained and was already under the influence of a "modern" thinker. Aspiring, at first, to be "the Alexander Hamilton of China," he studied economics at Clark University, 1918, and then attended Columbia University, 1919, where he studied political science and earned an master of arts degree. He was considered a "Bolshevik," according to Leo Ou-fan Lee, in the eyes of his classmates. Giving up his doctoral studies, he went to England with a view to studying under Bertrand Russell, "the Voltaire of the twentieth century." He discovered upon his arrival that Russell "had been dismissed from Cambridge partly because of his pacifism during the War and partly because of his divorces" (Leung, "Xu and Russell," 27). After this, Xu briefly studied at the London School of Economics, and then at Cambridge University in 1921. It is worth noting the Eurocentric labels applied to and adopted by Xu and other intellectuals in the Crescent Moon group, attesting to their identification with America and Europe. The nicknames signaled their divided selves and cultural identification at a time when such as association was suspect in China. Xu became "the Alexander Hamilton of China" when studying economics; he matriculated at King's College, Cambridge, with the name "Hsu Changhsu Hamilton," on the roster; and later when he turned to literature, he was dubbed, "the Chinese Shelley."

Xu wrote of his intellectual travels:

> My eyes were opened by Cambridge. My desire for knowledge was stirred by Cambridge. My self-consciousness took its embryonic form in Cambridge. I spent two years in America and two years in England. In America I was busy attending classes, listening to lectures, writing examination papers, chewing gum, going to the movies and cursing. In Cambridge I was busy with walks, punting, riding on bicycles, smoking, chatting, drinking five o'clock teas and eating buttered cakes, and reading at random. If I was a pure dunce when I came to America, I remained unchanged when I left the Goddess of Liberty. But if I was unenlightened in America, my days at Cambridge at least made me realize that previously I was full of ignorance. This difference is by no means little. (Leo Ou-fan Lee, *The Romantic Generation*, 132)

But what were the conditions at Cambridge that stimulated Xu Zhimo's exuberant expression? Cambridge University was peace to Chinese writers and intellectuals, an escape from the turbulent period of the warlords and the post-Republic cultural conflicts between the traditionalists and the iconoclasts in China, a tension that persisted from about 1919 to 1925. Xu was one of a growing number of Chinese supported by Boxer Indemnity Grants or private family funds that enabled them to leap over the geographical, cultural, and psychological "walls" of China and to begin literary and cultural conversations that sometimes had far-reaching effects. These Boxer funds—450 million silver dollars—were awarded to England and America in compensation for the damages to life and property during the Boxer uprising, and were used for educational, architectural, and even, according to J. M. Keynes and Archibald

Rose, the development of railways in China. Those Chinese students who could afford it with or without Boxer funds went to the United States or England or France; some, with Marxist political interests, to Russia; others with less money to Japan, geographically closer, as described in the previous chapter. Some Chinese returning from England, France, and America had new cosmopolitan eyes. Xu was one a group of Chinese who flocked to England—often Cambridge University, Oxford University, The London School of Oriental and African Studies, London School of Economics—and America—particularly Cornell, Columbia, and Clark University—after World War I to study practical subjects such as agriculture and economics or to write journalism. Willy-nilly, though this was not encouraged in history-centered China where fiction was considered "defective history,"[2] they were drawn into the study of British poetry or the novel. Interested in a New China, they were open to ideas from abroad, and the West offered an intellectual space where "fiction" was respected as a genre. And it is perhaps this British openness that allowed an influential group of Chinese writers to find validation for their alternate sense of "what is real" in the genre of "fiction" that was not encouraged in China. Those who pursued literary interests, however, were few. A Report of the British Government Board of Trustees for the Administration of the Boxer Indemnity Funds in 1934 indicates that twenty scholarships were awarded, most in fields such hydraulics, railway, civil engineering, and geography; only one was in English literature (7). There was also an allotment of 5000 pounds for professorship and 20,000 pounds for construction at Wuhan University. The numbers in the humanities increased as time went on.

Having the luxury of time and release from material concerns in Cambridge, Xu could develop personal relations, personal writing, explore East-West aesthetics, and enjoy the beauties of nature in the antique city of Cambridge. He was well liked by Bloomsbury. David Garnett wrote that "he came here once and won our hearts completely. Stayed with Roger" (Letter to Julian Bell, 1935, CHAO). Xu Zhimo, like Xiao Qian, a Chinese friend of E. M. Forster's, and, Ye Junjian, a student of Julian Bell's—both of whom visited a generation later in 1940s and 1950s—were enthralled by the idea of Bloomsbury and the idyll of Cambridge. Gaylord Leung, one of Xu's biographers, reports that Mr. Rolf Gardiner of Cambridge related that Xu was often seen chatting with G. L. Dickinson in his living quarters, the top floor of Gibbs, to which Dickinson welcomed the Chinese students on campus.

People observed Xu lingering by Dickinson's door in a strange state of mind. But, says Leung, they may not have realized that Xu was meditating. He writes that the penthouse

> was a place of serenity. Through the windows on the corridor, the green trees and the blue sky were visible. It was so quiet that we could hear time gliding by as the birds chirped. The corridor was quite spacious. Alone, Xu sat there quietly meditating under the influence of Dickinsonism. This literary man was completely absorbed in this state with unraveling the entangled threads of worldliness. (*The Complete Works,* 6)

Removed from the maelstrom of poverty and war in China, Xu wrote his farewell to Cambridge on the China Sea in 1925. What is of interest in this cliched poem is the traditional, extension of the borders of self into nature-characteristic of Chinese poets, reflected in lines such as "I'd be happy to remain a waterweed":

> Quietly I am leaving
>
> Just as quietly I came;
> Quietly I wave a farewell
> To the Western sky aflame.
> The golden willow on the riverbank,
> A bride in the setting sun;
> Her colorful reflection
> Ripples through my heart.
>
> The green plants on the river bed,
> So much and so gracefully swaying
> In the gentle current of the Cam
> I'd be happy to remain a waterweed. . . .
> (Twentieth Century Chinese Poetry, 84).

Xu Zhimo, according to T. T. Wang, "was China's greatest poet in the 1920s and 1930s [and] whose tragic death had been regarded as an [irreparable] loss to modern Chinese literature" (Wang to Leonard Elmhirst, 20 March 1964). Though other critics would say that Guo Moruo and Wen Yiduo were more talented poets and Xu, overrated. But there is no doubt that Xu was prescient about the modern literary values that would emerge in China the 1920s and then again in post-1976 literature. Xu eagerly embraced not only British romanticism but Thomas Hardy, modernism, and wrote home to his literary friends in China of James Joyce as early as 1922. He wrote in a forword to his own poem, his praise:

> The last hundred pages of his book [*Ulysses*] (which has more than seven hundred pages in all) are written in a prose, which is really pure: smooth as cream . . . It is not only free from capital letters, but it is totally unburdened with all those tiresome marks like,. . . . ?:-;-! ()" ". There is neither division of paragraphs, sentences, chapters or sections. Just a flow of limpid, beautiful, torrential text pouring forward, like a huge bundle of white poplin let loose, a large cataract coming down without any trace. What a great masterly art! (Jin Di, *Shamrocks and Chopsticks*, 16).

What a liberating observation of English: punctuation and capital letters and paragraphs as tiresome. Both e. e. cummings and Joyce shared this view. Xu's early affinity with Joyce is apparent here: classical Chinese was free of punctuation and spacing before 1917 and this, unwittingly, linguistically paralleled Joyce's experiments with the English language. But Joyce was repudiated in 1935 by the Chinese. Zhou Libo, a Marxist writer who opposed Western "decadence," labeled *Ulysses* "poisonous" and "obscene": "Who but persons with an excess of fat would need such a book?" (Jin Di, *Shamrocks and Chopsticks*, 17). This negative response to Western literature occurred again during the Cultural Revolution when Xiao Qian noted that China "traversed a Middle Age . . . in the 60s when to have studied British literature was a crime" (letter to the author). This political climate of repudiation influenced Yuan Kejia's literary positions on Joyce. In 1964, affiliated with the Literature Institute of Peking [Beijing] University, Yuan published an essay, "Survey of Stream of Consciousness Fiction in Britain and America," in which he also attacked *Ulysses* for its "nihilist, philistine and pornographic" tendencies. In 1978, after the Cultural Revolution when Western literature was reintroduced into China—no longer considered "criminal" by Marxist critics—Yuan Kejia changed his stance and included an excerpt of *Ulysses* in the eight-volume *Selections of Modernist Literature from Abroad* (see appendix C for listing of works included). Prescient about Joyce and other modernist writers, Xu Zhimo was welcomed upon his return to China in 1925 as one of its most flamboyant and influential poets and critics.

AN ENGLISH DON IN A CHINESE CAP: G. L. DICKINSON

A figure parallel to Xu, G. L. Dickinson, a Cambridge University don, visited China in 1910–11 and 1913–14, and expressed what was most extraordinary to him from a temple near Beijing. Writing to Roger Fry—"Dear Podge"—he exclaims:

> I feel so at home. I think I must have been a chinaman once. I'm now in a temple in the hills West of Peking [Beijing] . . . and a sense of a most dignified contemplative life that I have ever met anywhere else. . . . What a civilized people they have been. And how boundaries went in punishing them for it! But I won't [go into] all that, it makes me too indignant. Peking [Beijing] is amazing. . . . What I want to do is to take a room in a temple and spend a week there. (10 May 1913)

G. L. Dickinson, Cambridge don, in Chinese cap. By permission of the Provost and Scholars of King's College, Cambridge University, England.

In his later years, Dickinson wore a black silk Chinese cap, given to him by Xu Zhimo, around the quads of Cambridge when he felt a draught. Dickinson amused the students at King's College, Cambridge University, where he was a lecturer and then fellow in history, 1896–1920, with his mysticism. "I am speaking to you about China," he once told them, "not because I know anything about the subject, not because I once visited the country but because in a previous existence, I actually was a Chinese man" (Forster, *G. L. Dickinson*, 117). Dickinson's interest was affectionately parodied by the King's College Discussion Society and the Chetwynd Society in a 1912 issue of *Balieon H*.:

> Mr. Dickinson read a paper on "Is Life Worth Living" to a large meeting. . . . Mr. Dickinson said life, like a dome of many-coloured glass, stained the white radiance of eternity. . . . Mr. Bliss said he guessed it was clear that the reader of the paper had never seen the interior of a Christian Western home. (King's College, 16)

Parodying Dickinson's high-minded love of Shelley—"life as a dome of many-colored glass"—in juxtaposition with the poverty in the interior of a Chinaman's home, alluded to by Dickinson in his anonymously published *Letters from John Chinaman* in 1901, he is an easy target. Because of his temperament, he was drawn to the perceived romanticism (or is it "sentimentalism"?) in Chinese sensibility. A generation later when Harold Barger wrote to Julian Bell, who was teaching in Wuhan, China, he asked, "Do you feel about China as Goldie felt about it" (14 April 1936), alluding to the sentimental strain in Dickinson. Vanessa Bell also notes this in a letter to Julian:

> I always think Goldie had so much odd kind of romanticism in him—almost sentimental—that he swallows people whole once he took it into his head they were sympathetic and he ceased to be critical—in fact he was never very critical of people, was he. Perhaps he felt the Chinese attitude to life was fundamentally on his side—then he accepted all else. (25 October 1936)

The criticism—Dickinson's softness, idealism, other-worldliness, and his "different scale of values"—is mentioned by others in eulogies after his death. The same adjectives are often used to describe Xu Zhimo during this period, suggesting the temperamental affinities. Dickinson's gentleness, raptures about romanticism, and, sometimes, vagueness characterized other aspects of his personality. Virginia Woolf parodies it, writing "Goethe, Shelley, Goethe, Shelley, and then he loses his glasses." With a lifelong interest in Plato, Goethe and Shelley, giving lectures such as "Is Immortality Desirable?" and mystical talks on China, he was ripe for parody. And it was said that he had little skill with his hands, as anyone would attest who has tried to decipher his handwriting in letters now housed in the Modern Archives at King's College. Leonard Woolf perhaps best captures Dickinson in his description of his "thin vapor of gentle high-mindedness": an observer of English culture and politics temperamentally drawn to China.

Yet Dickinson's interest in China was propelled by a belief in the superior qualities of Chinese civilization: "I know of no other country which has regarded the trade of the soldier with aversion" (*Chinese Poetry*, 6). His stance was unusual in England at that time. T. S. Eliot, who studied at Harvard under Irving Babbitt, also was convinced that "Chinese civilization at its highest has graces and excellences which may make Europe seem crude" (Eliot, *After Strange Gods*, 43). But they were exceptions. Xu Zhimo mirrored Dickinson and Eliot in his admiration of British culture. E. M. Forster, G. L. Dickinson's best friend and biographer, characterized Dickinson's stance: "he came to her [China] as a lover, who had worshipped from afar for years. . . . China never failed him. She stood firm as the one decent civilization" (Forster, *G. L. Dickinson*, 117). To Dickinson—styled by Fry as "one of our most pacifist and progressive propagandists" (Letter to Charles Vildrac, February 1919)—China was a bellwether "civilization" to look toward to save Europe from its new imperialism and "barbarism." He admired its "most dignified contemplative life."

THE CULTIVATION OF THE ROMANTIC SELF: XU ZHIMO

It is always difficult to correlate British and Chinese concepts and literary terms and periods, as Earl Miner attests in his writing about comparative genres. Consequently, this book also reaches into earlier epochs of Asian art to identify "modern" qualities, traits, and cultural and literary currents that attracted twentieth-century British thinkers and writers. The British combed through Chinese aesthetic experience and used what they defined as modern despite its earlier age and with varying degrees of understanding.

Similarly, the Chinese culturally foraged British literature and culture for what would be useful in their society. An example of this cultural exploration involves the concept and expression of "self" in speech, writing, and visual art during the period of this study, 1900–49. In Republican China, the concept of "self" related to the Chinese artists' growing desire to express the individuality and subjectivity that marked the writings of Xu Zhimo and the May Fourth writers. The Chinese notion of "self," though, was enfolded in a long-standing tradition of Confucian and Daoist philosophy as well as incipient socialist ideology that promoted the value of collectivity, responsibility to others, and social obligation. For a British modernist, this seemingly undifferentiated "self" was hard to grasp: the borders between "it" and a larger landscape of nature or society blurred. The archaeology of the Chinese sense of "self" was yet to be unearthed as it was not articulated in such a way that it was recognizable to the British or the West. Its "genealogy," as Foucault might say, was "hidden;" the concept registered in another key as discussed in chapter 4, "Chinese Landscapes through British Eyes."

In traditional Chinese paintings, the individual figure is rarely focused upon as a subject (perhaps with the exception of dead emperors) as it often is in Western art since the Renaissance, particularly during the Neoclassical period that focuses on man as its subject. Also, as mentioned earlier, the Confucian philosophy that informs Chinese thinking places an individual in a hierarchy of ethical obligations to family, community and nation; to Daoism, in relation to nature and something in the universe; to socialism in relation to the people in the community; and to Marxism, in relation to the state. When the word "self" or "individual" is used in a Chinese context, we respond with our Western understandings. The "self" as a philosophical or psychological entity is delineated by our vocabulary of "subject" and "object" in Western philosophy from the time of Descartes ("I think, therefore, I am"), and in psychology since Sigmund Freud. We are deaf to the philosophical, cultural and economic dimensions in China where self and society, subject and object are less differentiated in the landscape. Even today, I am told, "individualism" in China is a neologism that sometimes connotes "selfishness," "do your own thing-ism," or "just consider yourself-ism," an individual who ignores social responsibility, whereas, in America, it is a valued trait. Exploration of the psychology of the individual state of mind may arouse suspicion given the value of collectivity in China. Consequently, socialist or capitalist principles can frame the "self" negatively or positively. What is important in the period under study is that the consciousness of the terms "self," "self-expression," and "individualism" developed and was articulated in the discourse of nation among Chinese writers in England and America, and then later in China. In the section that follows, I will trace Xu Zhimo's awareness and articulation of this term, "self," in relation to larger entities of family, community and nation, and the way that it enters into his literary thinking.

The emerging discussion of "self" during the period of this study in China can only be understood in relation to these larger forces, in a network of differences. In the first conversation to be presented here, the forces that act upon Xu Zhimo are no longer just those contained in traditional China but also England. His meaning as a poet and personality emerges from many Chinas at home and abroad. The literary, cultural, and political forces that swirl around him are those of the May Fourth literary movement which, in turn, incorporated the experiences of Chinese scholars abroad in America and England, as well as his own visits to England in 1918–25, 1927–29, and to India in 1928. In sum, the historical, philosophical, and cultural conditions that evolved in China in the early part of the twentieth century—moments in the consciousness of a nation—incorporate British and American (as well as Japanese, Russian, French, and German) thought, literature, and experiences, as well as the influence of Chinese scholars abroad. The notion then of "self" and its literary effects in "self-expression" and "subjectivity" evolves *among* cultures in the conversations such as those *between* G. L. Dickinson and Xu Zhimo as described by Zhang Longxi: "East-West Literature must be established in a third area, a mediating ground on which East-West comparative literature will acquire its own identity as different from either of the specialist branches" (*China in a Polycentric World*, 35). Such a mediating ground is presented in the recent criticism of Chen Xiaomei and Tani Barlow. We discover again in this conversation that what the West has viewed as "natural" or "universal" about the "self," "personality," or the "individual"—the philosophical and psychological basis of modernism—is a construct of our own culture and history. Analyzing this moment of exchange between Xu Zhimo and G. L. Dickinson makes us culturally and critically self-reflective. Uncovering the philosophical, historical, and cultural conditions that produce notions of "self" in the English imagination—conditions not replicated in China—we discover different perceptions and articulations of "subjectivity" and "interiority."

It is important to note, as Tani Barlow and Xiaomei Chen do not, that Western notions of the "self" and "landscape" (cultural and visual) at this time are modified by the growing British interest in Buddhist and Daoist conceptions of "self" and "ego" in Asian philosophy and art. While some Chinese intellectuals felt the lack of a convention and vocabulary for a growing consciousness of the "self" and the "individual," the British were burdened with it. They longed to lose the "ego" in philosophies represented in Far Eastern religions and culture, a trend that continues today in England and America. Each culture is drawn to what the other offers and to its own perceived lack.

Xu Zhimo's articulation of the "self" emerged from the British romantic poets who advanced a new kind of individualism considered revolutionary in China. In essays written during and immediately after his stay at Cambridge, 1920–22, he often used the word "romantic" to suggest a certain kind of experience. He spoke of a desire for a "variegated, dramatic life [to] . . . be treated as a piece of art, an artistic problem" (*Art and Life*, 15). The borders between life and art diminished. Xu's growing desire to express his self and subjectivity is marked in the poem "The Cricket" written upon his return to China in which he longs for a place where "dogma" cannot "cruelly ravish thought" (Kai yu-Xu, *Twentieth Century Chinese Poetry*, 91). Xu shored his notion of the romantic "self" and "individual personality" against the prevailing socialist politics. Such articulation became possible as Chinese society liberalized and allowed it to come into expression as a part of the May Fourth 1919 literary movement. British modernists, at the same time, wrote of the modern "self" articulated by Freud in the 1920s—a psychological entity, fragmented though it may be in the modernist conception.

Reflecting on one's "self," scrutinizing one's own "consciousness," or discovering through this process one's own body or sexuality was not a familiar way of thinking or being to Xu Zhimo's Chinese students at Qinghua University in 1926 where he returned to teach. Qinghua, nevertheless, was open to Xu's views as it prepared Chinese students to study abroad under provisions of the Boxer Indemnity. It was the first Chinese university to admit female students (Chen Heng-zhe, *My Childhood Pursuit of Education*, 45). Quoting Pater's dictum to "burn always with a hard gem-like flame," Xu argued "art-for-art's-sake" in his lectures to his students. In taking up this popular turn of the century British aesthetic slogan, Xu challenged the "traditional" Chinese dictum of "art for life's sake," another jingoistic binary adapted from fin de siècle terminology that frames this conversation. Returning from Cambridge and a different way of life and thinking, he echoed the sentiments of the aesthetic movement and the romantic poets. His notion of "artistic thrills . . . beauty and being alive" created a way of thinking in China that made possible the articulation and construction of a different notion of "self," reminding us again that the concept of "self" is historically and culturally constituted. At the same time as Xu heralded "art-for-art's-sake," the aesthetic movement was being parodied in England in Gilbert and Sullivan's *Patience* as the "aesthetic poet," Reginald Bunthorne proclaims "I'm an aesthetic sham."

But what was parodied, rejected, or "outgrown" from the point of view of British modernism was valued in China. While T. S. Eliot was shattering the pure exuberant "I" in "The Love Song of J. Alfred Prufrock," Xu was asserting its importance in his essay, "Art and Life." Xu urged students to join the age of revolt and rebel against the "cock-sure rationalism and baldheaded materialism" of eighteenth- and ninteenth-century China. He rebuked both "the Sanguine-colored Bolshevists worshipping their infallible God Karl Marx" ("Art and Life," 178) and a Confucius who "with a superb gesture, delimited man's sensual extension and enjoyment" (172). Feeling that the faculties of spirit and body had been deadened in Chinese society, he asserted the value of the body in passion in Greek and Renaissance culture: He reacted against Chinese Daoist and Confucian tradition in which romantic love and the senses were viewed as "distractive and destructive of one's innate energies." Sexuality, though a theme in some of writing of 1920s, does not generally surface in the canonical May Fourth writing as it does in Byron or British modernists like D. H. Lawrence, for example. Xu asserted:

> Love, therefore, like religion, which is but divine or cosmic love as the case may be, is transcendental and transfiguring, and being transfigured through that mysterious force one's mortal eyes are, for once to behold visions that belong to the spiritual realm and are commonly denied to matter-of-fact perception, and his ears are to be overwhelmed by the grand and sublime music that come like mighty waves in the sea, from the spheres. It is through that transcendental elevation of one's spirit that the creative energy heretofore inert and latent, begins to liberate itself. ("Art and Life," 174)

Xu claimed that this liberation of the body, reminding us of D. H. Lawrence, would lead to the liberation of the spirit in art, claiming the Chinese "have no art precisely because we have no life" (172).

Theodor Adorno explains the underlying politics of the rejection of romantic love in the thinking of socialists in China, and also the Fabians, Beatrice and Sidney Webb in England:

Petty-bourgeois hatred of sex, the common ground of Western moralists and ideologists of Socialist Realism. No moral terror can prevent the side the work of art shows its beholder from giving him pleasure, even if only in the formal fact of temporary freedom from the compulsion of practical goals. (193)

The idealized nude bodies in Greek and Italian art and the French academic painting of nudes and odalisques of the time—part of the Western tradition—was a new perspective to a Chinese artist whose own Asian tradition avoided painting the nude. The philosophical tradition of Daoism and Confucianism urged the renunciation of the senses and socialist ideology recommended the subordination of personal pleasure to the social good. Xu, nevertheless, urged, "Mind your life and art will take care of itself" (178). This new focus on the body and pleasure awakened in Xu the desire for a wife of his own choosing and he initiated unheard of divorce proceedings in China against his first wife, described by Pang-Mei Natasha Chang in *Bound Feet and Modern Dress*. Awakening a new idealism, he moved China toward the recognition of the right of the individual to complete self expression (177), and toward romantic love, a luxurious stance in China, as the most significant of experiences.

In using terms like "feeling," "self-expression," "enjoyment," and "true personality," Xu takes a stand that might be broadly termed "romantic," that challenged the prevailing philosophy and rhetoric of China. The "sentimental"—the emotional appeal of much of the Chinese poetry of the period—relocated the individual, his needs, and desires in literature, and it refocused long-repressed passion and love between individuals. Eschewing vaunted duty and loyalty toward family, community, and nation—part of the Confucian and then socialist ethic of social obligation—it pitted the individual artist against and outside the group. What is hard for the West to register is that the expression of the self, of individual emotion, of literary subjectivity, was then, and sometimes still is, transgressive in China—in fact, punishable at times. What we might label "banal," "weak," "emotional," or "sentimental" is a fledgling expression of a new language of self and identity and, sometimes, an act of bravery in Chinese society. It is a society in which the "I" has traditionally been lost in the "we," not only because of its core Confucian, Buddhist, Daoist, Maoist, socialist, Marxist, and communist philosophies, but also because, at various times in its history, the emperor or the state has repressed the subjectivity of the people in service to the nation. In fact, the views that Xu Zhimo expresses in his 1923 essay "Art and Life" are later recanted. Xu states, "I have written two essays in English: 'Art and Life' and 'Personal Impressions of H. G. Wells, Edward Carpenter, and Katherine Mansfield.' They look so disgusting that I refuse to publish them in my new book, *The Falling Leaves*" (*Complete Works*, 147). Why did Xu suddenly reject his narrative of feeling? This is another of the divisions of the artistic self required at times by Chinese politics and nationalism.

There is a long historical battle between the perceived narcissism and paranoia of Xu's stances just as there is a long literary battle in English literature about the place of feeling, emotional appeal and "sentimentalism" in the movement of modernism and in the culture. In both cultures in the twentieth century, there is a concern with how emotion is to be regulated, explained, and legitimated in life and literature. Suzanne Clarke states in her intriguing book *Sentimental Modernism* that modernism feminized "sentimentalism": "Sentimentalism is international, but each takes form in a way specific to each culture" (22). England feminized "feeling" and "sentimentalism" in the same way that it, at times, feminized China and its weak position in the world at the time. For the Chinese, feeling had to be repressed in certain cultural and political domains for individuals to better serve the community and nation; for the modernists (Ezra Pound, H. D., William Carlos Williams, T. S. Eliot) emotional diction and personal expression was something to be stripped from their poetry in reaction against Victorian excesses of sentimentalism about family and nation. Terms like "feeling" and "sentimentalism" take their own specific form as they migrate to different parts of the globe.

Like many of the Chinese intellectuals who studied in Cambridge and Paris and America, Xu Zhimo had moved into an international space that allowed personal liberation and the development of cosmopolitan eyes. Upon his return to China from Cambridge in 1923, Xu held an idea of the West in mind and challenged socialist notions of "reality" that continued to serve as the measure of literature in China in spite of the individualism and subjectivism fostered by the May Fourth literary movement. Like Wordsworth, Swinburne, Rosetti, Byron, Shelley, and Hardy before him, Xu heralded feeling, emotion, and energy as the wellspring of the imagination, the body and life. He became a leading poet as well as a translator of the British romantics (particularly Wordsworth, Swinburne, and Rossetti), as well as the Victorians, Elizabeth Barrett Browning, and Thomas Hardy. Formed in other cultural spaces—no longer, purely "Chinese"—Xu was a key figure upon his return to China in organizing the Crescent Moon group around 1925–26 with two poet friends, Wen Yiduo and Rao Mengkan, and the literary critic Hu Shi as well as Shen Congwen, Chen Yuan, and Liang Shiqiu. They also established the periodical the *Crescent Moon Monthly,* in 1928, as discussed in the previous chapter. The name of this society, one of hundreds in China at the time, was influenced by Xu's meeting and travel with the Indian poet Rabindranath Tagore, whose Bengali poems were known through English translations and whom he met in India in 1928 through Leonard Elmhirst. Xu himself wrote four collections of poems, *The Poems of Chih-mo* [*Zhimo*] (1925), *A Night in Florence* (1926), *The Tiger* (1930), and *Roaming in Clouds* (1931). The Crescent Moon group along with other literary groups such as the Creation Society and the Society of Literary Studies, advanced an emerging modernism in Chinese literature that challenged the "slogan literature" advocated by many "revolutionary" writers of the time (Tung, "The Search for Order and Form," 20). Xu Zhimo was increasingly perceived as anticommunist and anti-leftist in the literary and political spectrum of China.

Lecturing on "Art and Life" at Qinghua University upon his return to China in 1923, he criticized Chinese social conditions and upheld the virtues of literary England:

> One can speak neither of art nor of life without drawing, first of all, an indictment and one can't be too vehement at it—against prevailing social conditions to which we are all of us compelled to adapt ourselves. If the materialistic West is a civilization without a heart as we are accustomed to regard it nowadays, ours, on the other hand, is one without a soul, or at any rate with no consciousness of its ever having one. If the Westerners are being dragged along by their own machinery of efficiency, all bustle and hustle, to nobody knows whither, my almost brutal imagery of the society we know, would be a deadly stagnant pool of water, dark with mud and noisy with base insects and worms swarming over and about it, it smacks all but of decay and listlessness. (169)

Fresh from England, brandishing his sexually and socially liberated views, he utters his *j'accuse*. Attacking China's "lethargic habits," he rejected the "conventional trammelings" of the spirit in the sentimental Confucian education of the students:

The training of our mind and eyes from a very early age to adapt to the practical details and appropriate etiquettes of an unexciting living rather than opening up for them of the secret and enchanting possibilities of a great life, is the greatest failure in Chinese education and is responsible for the death of true personality and endless manufacturing of excellent mediocrities. (175)

Charging that the "spirit" and the faculty of the "imagination" have been forgotten in the education and formation of the Chinese soul, the scope of life shrinks, he said, to "an unattractive series of ethical platitudes." He charged artists with a "lack of consciousness" and "the death of true personality." China had crippled its artists: the spirit of British romanticism, both its literature and flamboyant artistic personalities (particularly Byron and Shelley), would rescue them. A certain popular aspect of British romanticism, not necessarily the importance of the imagination, molded one of the most important poets of China in the 1920s. From the leftist point of view, Xu was a sinister force on the literary scene of modern China, given his passion about British ideas of the self in literature and life.

One of Xu's most significant relationships would develop in 1926, when he met Leonard Elmhirst, a generous supporter of Indian and Chinese causes. Personable Elmhirst with his wealthy wife, Dorothy Straight (nee Whitney), was the founder of Dartington Hall in Totnes, Devon, a rural reconstruction project in a depressed area in southwest England. Here they formed a community of farmers and artists to implement Elmhirst's progressive agricultural reforms learned at Cornell University, and to develop Dorothy's interest in the arts. The Dartington community, founded in 1926, housed not only Tagore but harbored the Joos Dance Company in flight from Hitler and, when London was being bombed in 1940, the Sadler's Wells Ballet. Elmhirst was forward-looking and his generosity to those in whom he believed is documented in numerous letters in his archives at Dartington Hall. He wrote to Ling Shuhua in 1971 of three young men to whom he became attached in his visits to Beijing: Xu Zhimo, P. C. Zhang, and Little Zhu. He writes that he likes them all for different reasons: Xu for his "abundant charm, his sensitivity, his poetic imagination and his warmth of affection"; P. C. for his "philosophic calm and his abundant friendliness." Little Zhu, he said, had "an immediate understanding of the peasant farmer and of his outlook and problems so that when he and I went to a farmers' supply shop in the country side, not far I think from Qinghua, we could carry on an intellectual conversation with the local farmers" (Letter to Ling Shuhua, 18 June 1971).

Elmhirst made Xu Zhimo's acquaintance in China during his trip there with Tagore. It was during this time that Tagore led the historic mission from India to China with Leonard Elmhirst to meet with the scholars of Beijing. They were led by Hu Shi, the reformer who spent several critical years at Cornell University in America, and accompanied by Xu Zhimo; Nanalal Bose; Rabintiti Mohan Sen, scholar; Kalidas Nage, historian. Xu writes, "So we are to have the sage [Tagore] over at last! It would be a joy and delight to meet you here again" (Letter to LE, 22 January 1924). Tagore was interested in culturally connecting India and China, and it was during this trip that Elmhirst met Ling Shuhua at a painter's party at her home in Beijing in April 1923.

Xu Zhimo and Ling Shuhua were friends—probably lovers—and after his visit to England in 1922–23, he brought back to her a picture painted by Tagore and a small hand scroll that she had given him upon departure now

Leonard Elmhirst, Xu Zhimo, and Rabindranath Tagore, and unidentified men, at Dartington Hall, Totnes, England, 1928. By permission of the Dartington Hall Trust Archive, Totnes, England.

filled with a watercolor by Roger Fry and a number of poets, scholars, and artists of Beijing and London. Learning of this hand scroll in the middle of this project, I was delighted to have tangible evidence of the relationship between the artistic communities I was researching. Ling Shuhua also took this scroll back with her when she left Beijing for London in the late forties, and described it in a letter to Leonard Elmhirst:

> Both are unusual souvenirs and rare treasures, they were given to me by Hsu [Xu]! He was very generous to his friends indeed. I am very proud that I have them with me. When you come to London I should like to show them to you. (Letter to LE, 1964)

This scroll will continue to figure in relations between England and China. Just as Julian taught Bloomsbury in China, Ling Shuhua taught Xu Zhimo's poetry and Chinese modern literature in her lectures at the University of Toronto in 1966 and the London School of Oriental and African Studies in 1968. The lectures were partially based on information in Xu's letters to Elmhirst. Though Ling Shuhua had many letters that Xu had written to her, including love letters, they were lost.[3] In a 1971 letter to Leonard Elmhirst, Ling Shuhua remembered Xu's talent and noted that "the students today still are charmed by Xu's poetry and his charming character" (Letter to LE, 13 March 1968). Ling would write later that "it is a pity that I have lost during the war all the letters and poems Xu wrote to me" (Letter to LE, 12 June 1971). This is another example of the blanks in this study created by personal and historical upheaval in China.

    In June 1925, Xu was in Paris and then visited Dickinson in England again. During this period, he sent Elmhirst a characteristically exuberant message on the latter's marriage to Dorothy Straight: "O how I wish I could just jump across the ditch of the Atlantic and embrace you both!" (18 June 1925). He also writes at this time of the worsening conditions in China: "China is in a terrible fix and I have no longer any peace of mind. Both friends and family have sent for me" (18 June 1925). He writes to Leonard Elmhirst in July that a sudden departure for China is necessary, "Never before have I found myself in such an immensely difficult position; never before have I been so deeply worried; I hardly know what is going next to happen: it may be tragedy, it may be farce" (13 July 1925). The political and social upheavals caused by the 30 May 1925 incident, in which a conflict between Chinese workers and British and

Japanese authorities erupted, turned into a violent political movement. The Guomindang and the Communists were, at the same time, preparing for national unification, and in 1926 the Guomindang marched against the warlords in central and northern China. Shanghai was in turmoil.

Five months later Hu Shi writes Elmhirst an urgent appeal on behalf of Xu Zhimo, who despite national upheavals and "after some trouble" was married and "warmly received" by his parents in China. Hu Shi describes Xu's second wife, Lu Xiaoman, as a painter, singer, writer, and a speaker of French and English. Though she is "clever," she is, however, without systematic education. Hu Shi is worried not only about Xu's financial position, his father having lost his fortune because of a business depression and the war, but the place of intellectuals in a chaotic China of the late 1920s: "It will be ruinous to both Xu and his wife if they are to live long in these provincial surroundings. Their talents will have to be wasted and dwarfed.... You cannot fully imagine how ruinous it is to have to live with people of the older social habits who do not appreciate the individual development and who look upon their youngsters only as pleasant partners at a Mah-jong [Ma-jiang] game!" (26 December 1926). Hu Shi urged Elmhirst to financially support Xu and his wife's trip to England for two to three years to study. In January of 1927, Xu wrote from Shanghai of personal sufferings and then of the worsening conditions in China. Since his conversations with Elmhirst in the summer of 1926, he endured the rejection of friends because of his divorce, a time in which he says, "I suffered not the least, nearly everything except the sympathy of one or two friends [Hu Shi being one] being in my way. However I triumphed — triumphed against the deadly force of ignorance and prejudice in which all societies rest" (Letter to Elmhirst, 5 January 1927). He went on, however, to report that he and his wife, Lu Xiaoman, a woman who was often ill, were among the refugees in Shanghai because of the civil war "which burns everywhere like wild fire. Our province Zhejiang has so far enjoyed peace to the envy of all other provinces, but there is apparently no escape this time. Hangzhou has become half-empty and is just now under great terror of all manners of calamity which civil wars always bring in their wake. Poor West Lake! deserted and threatened" (5 January 1927). He noted, "We yearn to fly abroad but wings are yet wanting."

Elmhirst responded with characteristic generosity and asked Xu if he would like to pursue his studies in Europe and spend some time at Santiniketan, the model rural community that Elmhirst established in India with the help of Tagore. In a note attached to this letter, Elmhirst wrote to Dorothy that they should help the couple to come for a definite course of study in London or Cambridge, and that they should do something in cooperation with G. L. Dickinson to facilitate this: "I know they both want this and of course Hu Shi wants them back in China equipped to teach" (4 February 1927). This support of a leading poet by a sympathetic circle of British, including Dickinson, Elmhirst, and Arthur Waley, has been ignored in accounts of Xu's life. The conditions created by Elmhirst and Dickinson allowed gifted Chinese writers like Xu to escape from their own culture during turbulent times, to have significant contact with another culture, and to have time to write and develop as an artist. It also fostered important aesthetic conversations that would ripple into the stream of modernisms in China and England in the 1920s. In March of 1927, Elmhirst sent Xu 250 pounds to come to Europe; in September of 1928 another 300 pounds.

What is interesting in their correspondence are the on-the-spot accounts of conditions in China in the late 1920s during the turmoil of the civil war, a population helpless against the war propaganda, and on the move ahead of the Communists or the Guomindang or the advancing Japanese. English writers would experience the same demoralization during the blitz in the late 1930s and early 1940s. In 1927, Xu writes to Elmhirst what has become of China:

> Well, I am sure you wouldn't believe it. The whole country is fast rumbling into a nightmare of [?] passion and bestiality. And what is there to save the situation? The soberer forces are fast giving way, being trodden down, and will soon disappear altogether. Who are the present masters? Simple workmen, regular knaves and young boys and girls, mostly under twenty. (4 April 1927)

But Xu argues against those who held the Russians mainly responsible for this cultural and political upheaval in China:

> No don't you put too much on the Russians. They are no doubt the great designing genius; but this alone would not have insured their success. The native soil is fertile and ready for revolution; that is the secret. A curious and wonderful performance, indeed, this present upheaval in China. Something like a parody of the Russian Revolution. (Letter to Elmhirst, 4 January 1927)

This description foreshadows the treatment of intellectuals by the Red Guards during the Cultural Revolution. Xu, interestingly, held the communists responsible for "the fact of having actually created not only class distinction, but class hatred as well, which in former days had not the least semblance of existence in China" (Letter to Elmhirst, 4 January 1927). In despair, he felt that the intellectuals were powerless "against the turbulent flood of catch words and mob movements. All standards are turned upside down, all measures are reversed. Down with Reason! Down with wisdom! Down with those who dare independent thinking at all. This surely is no place for us." His disappointments reverberated in Virginia Woolf's writing in England as World War II approached and she too felt that war propaganda eclipsed daily life and serious writing in England. Two years later, he described more degradation, a situation in which Carsun Zhang, the brother of Zhang Youyi, Xu Zhimo's first wife, is kidnapped and tortured. He concluded that "in many ways we are worse off than India even. Ideals are dead. They have to be" (Letter to Elmhirst, 28 June 1929). But his resilient aesthetic ideals persisted and he informed Elmhirst that he was still pursuing "the Muses favor" and had helped to organize the first National Art Exhibition in China, June 1929. Though he despairs that there is not a single place in China "where law and order obtain at all," he carried in his mind's eye the vision and inspiration of the communities of Bloomsbury, Dartington, and Santiniketan in India. Such is the importance of artistic communities and the cultural contact of talented individuals whose travels East and West sustain them during times of transition and turbulence in their own cultures. Other cultures offer not only a physical haven, but also a place of the mind, alternative ways of being and seeing when surrounded by what Xu labels "the vicious forces of a maladjusted society" or "older social habits." (Letter to Elmhirst, 28 June 1929)

Elmhirst, being a man of global vision, however, was not only supporting a talented young poet but a member of a forward-looking generation of the new China. He encouraged the location of a site for rural reconstruction in China, and the establishment of a literary magazine that would encourage communication between Chinese intellectuals and writers. Always the practical and the aesthetic man, Elmhirst was pleased to hear that Xu was planning to meet with P. C. Zhang, S. Y. Zhu, and others in Shanghai to form a party to travel to the interior of Zhejiang and Jiangsu. There they would look into conditions and decide upon a tentative program for the rural experiment (XZ to LE, 21 October

1928). Xu was very impressed that Elmhirst had done for the Indian people "what no other foreigner has ever done. You have certainly contributed more than you are aware. And it is coupled with goodness knows what hard labor. You have exerted what is so very moving and cannot fail, I'm sure, to bring about results that will go a long way in solving the village problem in India" (Letter to LE, 13 October 1928). Xu's efforts to find a rural site continued into 1929, but the plans were never realized because of the civil war and growing Japanese incursions into China. What is remarkable is how forward-looking Elmhirst's rural development plans for India and China were. Recent U.N. schemes to deal with the problem of the "floating population" in China—rural men and women who travel to urban areas to earn an income and find work that does not exist in their economically depressed areas—resemble Elmhirst's plans. The social dislocation and alienation of these rural men, the conditions of their lives in the major cities of China, and their separation from wives and children thousands of miles away in the rural areas has brought their plight to

Chinese and British intellectuals, top, left to right: Ling Shuhua, Chen Yuan (Ling's husband), ZhaoYuan Ren (mathematician, linguist, composer); bottom, left to right: Bertrand Russell, Dora Russell, Yang Bu-wei (wife of Zhao Yuan Ren). Photograph taken in Russell's home, North Wales. By permission of Hsiao-ying Chen.

world attention. Newly announced plans for rural reconstruction in China, which move factories and development into the rural areas to insure the integrity of rural families in social and economic communities (as well as the much needed attention to the eighty percent of the Chinese population that lives outside major cities), bear remarkable similarity to Elmhirst's thinking in the 1920s.

In 1925, Elmhirst and Gardner encouraged Xu to develop a quarterly periodical, *English Review,* to encourage "direct communication between the new China with all her inspirations and aspiration on the one hand, and the rest of the intellectual world on the other" (Elmhirst to Xu, 15 July 1925). The civil war brought plans to a standstill; yet in 1926, Hu Shi was still discussing plans for Arthur Waley and Eileen Power to write on Chinese subjects, as well as Bertrand Russell and G. L. Dickinson, and a friend Y. C. Chin, a Chinese student of philosophy who had contributed to the *American Mercury.* G. L. Dickinson, E. M. Forster, Roger Fry, I. A. Richards, Bertrand Russell, Maynard Keynes, Archibald Rose, Beatrice and Sidney Webb, and other Cambridge humanists who admired China formed a resistant community in England. Had this succeeded, it would have been another document reflecting the cultural and aesthetic relation forming between these communities at this time. They supported projects such as the literary review Elmhirst was proposing and spoke out in different domains and various ways against British imperialism, the encroachments of businessmen, missionaries, and the Japanese in China. Xu, like other Chinese intellectuals visiting England, was pleased to meet Englishmen who did not envision a sick or weak China and was delighted when Russell was appointed to the Boxer Indemnity Committee (Leung, "Xu Zhimo and Bertrand Russell," 36). Each group of intellectuals returned to China (and perhaps left it) with a particular political and literary stamp, as discussed earlier in chapter 2.

Xu Zhimo was a man of sentiment and passion, often out of control. Leo Ou-fan Lee and, more recently, Natasha Chang have written of his passionate involvement with Lin Huiyin, the teenage daughter of his admired mentor, Lin Ch'ang-men [Lin Changmin], during his stay in Cambridge in 1920–22.[4] He had romantic adventures in Cambridge, and experimented with Western-style girlfriends as well as ideas. Though married to Zhang Youyi, he fell in love with Lin Huiyin, a young woman of delicate beauty, who was in Cambridge with her diplomat father in 1920, attending middle school. He sought advice from Bertrand Russell about his situation and, given his forward-looking views of love, marriage, and divorce, Russell supported the dissolution of his "loveless" marriage (Leung, "Xu Zhimo and Bertrand Russell," 29). However, Lin Huiyin, only sixteen years old (Xu was ten years older), was forced to return to China with her father to elude Xu and marry her intended, Liang Sicheng, who was to become one of China's most important architectural historians. Their marriage is described by Wilma Fairbank in *Liang and Lin*, the story of their difficult but happy life as architects struggling "to save old Peking [Beijing] as a wooded, leaf-filled city, to keep it free from industry, to preserve the wondrous walls and gates as public parts for all posterity to love and enjoy" (Fairbank, *Liang and Lin,* xi). After Lin's departure, Xu Zhimo initiated, nevertheless, spectacular divorce proceedings to sever his marital relationship in China undoubtedly influenced by Bertrand Russell's freethinking philosophy and the western concept of divorce. Sexual and personal liberation paralleled his aesthetic development in England. His contacts with another culture, another system of thinking, liberated him from the Confucian value of loyalty to family relations and allowed for the possibility, for better or worse, of the value of sexual freedom and personal happiness.

Xu achieved celebrity status in China because of his flamboyant reputation as a poet, lover, and personality. He also played a prominent role as interpreter on Tagore's tour of China. Recent scholarship reveals that while involved in these tempestuous and highly publicized relationships, Xu also had intimate relationships with Americans Pearl Buck and Agnes Smedley. Peter Conn in his recent cultural biography of Pearl Buck reports that she and her husband, Lossing, moved to Shanghai in 1927, escaping the political instability in Nanjing. Conn reports that Pearl Buck's marital relationship was unfulfilling, and that during this unhappy period, she was intermittently involved with Xu until 1931 (*Pearl Buck,* 103). In one of her memoirs, Buck describes Xu's remarkable hands, reminding one of Dora Carrington's votive representation of Lytton Strachey's hands:

> One handsome and rather distinguished and certainly much beloved young poet was proud to be called "The Chinese Shelley." He used to sit in my living room and talk by the hour and wave his beautiful hands in exquisite and descriptive gestures until now when I think of him, I see first his hands. He was a northern Chinese [actually he was from Zhejiang, which is in southern

China], tall and classically beautiful in looks, and his hands were big and perfectly shaped and smooth as a woman's hands. (Conn, *Pearl Buck*, 103)

In addition to her memoirs, the novel *Letter from Peking* (1957) also memorializes perhaps Buck's relationship with Xu in the figure of handsome Amerasian Gerald. He, as president of a major university, remains with his students in China, leading them westward during the revolution, and sends his American wife and son back to America. Gerald is described romantically:

> I saw Gerald run with his striking grace . . . the glint of the sun on his black hair, the lively glance of his black eyes, and the clear smoothness of his cream skin. The Chinese have some magic in the structure of their skin and even a little of the blood seems to purify the flesh. Rennie [their son] has the same faultlessness of skin. (90)

But Buck was not the only one attracted to the handsome Xu Zhimo. Agnes Smedley, a fiesty journalist active in Indian and Chinese politics, was drawn into a midsummer affair with him in 1927. In the 1930s however, Smedley switched her personal and political allegiance to Lu Xun, who was more of a "cultural guerrilla" (Conn, *Pearl Buck*, 254), and closer to her political positions. To enhance her cultural change of heart, it was observed that she dressed as an ordinary Chinese guerrilla when she was embedded with the Fourth Route Army at the beginning of the Sino-Japanese War to get her story (Xiao, *China but Not Cathay*, 133).

The development of Xu's Byronic personality, nurtured in England, paralleled his literary developments. Returning to China, dedicated to Western literature and ideas, he wrote to Roger Fry:

> I have always thought it the greatest occasion in my life was to meet Mr. Dickinson. It is due to him that I could have come to Cambridge and been enjoying all these happy days, that my interest in literature and arts began to shape and perpetuate itself & that I was enabled to know you—in whose large and sweet personality opened a new vision to me and has always been inspiring me to thoughts and feelings that are large, beautiful and noble. What a pleasure, what a charm, what a comfort, to be just near you and hear your melodious voice. (Fry Papers VII, 7 August 1927)

His personal effusiveness flowed into a style often described as sentimental and romantic by the British well into modernism. This style is evident in another letter to Roger Fry:

Your letter overwhelms me. Joys I have known; but what is this to compare with that unique feeling which your generous sympathy has caused to overflow my bosom this morning! How can I ever hope to convey to you my grateful thoughts that touch the deepest fibres of my heart? (7 August 1922)

A flamboyant and much-loved man and poet, Xu Zhimo died in a plane crash in 1931 at the age of thirty-six with the same spirit of wildness and adventure that he lived his life.

FEELING AS A TRANSGRESSIVE ACT: THE NARRATION OF "SELF" IN DEVELOPING CHINESE MODERNISM

In China, the "sentimental" or the expression of feeling was something to grow into; in England and America, it was something to outgrow. In both cultures, the "sentimental" was associated with the weakness of "feminine" or individual indulgence in emotion. In global terms, Chinese culture and Chinese men were represented in literature as "feminized" and, therefore, rightly subject to the West. The term "sentimentalism," as a locus for feeling in literature was then a nexus for both cultures. The terms loosely associated with "sentimentalism"—romanticism, self-expression, and subjectivity—are often juxtaposed with British modernism. Such terms, frequently used in the cultural and literary conversations of the 1920 and 1930s in China and England, form a network of meaning in the restless play of developing modernism. Ferdinand de Saussure's principle of meaning, again, importantly informs such explorations of difference in this book: "language is a system of interdependent terms in which the value of each term results solely from the simultaneous presence of others" (*Course,* 114). In developing a neglected aspect of international modernism, this book places Chinese texts (painting, calligraphy, fashion, porcelain, gardens, design, and writing) in the landscape of modernism, asserting its "presence" (and simultaneous "absence") in England and the West. It is unarticulated as a part of the developing aesthetic of modernism—unarticulated by the Chinese who were learning from critics like William Empson and I. A. Richards the ways of organizing and communicating their aesthetic thinking—and unacknowledged in writing of intellectuals and critics, in general, in the West. Though British, French, Russian, German, American, and Italian aesthetics of the early twentieth century were a part of a developing international modernist discourse, China, because of this lack of theoretical and critical articulation, and its linguistic, political, and geographical distance, was simultaneously present and absent in the aesthetic domain.

I foreground the Chinese aesthetic as a resistant artistic and intellectual community structured at a particular historical moment. In doing so, a new terrain is sketched for the play of modernism that captures the simultaneity and difference of concepts and terms used in both the British and Chinese context. In order to understand terms like "subjectivity"—so important in a discussion of modernism's project—used by both the Chinese and the British, we need to develop a terrain of "between-ness" where one neither fixes or denies the meanings of terms in one culture or another. Instead, a new terrain of understanding is developed "between" the literary thinking of different cultures using the "shadow language" that Edward Ardener recommends. We read anew then the cultural domains of the "self" (as expressed through the terms "subjectivity," "personality," "individuality," "consciousness") and the opposite terms by which they gain their meaning (according to Saussure) in China ("family," "community," "society," "nation," and "collectivity"). We read anew the term "expression" (of emotion, physical passion, speech, and literature) and the opposite within (nonexpression, silence, and repression), and we focus on the meanings of "civilization" and opposite terms in the field of meaning, "uncivilized," "barbarian," "savage," and "primitive" (though this last term is used more often in America in later decades, and less often in England at this time). In the late nineteenth and early twentieth centuries, some in England longed for the kind of humanity represented by old China and knew that the greatness of England would not be built upon railways and empires. What Edward Carpenter craved in "Civilization: Its Cause and Cure" (1889) was already present in the philosophy, though not necessarily modern practice, in China. What he and Dickinson created was a conversation of resistance. They challenged the Victorian notion of the social superiority of the English and the desire to spread "civilization" to less enlightened cultures, asserting that England's banner of material progress brought "uncivilized" behavior and spiritual bankruptcy.

Xu Zhimo is one of the first Chinese writers to passionately assert the beauty of the body, and to promote the importance of the self upon his return to China in 1923. His cry, however, was muffled by the rapid growth of the leftist literary movement beginning around 1928. Ding Yi suggests that the temper of the time was that "collectivism . . . ought to be the guiding principle of the writer's creativity; the hero in his work should be the mass not the individual" (Tung, "The Search for Order and Form," 18). Political consciousness and identity continued to outweigh individualism and literary values in Mao's talks on "Literature and Art" at the Yan'an Forum in 1942. After the death of Mao in 1976, the univocal voice—the master narrative of China—splintered and discourses of the "self" again emerged in writing. In a poignant dialogue between a journalist-father, Gu Gong, and a writer-son, Gu Cheng, we observe the differences in the views of two Chinese generations. The father writes from the viewpoint of the 1930s generation:

> I am finding it increasingly difficult to understand my child Gu Cheng's poetry. I am getting more and more angry. . . . I kept reading his poetry. I was disappointed, lost in thought. Finally, I exploded. I bombarded him with incessant lectures and questions: "What kind of eyes are you using to observe life?". . . "Why can't the giant rocks high above the river be swan's eggs instead of heads?" . . . "Is poetry the study of beauty or the study of ugliness?" But the son was no longer an obedient tool. He began a vigorous defense of his poems and his generation's poems. . . . The purpose behind portraying the world is to portray the self. Your generation sometimes wrote about "the self," but this "self" was always described as "a pebble used to build roads," a "gear valve," or "a screw." Is this "self" human? No, it's only machinery.

No longer content to be part of Mao's "machinery" or "cultural army" or to blend with community or nature in the traditional ways represented in the paintings of Ru Chen of Kung Xun, the Chinese writer began to break step with "the nation." The politician proclaims "You shall only practice your art . . . at our bidding. Paint us pictures, carve us statues, that glorify our gospels. Celebrate fascism; celebrate communism. Preach what we bid you to preach" (Woolf, "The Artist and Politics," 228). But new writers began to question the "materiality" of the conception of the artist. The merging of the self with a larger landscape, whether of the natural, social, or political world, is questioned, and the Chinese writer began to realize, as Virginia Woolf did in 1910, that "whether we call it life or spirit, truth or reality, this, the essential thing, has moved off, or on, and refuses to be contained any longer in such ill-fitting vestments as we provide" ("Modern Fiction," 153). Old models of being and consciousness no longer fit, and new literary language, forms, and genres were sought during the 1917 literary movement and the May Fourth literary movement. This is demonstrated in the literary views of Xu Zhimo and his colleagues in the Crescent Moon group (1925–33) among other literary societies. After the Cultural Revolution, the interrupted project of Chinese writers to find new "vestments" for the narration of the emerging subjectivity of the Chinese people continues.

Heralded by Xu, silenced for thirty years during Mao's leadership (1949–76), and now re-emerging is one of the Western concepts beginning with Descartes that, along with Marx and Hegel, has most profoundly influenced China: the literary and cultural split between subject and object or self and landscape. Though subject and object—the self in the landscape of nature and society—are traditionally presented in visual and philosophic harmony in Chinese thought, experience, and art, they become splintered in the May Fourth literary movement and the crucible of Mao's politics. We discover then that Chinese landscape painting, for example, sometimes expressed and sometimes disguised the spirit, brutalities, and schisms and problems in Chinese society. Song landscape painting or Tang poetry represents a culturally harmonious philosophy and society that writers like G. L. Dickinson embraced as the image of China in the West. Perhaps writers cling to forms of pastoral harmony during times of social chaos or war, but these forms are, nonetheless, responses to the war. Antique notions of China popularized in England at the beginning of the century revealed little trace of the social and political turbulence of modern China. Nor did these images reflect the Chinese trend to assert an individuality repressed in Chinese culture under various visual, philosophical, and political guises.

Xu Zhimo's exhortation to "cultivate . . . self-consciousness . . . and the natural resources . . . inherent in our nature" urged the construction of a "subjectivity." At the time that the terms "consciousness," "unconsciousness," "psychology," and "self" were surfacing in British culture in the work of Sigmund Freud, Carl Jung, and in writers of consciousness such as Joyce, Proust, James, Mann, and Woolf in the 1920s, such notions of subjectivity were discouraged by Marxist and Confucian thinkers in China. Yet Xu Zhimo noted the importance of Confucian thought in China. Though an admirer of Bertrand Russell, he criticized him on this point:

> Russell . . . does not fully understand the evolution of the Chinese culture and life to its present form. . . . He fails to gauge the influence of Confucius. He frankly admits in his book that he is not well disposed towards Confucius who insisted on excessive formalities . . . he presumes that the strength

of China has much to do with Lao Tzu [Lao Zi] and Chuang Tzu [Zhuang Zi]. (Leung, "Xu Zhimo and Bertrand Russell," 32)

Bertrand Russell, like G. L. Dickinson, Arthur Waley, and other British intellectuals, gravitated toward the non-militaristic and philosophical Daoist China of Tang poetry and Song landscapes. They do not speak of what others find distasteful: China's authoritarian and moralistic Confucian society, the privileging of family and society over values of "self" and "individuality," the famine then overtaking China, and the political turmoil of the civil war. Mao Zedong, in constructing what was to be the "revolutionary" modern literary history of China, states in his "Yan'an Talks" of 1942 that literature must "serve the people." Even today, the Chinese desire for socially engaged writing persists among a broad base of writers. This kind of writing does not espouse using literature to get in touch with "self" as defined by British modernists. "Self," rather, is a more inclusive term in China, a term that then, and now, includes the notion of community more starkly than in the West. Mao clearly makes distinctions between what might serve the "individual" but not the "state." But Mao's literary platform, seeking to develop writers into a "cultural army," is not motivated solely by the political. The notion of writing for family, community, nation is still part of a writer's sense of "being" in China, and it has been historically so during periods of historical crisis, including famine, Japanese imperialism, civil war, and postliberation. And during a life of sustenance and desperation—as can be gleaned from the stories written during the Republican era during which privation is a theme—personal feeling is sometimes anaesthetized.

In this discussion of Xu Zhimo, we observe that, at the same time that the terms "civilization" and "barbarism" surfaced in the political unconscious of Britain, Chinese intellectuals were preoccupied with notions of "subjectivity." China, in historical and social turmoil in 1911, placed a low value on subjectivity—the inner life, the individual imagination and private emotions. Later in the century, these states of mind were viewed as leading one to "individualism" and, perhaps, to challenges of national authority. But Chinese artists and intellectuals visiting Britain in the 1920s and 1930s became aware that change in literature and society must have its roots in the subjectivity of individuals—their dreams, desires, and passions. Reading modernist Virginia Woolf, the Chinese artists, shadowing the mind of Rezia, Septimus's wife, in *Mrs. Dalloway*, were drawn to depictions of the inner life: "he could feel her mind, like a bird, falling from branch to branch, and always alighting, quite rightly, he could follow her mind, as she sat there in one of those loose lax poses that came to her naturally, and, if he should say anything, at once she smiled, like a bird alighting with all its claws firm upon the bough" (222–23).

REDEFINITIONS OF BRITISH "CIVILIZATION": G. L. DICKINSON

At the same time that Xu Zhimo called for the assertion of the individual voice and spiritual revolution in China, G. L. Dickinson, the historian and teacher, praised China's traditional aversion to the use of force, its rational society, and its civilization. The term "civilization" was on everyone's mind in England, as was the Great War in which so many lives had been lost that the British could not help questioning its cost in the name of "civilization." British intellectuals were also anxious about the waning of British imperialism and the behavior toward the German "losers" after World War I; later, economists like J. M. Keynes attacked the thinking about authority and domination complicit with the rise of fascism and World War II.[5] Dickinson, well-informed about world affairs despite the vague persona that he projected to friends and students, wrote of the West's policy of "peaceful penetration" of the East (an expression also used later by Gertrude Stein to refer to the East) as a prelude to political absorption (276) in his well-received *International Anarchy*, written in 1926. Though events in the Far East were not directly connected with the outbreak of the Great War, Dickinson characterized the history of European relations in China as "one of continual aggression, military and financial. For China had committed the unpardonable offense of having a weak army, and of despising the soldier as compared with the official and the merchant" (*International Anarchy*, 276). Treaty ports and territories were conceded by the Chinese as a result of China's lack of military preparation and the continued subjugation of China by Japan, Russia, and Europe that began after the first Opium War, 1839–42. In the latter half of the nineteenth century, China experienced "humiliation" when various territories were granted to Germany (Shandong, Qingdao), Russia (Manchuria), France (Kwantung, Indochina, Annam), Britain (Weihaiwei, Guandong, Shandong, Burma, and Hong Kong), and Japan (Formosa and Korea).

"Civilization," was a word that became salient in British culture during this period when the "empire" expanded into so-called "uncivilized" parts of the world: India, China, and Africa. The use of the term "civilized" reassured the

British of their superiority during periods of economic expansion and exploitation. It was linked not only to culture but religion, Christianity. Hinduism, Buddhism, and Islam in the Far East—often considered "heathenism"—were a threat to the "true" faith, Christianity, and Yellow Peril cartoons often linked Europe's defense of the Cross to resistance to their influence. With the empire's decline, and war imminent or raging in the early part of the twentieth century, "civilization" became an organizing concept for the British struggling to hold on to a dying image of the nation. Given the "cost" of defending "civilization," particularly during World War I, it was on everyone's mind.

Definitions ranged from the levity of Clive Bell's "civilization is a lunch party at Number 50 Gordon Square" (Virginia Woolf's assessment) to Freud's juxtaposition of the terms "primitive," "barbarian," and "civilized" (*Civilization and Its Discontents*) to Leonard Woolf's jeremiad about the "barbarian" and "decivilizing" forces unleashed upon the world by Hitler and Mussolini in the late 1930s (*Quack, Quack!*), if not the "stink of civilization" that he detected during his days as a British administrative law judge in Ceylon. Much of the writing during this period circulated about the oscillating meaning of "civilization." It was a time, sadly, when the controlling myth of orientalism and the inferiority of the Chinese were not questioned, even in intellectual circles.

Sidney Webb; Beatrice Webb. Both by permission of the Picture Library, National Portrait Gallery, London, England.

Beatrice (1858–1953) and Sidney Webb (1859–1947), for example, described Chinese civilization as "barbaric" in their *China Diary* in 1911. Though one might expect them to identify with the Chinese revolution as Fabians, social reformers, and founders of the London School of Economics, they wrote little but moralistic and racist observations on the Chinese people after their travels, comparing them unfavorably to the Japanese, despite the positive reports they received from the English living in China. Focused on the social disintegration of China, they disagreed with G. L. Dickinson's idealized antique image of China. Visiting in 1911, the year of the fall of the Manchu Empire and the establishment of the Republic, they saw a different China. Sidney Webb, the main writer of their *Diary* account, was troubled with the "unnatural vice of homosexuality" in China as he was in Bloomsbury in England. Concerned with the "moral decay" of this "barbarian culture," Webb described the "vicious femininity" on the faces of Chinese men:

> With regard to sodomy, ever since I came to China I have been wondering whether the vice did not prevail extensively because of the expression on the faces of the men—the vicious femininity of many of the faces. We are told, on good authority, that in every Chinese town there is streets of "boys' homes," and that this form of prostitution is far more popular than the material and healthy one of men and women. It is this rottenness of physical and moral character that makes one despair of China—their constitution seems devastated by drugs and abnormal sexual indulgence. They are, in essentials, an "unclean race." (Webb, *Diary*, 140)

Racist remarks reoccur in the Webb's writing: "The country population, like the coolies of the towns, are most unpleasant to look on—dirty and undisciplined [and] with that same mocking smile on the faces of young and old—sometimes cringing, sometimes hostile" (133). Though socialists, they do not examine why the "hosts of men and boys [are] perpetually holding out their hands" (133). The moral and ideological cloak the "dirty" and "sexual" landscape that is salient to the Webbs. Self-doubt does enter, though, when Beatrice Webb puzzles about her stance compared to Dickinson's:

> What . . . is the cause of this fundamental difference in judgment between Lowes Dickinson, and us because I readily admit that he had an exquisite sense of beauty and that we have very little artistic faculty. Moreover his conception of the good is so completely different from ours, which I am

afraid is always based on the social value of an institution of law—that is, the way in which it will raise or lower the culture and development of what are called the common people. I imagine that Lowes Dickinson would loathe Soviet Communism which we think has discovered the root of the matter in its aims and methods. Then again Lowes Dickinson seems to have ignored science and its application to social organizations. (24 April 1934, *Letters*, 3: 393)

She is here describing temperament as well as a different worldview: she and her husband, politically focused on the development of social institutions; Dickinson, on philosophy and aesthetics. Beatrice Webb continued to demonstrate her lack of artistic facility, reporting to E. M. Forster on a conversation with a German art critic:

We saw very little beauty in modern China and its furniture or in the modern temples; and when I cross-examined the German expert at his Embassy, who had lived there twenty years buying [ancient] museum pieces, he told me that there had been no art in China for many hundreds of years, the last sign of it being some pottery about 250 years ago. (24 April 1934, *Letters*, 3: 393)

She recoiled at Chinese musical instruments—"two of which emitted horrible noises"—the music of China always presenting more difficulty than its visual images. When attending Chinese plays, she noted that they "seemed to us the last word of vulgarity and senseless noise" (*Letters*, 3:393). How different from G. L. Dickinson's response to a theatrical experience in the East when he writes of the unfortunate Westernization of an Eastern theater, in "A Malay Theatre":

And I remembered that everywhere, in Egypt, in India, in Java, in Sumatra, in Japan, the gramophone has made its way; that an inferior kind of harmonium is displacing the native instruments; and that the bioscope—that great instrument of education—is familiarizing the peasants of the East with all that is most vulgar and shoddy in the humor and sentiment of the West. The Westernizing of the East must come, no doubt, and ought to come. But in the process what by-products of waste and worse. (5 May 1913)

Though Dickinson is prescient in his observation that "the Westernizing of the East must come," he valued the culture. Because the Webbs polarized art and politics, they unfairly dismissed Dickinson's considerable influence on political thinking about China through his *Letters from a Chinese Official*. In fact, G. L. Dickinson, Maynard Keynes, Archibald Rose, and Leonard Woolf were integrally involved in creating Chinese "policy" and institutions through involvement with the League of Nations, the Fabian Society, and British government committees on China. Leonard Woolf's interest is revealed in the titles of some of the books in his library: pamphlets on *China's Position in International Finance*, published in London, 1919; Herbert Giles' *Chaos in China*, 1924; J. R. Chitty's *Things Seen in China*, presented to him by his sister, Bella, 1922; and Herbert Giles's translation of *The Travels of Fa-hsien* (399–414 A.D.); or, *the Record of Buddhist Kingdoms*, 1923. It is ironic, then, that Beatrice and Sidney Webb, visiting China as socialists (bringing coals to Newcastle, as it were), have little to say about the Chinese experiment with socialism and the establishment of the Republic in 1911, or the British responsibility for the sale of opium to the Chinese. They are so enamoured with the Russian experiment in communism that they repudiated China in favor of the "moral" coordinates in the West. They muse about Dickinson in 1933: "aesthete or social reformer, which is uppermost in him?" (*The Webbs in Asia*, 11 May 1933). After Dickinson's death in 1932, Beatrice Webb wrote to E. M. Forster about his biography of Dickinson:

> I have read it with very great interest, as I have always wanted to understand exactly what Lowes Dickinson meant by his vision of an ideal culture. Your account of his life and analysis of his writings has revealed to me why I was never able to appreciate him as a thinker, though I admired one or two of his books—John Chinaman and the Modern Symposium for instance. The truth is that our scales of value were mutually exclusive—perhaps they ought to have been complementary! This is brought out vividly by his impressions of India and China. (Letters of Beatrice Webb 3:392–93)

The Webbs' suspicions about Dickinson's commitments had some basis. He never delved into scholarship or looked too closely at the historical turmoil in China beyond the Boxer Rebellion and indemnity. His friends in Bloomsbury often commented on how his romantic imagination colored his view of China as he constructed a pagoda of the mind.

Dickinson did, however, find philosophical and aesthetic peace in China where the Webbs found none.

Letters from John Chinaman: G. L. Dickinson

The terms "civilized" and "barbarous" (paralleled by the American nineteenth-century term "primitive") were established and neatly compartmentalized in British thinking from the time of the Opium Wars, 1839–1852 to the Boxer Rebellion, 1901. Importantly, Dickinson and other British intellectuals and artists in this study reversed the value of the terms in imperialist British culture, reinvesting them with new meaning. "Barbarian" (i.e., nonaggressive China) was "good"; "civilization" (i.e., British imperialism) was "bad." Dickinson was not a typical Englishman. His sympathetic stance toward China was attacked by the Fabians, Sidney and Beatrice Webb, and his critical view of Britian's new imperialism led to the writing of the *Letters from a Chinese Official,* published anonymously in 1903. Dickinson, in the guise of a Chinaman, sketches China as a utopia in these letters in the tradition of sympathetic eighteenth-century Enlightenment observers like Voltaire and Goldsmith. In 1940, Xiao Qian influenced by the same example wrote in the voice of a Latvian to satirize

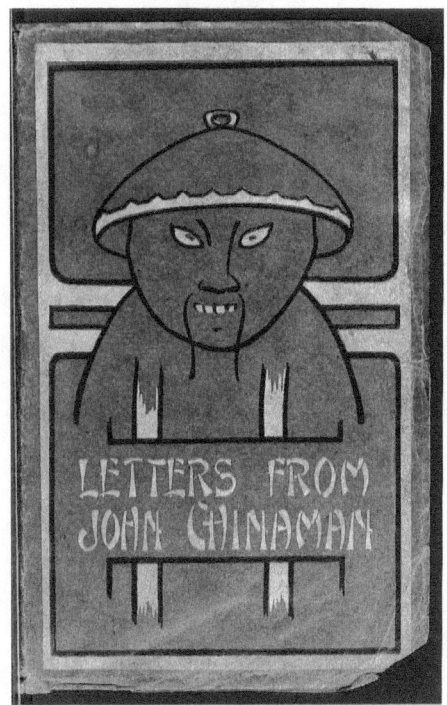

Cover of G. L. Dickinson's Letters from John Chinaman (1903). By permission of the Houghton Library, Harvard University.

China, *Long-Winded Remarks from a Red-Haired Barbarian.* Dickinson, however, writes in the persona of a Chinese gentleman, holding up a mirror to British habits of thinking about Chinese culture. R. B. Johnson published this book, with a rather menacing stereotypical picture of a Chinaman on the cover. This was the most popular of Dickinson's shorter works.

In 1900, the British sent expeditions to suppress the Boxer riots, a grassroots, antiforeign movement that especially targeted missionaries, their Christian converts in China, foreign embassies in Beijing. The rebel activity was widespread in North China with arson and the murder of thousands of Christians during the turmoil. In addition, the Chinese, as well as feeling defeated by a series of unfair treaties determined by Western powers in 1898, expressed their feeling about "foreign devils" as well as ongoing unrest in the North because of China's ever-present tragedies of drought, famine, and floods. The riot was apparently supported by the imperial courts, including the Empress Dowager, Cixi. Though an international military force of 2,000 was sent to protect foreigners during the rebellion, they were turned back and rail lines were destroyed. The siege, front-page news, was broken on 14 August 1901, by a second military force and the flight of the Empress Dowager Cixi and Emperor Guangxu from Beijing to Xi'an where the famous Xi'an stone warriors now stand. They once guarded the tomb of Emperor Qu, who has recently been made into a more benign figure in Zhang Yimou's film, *Hero.*

China resented the linking of religion, particularly Christianity, to the mission of *civilizing* the Chinese people. Catholic churches were destroyed, Catholic priests and their converts were killed and property was seized during the Boxer riots (Hinton, *Fanshen,* 60). The German ambassador was murdered, and England insisted on "revenge in the name of Jesus" (Dickinson, *International Anarchy,* 283), while the Chinese name of the rebellion, "Fists of Righteous Harmony," had as its motto, "Preserve the dynasty; destroy the foreigners."

This event was a turning point in the relationship between England and China. Two satirical literary voices arose in England soon after, that of G. L. Dickinson and Lytton Strachey, who mocked the British "Christian" and "civilized" response to the Boxer Rebellion. This next section will explore these two responses in greater depth.

In *Letters from John Chinaman,* published anonymously in 1901 (four of the eight letters having already appeared anonymously in the *Saturday*

Review), Dickinson chastises England for its materialism and heartlessness towards China in the wake of the recent Boxer Rebellion. In these letters, Dickinson assumes the persona of a Chinese official, a non-European traveling to England who describes China as a utopia in order to satirize England. Despite the reports of great civil disorder in China, his view was romantic and utopian. He writes in the enlightenment tradition of the letters of Voltaire, Montesquieu, Oliver Goldsmith[6] [as well as Li Ju-chen's (Li Ruzhen) *Flowers in the Mirror (Jing Hua Yuan)*], in which Europe is no longer positioned as the cultural center of the universe. Dickinson's Chinese official reverses the terms "civilization" and "savagery," and exposes the "barbaric" imperialist practices of "civilized" England.

Enlightenment "reason" has failed, and Dickinson joins an anti-nomian tradition that questions England's "progress." Dickinson's China, described in his 1913 letters from Beijing, is a pagoda of the mind, far off, antique, idealized, and mystical. Dickinson was angered by the British response to the insurgency: a harsh treaty, indemnities, and looting by the foreigners. He considered the Boxer Indemnity to be a form of English "looting" but "they loot with formalities" (*International Anarchy*, 284). He sided with the Chinese in emphasizing the imperialist stance that provoked the Boxer Rebellion; mainstream European politicians emphasized the rebellion, the looting, the murder of missionaries, and the flouting of international law. This discourse of scorn and ridicule documented in the British self-irony of the *Letters* is an example of the internalized critique that existed alongside the mainstream view of "Britannia rules." Dickinson's anti-imperialist and anticolonial satire exposes England's ethical weakness as a nation anticipating what we read in postcolonial theory today. In 1901, China was in the news because of the Boxer riots. It was the year that he published *Letters from John Chinaman* in England; when published in America in 1903, it was titled *Letters from a Chinese Official*, the title reflecting the concerns of a more racially-conscious nation.

Through this work, Dickinson critiqued England's new imperialism and made China a romantic site representing classical values. Lisa Lowe perceptively critiques this subject position in her work on Julia Kristeva's *Des chinoises:*

> The construction of China in *Des chinoises* conjured the oriental Other not as a colonized space but as a desired position outside Western politics and significance. Yet a final irony remains: this postdecolonization refiguration

of China continued to figure the Orient as the Other, no longer colonized but utopian, and this romantic regard for China permitted intellectuals in France to disregard the situation of actual postdecolonization peoples residing and laboring in France itself. (Lowe, "Des Chinoises," 161)

Following this logic, Dickinson's stance toward China, though admirable in the context of mainstream British thinking, blinded him to sites of injustice at home and in India. For example Dickinson, despite his Fabian identifications, opposed the admission of women and the working class to Cambridge University. In his contribution to the collection *The Woman Question* in 1918, he presents in "The Greek View of Women" a historical but equivocating stance in which he states his admiration for the "frankness" with which the Greeks describe sexual relations. Under the guise of presenting the Greek conception of the inferiority of women, he suggests his own. The Spartans, he says, view woman as "specially trained for maternity" and the State's view was that "there was little or no romance connected with the marriage tie" (1).

The letters of Dickinson written in the voice of a Chinese official are addressed to an English friend. The Chinese official, a longtime resident in England, brings into "new prominence at once the fundamental antagonism between Eastern and Western civilization, and that ignorance and contempt of the one for the other . . . in the face of the tragedy that is being enacted [British violence in the face of the Boxer Rebellion]" (*John Chinaman,* 3). The official begins his diatribe noting "his profound mistrust and dislike of . . . [English] civilization." "Our civilization," he observes, "is the oldest in the world . . . our civilization embodies . . . a moral order; while in yours we detect only an economic chaos . . . you profess Christianity but your civilization has never been Christian" (5*ff*). The Chinese, with no desire "to redeem or civilize the world" (11) or "to proselytize or trade" (71), have "a simple and natural character (when not maddened by the aggression of foreigners)" (40). Written just after the Boxer riots, the Chinese official blames the British for the tumult: "you are the cause . . ." (43). The Chinese official ironically refers to the claim that Chinese "mobs were barbarous and cruel." Alluding to the issue of British trade and the Chinese market and the forced territorial concessions to Britain in 1898, the Chinese official asserts that:

> Left to ourselves, we should never have sought intercourse with the West. We have no motive to do so; for we desire neither to proselytize nor trade

... the opening of this market is in fact the motive, thinly disguised, of all your dealings with us in recent years. (10–11)

The Chinese official reminds the British of the sorry history of forced relations with China. He observes that the first traders in China were the opium dealers, "pirates and robbers," selling a drug that destroyed many Chinese people in the mid–nineteenth century, closely followed upon by Christian missionaries that the Confucian and Buddhist Chinese were "compelled" to receive in 1840s. In the eighth and final letter, the official underlines England's "long course of injustice and oppression" and ends in an irony that rings with contemporary political significance:

> And—irony of ironies!—it is the nation of Christendom who have come to us to teach us by the sword and fire that Right in this world is powerless unless it be supported by Might! Oh do not doubt that we shall learn the lesson! And woe to Europe when we have acquired it! You are arming a nation of four hundred millions! A nation which until you came, had no better wish than to live at peace with themselves and all the world. In the name of Christ you have sounded the call to arms! In the name of Confucius, we respond. (55)

Again, it is the engagement with another culture that provokes Dickinson's self-criticism, and the enriching contribution of the other culture's perspective.

Since the letters were published anonymously and were addressed to Americans as well as the British, this led to an amusing and culturally revealing reception in America. Since the Chinese official was attempting to enlist sympathy by describing differences in culture, he writes not only of the category of "race" but also of religion. He contrasts "Christian" Europe with Asian Buddhism, Daoism, and Confucianism (48). This issue of religion enflamed William Jennings Bryan, the fiery American Christian who after reading Dickinson's letters, wrote his own *Letters to a Chinese Official* in 1906. When his own work was about to be published, Bryan discovered that the "anonymous" letters he read were not really written by a Chinese official but an Englishman. Publishing his response anyway, he acknowledges that "this nameless Chinese official has not only rendered real service but has also given our people a chance to prove their good intentions" (v). Acknowledging "our national sins" against the Chinese, Bryan nevertheless writes back (from the colony) defending America against the perceived hostility. Entering into the "struggle" between the East and the West, he composes chapters titled "Chinese Civilization Overrated," "Western Civilization Underrated," "The Folly of Isolation," "Labor-Saving Machinery," "Without a Mission," and "Christ vs. Confucianism." It is in this last chapter on the differences in religious belief that Jennings, the American, exposes the Christian-centeredness and prejudice of the Americans as well as the British who traditionally showed little respect for the "strange" and "nonmetaphysical beliefs" of Daoism and Confucianism. He rails at the Chinese official: "And can you be so blind as not to recognize the infinite superiority of the Christian creed? . . . Confucius dealt with rules and formulas; Christ dealt with substance and unchanging truth" (91, 87).

Returning to Dickinson, though he was not unmindful of China's own internal struggles between feudal and nationalist forces, he focused his sympathy for the beleaguered Chinese position on the issue of foreigners in China. This was not only salient in the imagined *Letters*, but in a series that he contributed to the *Manchester Guardian*, "Travellers' Tales," in 1913–14 after his trip to China:

> What do foreigners want? The Chinese may well ask. I am afraid the true answer is that they want nothing but concessions, interest on loans, and trade profits, at all and every cost to China. ("Tale on Nanjing," 8 April 1913)

This economic greediness might have been the long and the short of it before the war. Still, after the war, in 1919, Dickinson writes to Fry:

> England gives me the feeling of Babylon before destruction. Never did a nation so deserve destruction if that had anything to do with it. The frivolous, the coldhearted, the bestial ignorance and indifference is incredible. Of course, one always knew victory would ruin us, just as defeat is renewing Germany. I really see no life to England. (2 November 1919)

The use of apocalyptic Biblical language, "a Babylon," which Leonard Woolf uses twenty years later in his jeremiad *Quack, Quack!* attacking fascism in Europe, is typical of his generation. The irony in some of the definitions were not lost upon Dickinson.

Dickinson's letters followed a satirical tradition in which Oliver Goldsmith, a century and a half earlier, wrote *The Citizen of the World; or, Letters from a Chinese Philosopher, Residing in London, to His Friend in the East*, 1762. He too created a Chinese character, a mandarin, to voice his criticism of British missionaries and the establishment of factories in China, to praise the beauty of Chinese women, and to attack the sentimentality of the Chinese people as well as the British rage for chinoiserie. Using a foreign persona, as in Montesquieu's *Persian Letters* and Voltaire's *Letters to an English Nation*, gives force to the satire of England from within.

Dickinson shared in the criticism of England. As a historian and political scientist, he focuses on the image of China as an ancient civilization out of which foreign powers carve spheres of influence. He is perhaps more philosophically than politically concerned, as were many in Bloomsbury including Virginia Woolf and Leonard Woolf, with the fate of civilization. China stands with dignity and stillness but, as Dickinson stated in his 1930 BBC broadcast, he has, during his lifetime, "devoted much of . . . [his] time to the effort to understand and express other people's point of view" (*Points of View*, 21), working, for example, on the establishment of the League of Nations. In addition, he believes in the artists and poets who "give science a lead by giving imagination wings" (14). The two points of view—the aesthetic and the political—are the poles about which much discussion of China circulates, falsifying and distorting, at times, our cultural understanding.

Lytton Strachey's Son of Heaven

While Dickinson satirically lampoons the immorality of the British culture and government in its harsh repression of the Boxer Rebellion, Lytton Strachey goes "camp" with the imperial Chinese court that supported the Boxers in Beijing. His melodrama, "Son of Heaven," conceived of as a "thriller" in 1913, is the story of the usurpation of the throne by Empress Cixi from the Emperor, the "Son of Heaven," set in an opulent, oriental palace with numerous court intrigues. It remained a closet drama until 1925 when Strachey actually produced and staged the play with Bloomsbury friends for the benefit of the London Society for Women's Service, of which his sister, Pippa, was secretary. It has not been performed, to my knowledge, in contemporary times. What interests Strachey is not only the luxury of the Chinese court and the extravagant theatricality, but the gender play in the presentation of a strong even demonic ruling woman, Empress Cixi, with parallels to Queen Victoria. Fascinated by the cunning of the domineering Empress who dethrones the sensitive Emperor, Strachey concocts a kind of literary "chinoiserie" of empress,

Lytton Strachey and Virginia Woolf. By permission of the Provost and Scholars of King's College, Cambridge University, England.

emperor, princes, eunuchs, generals, Manchus, ladies-in-waiting, and an executioner in a palace melodrama containing elements of the tragic, romantic, lyric, and historical. Today, the acting by Bloomsbury friends, the inside jokes, the cross-dressing, the parody of men's and women's roles would be seen as high camp with the heterosexual matrix, as Judith Butler would say, inverted. Bloomsbury participated in the 1928 Scala production: Julia Strachey, half sister of Lytton, played Lady Ling; Stephen Tomlin, sculptor and first husband of Julia, played Kang, the reformer; Gerald Brenan, the writer obsessed with Dora Carrington, a guard; Angus Davidson, an assistant at the Hogarth Press after Dadie Rylands, Li Hong Zhang; Ralph Partridge, husband of Carrington who lived in a triangular relationship with Strachey and Carrington, the executioner; and Gertrude Kingston, a popular performer for whom George Bernard Shaw had written the play *Great Catherine.*

The play opens with sumptuous sets designed by Duncan Grant, the Winter Palace of the Forbidden City in Beijing, 14–15 August 1900, during the siege of the Boxer Rebellion. It is the spectacle that enthralls Strachey; it is the history that engages Dickinson. Though the tropes of the East for theatrical sets of the day were Gilbert and Sullivan's *Mikado* and Puccini's *Turandot,* in the Scala production, Duncan Grant's sets were created in the spirit of a Diaghalev ballet (traces of the sets cannot be found). The music of William Walton served as background. The setting in act one:

The Throne Hall of Heavenly Purity in the Winter Palace. Pekin. The great Dragon Throne with its elaborate carving, its steps, and its canopy, occupies the back of the stage. Pillars support the roof on carved beams. On each side of the throne are tables with china bowls containing pyramids of oranges. A few small seats in front. It is morning.

Strachey presents Empress Cixi as a monstrous usurper of the throne, emasculating the weak emperor, "the Son of Heaven," who has been a prisoner in his own palace for five years. Royal hi-jinks are revealed when the empress laments that Jung Lu [Rong Lu], commander-in-chief in Peking [Beijing], was a devoted lover five years earlier, but now has "changed so."

> Yes, we had fine times in those days, didn't we? Do you remember the masked ball we had once, when all the men were dressed as women, and all the women dressed as men? (act 1, p. 21)

The cross-dressing and the tradition of men playing women's roles in the Beijing Opera leads seamlessly into Judith Butler's notion of the "performance" of gender. Strachey intertwines his own love of acting (often in female roles, as the actors of the Beijing Opera) and Bloomsbury's delight in cross-dressing with an aspect of the melodramatic "mask" in Chinese culture. The gender play continues throughout the drama as Strachey makes sly comparisons between the Empress and Queen Victoria, who play at being "men" but are reviled for being weak "women." For example, Prince Tuan, a leader of the Boxer delegation, and Wang Fu, a provincial official, are critical of the Empress' reluctance to order Jung [Rong Lu] to fire on the "foreign devils." They resent her "shilly-shallying" and try to devise a way to put a stop to her actions:

> Tuan: After all, she's only a woman
> Wang: Yes, but with what a remarkable character!
> Tuan: Still a woman. And you know what that means: you yourself, my lord, are a married man. It means whims, caprices, hesitations, changes—in one word it means weakness... What we want is a man at the head of affairs.
> (act 1, p. 10)

Thinly disguising his own ambition to be emperor, Tuan advances his importance as a member of the imperial family and the need for the influence of a "man." Knowing what we do about the temper of the devouring Empress Cixi, we can only smile at his weak plots. The Empress herself is rife with identity confusions, worrying at one moment that she is "growing old" and is not attractive "as a woman"; at another time, when "vaulting ambition" reigns, she has her lackeys assert that she is "a man."

> Let's have a play to-night. They think they'll pinch me between them because I'm a woman. A woman! A woman! Am I woman? I say, am I woman? Whoever dares to say I'm a woman, I'll have them cut in pieces. I'm a man, a man. (act 1, p. 25)

"Can't you see," she says to the frightened Li, "that I'm a man. Tell me that I'm a man." "Certainly," replies Li. Here Strachey demonstrates Judith Butler's argument that "constraint is built into what the language constitutes as the imaginable domain of gender" (*Gender Trouble,* 9). It is the language—man or woman—that produces the binary thinking about sex and works against fluid identities where an empress can possess myriad qualities traditionally associated with both sexes. The empress is a despot but she is sensitive, vain, and, also, a painter like Queen Victoria whom she ironically describes as a "female barbarian." Reluctant to join forces with the Boxers and the ambitious Prince Tuan against the foreigners because she fears Tuan's ambition to be emperor, she refuses to order Jung-Lu to attack the foreign delegations. While the empress rants and reigns, the gentle emperor is involved in a palace intrigue with a beautiful young lady-in-waiting, Ta He [Da He], of whom the empress knows and approves. All view the "Son of Heaven" as weak, as he lacks the "manly" attributes, highlighting again the theme of the "femininity" of Chinese men that surfaces in British discourse of the time as well as Strachey's own gender spin.

Strachey plays with the fluidity of gender roles in a foreign space. China and the Far East allowed such cultural play. In a mock-heroic vein, much like Alexander Pope's *The Rape of the Lock,* he describes foolish eunuchs surrounding the empress who reductively respond to the tragedy of the Rebellion and deaths with silly domestic banter. One eunuch, hearing the explosions in the Forbidden City, announces that he was so startled that he "dropped a tea cup." And the Empress, while deciding upon matters of state—why Jung Lu [Rong Lu] does not use the arsenal and fire upon the "foreign devils"—interrupts matters of state with comments on the housekeeping of the palace: "That cloth is crooked and you haven't arranged the incense sticks" (act 2, p. 2).

When speaking with Jung Lu [Rong Lu], she laments, "Oh, politics, politics! Don't let's talk about politics. Let's talk about soups from the spleen of nightingales" (act 2, p. 6). The play represents a dying feudal culture in transition: an Empress with "small feet" who reigns like a man, and corrupt Manchu officials, like Wang Fu, who gives Lia a "loan" of $2000. Strachey parodies the corruption of a provincial official who announces, "I have worked for forty years in the service of the state and have never introduced a reform. May I count on your support?" (act 2, p. 7). The Emperor's plot to dethrone the Empress fails. Li Hong Zhang's troops desert him, and he and the empress take flight in disguise from the foreign troops massed to repress the rebellion. "The Son of Heaven" humorously trails behind in a cart. Old China emerges from Strachey's cornucopia of images: buddhas, tolling bells, swallow's nest soup, nightingales, almond trees, lotus lake, temples, and teacups. Anti-Western sentiments are rife throughout the play, as in Dickinson's *Letters from a Chinese Official*, with Empress Cixi as the mouthpiece: it is the "foreign devils" that bring "confusion and ruin to the Empire." It is yet another literary expression of Bloomsbury's sympathy for the antiforeign sentiments of the Chinese and impending sense of doom for Western interests.

In the early part of the twentieth century, as illustrated in this chapter, relations between England and China were defined not solely by trade, missionaries, or colonial forays, but by mutual assessment of the other's "civilization." In the hiatus between the demise of traditional British colonialism, the rise of its new imperialism, and the so-called ideological division of the world into superpowers in 1945, British and Chinese intellectuals and writers like G. L. Dickinson and Xu Zhimo assessed each other's traditions, literature, art, race, and religion. These reassessments of "civilization" were part of the political and cultural concern over world order. Public intellectuals like G. L. Dickinson, Leonard Woolf, and Woodrow Wilson talked about the demise of civilization and embarked on the construction of the League of Nations in 1919, while Virginia Woolf challenged women in 1938 to observe the actions of British men: "let us never cease from thinking—what is this 'civilization' in which we find ourselves? What are these ceremonies [of educated men] and why should we take part in them?" (*Three Guineas*, 73). The conversation about culture and civilization in the 1920s and 1930s was a national period of turning inward in which literature in England and China assumed some importance as the reflection of a changed consciousness. The issue was posed as the superiority of a civilization, the imperial power of England. This perception of a world organized by the "clash of civilizations" continues in the writing of Samuel Huntington today. But the thesis of clash is giving way, and this book follows rather the vision of Amartya Sen who suggests:

> Civilizations are hard to partition in this way given the diversities within each society as well as the linkages among different countries and cultures. . . . The main hope of harmony lies not in any imagined uniformity, but in the plurality of our identities, which cut across each other and work against sharp divisions into impenetrable civilizational camps. . . . The robbing of our plural identities not only reduces us; it impoverishes the world. ("A World Not Nearly Divided")

As Woolf says, when writing history or biography, it is not enough to say, "this has happened"; we must explore the pluralities of identity—to whom and when it happened—to introduce fragmented experience within history.

A constellation of historical, cultural, and literary forces swirls about the conversation between G. L. Dickinson and Xu Zhimo in 1921–22. In the letters and writings examined in this chapter, each looks at the other's culture and art and then critiques his own. Though often using the same words—"self," "self-expression," "conscious," "psychology," "civilization," and "barbarism"—continued exposure to these words reveals the sunken cultural and philosophical meanings in the minds of the English and the Chinese. Another culture or literature comes into existence, we realize, because certain conditions make it possible for one to see and reflect upon it.

THE UNWRITTEN *PASSAGE TO CHINA*: E. M. FORSTER AND XIAO QIAN

A generation after G. L. Dickinson, E. M. Forster was urged to write *A Passage to China* by a Chinese journalist and writer. Xiao Qian, who studied at King's College, 1941–42, reflected:

> *A Passage to China* had been behind [*sic*] my mind ever since we met. To Mr. Forster, China may be a land with a great deal of personal relationship left; to China, Mr. Forster would be an altogether different Westerner, neither pompous like the admirals, nor complacent like the diplomats, nor nagging as the missionaries, nor patronizing like the connoisseurs, but a sensitive, humane, understanding co-man. (*Friendship Gazette*, footnote to Letter No. 22, 22 September 1942)

E. M. Forster *by Dora Carrington. By permission of the Society of Authors, London, England.*

In 1934, Beatrice Webb had also encouraged Forster to write of China: "Why don't you write another great novel (analogous to *A Passage to India*) giving the essence of the current conflict all over the world between those who aim at exquisite relationships within the closed circle of the 'elect' and those who aim at hygienic and scientific improvement of the whole race?" (*Letters*, 392, 24 April 1934). Here the arch, self-righteous Beatrice Webb encourages the project, given Forster's international interests; nevertheless, she targets him (and implicitly Bloomsbury) for his "exquisite relationships" while Webb and other socialists work for the "hygienic and scientific improvement of the whole race." Nevertheless, though often asked to speak or write about China given the growing cultural interest in the country, Forster demurred, always feeling it was a subject beyond his scope: "so you see how ill prepared—alas!—I am to take my Passage to China as yet" (*Friendship Gazette*, 27 September 1941). In a letter to Xiao Qian, written in 1943, Forster remarked:

Now for your lecture [on his book, *China but Not Cathay*] for a minute. I much enjoyed it, thought it amusing and charming. It made me sad for I felt that I was too old to "take on" China, and that, better than Italy (my *first* lover), India, or France could it have been taken on by me. You must imagine that I have written a novel about China, the greatest of our age, but that unfortunately its pages have got stuck together during printing, so that it cannot be read. The clumsy big boy can hold it in his hands and even against his heart, but that is all. Do you think he will understand? (*Friendship Gazette,* 5 January 1943).

Sympathizing with Forster's stance, knowing what it means to take on a new culture as I write this book, I am aware, nevertheless, that his demurral, at that time, halted his expansion of the English novel into international domains. E. M. Forster and Xiao Qian, nevertheless, had a warm relationship as revealed in the collection of letters *Friendship Gazette.* These letters, as well as "A Week in London," talks delivered on the BBC during the London blitz of 1940 (and later printed in *The Listener*), give us a sense of the occasional literary thinking of two important writers from China and England.

Forster is drawn to "the foreign" and "other" ways of seeing. His close friendships with G. L. Dickinson, Leonard Woolf, T. E. Lawrence, Syed Ross Masood (he visited in India in 1912, 1921, and 1946), and later, Xiao Qian, journalist, translator, and writer, piqued his curiosity about the East. Though Forster did not personally preserve any of Xiao's letters, as far as my explorations in King's College Modern Archives reveal, he did pen a note in his *Locked Diary* on 31 December 1941, upon meeting Xiao and Arthur Koestler at a PEN Conference honoring Rabindranath Tagore, the Indian poet, in London (Forster, *Locked Diary,* 31 November 1941). The curious silence about Xiao on Forster's part is perhaps explained by Xiao's preservation of his letters to Forster in *Friendship Gazette.* In a personal letter, Xiao Qian revealed that "it was just by chance that King's Library preserved that *Friendship Gazette* which I made [copied his own letters to Forster] in the spring of 1944, just before I left Cambridge and became a war-correspondent attached to the U.S. 7th Army under General Patch. There were more letters exchanged after that, of course" (letter to the author, 2 June 1994). The letters Forster wrote to Xiao were destroyed according to Xiao during the Cultural Revolution: "I don't have whatever I had written in pre-1949 days, and if I had some those were lost during (and before) the accursed Cultural Revolution. I can't even tell you what I had written as it is so long ago and I have gone thru several hells, the worst being 1966" (XQ to the author, 15 September 1996). Interesting letters discussing Forster's *Howards End* were lost on Xiao's end, and Xiao speculates that Forster destroyed some of his letters:

> All my letters (I mean the originals) disappeared and my own guess has been: the old man simply tore them into pieces when he learnt in the early 50's that I failed to have a separate session with the friend, Professor Sprott, he sent (a professor at Nottingham University) and so failed to receive his letter and the book, which was to be delivered to me in person. I have often pondered, "suppose I were to be in the 50's again with the same Stalinist atmosphere, would I dare to have that separate session"? I am afraid the answer would still be NO, for during these 40 years I have seen too many people who were made counter-revolutionaries just by such a chance meeting. (XQ to the author, 2 June 1994)

Critic Timothy Tung confirms this in "Tragedy of a Literary Friendship," detailing Forster's disenchantment with Xiao because of his refusal to see W. J. Sprott in 1954 when he visited China as a member of a British cultural delegation. In a personal note, Tung stated,

> At the time (even three years before the Anti-rightist Campaign) Xiao Qian was already in the political dog house. He went to the official reception but did not dare to meet privately with Sprott (later admitting he was cowardly). Book and letter were returned to Forster.

Xiao went on to justify his decision not to meet Sprott:

> For during these forty years I have seen too many people who were made counter-revolutionaries just by such a chance meeting. In fact, I even congratulate myself for being dragged off the plane in 1950 when I was supposed to be the secretary to a group (official) visit to Britain, for a colleague of mine who studied in Cairo before 1949 and was included in a friendship mission to Egypt. He happened to return a friendly visit of a former collegemate and thus was branded a spy for 17 years! As to Forster's letters to me, amounting to some 80, including some long ones discussing his works, particularly Howards End, they were all burnt by the redguards in a fire set in the yard of my house in the evening of 23rd, August, 1966. (letter to the author, 2 June 1994)

Again, the historical turmoil in China seeps into the gaps and silences of this study. Shoring up my observations against the ruins of the Cultural Revolution that destroyed so many of the letters that would enlighten this study, I realize more fully the erasures of personal and literary relationships in literary history, and the need for narrative to fill the gaps. Nevertheless, Xiao Qian related to me in an interview in 1995 that Forster never forgave him for his inhospitable treatment of Sprott given Forster's own generosity to Xiao in Cambridge.[7] Is it possible that Forster had no idea that meeting Western visitors in China was a politically transgressive act in the 1950s for which Xiao would have suffered greatly? Did he believe that "personal relations" should prevail over Chinese political campaigns? Or was there another reason that caused the rupture, given that Sprott was a former lover of E. M. Forster's?

What *is* documented, however, is that even before the friendship with Xiao Qian, Forster was engaged with the East, and, more particularly, India. This can be gleaned in the letters of his good Cambridge friend and teacher, G. L. Dickinson, who was a great influence on him. Writing to E. M. Forster in 1911 during a visit to China, G. L. Dickinson allowed that China is a land of "human beings," but India is "supernatural" and "terrifying":

> China is a land of human beings. India, as it glimmers in a remote past, is supernatural, uncanny, terrifying, sublime, horrible, monotonous, full of mountains and abysses, all heights and depths, and forever incomprehensible. But China! So gay, friendly, beautiful, sane, Hellenic, choice, human. Dirty? Yes. Peking [Beijing], the last day of two is all but impossible even in a rickshaw—pools, lakes, of liquid mud. One understands the importance of the sedan chair and the wall side, 150 years ago in Europe. Poor? Yes. But never were poor people so happy (I speak with all the superficiality you care to credit me with). (in Forster, *G. L. Dickinson*, 122)

He goes on to describe the qualities of the Chinese people to Forster:

> A level, rational people—a kind of English *with* sensitiveness and imagination.... No reaches into the infinite; but a clear, nonrestricted perception of the beautiful and the exquisite in the Real. But the hand of the Powers, or rather the foot, is on her throat, I don't know whether she can pull through. Said one of them to me: "The Powers put their foot on China and say 'Get up you brute!' 'I'll get up' says China, 'when you take away your

foot!' 'No! You get up, and I'll take away my foot!'" The same gentleman remarked: "British rule in India is excellent—at water closets."

Many in the Bloomsbury circle were drawn to China, often remarking on the "sedate" Chinese temperament, and prejudiced against India, though Forster would be the exception. Julian Bell wrote a letter to his mother on his way back from Malaysia "confirmed in . . . [his] prejudice that the Chinese are charming and Indians unpleasant" (Letter to Vanessa Bell, 27 September 1935); Virginia Woolf wrote to Julian Bell in China that she believed that the English "are baked of the same blood as the Chinese." Another side of Bloomsbury is revealed in a letter from Eddy Playfair to Julian. He quotes Dennis Proctor—in responding to an article in the *Times* about an Indian professor—that "all niggers look alike" (25 January 1936). To this remark Playfair added that "that doesn't really apply to the Chinese, who are plainly human beings." The racial prejudice against the Indians was part of English colonial arrogance at the beginning of the twentieth century. The Chinese sympathy emerged perhaps from a combination of factors: cultural affinity, geographical distance from China, and England's less politically and culturally enmeshed relationship given that China was never a colony of England but in a semi-colonial relationship.

Against the grain, E. M. Forster wrote one of the masterpieces of English literature, *A Passage to India* in 1924, embodying his love of and insight into the Indian culture. Forster's early interest in the East was stimulated not only by his teacher and friend, G. L. Dickinson, but also by Leonard Woolf returning from his experience as an administrative judge in Ceylon in 1911, as well as Forster's own trip to Egypt with the Red Cross in 1915. Dickinson wrote of the tensions between the British and the Chinese after the Boxer Rebellion, siding with the Chinese in *Letters from John Chinaman* (1901); Leonard Woolf wrote *The Village in the Jungle* (1913) from the perspective of the Sinhalese, rejecting his past colonial role as judge in the Hambantota administration in Ceylon; and Forster wrote sympathetically of the Indian position in the cultural and spiritual clash between the British and Indian civilizations in his novel, *A Passage to India*, and his introduction to Eliza Fay's *Original Letters from India, 1779–1815* (1925). This interest in and constellation of relationships in the East suggest Bloomsbury's position outside mainstream British thinking that was a spur not only to Forster but to others in the next generation like Julian Bell, who was a student of Dickinson's at King's College.

Unlike India, China was never colonized by the British, but it did endure economic and territorial semi-colonization. The relationship with England began with an ideology in the eighteenth century and then the Opium Wars, the development of spheres of trade and influence, the building of railroads, the creation of economic concessions in major Chinese cities such as Shanghai, as well as the creation of legal extraterritorial status for Europeans in China. There were also incursions and economic concessions set up by France, Russia, Germany, Japan, and, after World War II, America.

E. M. Forster never wrote about China, but did form a close friendship with Xiao Qian, 1941–43, when he visited England. Xiao Qian described his relationship with Forster as his "one true friendship" in Cambridge, the intimacy of which was ruptured when Xiao returned to the historical cauldron in China. He entered during the middle of the Sino-Japanese War, the civil war between the nationalists and the communists, and, later, witnessed the founding of the People's Republic of China and endured the Cultural Revolution. Misunderstandings developed at a distance; letters were lost.

The literary effect of these "personal relations" is E. M. Forster's cultural openness. Forster welcomes other cultures into his novels and takes the genre beyond insular concerns with class and a narrow conception of what is "English." And it is this stance that draws Xiao Qian into relationship. Forster introduces in *A Passage to India,* for example, a new cultural and political range of Englishmen and women, some sympathetic and culturally sensitive to Indian problems and some not, as well as the presentation of educated Anglo-Indian characters. He admits the possibility of personal "friendship" as the basis for developing relations between nations—though in 1924, "No, not yet. . . . No, not there" (*A Passage to India,* 322). Though personally a shy man, Forster casts a bold and critical narrative eye on British colonialism in pre-independence India: he includes transnational issues and questions the new imperialism through the themes he introduces into the English novel. In *A Room with a View* and *Where Angels Fear to Tread,* he explores the themes of British and Italian sexuality, temperament, and sensibility. Transnational issues are in the foreground while insular class issues of the British are cast into the shadows after *Howards End.*

While Dickinson idealized other cultures in his writings, Forster grappled with personal and national issues with a more observant personal and cultural eye. He did, however, mysteriously stop writing novels after *A Passage to India* in 1924, though continuing a literary life until his death in 1970. Eddy Playfair in a letter to Julian Bell speculated, attributing Forster's much-discussed writing block to his desire and inability to capture more of the transnational or "universal" than the "psychological" in his novels: "Charles told us . . . that the real reason [for Forster's block] is that he will not be satisfied with a novel which more or less covers everything; it must be universal; and the psychological approach which is his style will not do for that" (Letter to JB, 13 November 1936). Forster was stuck. Was it a problem of narration? There were others who claimed that Forster's creative impulse was inhibited because of his inability to interweave the subject of homosexuality into his work because of legal and cultural taboos in England. Perhaps this is what Virginia Woolf alluded to in her 1930 letter to Ethel Smyth in which she observed that though Forster's books have influenced her, his work is now "impeded, shriveled" (*Letters,* vol. 4, 21 September 1930, 218). The literary effects of the suppression of homosexual experience in the genre of the novel in the early part of the twentieth century are still under examination.

E. M. Forster, in writing of his friend Edward Carpenter in 1944, articulated in personal and cultural terms the growing importance of other cultures and other races for British intellectuals and writers, and, in a veiled way, for homosexuals. In describing various countries in a letter to Xiao Qian as "lovers" or as "shits," Forster supplied a metaphorical background for his continuing emphasis on "personal relations," now projected as a metaphor for national relations. "Personal relations" would include, for himself and Edward Carpenter (the pioneer who "normalized" homosexuality), homosexual relationships across class, cultural, and national boundaries. Carpenter and Dickinson frankly accepted their homosexuality despite taboos in England of the time; other writers, like Siegfried Sassoon and E. M. Forster, were more conflicted. Other cultures like India and China, less culturally constricted or policed than England in the sexual domain, would provide other ways of being and places for homosexuals. Forster says of Carpenter that "as he had looked outside his own class for companionship, so he was obliged to look outside his own race for wisdom" (*Two Cheers,* 214). Carpenter, influenced by reading Walt Whitman's open sexual declarations in his poetry, and espousing socialism, closely allied himself throughout his life with working-class men, their causes, and their manual labor. This class alliance, according to Jean Moorcroft Wilson, was bound up with his homosexuality, easing conflicts experienced by Siegfried Sassoon, more conservative, and caught in the contradictions of the upper-middle class Thornycroft and Sassoon families (Wilson, *Siegfried*

Sassoon, 152). E. M. Forster also looked outside his own class and race for relationships. His first important love, Hugh Owen Meredith, fellow at King's College, and Syed Ross Masood, in India, intertwine to inspire *Maurice,* written about 1911–12, published posthumously in 1971. He dedicated *A Passage to India* to Masood and "the seventeen years of our friendship." In continuing the theme of movement from personal to transnational relations, it is important to note that Carpenter was not only a friend of Forster's and a lover of Dickinson's, but also that he had welcomed Xiao Qian into his home when Carpenter was about eighty years old. Gaylord Leung notes that Carpenter loved the culture of China, and spoke to Xiao of his ideas about liberty and "returning to nature."

"THE UNPOPULAR NORMAL": E. M. FORSTER'S EXPANDING NOTIONS OF TRANSNATIONAL SEXUALITY, CULTURE, AND THE BRITISH NOVEL

E. M. Forster and other British writers needed a more elastic and expansive form for the English novel. They sought a form that would encompass new cultural and sexual experiences and values, creating a new definition of "civilized" behavior in the nation of England. This new discourse of the individual and the nation, they speculated, would be embodied in a British novel that would someday include themes of cross-class and transnational homosexuality. That "cannibal, the novel," that Virginia Woolf describes was devouring other art forms ("Narrow Bridge," 18) and was a form open to introducing new spaces and themes in literature. In calling for new themes in literature beyond "love and battle and jealousy," Woolf observes in her essay "On Being Ill,"

> Literature does its best to maintain that its concern is with the mind; that the body is a sheet of plain glass through which the soul looks straight and clear, and save for one or two passions such as desire and greed, is null, and negligible and non-existent. (*The Moment,* 9–11)

Though Woolf was calling for a description of illness in literature, she also argued for descriptions of the body and a new hierarchy of the passions, issues that we see now in connection with the repression of the homosexual body in English literature. And because of this repression, there would be a "poverty of the language" for describing it. Though homosexual love and sex were being theorized in the novel at this time as transcending the categories of gender, race, nation, and religion, the boundaries of "civilized" behavior and national "identity" were clearly drawn. E. M. Forster and Edward Carpenter's theories remained in the "suburbs" of the sturdy land of England. Just as Julian Bell's personal friendship with Ling Shuhua inspired a constellation of letters, and cultural engagements that permitted Bloomsbury's prejudices to surface, Carpenter's, Dickinson's, and Forster's writing about homosexuality and transnational sexual relationships evoked, at times, the cultural narrow-mindedness, hypocrisy, and insularity of the waning British empire. As Forster would say when writing *Maurice*, "I am tired of what is very English" (*Friendship Gazette*, 7 April 1943).

Intellectuals and writers like E. M. Forster, G. L. Dickinson, Edward Carpenter, Lytton Strachey, and others in the Bloomsbury group asked questions that prepared the ground in the early part of the century for contemporary critical work such as David Eng's *Queer Diaspora*. Eng's study of the affiliation and transnational migration and communities based on sexuality connects with the communities described here. In treating themes that both questioned England's role abroad, and introducing the "international" through the representation of the "inner spaces" of the nation (Chatterjee, *The Nation and Its Fragments*, 147), the narration and themes of the British novel began to subtly shift. Virginia Woolf notes this in her essay "Mr. Bennett and Mrs. Brown":

> In or about December 1910 human character changed . . . All human relations have shifted—those between masters and servants, husbands and wives, parents and children. And when human relations change there is at the same time a change in religion, conduct, politics, and literature. (320–21)

Sexual affiliations and migrations and travel in relation to England's waning imperialism are also part of "the shift." But England was not ready to allow the public articulation of this shift. E. M. Forster's novel *Maurice* with its theme of homosexual relations, circulated underground, 1912–14, but was published posthumously in 1971. Woolf's prescient observation about the democratizing effect of World War I, a theme developed in the writing of Paul Fussell, cannot be ignored as men of different classes served in the trenches side by side during the war and relied upon one another. Women assumed so-called male roles in British society while the men were away fighting, and career opportunities not available in peacetime were realized as women organized to demand greater participation in education, employment, and government, as they had organized around suffrage before the war. After the war, the relations between the sexes and among the classes were never the same. The conditions of war had relaxed English gender and social categories, and this enabled people to more openly seek friendships with people outside of their class and culture. It was not, however, until the Wolfenden Report of 1963 that the House of Commons legally reformed Britain's archaic criminal statutes against homosexuality the following year. Then, for the first time since the era of Henry VIII, private homosexual acts between males over the age of twenty-one were not subject to prosecution.[8]

During this period of repression, clearly China and India, as well as other parts of the East, presented British men of a certain class and means with imaginative as well as erotic possibilities. The political and economic forces of British imperialism enabled the development of cultural "diasporas." Given that China and India were sexually open spaces, homosexuality, at this time, might be viewed as a transcultural force that leveled others. Since some of the homosexuals were also writers and travelers, their personal experiences of other cultures brought new variables into the then insular British novel, thus enriching its vision and content. It stimulated writing that questioned the cultural status quo, and broadened the definition of what was "English" and "civilized" in a field of growing international modernist influences.

At the same time, what was the perception of Asian men among the English? In the perceptions of some, Asian men were "feminized." Charles Lamb in his nineteenth-century observations on the popular willow-pattern plate had noted that he loved "the men with women's faces, and the women, if possible with still more womanish expression." Here Lamb may be referring to the tradition of Beijing Opera in which men acted and sang females roles. He might also be alluding to the Chinese male physique, seemingly slighter than the British, at the time. G. L. Dickinson in his 1913 visit to China discussed his wish for Chinese "boys"; Harold Acton lived in China, 1932–39, translating, lecturing and enjoying its permissive sexuality; W. H. Auden and Christopher Isherwood, lovers, traveled to China in 1939 before joining the Spanish Civil War. Ye Junjian, Julian Bell's student, translated for W. H. Auden during his trip to the warfront and described his behavior in China as "indiscreet."[9] In fact, when Julian Bell arrived in China in 1935, he too referred to the Anglo-Chinese community and the Chinese having "far better taste than non-Aryan aesthetic 'buggers'" like John Lehmann, who also visited China.

Adrian Wright's new biography of John Lehmann cruelly underlines Julian's assessment here. But Bloomsbury's frank acceptance of homosexuality united them in resistance to mainstream British discourse about sexuality and the search for erotic space abroad and at home. This book suggests that these cultural and sexual attitudes rippled into narrative forms and themes.

Brett Hinsch writes of the historical tradition of homosexuality in China that goes back, he speculates, to the Bronze Age. Expressions developed in the Chinese language, such as the "cut sleeve," and is revealed in literature such as *The Dream of the Red Chamber* (sometimes titled *The Story of the Stone*). Hinsch notes:

> In many periods homosexuality was widely accepted and even respected, had its own formal history, and had a role in shaping China's political institutions, modifying social conventions and spurring artistic creations. A sense of tradition lasted up until this century, when it fell victim to a growing sexual conservatism and the Westernization of morality. (*Passions of the Cut Sleeve*, 4)

Hinsch retells the traditional tale of "the cut sleeve." The Emperor Ai was sleeping with his consort Dong Xian stretched out across his sleeve. Sensitive to his lover, and not wanting to disturb him, the emperor cut off his sleeve as he arose (53). This image of gentleness and respect passed on to generations gives narrative space to the place of the homosexual in China. Xiao Qian also wrote to Forster in one of his letters of an Emperor of China who was known to be fond of "plucking the flowers in the back garden" (6 May 1943), a code expression for relationships with young boys. But, Xiao also informs Forster that there is no philosophical background that glorifies homosexuality in China "as in the West." If it happens, Xiao observes, it is "merely physical and it is more owing to circumstances than preference" (6 May 1943). Clearly, the tradition of friendship between men is a value in Chinese culture, as is documented, for example, in many of Arthur Waley's translations of poems, "Oaths of Friendship," "To Tan Ch'iu" ["Duo Dan Qiu"] "The Hat Given to the Poet by Li Chien [Li Jian]," "After Getting Drunk." Men are companions in courage, meditation, scholarship, chess, calligraphy, poetry, talk, and drink, and this is represented on numerous Chinese scrolls and porcelain. Romantic love, so central to the Western tradition, is displaced in Chinese poetry by the theme of wedded love and even more, friendship between men. Relations between men and women are here viewed as something commonplace, obvious—a need of the body, not satisfaction of the emotions. These he reserves entirely for friendship. I have been criticized for saying something like this; but the vast mass of classical Chinese poetry amply confirms my view. (A. Waley, preface, *Translations from Chinese*)

In 1913, G. L. Dickinson wrote from China of his embarrassment in being taken to a Chinese banquet of "sing-song girls" who he says are "very pretty little things, looking about ten, but being older." He assumed they were prostitutes, to be had for a price, but complained to Roger Fry, "Imagine me trying in great moral embarrassment, to act my part, and unsuccessful, I think I was. I wish they were boys!" (Fry, REF Collection III, 3 April 1913). Boys "got up as prostitutes" on the streets of China were described earlier by the Italian Jesuit missionary Matteo Ricci, who related his horror (as Beatrice and Sidney Webb would a century later): "there are public streets full of boys got up like prostitutes and there are people who buy these boys and teach them to play music, sing and dance. And then, gallantly dressed and made up with rouge like women these miserable men are initiated into this terrible vice" (Hinsch, *Passions of the Cut Sleeve,* 2.) Homosexuality then was flaunted on the streets in parts of China, often motivated by the poverty of the boys in the early decades of the twentieth century, when Forster's manuscript on the theme circulated underground in England.

Although Forster referred to homosexuality as "the unpopular normal," in a letter to Xiao Qian, he, nevertheless, observed the conventions. In 1934 when he wrote a rather colorless biography of his close friend G. L. Dickinson, he omitted any mention of Dickinson's homosexuality, a significant dimension of his personality. Forster left a blank in the middle of Dickinson's life, just as he does his own with *Maurice,* a novel that is autobiographically choked. Forster writes:

> [*Maurice*] was finished in 1914. The friends, men and women, to whom I showed it, like it. But they were carefully picked. It has not so far had to face the critics or the public, and I have myself been too much involved in it, and for too long, to judge. (*Maurice,* 250)

Looking more closely at *Maurice,* Forster's only novel that deals with the topic of homosexuality as an integral part of the British experience, we are reminded also that Harold Acton was in China, 1932–39. Acton taught, and immersed himself in Chinese theater and poetry, and later did translations with L. C. Arlington and Qin Shi Xiang. When Julian Bell arrived in China, Vanessa Bell urged him to get in touch with Acton, an Oxford poet, art connoisseur, and a friend of the Sitwells. Julian did meet Acton with Ling Shuhua and they visited Ch'i Pai shi together. Julian contacted him in 1936, and sent a copy of his recently published book of poems, *Work for the Winter.* Acton liked it, writing that "the poems are all astonishingly mature; and it is a joy to taste October pears after the sour berries of Auden and that school" (Letter to JB, June 1936). Acton was drawn to Julian's pastoral poems full of sensitive naturalist observations, resisting the "chasm in the road," the war that altered British consciousness and advanced the consciousness that became modernism. The associations between epicureanism in China, Acton's relationship with Carl Van Vechten, and black culture, curiously, come together as he continues:

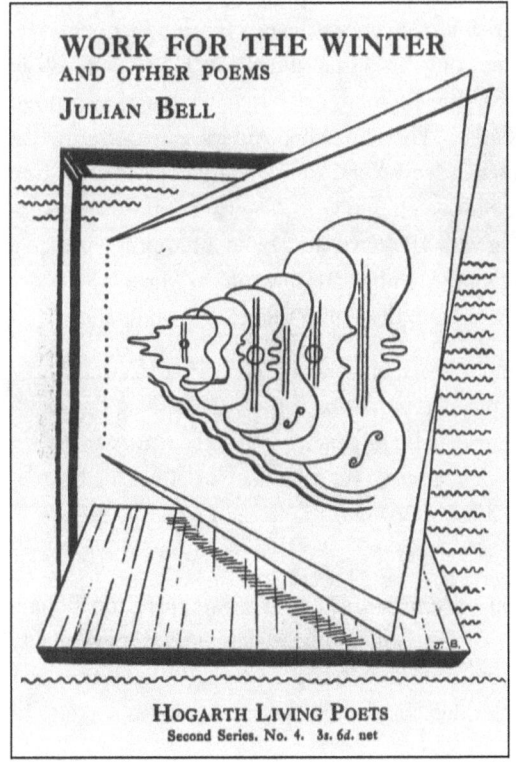

Cover of Julian Bell's collection of poems Work for the Winter (1936). By permission of the Society of Authors, London, England.

> Thanks for sending *Work for Winter* (though dear John Banting's cover seems to bear little relation to such visions and precisions of landscape and mood, and takes me back to nightclubs with negroes and the braceleted skeleton of Nancy Cunard. (HA to JB, 1936)

In 1977, Acton wrote to Ling Shuhua, "Ah Peking! [Beijing!] It was there that I spent the happiest year of my life. Consequently, I would be afraid of returning though one is told it is all for the best. I'm sure it has become sadly puritanical and I'm a shameless Epicurean in my 73rd year." In Beijing, he had also spent time with Julian and Ling Shuhua. In a letter to Ling Shuhua in 1977, he fondly remembered Xiao Qian, with whom he had spent much time in London during the war. He regretted that he had forgotten the Chinese he knew though he had translated "The Peach Blossom Fan" together with Chin-shih hsiang in 1948. He lived the life of an epicurean in China and left in 1939 just before the outbreak of the war in England.

Harold Acton's fascination with the Beijing Opera and theater brought him into contact with one of the great female impersonators of Chinese opera, Mei Lanfang. Mei Lanfang was not only an admired artist in China but also in America where he inspired Charlie Chaplin, in Germany where he inspired Brecht, and in Russia, Stanislavski. When he visited America, he performed at the Forty-ninth Street Theater in New York, Feb. 16, 1930, selections from his repertory, including "The Suspected Slipper," "The End of the Tiger General," and "The King's Parting with His Favorite." In an attempt to arrange a visit for Mei Lanfang to England, Archibald Rose wrote to Maynard Keynes and Lydia Lopokova, the dancer from the Ballet Russe, describing him:

> The most famous of Chinese actors, singers and dancers, is leaving for Moscow to give a series of plays. They will be entirely Chinese, in theme, music, dancing, decor and personnel. The general style of the plays suggests old Ming pictures, Buddhist legends etc. He plays the part of leading lady. The authorities say he is an artist of first rank. (Letter to Lopokova, Keynes Papers, 15/173)

Clearly, part of the attraction of homosexuals such as Acton to the Beijing Opera, was the tradition of males masquerading as females. Homosexuality was widespread among boy actors raised in troupes who were taught to wear cosmetics and delicate silk clothing, bind their feet and walk mincingly. In

Mei Lanfang, famous female impersonator in the Beijing Opera. By permission of the Dartington Hall Trust Archive, Totnes, England.

Chen Kaige's film *Farewell My Concubine*, we observe the imprisonment as well as liberation in this artistic and erotic space of the opera. Xiao Qian also wrote of boys playing feminine roles in dramatic repertories of the Imperial Court, describing how their own co-actors or men in the Forbidden City seduced the boys. The polite term "officials" was coined, according to Brett Hinsch, as the signal of "a passive man" who might meet a wealthy patron at "a tea gathering." During the Qing Dynasty, stories were told not only of "the scholar and the beauty," but also of the esteem that respected scholars had for actors. After Beijing Opera performances, some gentry hosted opera parties where the stars engaged in sex with the guests: a practice later criticized in May Fourth literature and neo-Confucian moral asceticism, according to Hinsch.

This is illustrated in the classical novel *The Dream of the Red Chamber* (1791). In this Chinese classic, Jia Zheng is annoyed with his spoiled son, Baoyu, when he is visited by some officers looking for a young actor, Qi Guan, who is an attendant of the Prince. Baoyu pretends that he does not know where the young actor is but the palace emissary asserts that he has "proof" of his presence. "Since you force us to it then, if you do not know who Qi Guan is, may we ask you how it happens that you have his red handkerchief hanging from your inner belt?" (Tsao, 166). Baoyu has exchanged "handkerchiefs" with the young actor, a sign of their homosexual relationship. The handkerchief with its history of intimacy in the West (e.g., Desdemona's erotically displaced "handkerchief" in *Othello*) also signifies homosexuality in the East.

Prostitutes were sometimes known as "sisters of the handkerchief." Ling Shuhua's short story "Once upon a Time," from her collection *Flowers in the Temple* (1928) and titled "An Embroidered Handkerchief" in an earlier translation, also presents the theme of the handkerchief and coded adolescent lesbianism. Two adolescent girls, Yunluo and Yingman rehearse the roles of Romeo and Juliet in a school play. On the evening of their final rehearsal, Yingman goes back with Yunluo to her dormitory:

> Sitting under the lamp, she watched Yunluo undo her hair and plait it into a loose braid, then change into her imported pastel pajamas with snowflakes embroidered along the cuffs and collar. Probably from the exhaustion of rehearsing, the tender rosiness of Yunluo's cheeks had risen to her eyelids, and she had to struggle to keep her pretty eyes open. She looked exceptionally delicate and vulnerable. (186)

Yingman offers to massage Yunluo's back and the narrator notes the "intoxicating aroma of Yunluo's powder, hair, or flesh" (186). Throughout the story, hints of sexual play appear, symbolized by the presence of the "handkerchief," the cultural cue of intimacy. Yunluo "throws down" her handkerchief at the beginning of the story when Romeo (Yingman) calls her to rehearsal. It reappears near the end of the story when Yunluo and Yingman wipe their eyes after crying together when Yunluo informs Yingman of her arranged marriage. Yingman, devastated by this news, expresses the wish that the two of them could live together for the rest of their lives:

> People make their own destinies. Why can't we be together forever? Look at the primary school instructors Miss Chen and Miss Chu, haven't they been living together for five or six years? My love for you is deeper and more permanent than any man's could ever be. . . . Can't you just consider this the same as being married to me? (191)

What distinguishes Ling Shuhua's story, written in 1928, besides the topic of adolescent physical attraction between women, is her delicate use of the language of intimacy and erotic suggestion. Yet a Chinese critic of the time, Qin Hongchun, speaks of the "sickness" that this story of bourgeois girls portrays—"their languishing" (264). Ling Shuhua's articulation of the theme of lesbianism, even sexuality, was new, a product of the new subjects introduced into literature after the May Fourth literary movement. It also entered into the stories of Lu Yin and Chen Xuezhao.

Lu Xun, one of China's foremost twentieth-century writers, in a curious essay "On Photography," written in 1924, writes of the popularity of the photo portraits of Mei Lanfang, the famous Beijing Opera female impersonator, doing "Celestial Maiden Scatters Flowers" or "Daiyu Buries Flowers." He describes these photographs as being "more elegant indeed than those of men of wealth and power, and . . . sufficient to prove that the Chinese do indeed have eyes with aesthetic sensibility" (Denton, ed., *Modern Chinese Literary Thought*, 201). These images of the "womanly man" are related to the tradition of men playing women in the opera and the homosexual practices in the opera world. All this, as Brett Hinsch suggests, is part of the silent homosexual tradition that drew some Englishmen to China as well as India. Lu Xun remarks ironically on the tradition of men playing women in the opera:

> Although I have only seen a few photographs of famous foreign actors and beauties, I never saw one of a man playing the part of a woman. . . . The art that is the most noble and eternal in China is the art of men acting as women. And yet, we can see that it is the "man who plays the part of a woman" who most causes anxiety and yet is most precious. This is because each of the two sexes sees this role as the opposite sex: men see a woman being acted, and women see a man acting. Therefore, this type of photography hangs eternally in the windows of photography studios and in the minds of our citizens. Foreign countries do not have this kind of complete artist. All they can do is give free reign to the will of their rock chiselers, blenders of color, and ink masters [artists]. The art that is the most noble, most eternal, and most universal in China is the art of men acting as women. (Denton, ed., *Modern Chinese Literary Thought*, 203)

Lu Xun makes an interesting cultural and aesthetic point about the fascination of "androgyny" in the photographs and of the "complete artist," Mei Lanfang. Virginia Woolf will also claim in 1927 in *A Room of One's Own* that the creative mind, the "great mind," is androgynous in combining the qualities of both sexes. In addition, the intertwining of gender and race politics is suggested in Lu Xun's tone of sarcasm.

Chinese works, as posited by Fredric Jameson, may more often reveal "a national allegory," writers longing to articulate repressed and interwoven personal and national desires. In some stories then, the Chinese male is "feminized" to express China's "weak" position in the world. In a puritanical culture, which China was at the time, where sex was rarely discussed openly, or affection displayed, the protagonist of Yu Dafu's short story "Sinking" cries out:

> What I want is love. If there were one beautiful woman who understood my suffering, I would be willing to die for her. If there were one woman who could love me sincerely, I would also be willing to die for her, be she beautiful or ugly. For what I want is love from the opposite sex. (Lau, ed., 49)

His despair over his own sexual detumescence, and inability to find and enjoy sex and love while living in Japan, is parallel to his "sinking" feeling about China, then subject to unequal treaties with the West and by Japan. The perceived humiliation of the Chinese nation by foreign powers is projected at this time into literary images of Chinese men being "weak" or "feminized." China being in a semi-colonial position, having to concede territories to England,

Russia, France, Germany, and Japan, is deprived of masculinist images in its literature. This despair over the "sinking" of desire reverberates in Ha Jin's recent lyrical novel, *Waiting*. Here too we read a national allegory into the novel, but it is not a foreign force or country that interferes with the fulfillment of desire as in Yu Dafu's "Sinking." In *Waiting*, the State, embodied in a provincial judge, controls the desires of a man, Lin Kong, who is bound in an arranged marriage (representing old China) to an illiterate woman he thinks he does not love. His wife, Shuyu, has bound feet—"Every pair of lotus feet come from a basket of tears" (206)—and the values of loyalty to him and his family. Marriage and divorce laws prevent him from entering into a relationship with a "city girl," Manna, based on individual choice and affinity (new China). After waiting eighteen years, he does finally achieve a divorce to marry his intended, it is too late, and his desire "sinks" again. At the end of the novel, he looks back to the comforts of his first marriage, based on loyalty to family. Yu Dafu's "sinking" and Ha Jin's "waiting" reverberate. Though, at first, it seems strange to an American reader, one learns to read the way that the personal and the national intertwine in consciousness in these stories—the consciousness that enmeshes loyalty to self and community that is an integral part of Chinese socialization.

This intertwining of the personal, sexual, and national is revealed in a painful letter from G. L. Dickinson to E. M. Forster that mentions the "beautiful brown bodies" of the Indians and the "ugly but fascinating" Chinese:

> If such a people [Indians] could be lifted onto a higher economic level, without losing these qualities, we should have the best society this planet admits of. Whereas I believe everything in India will have to be, and ought to be, swept away—except their beautiful dress and their beautiful brown bodies—there they do score off the ugly but fascinating Chinese. But their caste! And their whole quality of mind. No, it's all wrong. *C'est magnifique—mais ce n'est pas la vie*, any more than the Middle Ages were. Well, you did well in India. Does it seem like a dream, now you're home? (Forster, *Biography of G. L. Dickinson*, 124).

Not all, however, approved of G. L. Dickinson and his circle of intellectuals at Cambridge who seemed to have confidently accepted their homosexual preferences in spite of the cultural and legal restrictions. Dickinson and Forster had come to terms with their homosexuality in a period when Siegfried

Sassoon was fearfully skirting the issue, as described in Jean Moorcroft Wilson's wonderful new biography of the World War I poet. In fact, Dickinson's *A Greek View of Life* (1896) was viewed as a veiled defense of homosexuality, following upon the trials of Oscar Wilde as well as Edward Carpenter's publication of *The Intermediate Sex*. But Dickinson as well as Cambridge and Bloomsbury were often criticized for their morals. Beatrice Webb, writing to her sister Kate, complained of the "morality" of Bloomsbury and of the "catastrophe" of the separation of Alys and Bertrand Russell, holding Cambridge, in effect, responsible for Russell's libertarian conduct:

> I am sorry now that Bertie went to Cambridge—there is a pernicious set presided over by Lowes Dickinson, which makes a sort of ideal of anarchic ways in sexual questions—we have, for a long time, been aware of its bad influence on our young Fabians. (*Letters*, 372)

Her observations about the morality of the Chinese on her visit to Beijing juxtaposed the erotic "decadence" of the Orient,—the theme long popularized in the tradition of French paintings of, for example, Eugene Delacroix, Jean Ingres, and J. L. Gerome—with the "virtue" of the West.

Despite the cultural complexities of homosexuality in both Chinese and English culture, Forster shares with Xiao Qian the "almost publishable but not quite" manuscript of the novel *Maurice*, which he wrote 1911 through 1914 (*Friendship Gazette*, no. 27, 1 September 1943). Clearly interested in sharing this work with someone from a country where there was discreet tolerance of homosexuality, Forster wrote:

> I shall also be glad to hear any confessions that occur to you and also to hear whether there is anything parallel in Chinese literature [to *Maurice*]. I don't know of anything in English, and rather think so solid and out of door an attempt must be unique. (*Friendship Gazette*, 5 January 1943)

Xiao Qian responded that he had experienced an "infantile, platonic sort of Maurician life" before he was eighteen but that he soon "grew up." He reported a few early homosexual longings, the first being that he had a close male friend when a teenager to whom he wrote poems. But the close friend "grew up" before he did and Xiao felt that all his poems "became ridiculous like bank notes after the bank got broke. It did hurt deeply." He also reported that he was frightened by a French man once in Beijing, and that he knew a married school friend who used "to hire rickshaw men to go to his house" (6 May 1943). Nevertheless, he observed that there was no law forbidding homosexuality in China as in England, and that in Shanghai and Tianjin, there were brothels known as "rabbits." Given certain remarks, we can intuit that Forster was physically drawn to handsome Xiao. The ambiguity in their relationship is perhaps revealed in a passage omitted from the final version of Xiao Qian's autobiography, *Traveller without a Map:* "Our friendship [Xiao and Forster] was not really so coincidental. Now that I think back on it, we were attracted to one another" (Kinkley, "Autobiography as Therapy," 9). These personal communications interweave with a dialogue about Forster's *Maurice* manuscript, which was circulating as early as 1911–12 among his friends. Xiao apparently responded (the letters presumably destroyed) to the qualities of the character Maurice, and Forster replied:

> As you say, one characteristic of Maurice is his maturity. And another is his liking for happiness and his dislike for self-pity. If I had to end the book sadly or tragically for him, I should not have thought it worth writing. We have in England (as in France) good studies of immaturity, some tiresome self pityings, some tiresome proclamations of the Cause, and some pornography which, like most pornography, fail to be graphic.... This sturdy suburb search for an unpopular normal is probably new (*Friendship Gazette,* no. 34, 5 January 1943)

Note the coded words that describe his efforts in *Maurice:* the "sturdy suburb search," or in another letter, "so solid and out of door attempt," because the practice and representation of homosexuality, the "unpopular normal" (an ironic pairing) is illegal. The use of the word "suburb" is significant for its connotation in seventeenth-century England as a place outside the city for "inferior, debased, and esp. licentious habits of life" (*SOED,* 2066). The term is also associated with the word "ghetto," "where the Jews dwell as in a suburb by themselves" (*SOED,* 1950). The sunken meaning of Forster's chosen words connect the sexually licentious and the foreign outcast: the two themes discussed earlier, and often connected in the popular imagination, that he might have developed more fully in the English novel if conditions had been different. Forster continues:

> I have received your second and long letter this morning. I am very glad MAURICE moves you. As your using it, I'll see. I'd like you to use it, but the

West, and perhaps East too, being so ridiculous there are difficulties, and not only myself might be involved in them. I'll see. . . . Trying to judge the work, I am fairly well satisfied with Part 1, 2 and most of 3 but rather doubtful about Scudder. I could have created him better when I was elder; his nobility develops rather too fast. His two unprintable chapters are all right though and have the right amount of sensuousness—very difficult not to put in too much of this or too little—and the blackmailing chapter, which took a lot of rewriting, satisfies me too—When we meet I'll show you a critical letter Lytton Strachey wrote me about the book. Very intelligent. (*Friendship Gazette*, no. 34, 5 May 1943)

The novel begins with the young Maurice who "as he rose in the school . . . began to make a religion of some other boy" (24). This theme of "sacred" homosexuality reverses the heterosexual poles that D. H. Lawrence developed, and the "sacred" and the "profane" distinctions between heterosexuality and homosexuality in the church and society; such views became the basis for the theories of the contemporary critic, Judith Butler. Maurice meets a Trinity man, Risley, modeled on Lytton Strachey, but becomes "intimate at once" with another student, Durham. Both have sisters and mothers who are discussed and "despised" for their profession of religion or expression of emotion: "Home emasculated everything," observes Durham (52). Maurice, however, is allowed his sexual awakening in the yet unpublished English novel: "He had lied . . . he loved men and always had loved them" (62). England would not publish this awakening until sixty years later. Forster writes to Xiao Qian that Maurice seems "very English and there is no harm in that but for the moment, I am tired of what is very English" (*Friendship Gazette*, no. 32, 7 April 1943). India and the idea of China would offer Forster new psychological, cultural, and narrative spaces, as England had to Ling Shuhua, Xu Zhimo, and Xiao Qian. But Forster and his generation were not yet ready to take on the unknown China—"No, not yet."

SWALLOWING AND BEING SWALLOWED: POVERTY IN CHINA AND THE BRITISH NOVEL

Xiao Qian knew poverty and hunger, as many of his generation did. Born in Beijing in 1909, and raised as an only child by a widowed mother, he learned early about poverty and prejudice within and outside the East. A family genealogy in non-Chinese script indicated that he was an ethnic minority, having been born a Mongol, which amounted to "barbarian" in the eyes of the Chinese (see Jeffrey Kinkley's translation of Xiao's *Traveller without a Map*). Given the earlier discussion of the British use of this term, we note that the Chinese too have their ethnic prejudices against, for example, the Mongols and the Tibetans. Xiao described the poverty and loneliness that he endured as a child in the cold slums of Beijing in his wonderful early essay "An Album of Faded Photographs," in his short story "Under the Fence of Others" (*Chestnuts*), and in his recent autobiography, *Traveller without a Map*. In Beijing, he worked in a rug factory, a dairy, and the Beixin Book Company to support his early educational efforts. This sense of cold and poverty, suggesting the centuries of hardship that the Chinese poor endured, is captured in an Arthur Waley translation, "The Big Rug":

> That so many of the poor should suffer from cold
> What can we do to prevent?
> To bring warmth to a single body is not much use.
> I wish I had a big rug ten thousand feet long,
> Which at one time could cover up every inch of the City.
> (*Translations from the Chinese*, 239)

Self-conscious about the Western charge of "sentimentality" leveled against Xu Zhimo and other Chinese writers of 1920s and 1930s. Xiao Qian writes without self-pity or exaggerated emotional expression of a life of poverty that we in the West can only begin to imagine:

> But what left an even deeper impression of inferiority on my young mind was poverty; the years spent "under the fence of others." . . . The visits I frequently paid to pawnshops, the cries of second-hand dealers at our house, the queuing for charity porridge, even times when there was no food at all at home, these things were just material privation or physical hardship.
> (*Traveller without a Map*)

Though Xiao was born a Buddhist, "religion was a rice bowl," and he attended a Christian missionary school to get an education. Many Chinese stories are engaged with hunger and the rice that comes from heaven, diamonds of the gods. In 1935, Xiao transformed these experiences in the streets of Beijing and his missionary school into fiction in his stories "Cactus Flower" and "Conversion" (*Semolina*, 22–38). In the latter, he dramatizes the personal and cultural wrestling of a family trying to save a young woman, Niu-niu, from the "barbarian" (a derogatory term used by the Chinese to describe "foreigners") missionaries (*jiao shi*). Lured by the promise of work, white hands and soft voices, Niu-niu runs off to join the Christian parade to the sound of "drum beats." The girl's grandmother rails, "Oh you shameless brat! If ever the Boxers come back, I'll be the first to join and chop off your head" (34). Summoning the imagery of the anti-foreign Boxer Rebellion, her brother hurls himself upon the Christian generals who surround his sister:

> Who wants to be your friend? You—who tempt the poor Chinese, make them forget their mothers, neglect their honest self-supporting work to act in a mummers' show, and come here to be crazy. (37)

The Chinese experience of poverty and hunger turned many Chinese to Christianity and then Marxism, which, though, at times, insensitive and cruel, addressed, at various times, the terrible famine of the people.

Ethnic sensitivities nurtured in Xiao in China were awakened again during his time in England. From 1939–42, Xiao was a lecturer in the School of Oriental and African Studies of London University while at the same time serving as a British correspondent from *Ta Kung Pao,* the major government-run newspaper in Shanghai. When in London in the 1940s, he experienced "the color bar." He wrote to Forster of the prejudice against Chinese in housing: "Civil Liberties are taking up the question of Colour Bars in Flats, and getting a question asked about it in the House. My landlord will probably connect me with this and get rid of me if they can, so we may all be in the street together" ("Week in London," 16 October 1943).

Three decades later, Xiao brought the subject of poverty in the English novel to Forster's attention. He discussed *Howards End*'s "divided aim" in a letter, making Forster aware that he "had taken up poverty as a subject" (*Friendship Gazette,* 2 May 1943). Forster replies:

> I have been considering what you said about poverty and your misery and "crime" in China. Why am I ashamed to hear of such things? Not because I am shocked by them, as you suggest, nor because I feel I ought to have shared them, as Doestoevski might suggest but because I cannot IMAGINE them, because they emphasize a defect in my mental equipment. For an instant they become real, then they fall back again into words, "Barefoot and without a crust to eat, he . . ." etc. It is an extra barrier to raise that European poverty is nothing to Oriental.—I am very glad that you mentioned

this subject to me and I hope you will do so again. (*Friendship Gazette,* 7 July 1943)

Forster referred to Bob Trevelyan "who grew up in it" and said that "the poor are far too shy and wary to let one know." He also mentioned the poverty of John Hampson, George Gissing, and Charles Dickens of an earlier generation of novelists (*Friendship Gazette,* 29 May 1943). Yet Forster knew nothing of the dimensions of Chinese famine and poverty. Ling Shuhua, writing to Virginia Woolf during the Sino-Japanese War, said a "European person perhaps would not understand what I mean by amuse myself with misery, but here we are seeing everyday in the street . . . ruined houses . . . corpses . . . famine" (24 July 1938). Famine has been a continuing terror in the life of the Chinese, and William Hinton describes the conditions and misery of the Chinese in the town Long Bow during the period when Xiao Qian wrote. He relates the life story of one of the peasants that reflects the barbarity and cruelty of life in China, a part of "the chronic social tragedy that permeated the community and the society at large":

> There were three famine years in a row. The whole family went out to beg things to eat. In Chinchang city conditions were very bad. Many mothers threw their newborn children into the river. Many children wandered about on the streets and couldn't find their parents. We had to sell our eldest daughter. She was then already 14. Better to move than to die, we thought. We sold what few things we had. We took our patched quilt on a carrying pole and set out for Changchih with the little boy in the basket at the other end. He cried all the way from hunger. We rested before a gate. Because the boy wept so bitterly a woman came out. We stayed there three days. On the fourth morning the woman said she wanted to buy the boy. We put him on the k'ang. He fell asleep. In the next room we were paid five silver dollars. Then they drove us out. They were so afraid when the boy woke up he would cry for his mother. My heart was so bitter. To sell one's own child was such a painful thing. We wept all day on the road. (Hinton, *Fanshen,* 43)

As the details in this passage mount, it almost ceases to shock. It is an example of the extreme circumstances in China during Xiao's youth, the China that England never fully knew.

Xiao's hardships, later in life, became more political given the turmoil of the civil war in China between the communists and the nationalists. He described his difficult days in the 1960s when he was transferred from Mao Zedong's Thought Propaganda Team to the custody of the People's Liberation Army. Sent to a beautiful village in Hubei province with his wife and two children, Xiao soon discovered that this village is really "poor and blank" (249). As the editor and translator of his autobiography, Jeff Kinkley, explains, "'poor and blank' is a quote from Mao: 'China's people were poor and therefore ready for revolution, and blank, like a white sheet of paper on which any beautiful character could be written'" (*Traveller,* 249). Mao's powerful metaphor of a nation as a blank white sheet of paper, waiting to be inscribed can be "read" in many ways. The May Fourth and Crescent Moon group writers, including Xu Zhimo and Wen Yiduo's symbolic cry for the individual, had already written "selfhood" in invisible ink on the blank sheet of nationhood. Xiao Qian, relating the story of his difficult life and the crisis in China, championed "personal relations" as themes in his stories. He too inscribed "intimate expression" (literature) on the blank sheet of nation.

BRITISH MODERNISM THROUGH CHINESE EYES: KATHERINE MANSFIELD, D. H. LAWRENCE, JAMES JOYCE, T. S. ELIOT, AND VIRGINIA WOOLF

Another aspect of Xiao Qian and E. M. Forster's correspondence is their cross-cultural discussion of literature. Xiao notes in his autobiography that "literature had been my real calling" (*Traveller,* 181), though he was drafted, as were many Chinese writers, into the field of translation and journalism. The field of literary-journalism in China is indeed another mixed genre to be explored. Xiao's literary perceptions of British authors—Forster, Mansfield, Woolf, Lawrence, and Joyce—are revealed in his essays in *Etchings of a Tormented Age, A Harp with a Thousand Strings,* his autobiography, literary dialogues in his batch of Forster letters, and my interview with him in the summer of 1995. The British modernists presented literary and cultural challenges to the Chinese literary critics of the 1920s and 1930s, as they do to contemporary Chinese literature today. In addition, the concerns spill over into the postcolonial criticism of Edward Said, Homi Bhabha, Chandra Mohanty, Partha Chatterjee, Salman Rushdie, Sara Suleri, Haun Saussy, and Lydia Liu.

Xiao mentioned in an interview that Katherine Mansfield was the first foreign author that he read. Working at the age of sixteen, about 1926, as an apprentice in a publishing house, he was asked to go to the Beijing University library to copy a translation of Mansfield's stories by Xu Zhimo, discussed in the first part of this chapter. He said in the interview, "I think the story I translated was 'The Little Girl,' ["The Young Girl"] and it's about a girl who was maltreated by her own father and she watched the family next door, the father playing joyfully with his children so she fell into tears. And that brought my own lonely and painful childhood. So as I copied I ran tears" (1995).

Xiao Qian, acknowledging Xu Zhimo's earlier connection with G. L. Dickinson and Cambridge, noted that Xu didn't know Forster as he did. About twenty years earlier, though, Xu Zhimo did briefly meet and greatly admire Katherine Mansfield. John Middleton Murray, her husband, arranged a short twenty-minute meeting with Xu and Mansfield. Xu describes their meeting with his typical exuberance and with the visual imagination and nature imagery that characterizes much of Chinese writing:

> She is a wonder of nature: she is like the renewed mountains and lakes after the autumn rain, like the glowing sunset among multi-colored clouds, like the clear starry sky above the South Seas. . . . In my eyes, Mansfield looks like a pure and clear Indian jade . . . a transparent object . . . The beauty of her voice is another miracle. Through her vocal cords, musical notes tinkle and rest in my worldly ears. A miraculous phenomenon is revealed. The sound of her music is like the shining stars that appear in an azure sky. (Leung, "English Friends," 24)

Xu also notes that Mansfield advised him "never enter the political world. Angrily she criticized the political world as a mess of brutality and crimes" (Leung, "English Friends," 26). This was not advice that he could follow.

When I re-read Mansfield's stories with the Chinese eyes that I developed in the course of this book, I understood Xu Zhimo and Xiao Qian's complex attraction. Xiao and other Chinese readers were drawn to Mansfield's representation of poverty that flooded their lives in "The Young Girl," as they were to Mansfield's dying from tuberculosis, a "romantic" illness often represented in Chinese stories of the period. What is of interest in the discussion of developing modernisms is that her spare style has a "Chinese" quality. Her writing captures filigree emotions and nuances in a way that Ming painters or Song poets who often wrote beautiful, melancholy verse. She combines then the sentimental exploration of states of mind and a delicately nuanced poetic style. Her story printed in *Short Story Monthly*, among other places, is a fine example of the kind of sentimental and romantic literature to which the Chinese were drawn at that time, though we must not forget that her psychology and poetic style, subjectivity, was an aspect of modernism. Xu Zhimo would later label Ling Shuhua the "Chinese Katherine Mansfield," and others have compared her to Virginia Woolf, illustrating the Chinese sensitivity to and interest in British modernism's exploration of subjectivity. The popularity of this story as well as Alexander Dumas's *La Dame Aux Camelias* (*Camille*), the first European novel to gain a mass Chinese audience—a sentimental novel about a beautiful courtesan dying of tuberculosis—demonstrates the Chinese taste for this kind of expression. It must be remembered, however, that Chinese critics sometimes blurred the line between the expression of feeling in a story and the new narrative modernist modes for expressing feeling. Yet the short story form enabled authors to explore character and subjectivity in new ways.

Chinese writers of the Republican era were drawn to the genres of the short story and novel in British and Russian literature because they were forms that were highly valued in these cultures. There is, of course, a long history of interest in stories and storytelling beginning in the Han Dynasty and flowering in the development of the episodic novel in the Ming Dynasty. History and poetry, however, were always more highly valued than fiction which was often labeled "defective history." The characters for the term novel, *xiao shuo*, translate to "small talk," which reflects the way the novel was viewed in its origins: because of its subject matter, daily life, it was viewed as "low" literature as compared to the high literature of poetry. At the same time, the novel in England was embracing "the ordinary." "Look within," says Virginia Woolf,

> and life, it seems, is very far from being like this. Examine for a moment an ordinary mind on an ordinary day. The mind receives a myriad impressions—trivial, fantastic, evanescent, or engraved with the sharpness of still. From all sides they come, an incessant shower of innumerable atoms; and as they fall, as they shape themselves into the life of Monday or Tuesday. ("Modern Fiction," 154)

The three novels considered greatest in the Chinese tradition (*The Dream of the Red Chamber, The Adventures of Three Kingdoms,* and *All Brothers Are Valiant*), with episodic structures and multiple characters hard for an American reader to follow sometimes, tell these ordinary stories of daily life, love, intrigue, violence, and adventure, though the characters are often eminent and not ordinary. What is interesting in the Chinese form of the novel, however, is the interspersing of poetic passages marking moments of heightened emotion, thus elevating the genre of fiction. The mixture, creating a visual, musical, and emotional counterpoint, is missing from the European novel.

At the same time, there is a tradition of economy in the long tradition of Chinese poetry, the reigning force in its literature, with affinities to imagism in American poetry long before Ezra Pound and other American poets construct it. The British modernists are drawn to this quality in Chinese literature. Another aspect of "modernism" is that there are narrative and subjective qualities that exist in other times and literatures that later come to be salient and embraced in a particular culture and genre in a later literary period. Herbert Giles's, Arthur Waley's, Ezra Pound's, and Ernest Fenellosa's "translations" of Chinese poetry, often from the Tang period (7–9 A.D.) set modernists thinking about concrete images, grist for the modernist mill. The connection between Ernest Fenellosa's work and Ezra Pound was forged when Fenellosa's widow chose Pound to receive her late husband's papers, among them "The Chinese Written Character as a Medium for Poetry." Beginning then in 1913, Pound would become more of an "orientalist" and incorporate in his poetic pursuits research into Chinese characters and history, and, most importantly the development of the "ideogram method" as the basis for a new kind of poetry. It should be noted, however, that Pound in 1913 had already written the haiku "In a Station of the Metro," as well as other lyrics influenced by the Japanese and also based on the Chinese translations of Herbert Giles. It is important, therefore, to separate the two strains of developing modernism, in poetry and fiction, in China: certain Chinese fiction of the time, i.e., Butterfly literature, often favored the cultivation of sensibility, sometimes with stylistic and emotional, and later on didactic, excess; Chinese poetry embodied a spare style of minimalist language and an aesthetic of "leaving things out" that, along with Chinese art, greatly influenced the British and American modernists.

How do we resolve these tensions between the articulated sentimentalism and romanticism of the preferred stories and novels: British romanticism being a misunderstood part of this and viewed by the Chinese as mainly the release of emotion in poetry and life, and the unarticulated modernism present in Chinese poetry that inspired Ezra Pound, William Carlos Williams, and Wallace Stevens?[10] The forms of the short story, the novel, and the genre of literary criticism is what Bloomsbury perceived as its contribution to Chinese thinking about fiction and criticism. The new "personalism," sometimes labeled "sentimentalism," appealed to Xu Zhimo and Xiao Qian, writers who traveled to England and who understood the devaluation of the "subjective" life in China. There was a fear that such focus on the "interior life," the focus on the psychological, would eclipse the focus on "social" and collective life and thought, as expressed by Bakhtin in "Dostoevsky's Polyphonic Novel." But comparative reading and study teaches that the development and popularity of the romantic poets, and certain psychologically oriented British literature, were a challenge to the sometime repressive structures of Confucianism, socialism, and nationalism in China, just as Puritanism was repressive to writers in America in the eighteenth century.

Xiao Qian asserted in 1944, "Quite imperceptibly China has been going through an immense transformation. In the past, filial piety was the cardinal virtue and the family the unit of society. Today the individual has replaced the family, just as industry is taking the place of craftsmanship and agriculture" (*The Dragonbeard vs. Blueprints,* 61). This retreat from the collective allows for the expression of individual sexuality and romantic need in literature, but as in modern Chinese literature, there is still, from the viewpoint of an American reader, a more finely developed national consciousness and allegorical style. This is perhaps what C. T. Hsia has labeled "the obsession with China" in Chinese literature. Or is this consciousness in the mind and values of the American reader?

In stories written by women, their lives caught in the wheels of nation building, we find that in the 1930s some gladly sacrifice feeling and desire, and give their minds, hearts, and bodies to the state. For example, in Ding Ling's well-known story "When I Was in Xia Village," written during the harsh Guomindang period, the protagonist gives up her personal life to become a spy in Japan and is coldly received by her fiancé and provincial villagers upon her return. Her own story is lost in the nationalist discourse. But there are other female characters such as Xi Xi's "A Woman Like Me" who bewail their position and their "inability to express what . . . [they] think and feel [which leads] . . . to a habit of being uncommunicative" (Lau, ed., 316). In the 1990s, this value of expression is even more boldly questioned in a work like Wang Anyi's *Love in a Small Town.* Young dancers in this novel are sent down by the government to perform in a rural village during the Cultural Revolution and become involved in an obsessive sexual relationship that becomes destructive to others and themselves. The state, the story suggests, is no longer able to control desire, suggested in Ha Jin's recent novel, *Waiting* (1999), also.

Xiao Qian, influenced by Forster, cited some examples of how the writers of new China of this period become "aware of the value of personal experience to a resourceful novelist" (*Etchings*, 13). Discussions of this literature are confusing because of the different literary concepts and terms used in China and England. What the Chinese sometimes label "realism" in focusing on the content of the new literature Western critics label "romanticism" or "sentimentalism," focusing on the style. Xiao Qian cites an example of this "new realism" from Cao Ming's *Confessions:*

> In the first half of my ninth year, my pillow was seldom dry. I was the twenty-third child of a polygamous father, and my mother was his concubine. When I was ten years old, I was so peaky and thin that I looked like a girl of six. Often my mother clasped me tightly, playing with my queue and fondling my bony chin, saying, "It is hard to be a woman, and when one is thin. . . ."

In another autobiographical sketch, a young woman kneels before her Confucian father, imploring, "Father, give me a chance to study. Don't marry me off so soon!" She is betrothed to a boy she has never seen who is dying; she is beaten by her mother-in-law, runs away, and somehow manages to get into a school. But her parents discover and punish her. This literature, we sometimes forget, is born of extreme circumstances: poverty, orphanhood, and the abuse of women and children. Though we, and some Chinese, label it "sentimentalism," it is a cultural cry also heard in nineteenth-century American and British Victorian novels. Such literature might have been tolerated in the West in the twentieth century if the content had not been so floridly sentimental. During the same literary period that the Chinese were liberating the floodgates of emotion and self in these stories, however, a British and American modernism was developing in the novel in reaction against Victorian sentimentalism. It valued the concrete image, the conciseness of emotional statement, the repression of feeling, and simplicity of form, to be found, among other places, in Chinese poetry. Exploration of the newly "psychological" and fragmented notion of "self," however, accompanied the modernist style of minimalist imagery as it developed in the West. This is illustrated, for example, in the opening of T. S. Eliot's "The Love Song of J. Alfred Prufrock," which presents a stark image of the evening sky spread out "like a patient etherized upon a table," setting the psychological sky of Prufrock, the alienated protagonist in a dying city.

At the same time that T. S. Eliot was writing this poem, Xiao Qian was studying at Cambridge and learning about the modernism of Eliot and others under the tutelage of E. M. Forster and Dadie Rylands. After attending a poetry reading by T. S. Eliot, Xiao stated that he did not expect him "to be so affable and unassuming." He described him as being "of medium height and energetic, at first sight he seemed to have just reached middle age. But when he raised his very shortsighted eyes, his wrinkled forehead made him appear an old man" ("A Week in London," 8). The chairman of the meeting explained to the audience that socially minded Mr. Eliot had been up on air-raid duty last night, and might doze off. For Xiao, the experience of hearing T. S. Eliot read

> was the first inkling [he] . . . had of the music of modern poetry. T. S. Eliot's voice is not very resonant, nor did he raise and lower it or pause like an experienced lecturer. Yet in a subtle way his recital brought out meaning in the verse. When each poem ended you felt you had been listing to "a fountain flowing under ice." ("A Week in London," 8)

When listening to Eliot's last poem, a new composition, in which he described an old village, Xiao characterized it as being "like a chorale with a dialogue between a tenor and an alto. It's a pity that I've read so little of his poetry, and my memory is so poor that for three quarters of an hour I was like a Puritan immersed in a vat of wine" ("A Week in London," 9). He is intrigued by Eliot's furtive alliance with surrealists, a classification he gives to Joyce and Pound also. Six years earlier, in 1934, Bian Zhilin had translated and introduced Eliot's essay *Tradition and the Individual Talent* into Chinese, and this along with his translations of Henry James and E. M. Forster, were influential in the spread of British modernism. In the 1940s, after Xiao's return to China, Zhao Luorin would continue to translate Eliot's poetry for a Chinese audience.

E. M. Forster addresses Xiao Qian's "term of reference"—the cultural and stylistic conventions mentioned above—in remarks about Proust:

> Do you read Proust? He is not within your term of reference, of course, but he has had such an enormous influence on English novelists of the 20s and

the 30s that I expect you have glanced at him. I have invested in him. Taken much trouble with him that is to say, as have others with Balzac, and when one has done that one's judgment tends to be too favourable. Still I am fascinated with this enormous dream—for I think it to be—which keeps to the facts of place but plays the Dickens with time. I wished he hadn't such a monotonous and unfavourable view of human nature. Were he freer, with Miss Austen's freedom even, not to mention Tolstoy's, he would be the greatest novelist who ever flew. (*Friendship Gazette,* 31 January 1943)

Proust's "enormous dream" would appeal to Xiao and others in China, and be roundly rejected by others. The admission of the "psychological" into narrative was key. However, another "new term of reference" was introduced when Forster invited Xiao to a Rede lecture on Virginia Woolf at the British Institute on 5 March 1942, which would later be published in Forster's *Two Cheers for Democracy.* This term had to do less with the "psychological" and more with transnational themes and imperialism. Xiao was drawn to Forster and his censure of British colonialism in *A Passage to India* (as well as D. H. Lawrence's working-class origins) but, predictably, relegated Woolf to "an ivory tower." In his autobiography, he relates, "I, for my part, had long been interested in the English novel—I admired Woolf up in her ivory tower but almost worshipped Forster who welcomed the whole world into his books" (*Traveller,* 111). The cultural affinity with Forster, whose themes are more transnational, is apparent. It is his cultural expansiveness, along with the emphasis on personal relations, that appeals to Xiao and others of his generation. Writing to W. J. H. Sprott, a good friend of Forster's, about a talk he planned to give in Nottingham, D. H. Lawrence's Midlands, in 1943, Xiao asked somewhat ironically:

> I am very curious to know whether there are some people at Nottingham interested in Virginia Woolf's novels, and especially if there are people who have patiently read her and disagreed with her. She is so much a fact of Cambridge that to discuss her here often ends in collective eulogy. Her reaction to the Midlands, industrial, Lawrentian ought to be very fresh to me (I am doing a book for China next spring on E. M. Forster and Virginia Woolf). If you think it possible to gather a handful of people, I would be glad to pose as an ardent fan of Virginia Woolf before them and evoke their vehement antagonism and thereby reap a rich Harvest. (12 October 1943)

When Xiao returned to the ferment in China in the late 1940s, he was diverted from the planned work on Woolf and Forster, but he had expanded his literary lights, as others who traveled to England or read British literature, and changed his "terms of reference." This change in "terms"—comparative thinking—occurred when the Chinese traveled to England or read British literature; similarly, Lily Briscoe and other British artists began to see and read with "Chinese eyes" when they visited or imagined China. When Xiao read D. H. Lawrence, he complained:

> He has made me so unhappy, this hairy misanthropist. I have just read one of the dehydrated Lawrence, the Fantasia: he must have been very bitter when writing it. I did enjoy "A Man Who Died" which even reminded me of the Castle of Kafka. But so many of his characters are mere pegs on which hung all his queer ideas about life and the universe. (Letter to EF, 25 November 1943)

Forster responded, "Lawrence is certainly a change from Mrs. Woolf and myself. One's got to read him with the knowledge that he has a message, but never for the message" (*Friendship Gazette,* 16 October 1943). When Ling Shuhua was reading D. H. Lawrence in China in the 1930s, she noted that she read and enjoyed his short stories "greatly," though she did not like him as much as her favorites Virginia Woolf and Katherine Mansfield: "It is certainly the thing one likes to read in a lonely trip with an absent mind" (LS to JB, 4 January 1936). Ironically, though E. M. Forster is a solid part of the modernist canon today, in 1942, when invited to Cambridge University to speak on "Modern Writing" and its future for the young, he was uncomfortable because he was unable "to see that modern writing is a subject" (*Friendship Gazette,* October 1942).

Xiao never wrote the projected book about Forster and Virginia Woolf, another example of interrupted modernism in China. He reported in a letter that he did write some essays on Woolf upon his return to China in 1948, but he describes the repressive literary climate of that time:

> In the late 40s, I came back to a China deep in civil war and I had to earn a living both working as professor at a university and a leader writer for the liberal newspaper TA KUNG PAO [DA GONG BAO]. After 49, especially in the 50–60s, even Jane Eyre and Jean Christophe were condemned as "poisonous." To translate Woolf was unthinkable. (XQ to PL, 2 June 1994)

But when in England, he did write "a very satisfying essay" on Woolf and spent a weekend with Leonard Woolf in October 1943:

> In the evening he [Leonard] brought out a stack of Virginia's diaries and let me copy from them. Early the next morning, we went together with heavy hearts to the little brook where she had taken her life. I stood there on the bank, wanting to rebuke the gurgling waters. Then I felt perhaps I was wrong. The brook was just going endlessly on its way. Maybe it had simply relieved another transparent soul from further torment. (*Traveller*, 111)

Xiao places Woolf in the "ivory tower," the by now jingoistic juxtaposition of art and life derived from Marxist ideology that continues to circulate in Chinese literary discussion today. Forster, however, deconstructs these poles and places the world in the "tower" in a letter to Xiao in 1941:

> I am so muddled over this point, which you put to me so clearly. Sometimes I am for "art," sometimes against it. I am for it now, and feel that the world, not the artist, is in the tower that the tower is of the cheapest and most hideous materials and the artist as he wanders towards its base gets now a penny thrown at him now a brick and does well to receive them both with cynicism. I have rushed back to the Bohemian 19th century idea of the artist. (*Friendship Gazette*, 19 September 1941)

But this nineteenth-century conception of a forlorn individualistic artist working outside of society is not the Chinese conception of the artist who works within society that Chinese writers generally admire. This notion is best represented by Lu Xun, in the preface to his collection of short stories, "Call to Arms." Here he described his dream to attend medical college in Japan. Upon his return to China, he "would cure patients like my father, who had been wrongly treated, while if war broke out I would serve as an army doctor, at the same time strengthening my countrymen's faith in reformation" (Lau, ed., 4). One day, however, he saw a slide show of the Russo-Japanese War which showed "some Chinese, one of whom was bound, while many other stood around him ... the one with his hands bound was a spy working for the Russians, who was to have his head cut off by the Japanese military as a warning to others, while the Chinese beside him had come to enjoy the spectacle" (Lau, ed., 4). After seeing this film, Lu Xun left medical school thinking that it was not an important profession. He branded the people of China as "spiritually ill" and vowed to address this cultural disease through the writing of literature. "The most important thing, therefore, was to change their spirit, and since at that time I felt that literature was the best means to this end, I determined to promote a literary movement" (Lau, ed., 4).

Xiao Qian in Cambridge was fascinated with another kind of artist, James Joyce. E. M. Forster had urged him to turn his attention to Joyce: "never has so much been talked of a person whom so few understand" (25 November 1943). Xiao himself noted that his copy of *Ulysses* was nearly black with the notes of meanings of words marked in the hot, dreary summer of 1940. Little did he suspect then that about fifty years later he and his wife, Wen Jieruo, a well-known translator and editor of Japanese literature series in China, would become the translators of one of the two full editions of Joyce's *Ulysses* published in China in 1994. He wrote in a letter, "I had never dreamed that I would be translating *Ulysses*" (XQ to the author, 2 June 1994).

Xiao Qian in knickers, 1930s. By permission of Hsiao-ying Chen Chinnery.

In "A Week in London," Xiao mentioned that the British Museum, which had been bombed, reopened one morning, and he rushed over to copy out the titles of James Joyce's books:

> The museum's glass dome is beautifully constructed, but tragically vulnerable in an air raid. I found the big reading room lonely and deserted, and the hundreds of chairs surrounding the desks had all been turned upside down. (10)

Joyce and Woolf along with Mansfield were the modernist authors that Xu Zhimo had presciently heralded in the 1920s. Xiao made similar judgments, and while "plodding the labyrinth of Dorothy Richardson," he wrote to Forster that he felt the great achievement of Joyce who reconciled "two heterogeneous elements in writing: free flow (of consciousness) and external

Wen Jieruo, translator, holding English edition of Joyce's Ulysses *and Chinese translation. Courtesy of the author.*

shape" (25 November 1943). Dorothy Richardson, he viewed as "a faithful accountant of the world" who unwittingly demonstrated "how pointless, aimless, purposeless the stream can be without an external embankment." His judgment on Virginia Woolf's stream of consciousness was that it was "much too neat to be convincing," and he reserved his praise for Joyce "who seems to have treaded one dangerous zone, that of unintelligibility. It really seems to be the 'last test' whether writing can be on the level with music and paint; or not." Xiao, steeped in the social use of literature, was ambivalent about British modernism, and after reading Ezra Pound's anthologies and many issues of *Transition,* he began to loathe "modernism for modernism's sake" (25 November 1941).

Called back to China because of the Sino-Japanese War and civil war turmoil, his engagement with modernism was interrupted. However, in 1994, three years before his death at the age of 88, his translation of James Joyce's *Ulysses* with his wife, Wen Jieruo, appeared: the fruit of his early contact with Joyce's writings during his trip to Cambridge. In a 1995 interview, he noted that his wife had done a significant amount of translation.

Yuruo and Jin Di. Jin Di, James Joyce translator and critic, studied under I. A. Richards and William Empson. Courtesy of the author.

Xiao Qian. Journalist, writer and translator who studied with E. M. Forster and Dadie Rylands at King's College, Cambridge, 1941–44.

The second translation of *Ulysses* on the Chinese market is by Jin Di, a translator and critic, who began his translation in 1979 and worked on it in painstaking detail over sixteen years, completing it in 1996. In an interview with Jin Di in 1995, he related how he began his study of the English novel under the supervision of William Empson at Beijing University, 1947–49, interrupted by the Maoist revolution in 1949. Thirty years later he returned to the challenge of *Ulysses*, and he described the many merry linguistic paths that he followed in order to capture Joyce's remarkable sense of history and linguistic nuance. Jin Di found a parallel for Joyce's evolution of English styles in the "Oxen in the Sun" chapter, for example, by taking his Chinese readers on a similar historical journey from classical to modern Chinese dialects. In addition to the translation, Jin Di has also written a collection of essays, *Shamrocks and Chopsticks*, that details the difficulties of translation, the cultural and political atmosphere that prevailed over literature, and the reception of *Ulysses* in China over the past seventy-five years.[11] It is reported that 40,000 copies of *Ulysses* were sold in the first six months after publication of the two complete translations of Jin Di, and Xiao Qian and Wen Jierou, in 1996.

INTERRUPTED MODERNISM

The narrative style—so-called stream of consciousness, the psychological narrative of the inner life—that would interest Xiao Qian in 1941 in Cambridge intrigued other Chinese literati in the 1920s through the 1940s, and then again in the early 1980s. One could chart perhaps an interrupted modernism in China, beginning with May fourth 1919 and extending into various discourses during the 1920s and 1930s; a thirty year silence from 1949 to 1976, during which time Chinese sensibilities, consciousness, and narratives remained dormant; then a revival of the discussions of modernism with another sensibility in the early 1980s, blending with discussions of postmodernism in the 1990s. Why view the 1980s movement through the lens of postcolonial and nationalist critics as "a nostalgia for the past . . . a colonial nostalgia, not by the colonizer but by the ex-colonized" (*Lure of the Modern,* viii), as posited by the critic, Shi Shumei. Why not view the 1980s movement as an evolution from Republican-era literature interrupted and framed anew. International, migratory modernism takes on different shapes, colors, and connotations in different fields and places depending upon cultural and historical circumstances. European modernism was heavily influenced by the Industrial Revolution, Darwin's theory of evolution, and World War I; Chinese modernism, by the May Fourth movement, the 1925 demonstrations, and the beginning of the civil war. Now, we filter modernism through the Cultural Revolution as well as the international modernist movements. Whatever the present modernist–postmodernist state is in China, it "advances" still the sense of breaking with and rebelling against the values and authority of the past, as well as the present. There were so many different kinds of writers in the Republican era and not all are equally embraced today. Though some authors of this era were once viewed as "backward" or "decadent," and are now appreciated, what has happened in the arts is an "evolution" in terms of aesthetic, cultural, and political sensibility and narrative styles. The term "nostalgia" may freeze the fluid, zig-zag, back-and-forth eddies of any aesthetic movement in static language. Modernism–postmodernism does not just look back to an earlier period of political, cultural, and aesthetic freedom (though this is part of it), as it can never recapture the 1920s and 1930s "past" in the same way given that the experiences, sensibilities, consciousness, and narrative styles of the artists are different. For example, Wen Jieruo has just translated E. M. Forster's *Maurice* into Chinese, as well as the correspondence between her husband, Xiao Qian, and Forster in the 1930s. What *Maurice,* with its theme of homosexuality, means to readers in China of the new millennium, what it meant when it was written and circulated and read in manuscript form by Xiao Qian in 1912 in England, what it meant when it was finally culturally and legally acceptable to be open about homosexuality and was published in England in the 1960s are all different things. *Maurice* comes out of British modernism but migrates and means different things in different places—the comparative modernism advanced by this book. As we look at the arc of 1980s movements in China until today, what may be seen is modernist tendencies with an overlay of postmodern theorizing. Postmodernism pluralities, and avant-garde artists and styles in film, painting, and literature, in my view, can be seen as a fluid continuation of modernism's rebellions. Virginia Woolf reminds us of the spirit of modern fiction: "if we can imagine the art of fiction come alive and standing in our midst, she would undoubtedly bid us break her and bully her, as well as honour and love her, for so her youth is renewed and her sovereignty assured" ("Modern Fiction," 158).

In addition, a group of Chinese critics of the 1930s now living in China and America welcomed these British modernist works to Republican China but were alternately vocal or silent about their views, depending upon the political and cultural climate. A sample might include Professor Yuan Kejia

Qu Shijing, Chinese scholar of British modernism, and Quentin Bell. By permission of Qu Shijing.

(1921–2008), who published the influential *Selections of Modernist Literature from Abroad* (first volume, 1980), was a scholar at the Beijing Academy of Social Sciences, and is now living in New York City; Professor C. T. Hsia, who published the first important critical survey of Chinese fiction, 1917–57, in America, a *History of Modern Chinese Literature;* Professor Zhao Luorin, who translated T. S. Eliot in the 1940s, Whitman in 1991, and now works on the poet Robert Frost. Professor Qu Shijing, of the Shanghai Academy of Social Science, has had a long career of conversation about and contact with British novelists, particularly Doris Lessing and Virginia Woolf. He has translated several of Woolf's novels into Chinese, has written on her stream of consciousness style, and has collected criticism about her.

Melba Cuddy-Keane and Kay Ki, in reporting on new directions in Woolf criticism in China in 1998, note that many Chinese critics focus on her form and style, avoiding the content and feminism in her works. Han Minzhong, a professor at Beijing University, disagrees, underlining the different kinds of reception in mainland versus Hong Kong, China. Mainland Chinese critics, she says, "still focus mainly on political, ideological and moral aspects of Woolf, as they do with any writers" (note to the author). The critic Liu Shicong translated *Mrs. Dalloway* in 1997, and has written about "characterization" and the use of "stream of consciousness, including interior monologue and free psychological association," methods often noted in British and American scholarship. Woolf, then, is generally categorized as a stream of consciousness writer, along with Joyce, Proust, and William Faulkner in mainland Chinese reference works. Woolf, though, was vilified in the early 1980s for her stream of consciousness style, renamed "mud-rock flow." Stream of consciousness, a catch-all label, was considered to be an import from the West, not indigenous to China, and a style that some critics argued "negated rationality by upside down positions" with values that were "a reflection of the capitalist philosophy of life." Qu Shijing asserts that "to simply label a writer by stream-of-consciousness style is to simplify her complexity" (Interview by the author). Woolf in this critical conversation is rarely mentioned in relation to feminism or women's studies. Yiming Ren, a professor of literature at the Shanghai Academy of Social Sciences, reports that many new Chinese translations of Woolf's works began coming out in the 1990s, for example *Collected Essays* by Kong Xiaojong in 1993; *The Waves* by Wu Junxie in 1993; *Critical Essays* about Woolf edited by Qu Shijing in 1999; *Diaries* by Song Binghui and Dai Hongzhen in

1997, *Essays* by Liu Bingshan in 1999; and the first critical biography, *A Writer's Life*, by Wu Houkai in 2000. In addition, a new series of translations of Woolf's works is in process in the Shanghai Translation Publishing House. Given all these new translations, an intensive study of Woolf works is likely, and we wait for fresh critical treatments: perhaps a focus on her interest in women's issues or feminism with "a Chinese face" in China today, or, perhaps, a comparative study of the narrative style of Woolf and other Chinese women writers.

Fu Guangming, a protégé of Xiao Qian, reflects the renewed interest of a younger generation of scholars in members of the Crescent Moon group. He published a translation of Xiao Qian's biography in 1990 and Ling Shuhua's *Ancient Melodies* in Taiwan in 1991. He Fu, another modernist scholar and translator, has published the first complete translation of Yeats's poetry and is now working on John Donne.

C. T. Hsia, a very influential critic of Chinese literature in America, left China in 1947. William Empson, he reports, read his essay on Blake in a Chinese competition, and nominated him for a scholarship. When he arrived in America, he was beset with invitations to study at several universities: Kenyon, Berkeley, Oberlin, Harvard, and Yale. He spent the summer of 1948 at Kenyon studying with William Tate, Lionel Trilling, and William Empson, his mentor in China. Hsia, in his characteristic playful commentary, described Empson in an interview as "an absent minded person who drank on the boat home from China and all his money was stolen." Hsia described that heady moment in an Interview by the author in 2000. First, the critic Mark Schorer wrote to him from Berkeley and invited him to come but outlined what Hsia felt was a "discouraging" array of the additional English courses he would have to take. John Crowe Ransom wrote that he could come to Kenyon, but Hsia decided it would be "depressing to study with all men." Oberlin, because it was coed, seemed more attractive to Hsia. But then he heard from Matthieson, who had worked on T. S. Eliot at Harvard. Hsia said of Matthieson that he had "the appearance of being a New Critic but was a communist," and decided against Harvard. He was finally lured to Yale by Cleanth Brooks in the fall of 1948, and received a prestigious Rockefeller Grant to support his studies there from 1948 to 1951. Brooks along with F. R. Leavis and other New Critics influenced Hsia's critical perspective on literature. He never returned to China after having left on the eve of Mao's creation of the PRC, a period in which modernist interest in China was snuffed out. His position abroad, first as a student at Yale and then as a professor of Asian languages and literature at Columbia University until 1995, gave him the freedom to write the seminal *History of Modern Chinese Literature* that Hu Shi aspired to but never wrote—a work essential to all study of the period since its publication in 1961. David Der-wei Wang in the 1999 update of this work notes that Hsia

> "intervened" in the history of Chinese literature, and single-handedly "rewrote" a whole generation of fictional writings, "renegotiating" the way in which Westerners and Chinese view Chinese fiction (Hsia, Introduction, *History*, xiv)

While Hsia was publishing in America, a group of Chinese critics with an interest in European modernist literature in PRC were biding their time. Any expression of interest in the substance, translation, or publication of criticism of Western literature was criticized by the Communist Party during Mao Zedong's period of rule, 1949–76. In addition, the work and criticism by those who included themselves in a "modernist" school (for example, some writers included in the *Nine Leaves Anthology* of works of 1930s–50s) were not given recognition in critical works in 1949. These writers disappeared in Taiwan also during the first thirty-five years of nationalist rule, partly because their works were unavailable in the PRC to be exported. But in 1976, the post-Mao era, Professor Yuan Kejia (1912–), poet and an important critic of the 1940s, with an interest in Anglo-American poetry and modernism, compiled and published with Dong Hengxun and Zheng Kelu the groundbreaking *Selected Works of Foreign Modernist Literature, 1980–85*. These volumes re-introduced the modernist literature of Europe and America into China after a period of isolation under Mao Zedong. Chinese readers and scholars received British and American selections from, for example, Woolf's *Mrs. Dalloway,* Joyce's *Ulysses,* and Faulkner's *Light in August* (see appendix C). Since the field of "criticism" or "aesthetics" was yet undeveloped in China, these literary theories enabled Chinese critics to articulate a theory "to combat the leftist theory which subordinated poetry to narrow political needs" (interview with Yuan Kejia by the author). Again, the use of British theory and literature was invaluable to a resistant group of Chinese writers and critics, an important contribution to China's "interrupted modernism," 1919–49 and 1980–present. Having been freed from party-approved historical and literary assessments, literary scholars, writers, and students could learn anew of the legacy of both Chinese and Western modernist writers through these new anthologies. Yuan

Kejia was representative of that generation of 1940s critics who were influenced by New Criticism because of the presence and teachings of both I. A. Richards and William Empson in China, both of whom encouraged the Chinese to think more theoretically and rigorously about literature as critics and not just rely on intuition. Xiao Qian related in a 1995 interview that he attended the lectures of Richards, and added that "he was a saint to me ... he made me a critic." Some of Kejia's manuscripts on modernism, like some of Xiao Qian's and other scholars, were lost during the upheaval of the war with the Japanese, the civil war or the Cultural Revolution, 1966–76. Due to this historical maelstrom, much that happened is hard to document. Turbulent politics muted the production and preservation of the literature and criticism of the group of critics under discussion.

Another Chinese scholar of Virginia Woolf, Professor Qu Shijing, Shanghai Academy of Social Sciences, claims Julian Bell's introduction of Woolf's works in his courses at National Wuhan University in 1935 and 1936 was the impetus for some translations of Woolf in the late thirties and forties of varying quality. From 1949 to 1976, no one openly studied or translated Woolf in China, but in the early 1980s, one of the first stories to be translated in several versions was "The Mark on the Wall." In 1981, Qu Shijing, responsible for some of the early translations of Woolf in China, translated *To the Lighthouse;* in 1982, he translated some of her critical essays; then he gathered a collection, *Studies on Virginia Woolf by American and European Critics;* and most recently, *Virginia Woolf and Her Art of Fiction.* Professor Qu Shijing reports that *Orlando,* very much in the Western eye with the 1997 Sally Potter movie, is now in the process of being translated into Chinese by Zhu Naizhang.

Such literary discussions as those between Xiao Qian and E. M. Forster and the interactions of other critics with British authors are the missing story of modernism yet to be developed. Because of the politicization of literature under Mao Zedong, particularly during the Cultural Revolution, the transnational conversations and writings embodying literary and cultural tensions (harbinger of postmodernism), and represented in this book, were interrupted. Since it was more difficult to read Western authors (though departments of foreign language and literature and presses specializing in foreign literature existed), the kinds of literary relationships that form the basis of this book were not encouraged, and, consequently, there are only traces of China's participation in a developing international modernism.

Chapter Four

CHINESE LANDSCAPES THROUGH BRITISH EYES

China was far away from England—a nine-month journey for Lord Macartney on his first official trade mission to China in 1792, a three-month journey for Julian Bell on his way to teach at National Wuhan University in 1935—but, now, a day in my 1995 voyage. Yet the cultural and economic intersections with China appeared in everyday objects to be found in British homes, tea rooms, and department stores; in addition, the art of China, some of it looted, appeared in British exhibitions and museums. Beginning then in the eighteenth century, images of China became a part of English daily life—the glint of a blue and white willow vase or teacup, a fan or screen with a Chinese landscape, a silk dress with a pagoda pattern—a *mise en abime*. Traders, travelers, missionaries, architects, fashion designers, artists, photographers, and writers copied, adapted, or constructed images of China: pagodas in the moonlight, fish and water hermits in the mountains, clouds floating above mountains viewed from many perspectives, strange rock gardens, graceful willow trees. These images entered the popular imagination and appeared on scrolls, porcelain, fans, screens, wallpaper, silks, jade, lacquerware, and were reflected in *anglo-chinois* gardens. This was not only a new aesthetic to be found in the East but also a visual lexicon, what W. J. T. Mitchell describes as "a medium, a vast network of cultural codes" (*Landscape and Power*, 3). These "codes" first signalled "appropriation" and "exploitation" by the British, but later became "contributions" to and "enrichment" of the modernist discourse between China and England and the developing international modernist aesthetic.

   *Omega Workshop symbol*

This chapter explores what part these actual, represented, or imagined landscapes of China played in British culture, literature, and painting during a period of nineteenth-century expansion, the waning of the empire and expanded foreign relations with the "new" China after 1912. A guiding premise is that what is seen and represented in a natural or cultural landscape depends on who is "seeing" and "describing." Looking at the British representations of landscapes of China, one discovers certain colonial or imperial tropes emerging from a cultural reservoir. Addressing a critical need to attend to both the perspectives of politics and power as well as culture and aesthetics, I now address these dizzying landscapes within the context of nationalism, imperialism, colonialism, and aesthetics.

This chapter focuses on Chinese landscape through the eyes of painters and writers who are removed from mainstream British discourse about China. Vanessa Bell, Julian Bell, and Ling Shuhua look upon the landscape with "the painter's eye," and Virginia Woolf and Ling Shuhua with "the writer's eye," all helping to construct "the narrow bridge of art." I will begin, however, by sketching an economic backdrop to these views: China through the eyes of an artist on a trade voyage in the late eighteenth century; a photographer on the scene of the second Opium War in China in the mid–nineteenth century; and a British economist intent on building the Chinese market in the early twentieth century. Mainstream cultural values are encoded in these landscapes, and we find that British ideology is exported to the imperial periphery of China (Bunn, "Our Wattled Cot," 127*ff*). During these periods, the Chinese landscape is "seen as teeming with raw materials waiting to be turned into cash" (Horton, *Difficult Women, Artful Lives*, 154), the well-documented economic incursions connected with both imperialism and nationalism.[1] These economic and aesthetic views interweave then to further develop the critical conversation about Chinese landscape.

Visual tropes of China first begin to emerge in William Alexander's early eighteenth-century sketches of China made on Lord Macartney's voyage, the first English trade expedition to the embassy in the Beijing Court, 1792–94. Anderson brought back 970 sketches and water colors, to be found in *Picturesque Representations of the Dress and Manners of the Chinese* in three volumes, capturing the customs, the people, and the architecture of the walled city of Beijing, and reflecting the details of eighteenth-century Chinese life. Alexander later became the keeper of prints and drawings of the British Museum, a post also held by the translators of Chinese poetry, Laurence Binyon and Arthur Waley. Alexander's position as an artist juxtaposed with Macartney's mission to redress the imbalance in trade between China and England may well be a metaphor for this book. Given England's desire for Chinese silks, tea, and ceramics, Macartney was the first of a number of ambassadors and travelers set loose in China from the eighteenth to the twentieth century to establish treaty ports for foreign goods. Soon after this unsuccessful voyage (in which the Chinese expressed little interest in British exports) British decorative arts, designs, ceramics, fashions, gardens, sculpture, and architecture—inspired by the sketches, ideas, and materials acquired on this voyage—began to enter unobtrusively into the domestic and public spaces of British life. This was the beginning of "chinoiserie," for example, Chinese porcelain created from patterns sent by the Derbyshire porcelain firm to China, and hand painted by the Chinese or decorated with designs copied from European prints or engravings in combination with Chinese patterns. Even before this voyage, seventeenth-century Jesuit missionaries such as Matteo Ricci had traveled to China to inform and persuade the Chinese of the value of Western culture (see Spence, *The Gate*). The products and ideas brought home from expeditions and travel to China contributed to the construction of British tastes, and consequently, modernist perspectives. Eventually, economic contacts in Shanghai, Canton [Guanzhou], and Hong Kong were developed and the cultural fallout of trade was the long exposure of the Chinese to English ways, the growing British desire for Chinese products, and the circulation of products and visual images of China in British culture. At this time, before 1912, China was "a geographic and not political expression," as related by Professor William C. Kirby in a Columbia University China Seminar (summer 2000).

Such voyages were designed to seek trade and concessions for European investors who viewed China as a booming market. When interest in British goods could not be stimulated, the British worked to create a cultural need and market in China for opium, which the Chinese resisted and which led to the Opium Wars. Toward the end of the second Opium War (1856–60), Felix Beato, an Italian photographer, accompanied the Anglo-French forces in one of their military campaigns during which they seized Beijing and destroyed the Old Summer Palace at Wanshoushan, now an imperial park. Looking at Beato's photographs of the devastated landscapes, we see the Chinese as almost invisible, "props and corpses, further corroborating the power of the invaders" (Harris, *Of Battle and Beauty*, 9). Lytton Strachey ironically described this destruction of the Summer Palace as an act by which, "in the name of European civilisation," Lord James Bruce Elgin (son of Lord Thomas Bruce of Elgin Marble fame—now the Parthenon Marbles) "took vengeance upon the barbarism of the East" (*Eminent Victorians,* 226). Some of the looted Chinese art appeared in a 1910 British exhibition.

In the 1930s, England again cast its imperial gaze and sought the expansion of trade through the construction of railways in China. J. M. Keynes and Archibald Rose in the British Economic Advisory Council would analyze the means of cost and figure American capital and cotton fields, Lancashire textile mills and Chinese and British markets into the cost of "a Chinaman's shirt." They were savvy partners on this Commission: Keynes because of his economic sophistication and money-making talents, and Rose, his cultural knowledge and experience in China. Keynes was a politician, professor, author, journalist, patron of the arts, member of Bloomsbury, and, most importantly, an economic thinker who moved national economies. His works were translated into Chinese, studied by Chinese economists, and Shanghai Public Library holdings record the availability of his works in China beginning in the 1920s. Julian Arnold, the American cultural attaché who attended these meetings, observed that China had a population three to four times greater than the United States (it is now six times greater at 1.2 billion), and that China then (and now) would be important to America's agricultural, mining, manufacturing, and trade interests. Commenting on the development of rails, he observed that one-twelfth of America at that time, 1930, had railway mileage. The same rail development was advocated for China where men "function as pack-carriers at unit costs 10–15 times as great as those on American railways" (Rose, EAC). Arnold noted, finally, as both Rose and Keynes had, that "no single factor has contributed more toward economic advancement in the U.S. than railways" (Rose, EAC). Rose shared Arnold's economic analysis. He and Keynes jockeyed for access to the Sichuan market of 45 million people, one-tenth of the Chinese population that consumed one-hundredth of foreign imports. Since there was unemployment in Sichuan, he argued for the development of the railway. Politically and geographically, Sichuan was protected from the war between North and South China, and access to China was only through the dangerous Yangtze Rapids. Rose argued in the cool chambers of Britain's Advisory Council in 1930, harbinger of joint ventures today, that the Chinese "represent nothing so much as a vast body of consumers waiting to consume"

(EAC, 20 October 1930). It is interesting to note that Rose and Keynes argued that the Boxer Indemnity Fund, intended for educational purposes, could legitimately be invested in China's railway development:

> We do not accept the view of our colleagues on the Council arrangement by which, under the new agreement, a substantial portion of the Indemnity Funds should be invested in China's railways with a view to providing a permanent education endowment can be regarded either as a breach either in the spirit or the letter of the understanding given to the Chinese in 1922. (Rose, EAC)

Then and now, they are open to criticism for planning to spend Boxer monies to construct railways that would eventually develop a market for British manufactured goods in China, a mission that began with Lord Macartney in 1792. It is important to make this discourse of mapping and railway tracks visible as it modeled England's economic and imperial position in Chinese territorial space in the 1930s, just as earlier pink-red spaces on imperial maps modeled projected British colonies.

John Maynard Keynes *by Gwendolyn Raverat. By permission of the Picture Library, National Portrait Gallery, London, England.*

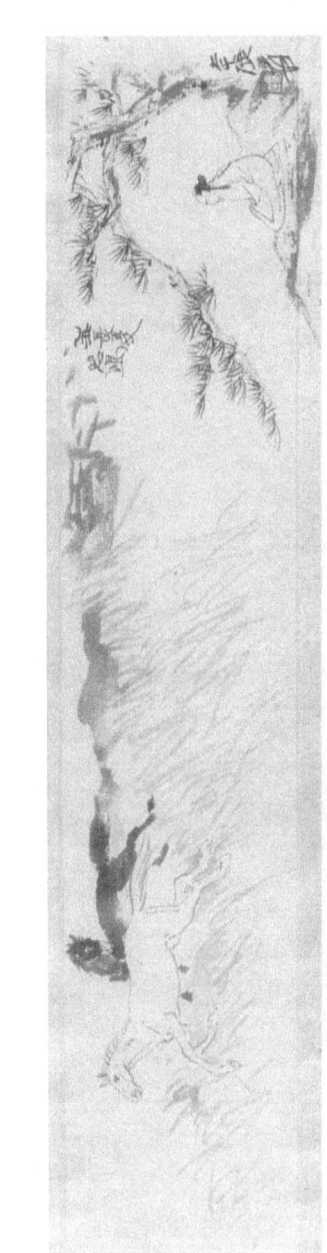

1–8. Ling Shuhua's Friendship Scroll, compiled 1925–58. By permission of the Khoan and Michael Sullivan Collection

1. Landscape (ink wash) by Roger Fry (1866–1934)

2. Two Horses Galloping through Long Grass (ink) by Xu Beihong (1895–1963)

3. "The dualism of mind and matter is essentially a masculine philosophy," inscribed by Dora Russell (1894–1986), and "Gentleman under a Pine Tree" by Zhang Daqian

4. Impression of Two Westerners (ink) by Lin Fengmian, 1926

5. Gentleman in a Boat among the Reeds *(ink) by Chen Xiaonan*

6. Tolstoy *(ink) by Wen Yidou (1899–1946)*

7. Child with Ball (ink) by Wang Daizhi and inscription by Xie Bingxin

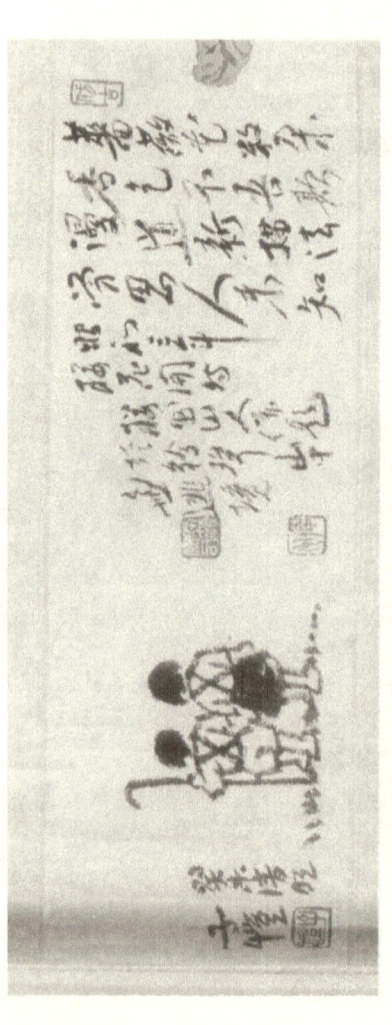

8. Two Children Walking Away by Feng Zikai. Painted in Szechuan, 1943, when Wuhan University had been evacuated to Loshan, south of Chengdu.

9–10. *Floral watercolors by Duncan Grant, gifts to Ling Shuhua. By permission of the Henry W. and Albert A. Berg Collection of English and American Literature, The New York Public Library, Astor, Lenox and Tilden Foundations.*

9.

10.

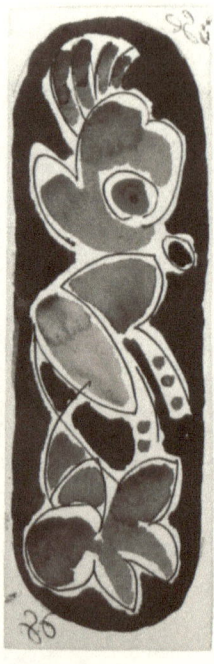

11. Bookmarks by Duncan Grant, gift to Ling Shuhua. By permission of the Henry W. and Albert A. Berg Collection of English and American Literature, The New York Public Library, Astor, Lenox and Tilden Foundations.

12. Silk fan and two boxes painted by Duncan Grant for Omega. © 1979 Estate of Duncan Grant, courtesy Henrietta Garnett.

13–16. Calendars by Vanessa Bell, gifts to Ling Shuhua. By permission of the Henry W. and Albert A. Berg Collection of English and American Literature, The New York Public Library, Astor, Lenox and Tilden Foundations.

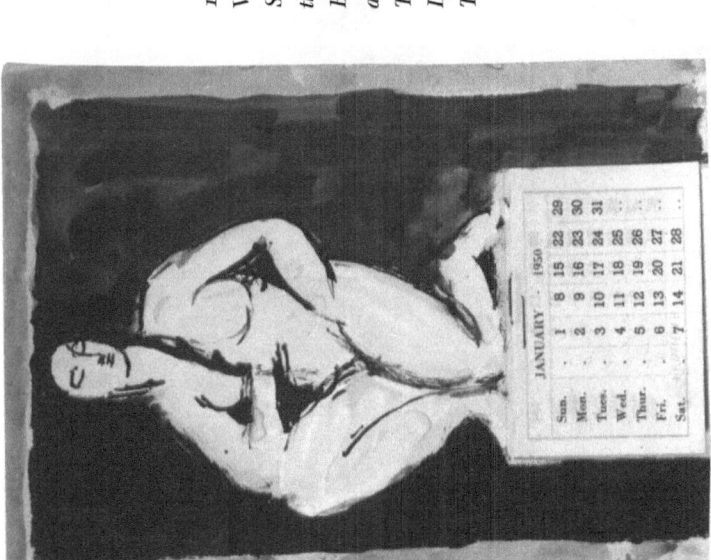

16.

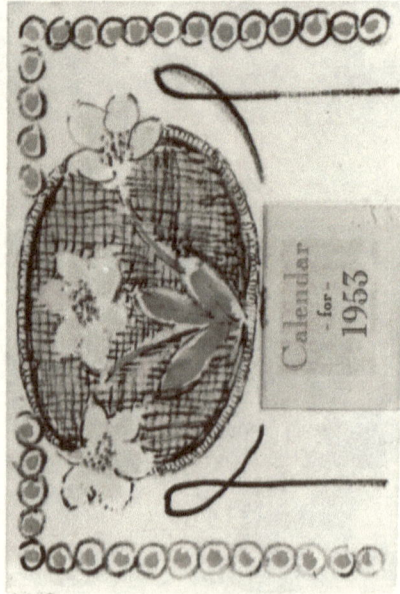

15.

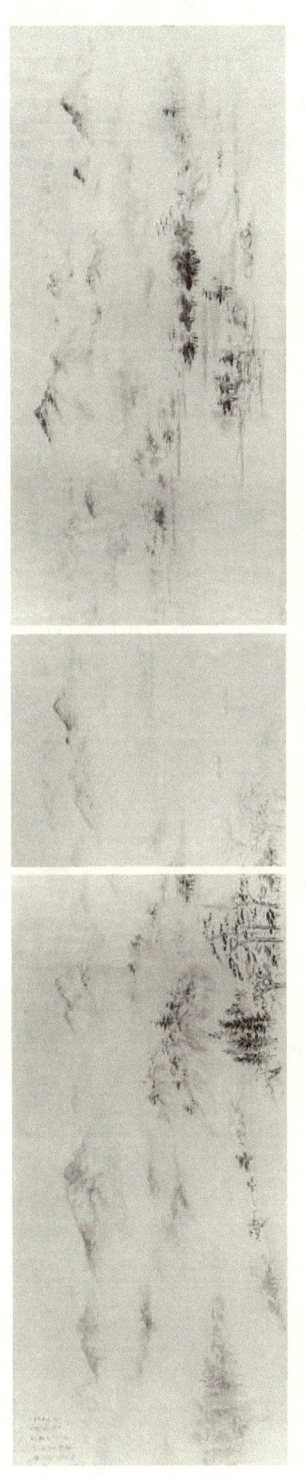

17. *From Geneva to Montreux, Switzerland, painting on silk scroll, by Ling Shuhua. Combines Eastern temples with Western churches and houses, ca. 1951. By permission of Hsiao-ying Chen Chinnery.*

18. Scroll of Sissinghurst by Ling Shuhua. By permission of Hsiao-ying Chen Chinnery.

19. Blue willow plate, adaptation of Chinese design

20. Daughters of Revolution, by Grant Wood, 1959. Art © Figge Art Museum, successors to the Estate of Nan Wood Graham/Licensed by VAGA, New York, N.Y.

This image appears in the cloth and ebook editions.

21. Cover of Ling Shuhua's autobiography, Ancient Melodies (1953). By permission of Hsiao-Ying Chen Chinnery.

22. Duncan Grant cover for Wu Chêng'ên's Monkey. © 1979 Estate of Duncan Grant, courtesy Henrietta Garnett.

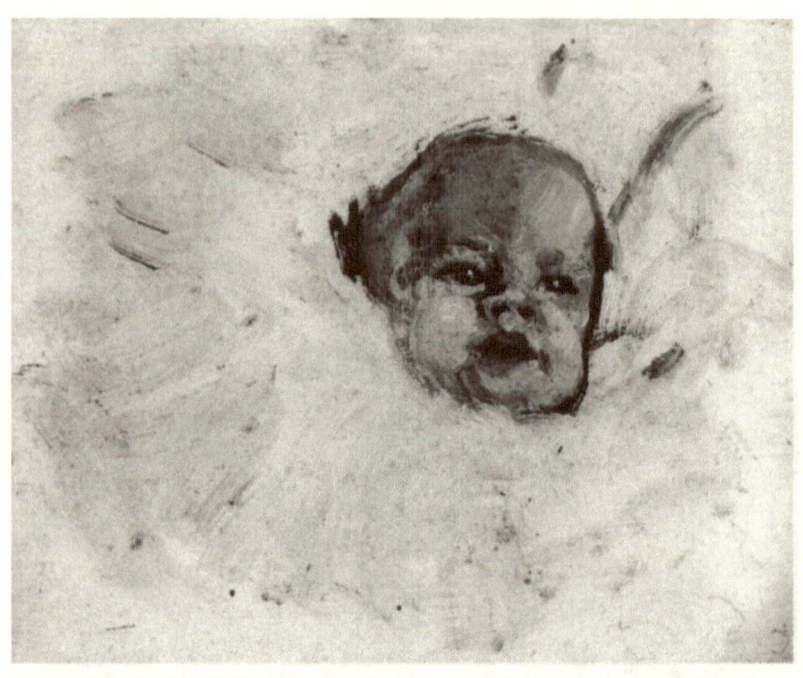

23. *Portrait of Julian Bell as an infant by Vanessa Bell (1908). By permission of Angelica Garnett.*

24. *Sketch of Julian Bell by Duncan Grant. Private Collection.*

25. *Julian Bell and Roger Fry playing chess*, painting by Vanessa Bell. By permission of the Provost & Scholars of King's College, Cambridge University.

Such were the economic forces being mobilized in England to develop the railways in China (many of which were destroyed during the Sino-Japanese War) at the same time that Waley's translation of antique landscapes in poetry floated across the British imagination. His poems bring into relief another world view:

> When the sun rises and the hot dust flies
> And the creatures of earth resume their great strife,
> You, with your striving, what shall you each seek?
> Profit and fame, for that is all your care.
> But I, you courtiers, rise from my bed at noon
> And live idly in the city of Ch'ang-an.
> Spring is deep and my term of office spent;
> Day by day my thoughts go back to the hills.
> (Translations, 139)

The thoughts of the painters and writers in this chapter—Julian Bell, Vanessa Bell, Ling Shuhua, and Virginia Woolf—also "go back to the hills," as they reflect on Chinese landscape and culture in conversation. Historically, painters and writers have no desire to own, exploit, destroy, or profit from the landscape as dictated by the imperialist motives just described. Yet the "encoded eye" (Foucault, *The Order of Things*, xxi) of intellectuals and artists may still harbor, unwittingly, "symbolic levels of violence" (Mitchell, *Landscapes and Power*, 9).

THE NATURALIST LANDSCAPE: JULIAN BELL

Julian Bell left England in August 1935, arrived in China three months later, in October, and stayed sixteen months, leaving in January 1937 after the discovery and scandal of his amorous relationship with Ling Shuhua, the wife of the dean who hired him. While there, a remarkable correspondence developed between him and his painter-mother, Vanessa Bell—she, writing every Sunday "like clockwork," letters composed over two or three days. Mainly she wrote about her daily life: the garden, the pets, the canceled Queen Mary mural contract, Angelica's dressing up as Ophelia, the new car, "the baby Austen," and Virginia Woolf's illness. What preoccupied Vanessa was relationship: both Julian's ultimately scandalous relationship with Ling Shuhua, and the unusual, perhaps, at times, cloying intimacy between mother and son. The word "lover" is used to describe it by Julian, Angelica, his sister, and Virginia

Woolf, his aunt. Julian wrote vividly describing the landscapes of China and his relationship with Ling Shuhua. But it was Vanessa's prodding—"describe it for me"—her ever-present desire to visualize the Chinese landscape and share it with Julian, that stimulated many of his vivid descriptions. Vanessa wrote:

> I always feel you. I see so many things in the same way but you've made it all much more vivid to me than anyone else has—you know I always think you have very much of a painter's eye—you notice colours, even the colour of night, in a way very few but painters do. Also you have the great advantage of being able to put it into words. So that all you tell me is alive and terribly exciting and I feel as if I'd almost seen it with you. (Letter to JB, 21 October 1935)

In another letter, she remembered G. L. Dickinson's romanticism about China (he visited 1911–12 and 1913–14) and how it gave way to the realities of Julian's naturalist description: "indeed you make me understand much more than I've ever understood before. Your accounts are like a fresh wind blowing on all these intensely subtle mysterious notions that Waley and most people seem to have about China" (25 October 1936). China was just opening up to the English and becoming more international since 1912. Julian wrote sensuous narratives of landscapes as he trekked, hunted, and sailed—with traces of imperial attitudes—but he enabled Vanessa to visualize a China that she had never seen. Parts of his letters are reminiscent of the genre of the landscape journal in China that consists of narrative and scenic description recorded by a finely-tuned observer. Yu Kuang-zhang, in an article on "The Sensuous Art of the Chinese Landscape Journal," offered this description: "Boundless mountains and hills, shadowy trees. An eyebrow of new moon hung above the towering cliffs, modulating its pace to the movement of man" (24). Julian shared this love of landscape with the Chinese. It was a quality of his poetry also that John Lehmann, the editor and publisher noted, "I like those poems best in which you have fewest sentences—without verbs, and in which you don't crowd your canvas too much. I feel it's important not to blur the picture in the particular sort of landscape painting which you go in for" (Letter to JB, 7 August 1928).

Though Julian Bell may not have been as unusually gifted as his Bloomsbury relatives, what he did possess was a painterly and poetic writing style. A few examples illuminate not only his descriptive gifts, but also the tropes of landscape shared by Julian and Vanessa. Importantly, they are based on the careful aesthetic observations of each: one in China sailing through gorges in a junk; the other, a painter in England making observations about another's observations. Vanessa wrote, "Your description of the river is so like the paintings one knows—oh how lovely it must be. I seemed to see it so clearly" (1 November 1935). He wrote to Vanessa one evening that "the world grows unimaginably beautiful . . . such blues of lakes and sky and mountain shadows" (6 December 1935); in another letter to Virginia Woolf, he describes "the blood orange moon rising through the clouds" (12 March 1936). In writing of a trip to Beijing with Ling Shuhua, Julian vividly described the Western Hills "that roll and heave like early bronzes of buffaloes":

> Our day in the Western Hills spent looking at temples. Some of them are very lovely, beautifully proportioned courts of white marble: lots of bas-relief that seems to me decent decoration, and some good statues. There's a colossal sleeping Bhudda in a sort of copper-gold who I fancy distinguished statesmen send him presents of colossal slippers. Then, as you'll see from the photos, we climbed a small mountain. I really lost my heart to the Western Hills. They're mountains—from the plain very jagged, but they roll and heave like early bronzes of buffaloes. And they're a superb size and colour. I really could live very happily in Peking [Beijing]. But I think I prefer Charleston. (JB to Vanessa Bell, 1 February 1936)

Vanessa imagined the China he described, and recounted for Julian her experience of the International Chinese Art Exhibition at the Burlington House in London, 1935–36. She wrote:

> My theory is that China—the landscape—is like their good painting—all subtle blues and browns and grays with suggestions of other colours and that people are always affected by what they live in. Not that they just copy it which of course they do, but somehow the general scheme gets into all their being and they cant escape it and always really think and feel within that range. (Letter to JB, 15 December 1935)

Julian Bell's descriptions of his experiences and perceptions reveal his love of the outdoor life. In one of his essays written at Cambridge, he described a naturalist as "someone who experiences certain definite and peculiar emotions about the physical world" ("The Naturalist's Point of View"). During his stay in China, he became a naturalist and took a rugged trip down the Yangtze River on a crowded boat to Kaiding, Chengdu (Sichuan province), and Kuling (Jiangxi province). It was July 1936, about ten months after his arrival in China, and he wanted, he said, to "really know something about China outside the respectable walls of Wuhan University" (Letter to Ling Shuhua, July 1936). Enduring all kinds of discomforts, he traveled with his student Ye Junjian, Derek Bryan, and Hansen Lowe, none of whom, he wrote to Shuhua, were "comparable as travel companions to seeing Pekin with you." Packed into small, airless, unhealthy boats with masses of people, he longed "for the mountains and cool winds and exercise" to make him feel well. But according to Derek Bryan, he was "very fit" and excited about purchasing a rifle and going to Kuling to shoot wild boar.

At other times, however, his "metropolitan aesthetics" moved from England and Europe to the "imperial periphery" of China (Bunn, "Our Wattled Cot," 126*ff*). The implications of his descriptions of the Chinese landscape emerge if we view them not only as an effusive response to a foreign place, but as "a system of aesthetic, conventional and ideological ordering" (127). Soon after his arrival in China, he wrote his early impressions of the "outside of China"

The Western Hills, near Beijing. Courtesy of the author.

when traveling to Wuhan in a bus. He "domesticated" the foreign, like most travelers. Observing boys loafing on the street, he saw China as something of "a Mediterranean country." In China's Wuhan and France's Marseilles, "people quarrel or bargain in the streets, and life appears to be preeminently social." Julian was drawn to this Mediterranean ambiance, but his painter's eye was also drawn to the "pagoda in its wood, or by the grey subtleties of rain and the brown or green landscape" which reminded him as an Englishman that "there is something of his own country about such a landscape." Viewing "the white and grey villages," he thought of Ireland; attending a performance of the Chinese theater with its masks, conventionalized dance of movements and chanted speeches, he noted that it gave "an effect that must be very like that of Aeschylus presented to a Greek audience"; seeing the social animation and life of the streets, he thought of people in Dijon or Marseilles. And yet he was open to the foreign, observing when arriving at Han Yang Men, "the most astonishing sight to the foreigner . . . the junks on the river" propelled by one sail on a mast that, he, a sailor himself, is surprised by for "it is more efficient than one might expect." Julian, aware of his generalizations, was not a blind traveler noting that "what seems to me the natural attitude is clearly not so to most of the people I meet" (Bell, *The Road to Wuchang*). Put into a cultural topspin like most travelers, he is forced to question as I did on my travels, how cultures represent each other. In reflecting on the so-called West's representation of itself as well as the Chinese representation, he observes that "the West of the publicists is a fiction." The countries of the "home, fortress and prison, of the fetish of cleanliness, respectability, reticence," images that had gained a foothold abroad in 1930s, only exist in the countries of the Protestant tradition, England, North Germany, Scandinavia, and America.

After Julian's imagination was piqued by the astonishing sight of the junks on the river, he had the opportunity to have a sailboat built and to sail on the lovely East Lake on the Wuhan University campus. He was drawn to the large clear space, as was Mao Zedong who was inspired by it to write a poem in 1956, "Swimming": "I have just drank the waters of Changsha / And come to eat the fish of Wuchang." Today, however, the campus is increasingly hemmed in by the thriving industry, business, and dense population of bustling Wuchang. This is very different form Innes Jackson Herdan's description in 1937. She was a Somerville College graduate working at Wuhan University at the same time as Julian, and she described the wonderful setting

Julian Bell and guide hunting in Tibet, 1936. By permission of the chief archivist, Wuhan University Library, China.

among the hills and lakes of beautiful clear water, and . . . far removed from the traffic of the neighbouring town of Wuchang. Because the whole area was so little developed, if one stood on one of the many hills, it seemed that the whole of China's plains and mountains, and behind them the rest of Asia, was stretching out to infinity. (Herdan, *Liao Hongying*, 78)

Descriptions of experiences on the lake, solo or with Ling Shuhua, emerge from the correspondence of Julian, Vanessa, and Ling Shuhua and soar with poetry. Often outdoors in China with a gun or a boat, Julian, a sportsman, wrote of the pleasure of sailing with "Sue":

The boats a great fascination—we're having windier weather, and last Sat. Sue and I sailed some yen [*sic*] miles or more—it must have been more like twenty in distance covered, of course—into a fascinating green country with empty mountains coming right down to water's edge, and farm houses and gazebos and ruined temples and fishing families—it's the best way I know of seeing the country. (Letter to VB, 16 June 1936)

In a later letter to Shuhua, he described another sensuous sailing venture on the Wuhan lake:

Well, I didn't go to the dismal party after all. Because I went sailing that afternoon. . . . I slowly drifted back, bathing, and just as I was going to anchor and go in a little wind came up. It rose very fast and after a tack or two across the arrows it was blowing half a gale and it seemed silly to go in. So I went on sailing and sailing with a lovely warm wind. All my clothes got wet, so I took them all off; the wind was warm enough. The moon came up almost as bright as day and I sailed right up its path on the water, over to Mo San with the boat putting her lee bow right down into the waves, and white foam and spray shooting up. It was one of the most romantic things I ever did. (September 1935)

This sensuous prose sometimes seems like an unwritten poem. The correspondence reveals Julian's gift for description—letter writing being his most prolific genre—and his poetic "eye" that never brought him the more obvious successes as an artist in life. As a sportsman, stalking, desiring "to shoot a boor" in the wilds of China, he is at one with the landscape with a different set of values. The tropes of temples, pagodas, buddhas, lakes, and mountains appeared frequently in Julian's letters as well as the writings of G. L. Dickinson and Dorothy and I. A. Richards, who visited China several times and scaled the mountains. If one aspect of the myriad definitions of the "orient" is exotic landscapes, then Vanessa's curiosity and Julian's descriptions are no exception.

When Julian wrote to Vanessa from China about his continued interest in the Spanish Civil War—he had wanted to go to Spain, not China initially—she tried to discourage him. Yet in October 1935 in China, he wrote to Ling Shuhua, who was in Beijing convalescing, that "it means a lot what happens in Spain," relating that he would feel as "wretched if fascists win as you would be about the Japanese." Writing of Felicia Brown who had been killed in the Spanish Civil War, Vanessa Bell observed in a transparent letter to Julian:

[It] does seem a terrible waste of someone gifted, as she evidently was. I understood your wanting to go and see what war was like, and perhaps I should understand your wanting to go to Spain if you were here, only I do think nearly all war is madness. It's destruction and not creation, and it's mad to destroy the best things and people in the world. . . . I see one couldn't help joining anti-fascists if fascists started attacking, as they have in Spain. . . . Of course going as a war correspondent is different, but I am glad, my dear, that I don't have to try to reconcile myself to your rushing off to Spain. (Marler, 10 October 1936)

Later, Julian wrote more, as recounted in letters and in Stansky and Abraham's original study of Julian in this period. He wrote to Charles Vildrac in France that he wanted to go "at once" to Spain from France, after his arrival from China. Vanessa was sent into a panic. She prevailed and he returned to England, but left on 6 June 1937. When he arrived in Madrid to serve as an ambulance driver, Vanessa wrote, "You seem more remote than in China. The only consolation is that you are with people you like and leading a life you like" (Marler, 7 July 1937). Julian died from shrapnel wounds eleven days later, 18 July, and was buried at Furencarral, north of Madrid. Vanessa reported that "the wound was so terrible that he could not have lived. The doctor told me how much good Julian had done, that he had brought in hundreds of wounded men." Vanessa wrote to one of Julian's good friends after his death:

> I think there is one thing I want desperately to say to any one who will listen—if only I could—and that is simply that I am quite sure, reasonably and definitely sure, that the loss of people like Julian is a waste. . . . I am old enough to know a little what he might have done and been if he had lived. I know that if life would have given infinite good and possibilities to the world which are now lost. . . . Fascism wants to destroy intelligence—we must not let it do so. (Marler, 440n. 2)

THE PAINTER'S EYE: VANESSA BELL AND LING SHUHUA

There is, when looking at landscape, "something in the universe that one is left with," writes Virginia Woolf in *The Waves*, place having a more lasting identity than we have. Just as Julian Bell's sensibility and admiring descriptions of the Chinese towns, lakes, and countryside remain with us in his letters and poems, so do Ling Shuhua's verbal and visual landscapes. Writing and painting last. After his death in 1937 in the Spanish Civil War, a correspondence and intimacy developed between his mother, Vanessa Bell, and Ling Shuhua, though they had never met. Vanessa, according to all accounts, was devastated by the death of Julian. Roger Fry spoke of her as "such a virtuous mother . . . she's absorbed by domesticity whenever she isn't painting" (Letter to VW, King's College archives, 24 October 1921). Upon Julian's death, Virginia Woolf wrote in her *Diary*:

> Vanessa looks an old woman. . . . Julian had some queer power over her— the lover as well as the son. He told her he could never love another woman

as he loved her. He was like her; yet had a vigour, a roughness, and then as a child, how much she cared for him. I mean he needed comfort and sympathy more I think than the others, was less adapted to get on in the world—had a kind of clumsiness, of Cambridge awkwardness together with his natural gaiety. And that all lost for the sake of 10 minutes in an ambulance. I often argue with him on my walks. (17 September 1937)

Formalized, Virginia Woolf's argument with Julian for joining the Spanish Civil War became the anti-war polemic, *Three Guineas*. Vanessa coped by openly expressing her loss to Ling Shuhua, having to be stoical around her family. A faraway China of the mind inhabited by her son's lover provided a place for her feelings as she confided her sadness, frequently, in letters that began about two years after Julian's death. In an early letter in 1939, she writes, "I feel you would understand more than most people, though I cannot express myself clearly" (13 June 1939). Her correspondence continued for about sixteen years, ending in November 1955, though the letters become less frequent and more perfunctory after 1951. Even in 1947, ten years after Julian's death Vanessa still wrote that she could not talk of Julian easily, "but he is so often in my mind and I wish continually that he were here with you. But it is no use—one has to be without him and all we can do is work and try to be sensible" (20 April 1947). In 1952, the new generation seemed to offer some comfort as Vanessa related that Quentin and his wife were visiting: "The baby is really very beautiful with large eyes far apart and a most attractive smile. He is called Julian as perhaps you know. It seems strange at first to have another Julian but I am glad they have given him that name" (28 December 1952).

"Seeing together" also first formed the bond between Julian and Shuhua. Julian wrote to Ling Shuhua as he sailed back to England after their turbulent affair, "you're the only human being I really enjoy looking at scenery with" (17 March 1937). Julian had always promoted Vanessa's relationship with Ling Shuhua. In one letter he wrote, "She's . . . the only woman who would be a possible daughter in law to you" (Letter to VB, 22 November 1935). Though Vanessa could not forget the anxiety and sadness of two years earlier when Julian had to leave China in a whirl of scandal because of his illicit relationship with Ling Shuhua, she, nevertheless, wrote sympathetically to Shuhua in September 1938:

Vanessa Bell, 1932. By permission of the National Portrait Gallery, London, England.

Ling Shuhua, ca. 1930s. By permission of the Henry W. and Albert A. Berg Collection of English & American Literature, New York Public Library, Astor, Tilden & Lenox Foundations.

Your letter is very sad. I am glad that you write what you feel to me—please always do so. Then it is possible for me to do the same to you and so we can have intimacy with each other. I think Julian had made something between you and me possible by his death that perhaps we could not have had if he were alive—so let us make the most of it dear Sue. (16 October 1938)

Vanessa, haunted by the death of Julian as well as the isolating effects of the war, did encourage Shuhua as an artist to be thankful that she had work during a time of war. "I really pity people," she wrote, "who are not artists . . . [with no] refuge from the world . . . life would be intolerable if one could not get detached from it" (13 June 1939). Ling Shuhua, living with her own memories of Julian in the midst of the brutal Sino-Japanese War and the civil war, tried to salvage her art but wrote little because of the turbulence of her life.

Shuhua, a painter, calligrapher, poet, and collector, is part of the world of "art" that Julian and Vanessa also shared. "Seeing"—the aesthetic gaze—is what brings the three of them together across cultural boundaries, continents, and even death. Vanessa and Shuhua had a shared delight in discussing colors and looking at and painting landscapes that is documented in their correspondence. One can understand this affinity when reading Ling Shuhua's refined description of the color of a Chinese red lacquer table, a "red" that was a brown mixed with red and orange. She writes:

> The best red lacquer in Peking was something beyond words to describe, it was not like the sort of red paint which made one's eyes feel sore. . . . This was a kind of red colour which gave one [a] feeling of superb beauty though without the suggestion of attractive charm or dashing prettiness. If it were placed among black or wood coloured furniture, one [would] . . . not feel it unbecoming." (*Ancient Melodies,* holograph)

Vanessa Bell and Ling Shuhua often wrote with "a painter's eye" of Julian, of Virginia Woolf, and of the landscapes Julian enjoyed in China and in England. In September 1938, Vanessa Bell wrote of how she felt closer to Julian in the garden at Charleston and how "Julian seems nearer here than anywhere else. Even now I could so easily expect to hear his voice or find him sitting on the lawn" (Letter to LS, 16 September 1938). In another letter to Shuhua, she noted, "do you remember how Julian liked the bare trees?" (Berg, 7 December 1950). She also imagined the landscape of China, noting that "Julian always said China reminded him so much of the south of France" (Letter to LS,

9 December 1938). When the memorial volume of Julian's writing was published in England and China in 1939, Ling Shuhua wrote with some anxiety, since the relationship was alluded to in the volume. Vanessa assured her, "surely people wont bother very much about a scandal already more than 2 years old. People's memories are short in such ways and they easily get confused. Surely not too very many people will read the book, for as you say it is expensive, I suppose more for the Chinese than the English" (13 June 1939). Here, Vanessa seemed culturally insensitive to Ling Shuhua and Chen Yuan's potential "loss of face" in China. In a letter written in 1941 after Virginia Woolf's suicide, Vanessa brought this death and Julian's together to portray her own sense of desolation:

> The news you saw about V. was only too true—It has been very terrible. She had been getting ill for some time and felt that she was going out of her mind—I think it was true that she was very near it but if only we could have kept her safe for a time she would have got better . . . Life was sad enough without that and to me the loss of Julian is greater than ever for he would have helped. (Letter to LS, 27 May 1941)

In October 1946, Ling Shuhua left China for London with her daughter, and Vanessa helped her professionally when she arrived in England. Leaving, Ling wrote of the "sensitive position of the Chinese nation" as it geared up for the establishment of the People's Republic of China and Maoism. In 1948, Vanessa wrote that in hearing news about China's political turbulence, she was glad that Shuhua and her daughter were not there. In 1949, Chen Yuan, Ling Shuhua's husband, became China's permanent delegate to UNESCO in Paris, and Ling Shuhua spent time in London before going to Paris. The correspondence with Vanessa begun in 1937 after Julian's death continued when Shuhua was in London and Paris—punctuated by occasional visits and much gift giving. The gifts are a revelation of her many artistic talents: illustrated calendars, designs on handkerchiefs, paintings on silk scarves, prints of Chinese gods on thin paper, ginger plants, a brooch, chocolate, a pin cushion, even pottery and a lamp that Quentin Bell fired in his kiln. Shuhua also mentions "a fan book" in which Duncan and Quentin would draw, a friendship token like the scroll that Ling Shuhua had given Xu Zhimo. But gift giving was an aspect of the Chinese cultural tradition that made Vanessa uncomfortable, and, after awhile, and she protested that Shuhua was sending "too many presents" (Berg, 24 December

1948). Though they had been brought together by Julian's death, one senses that she and others in the Bloomsbury circle began to tire of Ling Shuhua's attentions, and Vanessa felt that she could no longer really assist her in her adjustment to life in London.[2] Yet as late as 1960 when Vanessa was ill, Shuhua wrote that she had sent some postcards from Wuhan University "where Julian had spent a number of happy days."

Vanessa was always sensitive to the beauty of what Shuhua sent, particularly during the war. Thanking her for a letter that contained Chinese New Year's pictures, she exclaimed:

> They are lovely. Especially I think those on their paper which I suppose are those of the different gods. I had never seen anything like them before. I wonder if other people in England who know about Chinese things, such as Arthur Waley have seen prints like these. I think I must try to show them to him. They are such exquisite colors and drawings and we have all been looking at them again and again and thinking how wonderful it is that such a present should have reached us here in the midst of the war, where one seems to be completely shut out from the outside world. (Letter to LS, 17 March 1940)

Upon receiving a Christmas card with a painted calendar by Shuhua, Vanessa noted that "it is like Matisse yet purely Chinese" (4 February 1940), suggesting the appeal of the antique to the modernists, the reciprocal aesthetic nurturing, a theme to be further developed in chapter 5, "Developing Modernisms." In 1950 when Shuhua made plans to visit Italy, Vanessa suggested that she see the Venice Accademia Padua near Venice, the Arena Chapel by Giotto, the Tintorettos and the Fra Angelicos in Florence and the Botticellis in San Marco (VB to LS, 27 April 1950). Vanessa observed that "Sienese paintings have a great deal in common with the Chinese" and advised Shuhua to write about them (Berg, 1 July 1950). Her comparisons of Chinese art with perhaps the "flat" qualities of Matisse and Sienese paintings, and Roger Fry's with Botticelli, enlarge our definitions of the "modern." My own "eyes" changed in observing the dancing figures in a "Sagdian whirl" on a tomb from the Tang Dynasty in the recent Asia Society exhibit on the Silk Road. Suddenly, I could see the same flowing lines as Matisse.

Given that they were both artists, however, Vanessa's letters often reflect on Shuhua's efforts to paint during a time of war and civil turmoil in China: "write, paint, don't waste gifts" (Berg Collection, 17 March 1937). Given Julian's close relationship with Roger Fry, Vanessa asked Shuhua if she had "read Fry's last lectures on Chinese art" (5 December 1939), and sent her Virginia Woolf's biography of Fry, but they were lost in the mail. Vanessa, obsessed with Julian, wrote in 1940 that she had just finished reading Virginia's biography of Fry and noted, "Reading it too has made me think how Julian would have enjoyed it—there are a few things said about him to show what Roger felt about him and what their relationship was" (Letter to LS, 17 March 1940). The refrain was advice to herself as well as Ling Shuhua: "you must work. You must write your book and paint too." She continued, "it would be terrible to waste your gifts and someday I expect they will bring you happiness. I like your description of your garden with its fruit trees and the two large old trees by the gate. . . . How I should like to see your home and the Western Hills" (17 March 1940). Vanessa Bell encouraged Shuhua to arrange for an exhibition in Paris or America where Shuhua's sister lived and advised, "don't let lack of success discourage you" (5 February 1947). After Shuhua's exhibit at the Zwemmer Gallery, Vanessa observed sympathetically that it was "difficult to sell or get recognized unless they are quite young and in the fashion" (Berg, 15 February 1953). Eventually, Ling Shuhua had several shows in Europe: one of her own paintings with two other women in London in 1947 (Berg, 17 February 1949); another at the Adam's Galleries in 1949 when Vanessa urged her to include "paintings of London and the river and the scenes of Switzerland, particularly 'Between Geneva and Montreaux.'" (Berg, 25 August 1949); another at the Zwemmer Gallery in 1953; and her own collection of literati Musée Cernuschi, Paris, 1962. She also exhibited in America in her travels in Indianapolis, and at the Doll and Richards Gallery in Boston. She noted that "Boston is the place in which Oriental art is considered to have the best standards in America. Its art museum [the Boston Museum of Fine Arts] has the first collection of Chinese paintings" (LS to VB, July 1960).

"It is most interesting . . . to see European landscape through Chinese eyes," wrote Vanessa Bell to Ling Shuhua in 1949 upon viewing her exhibition of paintings at the Adam's Galleries in London (13 December 1949). She hinted here at the postmodern value of "defamiliarization," pointed to by the Russian formalists. Having earlier encouraged Ling Shuhua to paint London scenes, Vanessa wrote, "I am sure people will be interested in seeing how London looks to a Chinese artist. One has seen so many paintings of Chinese scenes, but very seldom any of one's own familiar surroundings" (11 July 1949). Duncan Grant agreed and said of her Alpine painting in the same exhibit that "some of the smaller landscapes done in Europe have a strange fascination" (Letter to LS, 15 December 1949). While in England, Ling Shuhua painted what she termed "Easternized" landscapes that she discovered to the north of London, in the smog of the Thames, the Scottish lakes, and Vita Sackville-West's Sissinghurst. But she did not, as André Maurois wrote in the introduction to the Musée Cernuschi catalog, "seek to give by some artifice an oriental strangeness to these Western landscapes. Rather, she paints them as she sees them and this is sufficient for her originality because she discovers in them a thousand-year experience" (Shuhua, exhibition pamphlet).

Vanessa cast her eye in the direction of the East belying Bloomsbury's reputation for cultural narrowness; similarly, Ling Shuhua gazed at English landscape. Vanessa Bell and Ling Shuhua, modernists, foreshadowed the different cultural and aesthetic perceptions now vaunted by hydra-headed postmodernism. When Lily Briscoe hints at postmodernism—"One wanted fifty pairs of eyes to see with" (Woolf, *To the Lighthouse*, 294)—she reflects not only on the complex character of Mrs. Ramsay, but announces the "plurality" of cultural perspectives to be entertained as a part of modernism and, then, postmodernism. Lily Briscoe and Vanessa—along with a loosely defined first generation of Bloomsbury, G. L. Dickinson, E. M. Forster, Roger Fry, Lytton Strachey, Arthur Waley, as well as those closer to her in age, Virginia Woolf, Leonard Woolf, J. M. Keynes—were spinners of the modernist line that was cast into the twentieth century out of the dissolution of Victorian waters. They became fascinated with foreign landscapes that helped to define their own and themselves as well as another place; at the same time, Chinese culture and literature developed an international dimension.

Vanessa's attraction to Ling Shuhua's paintings and "seeing" European landscape through "Chinese eyes" connects with Roger Fry's interest in "hybrid painting" revealed in his "The Double Nature of Painting," 1923. This interest in doubleness—whether of two cultures or of form and subject (see Woolf's essay on Sickert)—is a modernist drift with eddies in Bloomsbury in the 1920s and 1930s, a current that critics have largely ignored in their emphasis on the formalist aesthetic principles in Bloomsbury that prevailed largely before World War I. Vanessa Bell's interest in French art, as revealed in Mary

Ann Caws and Sarah Bird Wright's *Bloomsbury and France,* and her openness to Chinese art, separated her from mainstream British art circles—she, ready and open to other aesthetic conventions and ways of seeing. At the same time, British art and aesthetic conventions were being absorbed in China, Africa, and India.

Though Shuhua had considerable support from Vanessa and was encouraged in 1949, seven years later in 1956, she wrote:

> It is a bitter experience to be able to paint but not allow to go on working simply because it is not wanted. People in this country, most of them are unwilling to accept new ideas and new kind of arts unless they are something like their own. (LS to Leonard Woolf, 9 February 1956)

Shuhua's observation about different aesthetics in different cultures was correct. England was still getting used to "seeing" and appreciating Chinese art; the first major exhibit of Chinese art having only been mounted about twenty years earlier. Shuhua reflected:

> Most Chinese pictures sold here are a mixture of the East and the West. The subjects or pictures must suit the taste of the Westerners. I hate to think of this unavoidable failure but what can I do? (Letter to LW, 9 February 1956)

In fact, she had already been spurred on by Vanessa's advice and had painted some mixtures of East and West, English landscapes through Chinese eyes. She wrote to Leonard in 1953 that she had painted pictures of Monk's House and Sissinghurst Castle.

The years 1953 and 1954 were the high points in Shuhua's career in Europe. She published her autobiography, *Ancient Melodies,* through Leonard Woolf's Hogarth Press in 1953, and had a very successful exhibit of her paintings at the Musée Cernuschi in Paris in 1954. Though she had already mounted one exhibit at the Adam's Galleries in 1951 with the help of Dorothy Woodman, and had sold eleven of thirty-seven paintings, she felt that she needed more advice to mount a professional exhibit. Leonard Woolf assisted in trying to enlist first Ben Nicolson, Vita Sackville-West's son, and then Anthony Blunt, a good friend of Julian's at Cambridge who was now a professor of art and head of the Courtauld, to look at the pictures. Dorothy Woodman also looked at Shuhua's art again and Shuhua reported that she was "especially interested in my drawings which emphasize rhythms which in some way have some original quality like what is music. I draw nearly seventy different orchids (flowers and leaves) all in different forms to illustrate my visions" (Letter to LW, 18 June 1953). Though nothing happened in London, Shuhua was invited at this time to have a one-woman show at the Musée Cernuschi in Paris, with a promise to introduce the show to other museums in European countries. André Maurois wrote a foreword to the catalog with the dedication, "To Shuhua who has all the talent." Her show was so popular that it was held over for an extra three months in Paris, and she noted that an American museum might exhibit her also. There was also talk of an exhibition at Harvard. Typical of her tendency toward self-aggrandizement, Shuhua spoke of her luck and getting "famous" if introduced in America.

She was grateful to Vita Sackville-West for writing the introduction to *Ancient Melodies,* the autobiography of her early years, a connection made through Virginia Woolf's friendship. In 1966, she engaged Quentin Bell to look at some Han rubbings (200 B.C.–200 A.D.) that she owned and, he, "enchanted" by them, encouraged her to find a museum in which to exhibit them. The other shows that Shuhua mounted were in London, Paris, and Boston, and she mainly exhibited Chinese paintings from her personal collection that she had brought to England with a few of her own paintings included.[3] André Maurois in his introduction to her catalog wrote of Shuhua's "honest and sensitive heart" as expressed in her paintings, and he gives an idea of her standing in China:

> Shuhua thus continued the tradition of a family "embalmed with books." She practiced calligraphy, painting and writing simultaneously. Novelist, poet, she directed a renowned literary journal and has a distinguished place in contemporary Chinese literature. . . . In painting, her style is what the Chinese call, "Wen-Jen Hua," the painting of literary people who strive to express the soul of the painter as much as what is being painted. In this lyrical painting, mountains, rivers, bamboos, and flowers are both objects and thoughts. The silences and the whites are as expressive in the paintings as the lines. "It is often difficult," says Dr. Kuo Yi-I Shou, "to discern if the painting is the illustration of the poem of if the poem illustrates the painting. It is this triad of verses, calligraphy and the painting that makes poetry." (Shuhua, exhibition pamphlet)

He also mentioned the episode that she described in *Ancient Melodies* when at the age of six she was observed drawing by a friend of her father's. Marked as talented, he spoke to her father and she became the pupil of the famous artist, Miao Su-Yun. Maurois described "her foggy mountains, her rivers which hardly delineate the line of the riverbank or the reflection of the water . . . white clouds, vaguely patterned with gray . . . [forming] a universe which is clean and right and which seems to emerge from the fog of a dream." He noted the way in which "the vigor" of her brushstrokes created in just a few strokes, an orchid, a magnolia stem, an apple blossom. He spoke of what appealed to the modernists, her "abstract style." In addition, Duncan Grant mentions that Shuhua will have exhibits in New York and Boston, "where I have always heard there is a great appreciation of Eastern art" (Letter to LS, 25 June 1955), and that the Boston Museum bought one of her paintings.[4]

Ling Shuhua mentioned in a letter to Leonard Elmhirst in 1967 that the painters she had exhibited in "A Painter's Choice," and whom Elmhirst met when in Beijing with Xu Zhimo and Rabindranath Tagore in 1924, occupied a very important place in Chinese art. Noting that Elmhirst is the only person in the West to have met some of these painters, she said that the "paintings become more and more valuable as the years go by" (Letter to Elmhirst, 26 June 1967, LKE 3). She sent him an article to be included in the catalog of the show mentioned above and asked if he would write something about that gathering in Beijing. In London preparing for her exhibit in 1967 at the start of Mao's Cultural Revolution, Ling Shuhua was nostalgic for the "old China." She writes to Elmhirst that

> any beautiful association or recollection about old-day-Peking [Beijing] would help the West to understand that all the things, such as the purge, the Red-guard, the party line and all the posters to purge some body in the beauty sight of China are imported stuff chiefly from the Russians—they are brought in by force. The Chinese don't like such things at all! Don't you think so?" (26 June 1967, LKE 3)

Deeper into news of the Cultural Revolution, she again writes in 1971 of her memories of the cultural circles in Beijing captured in two lines in Chinese poetry: "Remembering her green skirt, I would lose my heart on the lovely grass wherever I go" (Letter to LE, 25 June 1971, LKE 3). Shuhua's China is not Mao's and Elmhirst warns her of the problem in being invited back to

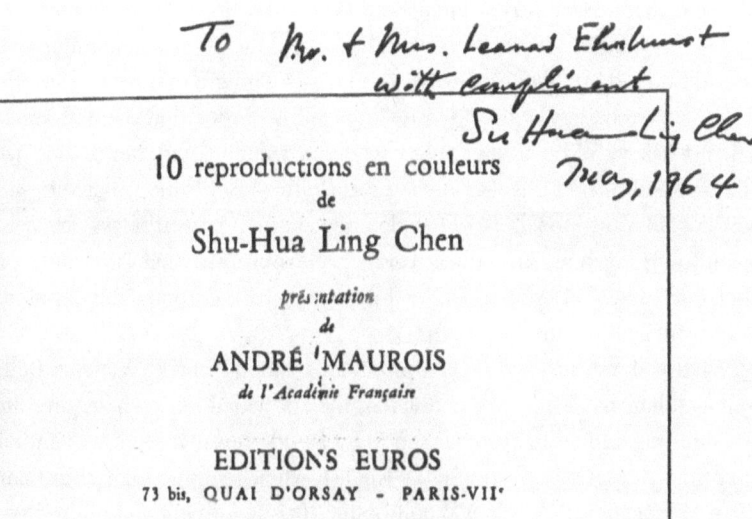

Invitations to Ling Shuhua gallery openings. By permission of the Dartington Hall Trust Archive, Totnes, England

China in 1972: "A country so changed that you may find you have made a mistake in returning . . . I wish that even a handful of the present generation could realise through and from you what the past of Chinese culture had to offer" (LKE, 7 March 1972). She did visit China and recorded that she had "a heart to heart talk with Mrs. Zhou En-lai," who was a student with her in the 1920s. She asserted during this visit during the Cultural Revolution that she might never again return to China: "They do not want me." Nevertheless, she visited beautiful Hangzhou, saw Mao's bridge, and observed that "no one writes poetry anymore" (Letter to LE, 7 July 1973). In the 1990s, her reputation would rise again in the Deng era.

What is important about Ling Shuhua's relationship with Vanessa Bell as well as Julian and Virginia Woolf is that they provided her with another literary, cultural, and sexual standard to place beside her own. She was emboldened to write an autobiography in English when few women did in China. Even in England, as Virginia Woolf notes, "It is less than two hundred years since people took an interest in themselves; Boswell was almost the first writer who thought that a man's life was worth writing a book about" (*The Moment*, 129). The cultural contact was important. As Hu Shi, one of the thinkers behind the May Fourth movement, stated:

> Contact with strange civilizations brings new standards of value with which the native culture is re-examined and re-evaluated, and conscious reformation and regeneration are the natural outcome of such transvaluation of values. (*Renaissance*, 46)

CONSTRUCTING THE "NARROW BRIDGE OF ART": VIRGINIA WOOLF AND LING SHUHUA

It was left to Ling Shuhua and Virginia Woolf to develop this aesthetic conversation, further linking Bloomsbury and the Crescent Moon group. When I came upon their letters—Shuhua's words overlay red traces of grasshoppers, bees, and leaves on delicate rice paper—I entered an intimate space between women writers of different cultures confiding during a time of war. There is a lyric quality in the sixteen-month correspondence, 3 March 1938–16 July 1939, much as if each is trying to walk over a fragile bridge on a willow pattern plate. The bridge is personal, cultural, and national: the bridge is art. As Eudora Welty reminds us, "Art though is never the voice of a country; it is an even more precious thing, the voice of the individual, doing its best to speak, not comfort of any sort, indeed, but truth" ("Place in Fiction," 2).

Woolf began this correspondence after Julian Bell, her nephew and Ling Shuhua's paramour, died in the Spanish Civil War in 1937. War surrounded them. As Shuhua wrote in her first letter, "beside the general disaster, I have my personal deep sorrow which I never can get out of my mind" (1938). They suffered both from the effects of war and personal sorrow over the early death of a vibrant young man of twenty-nine.

The bridge of art is "narrow" because a cultural gate had just opened between England and China after the establishment of the Chinese Republic in 1911; "fragile" because Virginia Woolf and Ling Shuhua never met and wrote during a turbulent period of the war across personal, linguistic, cultural, and national walls. Yet they are drawn together as writers, women writers trying to write, living through a time of personal and historical struggle, the Sino-Japanese War in China and the beginnings of World War II in England. Both were of the same class, the "daughters of educated men": Ling Shuhua, the daughter of the mayor of Beijing; Virginia Woolf, the daughter of Leslie Stephen, the well-known literary figure and editor of the *Dictionary of National Biography*. Ling Shuhua's life as the daughter of the mayor was perhaps even more privileged than Virginia Woolf's, reversing the usual "assumption of privilege" of the Western woman in postcolonial studies. Nevertheless, Woolf was the more established writer, about eighteen years Shuhua's senior, and had published all of her major works except *Three Guineas* (1938), and *Between the Acts* (published posthumously in 1941). Ling Shuhua, known mainly as a painter and writer of children's stories and short stories in China, was venturing into the field of autobiography in 1937.

She was also experimenting with writing in and translating into English, preparing her stories for an English audience. The critic Shi Shumei asserts that Woolf's "subtle Eurocentric attitude" had led her to advise Ling to write in English, thus placing Woolf in a Procrustean bed of postcolonial hegemony:

> The unspoken presumption behind Woolf's suggestion seems to be a hierarchical conception of language and audience, that English, the language in which she herself wrote in, is the authentic, if not superior, language for creative endeavors, and that the Western audience is the one worth writing for. (*The Lure of the Modern*, 216)

Virginia Woolf *by Man Ray.* © 2003 Man Ray Trust/Artists Rights Society (ARS), New York/ADAGP, Paris.

The facts of this situation, validated in letters, are that Julian Bell, beginning in 1935, had suggested that Ling Shuhua publish her short stories in England, and the following year he collaborated with her in translating her stories. He had sent the translated stories to his mother in England, and they were then sent to the *London Mercury*, where, he discovered when he returned to London in 1937, they had been rejected by the editor, R. A. Scott-James. Shuhua was drawn to English culture and literature—as was her husband Chen Yuan— even before she met and fell in love with Julian. After Julian left Wuhan in January 1937, they spoke of reuniting and living together in England. Though some critics would have it otherwise, this was part of her complicated identity as a cosmopolitan Chinese artist who identified deeply with the nation of China, whose imagination freely connected with different people and different parts of the world. Undoubtedly, Virginia Woolf, like many who are foreign to the culture of China, understood some things about it, misunderstood others, and may have been culturally ignorant or insensitive, at times, as described in this chapter. Similarly, Ling Shuhua misunderstood things in her relationship with Julian Bell and English culture and literature, but she was bent on reinventing herself. She was involved in an unhappy marriage, and intent on creating an imaginary English audience and another way of writing during a troubled period in China during the Sino-Japanese War. Undoubtedly, Woolf was the established writer, and Ling Shuhua was asking for writerly advice. The "unbalance" and "asymmetry" that Shi Shumei notes in this relationship may, however, be based on the experience and talent of Virginia Woolf and the drive of Ling Shuhua, rather than an imperialist, Eurocentric plot. Transnational aesthetic encounters, as Yip Wai-lim has explained, will often mobilize the prejudices and ideologies of each culture, and limited understanding and misunderstanding will, at times, be a part of the experience. But the experience must be had, the venture taken. Otherwise, the use of fashionable words like "transnational" and "global" in contemporary cultural and literary criticism will ring hollow.

In their correspondence, Woolf and Shuhua do not adopt the tone, stance, or vocabulary of "domination" and "subordination" or "master" and "oppressed," terms of relationship that postcolonial critics like Gayatri Spivak have defined as the norm. Researching their historically specific circumstances as urged by Chandra Mohanty, I found that they identified as women writers struggling to sustain an aesthetic vision during wartime as they suffered personally from the death of Julian Bell and the effects of the war around them. Their sense of themselves as women and writers deconstruct the mainstream cultural certainties, the official stories of a nation at war. Economic, political, and social analysis, which present categories of the oppression of women based on poverty, illiteracy, reproductive rights, nutrition, and overpopulation, represent one order of women's reality; the other is what we find when we look within to the writing of women, created in resistance to this cultural monolith. We need to counter some Western feminists' views of Ling's "feudal" thinking as well as some Asian critics' views of Woolf's "subjugation." Virginia Woolf and Ling Shuhua's correspondence generates not imperialist and capitalist moves—as some neo-Marxist would have it—but relationship—as they realize their place as women and writers in their society during wartime. They transform paradigms as Isak Dinesen and Olive Schreiner do in Sue Horton's account of remarkable women writers who reinscribe modernism and colonialism with different meanings than the men who have largely created such systems. Each brings to the conversation, however, a different aesthetic and culture, expressing in her correspondence both the mutual reflection and cultural tension of their respective literary communities, as described in the earlier part of this chapter.

The relationship, therefore, does not fit the postcolonial model, which Chandra Mohanty describes as the five ways in which "women" as a category of analysis are generally incorporated into Western feminist discussion: 1) women as victims of male violence; 2) women as universal dependents; 3) married women as victims of the colonial process; 4) women and familial systems; 5) women and religious ideologies (Mohanty, *Third World Women*, 56–62). Ling Shuhua and Virginia Woolf are privileged women artists who share the "miserable mind feeling" of war and some social constriction because they are women. Shuhua fled Wuhan for Sichuan with her daughter to avoid the frequent bombings of the Sino-Japanese War and a society in chaos; nevertheless, Ling Shuhua was still a "subject," a more or less independent agent, as represented in the letters and writing. Woolf never suggests otherwise. There is a hegemony in that Woolf, as the older more established writer, was respected as the "laoshi" (the teacher). Shuhua writing in her second language consistently asked for help and advice as any novice writer writing in another language would: "tell me mistakes I have made." But Woolf says little about her syntactic errors in English, and advises her "to keep the Chinese flavour" (28 February 1939). This stance can be viewed unsympathetically: as the postcolonialist critic, Shumei Shi, remarks, "Woolf was calling for Ling to exoticize herself in the gaze of the West" (*Lure of the Modern*, 218). Woolf, however, like a good teacher, was trying to address Ling's fear of error in writing in English as well the fact that she had little tradition behind her in

China in the writing of a female autobiography. In discussing the difficulties of nineteenth-century British women writers, Woolf speculates:

> Whatever effect discouragement and criticism had upon their writing—and I believe that they had a very great effect—that was unimportant compared with the other difficulty which faced them . . . when they came to set their thoughts on paper—that is that they had no tradition behind them, or one so short and partial that it was of little help. For we think back through our mothers if we are women. It is useless to go to the great men writers for help. (*A Room of One's Own*, 79)

Who were Ling Shuhua's literary mothers? Woolf did offer advice, and they did correspond in English; nevertheless, she urged Ling Shuhua to write and to represent herself and the Chinese society she knew. Shuhua's use of the English language did not "subjugate" her to English culture but enabled her, unlike most of the English in this study, to traverse cultural boundaries with her linguistic gifts and to communicate with a great modernist writer in another country. Looking at Ling Shuhua's lyrical letters and writing now, it is remarkable to me, a teacher of English language and literature, how proficient and talented she was. Though polarized thinking about East and West often sets up what Mohanty labels a "negative relation" (*Third World Women*, 71), Woolf and Ling Shuhua's experiences are constituted differently. Their relationship and others like it challenge Mohanty and Gayatri Spivak's position that "the subaltern cannot speak" (Spivak, *The Post-Colonial Critic*, 308), altered, as it is, by the variables of class, education, language learning, political sympathy, personal affinity, and dedication to art. Whatever forms, methods, or cultural and publishing outlet that Ling Shuhua could not find in her own literature and culture at a particular literary and historical juncture, she found in another and this nurtured her own well of experience in China. These reservations, however, do not mitigate the importance of the work of Mohanty and Spivak, as well as the works of Leila Ahmed's *Women and Gender in Islam*, Abu-Lughod's *Veiled Sentiments*, and Lisa Lowe's *Critical Terrains*. They express the complexity and variety of experience, including being a woman, beneath the totalizing label, "East."

Despite cultural differences, Ling Shuhua and Woolf connect as women writers writing from a site of change and war, the British under the threat of World War II and the Chinese in the midst of the Sino-Japanese War and the civil war. They pose the question of how women writers should behave during times of national crisis. Ling Shuhua writes of the horror of the "colonial condition," China under siege by the Japanese imperialists. Both the personal and the national flow into the space of their letters bringing into relief "the obscure recesses of national culture from which alternative constituencies of people and oppositional analytic capacities emerge" (Bhabha, *Nation and Narration*, 3). They express their ambivalence about war, what Ling Shuhua terms "the miserable mind feeling," and their feelings of powerlessness as women to stop it. At the same time that they are discussing their powerlessness, Woolf is writing about women's desire to participate in decisions about war in her polemic *Three Guineas*.

Two discourses then, marginal to mainstream discourse in China and England, emerge in these letters: women struggling to claim their feelings and subjectivity as writers eclipsed during a time of war; women writing against the pro-war national trend in their own countries; women countering stereotypes of "feudal" or "imperial" thinking. The letters are fragmentary but they are forms of personal art that contribute to the shape of nation. Partha Chatterjee reminds us that the kinds of subjective exchange represented by Virginia Woolf and Ling Shuhua are "discourses situated within fields of power" (*The Nation and Its Fragments*, 137). The dominant discourse of the nation may challenge Woolf and Ling Shuhua's version of history in their letters, yet, as Foucault states, both "power" and "subjectivity" are part of the dialogue of any nation, a necessary struggle, a necessary "relation" for "power" to exist. Ling Shuhua and Virginia Woolf poised between the personal and the political— loyal to the subjective, to art, and to feeling for nation, and between the cultures of China and England—offer a rich "*inter*national dimension both within the margins of the nation-space and in the boundaries in-between nations and peoples" (Bhabha, *Nation and Narration*, 4). They both fear, as Ling Shuhua expressed, that "there is no one [who] care[s] to read something personal, for there is [are] many important things in the world that one [might] want to read" during a period of national crisis. Such conversations move us to an articulation of differences that create new kinds of narration about nation.

The correspondence began after Julian Bell's death in 1937. Woolf sent Ling Shuhua copies of *A Room of One's Own*, *The Years*, and *The Waves* as Julian had earlier requested. Ling's response to these modernist works is recorded in a short *Memoir*, particularly Woolf's feminist manifesto *A Room of*

One's Own: "One day I happened to come across and read Virginia Woolf's book *A Room of One's Own*, and I was quite carried away by her writing, so suddenly I decided to write and see if she were in my situation what she would do." Addressing the despairing woman who was caught in the turmoil of the Sino-Japanese War as well as the civil war in China in 1938, Woolf wrote, "think how you could fix your mind upon something worth doing in itself. I have not read any of your writing, but Julian often wrote to me about it. He said too that you have lived a most interesting life" (5 April 1938).

Often generous toward younger women writers (though not always with her competitors like Katherine Mansfield), and curious about where the accent falls in the language of foreign authors, Woolf makes up "the foreign" and "woman" in her writings, "made up, as one makes up the better part of life" (*Mrs. Dalloway*, 81). What interests her about foreign authors is their aesthetic practices—the "foreign tongue," the "angle" of vision, the "accent," the "stamp," the "emphasis laid upon such unexpected places that at first it seems as if there were no emphasis at all" ("Modern Fiction," 157). She does not pretend cultural knowing, enjoying like other modernists the state of "not knowing." It gives space to desire, to imagine and to create. In *A Room of One's Own*, Woolf notes that the novel "is a structure leaving its *shape* [emphasis added] on the mind's eye, novels build in squares, now *pagoda shaped* [emphasis added] now throwing out wings and arcades" (74). China, South America, and Africa contribute to the British creation of new shapes and spaces for modernists. Looking at different shapes of ceramics, for example, in China—I found saucers without cups, irregularly shaped bowls, large rain basins, jars with tripod bases—I began to understand the culture in shape. And, as Woolf presciently suggests, a culture in new shapes of the novel. Woolf says, "let us imagine a blazing South American landscape," in her essay "The Plumage Bill" (*Collected Essays*, 3:242), a landscape that is then realized in her novel *The Voyage Out*, though she has never traveled to South America. The "East" is then both a geographical place and a place of the mind and desire that Woolf and other English authors and artists invent at the beginning of the twentieth century. As Haun Saussy perceptively writes, "China has always been and still is in the process of being invented" (*The Problematics of Chinese Aesthetics*, 4).

Woolf constructs an image of the East. In this chapter then, we follow her making up "woman"—herself and Ling—at a particular moment and place in history, as well as in Julia Kristeva's supranational, "monumental time" as she travels across cultural and ideological boundaries to connect briefly with a writer and the aesthetic of the East. Her ideas of Asia begin, perhaps, with her reading of letters from traveling friends. She also does some literary reviews of translations of Chinese and Japanese works (including a 1925 review in *Vogue* of Arthur Waley's translation of Lady Murasaki), as well as poetry just becoming popular in England before World War I. In a 1913 review of Pu Songling's *Strange Stories* (*Liao Zhai Zhi Yi*), written in the second half of the eighteenth century, she alludes to their "queerness," particularly when compared to the robust English fiction of Henry Fielding and Samuel Richardson being written at the same time (*Collected Essays*, 2:7–9). To give an idea of the "slightness" of the stories, she suggests that "one must compare them to dreams, or the airy, fantastic, and inconsequent flight of a butterfly." One can sense the early attraction to both the poetic imagery and the taking of the strange to be true in these Chinese stories that will also draw her to Shuhua's writing. The fictional and cultural world of Pu Songling, says Woolf, is "topsy-turvy," and after reading them, she remarks, one feels "much as if one had been trying to walk over a bridge in a willow pattern plate" (*Collected Essays*, 2:7).

The Daughters of Educated Men: Ling Shuhua and Virginia Woolf

Virginia Woolf and Ling Shuhua were, as Shuhua said, the daughters of mandarins, or as Woolf would say, the daughters of educated men. Both were "the unconscious inheritors" of the cultural traditions in their respective countries; both resided in the figurative "tower" that Virginia Woolf described as "leaning" (*The Moment*, 139), or the "ivory pagoda" alluded to by Chinese critics. Both realized their privilege but also their disadvantages in not having access to the same education as men of their class, culture, and generation. In a paper she delivered at the Brighton Workers' Educational Association, later published as "The Leaning Tower" in 1940, Woolf describes the social confusions that the threat of war brought to England in the spheres of education, gender, class, and 1930s literature. She writes, "Then suddenly, like a chasm in a smooth road, the war came" (136). Woolf positions herself and other women of her generation as outside of or unable to come down from the English "tower" that is leaning more and more to the left in the 1930s. She separates women from the men of her generation:

> We are not in their position; we have not had eleven years of expensive education. We can cease to imagine. We can come down. But they cannot. They

cannot throw away their education; they cannot throw away their upbringing. Eleven years at school and college have been stamped upon them indelibly. ("Leaning Tower," 141)

Though in *A Room of One's Own,* Woolf will argue for women's access to education at Oxbridge, in *Three Guineas,* she begins to appreciate the unique psychological and cultural position of women who have been deprived of this education. Being both "inside" and "outside" the culture, members of the "outsider's club" can critique it. This notion of being "outsiders" as women but "insiders" as privileged inheritors of the cultural traditions of their nations informs the letters of Woolf and Ling Shuhua.

The psychological and cultural constriction of feminine space that Woolf describes in *A Room of One's Own* was familiar to Ling Shuhua. Though there are critics who might say that Shuhua's is "a Western-mediated feminism" (Shi Shumei, *Lure of the Modern,* 220), the fact is that Ling, as the daughter of a concubine of the Mayor of Peking, had ample opportunities as a child to observe the sad lives of women in the feudal concubine system. The holographs as well as the autobiography of *Ancient Melodies* demonstrate that she was a listener to the stories of the six mothers who were her fathers' concubines. Statements like "I listened to their gossip" and "I enjoyed listening to a story" that her mother told about Second Mother mark the narrative. She heard different points of view on the same stories as she stated that she would sit quietly beside her maid in the servants' quarters after supper when they would chatter about the appearance, characters and jealousies of the six mothers. One day, she heard of a new mother coming into the house, "but why should Fifth Mother weep the whole day?" (*Ancient Melodies,* 51). At other times, she would watch her father's face "unmoved" as he sat at a big black table in his study, calmly writing characters as part of his lifelong practice of calligraphy, while the crying and "abusive words" of the mothers could be heard in the background. She gazed at him and wondered if he felt sorry about their quarrels, surely about him: "but I did not dare to ask" (97). Observing his neglect and the frustrating lives of the mothers, she wryly observed, "that Father had something to do with it" (*Ancient Melodies,* 97). That was his habit." What better training for a writer? Woolf has remarked that "all the literary training that a woman had in the early nineteenth century was training in the observation of character, the analysis of emotion" (*A Room of One's Own,* 70). Ling Shuhua could be Jane Austen "listening" in the common sitting room or Eudora

Welty sitting on the porch "listening" to the conversations of her southern family, in training to write. It was mainly the daily stories that she heard about her mother's life as well as the other mothers that probably fashioned the feminist subjectivity, evident in her stories and autobiography. Where does the feeling of "unendurable shame" (*Ancient Melodies,* 100) come from when she hears her father apply the word "silly" to her pretty and wise mother? Why is she so curious about Cousin Feng who, she records in her autobiography, will make a "new fashioned marriage," a modern couple rather than the concubine arrangement that Ling Shuhua observed as a child? (*Ancient Melodies,* 246*ff*) It cannot be denied, however, that Woolf's feminist slant reinforced her attitudes and encouraged her to think along certain feminist lines, as discussed in this chapter.

In one of the stories in the holograph, Ling Shuhua, a listening child, learns that Second Mother wants to make father neglect her mother and Fifth Mother, and is working hard to get a Sixth mother in the family, so that father's property will be held by her. Motivated by economics and jealousy, Second Mother tries to displace father's affection for Fifth Mother. As I read of the complex and byzantine family intrigues among the mothers, I understood why Julian Bell compared Shuhua's stories to Russian novels, and why she herself struggled in her writing with keeping all the characters straight for the reader unfamiliar with the traditional family structure of the wealthy men of the time. In Ling Shuhua's extended family, First Mother has died; Second Mother is mean-spirited and always trying to psychologically and pragmatically outmaneuver the other wives so that she can inherit the father's property; Fourth Mother, her own, often tries to negotiate squabbles; Fifth Mother is a gentle soul abused by Second Mother; and Sixth Mother, the addition to the family at Second Mother's urging, is married, has a son, but according to Ling Shuhua's mother, is being "bought" from her husband by Ling Shuhua's father. The mothers do not like her, consider her commonplace, as "she looked like a maid to others." There was much erotic intrigue, Ling Shuhua hinted at in *Ancient Melodies,* probably because Julian Bell had urged her to write openly about sexuality against the current of Chinese tradition. It was not Bloomsbury, because most of the freedom belonged to the men, but Ling Shuhua slyly includes the ways in which the women retaliate against father and the social system that oppresses them. Second Mother, one of the most aggressive, lures father from Fourth Mother's room one night, which is against the feudal custom. According to Ling Shuhua's mother, Second Mother was "beating on a night watchman's wood" one night (generally there was a night watchman in large houses in Beijing who beat this wood to give warning to thieves). Father was sleeping with Fourth Mother, and heard the banging, and yelled for it to stop. It didn't. Second Mother called out, "I can't go to sleep alone," and told father that if he did not come to her room she would "go out with another." Father was challenged and went to her room. Shuhua's mother simply observes, "A man simply go [went] after her like a cat." The other mothers, disliking Second Mother, speak of her as a "fox," not minding the gossip about her aggressive breaking of the sexual code and "losing face." We see in this society of women concubines that they had their own conventions and loyalties among themselves, and were on "better terms . . . when Father was away from the house" (158). Second Mother, after this incident, according to cultural cue ironically "felt sorry for father because he was bullied by Second Mother." The "face" of father in this world was the one that counted the most.

The challenge for Ling Shuhua in capturing this complicated family relationship is to shape her life and control the characters. Shuhua's considerable gift for description, her painter's eye, is evident throughout the autobiography but her ability to plot, to control the many characters in her narrative, to develop mature themes, and to sustain interest in the "interior" sometimes falters. The issue of writing an autobiography given the multiple characters, so many wives and mothers in the traditional Chinese family, as in the traditional Russian novel, is a narrative challenge.

In another part of the autobiography, father tells a story about his friend Chiang, who is being beaten, "tortured to death," and forced to "kneel down on the handkerchief for three days" by his concubine. Father goes to the rescue and advises Chiang to openly confess his infidelities to his concubine to ease the tension in their relationship. When the mothers listening to father's story ask him, "But what is your magic to deal [in dealing] with women?" He answers:

> Women are most practical creatures, they only yield to fact. If you could make them see the facts, and don't hide anything from them, they will do anything. . . . They don't like to bother themselves about this mistress thing.

Shuhua then continues, writing from the perspective of the child-observer, "What do you mean by fact? I forgot who asked this question which I too wanted to know very much but didn't dare put. 'Fact is the thing you have done.' Father gave a very clear answer but I did not quite get the idea of his meaning for a very long time" (holograph, *Ancient Melodies*). And so the stories continue about father, the wealthy mayor of Beijing, about fifty years old with his six concubines all under the age of twenty-five, according to Ling Shuhua. When tear-stained Second Mother laments to Fourth Mother that she is depressed and worried about her future in this configuration of women, Fourth Mother pauses and tells her that she used to sing a ballad, "Pretty flowers never think of their future. Shortest song, the sweetest, bright moon, the shortest." She urges Second Mother to look at her life in a way that will not bring too much unhappiness to herself and others. The prevailing philosophy among the concubines was that "a man's heart is like a needle in the sea, one never captures it." Is it any wonder then that Ling Shuhua with this well of stories about women living under repressive old-style feudal conventions would seek to write about liberated women, and, indeed, be one herself?

Ling Shuhua was also fascinated with stories of women getting an education in a system that excluded them, echoing Virginia Woolf's argument in *A Room of One's Own*. But unlike Virginia Woolf's father, Shuhua's did not invite her into his study to read freely. Shuhua writes:

> In his study, along the walls there were shelves, full of big books. I always wondered what could be printed in them. . . . Sometimes I almost made up my mind to go ask father to let me have a look at those neglected books, but as soon a 6th mother's long face covered with dead-white powder appeared in my mind, it was like a white wall standing in the way, which at once stopped my going. (*Ancient Melodies*, 66)

Later in her autobiography, she fantasizes manly disguises that will enable her to take Imperial Court examinations, laborious tests that required long years of preparation that qualified scholars for important government posts, and which were abolished in 1902. Arthur Waley translated a poem, "After Passing the Examinations," written in 800, during the Tang Dynasty, reflecting this long tradition:

> For ten years I never left my books;
> I went up . . . and won unmerited praise.
> My high place I do not much prize;
> The joy of my parents will first make me proud.
> Fellow students, six or seven men,
> See me off as I leave the City gate.

My covered couch is ready to drive away;
Flutes and strings blend their parting tune.
Hopes achieved dull the pains of parting;
Fumes of wine shorten the long road . . .
Shod with wings is the horse of him who rides
On a Spring day the road that leads to home.
(Translations, 138)

Ling Shuhua's uncle assures her that when she is grown up, "examinations of all kinds will be open to women" (*Ancient Melodies,* 149). Like Woolf in *A Room of One's Own,* Shuhua desires to enter institutions then forbidden to women. But significantly, the "white wall" that shuts out the view is the powdered face of her powerful Sixth Mother, not the flapping black wings of the male beadle on Woolf's Oxbridge lawn. Though the alarm about women's learning is sounded in both cultures, it is important to note the differences. In a society where the father is absent and the female concubines (his six wives) socialize young women into the male-dominated culture, it is the "white" female face that collaborates with patriarchy and that shuts out the view: male power remains hidden.

Ling Shuhua grew up in a wealthy, cultured Chinese household in which artists and writers gathered. She was the fourth child of the fourth concubine, and tenth daughter of the mayor of Beijing during the period depicted in Zhang Yimou's movie *Raise the Red Lantern.* Her father was a member of the Hanlin Academy in Beijing and secretary at court, and was chosen to go to Japan as an ambassador to inspect improvements made during Meiji reform. In the story "Childhood in China," which later appeared in *Ancient Melodies,* she describes how on certain days of each month her father as mayor of Beijing would sit as the judge of final appeal in the courts. Hiding behind a wooden screen, Shuhua would witness his treatment of the prisoners. She describes his "womanly kindness" in these proceedings, and says, "his voice sounded as kind as when he spoke to his own children." Her interest is piqued, however, by the case of a young woman who had murdered her mother-in-law. Shuhua's compassion for the plight of the woman, known as a "dashing beauty" in the district, is evident as she describes her address to her father, the judge:

"My blue sky lord"—the woman prisoner addressed father as other prisoners did, but her voice seemed so powerful that the court became silent suddenly—"to tell the truth, I am not the person who has killed my mother-in-law, for she had been killing me . . . My mother-in-law actually had tried to kill me many times before I killed her. Any one of our neighbourhoods could be my witness. All of them have seen how miserable I have been in my house. I work as hard as a cow or a donkey day after day, sometimes even worse than these animals, because they are allowed to meet their husbands, while I. . . . ." ("Childhood in China," 724)

Culturally prescient, Shuhua highlights the fraught relations between mother and daughters-in-law in China, as did her enlightened friend and dramatist Yuan Changying, one of the three talents of Luojia, in her drama *Southeast Flies the Peacock*. But the incident in the story has a Rashomon-like quality rippling into Ling Shuhua's home and imagination, meaning different things to different people. Shuhua remarks that whenever she sees a young woman "with a pale think face, and a pair of bright black eyes, walking like a willow branch shaking in the wind, I think of the woman prisoner." Poetic, visual images distinguish her writing: a woman "walking like a willow branch shaking in the wind" in this story, or her mother and her aunt dressing hair, "their pretty white hands moving up and down on the black hair like magnolia petals as they fall" (*Ancient Melodies,* 141). Aware of the jealousies and tensions among her father's six wives, Shuhua's mother tells another version of the story years later. Her mother asserts that the "fox-like" woman prisoner was trying to seduce the mayor. When Fifth Mother asks if the prisoner was pretty and the mayor assents, Fifth Mother hurls an insult, and father throws a cup of hot tea at her. That night, Fifth Mother takes an overdose of opium but is saved by a doctor. The fears about the mayor taking a new mistress had caused panic among the concubines of the house. When Shuhua later asked her father about the beauty of the prisoner, he remarks:

> I think she was a great beauty. But she was like the flower in the mirror and the moon in the water. Your fifth mother made a mistake, for I never would be such an idiot as to try to pick the flower in the mirror, although it is true I feel enjoyment when I look at it. ("Childhood in China," 724)

The repressive roles of the mother-in-law and the patriarch, and the helpless position of the several wives in the traditional family structure of China are cultural targets in Shuhua's retelling, as is the brutal mother and daughter-in-law relationship. Vanessa Bell, after reading this story in the *Spectator*, observed that Ling Shua had "managed to make something lovely out of a rather horrible experience," and she praised her ability to "make one feel it from the child's point of view which is very rare" (Letter to Ling Shuhua, 7 November 1950).

Aware that she does not bear the value of a son, Ling Shuhua, is, nevertheless, like Woolf lifted by her father from the domain of women because of her talent at painting:

> Being the fourth child of my mother and tenth daughter of the family, I was naturally neglected. . . . I often felt unhappy when I considered that I was only a girl . . . [but] when my father knew I could paint, I suddenly became his favourite child. (*Ancient Melodies*, 201)

She also spoke nearly all of the dialects of China (LS to LW, 28 September 1953). In the end, much is left out of the autobiography, including her relationship with her sister Mei, who is briefly mentioned. Mei, the fourteenth daughter of the family, according to Shuhua's daughter, Ying Chinnery, was born in 1903 and moved to San Francisco, where she married K. K. Chen, a successful businessman in pharmacology. Later when the scandal of her relationship with Julian Bell broke out in November 1936, Ling Shuhua thought of visiting her sister in America. It must be remembered that Shuhua was not only writing under the constraints of what was acceptable for a woman to write of her life and loves in this autobiographical form (from the late 1930s to mid–1950s), but she was also repressing information about her life that might be damaging to her daughter or husband's reputation. For Ling Shuhua to begin to write as she did in the late 1930s about herself was a daring act; nevertheless, she confined her autobiographical narrative, which was not published until 1953, to her childhood and college years, avoiding the more complex experiences of her adulthood. Her writing is constrained, though revealing at times. Her silence is based on her family feeling, the political and cultural transgression of having a relationship with a Westerner, and the personal need to "save face" after the "scandal." Vanessa Bell used this word to describe the end of the affair in a letter to Ling Shuhua (13 June 1939). This personal motivation, more than Janet Ng's postcolonial assessment—"her feelings of frustration writing as a foreign writer from a politically subjugated nation for an audience of the subjugating nation"—probably determined her "speaking in a clipped tongue" (Ng, "Writing in Her Father's House," 239).

Though Bloomsbury wrote (more or less) freely of erotic life, Shuhua, as a Chinese woman, had no precedent for this, though she was of a generation of women writers bred in the liberalizing May Fourth literary movement. She adopted the traditional stance of the naïve observer like many women writers of the time who had been writers of children's stories. It is a "safe" viewpoint to adopt as part of a transgressive literary and cultural strategy: a child can reveal the corruption, injustice, and violence in society under the cover of being a child without the social accountability of a mature adult. Despite the fact that much is left out of her autobiography, *Ancient Melodies,* cracks of feeling develop and the words "misery" and the "fate of women" are repeated. Remarking that she learned to understand these words from her mother, she writes of Ju-lan's life. Her mother refused to "marry a man who could only read half a page of Chinese characters" (*Ancient Melodies,* 28): a marriage was then arranged to one of the wealthiest men in Beijing. The scenes of heightened jealousy among the concubines—jealousy is the "breaking of their vinegar jars"—are particularly vivid. Though her mother was positioned for jealousy, Shuhua describes her as a good friend to the other wives. Wryly, she observes that her "charming" father was "a type of Chinese gentleman who never missed a chance of enjoying life, and he was lucky, he got it all."

The question remains: who is Shuhua? Her relations with Bloomsbury began because of Margery Fry who visited China in 1934 and "the great connector" and poet, Xu Zhimo, years before she met Julian Bell. Xu Zhimo, as discussed earlier, was a good friend of Chen Yuan (her husband) and Shuhua's, and when he visited Cambridge from 1920 to 1922, he carried Ling Shuhua's friendship scroll. T. T. Wang, in a letter to Leonard Elmhirst, notes Chen Yuan's relationship with Xu: "Of his very close friends in those days [1920s–30s], however, one is still living in London. He is Professor Chen Yuan, China's permanent delegate to UNESCO" (20 March 1920).

When she first writes to Margery Fry in January 1934, she connects personally and aesthetically with the margins of Bloomsbury. But we get our sense of Shuhua—a new figure in the Bloomsbury constellation—through letters. Previous to some letters made available after her death in 1990, discretion dictated that she not be named. In 1953, Aileen Pippett notes that "a friend from China recognized at Monk's House . . . objects that she had helped Julian Bell to buy at a fair in Beijing in 1936." And, as mentioned earlier, Peter Stansky and William Abrahams discreetly refer to Shuhua as "K" in "Julian Bell in China" in *Journey to the Frontier,* the important book that began the exploration that this study continues. This cryptic initial "K" then becomes the title of a novel by Hong Ying published first in Chinese about which there is a lawsuit questioning the borders between fiction and biography. In addition, Francis Spalding wrote to Ling Shuhua in 1982 when writing her biography of Vanessa Bell that she had "altered the passages you wish me to change." She also sent her a copy of an article about Virginia Woolf and Ling Shuhua that appeared in the *Virginia Woolf Miscellany* (Spalding to Ling Shuhua, 4 October 1982, Berg).

But in Ling Shuhua's letters to Virginia Woolf, we read of her aspirations to write an autobiography in English, her "miserable mind feeling" during the war, and hints of suicide; in her correspondence with Vanessa, of her painterly interests and her relationship with Julian; in the few available letters to Julian, her self-torture and passion; and in the letters to Leonard Woolf after Julian's death, her pragmatic drive and desire to succeed as a writer in England. To be responsible to the genre of the letter, however, we must pay attention to dialogue. To whom is the letter written and what is the recipient's response? Both are part of a letter writer's flickering aspects of self, revealed to different people. Since few of Shuhua's letters are available, the portrait sketched here is constructed from "scraps, orts and fragments": her writings, some Chinese commentators, and Bloomsbury responses to her letters. We observe her mostly through English eyes—each unveiling a different facet of her culture or personality. Occasionally, we read her own representation in her autobiography or in the few letters we have. And we have impressions from a contemporary, Ye Junjian, one of Julian Bell's favorite students at National Wuhan University when he taught there 1935–37. Ye Junjian knew not only Julian, but also the dean of Humanities, Chen Yuan, who was also his teacher and Ling Shuhua's husband. In an interview, Ye Junjian revealed that he knew Shuhua and Chen Yuan very well, and that indeed the dean had hired Julian to teach at Wuhan. He described Ling Shuhua as "a painter, then a story writer that even the people of the Progressive group [leftist]—like Mao Dun—also appreciated her writing" (Interview by the author). Later on, when Ling Shuhua and Ye Junjian were in England in the late forties, they used to meet. When asked if she was beautiful, Ye replied, "Well, not beautiful, but she was cultured. It was quite enjoyable to have a conversation with her about everything but politics. A quite enjoyable pastime. She was also vivacious." (interview with Innes Jackson). Shuhua sparkled at conversation and gossip, the mainstay of Bloomsbury.

Shuhua, when living at Wuhan, was also considered one of the "three talents of Luo Jia," along with Yuan Changying, a writer who died towards the end of the Cultural Revolution in 1976, and Su Xuelin, a writer and professor of literature at Wuhan who published an essay on Shuhua after her death in *Luo Jia,* July 1990. Xu Zhengbang, archivist at Wuhan University, described Shuhua as the youngest of the talented three and "open and beautiful" (Interview by the author). Su Xuelin agrees, describing Shuhua in 1926 at her first meeting as "really beautiful and elegant like her literary style." But Su had reservations about her honesty. In her 1990 essay, Su corrects some of Shuhua's misrepresentations, stating that she never taught at Wuhan University, though she claimed she did, asserting that she got a job at the University of South Asia teaching Chinese only because Su herself had recommended her, and that she taught for only one year, not four. She concluded that Shuhua probably had difficulties in performing as a teacher. "That's why her husband Chen Tongbo [Chen Yuan] did not let her teach even for an hour when he was dean of Humanities at Wuhan University," Su Xuelin wrote for *Luo Jia.* Despite these peccadilloes, Su Xuelin acknowledged Ling Shuhua's talent as a writer of elegant prose and as a painter, though Ying Chinnery, Shuhua's daughter, asserted in an interview that "Su Xuelin disliked my mother." Sadly, Su Xuelin reported that Shuhua lived a rather isolated life in London in her old age and was robbed of precious personal possessions by a "house robber" boarder, perhaps some of the letters pursued in this study. In her lifetime, her literary reputation was small compared to Ding Ling and Bing Xin, and other women writers of her generation (partly due to the censure of educated, western-identified writers), though her literary position, as well as that of the Crescent Moon group, has been reaffirmed by recent scholarship in the PRC.

The "three talents of Luojia," the local reference to Ling Shuhua, Su Xuelin, and Yuan Changying at Wuhan University, were an interesting triad of women writers drawn to European thinking and writing in the 1930s. Luojia, a hill in Wuhan, has long been a landmark of Wuhan. Yuan Changying was considered one of the most talented dramatists of the May Fourth era, but her literary reputation suffered the death of so many others during the Cultural Revolution. Born in Hunan to a wealthy family, she, like Ling Shuhua, was sent abroad for her education, 1916–21 at Edinburgh University, receiving a master's degree in English drama. While abroad, she met Chen Yuan, and eventually some of her work appeared in his journal, *Contemporary Review.* She focused on literary translation and criticism after a period of writing drama. Her play *Southeast Flies the Peacock* (1930), translated by Amy Dooling in an anthology of women's literature, *Writing Women in Modern China,* and later produced by John Weinstein in Cambridge, Massachusetts, 1997, reveals that there is not "anything more difficult in life than being a daughter-in-law" in China during certain periods. This play, set in the Han period with anachronisms from the 1930s, portrays a mother's extreme, cloying love for her son, and jealousy of her daughter-in-law. Though one finds cloying mother-son relationships in the British tradition, in, for example, D. H. Lawrence's *Sons and Lovers,* what alienates a modern reader is the extremity of the situation, the brutality of the mother, and the psychologically unbelievable dutifulness (to the point of death) of the son. A contemporary American reader reads for the psychology and credibility of such a family; the Chinese reader of the time for a moral or national allegory. In these different ways of reading lie many misunderstandings. Though the beautiful Miss Lan "cures" the son's illness, a kind of anomie, she earns the undying hatred and abusive treatment of the mother-in-law, and the dying love of the ineffectual son. Using a Bakhtinian analysis, one can hear, throughout the play, a dialogue between the feudal thinking of the mother and the modern thinking of the young people. This is illustrated in the mother's discussion of women's "virtue" and criticism of Mei, the daughter-in-law, because "the less talented a woman is, the more virtuous." The son and daughter, unable to cope with the circumscribed and cruel lives they lead, seek, as in many Chinese stories, a romantic resolution. They commit suicide together by drowning. When the mother finds the body of her son, she becomes a King Lear figure (with a strain of nationalism). The mother rails as "a fierce gust of wind blows her disheveled hair like the tattered flag of a defeated army, surrendering to an invisible enemy. The mournful sound of the wind is like the wailing of defeated soldiers" (Yuan, *Southeast Flies the Peacock,* 252). This drama, focusing upon and exposing the treatment of a daughter-in-law, ventures to question traditional family relations and the role of young wives. When it was performed at Wuhan University in 1935, according to Su Xuelin, another of the "talents," it received "hostile reviews from leftist critics who felt the play lacked relevance to China's struggle with Japan" (Dooling, *Writing Women in Modern China,* 210), despite the buried national metaphors. Though there is some powerful imagery in the drama, it appears to be literature written for a modern didactic purpose. Leftist critics considered this focus upon the familial and the personal a national betrayal in the 1930s.

The "three talents of Luojia": Su Xuelin, Ling Shuhua, Yuan Changying. By permission of the chief archivist, Wuhan University Library, China.

"The Miserable Mind Feeling": The War and Women's Writing

In 1937, Ling Shuhua wrote to Virginia Woolf from China to also express her interest in the personal—the individual life—and what was considered to be shameful in a time of national crisis and war—the desire to write. Yet for both women, language mediated their sense of loss. Shuhua lived through incredible cultural change from 1900 (though she would sometimes record her date of birth as 1904) to 1990. Born in the year of the Boxer Rebellion, she lived through China's transformation from the Qing Dynasty to republic in 1911, the Sino-Japanese War, 1937–45, the civil war between the communists and Guomindang, and she left in 1947, just before the establishment of the People's Republic of China in 1949. In the context of China's collective national needs, when every aspect of personal life was under attack, "feeling" and writing about the displacements of war was considered a luxury. They sensed the monstrous, depersonalizing effects of the war machine that threatened to silence the writer's personal voice in a world dominated by the "loudspeaker voice" of the government, the radio and the newspapers. "These years," said Elizabeth Bowen, "rebuff the imagination as much by being fragmentary as being violent." Woolf and Ling Shuhua's lives and communication were interrupted by the movements of the war, yet the letters dramatize the value of personal, cross-cultural conversation in which one artist may answer the needs of another who is oppressed by certain personal, cultural, or political conditions in her own country. They spoke, as Eudora Welty would say, not in the voice of countries but "individual" voices. Shuhua, traveling through war zones from Wuhan to Sichuan, was often in a state of nervous tension, a "refugees fate." She was in the actual midst of a brutal war that was still remote to Woolf, though later the incursions of war into British daily life would be noted in her *Diary*: the gunfire in the Channel; Hitler's voice on the wireless (see Laurence, "Facts and Fugue," 227*ff*). Woolf's encouraging letters— "don't despair"—that focus upon Shuhua's writing enabled her to sustain the effort psychologically during the geographical and cultural displacements of the war. We can hardly imagine the meaning and importance of Woolf's letters and books that were sometimes lost, and yet eventually found their way through personal contacts with missionaries and friendly postmistresses. Woolf herself feared, as the airplanes growled overhead, whether the book she was writing would be "like a moth dancing over a bonfire—consumed in less than one second" (*Diary*, 5:142). Virginia Woolf and Ling Shuhua lived and wrote under the influence of enormous change and the threat of war, and this as well as their birth and education brought them together.

Yet Ling Shuhua's autobiography and early letters also reveal the way in which we imagine and create ourselves and one another in cultural and literary conversation, as posited by Benedict Anderson. In the opening letters, we find in the style of Woolf, a certain quaintness, a stylized representation of the Chinese. As the correspondence develops and Ling Shuhua writes of the cities and people ravaged by the advancing Japanese, the bombings, the death, the sickness, the famine, the dislocation during the Sino-Japanese War, this quaint image of China shatters in the British imagination. The willow plate represented on the 1942 cover of the *New Yorker* is cracked, and writing under the threat or actuality of war, Shuhua and Virginia and Vanessa, artists in despair, connect. The *New Yorker* cover represents the shattering of the West's idyllic representation of China, a visual trope that had been salient for at least a century. China's new landscape included a Japanese flag and planes that fly above the romantic twin doves described as star-crossed lovers in antique Chinese iconography. It is this period of cultural flux and reflection that this study represents.

Shuhua wrote to Woolf to express her "miserable mind feeling" about the Sino-Japanese War. As the correspondence continued, Shuhua wrote in 1938 of the "ruined houses" in China, reminding us of Woolf's descriptions of photos of the "dead bodies and ruined houses that the Spanish government sends almost weekly" noted in *Three Guineas* (68). Ling Shuhua's scene of war reverberates in China:

> During these last weeks as all bad news brought out at once; we lost [Guangzhou] unexpectedly and Hankow [Hankou] had to withdraw our troops, and the West being in a helpless condition. . . . As I understand that it is useless to go to the front to fight for we cannot find our enemy, we only see the machines . . . I dream . . . I saw my house in the ruin and broken furnitures, outside the house the laying corpse, the unburied corpses smelling badly, I think perhaps you would like to know a bit of extreme miserable mind feeling so I wrote this to tell you. (Letter to VW, 16 November 1938)

She writes of having to face this "helpless condition" every day: "Japanese aeroplanes had come to visit West China 3 times a week recently. I feel quite the same as a month ago. Death does not make any difference to my thought now" (1938). She hints at suicide in a few letters, prescient about Woolf's own predisposition. Continuing her description of the effect of the war on women, she mentions a Wuhan college girl's suicide, just as Woolf had alluded to the rape of a girl by soldiers in her novel, *Between the Acts:*

> Just a few weeks ago, a college girl of the Wu Han [Wuhan] University had committed suicide. . . . She dies because Hankow [Hankou] was occupied by the Japanese and she could not hear from her family. (12 December 1938)

She continues the description of the girl in another letter: "Her death gives me a surprise because I know I have been much unhappy than what she has had, but she had courage to put an end to it" (12 December 1938). Here she hints at suicidal thoughts, another feeling shared with Virginia Woolf, who committed suicide in 1941.

Su Xuelin, a writer, professor at Wuhan, and friend of Shuhua's, also wrote of this period of turmoil when the university moved to Sichuan in 1939:

> As the War of Resistance against the Japanese Invaders broke out, Wuhan University moved to Leshan, Sichuan province, so did we. . . . In 1939, enemy airplanes threw bombs, turning Leshan into ashes, thousands of

people died. . . . Later enemy planes often flew over. We were concerned with sirens and the rising price of daily accomodations, let alone having time to write and research. (*Luo Jia*, no. 104, 1990)

During this period, Ling Shuhua made a distinction, as we often do today, between the people and the foreign policy of a country. Having fled to West China where she continued to endure the Japanese bombings, she, nevertheless, claimed, "In my heart, I often feel I love Japanese ordinary people not less than I do Chinese. But why do we have to fight?" (12 December 1938). Ling Shuhua spent 1927 in Japan with her family and had developed cultural sympathies: one can appreciate the sentiment, though politically volatile at the time, and later damaging to her reputation. The imagery of the "machine" surfaces in these letters written from a sixteenth-century village with small temples where the people worship gods and ghosts, making us aware of how modern weapons of destruction were perceived in China at the time. She observes "little children who never had the pleasure to ride on a train or a motor car" who could tell you the difference between the Chinese and Japanese planes. She tells of soldiers who "never saw a tank or machine gun" being confronted by these modern armaments in the front lines of the Japanese. Seeing the corpses of the conscripted soldiers piling up, she thinks of their lives as "too sad to tell."

Vanessa too wrote to Ling Shuhua during this period and observed from England how "the war seems to cut one off from the rest of the world . . . one can hardly believe now in a world in which there wont be war or the fear of war." She described their daily life at Charleston to Shuhua:

> Here we are just at the beginning [December 1939], yet so far there have been none of the horrors one was told to expect and perhaps they wont come at least not to England . . . [Angelica] and I and Duncan who is here too all do a good deal of painting. Also we do a certain amount of work in the garden and keep chickens and ducks and generally lead a country life with occasional visits to London. But London is rather gloomy with all in the pitch dark. . . . Please be as happy as you can manage in spite of all—I know Julian would have told you the same. (5 December 1939)

Shuhua traveled to Leshan in Sichuan Province, Western China, with her daughter, Ying: "we think we are safe from bombing by our enemy but we might be killed by several kinds of special diseases. It's alright for us at present, because I always think being a Chinese, one has to look for hardship, preparing the worst of luck, then by and by one may learn to amuse oneself with misery" (24 July 1938). She mentioned Hitler also, stating that he "would never believe that his dam policy even brings distress to a poor little woman in the Far East" (16 November 1938). A year later, Shuhua wrote, "everybody wants peace, but nobody dares tell it. It is said Japan is going . . . to bomb. . . . The most ugly and painful scenes are those conscripted soldiers in Sichuan I see every day . . . prisoners . . . hungry" (11 January 1939). Earlier, in 1936, Mr. Xu Zhengbang related in an interview that Ling Shuhua had made clothes for needy Chinese soldiers and donated money for their well being. Woolf responded that she and Leonard were going down to Sussex "waiting for what Hitler may do next. People are tired of talking about war; but all the same we do nothing but buy arms. The air is full of aeroplanes at the moment." Woolf reported in another letter that she and Leonard were considering moving the Hogarth Press from London and shutting it up altogether during the war because "nobody will read anything but politics" (17 April 1939).

Woolf's state of mind in these little-known letters echo Beckett's stance, "I can't go on. I'll go on." They reveal the despair that Woolf also experienced at the end of her life as an artist struggling with her art to resist the depersonalizing effects of the war and the collapsing civilization around her. The words "I wish I could help you" reverberate throughout her letters to Shuhua as they do in Vanessa's. Importantly, Vanessa's letters were healing as she referred to Julian whom they both loved. She visualized her Charleston garden for Shuhua who loved plants and flowers in descriptive words for a painter: "It's full spring here and our garden has blue, pink, white flowers—and all the hills are deep green; but very small. Our little river is about the size of a large snake; Julian used to wade across it and sail a tiny boat" (17 April 1939).

In Woolf's next to last letter to Ling Shuhua, 16 July 1939, she related that Harold Nicolson, who was then a Labor member for West Leicester in the Parliament, stated that the war "must come next month." She wearily commented on the refugees, the airplanes and the shelters in England and expressed great despair: "one is so numb that it seems impossible to feel anything, save that dull vague gloom." Nevertheless, she said that the British were getting used to things, but noted that "it will be different when it comes. Like you I find work the best thing." Writing to Shuhua, who was already in the midst of the horrors of war in China, Woolf prepared herself. She ended her letter, "With my love and believe in my sympathy, futile as it seems." Each of their letters suggests the tensions of war, the temperamental and psychological vulnerabilities and the need to write. In spite of all, Woolf encouraged the progress of Ling Shuhua's autobiography and sent books to set her thinking about the genre.

Woolf's advice was—*work*—the stance that always saved her and Vanessa in times of distress. She notes in one letter that she and Vanessa are meeting to talk: "These little meetings are the best things we have at present. We talk about pictures not about war" (16 July 1939). To Shuhua, she says, "think how you could fix your mind upon something worth doing in itself" (5 April 1938) during this period of turmoil. Shuhua wrote and remarkably learned to type, and despite the vagaries of the mail during this period, sent chapters of her autobiography to Woolf over the period of their year and a half correspondence. She asserted that "among many women, I think I am a fighter" (31 December 1938), and brandished her work as

> the only single sparker which gives me fire and strength to linger upon life. Being faced with the great disaster of a whole nation, one feel personal sorrow is not something worth mention, yet it is the very thing one has to taste every day and night. (Letter to VW, 12 December 1938)

It was this sense of individualism, this sense of herself as a writer, that saved Ling Shuhua, though such "detachment" and alignment with art was considered *criminal* during this period of desperation, as discussed in the last chapter on literary communities. Though she sadly reported that "the war in China seems last longer and longer than anyone could think about it only half a year ago, one cannot help feeling it might be by God's will that he intends to put an end on the yellow race" (12 December 1938). Nevertheless, Ling Shuhua wrote and rewrote her autobiographical chapters.

In 1936, Julian Bell had sent some of her short stories to David Garnett in England to circulate, but R. A. Scott-James of the *London Mercury* rejected them in August of that year. A decade later China was in the news in England because of the Sino-Japanese War and the civil war between the Guomindang and the communists. This new political and cultural interest perhaps helped the publication of one of Shuhua's stories, "Childhood in China," in the *Spectator*, 22 December 1950. Vanessa Bell mentioned reading the story that recounts a father's judgment of a young woman who is put on trial after murdering her mother-in-law, a revolutionary topic, given the general "dutiful" behavior of Chinese daughters-in-law to the oft represented brutality of the mother. Given the mistreatment of many young women culturally condoned as part of a Confucian system of family hierarchy, Shuhua's story blasted what was a "horrible experience . . . from the child's point of view" (Berg, 7 December 1950). A year later, Vanessa thanked Shuhua for the copy of *Country Life* which contained "your charming account of your old gardener and drawings" (part of her autobiography) noting that it was "unusual in England for anyone to do both" (Berg, 28 February 1951).

Ling Shuhua's Writerly Self

In her letters, Ling Shuhua cast Virginia Woolf in the role of *laoshi*, "teacher." After five months of correspondence, Shuhua wrote to Woolf from Leshan, Sichuan, Western China, where she had fled with her daughter:

> When you tell me I'm not hopeless in writing will you allow me to call you my teacher or my tutor when I next write to you? A teacher to a real Chinese's mind (I mean who have not been changed by Western influence) is equally highly respect and intimate as well as parents and brothers. I am not certain what this word means to English people. (24 July 1938)

Woolf responded, not understanding the title of respect in China, "Please call me Virginia. I do not like being Mrs. Woolf" (27 July 1938). Shuhua avoided using the name "Chen" (her husband's name) in her correspondence also, requesting in an early letter to Woolf that she call her "Sue" as "I feel it's not becoming being a Mrs. Chen to write this letter to you; she also used her pen name "Ling Shuhua." Shuhua changed her form of address, and sent chapters of her autobiography over the period of a year and a half. Struggling with and writing in her second language in the genre of autobiography, new to her, she wondered about her "tools," making a charming comparison between cooking with foreign implements and writing in a second language:

> I know there is very little chance for me to write a good book in English for the tool I use to do my work is something which I can not handle well. It is true in cooking too, if one uses a foreign pin [foreign pan] or stove to cook a Chinese dish, it won't come out the same as the original. It often loses some good taste. In writing I don't know how far it counts. When I read a

good translation, I feel a relief at once . . . Dear Virginia, I want you to tell me what shall I do since I am in a state of nervous tension. Oh, yet, how I hope you would be as kind as before to tell me to try it, don't despair. (31 December 1938)

Woolf appraised Shuhua's chapters, noting "a charm in the unlikeness. I find the similes strange and poetical" (Monk's House, 15 October 1938). Woolf valued the "foreignness" in her style, and urged her "to keep the Chinese flavor" (28 February 1939):

> Please go on; write freely. Do not mind how directly you translate the Chinese into the English. In fact I would advise you to come as close to the Chinese both in style and meaning as you can. Give as many natural details of the life of the house, of the furniture as you like. And always do it as if you were writing Chinese. (Monk's House, 15 October 1938)

Countering the advice of most teachers of English as a second language today, Woolf encouraged Shuhua to "think" and write in Chinese, then translate into English. She dismissed Shuhua's worry about English grammar, and told her to resist the common practice of putting her work into formal English prose. She countered that if the manuscript were, to some extent, "made easy grammatically by someone English I think it might be possible to keep the Chinese flavour and make it both understandable and yet strange for the English" (Monk's House, 15 October 1938). Woolf valued the "strangeness" of the writing, working with Shuhua to preserve it, much like the Chinese-American writer Gish Jen, rather than urging her to deny differences.

After reading Shuhua's autobiography, Vanessa also wrote how "charming" she thought it was, particularly "the fact" that life in a Chinese household is described by an artist. "How splendid to be able to both paint and write," she remarked as she looked over the sketches to be included in the 1953 autobiography, *Ancient Melodies.* Shuhua herself aspired to write something "true of culture, of things in themselves":

> If my book could give English readers some picture of real Chinese lives, some experience about Chinese who are as ordinary as any English people, some truth of life and sex which your people never have a chance to see it [is] even seen by a child in the East, I shall be contented. (Monk's House, 24 July 1938)

She distinguished herself from Pearl Buck, writing of her dislike of *The Good Earth*. Even though she has written "a good story to satisfy her readers," it is written according to stereotype and readers' expectations. In a letter to Leonard Woolf in 1952, Shuhua related her literary aspirations:

> I hope I could write a book which would express China and Chinese well. There are many books about China in the West most of them were written to satisfy the curiosity of the West. The authors sometimes tried to make stories about Chinese people from their imagination only. Their attitude towards their readers is not honest. Chinese people then appear to be sort of half ghost and half man beings in the West. (6 July 1952)

During the same period, Shuhua read Wang Suling's *Daughter of Confucius* and noted that Wang's American teacher "cooperated" with her in the writing of the book, and Shuhua prided herself on doing her own writing, allowing editing for her English or cultural information. "It is quite a different thing," she says of Wang Suling's work. "It is only a story in report-style. There had been published hundreds of books like that before. I'm afraid very few people want to read this kind of work. The style and the way of telling it is very ordinary" (Letter to LW, 10 September 1953). Such commentary reveals Shuhua's sensitivity to matters of style and her aspiration to experiment with the narration of her life. The holographs of her own autobiography reveal her attentiveness to word choice and style as she changes words like "embarrassing" to "ashamed" or "every" to "each" or to achieve the right tone, "children" to "little lords and ladies."

Vanessa also encouraged Shuhua to write her autobiography, assuring that "the English love autobiography and they are all the fashion" (VB to SL, 9 December 1938 or 1939). She also remarked that she was reading *The Good Earth*, testifying to Pearl Buck's influence on English and American perceptions of China as claimed by Peter Conn in his wonderful new biography of Buck. But Vanessa also wondered "if it gives any idea of China or a little of it" (Letter to JB, 4 September, 1936?).

When Virginia Woolf first wrote to Shuhua, she stated, "I often envy you, for being in a large wild place with a very old civilization" (17 April 1939). Here the tropes of China as antique, undeveloped, and geographically far away play in Woolf's imagination. Distance—geographical and cultural—is something that informs Virginia's early letters. But Julian, close by in China, responded differently. Shuhua recorded Julian's version of her in an early letter to Virginia:

> When Julian was in China he often told me that my life is a poem. I said because of the sadness and the character of my strong personality make him think so. He smiled. (*Memoir,* Berg)

Later, when Shuhua's husband discovered the affair between them, he denied Julian's knowledge: "I really don't think you really know her" (Yuan to JB, 29 January 1937). Shuhua, however, goes on to give a different version of herself to Woolf: "Among many women, I think I am a fighter" (31 December 1938).

After the war, Ling Shuhua found some peace for creativity. Su Xuelin described how Shuhua made a retreat, an attic room within a newly built house in Leshan:

> Opening the window of the clean attic, we enjoyed the faraway scenic beauty. At that time General Chen led his battalion, defeated the enemy several times, and the Japanese army was at its end. Without the enemy airplanes, we spent quiet, peaceful days here. Seizing this opportunity, Shuhua drew and painted, and she opened several exhibitions in Chengdu, Leshan very successfully and widely acclaimed. (*Luo Jia,* no. 104, 1990)

It should be noted that when Shuhua wrote to Virginia Woolf, she was already established as a short-story writer in China as well as a painter, but her reputation was minor compared to Woolf's. In her three short-story collections, *Flowers in the Temple* (1928), *Women* (1930), and *Two Little Brothers* (1935), Shuhua wrote of women's position in Chinese families and society—the married, unmarried, female students—relations between men and women, women's friendships, children, and deteriorating domestic situations. Her female characters "still have ghosts to fight, many prejudices to overcome" as does Woolf's "angel in the house." But it is not only the subject matter but also the narrative techniques that engage us. One of her stories, "What's the Point of It?" goes furthest in representing not just the material conditions of a woman's life but in rescuing and narrating her inner life, a new psychological and narrative exploration in China. In this story, she also represents women in relation to other women and not just men (as Virginia Woolf advises in *A Room of One's Own*). She represents the bored, pointless feelings of Ru Pi, an educated woman, as she reflects on her life in relation to women who cross her path during an ordinary day. The innovation of Shuhua is her focus on the "ordinary" and narrative technique as she tries to represent the consciousness of the woman through thoughts and conversation. She begins the story in the mind of Ru Pi:

> " . . . What an irritating sky. Its been raining for a week now, and as if that were not enough, it was black and gloomy again early this morning, and look, its already starting to rain." Ru Pi grumbled to herself as she got out of bed. Outside it was all right; the peach and pear blossoms had all fallen, and the trees are covered with young green leaves. But in the room there was a smell of damp and mold (1).

Compare the opening of *Mrs. Dalloway* on an admittedly finer day in June, which also begins with morning ruminations and is also narrated as an inner colloquy:

> Mrs. Dalloway said she would buy the flowers herself. For Lucy [her servant] had her work cut out for her. The doors would be taken off their hinges; Rumpelmayer's men were coming. And then, thought Clarissa Dalloway, what a morning—fresh as if issued to children on a beach. (1)

In Shuhua's story, Ru Pi then listens to some remarks about waste from her frugal maid, and reflects, "What she says is true. . . . " Later, she "thinks" as she looks at a neighborhood woman in her rickshaw,

> What made her look so haughty? There seemed to be no early reason for her coming. . . . When she went back up stairs, she still could not calm her mind. Looking over the roofs she saw that the tiles still lay as they did every day, firmly, one overlapping the other. Outside the flowers of the Chinese plants had already been replaced by the fruits. From the house on the East side came the sound of a woman crying (5).

Ru Pi then reflects on the roles of other women in Chinese society, particularly her maid. Cheng Ma, she observes, is intrusive in treating her mistress's property as if it were her own, and in choosing to keep moldy things in the cupboard that she has been directed to throw away. She is also both repelled and admiring of Mrs. Pai, the busy mother of six "monkies." She hears a young woman crying next door after having a scene with her husband; and she sees women shopping and discussing the prices of things. She responds cynically to the value of their lives, as well as the "laziness" of her own:

Looking at the neighbouring households she thought there was a great deal to be said for the scholar who had explained that the word for "home" (jia) is the same as that for "chains," and that the character is written as a pig under the roof.

But why should a reasonable person be chained, and why should someone whole and sound have to be fed like a pig? The more she thought about it the more depressed she felt, and at last she left the window and sank heavily onto a chair. It was true, though, a pig's life was pointless, except for eating and begetting and sleeping, sleeping and begetting and eating again; what more could you expect. Pig be calm and peaceful, stay in your pen! (6–7).

Feeling the pointlessness of her life, she looks at herself through the eyes of those of another class, her maid and a rickshaw driver (there were about 70,000 licensed and unlicensed rickshaw drivers in 1919). Shuhua's characterizations of women hardly represent an uncritical bourgeois stance, what the "realist" Chinese critics of the day had attacked in her writing. Ru Pi overhears a conversation of her maid with another maid, saying that she couldn't see the good of a woman sitting in her study. Feeling the sting of her maid's observation, Ru Pi pulls out a book she had begun to translate but let lapse a month ago. She works on a chapter of the translation and feels "her heart grow lighter" for a moment as she grasps the meaning of the book. But the pleasure doesn't last. When she goes out to shop in Hankou, the people who serve her in stores and the rickshaw driver classify her as "rich" and "important." She, however, notes the irony of being pulled along at full speed by a rickshaw driver and going nowhere important. "There was no reason at all that this young man should waste so much energy; it was a shame, a crime." Such ennui with its Chinese inflection is the state of mind explored by Flaubert in *Madame Bovary*, another bored, modern, married woman.

Interestingly, Ru Pi looks upon foreigners with admiration, something for which Chinese critics of the time excoriated her and the Crescent Moon group, an issue discussed in chapter 2, "Literary Communities in England and China." She notes the beauty of the places where foreigners live, "just like a garden," while "we Chinese never spend money on planting trees and flowers, and so the houses with their black smoky walls looks like pieces of rotten black stuff." Tired of the frugality and good advice of her servants, she longs for the beauty of the foreigner's university compound, but realizes too that "if there's trouble in China they [the foreigners] all run away." Such split attitudes toward the West—the attraction to the life style and the repulsion by some of the values—are an example of what Shi Shumei describes as the "bifurcation of the West as a discursive and a material presence in modern Chinese intellectual discourse" ("Gender, Race, and Semicolonialism," 953). Ru Pi, cosmopolitan, is drawn to the aesthetics and material living conditions of "foreigners" (Westerners), but is skeptical about their political loyalties to China. She is drawn to the "Western" aesthetics and lifestyle but is disgusted with the insensitive behavior, and illustrates in her attitude the two "Wests" that she perceives. Shuhua here deconstructs the notion, as other authors will, that there is a monolithic narrative about the West in Chinese culture and literature of the 1920s and 1930s. Ru Pi goes on—she thinks, sees, feels, sighs, and reflects on the meaning of her life as a "bourgeois" woman. But like Woolf in *Mrs. Dalloway*, Shuhua does not sketch the woman just to criticize a certain social class, but to reveal the inner life of a woman who feels that her life has become pointless. As in all good writing, we are above or beneath or beyond a simple categorization of "class" in Shuhua's stories. Chinese critics then and now who work to "socialize" or enforce predominant political or patriarchal values in the reading of Chinese literature neglect Virginia Woolf's idea of rescuing women in literature in *A Room of One's Own*:

> For I wanted to see how Mary Carmichael set to work to catch those unrecorded gestures, those unsaid or half-said words, which form themselves, no more palpably than the shadow of moths on the ceiling, when women are alone, unlit by the capricious and coloured light of the other sex. (88)

Shuhua, like Woolf, wrote on the borders of poetry and prose: traditional generic categories do not always apply to their writing, though critics continue to prepare these Procrustean beds. It is then the mixture of poetry and prose, the heightening of visual metaphors, the exploration of autobiography, the representation of "unsaid or half-said words" of Chinese women, and the fascinating culture of Chinese family life that Julian Bell and, later, Virginia Woolf, had encouraged in Shuhua's writing. What distinguishes her from other Chinese women writers of the time like Ding Ling and Bing Xin? It is the quality of her visual and poetic language (made from a judgment of her edited English, not a translation), her more frequent presentation of women in relation to other women, and her incipient exploration and narration of states of mind. Shuhua, modestly, like other women writers connected with the liberalizing May Fourth literary movement, moved Chinese literature from one stage to another as she began to look at her female characters the way Virginia Woolf looked at the infamous Mrs. Brown, subjectively, from within, and to question the cultural systems that controlled them, from without.

Critics, however, have interpreted her stories in different ways depending upon politics, and the place and time of reception as outlined in chapter 2. Chinese critics contemporary with Shuhua often negatively interpret her stories and her representation of women, predictably, in relation to nationalist or socialist principles in literature. Today, many Chinese-American and PRC critics find value in the beauty of her poetic style and her questioning of women's roles in the China of the time. Xingcun Qian, a critic contemporary with Shuhua, credits her "clear and beautiful style" but criticizes the "rich ladies" that inhabit her stories. He views her as a progressive bourgeois intellectual describing bourgeois females. Among the twelve stories in *Flowers in the Temple*, half of them, he claims have taken rich ladies as their heroines: "Some of them are high bourgeoisie and others belong to the impoverished middle bourgeoisie. But their feudal minds and degenerate lives are the same" (260). He concedes, however, as do the social critics of Woolf's *Mrs. Dalloway* that,

> The author expresses the innermost beings of these bourgeois ladies or progressive rich ladies. And she also expresses that the extended bourgeois family is unhealthy. She has achieved great success in describing bourgeois ladies, their life in a patriarchal society, their morbid psychology and their desire for sexlove. (263)

The critic, in 1928, also expresses ambivalence about Ling Shuhua, but his criticism also contains considerable distortion of the story based on his assessment of her "as a modern intellect in the capitalistic class" (259). He praises "the clarity and beauty of her language" and notes that her "style is simple; her language is profound and fluent" (254). At the same time he writes that Shuhua expresses "her discontent with female capitalists" and their lifestyle, exposing "their ugly and vulgar inner side and their dull and dry souls" (254). He adds, "we may find the desire of those young ladies . . . confined in the feudal . . . [the] thirst for sexlove" (255). Not acknowledging Ling Shuhua's implicit critique of a Chinese society that cripples women's development,

Xingcun Qian can only assert that Shuhua is criticizing, for example, the "irresponsible wives of vanity" in a story like "The Mid-Autumn Festival" (one of her most widely anthologized stories in the West). Here the critic ignores the husband's overreaction and harsh punishment of his wife for her suggestion that he finish their festival meal together before visiting his dying sister: a suggestion that he could have rejected if it were against his better judgment. The critic is also suspicious of the sexual interest in Shuhua's stories and claims that among these "capitalist" and "bourgeois" men, "the wives are but sex-machines and exquisite toys; the husbands are merely providers of living and supporters of vanity" (255). In short, he says Ling is "a modern intellect of the capitalistic class" (256). What Woolf says of certain novelists, we may say of certain critics: "they have made tools and established conventions which do their business. But those tools are not our tools, and that business is not our business. For us those conventions are ruin, those tools are death" ("Mr. Bennett and Mrs. Brown," 330). It is difficult to fully understand that the intertwining of social assessments of the class and class sympathy of the author with the assessment of the author's art is a *given* in official Chinese literary criticism of the time. But both Virginia Woolf and Ling Shuhua will question women's social conditions and become, through their individual voices, a "gadfly to the state," a position hitherto only occupied by men.

When we compare the new critical and cultural tools—gender analysis—of Rey Chow, a contemporary Chinese-American critic, to those of the aforementioned socialist-nationalist critic, we find a considerably different slant. Though Ling Shuhua sharply observes women's collaboration with their own victimhood, she also demonstrates that the cultural cards are stacked against women. Rey writes of the "virtuous transactions" of the women in Shuhua's stories, releasing them from the anaesthetizing drone of the class issues that concern Xingcun Qian. Rey Chow speaks of the "virtuous transaction" as the typical social contract of a Chinese woman of the period, and she demonstrates how Shuhua's stories mimic "closed ideological structures" ("Virtuous Transactions," 81). For example, the story "Embroidered Pillows" illustrates the futility of a young woman's half-year project to embroider cushions—a traditional feminine activity in China—in which she painstakingly interweaves thirty or forty different and beautifully colored threads into an intricate design. The pillows, however, are trampled and vomited upon by drunken and careless guests soon after she completes the task. A reader is left with a sense of irony, futility, and rage about the position of this woman and her traditional needlecraft activities. It is time, the reader of such a story says to herself, that women give up such roles. Rey Chow reveals how Shuhua's stories demonstrate

> the horror of ideology's normal functioning from within. Thus it is when the woman's virtuous transaction with her society is most complete—when the self-sacrifice is most unreasonable—that the narrative point is most poignant, and most suggestive of the need for social change. ("Virtuous Transactions," 81)

Though on the surface of these stories, women dutifully perform traditional tasks exhibiting Confucian family values, there is always a crucial moment when the whole enterprise is trashed or questioned in her stories. And it is in this rupture of the domestic virtues and verities that a new kind of Chinese women's literature will develop in China.

Experiments with Genre: Short Story and Autobiography

The issue for Ling Shuhua in China in the 1930s was how to write a woman's life. Women could find a place in the biographies of men as mothers or wives, or as exemplars of virtue, but other cultural spaces and narratives were closed off. Coming from Chinese culture where the genre of biography or autobiography was most closely identified with the lives of notable Buddhists or emperors or virtuous women, there were few models to follow.

In fact, autobiography was often defined as biography written by the subject himself, since the notion of writing about another person's life was more common. Though, according to Wu Pei-Yi, men had been writing in some version of this genre from before the Qing Dynasty, few women had inscribed themselves into texts. In addition, since the sixteenth century, according to Wu Pei-Yu, there was a strong taboo against self-expression and revelation in Chinese biography unless it was in a religious or a national context, i.e., the spiritual biographies of Buddhists or, later, the individual life inscribed into the narration of the nation.

The social history and material conditions in England encouraged the development of the genre of autobiography, which relied upon the entity of the self and the spaces of psychology and personality. In developing countries, as Partha Chatterjee notes, the individual could only "represent the history of his life ... by inscribing it in the narrative of the nation" (*The Nation and Its Fragments*, 138). During times of crisis—war, famine, nationalism—the individual was subsumed in the collective of family, community, and nation. Ling Shuhua, during a period of war and heightened Chinese nationalism, sought not to escape the story of nation, but to transform and tell it through the individual voice of the individual writer. Similarly, Virginia Woolf suffered the same loss of voice—the individual writer's voice—by the public voice that "preached" in the newspaper or on the radio before the outbreak of World War II. She called it the "loudspeaker voice," an unconscious trace of the growing physical presence of loudspeakers on the streets of China. As World War II approaches, says Woolf, "the public world very notably [invades] the private" (*Diary*, 5: 131).

This study illustrates the misunderstandings that emerge in personal and cultural relationships and genres—the short story, autobiography, and biography—in China and England. The genre of self-disclosure, autobiography, however, was established in England for about two centuries; in China, at the time, "such disclosure of self remained suppressed under a narrative of changing times" (Chatterjee, *The Nation and Its Fragments*, 138). Shuhua's literary conversations with Julian Bell and then Virginia Woolf were "transgressive" in China because such exploration of individuality and self-disclosure was associated with the "demon" West. Bakhtin reminds us of the different cultural "strains" that we can hear in such a conversation. Woolf, in correspondence with Shuhua who was culturally ignorant of the archaeology of the genre in China, simply urged her to write of her life in English, as Julian and Vanessa Bell had. Nevertheless, as in many transnational literary relationships, Woolf's "foreign" advice challenged Chinese norms. In elevating the status of autobiography, the telling of the individual life, Woolf helped Ling Shuhua liberate the early parts of her life. Encouraging her to send the chapters of her autobiography one by one, Woolf created a shadow English audience to whom Shuhua could write—one more culturally open to a woman and to this form of writing. Freed from the generic and ideological constraints of her time and place—"self" hidden under the narrative of "changing times"—Shuhua revealed her own textual strategy. It would differ from the male-narrated lives in China in its use of a child-narrator, its preoccupation with, and critical stance toward, the domestic lives of women and children, and a poetic, lyrical style.

Woolf sent Shuhua books throughout the war, stating that "the English in the eighteenth century wrote in the best way for a foreigner to learn from"

(VW to LS, 27 July 1938). One wonders, however, given Shuhua's inquiry about genres in a later letter—and the fragmentary Chinese tradition of autobiography and view of history—what her conception of autobiography was. Is it any wonder that Shuhua asked for recommendations of biographies and autobiographies from the West that Woolf supplied, modeling her thinking as Julian Bell had done a few years earlier in the genre of the short story? Shuhua asked for recommendations stating that "for years I have read blindly, it is a vast, I suppose " (LSH to VW, 24 July 1938). Among other books, Woolf sent William Cowper and Horace Walpole's letters; Lamb's *Essays;* moving into the nineteenth century with Scott's *Rob Roy,* Jane Austen, and Mrs. Gaskell's *Life of Charlotte Bronte.* These latter books, she thought would give "a feel for the lives of women writers in the nineteenth century—their difficulties, and how they overcame them" (VW to LS, 27 July 1938). Among the Moderns, she sent George Moore's novels. About six months later, Shuhua wrote that she was reading autobiographies in English—Mark Twain, Lincoln Steffans, and H. G. Wells—and characterized them as "things written by successful men," revealing her awareness of the different traditions that women will develop in this genre in China and England. In one letter Shuhua wrote that she had difficulty distinguishing between the genres of autobiography and short stories. As she wrote chapters for the autobiography, she said that they felt like short stories: "My eyes is high, my hand is low" (Berg, 20 January 1939). She wrote many short stories before coming to autobiography and feared as she wrote the short chapters that "they are still like short stories: they don't connect well. But I don't like to write an autobiography like a novel" (20 January 1939). Her self-criticism is valid as the chapters in the autobiography do lack a fluidity.

Chinese writers, we remember, became engaged with the literary form of the short story developed by the Russians and the British in the early twentieth century; they were reading Chekhov, Gogol, Katherine Mansfield, among others. A new periodical, *Short Story Monthly,* was founded at this time and attested to the new interest. Many women writers were drawn to this form hovering between memoir and story. Moving away from the broad presentation of social realities or history, a single character often became the subject matter of the short story. Not as preoccupied with plot as the novel, a short story could glancingly reveal a character's mind. With the change in the use of colloquial Chinese rather than the classical Mandarin in literature introduced during the May Fourth movement, and the expression of long-repressed cultural discontents, for example, in the student demonstrations against the British in 1925, came the desire to expose and dramatize the inner conflicts of characters. Exploited workers with grievances, the elderly who felt neglected, shopkeepers frustrated by official bureaucracy, and women with domestic problems became the new subject matter for this new form. Since Shuhua had written in the short-story form first, its requirements were salient, and it became confused with her autobiographical writing. Contemporary critics and theorists in China, England, and America, however, continue to grapple with the shifting borders of fiction, memoir, and autobiography as Shuhua had.

The draft of the autobiography that Shuhua sent to Virginia Woolf—which eventually became *Ancient Melodies* published by Leonard Woolf's Hogarth Press in the winter of 1953—is an interesting cross-cultural production. In the manuscript of a brief seven-page *Memoir,* Ling Shuhua wrote that soon after she came to England in 1947, she was homesick. She became interested in a series of articles in the *Observer* titled "In Your Garden," by Vita Sackville-West. Enchanted by the fact that Vita talked about Chinese plants, Ling Shuhua wrote to her. Eventually she was invited to see the glorious gardens at Sissinghurst Castle, and, at that time, Vita asked, given Shuhua's interest in literature, if she had ever written anything in English. Ling Shuhua related her earlier correspondence with Virginia Woolf about the autobiography of her early years. Surprised at this coincidence, Vita said, "You must finish your book." This autobiography was then nurtured by Bloomsbury: encouraged in its early stages by Julian Bell and then Virginia Woolf, edited by Marjorie Strachey, and encouraged and brought to closure with an introduction written by Vita Sackville-West. It was then read by C. Day Lewis, published by Leonard Woolf's Hogarth Press, reviewed by Harold Acton (unsigned) in the *Times Literary Supplement,* J. B. Priestley named it book of the year, and, according to Henrietta Garnett (Angelica Bell and David Garnett's daughter), was read aloud to her by her grandmother Vanessa Bell.

The child narrator of this autobiography seems stilted today, but it was a persona that Shuhua was drawn to in the 1930s along with other women writers like Bing Xin, who wrote children's stories in the 1920s. Ye Junjian reports that Ling Shuhua was mainly known as a painter and a short-story writer in China, particularly for her children's stories in the 1920s. He describes her as "a kind of humanist. She was not interested in politics" (Interview by the author). She wrote, in fact, a collection of stories called *Children,* edited by her husband during the years they lived in Japan. It was also in Japan that she gave birth to her daughter, Ying, she said, in 1938 (though this date is debated). Given what is now known about her romantic life, the silences about her adulthood in the autobiography are eloquent. Nevertheless, she writes beautifully about her childhood and her mother's life as a concubine of the Mayor of Beijing—her mother was one of six—in the traditional Chinese family style of the time. What is most arresting in her writing are the poetic and visual metaphors, particularly in the sections on the life of the concubines and the old gardener. Undoubtedly, her visits with Vita Sackville-West, who helped with the publication of her story "The Gardener," also inspired her painting of the gardens of "Sissinghurst." She spoke of Vita as "clever and beautiful, easy to get on with and kind and approachable" in her *Memoir.*

Shuhua wrote simply with the eye of an artist and poet and produced a restrained yet lyrical autobiography of her early years. The viewpoint of the naïve observer, developed perhaps during the years she wrote stories for children, was a popular narrative stance at the time, not only in literature but movies. Children and ideological youth represented a socially and philosophically intact concept of the nation in the 1920s and 1930s. The child's viewpoint, which was perhaps adopted more by women who were on the margins of the writing culture in China, allowed the "naïve" observer to make observations about the injustices and corruption in society without bearing the full political responsibility. The device of the child narrator permits the juxtaposition of innocence of voice and violence of observation without consequence. The naïve and sentimental child can create a voice in opposition to society, and yet it will be a voice that will lull the authorities. Somehow the "child," beyond the arm of the law, cannot be held accountable for observations that a more mature persona (that could be confused with the "author" by the authorities) could not. So, for example, in Shuhua's autobiography, the deadly marriage contracts that women were forced into in China or the jealousies among the concubines could be openly discussed. The child also played into the sentimental strain of the time. The child or female narrator is a literary device that can reveal the feelings, thoughts, fears, and anxieties—the inner workings of psychology—in a nation that does not always tolerate free expression with impunity. Children and women can become narrative agents of change.

You Are as Humble as a Chinese Gentleman: Leonard Woolf and Ling Shuhua
It was left to Leonard Woolf to build practical supports for Ling Shuhua's autobiography, the transnational bridge that Virginia Woolf had begun. After

Virginia Woolf and Julian Bell's deaths, their legacy to Ling Shuhua was their Bloomsbury network. Correspondence with Vanessa Bell ensued, and she became a figure of interest, not only because Shuhua was Julian's friend, but because she was both a writer and a painter—a combination not uncommon in China which joined the sisters'—Virginia and Vanessa—arts (see Diane Gillespie, *The Sisters' Arts: The Writing and Painting of Virginia Woolf and Vanessa Bell*). As Julian said, "she is really of our world," and her promotion by Bloomsbury upon her arrival in London proved him correct in his judgment. Though Shuhua often wrote of visiting England, it was the Sino-Japanese War, the civil war, Chen Yuan's anticommunist sentiments, and his appointment as the first Chinese representative to UNESCO in France that spurred them to leave the country in 1947. Chen Yuan was familiar with European culture and had spent ten years in London as a young man, had studied at the London School of Economics, and worked with H. G. Wells. During the war, he had visited Leonard Woolf with Xiao Qian (LS to LW, 20 September 1952). Leonard, always engaged in international politics, had some interest in China. Diane Gillespie reports that he had several books about China in his library, now housed at Washington State University, Pullman: *China's Position in International Finances* (Allen & Unwin, 1919); J. R. Chitty's *Things Seen in China* (London, 1922); and Herbert Giles, *Chaos in China* (W. Heffer, 1924).

Chen Yuan left China before Ling Shuhua at the end of 1942 and spent 1943–44 in London, also traveling to San Francisco in 1946. Ling Shuhua arrived in London with her daughter after the war in 1947 at which time she developed a correspondence sprinkled with meetings for lunch and walks in gardens, most extensively with Vanessa Bell, Vita Sackville-West, and Leonard Woolf. Mostly, it was a circle of friendships with women that sustained her during this period, some in Bloomsbury finding her "tedious" in her fawning and seeking favors.

Ling Shuhua's documented correspondence with Leonard Woolf began in May 1952, and it continued until 28 February 1969, a month before Leonard's death. Shuhua respected Leonard's practical advice and often consulted him on contacts to pursue for publishing or art exhibitions. "You are as humble as a Chinese gentleman," she exclaimed after hearing him speak modestly about the last volume of his autobiography, *The Journey not the Arrival Matters*, on the BBC in the late 1960s. Indeed Leonard, restrained and decorous, did seem a repository of Chinese values. Though Vanessa and Virginia encouraged Ling Shuhua to continue to work during a time of war and psychological stress in the 1930s, it was left to Leonard to deal with the practicalities of bringing it to fruition in the fifties after her arrival in London. She wrote to him in 1952 to ask if he would read her reminiscences:

> My plan to write this book started at the time I first wrote to Virginia [in 1938]. She was the first and only person who encouraged me to go on writing at the time. When I heard she die [sic], I could not continue writing this book. As you know the Second World War spreaded over China, I had to face all the difficulties and to take up all the duties of a Chinese. I had to put off writing till the war ended. (29 May 1952)

Though her remark about not being able to go on writing appears somewhat melodramatic given that she had never met Virginia Woolf, Woolf may very well have been responsible for her continued development as a writer *in English*. She accepted her work chapter by chapter, commenting upon each that she received in a letter. As Shuhua informed Leonard in 1953, she sent eight or ten manuscripts to Virginia to read during the Sino-Japanese War, particularly during 1938–39. Virginia promised to keep all the chapters together. And she did. When Shuhua arrived in London in the late forties after the turmoil of the Sino-Japanese and civil wars, she had lost her manuscript. Leonard Woolf found it in the files. After a visit to Monk's House, viewing Virginia's sitting room and garden with Leonard, Shuhua remarked, "she certainly has a great heart; she even tried to help some one who lived thousands of miles away and led a life which was so different from her own" (Letter to LW, 29 August 1952). In her *Memoir*, after she saw Edna O'Brien's play *Virginia Woolf* in London, she wrote:

> During the last two decades, Virginia Woolf has often been written about. That people saw her as a brilliant writer, very high-brow and even spiteful, at times. Few people realize that she was basically kind-hearted and anxious to help others.

Virginia Woolf's method of reading and responding to each of Shuhua's chapters was an unusually nurturing method, and one that would not be practiced by most readers and publishers as Shuhua found out when she sent Leonard a chapter of a new book. He responded, "so far as it goes it is interesting but it is really too short for one to be able to say definitely, one way or another whether it would make a book" (25 October 1961). Leonard, a publisher, did not assume the same mentoring relationship to Shuhua as did Virginia Woolf. But *Ancient Melodies* was an interesting cross-cultural product nonetheless.

She wrote little after *Ancient Melodies,* and perhaps her inability to find someone to be a reader in England inhibited her writing career. Given her unfamiliarity with the genre of autobiography and her insecurities with the English language, she needed reassurance and more frequent feedback on smaller bits of writing to sustain her. When this was lacking, it was difficult for her to produce. As she noted in one of her letters to Leonard, she often worried about her English, "which often let her down," and though she sometimes worked with Marjorie Strachey, she was ill and unable to help her in November 1953 when she was trying to make headway on her new book.

In Shuhua's letters to Leonard, she relates her love of gardens, a love that she also shared with Vita Sackville-West, whose Sissinghurst gardens are well known and who promoted her story "The Gardener." It led Shuhua to reflect that "one day the [English] rose may take the place of the Chinese orchid in my heart" (Letter to LW, 5 July 1954). Using the Bloomsbury network with tact and determination—what the Chinese would identify as *guan xi*—Ling Shuhua forged relationships that advanced her career. Her relations included Vanessa Bell, a mainstay, Vita Sackville-West, Leonard Woolf, Quentin Bell, Clive Bell, A. O. Bell, Nigel Nicolson, André Maurois, Harold Acton, J. B. Priestley, Joseph Needham, Angelica Garnett, Trekkie Parsons, Dorothy Woodman, Kingsley Martin, Marjorie Strachey, Arthur Waley, and Anthony Blunt. During this period, she mounted exhibitions of her own collection of paintings, Wen-Jen Hua painters (literary painters of the Yuan and Sung dynasties), and Han rubbings; completed and published her autobiography, *Ancient Melodies;* did translations from modern Chinese literature and tried to advance a book; wrote an essay and planned a book on Chinese painting; wrote nine plays for the BBC on "overseas Chinese people's lives" (Letter to LW, 1 July 1968); and taught in Canada. She also was invited to lecture at the London University School of Oriental and African Studies. André Maurois offered to assist in getting *Ancient Melodies* translated into French, and there was also talk of publishing it in America. But the latter made her anxious, perhaps because of remarks about Amy Ling Chen, the fourteenth daughter, who lived in San Francisco. Shuhua was characteristically silent about her personal relations and family life, but clearly she was concerned about things she had said: "There are many problems which will rise if I publish my book in America. I have to think about it carefully and see how far I can manage to leave out some parts yet without any bad effect on the book" (Letter to LW, 4 June 1954). One suspects that there were fictions in her autobiography.

On or about May Fourth 1919

Shuhua, like other women writers connected with the May Fourth literary movement, moved Chinese literature from one stage to another as she began to look at her female characters and her own life in the way that Virginia Woolf looked at the infamous Mrs. Brown—from within. As mentioned earlier, Shuhua, while at Wuhan, was considered among the "three female talents of Luo Jia," which also included Yuan Zhangying and Su Xuelin. These women writers were considered major contributors to May Fourth writing, and like the present generation of young intellectuals in China, they were drawn to the cultures of Europe and North America.

Unexpected political events carried the May Fourth literary movement into the foreground of events in China. After World War I, when the Versailles Conference handed over Shandong Province to the Japanese in 1919, Chinese students were enraged by feelings of national "humiliation" and betrayal. They went to the streets to demonstrate against the weak Chinese government, and their political issues joined with rebellion against Confucian values, the classical written language, class hierarchies, social practices, and literary norms. Ideas from abroad nurtured the growing discontent at home, and a national discussion developed from the correspondence of Hu Shi, a literary reformer studying at Cornell University in America, and Chen Duxiu, who issued literary manifestos in China, part of the flourishing interest in literary theories and the West. Together they helped to create a literary movement that was a conscious articulation and rebellion against the force of the classical literary tradition in China. May Fourth 1919, might be compared to December 1910, the period just before the war, when there was agitation in British society about class relations. Gender and class relations began to shift. As Virginia Woolf said in her essay "Modern Fiction," "human relations changed." Peter Stansky describes in his book *On or about 1910* the labor unrest, women's agitation for votes, Irish turbulence, and rumbles of war that disturbed England and moved the society toward more egalitarian positions in society and literature. In 1919, the democratization of literature occurred in China as writers moved away from feudal thinking and the use of the classical Chinese language thus making possible the reconceptualization, historically and linguistically, of culture and literature. Shuhua attended Yanjing University with her sister Mei. Yanjing University evolved from the American Board Mission School for Beggar Girls, founded in 1864 by Eliza Bridgman, and became Yanjing College in 1920; then it merged with three other colleges, and later became China's premier Beijing University, Beida. At Yanjing, Shuhua observed the upheaval:

> Not long after we entered the school, there was the tide of the well-known May the Fourth Chinese Student Movement sweeping over China. We learned in those days that China after the Great War had been most unfairly treated by the Great Powers; these were Great Britain, the United States, France, Italy and Japan. China had joined them to fight against Germany during the war; but what did she gain? Worse than nothing. Japan was then enjoying more privileges than Germany had before: she occupied Tsing Tao [Qingdao, a peninsula in North China] when Germany withdrew. Beside this, she took advantage of our civil war: she stole our lands, and made the Chinese warlords sign agreements secretly to give her privileges over a number of important industries in China. (*Ancient Melodies*, 231)

At the Peace Conference in Paris at the end of the World War I, the Western powers decided to sacrifice China's claims to Shandong. The students of Beijing University found out that the minister for Foreign Affairs, Cao Yulin, had made a secret agreement with Japan. They called up ten thousand young men and women, all anxious to do something to save China from political humiliation. These students rose to a position of national leadership as they wildly protested, breaking into the home of the pro-Japanese minister and beating the Chinese minister to Tokyo almost to death. The Chinese delegation at Paris was warned not to sign the treaty and they obeyed. This first victory of the student movement was without precedent in Chinese history. And so the May Fourth literary movement began as a student demonstration against a "weak" Beijing government making concessions to Japan after World War I. This led to changes in personal and national consciousness that evolved into a literary movement. Hu Shi, the literary reformer, announced, "The greatest contribution of the recent literary revolution was to supply this missing factor of conscious attack on the old tradition and of articulate advocacy of the new" ("The Chinese Renaissance," 62).

Ling Shuhua related that when they returned to school from the demonstration, her "Chinese teacher, Chang Ko-Yu, told us to write an article about it. The best article was selected and sent to the *Tianjin Daily*. . . . Next morning Mr. Chang Ko-Yu brought a paper to the class . . . I realised it was my article" (*Ancient Melodies*, 233–34). Mr. Zhang told her that someday she might become a writer, and told her to treasure her first printed article. During 1919–20 about 400 small periodicals, all published in the spoken language of the people, *bai-hua*, became the literary medium. The politics of the day brought a new literary language into expression.

Much has been written about the May Fourth literary movement and its effects on the formation of Chinese modernity or interrupted modernism. It is an important moment in the intersection between England and China. There are two issues that arise again and again in literary discussions of the 1920s and 1930s in China, as well as today. One is the oversimplified categorization of writers, critics, and literary societies as being of the "art for life's sake" or the "art-for-art's-sake" school, the latter associated with the West, the "foreign," the "alien," the "decadent." China's advancement of the "art-for-life's-sake" may be understood in the context of the times. China was often under siege by forces from within—the civil war, famines, drought—or without—the Japanese and other foreigners—in the first half of the century. The "art for life's sake" slogan reflects the sense of urgency in the culture and the state's cultivation of "duty" in people and artists. Yu Dafu of the creationists in "Class Structures in Literature" (1923) astutely wrote of the Chinese construction of the terms "class" and "art." He speaks of critics who are

> Unable to see through to the pain and anguish of their predecessors (writers who created Utopias) and created instead such terms as "art-for-art's-sake" and "art for life's sake" to calumniate them and deny them a salutary role in human history. In my view, the French critics who first created the terms should have died a thousand deaths. Art is life, and life is art and nothing is served by making them antagonistic. (Denton, ed. *Modern Chinese Literary Thought*, 264)

Mao's historical goal of eliminating class barriers that separate humanity sometimes made Chinese literature into what Hu Qiuyuan called "a gramophone . . . to lower art to the status of a gramophone is to turn our backs on art" (Denton, 376). "Loudspeaker voice" was the term, interestingly, that Virginia Woolf also applied to the political voices that drowned out the personal artist's voice in the late 1930s in England. Starkly contrasting one writer or one critic as "good" with the label of "art for life's sake" has often falsely calumniated and denied a particular writer his place in literary and human history, as Yu Dafu claimed. Literary works are made to fit political procrustean beds. Today, we, in America, view art and politics as intertwined and find the separation theoretically difficult, a false debate. Yet writers have been tortured or killed in China over this issue, particularly during the Cultural Revolution.

Another critical issue that preoccupied Chinese critics during the May Fourth period was whether developing modernism in China was a continuation of past literary practices in China or the interjection of Western thinking and practices and, therefore, a rift in the tradition. This same kind of dichotomized thinking pervades discussion of British modernism: was World War I the cultural divide between Edwardian literature and modernism? Is modernism a development or continuation of the symbolism of Baudelaire or British Victorian trends? If Virginia Woolf says that on or about December 1910, something happened that changed the course of English culture and literature, could we say of China that on or about 1919, something happened to change Chinese literary directions? In England, the unrest of the working classes, the formation of unions, the development of the Labor Party heralded the change in class relations that would bring a new voice into literature; the same was happening in China in 1919 with different historical underpinnings.

There are those critics like Bonnie McDougall who pinpoint 1919 as the cultural and literary moment that divides traditional and modern Chinese literature; there are those like David Der-Wei Wang who see this moment as a continuity with past literary movements begun during the Qing dynasty (1644–1911). And there are those like Hu Shi, the Chinese scholar who spent time at Cornell University, who assert another definition of the "modern" beginning in the Song and Yuan periods, when novels and plays were first written in the vernacular:

> The great novels and the great short stories were produced throughout many centuries, and the great novels were not written down, in their final superb form until the Ming dynasty. But at that time Mr. Chen Duxiu agreed with me that the tide of revolution that was going strong in the Yuan period was set back by the eighteen demons (the shih-pa yao-mo) in the Ming and Qing dynasties. ("A Lonely Literary Experimental Work," 154)

One of the eighteen demons was the use of the classical rather than the vernacular Chinese language. Hu Shi's definition of "modern" fits with Roger

Fry's who also looked to earlier periods of Chinese art—Han, Tang, Song—to define the "modern" qualities in ancient Chinese art that contributed to the British discussion of modernism. Translation made it possible to have this discussion of modernism in the early twentieth century.

Translation of British Literature

The origin of Western literary translations began in the last decade of the nineteenth century when Liang Qichao, an eminent Chinese intellectual, and a group of literati created a literary magazine in Japan named *New Fiction*. They underlined the importance of novel writing and demonstrated this with foreign works and their own writings, encouraging the publication of new novels, East and West. Mao Dun, Lao She, Ye Shengtao, and Ba Jin, among China's first novelists, were undoubtedly influenced by the new availability of these translations of Western works.

It has always been difficult for Chinese scholars to locate and engage with English literature because of the paucity or the quality of translations. The first translations of European and American literature, as noted above, were made from Japanese translations into the Chinese classical language. Translators like Lin Shu, one of China's most prolific translators, translated Western works and in twenty years more than 200 English and European novels, many nineteenth century "realistic" works of social reform, into classical Chinese: Charles Dickens, Charlotte Brontë, Rider Haggard, Arthur Conan Doyle, Walter Scott, Jack London, Victor Hugo, Alexander Dumas, Honoré de Balzac, Leo Tolstoy, Washington Irving, Harriet Beecher Stowe (McDougall, 8). Hu Shi commented that it was humorous to read of figures in the novels of Charles Dickens speaking in a dead language, classical Chinese, written 2,000 years ago. Though the quality of the translations was poor, it was the beginning of cultural contact. The translation methods of Lin Shu, however, should be noted. Knowing nothing of foreign languages, Lin Shu had an assistant create a literal translation of the text (usually a Japanese translation of the English text) into spoken Chinese. Then Lin freely retranslated the plots of the well-known Western works he heard into classical Chinese, making sure to preserve Confucian values in the telling. With the exception of S. T. Wei, who occupied a position of importance in translating, Lin Shu's translations with all their shortcomings were all the Chinese had. Though Hu Shi placed Lin Shu among "the blind forces of reaction" ("Tentative Thoughts," 54) because of his use of the classical language that denied literary access and cultural contact with the masses and his ideological tampering with the plots, he nevertheless promoted cultural contact in a seminal period through his work in the 1920s.

After the May Fourth literary movement and the adoption of the vernacular in China, the new literati found an easier medium to translate Western authors. Translation of global literature began to assume a more serious position in China as literary translators gained more respect and critics enlarged their vision. Along with translations of British and American works were translations from the German, Austrian, Russian, Scandinavian, Polish, and Italian (Tsung Hyui-puh, 372–77).

At the same time that Western prose works were being translated, Bian Zhilin translated the poetry of Baudelaire, Mallarmé, Valéry, and Rilke in the collection *Window to the West,* and the poetry of Yeats, Eliot, and Auden in *Translations of English Poetry,* which influenced developments in modern Chinese poetry (Yip Wai-lim, *Lyrics,* 62*ff*). Not only did translators negotiate the language, but also politics. It is reported that during W. H. Auden's trip to China in 1938, he read Sonnet XVII from his sequence "In Time of War" at a reception in Hankou. The poem was translated and appeared in *Ta Kung Pao* the next day. The second line of the poem, "Abandoned by his general and his lice," was translated as "The poor and rich combine forces to fight" (Yip Wai-lim, *Lyrics,* 62), a deliberately inserted political slogan.

At the same time that the Chinese were beginning to translate Western works, the translators James Legge, H. A. Giles, Witter Bynner, and Arthur Waley, in successive generations, began to translate Chinese literature. The impact of these translations in opening up the Chinese culture and aesthetic cannot be underestimated. H. A. Giles (1845–1935) studied Chinese language when he joined the China Consular Service in 1867 and was a well-known Sinologue when he retired from public life in 1893. He was elected to the chair of Chinese in Cambridge, following the Reverend James Legge (1815–97) and published important works such as "Some Truth about Opium," *A Chinese-English Dictionary,* and the popular *Gems of Chinese Literature.* It is known that the Woolfs had two of his books in their library: his translation of *The Travels of Fa-Hsien* (399–414 A.C.E.) or *Record of the Buddhist Kingdoms* (1923) in which Leonard Woolf made notations, and *Chaos in China* (1924). The linguistic, cultural, and theoretical issues of working in two languages like Chinese and English faced by all of these translators has recently come under the scrutiny of Lydia Liu. In *Translingual Practices,* she asserts the importance of reconsidering the conditions of contemporary translation theory in terms of "contestation of languages" on a literal level. As noted earlier in the discussion of I. A. Richards's views of translation, it is not only words but also cultural, literary, and conceptual categories that are "translated." Meaning exists in a network of differences, and the concepts—*self* and *individualism*—mean different things in different historical periods depending upon the meanings of "family," "community," "society," "nation," as well as economic forces and systems. They exist in relation to other concepts for, as Ferdinand de Saussure asserts, there are no positive meanings in language. Lydia Liu reminds us of the network of historical and cultural differences that recreate the meanings of these terms in relationship in the work of translation.

Chinese translators who knew English did later translations of Western works after the 1980s thaw. The critic and translator Jin Di, for example, began working on a translation of James Joyce's *Ulysses* from the English in 1980. Four episodes translated by Jin Di appeared in the Chinese journal *World Literature* in 1986; continuing his work at Yale and the University of Virginia, he completed the first volume consisting of twelve chapters in 1992, and the rest in 1995. He has written of the process and politics of this translation in *Shamrocks and Chopsticks: James Joyce in China* (2000). Another translation of *Ulysses* done in partnership by Xiao Qian (1910–99) and his wife, Wen Jieruo, employed a Japanese translation as well as the original English. Xiao, a friend of E. M. Forster's in the 1930s at Cambridge University, and his wife began work on their translation around 1990, published in three volumes in 1994. In a March 2000 interview, Wen Jieruo explained their process of translation, allowing that they "did it quickly." She did the whole first draft of the translation using four Japanese versions of *Ulysses*, as well as Hans Gabler's notes and others when there were discrepancies, and the occasional assistance of the Canadian scholar, Patrick Kavanagh. Her background in Catholicism as well as Shakespeare, Homer, and the Bible, she said, aided her translation. Working fourteen hours a day for two years, she said that her friends wondered if she had left Beijing. Episode 13, "Nausicaa," she said, was the easiest; episode 14, "Oxen of the Sun," with its recapitulation of prose styles in English history, the most difficult, as they could only reproduce two styles. Xiao Qian, she explained, then edited her first draft, comparing the Chinese to the 1922 Shakespeare & Co. English edition, working on matters of style and making it into a "literary work." Though 10,000 copies of their translation, published by Yi Ling

Publishers in 1994 (parts) and 1999 (whole work), were sold, she acknowledged that "people sometimes put *Ulysses* on a shelf for show."

In discussing modernist tendencies in China, then, we need to look at the relations between literary periods, groups, and political currents in England and China. Cultural and historical relations extend from group to group; writers form groups in the same way as books: "We can only hope," as Woolf observes in "The Leaning Tower," "to single out the most obvious influences that have formed writers into groups. . . . Books descend from books as families descend from families" (Woolf, *A Room of One's Own*, 130).

CHINA ON A WILLOW PATTERN PLATE: CHARLES LAMB, GEORGE MEREDITH, AND ARTHUR WALEY

Julian Bell's descriptions of China are those of a naturalist and a poet; Ling Shuhua's and Vanessa Bell's, painters; J. M. Keynes's, an economist; Felix Beato, an imperialist photographer. Their descriptions differ from the idealized and poetic landscapes present in late Victorian and early modern England, those found in a Charles Lamb essay, George Meredith's *The Egoist*, or Arthur Waley's well-known translations of Chinese poetry or, conversely, the descriptions of territory and landscape associated with English imperialism.

Xiao Qian and his wife, Wen Jieruo. By permission of Xiao Qian

Growing familiarity with the landscapes of China and Japan in literature, paintings, gardens, and products imported from China began to imperceptibly structure English ways of seeing, now being acknowledged in contemporary criticism. In the translations of Chinese poetry, for example, a blending of subject and object, of what is inside and outside the artist is represented: an undifferentiated state of being and aesthetic perception for which some of the English modernists longed.

> Ever since the day I was banished to Hsun-yang
> Half my time I have lived among the hills.
> And often, when I have finished a new poem,
> Alone I climb the road to the Eastern Rock.
> I lean my body on the banks of white stone:
> I pull down with my hands a green cassia branch.
> My mad singing startles the valleys and hills:
> The apes and birds all come to peep.
> Fearing to become a laughing-stock to the world,
> I choose a place that is unfrequented by men.
> (Waley, "Madly Singing in the Mountains," *Translations*, 197)

Traditional Chinese critics also depersonalize poets in descriptions of their qualities. For example, Shen Ming-chen says, "Li Po [Li Bai] is like the Spring grass, like Autumn waves, not a person but we must love him. Tu Fu [Du Fu] is like a great hill, a high peak, a long river, the broad sea, like fine grass and bright-coloured flowers, like a pine or an ancient fir, like moving wind and gentle waves" (Ayscough, lxxxiv). Chinese perception, as represented here, erases the borders of self that somehow enters the landscape, as well as the borders between literature and painting. Tao Kai-yu says of Tu Fu's [Du Fu] poems that they are "like pictures, like the branches of trees reflected in water—the branches of still trees. Like a large group of houses seen through clouds or mist, they appear and disappear" (Ayscough, *Fir Flower Tablets*, lxxxv). Philosophically, this way of seeing and writing dissolves the Cartesian formulation of subject and object as well as distinctions between the animate and inanimate, maintained in the Western intellectual tradition. In addition, in China at this time, as Eudora Welty has noted, "painting and writing, always the closest two of the sister arts . . . in ancient Chinese days only the blink of an eye seems to have separated them" ("Place in Fiction," 3). This way of seeing appealed to the modernists; England was a culture mired in what Roger Fry labeled "realism" in his lectures on Chinese art. Interestingly, the Japanese, going through their own cultural reassessments in relation to China as well as the West, labeled Western-style realism "copy-reality-ism" (Karatani, *Origins of Modern Japanese Literature*, 26). Arthur Waley's translations of Chinese poetry extended these changes in visual sensibility into the literary. The Chinese landscapes present in England since the eighteenth century—the scrolls, fans, gardens, and porcelains representing Eastern perceptions of flowers, birds, willows, moonlight, pagodas, teahouses, footbridges, scholars, monks, and poets—became part of the landscape of modernist British literature, a *mise en abime* that suggested the "foreign," the "strange," the "exotic."

One of the landscapes or tropes of China in the British scene was the popular blue and white willow pattern china. Socialized like many of the British into a notion of Chinese landscape represented on blue and white willow plates, Vanessa and Julian Bell as well as other British artists were well aware of the traditional motifs of pagodas, weeping willows, footbridges, and junks on the river. This product more than any other is an example of the British embrace and construction of the "mysterious orient." In its myriad forms over two centuries, it represents a cultural negotiation in which England often portrayed itself as the "civilized" nation simply drawing upon the arts and wares of a "primitive" nation. In actuality, the British "appropriated" the rich blue and white, and other ceramic, arts of China "liquidating" the reference to China along the way, and then using it to enrich its own porcelain arts.

The blue and white willow plate represents one of the best-known expressions of the British encounter with Asian culture. The plate, a regular part of Victorian households, had the familiar "oriental" landscape characterized by a willow tree in the center, the footbridge with three figures, the blossoming orange tree behind the tea house, the pagoda, the boat, the doves, and the fence running across the foreground. The romantic story represented on the plate appealed to the British notions of the "primitive" society of China evolving in ethnographic reports and geographical explorations of the time. The popularity of this particular pattern and its story presents a progressive British society looking upon a simple and static Chinese society. The Chinese designs from which the popular manufactured versions were adapted were hand-painted, free-style representations of sprays of leaves, flowers, lotus blossoms, birds, berries, peonies, dragons (good luck symbols of the emperor), chrysanthemums, phoenixes, and Chinese good-wish characters concealed in the decorations. This Chinese porcelain was the most widely publicized Chinese product in the Liberty catalogs, its cobalt blue color and poetic pattern having won the hearts of the British. The willow pattern in England went through many transformations, and is now the best-known expression of eighteenth-century Chinese porcelain art seen through Western artists, craftsmen and manufacturers' eyes.

Liberty catalogs describe a variety of blue and white vases, "old Nankin [Nanjing] Blue and White Cisterns decorated with a design of white hawthorn cluster upon a blue ground," Nanjing blue and white bowls and covers, flower vases, and altar candlesticks. Antique, modern versions, and reproductions of Chinese blue and white flooded the British market. But the social history of the popular blue and white willow porcelain in England—or what Igor Kryptoff terms "the biography of an object"—is well documented. Here we briefly trace the construction of China on this porcelain as it appears in department stores, British homes, art collections, literature, and painting. It serves as the mute cultural and aesthetic background of this chapter as it holds the cultures of China and England in aesthetic tension. First, we observe that traders and missionaries brought back hand-painted Chinese versions that appeared in the culture; then it became an aesthetic object imported to England for elegant department stores like Liberty; then copied or adapted and manufactured by fine porcelain makers like Staffordshire, sometimes with the addition of British family crests; then mass produced in inexpensive versions for the general population. At the same time that it evolved as an aesthetic and consumer product, it became a motif in British literature and a quotation or window on the East in American and European postmodernist paintings.

Briefly, its cultural life begins with Marco Polo, who reportedly brought back the first porcelains from Kubla Khan to Venice. The term "porcellane," meaning "little pigs," was first applied by the Italians to cowrie shells with smooth white surfaces. The meaning later extended to the white porcelain that Italian Jesuit missionaries brought back from China, the Italians being the earliest among the Europeans to have cultural contact with the Chinese due to the intense Jesuit activity in the Far East. Porcelain was reportedly invented by the Chinese—though there are some sources that claim it was the Persians—sometime during the Tang Dynasty (sixth to ninth century), and its process kept secret by the Chinese for about a thousand years. The Persian cobalt blue influenced the Chinese product and William Chambers, the eighteenth-century designer, reports that sometime around the fourteenth century, the Persian product gained in popularity over the Chinese celadon (green) of the period. The porcelain captivated the Chinese and European market: from the time of the Ming Dynasty (1368–1644), when the Chinese introduced some of its finest blue and white decorated products and furniture, through the Qing Dynasty (1644–1912), the period when the British East India Company stimulated the exportation of these wares. It was in demand and became a trope in English and European writing and art from the eighteenth century on. The visual and literary transformations of the familiar blue and white serve as an excellent example of the thesis of this chapter: that European modernist art fed upon and, at times, followed upon trade with China and an increasingly global culture of developing consumerism. Then, as now, global relations, encouraging trade and business contact, led to cultural and aesthetic contact that enriched the images, objects, and ideas afloat in a cultural bricolage, from which the artist shapes his art.

After years of importing the blue and white landscapes perfected by the Chinese, the British began their own manufacture, juxtaposing various bits and pieces of these designs to construct their own "orient." James McNeill Whistler in his "Ten O'Clock" lecture observes how "art happens" and, "cruel jade" that it is, feeds upon materials from anywhere in the world:

> Art, the cruel jade . . . hies her off to the East to find, among the opium eaters of Nankin [Nanjing], a favourite with whom she lingers fondly—caressing his blue porcelain, and painting his coy maidens. (*Mr. Whistler's "Ten O'Clock,"* 27)

What is of cultural and aesthetic interest about the blue porcelain is that the British appropriated the ceramic technique and then familiarized the willow landscapes by attaching a story to it. The British, as Whistler observed, were rather "literary" artists in the nineteenth century often viewing their art as a symbol of or a telling of a story. The willow plate in China had many hand-painted variations, but no anecdotes attached; in England, however, the plate had the secondary willow legend, a narrative that the British developed that was retold in many Victorian articles in the popular press, theatrical entertainments, fiction and poetry.[5] The Victorian legend tells the story on the manufactured British plate: it concerns Koong Shee [Kang Xi], the daughter of a wealthy mandarin who loved Zhang, her father's secretary. The mandarin wished his daughter to marry a wealthy suitor, forbade the marriage, and locked her up in an apartment on the terrace of the house, which is to the left of the temple. From her prison, Koong Shee "watched the willow tree blossom" and wrote poems in which she expressed her ardent longings to be free before the peach bloomed. Zhang managed to communicate with her by means of writing enclosed in a small coconut shell attached to a tiny sail, and Koong Shee replied, "Do not wise husbandmen gather the fruits they fear will be stolen?" Zhang disguises himself and carries off Koong Shee. The three figures can be seen on the bridge:

> Koong Shee [Kang Xi] with a distaff, Zhang carrying jewels and the mandarin carrying a whip. The lovers escaped and lived happily for many years, but were found by the outraged wealthy suitor who burnt their home, and from the ashes of the bamboo grove their twin spirits rose, Phoenix-like, in the form of two doves. (Talfourd, *The Mandarin's Daughter*)

This story had many different versions in nursery rhymes, children's tales and even popular drama of the late nineteenth century. In an 1865 drama titled *An Original Chinese Extravaganza Entitled The Willow Pattern Plate*, performed in the Prince of Wales Theater in Liverpool, the backdrop is a giant willow pattern plate and characters act out the willow legend before it—as a parody. The names of the Chinese characters are ridiculed: Chim-Pan-See is "a powerful Enchanter—a Chinese puzzle in one piece"; Koong Shee, the runaway maiden, is described as "He-sing's only daughter, all the rage in China, and the particular passion of Zhang"; Zhang, the secretary with whom she is in love, is described as "He-sing's secretary, whose absence from his employer's good books leads to his own dis-missal and mizzle"; Lo Spi is a Chinese detective who pursues the lovers over the traditional footbridge; So-Sli is Koong Shee's Waiting Maid. The place is "Somewhere in China"; the time is "Out of Mind." Cultural stereotyping, ridicule of Chinese "barbarism," parody, and double entendres pervade the play. It is a culturally smug presentation of the story of the lovers in the willow legend, now part of the English popular imagination.

The English were fascinated like the Persians, Dutch, Americans, and Germans with this narrative and the familiar landscape on the familiar plate. They were also, however, insensitive and indifferent to the world view and the aesthetic sensibility of the Chinese as the reproductions of the plates and the drama above documents. The commodification by English potters is clearly a "translation" set loose from its cultural moorings. There was little effort to understand the complex meaning of the landscapes in the Chinese versions. But it is what looms in the British imagination in Victorian times—what was popularly called a Cathay landscape. Charles Lamb in the early nineteenth century describes his nostalgia for and a scene on a blue and white willow plate in the essay "Old China":

> I like to see my old friends—whom distance cannot diminish figuring up in the air (so they appear to our optics) yet on terra firma still—for so we must in courtesy interpret the speck of deeper blue, which the decorous artist, to prevent absurdity, had made to spring up beneath their sandals. (291–92)

Here Lamb observes his old friends, figures in a floating world without perspective, or as he says, "without our optics." He reveals Peking [Beijing] Opera gender reversals, observing "men with women's faces, and the women, if possible, with still more womanish expressions." Then he remarks on the sense of Chinese space, the distances between figures, and summons up the images of Mandarins, and the "dainty mincing" foot, undoubtedly once "bound," of the lady:

> Here is a young and comely Mandarin, handing tea to a lady from a salver— two miles off. See how distance seems to set off respect! And here the same lady, or another, for likeness is identity on teacups—is stepping into a little fairy boat, moored on the hither side of this calm garden river, with a dainty mincing foot, which in a right angle of incidence (as angles go in our world) must infallibly land her in the midst of a flowery mead—a furlong off on the other side of the same strange stream! Farther on—if far or near can be predicated of this world—wee horses, trees, pagodas.[6]

Figures float in a world "uncircumscribed" by our rules of perspective. The concepts of far and near established in Western art in the Renaissance are abandoned in Lamb's description of this strange world viewed on the plate. The suggestion that this is primitive culture appears in the word "lawless," as this narrative reveals that the Chinese treat space as "flat," inviting the viewer to find his own angle of vision similar to modern "flat" paintings.

Where do we enter this landscape, Lamb seems to ask. Must our cultural sympathies change and relate to the whole of nature and society instead of the lone human figure into which we are socialized in Western art? The Chinese landscape presents us with a different world view, and consciousness of nature and man. To Lamb's British eyes, the three small figures on the bridge are dwarfed by nature and fate. To the Chinese eye, the human is a small part of the whole, and multiple perspectives are presented in one glance. The blue and white willow pattern plate, a Chinese landscape through British eyes, is an unsuspecting commodity of the cultural layers that it represents.

When a flash of blue and white porcelain appears in modern paintings of Grant Wood, James McNeill Whistler, Matisse, Duncan Grant or Redon, it becomes a window on the "foreign." Similarly, Far East textiles in paintings like Renoir's *Madame George Charpentier and Her Children* intimate China or Japan in the midst of representations of European domesticity. This "trace" or "quotation" of China in nineteenth- and twentieth-century art suggests that certain tropes of the East—the blue willow ceramics, fans, screens, Chinese lanterns, pagodas, kimonos, landscape scrolls—are incorporated by British and American art. For example, Grant Wood's painting *Daughters of the American Revolution* represents a proper-looking, white-haired American woman toasting the viewer with a clearly represented blue and white willow teacup. Though America rebelled against being a colony of England by throwing its tea and figurative tea cups into the Boston harbor in the eighteenth century, we see America in this painting paying homage, quoting the British quoting China. A *mise en abime*, the blue and white willow teacup looming in the foreground of Wood's painting opens up one historical and cultural scene after another. Similarly, James McNeill Whistler's *The Princess from the Land of Porcelain*, dressed in a flowing kimono, holding a fan, with a flowered screen in the background, blue and white standing vase, and lovely rug, projects the East (Japan) into Europe. In addition, Whistler's design of the Peacock Room in 1877 (now in the Freer Collection of Art in Washington, D.C.) for Frederick R. Leyland, a wealthy shipowner from Liverpool, reveals his cultural fascination with blue and white ceramics and design of the East in nineteenth-century America. When his patron was away, Whistler could not resist covering the ceiling of the room he had been commissioned to design for the porcelain with gold leaf and peacock feather designs—to the dismay of Leyland. Similarly, Matisse's *Anemones and a Chinese Vase* and Redon's *Flowers in a Chinese Vase* have a glint of the Chinese blue and white. Importantly, we note the influence of the East on some of Duncan Grant's paintings and

Still Life, the Sharuku Scarf *by Duncan Grant.* © 1979 *Estate of Duncan Grant, courtesy Henrietta Garnett.*

objects (boxes and fans). The blue and white porcelain in British and American art becomes a window on the foreign and the exotic in the midst of American and British representations of domesticity and womanhood. It is interesting to note, however, that in Chinese paintings women often are portrayed with a fan, while portraits of women in the West sometimes include a woman with a book with pages spread open, a trace of the fan.

By the nineteenth century, the blue and white willow pattern was in most British households. Its presence is documented in accounts of British childhoods, and numerous literary and artistic associations. Virginia Woolf notes that she used to learn Greek from Clara Pater, her home "all blue china, Persian cats and Morris wallpapers" (*Letters,* 4:411). George Meredith in *The Egoist* (1879) plays on the "willow pattern" with the name of Sir Willoughby Pattern, the protagonist and egoist. The willow pattern legend adapted by the British that informs the design of the plate is the story of lovers who rebel against parental matchmaking. This legend is mirrored in the plot of Meredith's novel as Clara Middleton also rebels against her father's wishes in choosing a mate. Perhaps the willow pattern also suggests the social patterning of Willoughby's despotic plot to ensnare Clara, the "dainty rogue in porcelain," the oppressed feminine (and China), who shatters his plot.

Arthur Waley also captured the delicate designs of Chinese landscapes such as those represented on blue and white china in his translations of poetry, his first important volume appearing in 1918, *170 Chinese Poems.* Though visual objects led the way, it was through Waley, then curator of prints in the Oriental Division of the British Museum, that most of Bloomsbury, indeed pre-war England, gained its literary sense of "poetic" and "misty" China. Waley translated poems in which the reader had the visual and psychological freedom to move mysteriously in and out of the poem as an "I" or "a single grain of rice":

Mounting on high I begin to realize the smallness of Man's Domain;
Gazing into distance I begin to know the vanity of the Carnal World.
I turn my head and hurry home—back to the Court and Market,
A single grain of rice falling—into the Great Barn.
("Climbing the Ling Ying Terrace and Looking North," *Translations,* 258)

Familiar with Chinese landscape scrolls circulating in England since the voyage of Lord Macartney, the British received Waley's translations with ready perceptions and images in mind. The paintings and Waley's translations of Chinese poetry—really the first Chinese literature after Confucius and Mencius (I. A. Richards translated his philosophical ideas) to become widely read in England—became a chord in English culture and informed contemporary perceptions. The literary and the visual worked together to prepare the English public for Chinese art.

Arthur Waley's translations enabled the British to experience the mingling of heaven and earth, the cassia trees, the pines and bamboo, and the mountains of China:

> In the Mountains on A Summer Day
> *by Li Po*
>
> Gently I stir a white feather fan,
> With open shirt sitting in a green wood.
> I take off my cap and hang it on a jutting stone;
> A wind from the pine-trees trickles on my bare head.
>
> Self-Abandonment
> *by Li Po*
>
> I sat drinking and did not notice the dusk,
> Till falling petals filled the folds of my dress.
> Drunken I rose and walked to the moonlit stream;
> The birds were gone, and men also few.

These compelling and haunting landscapes found in Waley's 170 *Chinese Poems,* 140 of which had never been translated before, and later in *More Translations from the Chinese,* in 1919, created a powerful sense of Chinese landscape along with representations on scrolls and paintings. And there were also Herbert Giles's translations, particularly of Pu Songling's strange eighteenth-century stories described in a 1913 review by Virginia Woolf as "queer" and "topsy-turvy." Though the Chinese consider Waley's translations a part of "English" literature, not Chinese, he brought new landscapes, visual and poetic, to a people who had known China mainly through its handicrafts and arts, imported or adapted through trade. Though Waley, preferring his idealized vision, never set foot in China or Japan, G. L. Dickinson "had sowed the seeds of his [Waley's] achievement," according to Dadie Rylands (letter to the author, 13 March 1996), and was the most widely known translator of his time.

Lopokova Dancing *by Duncan Grant.* © 1979 *Estate of Duncan Grant, courtesy* Henrietta Garnett.

He was referred to by the charming Lydia Lopokova as "the Chinese Bloomsbury." His translations probably had more to do with the interest in and poetic ideas of China (from the Tang Dynasty, 600–900, in particular) than any other writings in England. In addition, the British were drawn to Chinese domestic arts (folk art, fans, fashion), paintings on scrolls, porcelain, garden design, and architecture from the late 1700s to the modern period. Modern China, in a state of political and creative atrophy, was largely ignored, but British Modernists loved the art of the Zhou and Han dynasties, and turned, particularly, to the Tang and Song for inspiration. China during this period registered in the sensibilities of British intellectuals, writers and artists, and another discourse, beside the imperialist, emerged.

Arthur Waley's main task, to introduce Chinese and Japanese landscapes and literature to the general reader in the West, never flagged, and he published a steady stream of translations of both Chinese and Japanese classics over thirty years. He became a distinguished if reticent figure in Bloomsbury. Virginia Woolf wrote of finding Waley "a little demure and discreet" (*Letters*, 3:183), but, nevertheless, wrote a positive review of his Japanese translation of *Tale of the Genji* in *Vogue* in 1925. All aesthetic and translation questions relating to the "oriental," were referred to him. When Vanessa received a letter with New Year's pictures from Ling Shuhua, she exclaimed:

> They are lovely. Especially I think those on their paper which I suppose are those of the different gods. I had never seen anything like them before. I wonder if other people in England who know about Chinese things, such as Arthur Waley have seen things like these. I think I must try to show them to him. They are such exquisite color and drawing and we have all been looking at them again and again and thinking how wonderful it is that such a present should have reached us here in the midst of the war, where one seems to be completely shut out from the outside world. (Letter to SH, 17 March 1940)

Waley was born into an agnostic Jewish family, the eldest son of Sigismund Schloss (1813–87), a cotton broker in Manchester who had been born in Frankfurt, and Rebecca Mocatta, part of a Spanish-Jewish family living in England since the seventeenth century. During the war, the family changed its name to Waley, his mother's maiden name, fearing German prejudice. He was a brilliant student of classics at King's College, Cambridge, but a disease that caused the loss of sight in one eye ruled out the career of a scholar. When traveling in

Spain in 1913, he heard of a job in the Oriental Prints and Drawings Department of the British Museum working under Lawrence Binyon, the poet and translator. Binyon hired him and encouraged his study of Chinese and Japanese to understand the content and literary background of the paintings, and soon Waley was engrossed. An excellent student of language, Margaret H. Waley, the wife of his brother, Hubert, wrote in an unpublished essay, "A View of the Family from Within," that Waley loved music and had an "excellent sense of pitch which allowed him to assume the tone (as well as the accent) of any language at will and must have been particularly valuable in the study of a tone language like Chinese" (Rutger's manuscript). Interestingly, Waley became friends with Ezra Pound through his interest in Chinese because, though Pound knew no Chinese, his versions translated from the French were published in 1915 in *Cathay*. This prompted Waley to do the same to convey his vivid sense of the beauty of this literature to others. In 1916, he printed about fifty copies of a booklet of Chinese poems that he had translated and distributed them to friends, among them G. L. Dickinson, Ezra Pound, Clive Bell, Laurence Binyon, Roger Fry, Dora Carrington, Bertrand Russell, T. S. Eliot, Leonard Woolf, and W. B. Yeats (noted in "Description of the Arthur D. Waley Papers," Rutger's manuscript). The interest of early modernist poets and writers in Chinese and Japanese culture and literature reveals again the role of China in a developing international modernist aesthetic.

In 1918, Waley met Beryl de Zoete, whose admiration for him and his career enabled them to create an unusual lifestyle—neither marriage, or children, or a shared flat. Beryl too was gifted with languages, a dancer, a pupil of Dalcroze, who wrote books on dancing in Bali, India, and Ceylon. Her interests led them to Dartington Hall in Devon in the summers, and there Waley met Leonard and Dorothy Elmhirst, who had an interest in India and China. Beryl de Zoete easily became part of the vital artistic scene at Dartington Hall and was often accompanied by the rather withdrawn Waley in the 1940s. She was an author of works on Balinese, Indian, and Ceylonese dancing, and gave a lecture on this at Dartington. Later, through Leonard Elmhirst's patronage during a critical period in China, Dartington Hall figured in the support of the well-known Chinese poet Xu Zhimo as described earlier. During World War II, 1939–45, Waley worked in the Japanese Section of the Censor's Office, loathing Hitler and his treatment of the Jews. Though entangled in the war and his mother's death, he did finally during this period translate and publish Wu Cheng'en's *Monkey* (Xi You Ji), which was illustrated by Duncan Grant

Dartington Hall, Totnes, England. By permission of the Dartington Hall Trust Archive, Totnes, England.

and which Waley dedicated to Beryl de Zoete and Harold Acton. After the war, the British government, realizing that they had too few experts, began to encourage the study of China and Japan. During this time, Waley worked at the London University School of Oriental and African Studies, located in Bloomsbury, as a fellow.

Illustration from Wu Cheng'en's Monkey *by Duncan Grant. © 1979 Estate of Duncan Grant, courtesy of Henrietta Garnett.*

Most of Bloomsbury knew Waley. Mrs. Hubert Waley notes his early connection with this group when he was at King's College, Cambridge, where he studied with G. E. Moore and G. L. Dickinson, who became a lifelong friend, and introduced him to Roger Fry. But Waley was not bound to one community and had connections with the Vorticists and Chinese groups also. Interestingly, Waley in his BBC talk, "Blake the Daoist," documents his meeting with the Chinese poet Xu Zhimo, an important force in Chinese poetry already discussed in chapter 3, "East-West Conversations":

> Some twenty years ago the Chinese poet Hsu Chih-mo [Xu Zhimo] took down a book from my shelves and after reading a few lines he acclaimed, "This man is a Daoist." The book was the long prophetic poem *Milton* by William Blake. ("Blake the Daoist")

Both Waley and Xu were reminded of the second book of the *Taoist Book* by Chuang-Tzu. When an exhibit of Blake's graphic work appeared in Beijing in the 1930s, Waley wrote from the British perspective, "Too few students of Daoism have been familiar with mystical writing produced in other parts of the world" ("Blake the Daoist"). He hoped that the exhibit would lead Chinese students of Daoism to study Blake's mystic writings.

Though the Chinese, according to Ye Junjian (Julian Bell's friend), considered Waley's translations "creative . . . a part of English rather than Chinese literature" (Interview by the author, 1995), they, nevertheless, represented—perhaps mitigated—the sensibility, philosophy, and landscapes of China to England early in the century. Roger Fry wrote to Rose Vildrac 1917 that Waley, one of his friends, had just finished translating "very beautiful poems of the Han period. They have such simplicity and absence of rhetoric that they are quite in keeping with today's taste" (*Letters,* 408). It was the simplicity and line of the Han period in sculpture and poetry that appealed to British modernists, a quality to be discussed further in chapter 5, "Developing Modernisms."

The Chinese saying "he regards a camel as a horse with a swelled back" may be used to illustrate the larger cultural framework that creates what each of the intellectuals and artists in this chapter sees. For, like all of us, they "see," but they cannot see what makes them see. What is familiar to them from the culture of England shapes what they see elsewhere.

It is important to note, however, that the gaze of G. L. Dickinson, Julian Bell, Vanessa Bell, and Arthur Waley is not "neo-imperial" as is Archibald Rose and Maynard Keynes in their reports on the development of British railways in China during this period. Julian's is a naturalist or an aesthetic gaze—sometimes a shopper's gaze—a reality as present at this time in England, and sometimes forgotten in critical texts like Edward Said's. Historical reality is one order of reality, but there are other orders too. The cultural, political, economic, imaginative, and aesthetic realities represented in this chapter constructed by intellectuals and artists seeing together—Vanessa and Julian Bell, Ling Shuhua and Virginia Woolf, Beatrice and Sidney Webb, Arthur Waley, J. M. Keynes, Archibald Rose—create a rich cultural, political, and artistic *bricolage*.

EXPANDING "ENGLISHNESS": *LE JARDIN ANGLO-CHINOIS* AND THE KEW GARDENS PAGODA

Chinese gardens also inspired the eighteenth-century *le jardin anglo-chinois*. This designation—the English-Chinese Garden—and the incorporation of the Chinese pagoda and architecture into English landscapes was an aesthetic solution to what William Chambers, the eighteenth-century architect, bewailed as the "dullness" and "boredom" of an English garden. W. J. T. Mitchell observes that "the geographic claim that landscape is a uniquely western European art falls to pieces in the face of the overwhelming richness, complexity, and antiquity of Chinese landscape painting" (9)—and, I would add, English gardens. Wonderful descriptions of garden design by William Chambers, *A Dissertation on Oriental Gardening* (1772), and Chinese landscape painting by Michael Sullivan, *The Birth of Landscape Painting in China*, document the important role that landscapes played during periods of imperial grandeur in China—centuries before England's nineteenth-century development of the genre. This is another example of the hybridity and transnational aesthetic dialogue that enriched British art.

Two schools of thought, however, prevailed in the middle of the eighteenth century on whether the addition of Chinese features to an English garden made it an "Eden," as William Chambers said, of "what was once a desert." Or as Horace Walpole believed, "the Chinese garden was simply silly and spurious 'Orientalism' in the middle of England" (Hunt, 33). Chambers, a venturous and prescient designer and architect who was drawn to the Chinese aesthetic, noted early that "the creation of gardens is determined by intellectual, social, economic, political and artistic forces which in their turn are mirrored in gardens" (Hunt, *The Genius of the Place*, 3). Even gardens are not ideologically innocent.

When Chambers wrote and designed, the English garden was again in the process of reforming itself as it had been since the seventeenth century when first Italian and then French styles were incorporated and, later, rejected. In the early part of the seventeenth century, Italian Renaissance gardens, described by Andrew Marvell and John Milton who had traveled to Italy and captured this in their poetry, had a shaping influence on the English. The feature of the "ha-ha" apparent in English architecture and landscape as well as Jane Austen novels was also a part of the Italian Renaissance castle. The "ha-ha" was a boundary separating a house from a garden or the surrounding countryside without a formal fence or obstruction of the view. Defined by the *OED* as a "sunken fence," French etymologists claim that the term "ha-ha" evolved from the expression of surprise at seeing a fence or boundary when approaching closely. Such modifications as the "ha-ha" in English landscape design were judged by William Chambers to be uninteresting features, and little else but ways of differentiating fields. William Mason, representing mainstream views of the time, satirizes Chambers' rejection of English taste in a "Heroic Epistle to Sir William Chambers" (1773):

> O let the Muse attend thy march sublime,
> And, with thy prose, caparison her rhyme;
> Teach her, like thee, to gild her splendid song,
> With scenes of Yuen-Ming, and sayings of Li-Tsong;
> Like thee to scorn Dame Nature's simple fence;
> Leap each Ha Ha of truth and common sense.
> (quoted in Hunt, *The Genius of the Place*, 323)

After the Italian Renaissance influence, the French Cartesian philosophy of a priori systems influenced the English design of gardens by "rule and line." French formality, enclosing walls, and the careful "disposition" of nature, was practiced in stiff Tudor and Stuart gardens. William Chambers entered into this history and wrote that the Chinese aesthetic in the temples and gardens of the East was the solution to the boredom and dullness of the "regular" English garden (more under French sway at this time). A poem by William Cawthorn, "Of Taste," written in 1756, confirms again the British shift from European to "Mand'rin" taste in the mid–eighteenth century, and the fetching of "models from the wise Chinese." The description of the emerging hybrid aesthetic is the forerunner of modernist and postmodernist theorizing:

> Of late, 'tis true, quite sick of Rome and Greece,
> We fetch our models from the wise Chinese:
> European artists are too cool and chaste,
> For Mand'rin only is the man of taste;
> Whose bolder genius, fondly wild to see
> His grove a forest, and his pond a sea,
> Breaks out—and, whimsically great, designs
> Without the shackles of rules and lines.
> Formed on his plans, our farms and seats begin
> To match the boasted villas of Pekin.

Presenting pictures of China in the English landscape and home and emphasizing the "zig-zag" line or "irregularity" of Chinese design, Chambers's interest and encouragement of the "use" of "authentic" Chinese features of architecture and wares (that he or Chinese artists carefully sketched for him on his visit to Guandong) would develop later in the century into the aesthetic of the "picturesque" in English gardens. The qualities of English "picturesque" emerge from the Chinese and Indian aesthetic: the temples, the decorations of serpents and bells, the Chinese idol or porcelain elephant on the mantle. William Cawthorn captures this in a poem:

> On every hill a spire-crown'd temple swells.
> Hung round with serpents, and a fringe of bells:
> Junks and balons along our waters sail,
> With each a gilded cock-boat at his tail;
> Our choice exotics to the breeze exhale
> Within th'enclosure of a zig-zag rail
> In Tartar huts our cows and horses lie,
> Our hogs are fatted in an Indian stye;
> On ev'ry shelf a Joss divinely stares,
> Nymphs laid on chintzes sprawl upon our chairs;
> While o'er our cabinets Confucius nods
> Midst porcelain elephants and China gods. ("Of Taste")

Here the intermixing of Chinese, Tartar, and Indian tastes define the "British" style. On the other hand, essayist Joseph Addison (1672–1719) returns the gaze and presents the Chinese perception of the European aesthetic (just as

G. L. Dickinson had presented a Chinaman's view of English culture in *Letters from a Chinese Official*):

> The inhabitants of that country laugh at the Plantations of our Europeans, which are laid out by Rule and Line; because, they say, anyone may place trees in equal rows and uniform Figures. They chuse rather to show a Genius in Works of Nature, and therfore always conceal the art by which they direct themselves.
> (quoted in Hunt, *The Genius of the Place*, 140)

In spite of cultural and aesthetic resistance suggested above, under the influence of architects like William Chambers, a style labeled "Orientalism"—which included elements of the Chinese, Japanese, Indian, Arab, and Russian aesthetic—arose during the period of British economic expansion and contact with the East in the latter half of the eighteenth century. And the "Anglo-Chinese" garden emerged. The Chinese philosophy of the harmonious relation between man and nature is mirrored in the garden and the architecture (pagodas, teahouses, bridges, moon-viewing platforms) that are spaces for meditation. Since styles of meditation are learned inside gardens or moon-viewing terraces or teahouses, the paths, bridges, water, flora, fauna, temples, pagodas are varied spaces constructed to fit or enhance the state of mind of the meditative garden dweller. The basic states of mind to be cultivated in a Chinese garden are "pleasing," "horrid," or "surprising." Instead of the tyranny of French "rule and line," Anglo-Chinese gardens evolved into local spaces containing a variety of visual landscapes: grassy areas that lead to a small area of water, surrounded by rock formations, around which there may be trees, an arching bridge, a sculpture, and cattle or deer on the surrounding slopes. Chambers explained that since the Chinese are not fond of walking, they rarely created the grand avenues or expansive walks to be found in Europe:

> The whole ground is laid out in a variety of scenes, and you are led, by winding passages cut in the groves, to the different points of view, each of which is marked by a seat, a building, or some other object. The perfection of their gardens consists in the number, beauty, and diversity of these scenes.
> (*Designs of Chinese Buildings*, 15)

Two of the features that distinguish the Chinese garden, then, are the "asymmetry," the irregularity in the arrangement of plants, rocks, trees, and structures, and the variety of "scenes" to be encountered as one walks through it, each one representing a different affect or point of view. If the garden is small, objects are placed so that they can be viewed from different points of view: a rock might be the backdrop for a waterfall from one perspective, a looming mountain from another angle. If the grounds are large, different scenes may be constructed for morning, noon, or evening views when the sun or moon casts a certain kind of light over a bridge or building or a weeping willow tree. For example, one might position stepping stones on a path so that at a particular time in the evening, from a particular stone, one can view a pagoda next to an arching bridge, a mountain behind it and the moon at a certain height in the sky. Such gardens still exist in China today, and there are particularly beautiful ones in Suzhou and near West Lake in Hangzhou. It is the multiplicity of scenes, views, perspectives, and surprises in the garden as well as painting and poetry that drew European modernists, sometimes unwittingly, to the Chinese aesthetic. This fluidity and multiplicity of perspective infiltrated the British gardens, visual arts, and, eventually, literature.

The formula of three kinds of scenes—the pleasing; the horrid, or the terrible; the enchanted, surprising, or romantic—is achieved, according to William Chambers, by the Chinese with the special effects of winding rivers, lakes, vessels, sculptures, aquatic plants, and flowers. The *pleasing* scenes are achieved by simple lakes, fountains, hills, woods, gay plants and flowers, and contrasts of light and dark that create a picturesque scene. *Horror* is achieved with dark caverns, gloomy woods, rushing cataracts, barren rocks, ill-formed or shattered trees, burnt buildings, bats, owls, vultures, and birds of prey as well as howling wolves and growling tigers. Sometimes descriptions of local tragedies are inscribed into the stone to add to the gloomy mood of the *horrid* garden. Walking in the gardens of Suzhou and the West Lake as well as gardens found in the middle of cities like Beijing and Shanghai, I too experienced the variety of scenes that Chambers described. There is a wonderful surprise and variety in the small landscapes presented in a walk that was foreign to me, used, as I am, to the formal gardens of the French or the wilder look of contemporary British gardens. As suggested, these scenes contributed to the development of the Gothic in British eighteenth-century literature and art. The *enchanted* or *romantic* scene is constructed with surprise streams or

The Chinese pagoda, Kew Gardens, London, built 1761–62.

torrents passing underground with strange, gurgling sounds as well as the weeping willow, one of their favorite trees, as well as plants, flowers, and birds. The Chinese are also expert at creating scenes that are formed from the soft, bluish limestone that I discovered in my trip to southern China, Guelin on the River Li. Limestone mountains are formed into strange surrealistic shapes by the erosion of waves or rain. In some gardens, the Chinese create artificial rocks from these limestone forms by the addition of cement. "Irregularity" is preserved and, as Chambers notes, "artful confusion" reigns with "no appearance of the skill which is made use of" (*Designs*, 189). Because parts of China are quite hot in summer, water is always a part of the gardens and the streams or cascades constructed are never regular but sinuous in design. Trees may obscure the end of streams; dark passages in caverns excite suspense in the spectator. Parts of the composition of a garden may be obscured by mountains or buildings or mist or appear in moonlight stimulating the viewer to imagine what is held back (han xu) or what is left out or unseen. Such gardens, like Chinese poetry, leave room for the imagination of the observer, another element that relates to twentieth-century modernist principles outlined in chapter 5.

Kew Gardens: The Chinese Pagoda

Another striking design that helped to create the vogue for Chinese landscape is William Chamber's eighteenth-century Chinese Pagoda that still stands in Kew Gardens, London. This Anglo-Chinese style became fashionable for a while in decorative buildings as well as the gardens described earlier about the middle of the eighteenth century. Architecture inspired by the East—particularly the pagoda and rotunda—were present in the British gardens established at Ranelagh, Vauxhill, Brighton, and Kew. Contemporary reports of Ranelagh, a fashionable public resort in Chelsea that opened in 1742, state that it was designed to rival Vauxhall with its Eastern garden, canal, bridge, and Chinese buildings and rotunda (Bloom, *Evelina,* 407). And the Royal Brighton Pavilion in Sussex is a fanciful collection of buildings that embody Chinese, as well as Moorish and Russian architectural features.

Kew Gardens or the Royal Botanic Gardens is England's leading botanical institution consisting of over three hundred acres of lands and royal residences. William Chamber's work for Prince Frederick, Prince of Wales, and Princess Augusta during this period reveals the awakening of British interest in the Chinese aesthetic at least forty years before Lord Macartney's official trade mission, 1789–92. William Chambers, when introduced to Prince Frederick in

1749, drew up plans for a "House of Confucius," which he described as a "new Chinesia Summer House painted in their stile." Chambers, *Plans, Elevations, Sections, and Perspective Views of the Gardens and Buildings at Kew in Survey*.

The Chinese Pagoda, built 1761–62, was considered at the time to be the most accurate imitation of a Chinese building in Europe, commissioned by Princess Augusta, the mother of George III, who later stimulated trade with China. It was constructed according to the Chinese fashions of the day through British eyes: a ten-story octagonal structure, the walls constructed of multi-colored greystock bricks, fifty meters high. The *Universal Magazine* commenting on its size compared it unfavorably with the "stupendous originals" noting that "we must look upon that at Kew almost in the same light as the little models of the latter that we see in the toyshop" (Kew Information Sheet). An interesting detail in the history of the Kew Pagoda is that the roofs were originally covered with varnished iron plates with an iron dragon. Each of the eighty dragons (a symbol of the emperor and good luck) was covered in colored glass and held a ball in its mouth. This roof feature was double gilded and chimed in the wind. Later, however, George IV replaced the metal plates with slate when he sold the dragons to pay his debts, according to Joseph Hooker, director of Kew Gardens 1865–85 (Kew Information Sheet). A visitor to the Pagoda now will see holes puncturing each floor. These were made during World War II so that British bomb designers could drop models of their inventions from the top of the pagoda to test their flight.

Images of Kew and its Chinese pagoda have entered English literature. Virginia Woolf's 1919 story "Kew Gardens" describes the beauty of a July afternoon in the gardens and summons the Chinese tropes of pagoda, tea, orchids, cranes, and crimson colors:

> Wherever does one have tea? she asked with the oddest thrill of excitement in her voice, looking vaguely round and letting herself be drawn on down the grass path, trailing her parasol, turning her head this way and that way, forgetting her tea, wishing to go down there and then down there, remembering orchids and cranes among the wild flowers, and a Chinese pagoda and a crimson-crested bird.

Originally, the Kew Pagoda, on a site near the Orangerie in Kew Gardens, was next to the Turkish Mosque and Alhambra, also designed by Chambers, reflecting the fashionable interest in Eastern styles among the landed gentry in the middle of the eighteenth century. Queen Louisa Ulrika of Sweden was reported to be downcast because she did not have a "Chinese folly" in her garden at Drottningholm Palace outside of Stockholm as did her mother, Queen Sofia, and her brother, who later became Frederick the Great.

The style, "chinoiserie," was loosely based on Chinese designs and descriptions and sketches from travelers like Chambers. The Kew Pagoda, though considered by the British to be authentic, should have had an odd number of stories—not ten—to be really accurate. But there were other pagodas built in Europe before the Kew version. Louis XIV, the Sun king, built a Chinese Pavilion (Trianon de porcelain) at Versailles during the winter of 1670–71 (just before the Kew construction); Elector Max Emanuel built a two-story Pagodenburg at Nymphenburg, 1715–18. In England, the Kew Pagoda inspired a three-story interpretation at Alton Towers in the 1820s, and another pagoda was built in St. James Park in 1814 in honor of a victory in the Napoleonic wars but was burnt down by a fireworks display during the commemoration.

Though Chinese features were presented to the English in engravings before William Chambers—the gardens at Kew were never fully accepted by the British. There was resistance to the admission of the "foreign"—the Chinese elements—into the definition of the English garden art: critics feared the dilution of pure "Englishness" in the garden and the culture. William Mason satirized the "Barbaric glories" of Kew using the category "uncivilized" to condemn difference as discussed in chapter 3, "East-West Conversations":

> August Pagodas round his palace rise,
> And finish'd Richmond open to his view,
> "A work to wonder at, perhaps a Kew."

Reacting against the "extravagances that daily appear under the name of Chinese" (preface, *Designs*), Chambers visited Canton [Guanzhou] twice in the eighteenth century as an employee of the Swedish East India Company. While there, he made drawings of typical buildings, boats, furniture, and gardens that he later used in his landscape and building designs. Like an early-day Roger Fry, he realized the potential contribution of the new Chinese aesthetic to English arts and asserted that "the architecture of one of the most extraordinary nations in the universe cannot be a matter of indifference to a true lover of the arts" (preface, *Designs*). Chinese gardeners, Chambers says, are "like the European painters" who inspire English practice (Hunt, *The Genius of the Place*, 283). But his boldness was ridiculed by Walpole, who wrote that his *Dissertation on Oriental Gardening* (1772) was "more extravagant than the worst Chinese paper . . . : the only surprising consequence is, that it is laughed at, and it is not likely to be adopted" (quoted in Hunt, 33). Despite this resistance, the aesthetic of Chinese gardens filtered into British perception and practice and influenced the developing British modernist aesthetic.

William Chambers, though fascinated with Chinese arts such as those presented in the Brighton Pavilion, nevertheless, feared "to be numbered among the exaggerators of Chinese excellence" (*Designs,* 1). Suspected of placing Chinese architecture "in competition either with the ancients, or with the moderns of this part of the world," he employs the words most often applied to Chinese arts, "curious," and pro forma, acknowledges their "inferior taste" (*Designs,* 2). In his work, as in Roger Fry's, the word "useful" appears in relation to Chinese arts, each foreseeing that the "variety" to be found in foreign arts will be a contribution to the British aesthetic, which each in his time—two centuries apart—sees as insular and dull. Chambers continues that "generally speaking, Chinese architecture does not suit European purposes; yet in extensive parks and gardens, where a great variety of scenes are required, or in immense palaces, containing a numerous series of apartments, I do not feel the impropriety of finishing some of the inferior ones in the Chinese taste." In the context of eighteenth-century regularity of "rule and line," Chambers is treading in dangerous territory. Defensively he notes that he looks upon Chinese buildings "as toys in architecture . . . on account of their oddity, prettiness, or neatness of workmanship, admitted into the cabinets of the curious, so may Chinese building be sometimes allowed a place among compositions of a nobler kind." Chambers is clearly impressed that the Chinese "formed their own manners, and invented their own arts, without the assistance of 'example,' and far from all civilized countries" (Preface, 2, *Designs*). Though observing in his aesthetic discussions the familiar dichotomy between the "civilized" and the "antique," the West and the noncivilized and barbarous East, he refrains from using the debasing vocabulary of other British observers. He notes only that China has been geographically and linguistically isolated for thousands of years, and therefore has developed an aesthetic untouched by the West.

There was a professional cost to Chambers' embrace of China's aesthetic. He apologizes for his travels and taste in his preface to *Designs of Chinese Buildings, Furniture, Dresses, Machines, and Utensils,* and asks "why it should be criminal in a traveler to give an account of what he has found worthy of notice in China." Anticipating a loss of reputation as an architect, he is clearly aware of his cultural transgression as an aesthetic "criminal." Though commenting on what is "novel," "odd," "pretty," or "curious" about the Chinese, his main strategy, nevertheless, was to familiarize the British with the Chinese aesthetic by comparing it to what they did know, the art of the ancients. He compared the "ting," the great entrance hall of a Chinese house to the Atrium, the Peripteros of the Greeks, and the Monopteros and Profsyle temples. He noted the use of the "pyramid" figure in antique Greek and Chinese architecture, as well as columns for support, fretwork, and the manner of putting up walls. But he found the affinity "surprising" because "there is not the least probability that one is borrowed from the other" (Preface, 2, *Designs*).

The Royal Brighton Pavilion in Sussex, England, is another British fantasy of the Orient. Here we see what Baudrillard terms "the liquidation of reference." Its wondrous collection of buildings contains the Chinese influence that Chambers appreciated as well as Moorish, Indian, and Russian influence. Designed by Henry Holland in 1787 and expanded with the fantastic minaret design of John Nash, the Pavilion was completed in 1820. It soon became the center of Brighton's international social scene, as we read in Jane Austen's novels.

Many of the objects inside the pavilion are featured in the grand rooms revealing the popular "Chinese taste" in seventeenth- and eighteenth-century England. They were made by the Chinese for the British market or were British adaptations of Chinese design: Chinese lacquered furniture, flowered wallpapers, Spode blue and white porcelain lamps flanked by dragons, beech chairs simulating bamboo, and huge crimson doors with gilt decorate many of the rooms in the pavilion. The taste was not new in the mid–eighteenth century almost every large English house had its Chinese room or what was called "Chinese Chippendale" furniture. The tropes of Chinese design—the pagodas, butterflies, peacocks, dragons, bamboo, serpents, goldfish, flowers—are everywhere. And the large murals represent the benign aspects of Chinese culture: children playing with a harmless snake; women with regal bearing gesturing gracefully or wafting fans; children holding banners and parading with cymbals and lutes; a man and child gazing at a goldfish; a child bestowing flowers upon a woman. Interestingly, many of the figures in these murals wear Chinese costume but have the rosy faces of the English. This blending of cultures defines chinoiserie. The whole building is a flight of fantasy that expresses the poetic interest in and desire for the "mysterious" Orient. Dazzling though it is, we are reminded that that Pavilion is a British conception of the Orient, the decorations of which became the "simulacra," the substitute for the actual China living through brutal famines and battles among the warlords during its construction in the eighteenth century.

The Hybrid Vision

Why do these multiple British constructions of China matter? What does the cultural and aesthetic contact described in this chapter yield? Julian's travel letters and the art he sends back from China; Vanessa and Ling Shuhua's correspondence; Virginia Woolf and Ling Shuhua's letters; Lamb and Meredith's use of the trope of the blue and white willow pattern plate in literature; Waley's translations of poetic scenes of far-off China; William Anderson's eighteenth-century sketches of China, its landscapes, and people; the Anglo-Chinese garden; Felix Beato's photographs of the Second Opium War; and Keynes' maps of networks of British Rail. Each landscape contains its own ideology and worldview and all contribute cultural knowing to the whole. Through cultural contact, imaginings and art, the British gain a more complex vision of "reality" that incorporates Chinese visions that become an unacknowledged part of an enriched modernist British art.

Fantasizing about a life in England with Shuhua in an intense period of their relationship, Julian Bell creates a "hybrid" scene. He writes to Shuhua that "we will walk down the garden path and you shall write Chinese poems and paint Chinese pictures about English scenery" (17 December 1936). Later Vanessa writes to Shuhua during her visit to London in 1949 to mount her show of paintings at the Adam's Galleries. Vanessa, like Julian, was drawn to the "hybrid" vision of a Chinese artist in London. Before Lily Briscoe, the English artist character in *To the Lighthouse,* incorporates Chinese eyes that become part of the modernist aesthetic vision, we find the British fascination with Ling Shuhua's hybrid vision in a letter that Vanessa wrote to Shuhua:

> I am sure people will be interested in seeing how London looks to a Chinese artist. One has seen so many paintings of Chinese scenes, but very seldom any of one's own familiar surroundings. (Berg, undated)

When Shuhua did paint such scenes and they were exhibited at the Adam's Galleries, Vanessa admiringly wrote:

But when we [Duncan and Vanessa] came to look at them more carefully I was really very much impressed by your qualities as an artist. It is most interesting of course to see European landscape through Chinese eyes and I thought some of the most successful were those of Switzerland. (Berg, 13 December 1949)

Such "hybridity" now theorized by critics such as Homi Bhabha, Stuart Hall, Arjun Appadurai, and Sara Suleri[7] was present in people's observations and in cultural constructions in England and China in the 1920s and 1930s, hinting at what has developed into modernism and postmodernism. Another artist and writer, Chiang Yee [Jiang Yi], was similarly looking at London, Paris, and other European cities through Chinese eyes about the same time and wrote a series of *Silent Traveller* books. When we look at people looking at landscapes together at a particular moment in cultural history, it is rather like a visual chord in which we see many things at once. For the landscape of China—as Virginia Woolf's lighthouse—is not one thing.

Chapter Five

DEVELOPING MODERNISMS

INCORPORATING "CHINESE" EYES

Virginia Woolf confers "Chinese eyes" upon Lily Briscoe, the English artist in *To the Lighthouse,* suggesting a new mode of perception that had been developing in England from the import of blue willow pattern to *le jardin anglo-chinois.* Imagining the state of mind and perception of an English artist aesthetically foraging between cultures in remote regions of the world in the twentieth century, Woolf lacks familiar models. She glancingly presents an artist enriched by the "foreign" or more specifically, "Oriental" discernment, for Lily's eyes are "fine, Chinese, oriental." Just as the Chinese writers described in previous chapters—Ling Shuhua, Xu Zhimo, and Xiao Qian—forage British culture and literature for inspiration, Lily's perception is honed on that of eighteenth-century British travelers, artists, and poets who professed to learn from the aesthetic creed of the Chinese. "My eyes and my taste, since I have been in China," says the writer Attiret, "have become a little Chinese" (Lovejoy, *The Grand Chain of Being,* 119). Following Lily Briscoe's eyes, this chapter suggests new directions in the study of modernism as an aesthetic, an ethos and a mode of perception that has been defined many times. Modernism, confined for the purposes of this study from about 1890 to 1940, constructs itself not only from European sources, but as advanced in this chapter, a greater range of cultural phenomena including Chinese art, literature, and culture at the forefront of change. Astradur Eysteinsson asserts in his study:

> While everyone seems to agree that as a phenomenon modernism is radically "international" . . . constantly cutting across national boundaries, this

Artist at Work, Chinese stamp

quality is certainly not reflected in the majority of critical studies of modernism. Such studies are mostly restricted to the very national categories modernism is calling into question, or they are confined to the (only slightly wider) Anglo-American sphere. (*The Concept of Modernism*, 89)

It has not been fully acknowledged that Chinese art and decoration in England intertwined in the development of British modernism. Yet the tradition of valuing the beauty of Chinese porcelain, silks, scrolls, fans, furniture, fashions, gardens, and objets d'art is a long one. Even the British who did not travel became "a little Chinese" in their domestic and aesthetic tastes, beginning in the eighteenth century. The vogue for chinoiserie (at its height between 1890 to 1935) that could be observed in the Chinese Pagoda in Kew Gardens, the Brighton Pavilion, or in London's Liberty department store was a preparation for later more serious engagement in the visual and literary aesthetics of China in the twentieth century. The visual and aesthetic principles embodied in arts and wares kept China in the eye of the British, preparing for the ethos of modernism.

Among Roger Fry's own collection were his coveted Tang horse and Kuan Yin, a 6th century stone goddess of mercy. Through commercial institutions like the Liberty department store, founded by Arthur Lasenby Liberty in London in 1857, and later Roger Fry's Omega Workshop, 1910–14, the taste for the designs, patterns, forms, and materials of "the foreign" was encouraged. His Omega workshop produced a copy of an eighteenth-century, grey-glazed, Chinese vase. Foreign objects representing a mass of different aesthetic tastes appeared in British homes. And Liberty & Co. became a kind of mini-museum, an exhibition space for beautiful wares selected on the basis of their ethnographic interest and artistic merit. One catalog described the spaces for the bazaar at East India House and Chesham House, where most of the art and products of the East were introduced, as "arranged for the display of specimens." This vocabulary is curiously scientific, following the ethnological drift of the time, giving us a sense of the foreign goods and peoples as objects of study. The "specimens" were the objects imported from these countries, at the end of the nineteenth century: later British adapted and became "familiar" with these foreign objects and the vocabulary transformed. "Curios" or "specimens" became "craft," "objets d'art," and "art," helping to create a modernist aesthetic that knowingly or unknowingly incorporated the "foreign."

An 1898 catalog, "The Liberty Bazaar: A Permanent Exhibition of the Most Characteristic Decorative Objects and Artistic Manufactures of Europe and the Far East," validates the department store's status as a kind of mini-museum on its opening page. It states that the store contains permanent and practical art and that the viewer can see the "most famous modern decorative manufactures of Europe and the Far East." The "rules" of the "exhibition," often held in Liberty's East India House or the basement of Chesham House on Regent Street separate from the main store, are contained in an 1892 catalog that states "The former Exhibition was held under the more usual Exhibition rules—that is to say, visitors were not so much desired to purchase as to take note for future use of the great advance made in the British silk industry." Some exhibitions were produced to familiarize the public and create an informed consumer.

It is said that when Arthur Lasenby Liberty opened his department store, he began to stock his store with oriental objects after he had seen an international exhibit of Chinese art at the Victoria and Albert Museum. Before he established the first Liberty department store and transformed shopping into an Oriental "bazaar," people purchased goods in small specialty shops. The "space" of London expanded geographically and metaphorically. Liberty catalogs at the turn of the century present images of bazaars, an "oriental" world that presents an array of goods from all over the world in one place, displaying objects—sometimes for exhibit, sometimes for sale—from countries like Japan, China, and Persia. One of the Liberty catalogs described the "fanciful products of the Eastern World. The Bazaar, indeed, is a veritable realization of the Palace of Aladdin, with the xix century supplemental advantage of brilliant electric illumination" (Eastern and Misc Bric-a-Brac Liberty & Co., 1891). Turn of the century catalogs describe "Japanese coloured antimony metal ware; Indian hand-engraved solid red-copper wares; Benares trinkets, finger bowls, bells, and trays; Byzantine hanging lamps; Arab smoking-room hanging lamps, mosque lamps of brass; bronze Persian dishes; Rouen Faience; Sarceic and Hindoo carved inlaid furniture; Damascus hand-wrought metal work; Turkish artistic metal work hanging lamps; Swedish tubs; Hispano Mauro Metallic Lustre-ware; and English Florian Ware and Green Ware."

An 1896 Liberty catalog, "History of Feminine Costume," traces the evolution of female fashion from the earliest times to the present. Influenced by designs, fabrics, and trends from other parts of the world, the narrative claims,

"In addition to marking an era of Renaissance in female costume, [the developments] . . . have beneficially influenced, and well-nigh revolutionized the textile and decorative manufactures of the *civilized* [emphasis added] world." Designers and artists may forage for ideas of form, color and design from "uncivilized" nations—see Liberty products from China, Turkey, Africa, India—but it is only the "civilized" world that knows how to develop and innovate with this "raw" material in the British fashion market. In the background of this discourse to be found in the Liberty catalogs is the narrative of the new institution of the department store that embodies the Victorian social evolutionary theory of Darwin that cultures develop from the "primitive" to the "civilized." This same phenomenon can be observed in department stores in Europe and America today. The introduction of the culture, for example, of Mozambique in Paris's Galleries Lafayette or New York's Bloomingdale's presentation of Chinese-influenced products after the exhibition "Treasures from the National Palace Museum, Taipei" at the Metropolitan Museum of Art in September 1996 is continuing evidence of the relationship. Chinese silks, designs, patterns, themes, porcelain, ceramics, tea, bibelot, lacquer boxes, wallpapers, and embroideries were marketed by the department store, and through this the British public was familiarized, socialized, and educated into a Chinese aesthetic emerging from an "uncivilized" world.

What objects were on view reveals much about British politics. One catalog stated that the British market was flooded with "the textile treasures of Turkey after the war of 1887," suggesting the aesthetic "looting" that accompanied England's wars. Once again the question of what is "civilized" surfaces in the discourse of the department store and museum as in the earlier dialogue between G. L. Dickinson and Xiao Qian. The "civilized" world's configuration and representation of its care, possessiveness, and, sometimes, appropriation of the arts, products, designs, and forms of the "primitive" world remains complex. In the "Eastern antiquities, 1897–1900" Liberty catalog, the cover depicts an Asian figure with clawed toes, punk hairstyle, and a wild facial expression, lifting a hatchet-like tool. On the other side of the page is a generic Persian, Turkish, Indian figure with a fez-like hat kneeling on a straw mat forging a metal object on a fire. Summoning up stereotypical images of the "primitive" makers of the products displayed within the Liberty catalog reinforced England's comforting polarities of the "civilized" and "uncivilized" world. Nevertheless, we note in the new millennium the cultural riches that England absorbed from the East. Though propelled by economic motives, the Liberty catalogs document the British trade with, interest in, respect for, and engagement with Eastern arts, products, and cultures. In its images and descriptions, the department store and catalogs reveal British prejudice but also the attempt to familiarize the foreign and the exotic in forming itself. The ideology of the British is reflected in the choice of adjectives used to describe products that were "appropriated" and "looted," but "enriched" the culture.

The narrative within the Liberty catalog contains descriptions of products like "A *grotesque* Japanese Bronze Kylen formed as an incense burner"; "a *quaint old* Chinese bronze goat"; "a pair of *rare old* bronze candelabras in the form of lotus flowers and leaves. An *exquisite* group producing a fine effect"; "a figure of a Chinese mendicant in Sang de-boeuf pottery. *Very quaint*"; "A *curious* old Malay Kreese with a quaint ivory handle carved in a *very grotesque* style with the head and shoulder of a myth"; "A *quaint old* Japanese helmet of black lacquered wood, having the crest of a Daimes in gold upon the front. Messr Liberty & Co. Ltd. have a *choice* collection of Japanese Helmets which

Liberty catalog cover, "Eastern Antiquities" (1897–1900), emphasizing the "primitive." By permission of the Victoria and Albert Museum, National Art Library, London, England.

are well worth a visit of inspection." Adjectives like "grotesque," "quaint," "exquisite," "uncommon," "rare," "curious," "old," "fanciful," and "original" code the East as obsessed with the "miniature," the "curiosity," the "ornament." The "foreign" both intrigues and threatens the British aesthetic imagination. The cultural irony is that these new products and arts imported from China, Japan, and India—and initially described as "primitive" or "grotesque"—were domesticated by the British in the department store. As time passed, these products were endowed with more value and class, as can be observed from the history of changing adjectives. For example, we begin to observe the use of the French language, *"crepe de chine"* or the *"anglo-chinois jardin"* to familiarize and domesticate the "grotesque" and "primitive" and "curious"; and, in some cases, these objects eventually earned the label "art." Such products not only contributed practical and artistic elements to the marketplace of England, but transformed taste, homes, and the modernist aesthetic.

These department store catalogs, then, are important cultural documents that reflect the ambivalence of the British culture, its receptivity and resistance to Chinese art and culture. The British sense of self, others, and art is negotiated in the descriptive words on the page. From this cultural and aesthetic negotiation beginning in the middle of the nineteenth century, elements of the "foreign" became incorporated into British aesthetic, surfacing in the modernist period. Often this contribution is unacknowledged. However, it cannot escape a reader that in the 1896 "History of Feminine Costume" catalog, the British costume of 1789 consists of "a large hat a la chinoise, trimmed with ribbons and bunch of light, green feathers, in the midst of which a black wing stood up, the crown being covered with striped yellow and black silk" (Liberty Catalog). Feathers imported from China as well as hand-painted and finely spun silks of all kinds flooded the British market. The skirt of this outfit is described as being made of bright blue silk and the corsage is "pointed and made of striped lavender and white pekin" (Peking silk). "Sirang," printed silk, is mentioned along with "chrysanthemum silks" suitable for tea gowns. During this high period of chinoiserie, the 1936 catalog describes handmade knickers in "flesh pink crepe de chine" and Golden Bird silk "printed in a variety of Chinese designs and fast to washing colors on a lightweight Chinese Tussor Silk."

The attention to Chinese art and wares was significant, but it should be noted for future explorations that there was also a considerable display of Japanese products—the enamels, bronzes, lanterns, Kaga ware, Bishui ware,

Imari plates, Raku figures, Satsuma ware, and Nagoya blue and white—their "consummate skill" noted in commentaries. Japan, considerably more open to the West than China since the Edo period, was culturally and politically closer to imperial England, and, undoubtedly, more receptive to trade. Nevertheless, the products of China were featured in the Liberty catalogs: the Canton Gongs; sunshades and glass lanterns; blackwood carved stands adapted for the display of porcelains, bronzes, jardinieres; joss sticks, the pastilles used in the temples and the joss houses in China, and a reputed disinfectant and a fragrant perfume; and fans.

Another aspect of the British presentation of Chinese products is that some of the objects made available in Liberty may fall into the category of "looting," a hotly contested issue in art museums today as discussed in the writing of James C. Hevia. European "ransacking" of Chinese art is validated in a letter that Roger Fry writes to G. L. Dickinson from Paris in 1913. He observed:

> The East is thoroughly ransacked by arts dealers and . . . one can learn more about the best things in Paris than in Beijing. I've just seen a show in Paris full of the most amazing things among them the finest Wei dynasty statues from somewhere away in the West of China as fine as any ever done. The Chinese pictures Bob's got aren't much (tho' they're pleasant pretty things) but it's evident that the really big things are never accessible. The Chinese know too much about it for that. (1 June 1913, Dickinson, King's College)

In addition to the shopping rituals in department stores, the British were also drawn to tea drinking and the social rituals surrounding it, which, led to the importation of teas from China and India and an interest in importing and producing beautiful china in which to serve it. The British, tea drinkers like the Chinese, had been importing tea from India, which had been importing it from China since at least the establishment of the British East India Company in the seventeenth century. There was a long tradition of tea drinking in China, its rituals and forms blossoming during the Tang period when tea was advocated not only for traditional medicinal purposes, but also for mental alertness during Buddhist meditation (Blofeld, *The Chinese Art of Tea*, 3*ff*). The Chinese written character for tea is pronounced "cha" (sometimes "tei"), and "cha" or "chai" is still the term used in India and Russia while many European countries use their term "the" or "tea." Like the French, the Persians, and the Dutch, the British were drawn to the beautiful, hand-painted tea sets with representations of birds, animals, insects, flowers, and trees that were imported or adapted from Chinese patterns, particularly the blue and white willow pattern.

The habit of stopping for tea in a teahouse—some still to be seen in Suzhou, Hangzhou, and Yangzhou's beautiful private and public gardens— was a custom in China, and became one in England's department stores and tea shops. Teahouses on Chinese scrolls were solitary in a landscape composed of a lotus pond, a willow tree, a rock garden or a bridge. Shaped like squares, circle, hexagons, some had windows or movable screens made of rice paper that could be folded back so that the landscape or the moon could be admired as part of the meditative moment of tea drinking (Blofeld, *The Chinese Art of Tea*, 53*ff*). Though Roger Fry, writing of Chinese culture, felt that one must be on guard with a people who created the "tea ceremony," people who developed "this hypnotic business of walking along the garden path in silence to the tea house" (*Transformations*, 69), he too was in awe. The teahouses were used for contemplation, scholarly pursuits, playing chess, listening to music, or communing with nature on the moon-viewing platform. It was a place where the Chinese learned to put themselves into a good state of mind.

Adapted from Chinese culture then, tearooms proliferated at the turn of the century in Great Britain. Shopping and working women developed the habit of stopping for tea, helping to create a gendered cultural space for rest and relaxation in the public rooms still to be found all over England. ABC tea shops were founded in 1885 and Lyons in 1894. Consumers could obtain special blend China and ceylon teas, pure China tea, lotus blend choice Indian and China teas, Yang-yin blend, pure ceylon tea (as well as some of the fine teas from Fujian and Zhejiang provinces) along with teapots and accessories. The Glasgow and Willow Tea Rooms in Edinburgh, designed by Charles Rennie McIntosh and his wife, Ms. McDonald, about 1896–1910 and reassembled for a recent exhibit at the Metropolitan Museum of Art, were a response not only to the love of tea imported from India and China, but also the Temperance movement. Tea replaced spirits. More women—socializing after shopping at department stores or as part a growing number of women who were entering the office work force during a time of booming economy—needed tea breaks. Miss Catherine Cranston in Glasgow enlisted architect McIntosh and his wife to decorate four suites of elegant tearooms that thrived in Glasgow. These interiors were designed holistically and combined architecture, furniture, design, and porcelain in new ways. One of these rooms, "The Ladies Luncheon Room," was reassembled and on view in the Metropolitan Museum of Art in 1999 after being dismantled in 1971. It featured beautifully designed wood paneling, art nouveau windows, elegant high-backed chairs, and the ever-popular blue and white willow pattern porcelain, set off by crisp white tablecloths and flowers. It remained open into the 1940s on a street named the Scottish Alley of the Willows. These tearooms drew the attention of the continental avant-garde—Wiener Werkstatt—rather than the British, but the inspiration of the custom of tea drinking and the blue and white porcelain remains in these glorious rooms.

On the utilitarian, cultural, and aesthetic level, the British were culturally ready, as Yip Wai-lim would say, for the absorption of the "foreign" into the "domestic." In this culture of tea, the earliest porcelain was imported from the southern provinces of China in the early eighteenth century—mainly the marked wares of Nankin [Nanjing], Canton [Guanzhou], and Koongsi [Guang Xi]. These hand-painted plates, the designs in all likelihood derived from Song porcelains, were painted free style with leaves, birds, phoenixes (the empress), dragons (the emperor), and particular flowers like the lotus, chrysanthemums, peach blossoms, peonies. Sometimes, Chinese good-wish characters like "fu" (the character for "bat" and "happiness") were concealed in the design as well in the Chinese versions. The English were fascinated with the finely observed details of the natural world on the blue and white, and in 1760, Thomas Minton adapted the first blue willow pattern for English consumption from Chinese design, just as the Dutch developed Delftware. Later, Spode-Staffordshire, Wedgewood, and Adams and Davenport created their own variations on the theme of Chinese landscapes, and the competitive, mass production of blue and white porcelain followed and were adapted to the manufacturing process then developing in England. When the British East India Company became involved in its manufacture, the domestically produced, manufactured willow ware offered a hybrid vision of Chinese landscape seen through British eyes. There were as many as fifty British firms that were manufacturing willow ware at one point. The cultural and aesthetic representations of the gardens of China on the willow ware and in the construction of actual *anglo-chinois* gardens in the landscape of England evolved during this period. The blue and white china became part of British "chinoiserie," the European adaptation of Chinese ceramics and art that fit their notions of "quaint" Cathay.

CHINOISERIE AND THE INTERNATIONAL CHINESE EXHIBITION

"All London has gone Chinese," wrote Vanessa Bell to Julian Bell in China in 1935. With the coming of the first International Chinese Exhibition of Art at Burlington House, London, Vanessa announced "that all the great dresses are going to be Chinese and no one talks of anything but Chinese art" (Letter to JB, 7 December 1935). The mention of fashion and Chinese "high" art in the same sentence records the parallel streams of consumerism and aesthetics in Vanessa's thinking, and British culture at the time, suggested by the earlier

The pagoda dress, Chinese fashion in England. Credit: Metropolitan Museum of Art

discussion of the Liberty department store. Beginning in the late eighteenth century, England's trade with China through the British East India Company stimulated the vogue for antiques, goods, and fashions imported from China and India. Out of this trade arose a European style in art, crafts, porcelain, and objets d'art that was labeled "chinoiserie," a style that conjured a fanciful and poetic notion of China. This style became part of the department store, museum, and tourist culture representing China in England, and shaped the way the British thought about Chinese culture.

England had been interested in Chinese art, objets d'art, and monuments since the first trade missions in the eighteenth century. Museum and personal collections of art and objects from "antique" China were developing rapidly in the 1920s and 1930s and were made possible by England's "nineteenth-century colonial archaeology" (B. Anderson, *Imagined Communities*, 177). The Liberty department store, and art and archaeological exhibits presented in England beginning in the 1850s exhibited a "museumizing imagination" that was, as Benedict Anderson asserts, "profoundly political" (178). Britain's commercial empire, waning after the collapse of the East India Company and the Indian mutiny in 1857, was a sign of its weakening influence around the globe. What was on the rise, however, was the metropole. England, pulling out of India, redirected its commercial attention to aesthetic and historical work within its own culture or symbolically or pragmatically connected to its colonies abroad. It turned its attention to the art, archeology, and ethnology, the study and classification of peoples and objects in the early twentieth century that would be linked to scholarship and tourism. In my recent trip to the Yungang Caves in Shanxi Province, I viewed a few caves where Buddhist sculptures and carvings in niches were looted and carried off to the British Museum. The art objects were not only looted by England but studied, described, and classified in schools of archaeology, art, and "oriental" studies according to British styles of thinking and classificatory grids. In 1909, the School of African and Oriental Studies was founded upon the "fact" of England's firm imperial position (Said, *Culture and Imperialism*, 213). Educational institutions, maps, and museums metaphorically expanded England's domain.

Within Bloomsbury, however, the response to China was largely domestic and aesthetic. Vanessa urged Julian Bell to send objects home—silks, porcelain, and, particularly, ceramics. Crates of folk art, silks, pewter, earthenware bowls, Han pots, and celadon green pottery arrived at Charleston with Julian noting that "the Chinese don't go in for plates and not at all for saucers." Julian was particularly attentive to Chinese ceramics:

> Did I tell you she [Shuhua] bought me some superb cheap stuff the other day—one great Han pot, cracked . . . thick in the bottom, hand-turned, a little black decoration, something pressed into the clay (under the glaze) with the finger, thumb marks showing. Hand thrown of course. (Letter to VB, 6 December 1935)

A month later, he writes again that he will send silks, and notes again that he has bought a great quantity of pots:

> Very cheap all and I can't help thinking you'll like them: deep, irregular, Crackled, glazes, green, dull yellow, and black, with a few simple patterns in black, made locally and bought by Sue from peddlers who come to the door. One rather superb yellow one with figures of sages 18" height, very primitive looking. (Letter to VB, 7 January 1936)

Leonard Woolf was sent a jade fish that remains at Monk's House in Sussex today, and Vanessa was delighted one morning to receive blue and green glass earrings. Julian shopped with Ling Shuhua, and Vanessa longed to be there: "If only I could go out with you into the villages you describe I'm sure I could get lovely things . . . pottery, greenglazes, stuffs—and pewter . . . bring back lots of things" (Letter to JB, 7–8 November 1935). After Julian's death, Vanessa wrote to Shuhua that she would have an exhibition of pottery that Julian brought back from China to be sold to help Chinese students (Letter to LS, 9 December 1938).

At the same time that Vanessa Bell urged the purchase of Chinese ceramics and folk art, she wrote of the International Exhibition of Chinese Art at Burlington House, where she observed official Chinese art. There she saw Chinese bronzes, sculptures, textiles, red lacquers, jade, pottery, fans, and more than 150 paintings from Chinese imperial palaces representing the Tang, Song, Yuan, and Ming dynasties (ca. 618–1644). It is of political as well as aesthetic significance that this was the first comprehensive collection of Chinese art lent to England by the Chinese Government (about 900 of 4,000 pieces of art). R. L. Hobson, a contemporary art critic, observed of the exhibit:

> From the cultural point of view—and cultural relations are now recognized as having a profound influence on political—it is of the highest importance,

in that it will help us, as nothing else can, to appreciate the genius of a gifted race which is separated from us physically by the width of the world and intellectually by a formidable language barrier. ("The International Chinese Exhibition," 311)

England, America, Belgium, France, Germany, Holland, India, Japan, Russia, Sweden, and Turkey also made contributions to this exhibit. It was said that twice as many Chinese art objects were on view as in any previous British exhibition. The Chinese paintings it contained—particularly pre-Ming paintings—were rarely shown in Europe at that time. But landscape painting, always dear to English hearts, drew them to China. Though this interest developed in England late in the nineteenth century, it was not lost upon them that the Chinese had been painting landscapes since the Song Dynasty (960–1279). It followed upon England's earlier fascination with ceramics, porcelains, bronzes, jades, and sculptures. And though these arts were an earlier development in China than painting, the Chinese themselves considered painting and calligraphy to be their most valuable arts.

It was curiously remarked upon by one reviewer that the painters who were most strongly represented in this international exhibition had "worked under the influence of the Jesuits" such as Qing Ting-piao and Castiglione in "the hybrid style." Basil Gray, an art critic, remarks upon the case of the jesuit painter Castiglione, who "used the materials of the Oriental painter, silk and Chinese brush, and took a Chinese name, Lang Shihning, [and who] is really a European painter" (317). Han pottery, Zhou bronzes, jades, sculpture, and, of course, porcelain were the more popular and studied forms in England, as documented in Vanessa Bell's letters and Roger Fry's writings. In the beautifully reconstructed Shanghai Museum, my eye like Vanessa's was drawn to the ancient Zhou bronzes (ca. 1122 B.C.–249 A.D.), the strange and magnificent vessels and delicate tripods. She noted, "The early things are simply lovely, the bronzes and pots" (Letter to JB, 15 December 1935, Tate). At the same time, she observed that the art of China was strange and unfamiliar as we might feel upon first viewing:

> It seems to be something like music using another scale—we're not used to the harmonies and relationships they use (one has to get into their world that seems oddly faint and remote in some way—perhaps, in its own scale, so to speak, it has as much to do with actual appearances as European art. I

suppose the poetical suggestions are in a way rarified, as their poetry seems to be). (Letter to JB, 7 December 1935, Tate)

Despite this unfamiliarity, record attendance at lectures and the publication of simple books on Chinese art during the period of the Burlington exhibit, November 1935–March 1936, attest to the British curiosity about the Chinese artistic tradition. Vanessa's dialogue with Julian—she, a representative British artist in the thirties—suggests that imported commodities, as well as the fashionable adaptations being created in London, inspired, in part, by exhibitions such as that at the Burlington House, helped to prepare the way for England's engagement with Chinese aesthetics.

There was much, however, that was strange in this international exhibit at the Burlington for the Chinese as well as the British. The cultural framing of art for the "exhibition" or "museum" alone was a new concept of presentation just coming into vogue in China in the 1930s. Traditionally, works of art were kept at home in treasured closets or drawers, and scrolls were unrolled in part and shown privately to guests, one by one, on certain occasions. Viewing someone's art was considered an honor, a private rather than a public experience. The scroll, whether paper or brocade, is unrolled slowly, its meaning revealed over time, section by section, in several visits, and not taken in at one glance, as is Western art. The concept of a museum, a public space in which art is not handled but placed on view and distanced behind glass, was a Western concept unfamiliar to the Chinese. One does not view a Chinese scroll as one does a Western framed painting in a moment of time, but over time, as a Torah scroll. A viewer returns to the scroll, viewing short sections with accumulated perception and understanding, holding it in mind and spirit. Vanessa Bell understood this. She writes to Julian asking, "Do they have any kind of picture gallery in China? Or would they consider it barbarous?" (6 February 1936, Tate). The Burlington House, presenting all the Chinese treasures at once, nevertheless, tried to respect the cultural and aesthetic differences by isolating small groups of art objects with screens to sequester the viewing experience. Thus the exhibition space was as much a cultural construction as any interpretation of the Chinese art.

Orientalism and English Reflexivity

Much has been written about the images and tropes of China and the East, present in British culture from the eighteenth century to the time of these conversations in the twenty-first century. Edward Said has argued that "orientalism" is "a Western style for dominating, restructuring and having authority over the Orient" (*Orientalism,* 3) that emerged in the eighteenth century. The cultural fallout was a panoply of goods and images in nineteenth- and twentieth-century England that bore the mark of the British Empire, and that would later be represented in English art and the novel. Said accurately describes eighteenth- and nineteenth-century British expansionist designs upon the Orient; however, the emphasis of this book is on the "contrapuntal perspectives" (*Culture and Imperialism,* 32), the different constructions of the "Orient" by resistant intellectuals, artists, and communities. Chinese art, gardens, fashions, and individuals were set free from historical and political moorings and "set loose" in Britain's cultural, philosophical, and aesthetic domains. Works like G. L. Dickinson's *Letters from a Chinese Official* then became "an occasion for [England's] reflexivity in the form of satire" (Stewart, *Crimes of Writing,* 39).

It is then the premise of this chapter that Chinese art, products, and ideas are marked in several ways: 1) historically, as evidence of British imperialism and signs of markets abroad; 2) culturally, as foreign objects of desire and interest; 3) anthropologically, as objects that revealed information about cultures abroad and that sometimes implied criticism of the British home culture; 4) aesthetically, as contributions to the construction of British culture and international modernism.

Artists, architects, gardeners, and designers everywhere, then as now, cast about for other ways of seeing. William Mason satirically notes the influence of the culture and arts of the East—China, Japan, Tibet, India, Africa, Turkey—on English gardens in "An Heroic Epistle to Sir William Chambers, 1773," who was one of the leading proponents of Chinese taste in the eighteenth century:

> Nor rest we here, but at our magic call,
> Monkies shall climb our trees, and lizards crawl;
> Huge dogs of Tibet bark in yonder grove,
> Here parrots prate, there cats make cruel love;
> In some fair island will we turn to grass
> With the Queen's leave) her elephant and ass.
> Giants from Africa shall guard the glades,
> Where hiss our snakes, where sport our Tartar maids.
> (quoted in Hunt, *The Genius of the Place,* 324)

Images of Eastern landscapes abounded in picture books, literature, art: menacing serpents and lizards, monkeys and parrots in the trees, startling birds, fragrant flowers, strange fruits, and women dressed in the flowing robes of Turkey or China. The requisite blue and white Nanjing vase or the Japanese screen or fan from Liberty's was, as Lionel Lambourne states, a stage in the pursuit of a new aesthetics. Oscar Wilde quipped, "how often I feel how hard it is to live up to my blue China" (Ellman, *Oscar Wilde,* 45).

Images and cultural representations of the East multiplied in British culture during the Opium Wars, 1839–42. The British were always seeking to address a trade imbalance with the Chinese, having developed tastes for imported Chinese silks, tea, and porcelain. Starting with Lord Macartney's 1786 trade expedition, the British sought to correct the imbalance by creating a market and cultural need for opium in China. With opium grown in India and shipped to China by the British East India Company, the market was created over Chinese objection on moral grounds and is an example of one of the most shameful cultural and economic manipulations in British history. Britain's early economic exploitation had cultural fallout—the early association of vice and the East. Images of drugged, criminal, salacious Chinese abound in nineteenth-century British literature, movies, and art, linking degradation and drugs with the Chinese in the popular imagination. The damaging effects of opium in China serves as a background to films such as William Wyler's *The Letter* (1940) and, more recently, Zhang Yimou's *Shanghai Triangle* (1998).

The constructions of the Orient in literature had little to do with the information gathered in travel to China or from those Chinese who visited England. British literary works of Samuel Taylor Coleridge, and, for example, Thomas DeQuincey, describe the consequences of the availability of this drug and its marginal effects in England. Coleridge, like Lord Byron, Percy Shelley, and Robert Southey, imported the imagery of the East into his poetry, leaving us with the quaint opium dream of "Kubla Khan": "In Xanadu did Kubla Khan / A stately pleasure dome decree: / Where alph, the sacred river, ran / Through caverns measureless to man / Down to a sunless sea" (44). In China, the effects of opium were devastating.

"THE LIQUIDATION OF REFERENCE"

Some imported products from China found in Liberty's turn-of-the-century catalogs—for example, Buddha sculptures, Cantonese gongs or joss sticks—

which, in origin, served a ceremonial or ritual purpose, later became decorative objects in British homes belying their makers' "intentions." They participated in the "hyperreal" or the "liquidation of reference" as described by Jean Baudrillard: the erasure of historical origins or cultural references. British consumers then and now did not know or care from where the products came. In observing this phenomenon encouraged by global trade, travel, and exchange of ideas through new technology, we abandon the romance of "intention" or "origin," and consider it one variable among many that determines what a product becomes. Products in the marketplace, not subject to national or racial loyalties, develop into aesthetic bricolage. Commercial products as well as art entered unobtrusively into domestic spaces in other countries and subtly began to influence public taste.

Observations on the popular blue and white willow pattern designed for use in England confirm the way the British were "educated" about Chinese aesthetics. Blue and white porcelain is an example of what Jean Baudrillard terms the "hyperreal" (*Simulacra and Simulation*, 4): "models of the real without origin or reality . . . a question of substituting the signs of the real for the real" (2). The architect, William Chambers, traveled to Guanzhou (Canton) in 1757 because he was concerned that the Chinese products in England lacked this quality: "the merit of being original" or "authentick." In bringing back his own and Chinese painters' sketches of the products he hoped to put "a stop to the extravagancies that daily appear under the name of Chinese, though most of them are mere inventions, the rest copies from the lame representations found on porcelain and paper-hangings" (Preface, *Designs*). At this time, about 1740–80, England had small factories in Chelsea, Liverpool, Plymouth, and Bow creating Chinese-inspired porcelain, but most English factories were unable to compete against the inexpensive Chinese export. Jill Weitzman Fenichell, an English porcelain expert, noted that the "English porcelain was a lot more expensive than Chinese. Even though you might have to wait two years for delivery, you could buy an entire service of Chinese porcelain for the price of a few pieces of English porcelain" (Moonan, "Diverse Styles at the Birth of Porcelain," 38). The artistic style, however, was a blend of the English and Chinese, chinoiserie, and though rejected as "inauthentic" during the eighteenth century, collectors in the nineteenth century and nowadays—abandoning (like literary theorists) the notion of "original"—coveted the "naïve appeal" of borrowed motifs. The English copied waterside scenes, the small boats, junks or clippers in port, the pagodas, the footbridges. And to distinguish their wares from the Chinese, plates and sauceboats were often shaped differently. Teacups and plates or saucers were different in form from the Chinese porcelain: they used wide shallow bowls; handleless small cups, smaller than British tea cups; or somewhat larger cups with lids and, occasionally, saucers, or scallop-shaped plates. The blue willow tradition in England participated in the "hyperreal": an independent cultural and aesthetic history that was loosely connected to its "origins" in China and that became an aesthetic intersection of many forms. We might find any of the following "models" of this popular plate in British homes: the plate could be imported from China and hand painted according to Chinese aesthetics—a Chinese export; or hand painted in China according to British specifications of pattern or design; or hand painted in England by British artists with Chinese inspiration, manufactured in England by Worcester (founded 1751), Derby (founded 1750), Spode, or by a mass production firm like Staffordshire. Baudrillard would say that the ever-popular blue willow plate is without "origins":

> We are in logic of simulation, which no longer has anything to do with logic of facts and an order of reason. Simulation is characterized by a precession of the model, of all the models based on the merest fact—the models come first, their circulation, orbital like that of the bomb, constitutes the genuine magnetic field of the event. (16)

In addition, the blue willow story, a fanciful British tale of Chinese lovers adapted from a Chinese story, accompanied the plate in its cultural history. This story, like the design, is unmoored from China.

In this new international aesthetic, notions of identity, nation and race are in flux. What then does it mean to be "Chinese"? What does "Chineseness" or a "Chinese quality" mean aesthetically? What aspects of identity and aesthetic will be held dear and preserved, which cultural and aesthetic boundaries dissolved and which aspects yielded, willingly or unwillingly, as mass global culture spreads?

Observing this consumer development, the question is whether the interest in chinoiserie—fashion, furniture, and decorative arts—is aesthetic evolution or devolution, whether the presence of consumer products imported from China or manufactured at home prepare or confuse the British "eye" for later aesthetic contacts. Though relatively untroubled in England, this relationship—between consumerism, chinoiserie (the products of popular culture) and art—has a long history of conflict, articulated as a "desecration" or a "commodity fetishism" by the Frankfurt School. Theodor Adorno represents this conflict when he observes that art and consumerism "desecrate each other":

> There are two "positions on objectivity" which are constantly at war with one another, even when intellectual life falsely presents them as at peace. A work of art that is committed strips the magic from a work of art that is content to be a fetish, an idle pastime for those who would like to sleep through the deluge that threatens them, in an apoliticism that is in fact deeply political. For the committed, such works are a distraction from the battle of real interests. (*Commitment*, 177)

On the other hand, Roger Fry, Vanessa Bell's contemporary, would probably consider "chinoiserie" a "training of the eye." Though some twentieth-century observers might view it as "mere frills," contemporary art critics like Christopher Reed affirm the importance of the decorative in the production of the domestic arts.

In recent British and American criticism, evolving out of Ruskin and Fry, critics collapse the distinction between popular products and art that Theodor Adorno maintains. New theories assert the agency of the consumer who "chooses" products rather than being "manipulated" or "victimized" by the market, or, as Rita Felski claims, the consumer has the "potential for active negotiation" or as Ruskin notes, the "power" to educate (*The Gender of Modernity*, 111). Given that the "consumer" from the late nineteenth century on is represented as a woman (61), Adorno's charge that consumers "sleep through the deluge that threatens them" has a gender component. Felski notes:

> The figure of the consuming woman was thus to become a semiotically dense site of cultural imaginings of the modern and its implication for the relation between men and women. (65)

Recent studies focus upon and reveal the influence of consumerism—and gender—on the development of aesthetic taste. Men represent and cloister "high" art; females enhance the growth of consumerism, and are represented as buying-machines, fetishists, susceptible to, indeed victims of, the temptations of mass culture and the new institution of the department store. The gender bias in associating women with "passivity," "inchoate desires," and "susceptibility to the commercialization of pleasure" has a long if unspoken tradition in our culture (61).

At the same time, they were, as Ruskin said, the first "aesthetic missionaries" to promote Chinese culture. In Woolf's short story "Mrs. Dalloway in Bond Street," as in *Mrs. Dalloway*, we observe Clarissa buying the flowers and visiting hat shops and the tailor. Women, then, traditionally consumers and decorators of the home, were largely responsible for the early viewing, spreading, and popularity of Chinese arts and products. Christopher Reed notes that even in attacks on Bloomsbury art today, "domesticity becomes equated with femininity (or even castration and perversion) in a culture where the real and the important are conceived as prerogatives of masculinity, and the homey is, by definition, insipid" (*Not at Home*, 158). He notes that in Germany as well as in England "a decorative ideal of modernism . . . came to seem tainted with connotations of women's work and popular success" (14). The domestic aesthetic—products for the home, Chinese inspired or otherwise—becomes a space that is denied in a developing "muscular modernism." "Rhetorics of masculinity and femininity work powerfully to structure the experience of both sexes, perhaps most acutely in professions associated with art and interior design, which have historically been feminized, though most of their practitioners are men" (16). This gender analysis encourages us then to pay more attention to the domestic undercurrents of the Chinese aesthetic in developing British modernism.

Chinoiserie then became popular in homes and lives of the English, and what began as "curiosities"—strange foreign objects or materials that piqued the popular imagination—transformed into the descriptive category used in Liberty catalogs as "curios." This term evolved from the notion "a cabinet of curiosities" that early European travelers and art collectors developed. Such cabinets can sometimes be observed in seventeenth-century paintings, for example, Frans Francken Il Giovane's *La Bottega di un Antiquario*. Here one sees a collection of objects, some natural wonders such as odd seashells or sea creatures, or exotic flowers or objects from foreign places, arranged in a wooden cabinet, in the room of an art collector selling paintings to a client. Similarly, in England at the end of the nineteenth century, travelers and collectors, and then merchants, fascinated with foreign art and culture, began bringing home or importing foreign ceramics, materials, rugs, and would display them. Once the "oddities" were accepted, culturally and aesthetically, value was attributed to them. The descriptive word then became "art" rather than "curios," as can be gleaned from a perusal of London newspapers and magazines in the 1930s when there was a market for chinoiserie. Until recently, however, consumerism—encouraged by the establishment of the commercial institution of the department store that markets personal and domestic objects—has been considered something "outside" the borders of "art" or "modernism." This study illustrates the way in which the British culture transformed Chinese "curiosities" or "curios" into consumer products, and, eventually, the cultural construction of what is nowadays known as "art."

THE AESTHETIC GAZE

It is perhaps significant that it is Mrs. Ramsay who describes Lily Briscoe's eyes as "Chinese." Lily is perceived as an artist who looks afar and contemplates beauty. She is a woman who chooses not to heed Mrs. Ramsay's anxious advice that "women must marry." As a new woman and an artist, she is "other." But Lily is not the only character with "Chinese eyes." Woolf also confers "oriental" eyes upon Elizabeth, Mrs. Dalloway's independent daughter: "Chinese eyes in a pale face; an Oriental mystery" (186). Elizabeth, like Lily the artist, is an unreadable sign, having some Mongol blood in her lineage. Neither her mother nor Miss Kilman can "read" or possess her. This trope of "oriental" inscrutability and otherness is, however, not only assigned to women in Woolf's work. She extends it to the poet John Donne, described in an essay as a young man "gazing from narrow Chinese eyes upon a world that half allures, half disgusts him" (*Essays*, 3:463). Woolf's admiration for Donne is captured in a trope that applies to individuals who travel to distant psychological or aesthetic regions, "point zero," where they attempt to empty themselves of their culture. Such discerning "eyes" signal not only a distant geographical place, China, but the unfolding of an immaterial philosophical space where "it is once more possible to think" (Foucault, *The Order of Things*, 342).

Looking at English landscape with Chinese eyes, Lily, the English artist, will discover a new aesthetic space and transform what is seen. New structures of perception will emerge and contribute to the modern visual sensibility which, in turn, will affect the "literary." Culturally, the fictional Lily Briscoe's and the poet John Donne's gazing at English landscape with "Chinese eyes" will evolve into the post-empire literary rewritings of England and English works by postmodern children of colonialism from India, Africa, and the Caribbean. For example, Salman Rushdie will rewrite *Tristram Shandy* through Anglo-Indian eyes in *Midnight's Children;* Caryl Phillips will view the empire through the eyes of St. Kitts in *Cambridge;* Derek Walcott will rewrite the *Odyssey* though Trinidadian eyes in *Homeros;* Chinua Achebe will write of his divided self through Nigerian and British eyes in *No Longer at Ease;* Kazuo Ishiguro will see through Japanese and English eyes in *The Remains of the Day,* Zadie Smith will gaze through Jamaican and Bengali eyes in *White Teeth.* Postmodern Indian and Caribbean writers will expand "Englishness": they will travel to England, sometimes to be educated; then home, away from England; then back to England to look at culture and aesthetics anew. This is the new transnational space of the migrancy and contemporary novel that reveals new and malleable identities constituted through travel and suggested in the conversations in this study.

As one of the most important creators of British aesthetic taste in the early twentieth century, Roger Fry incorporated "Chinese eyes" and sought in other cultures the forms that would have a bearing on the visual and, eventually, the literary sensibility of modernism. Urging openness to "a new mass of aesthetic experience," he warned the English:

> We can no longer hide behind the Elgin marbles and refuse to look at the art of China, India, Java, and Ceylon. We have no longer any system of aesthetics that can rule out, a priori, even the most fantastic and unreal artistic forms. They must be judged in themselves by their own standards. ("Oriental Art," 794)

Roger Fry turned to foreign art. While E. M. Forster was traveling to Egypt and India, Fry and other artist friends in the broadly defined Bloomsbury circle were also intellectually and aesthetically voyaging in other places. First, Fry celebrated the French postimpressionists as described by Mary Ann Caws and Sarah Bird Wright in their beautiful volume, *Bloomsbury and France* (1999); later, he became fascinated with the "line" and "rhythm" of Chinese art, knowing that these different ways of seeing would bear on modernism, both visual and literary. He had met Xu Zhimo when he attended Cambridge as a visiting student in 1921, was drawn into a discussion of Chinese art and introduced Xu to European artists such Cezanne, Matisse, and Picasso. Xu, in fact, invited Roger Fry and G. L. Dickinson to visit China to talk about modern art. When he left Cambridge, Fry gave him a large portrait of Dickinson and some sketches to take back, as well as a painting for the president of National Wuhan University (Leung, "English Friends," 6).

Though mainstream British art critics did not embrace Fry's views, he was the leader of a younger generation of painters. Known best as a critic of postimpressionism, he believed that "it's always in France that the future takes shape" (RF to Charles Vildrac, 17 February 1916). Fry was also a painter and began his artistic career drawing closely observed forms of nature after giving up the study of science. As an art critic, his aesthetic judgments were instinctive and he was drawn to Chinese ceramics, particularly of the Han, Tang, and Song Dynasties, as well as the art of Japan, India, Java, and Ceylon that Laurence Binyon describes in *Chinese Art*. He looked to Chinese ceramics, South American sculpture, Mayan art, Byzantine tiles, African sculpture, Florentine Giotto's, and French postimpressionists for "essential principles." Even in 1910, Fry sensed that "the greatest practical value of Eastern art lies in the fact that those essential principles which, in our thirst for verisimilitude, we have overlaid, have been upheld with far greater constancy by the artists of the East" ("Oriental Art," 802). Fry understood the long aesthetic tradition of nonrepresentation in China, a culture that was inscribing bronzes when the West was in the Stone Age. Glazed ceramic art emerged about 1000 B.C., the development of glass in 300 B.C., and the creation of patterned silk in 200 B.C.

Roger Fry's "Essay on Aesthetics" in 1907 provides evidence of his early interest. His tastes developed, perhaps, in his discussions with Denman Waldo Ross in Boston or, as with many in Bloomsbury, the popular translations of Tang (6–9 A.D.) poetry by Arthur Waley, *170 Chinese Poems,* 1918, or Laurence Binyon or the translations of *Mencius* by I. A. Richards. In this turn toward the expressiveness and the economy of the aesthetic concepts and vocabulary of the Chinese—particularly "rhythmic line" and "plastic values," elusive concepts to be discussed in this chapter—British modernists sought a new aesthetic.

The period in which Fry began to champion Eastern art, about 1906, and then postimpressionism in the 1910 and 1912 exhibits in England, was one of personal difficulty. After these controversial exhibitions, his granddaughter Pamela Diamand recollects that

> his wife's illness, against which he had struggled indomitably, was declared hopeless, his connection with the Metropolitan Museum of New York, for which he had turned down the possibility of becoming the Director of the National Gallery and which was his main financial stay, was ruptured and his reputation as a learned exponent of Italian art was shaken as a result of his championing the Postimpressionists. (REF, 4)

The personal blows, his wife's mental illness, and professional rejection by the official art world, she suggests, made him a bit reckless. He was ready to personally and culturally act up, and he wrote to his friend Simon Bussy in 1911, "I am now become completely Matissiste" (*Letters*, 348).

To Julian Bell, who had a close relationship with Roger Fry (as documented in his own and Vanessa's letters and in his unpublished "Hogarth Letter" on Fry), he was "first and foremost an eccentric in the grand manner of the English eccentrics, and it is thus that I most often remember him—as a child's vision of the White Knight come out of the Looking Glass World" ("Hogarth Letter," 44). Leonard and Virginia painfully rejected this "Letter" which Julian wrote about Fry after his death in 1935–36 when he was in China for their Hogarth publication series. This was not only because Julian had a careless writing style, and difficulty writing on argument, but also because the letter was mostly about Julian. When Virginia Woolf received Julian's first draft in December 1935, some pages of which he said "flew in to the China seas," she asked him to "rethink them" and asked for more information on childhood stories and Fry's work. Julian, in the end, never wrote an acceptable, publishable, or public letter. After this rejection, Vanessa Bell wrote protectively to Julian about Bunny Garnett's theory of Virginia Woolf who "lives so precariously (in nerves and brain) that she can't face any other writer of any real merit. The responsibility and strain of accepting them would somehow upset her own balance, he thinks. That is why she always gives absurd praise to obscure females and one never hears her really enthusiastic about any of her own generation" (10 October 1936). Julian, nevertheless, wrote lovingly of Fry as an aesthetic mentor, and Woolf credited him with capturing "the feeling of him" (*Letters*, 5:447). In the same letter to Julian, Woolf wrote that, as she was reading through Fry's 1926 letters in preparation for writing her biography, she came across Fry's compliments on Julian. Quentin, Julian, and the Keyneses had been to dine, and Lydia, J. M. Keynes's wife, was talking on and on. Fry writes:

> I felt hardly able to play up and relapsed into talk with Julian and Quentin who accompanied us. Julian's very beautiful, and very charming and extremely intelligent. He's got much of Clive but is a more serious character with bigger ambitions and altogether more to him. I've been teaching him chess and he's got on with astonishing rapidity so that I have to reduce my handicap every day. (Woolf, 1 December 1935, *Letters*, 5:449)

Vanessa captures this moment of mentoring and chess in her painting of Julian and Roger still on the stairwell at King's College, Cambridge.

But at first, Fry, the art critic—with whom we can identify as American and British viewers of Asian art—was bewildered by the strangeness of the new art. It was art, it should be remembered, that swirled into British aesthetic consciousness in the twentieth century because of England's eighteenth-century imperial and commercial ventures. Always adventurous, Fry felt that the British public were "such sheep" (Letter to Robert Bridges, 20 November 1920). Vanessa Bell, whose aesthetic views were very much influenced by Fry, was also open to other ways of seeing. She wrote to Julian in China in 1935:

> My dear (we've never heard of the old man of Peking [Beijing] who paints like Matisse—can one see his works?) It seems to me something like music using another scale—we're not used to the harmonies and relationships they use (one has to get into their world which seems oddly faint and remote in some way). Perhaps, in its own scale, so to speak it has as much to do with actual appearances as European art. (7 December 1935)

She added then that George Duthuit raved about Chinese painting and said that all they "leave out they leave out on purpose because they know better" (7 December 1935, Tate). Fry's views, which inform this chapter, reveal not only his curiosity and receptivity to Chinese and French art as a part of developing modernism, but also implicit criticism of the conservative nature of British art and aesthetics. He believed "we English decide about everything—even art—(alas) according to morality" (Letter to Charles Vildrac, 17 February 1916). In a 1910 review, he writes of how, scarcely a hundred years ago, art meant for the cultivated European was that of Greek and Roman sculptures and paintings of the Renaissance. He articulates the English crisis of representation in a review of Lawrence Binyon's *Painting of the Far East*. He states that once critics acknowledge that these views of art are not the only ones, then "we have admitted that artistic expression need not necessarily take effect through a scientifically complete representation of natural appearances" ("Oriental Art," 794). Fry here intellectually worked through his own scientific notions about observation as well as one of the basic tenets of modernism: that verisimilitude or lifelike quality is no longer a value in art or literature. The future of English art for Fry was in viewing of the art of France, Africa, and Asia.

Fry's "Chinese eyes" developed in a series of reviews and essays around 1907 and in his well-received Slade Lectures on Chinese art at Cambridge in 1933–34. One of the most likable and generous of English art critics, Fry was intellectually open and always aesthetically venturing into new spaces. Like Virginia Woolf in the literary domain, he was eager to break old aesthetic molds. The civilizations of East and West had developed almost independently from 2000 B.C. Nevertheless, we witness their joining in Fry's writings and observations, drawn as he is to ancient Chinese art as a harbinger of modernism. He spurred cultural and aesthetic discussions in the twentieth century as did William Chambers in the eighteenth.

Roger Fry was a bellwether for English art, ready around 1910 to abandon the Western thirst for "lifelikeness," an antimimetic stance that the Chinese of earlier epochs (though not necessarily contemporary China, which was then in turmoil) had adopted. He was ready to embrace "a vast mass of new aesthetic experience" ("Oriental Art"). Literature was always England's greatest art; Fry, in observing an exhibit at Burlington House, writes that it is no wonder that English art has also tended to be literary: "an art that tells stories, an art of illustration—the picture book" (Burlington House, 2). The exhibit, he says, "offers plenty of entertainment for those who like pictures but do not care much about art." Such pictures taught morality or edified the reader. But in a 1925 essay, Virginia Woolf urges painters, as she later will advise authors in *A Room of One's Own*, that they should not contaminate their art with "storytelling" but "say what they have to say by shading greens into blues posing block upon block." She notes in a letter to Richard Braithwaite that in *The Waves,* she did not "aim at character or story" but "beyond all that . . . O the difficulty I had till I got them to think in soliloquy at a certain pitch" (Letter to RB, 21 January 1932).

THE EPISTEMOLOGY OF BOUNDARIES: SUBJECT AND OBJECT

British modernism turned away from the representational and sought an abstract reality, for example, Lily's "triangle" to represent the Ramsay family or the "line" in the center of her painting that may represent the lighthouse or a marker of time. The Chinese had been preoccupied with the calligraphic line in painting for centuries. If we begin with a traditional notion of landscape painting in the East and West—an artist in a physical place, meditating or gazing upon and representing a scene in nature—we find different stances, experiences, artistic materials, notions of process, and representations of the scene in twentieth-century China and England. The relations among the painter, nature, and art materials are experienced and represented differently in the painterly tradition of East and the West. As has often been observed, the human figure dominates the British landscape, while, for example, a Song landscape represents man as a part of the whole of nature: mountains, sky, rivers, and trees. The "place" of man and the relation of the painter, the "subject," to the landscape, his "object," is experienced differently in each culture. Chinese Daoist notions lead artists to perceive subject and object as one, the artist in harmony with the contemplated object—or as I. A. Richards, fascinated with the philosophy of Mencius, says, "the mind was not so split" (*Mencius on Mind*). Chinese artists often present flowers or vines on ceramics or scrolls not just as "still" designs but more often as part of an organic branch or tree, growing. British modernism, more troubled about such harmony, announces and represents a "split" or fragmentation of subject and object.

For example, Virginia Woolf in *To the Lighthouse* presents a woman artist with "little Chinese eyes" standing at the edge of a lawn, painting. Lily Briscoe sees

> the jacmanna was bright violet; the wall staring white. She would not have considered it honest to tamper with the bright violet and the staring white, since she saw them like that, fashionable though it was, since Mr. Pauncforte's visit, to see everything pale, elegant, semi-transparent. Then beneath the color was the shape. She could see it all so clearly, so commandingly when she looked: it was when she took her brush in hand that the whole thing changed. (32)

Woolf focuses on Lily's "process" of seeing the abstraction, the "shape" beneath the "color," "the lines running up and across" (310) that preoccupied the European postimpressionists. But Woolf, the modernist, captures not only the "seeing" but the performance, the process of painting:

> With a curious physical sensation, as if she were urged forward and at the same time must hold herself back she made her first quick decisive stroke. The brush descended. It flickered brown over the white canvas; it left a running mark. A second time she did it—a third time. And so pausing and so flickering, she attained a dancing rhythmical movement, as if the pauses were one part of the rhythm and the strokes were another, and all were

related; and so, lightly and swiftly pausing, striking, she scored her canvas with brown running nervous lines which had no sooner settled there than they enclosed (she felt it looming out at her a space). (235–36)

Woolf presents Lily's process as she paints—the pausing, dancing, flickering, striking—and achieves in one stroke the union of subject and object.

Similarly, the long tradition of Chinese painting has never concealed its process, often revealing traces of brush strokes on the canvas. In English art, techniques and process often hidden in nineteenth-century Victorian "finished" paintings become more valued and visible in the twentieth century. The very materials the Chinese painters use—the unprocessed paper, the silk, and water-based ink—become one with the paper as the artist becomes one with nature: the ink and the paint, materials, dissolve into the paper or silk in the way that the artist's consciousness dissolves into nature. And because the artist works quickly with these materials, the fleetingness and spontaneity of the brush stroke is captured. As demonstrated here, the Chinese artist is not "belated" (Liu, *Translingual Practice,* 183) but "early," preceding the "modernist" in letting the viewer know just how he achieves his artistic effects on the canvas—his brush strokes and process visible—long before Western artists do. And this focus on process both in literature and painting will become an expression of English and American modernism and postmodernism.

About ten years after Woolf created Lily Briscoe, Ling Shuhua in China wrote a short story, "A Poet Goes Mad," in which she represents a male poet-artist:

> As the sun came out, Chu Lung Shan filled the centre of the picture very clearly, the ridges stretching away in shades of brown and green one behind another, the farthest seeming as insubstantial as silk gauze, and as if one could see the sky through them. It was very clear now at the foot of the mountain, and a long bright line looking like a river lay curving round them; beside it was a long belt of trees, stippled with deep red and white powder, like peach or almond blossom. At the foot of the hills were clumps of pale yellow willows, matching the yellow thatch roofs of a number of houses, and from these the snow white smoke rose straight, blurring the distant colours of hills and trees.

Painting in China is closely related to poetry: both are defined along with calligraphy as "literary" arts. A painting does not just represent a scene but holds the life of the contemplative artist—the imagined colors, concept, thought, emotion, and philosophical notion that has moved the artist to paint. This poetic thought becomes part of his design of a painting in the form of a calligraphic verse inscription, and the written word intertwined with line is honored for its inherent beauty. To the Westerner, this calligraphic inscription may be peripheral—it is writing not painting—but to the Chinese, the painting is enhanced by and is indistinguishable from the strokes of the characters. Quentin Bell in a foreword to Ling Shuhua's Wen-Jen Hua catalog (Qing literary school of painting) wrote:

> Here the picture is united to a poem, united often enough by the *actual intrusion of the written word in the picture space* [emphasis added], by the quality of the calligraphy, and, we suppose, by a harmonious agreement between the verbal sentiment and the image. How then can we get the full flavour of the works, even though we may be served by the best of translators? Speaking for myself, I am not much helped by those who furnish philosophical explanations; there is, whatever the expositors may say, an enigma, which in the end leaves us baffled. (Ling Shuhua, *Painter's Choice*)

Baffled, this Western artist, Quentin Bell, finds the calligraphic verse an "intrusion" on the picture space.

The Chinese artist as represented in Ling Shuhua's story blends the act of painting, the observation of nature, and the reciting of poetry. This produces a "contemplative" state of mind rarely described by Western artists as a prelude to the act of painting. Painting a "mountain and river picture," considered one of the noblest branches of Chinese painting, Chu Lung Shan unites painting and calligraphy and poetry. The painting is "literary" in that his perception and performance are conditioned by the refrains of the poem—"he heard someone singing the poem while he stood there looking." The sensation of hearing a poem or looking at a landscape is blurred. He paints in color, though most Chinese have painted largely in ink to express emotion without the aid of color. The portrait of the artist develops:

> Che Hsing [Zhe Xing] watched it [the landscape], rapt, and without thinking of moving. "I never thought there was such a place in the Western Hills. It looks as if it were the Peach Blossom Source [The Earthly Paradise of a famous Tang poem] itself." He heard someone singing the poem while he stood there looking. (Ling Shuhua, "A Poet Goes Mad")

There is not only the sense of Che Hsing's [Zhe Xing] raptness, but his stillness—watching "without thinking of moving"—so that he becomes a part of the nature that he paints. As Roger Fry describes it, the Chinese artist's exalted feelings in nature lead to a silence, a contemplative state that produces a "receptivity" (*Transformations*, 69*ff*), and a state that suggests "listening." The Chinese painter is not "representing" or "depicting" nature—terms that suggest a split between the artist (subject) and the painting (object) in the West—rather he is "engaging" or "harmonizing" his emotions in the natural world, or through "contemplation" or "meditation" becoming a part of the rocks, trees, streams, and mountains. The vocabulary is apt. As Lydia Liu reminds us, such distinctions—our "translingual practices" of naming and our discursive formations—are crucial to our honest attempts to describe Chinese aesthetic practices (xviii). Ling Shuhua describes the artist's state further: "his mind is free to wander in a state of complete peace and forgetfulness. When it passes this state, it achieves a state of transcending, out of this world" (introduction, *Painter's Choice*). This state, described by James Liu, is one of "reception" where the poet/painter "'empties' his mind and keeps it 'still' in order to be receptive of the Tao" (*Chinese Theory*, 49). In the Chinese metaphysical theory, the poet-painter is the "instrument of some supernatural force of which he were unaware and over which he had no control, but as spontaneously manifesting the Tao, in the 'transformed state' of consciousness he has attained in which there is no longer any distinction between the subjective and the objective" (49). The "self" blends with other states of being and is not "lost" in the process. Interestingly, Liu notes that the "mirror" in Western art is a metaphor for art as a reflection or imitation of nature or the idea behind it, whereas in Chinese art, the mirror signals "emptiness," freedom from oppressive rationality or feelings.

The Chinese painter fills his central space clearly with color, and the borders shade away—"the farthest seeming insubstantial as silk gauze"—articulating none of the "white spaces" and "emptiness" that Lily confronts on her Western canvas. The landscape, which serves as the background for man in eighteenth-century British art, is the foreground for the Chinese painter. Impressionistically, the Chinese painter paints what he sees from the foot of the mountains, to the hills, trees, thatched roofs, smoke—blurring all in his haze of colors. He is not bound to the principles of linear perspective or shadows. His "position" is what he can apprehend of the relationships between all that he sees and meditates upon. Reciting poetry and meditating, he stares beyond the object and paints what is in his mind's eye—something transcendental. As Kojin Karatani says of the Japanese culture, "landscape is not simply what is outside. . . . It is only within the 'inner man' who appears to be indifferent to his external surroundings, that landscape is discovered. It is perceived by those who do not look outside" (*Origins of Modern Japanese Literature*, 25). As an example, Karatani notes that Basho, the Japanese poet, experiences landscapes but writes not a single line of description.

This blurring of the distinction between what is outside in external surroundings of nature and what is inside in the perception of the artist is perhaps best illustrated in some Chinese landscapes and modernist canvases like Picasso's. In both Chinese and British modernist art, multiple perspectives, what is outside and what is inside, are presented in a glance at the canvas. For example, in beautiful Song landscapes (960–1279 A.D.), artists simultaneously expose the different sides of mountain scenery. Rocks may be represented as seen at different times of the day, from different positions (looking up, down, across), from different perspectives (on top of the mountain, from a cloud, from a river). It is said that certain monks spent five years in the mountains, learning to understand the essence of "zhi" (spirit) of rocks, painting them from inside, outside—multiple perspectives. Similarly in viewing Gai Qi's hanging scroll, "Reading in the Studio Douqiu," painted during the Qing Dynasty, we see a willow tree from above as if we are looking down upon it; at the same time we view a man reading through a window in a studio as if we are on a level plane with him: perspectives are multiple and simultaneous as in European modernist art. This desire to blur the inside and outside is an impulse that we also find in other modernists like the architect Frank Lloyd Wright. In the landscape of a house, he attempts to create a continuum from the inside to the outside so that one cannot clearly draw a line between the two. This collapse of outside and inside in the psyche and art leads modernist writers and painters like the earlier Chinese artists to present "reality" on one plane from multiple perspectives, one folding into the other, as, for example, in a Picasso's "Les Demoiselles d'Avignon."

The Chinese painters and the European modernists in these examples no longer draw the line between inside and outside in consciousness and perception—like a Moebius strip—and begin to present it all on one plane in their art. The painful splits that Lily Briscoe experiences are expressed less often— either those of the modernist artist who is self-conscious and preoccupied with being a subject (in this case a woman artist surrounded by men who assert that women "can't paint, can't write") or the separation of the artist from the "white canvas." It must be remembered that the sense of place of a male painter in Chinese society is different from a woman in England like Lily Briscoe: he is often a male scholar or poet who also paints; he works in isolation; he is not concerned about what other people think. Gender does not intrude in his scene. And the places in which he works are no-place: "Living deep in the mountains . . . painted in the studio of the Deep Willows."

The long tradition of the Chinese painter might be compared to eighteenth-century British watercolorists who moved away from the mimetic representation of nature. The great English watercolorist, Alexander Cozens (1717–86), experimented with the technique of the "blot," using random dots of color on paper as a method of dissociating the mind from references to place, color, shape, and other effects. And in the nineteenth-century, J. M. W. Turner further developed wonderful atmospheric effects with watercolor and light in actual landscapes, and this later was infused into French postimpressionist landscapes that become more abstract. It is in observing these artists as well as Chinese painterly values that the differences in the articulation and vocabulary of landscape art are noted. Chinese terms, as this chapter demonstrates, are more abstract, at least to our perceptions—rhythm, line, spirit, life—while the nineteenth-century British artists experimenting with new techniques in landscape use words that point to light, color, sky.

Lily also ruminates as she paints, but it is not on the topic of poetry that inspires the Chinese artist Che Hsing [Zhe Xing] in Shuhua's story. She thinks about herself, woman artist as subject or the Ramsay family expressed as a triangle. Woolf's narrative experiment and her major contribution to modernism was her wonderful mix of the inner being of women with reflections about externally defined social roles and expectations. Woolf's artist has the anxieties of the world in her fingertips: she does not achieve the contemplative state described earlier in the Chinese artist. Woolf represents the artist as a "new woman," a female "subject" with psychological and social "demons" alighting on her paintbrush:

> It was in that moment's flight between the picture and her canvas that the demons set on her who often brought her to the verge of tears and made this passage from conception to work as dreadful as any down a dark passage for a child. Such she often felt herself—struggling against terrific odds

to maintain her courage; to say: "But this is what I see," and so to clasp some miserable remnant of her vision to her breast, which a thousand forces did their best to pluck from her. (*To the Lighthouse*, 32)

Lily's painting is minimalist and abstract. Woolf's description of her painterly style moves like no other, including Shuhua's, in and out, up and down, in the mind of the reader: "up" (surface, society, events), "down" (depths, core of being). She represents Lily's thinking about her painting and glancing at Minta being charming to Mr. Ramsay:

> At any rate, she [Lily] said to herself, catching sight of the salt cellar on the pattern, she need not marry thank Heaven: she need not undergo that degradation. She was saved from that dilution. . . . She had been looking at the tablecloth, and it had flashed upon her that she would move the tree to the middle, and need never marry anybody, and she had felt an enormous exaltation. (154, 262)

The interweaving of the process of painting and social narrative beautifully captures the flickering thoughts and consciousness of Lily. Society might view her as "a skimpy old maid, holding a paint-brush," but she has clearly stepped into "the waters of annihilation" (269). Lily as a troubled "subject" is separated from the "object," the landscape and the painting: there is a gap. She is a woman painter and she openly grapples with issues of confidence. The Chinese artist as represented in Shuhua's story is in harmony with his own contemplative state and the landscape: "subject" and "object" are one. But as the East "modernizes," critics note that subjects are delineated in new ways and the transcendental state of the artist described above is abandoned. When a brush painter of the East paints a pine grove, Kojin Karatani says, the artist means "to depict the concept signified by the pine grove, not an existing pine grove. This transcendental vision of space had to be overturned before painters could see existing pine groves as their subjects. This is when modern perspective appears" (27).

THE CRISIS IN REPRESENTATION: AESTHETIC RECIPROCITY

This discussion of landscape and painting reveals that in both England and China there was a crisis of consciousness and representation in the early twentieth century. The aesthetic economy and restraint that the British found in the poetic and visual practices of Chinese art reinforced the direction of British modernism. The individual voice and expressiveness of the romantic poets, as well as some of the moderns, attracted some Chinese writers in Beijing to the British aesthetic. In the rather confusing debates that surrounded the revived discussion of modernism or *mo-deng* in China in the 1980s, literary critics—rather than recognizing this mutual receptivity—continued to be preoccupied with "old think," with Chinese cultural "purity." "Will the stream of consciousness flow into China?" was a question posed in a modernist forum by Marxist critics who feared contamination from the "impurities" in Western perceptions and literary and cultural values (Li, "Modernism and China," 41). This assertion of national "purity" against "foreign" influence continues, inspiring ennui then and now. Cultural and literary crossings have occurred and cannot be stemmed. Less xenophobic critics like Ba Jin and Xia Yan observed in the same modernist debate that intellectual travel and literary dialogue begun in the 1920s and 1930s would continue: aspects of British literary aesthetics might reinforce tendencies already developing in China; aspects of Chinese visual and poetic art might reverberate in British visual and literary modernism. Rather than employ an outworn model of political dichotomies to polarize aesthetics, or label "modernism" a western movement, we should perhaps transform our vocabulary to terms like interrupted modernisms, multiple modernisms, migratory modernisms, or an evolving international modernism.

A more useful critical discussion would emerge if it was simply observed that the ethos and perceptions of modernism began to consciously take shape in China in the 1920s and 1930s as the authors and cultures of Russian, India, France, Germany, and England encountered one another and the circumference of aesthetic consciousness widened. The question for the Chinese, as it is for the English, is what shape modernism would take as it is evolved in different places and migrated to other countries and then back again. In the 1920s and 1930s and now, the national "state of mind" is in flux: notions of "Chinese" identity, culture and literature from the mainland, Taiwan, and Hong Kong have become more fluid as people travel in actuality or cyberspace, and as economic systems like socialism, Marxism, and capitalism lose their clearly defined boundaries. Such movement and travel changes the construction of social and literary reality. Sometimes a literary technique like surrealism or stream of consciousness (catchall labels that have more refinements than such static labels suggest) are adapted and used as they fit the needs of the artist or culture regardless of politics. The contemporary Chinese writer Can Xue, for example, uses surrealist techniques to capture her sense of the actual and the imagined China. The doubleness of the technique contains a tension that fits the cultural and literary reality she wants to create. She has her own aesthetic grounding, and as an artist would rightly resist a critical interpretation that tacked, for example, "French surrealist technique adopted from the West" onto her cryptic stories. In spite of political labeling, artists will find methods of evasion, and ways out of cultural divisiveness, achieving individual aesthetic resolution.

Questions of representation thread this book. Edward Said has asked, "How does one represent other cultures?" "What is another culture?" How do different intellectual communities with different historic and aesthetic groundings represent themselves to themselves and to others, given that representation is both an ideological and aesthetic act? Why do some individuals focus on stereotypical or political or racist views while others explore multiple voices in a culture? Why do some critics herd books into jingoistic categories of "imperialist" or "Marxist" categories alone? How are communities represented by contemporaries and in retrospect by literary historians and critics?

Though the aesthetic history of the British and Chinese cultures were fundamentally different, they were also serendipitously complementary. In the 1920s, both cultures questioned their representations and aesthetic stances. Critically, little has been said about this; rather, it is the polarizations that are salient in critical and historical discussion as revealed in chapter 2, "Literary Communities in England and China." The mutual aesthetic foraging, the articulated and unarticulated needs, and the cultural reciprocity marked in the writings and dialogues of these artistic and intellectual communities in the Republican period of China (1911–49) may be the new paradigm for studies of interaction between multiple Englands and multiple Chinas. Some of these were Englands and Chinas of the mind in which, as Jonathan Spence notes, "the country itself begins to fade into another mode of discourse" ("Chinese Fictions," 101). And yet the British modernist movement toward simplicity of diction and economy of line struck a historical Chinese cord.

What British modernist critics have neglected is England's renewed dialogue during the modernist period with the visual and poetic aesthetics of an earlier Asia: the art of the Han, Tang, and Song Dynasties, and Chinese poetry through the translations of James Legge, Laurence Binyon, and Arthur Waley. Though it is now widely acknowledged that the term modernism encompasses a number of historically related movements—impressionism, post-impressionism, expressionism, cubism, dadaism, surrealism, vorticism, futurism, suprematism, orphism—the imagism of China and Japan has been largely undiscussed. The relationship between British and Chinese aesthetics was a conversation begun, however, in the eighteenth century in the writings, for example, of architect William Chambers, and was a narrative submerged in the economic and political discourse surrounding the British empire's expansion into opium, trade, railroads, and foreign concessions into nineteenth-century China. In the early twentieth century, the focus of this study, the activities of trade and economics faded and an aesthetic narrative surfaced. The British acknowledged that the "simplicity," "decorum," and "sedateness," of Chinese culture and art was more compelling than the Indian. This affinity is expressed in their ceramics, porcelain, poetry, architecture, gardens, furniture, objets d'art, home decoration, and fashion, the forms of Chinese art that had been circulating in England since the eighteenth century. Roger Fry asserts that

> Chinese art is in reality extremely accessible to the European sensibility.... A man need not be a Sinologist to understand the esthetic appeal of a Chinese statue.... And it so happens that both the principle of design and the nature of their rhythms are not half so unfamiliar to the European eye as Chinese musical rhythms are to our ears. (*Transformations*, 68)

Their art, though remote, evoked a cultural sympathy, a feeling that this art would not be too "foreign" in a British home. The values inherent in Roger Fry's choice of descriptive words for Chinese objects, for example, are evident as he speaks appreciatively of the qualities of politeness, restraint, understatement, and sedateness (he might almost be describing traditional British cultural traits):

> These Chinese objects have an air of belonging to people who were polite, traditional and sophisticated, and that brings them near to our own ways of living and feeling, more so, I think, than is the case with those of athletic beings who drank out of the black and red Greek vases. With them we hardly know when Epicurean habits might not suddenly give way to explosive irruptions [*sic*] of passion. But with the Chinese, I feel sure that even if one had been put to death at the end of a feast with a dignitary of the Zhou Empire all would have been conducted with reassuring decorum to the very last, for the Chinese have something very safe and comfortable about them which even the grinning monsters' faces on their bronzes do little to dispel. (*Transformations*, 69)

Chinese decoration and art was present in British homes and culture. Even modernist movements like art nouveau selected the simple, elegant lines of Ming furniture made from beautiful huanghali wood, popular in sixteenth- and seventeenth-century China as part of their international exhibits.

The Chinese contact with and interest in European art, and the comparative thinking it spurred, led to the creation of a new field of study in China—aesthetics. Urging G. L. Dickinson and Roger Fry to visit China in 1922, Xu Zhimo advises, "You will have to bring over a lot of books as well for we are unspeakably ignorant in aesthetics as a serious and organized study" (Letter to Roger Fry, 15 December 1922). How aesthetics relates to the categories of literature and history in China is complex, as are the concepts of "literature" that emerged in England in the eighteenth century. Just as the category of "criticism" was developing around the study of "literature" in the 1930s in England, Chinese writers and intellectuals began to anticipate the separation of "literature" from "history," and the creation of the field of study of "aesthetics." Julian Bell had observed that the Chinese rarely "articulated" their aesthetics in discussion. These shifting terms and entities, it must be noted, are part of the emerging cultural and aesthetic "codes" in China at the beginning of the twentieth century.

Another aspect of the crisis of representation in both England and China was a new interest in the concept of a "subject" of a painting in China. Though the understanding of this term was different in England and China because the distinction between *subject* and *object* was not experienced or articulated in the same way as discussed earlier, it should be noted that the Chinese, nevertheless, have always been unselfconsciously "subjective." The treatment of landscapes, mountains, trees, sky, rivers, teahouses, and scholar figures in painting and poetry had always been "subjective." For example, one could discern the subjective signature of the Chinese artist, always, in his brush stroke, though paintings appeared to be of similar "subjects." As Ling Shuhua observes, "The brushwork is sometimes as heavy as a piece of rock; and at other times it is as delicate as a white cloud floating in the autumn blue sky" (*Painter's Choice*, 6). In addition, in the constellation of terms surrounding the "subject," contemporary discussion of "subjectivism" in Chinese literature still suggests broad yet useful distinctions between the "expressive" emphasis in traditional Chinese literature and the "representational" orientation of Western art (Denton, *Modern Chinese Literary Thought*, 8).

When Chinese artists began to focus on the "subject" in a new way or upon different subjects for painting, they did not bring to bear the observational style of the West, influenced by science or the metaphor of the lens. Our metaphors were those of the microscope, the telescope, x-rays, and now laser, sound waves, and cyberspace. The West's development of subjectivity, prompted partly by habits of thinking of the enlightenment, science, and Freud, turned the "lens"—the power of observation—inward, to reveal the hidden parts of human beings—psychological and physical. Roger Fry, as an example, transferred his powers of observation from science to art in analyzing "pleasure" in his responses as an art critic. Other visual artists became scientific in their representation of anatomy and the musculature of figures. The art of China, however, expresses different attitudes toward subjects such as human figures and animals in art. The Chinese artist never loses sight of individuals or animals as a part of nature or society—some larger landscape beyond the individual figure, as discussed in the previous chapter, "Chinese Landscapes through British Eyes." Animals are elevated in Chinese art, as Fry discovered in his observations of the Zhou, Qin, and Han bronzes (ca. 1000 B.C.–220 A.D.). The Chinese, for example, welcome the new year with an animal from their zodiac, while the West presents a human, Father Time, on New Year's Eve. Viewing the culture and art of West with man at its center as "arrogant," Fry praised the Chinese whose world embraced mountains, plants, animals, and sky. They seemed to say through their art:

> We can afford to play. We can play with the offspring of our imagination. . . . We need not take even them too seriously. If we like to imagine monsters, we will, but however real we make them, we need not be frightened by them. . . . Even the beast of the Zhou dynasty, like the Buffalo, do not in spite of a certain clumsy ferocity, really belie this attitude. Everywhere I find, underlying the actual invention, this strain of sly, discreet humor. (Fry, *Transformations*, 80)

It is this quality of "happy disinterestedness" (*Transformations*, 80)—play and humor—that also draws the moderns and postmoderns to Chinese art. In his Slade Lectures, Fry notes how artists of the Zhou Dynasty "play with the idea of an animal's ferocity" (117). Even monsters, the Chinese seem to say in their representations, are only "terrible" in play, and we can often find a smile on the face of the tiger or a forthright fish who gazes out at us from the canvas.

Do not take the world or men too seriously, they seem to say. We remember the three Chinamen carved in lapis lazuli in Yeats's poem: "Their eyes mid many wrinkles, their eyes, / Their ancient, glittering eyes, are gay" ("Lapis Lazuli," 293).

And it is in these Zhou and Han animals that Fry finds the quality of "rhythmic line," or what William Chambers labeled "litheness of form and vitality of movement" (Hunt, *The Genius of the Place*, 230). To Fry, the Zhou bronzes retain, "perhaps from more primitive times, that peculiar instinctive grasp of a vital rhythm which seems so often to disappear from a civilized and self-conscious art" (*Letters*, 87–88). He notes how a bronze elephant "is conceived with such a continuous and consistent movement that he becomes very real and alive" (115) and how the representation of a camel "keeps touch with inner life" (141). Kneeling Eastern Han figures and horses seen in the newly renovated Shanghai Museum and in the Boston Museum of Fine Arts would confirm for me Fry's perceptions. Certain words and phrases play throughout his lecture: spontaneity, intuitive, instinctive feeling, greater psychological expression, revelation of the inner life, rhythm, alertness, and vigor of line. Fry takes the words "barbarian" or "primitive," often used as negative cultural and aesthetic assessments, and creates a positive topspin that transforms meaning.

England and China exchanged during this period new categories of perception as well as a new vocabulary to articulate the changing boundaries of art as determined by differing world views. Words were needed to describe changing aesthetic and philosophical boundaries, perceptions of representation, traditional practices, and new aesthetic experiments. Yet once the words were found and roughly translated, I discovered that they also eclipsed the philosophical "archaeology" of the cultural concept. The truth of Derrida's assertion that "language bears within itself its own critique" is one that is always before us. Words like "rhythmic line," "plasticity," "flatness," or "intervals of space" used routinely in discussions of Chinese art, translated from the Chinese, did, on the one hand, help the British modernists to relocate objects in modernist space. Since the use of white space and perspective were different—presenting figure and ground on one plane—figures sometimes appear to be floating in space in a Chinese painting, or, as Lamb remarks in his essay, "lawless." But what do these perceptions and words mean in the East and the West? I. A. Richards warns of "the concealed ambiguity" in words in his examination of translations of Chinese to English words and concepts in *Mencius on Mind.* Words are, after all, part of traditions of perception, experience, and thinking in different cultures. We know from translation theory that the same words or translations of words and concepts from one language to another can generate considerable ambiguity and misunderstanding. How do we then, Richards asks, separate translating "mistakes" from acceptable differences in interpretation? We include, wittingly and unwittingly, as Richards acknowledges, the mistakes and misunderstandings as part of the dialogue. Using Foucault's "archaeological" analysis of culture, we find that there are, at this time, similar cultural and aesthetic categories and formations in England and China: the articulation of the subject in China or the dissolution of the subject or figure in British modernism; the separation in England or the at-oneness of the artist with his materials in China; the individuation in England or dissolution of the ego of the artist in the universe in China; the separation or the invitation of the reader or viewer into creative partnership with the artist. All these categories reveal the preoccupation with the relation between subject and object (the artist and his materials, the artist and the work of art, the reader or viewer and the work of art)—a defining and important issue propelled by this book—with which both cultures grappled.

Roger Fry believed that science is the antidote to "the unendurable obsession of the ego as the center of things" and tried to incorporate this stance into the words he chose to describe art. In a letter to Percy Wyndham Lewis—whom Fry had invited to be part of the Omega Workshop in 1912 and from whom he separated when Lewis became a vorticist—he writes about Leon Bloy's *Mendiant Ingrat* and the concept of Western "ego." Overwhelmed by "the satanic beauty" of the work, he comments:

> It is fascinatingly interesting to me because I hardly thought that Christianity was made to fit the peculiar arrogance (egomania) of certain Western people in whom the illusion of self-importance is so colossal that they have never had the faintest possibility of understanding what the universe is like. The miracle is that it is the West that has discovered science, the only possible antidote no doubt, to a Western mind, for this unendurable [opinion] obsession of the ego as the centre of all things. . . . Eastern people who alone have had enough humanity to see more or less what things were like have never needed it and of course accept it the moment it is presented to them.
> (Letter to Percy Wyndham Lewis, 5 March 1913, *Letters*, vol. 6)

Never acknowledging Thomas Kuhn's assertion that "there is no neutral observation," even in science, Fry is misled. A critic observing and describing his own perceptions of a work cannot be "objective." But what is relevant is Fry's interest in the East's ability to diminish the force of the "ego" and to enhance the quality of "disinterestedness" in art. This quality draws him and other modernists to the dissolution of the subject (the "ego") in the object (or landscape) to be found in the Chinese aesthetic practice which has an absence of anthropomorphism. One has to look hard and long to find the human figure in the center of a scroll (with the exception of paintings of dead emperors), and rarely a female nude, a common subject in Western paintings. Occasionally, one finds an artist like the now popular Sanyu, who studied in Paris and then painted female nudes with Chinese calligraphy techniques.

The Chinese placement of "man" in the context of landscapes in art is a sign of "disinterestedness." Looking at a typical landscape, we see a monk, mountains, sky, trees, water, footbridge, and a pagoda related in space so that all are a part of the *ground* of the picture and the universe: he is not the unliberated, trapped "Western man" of whom Foucault writes. And in writers like Samuel Beckett and Harold Pinter, we sense the development of this modernist notion of the "disinterestedness" of the universe, even its "indifference." This relates, then, to the unimportance of man in the landscape. Fry notes in his writing,

> The Greek or the Western arrogance about the species of animal to which we happen to belong. We have, therefore, devoted a quite special and intensive study to the forms of our kind . . . the Chinese have never, apparently, focused their attention so narrowly on their own species. They have never lost sight of its relative position in the schemes of nature. As a result we are likely often to feel the inadequacy, and from our point of view, the relative insignificance of their figure imagery. (*Transformations*, 77)

In questioning man's place, Western anthropomorphism, as the center of a philosophical or artistic landscape or the center of perception, Fry, like Virginia Woolf and Italo Calvino, creates a rift in the deepest strata of Western culture. If artists attempt to represent themselves in relation to nature or the cosmos and not just in relation to themselves or other people, they shift the place of the human being in the universe philosophically and aesthetically closer to the Chinese. Chinese philosophy and aesthetics place man in relation to a universe of nature—as visualized in their landscapes—and though man is portrayed as being small in scale, he is, nevertheless, a part of the harmony of the universe. Though Western modernist writers also encompass the universe in their vision, they portray their insignificance in or the indifference of the universe. Rather than being in harmony with nature as in the Chinese world view, they are out of joint and withdraw or become recalcitrant, as in Samuel Beckett's plays or T. S. Eliot's poetry. In the Chinese conception, human beings have a weakly bordered "self" that dissolves into other things. Italo Calvino, just before his death, writes of the same relationship and his desire to give voice to it:

> Think what it would be to have a work conceived from outside the self, a work that would let us escape the limited perspective of the individual ego, not only enter into selves like our own but to give speech to that which has no language, to the bird perching on the edge of the gutter, to the tree in the spring and the tree in the fall, to stones, to cement, to plastic. (*Six Memos for the Next Millenium*, 124)

Sometimes we see a fish smilingly looking out of a Chinese scroll "giving speech" to this subjectivity of which Calvino writes. Virginia Woolf also aspires to enter other selves, into, for example, birds or nature, in the preludes of *The Waves*. She, in fact, writes in her *Diary* at about the same time that she is writing *The Waves* of a play she would like to write with "voices speaking from the flowers" (*Diary*, 4:275). Chinese representations of animals—intuitive Zhou grasshoppers, intelligent fish or ferocious dragons—emerging from the live relationship between the artist and the animal and that often give voice to nature in a manner to which Woolf aspires or which Bertrand Russell hypothesized: the existence of a reality outside the self, a subjectivity possessed by objects in nature. It is a perception that the Chinese had arrived at centuries before.

LEAVING THINGS OUT: THE LINE

Concepts like "line" bring the aesthetics of China and Europe together. The Chinese concept of "wen"—a broad notion of "writing"—explodes the concept of "line" into myriad meanings in the twentieth century. As J. Gernet has noted:

The word *wen* signifies a conglomeration of marks, the simple symbol in writing. It applies to the veins in stones and wood, to constellations, represented by the strokes connecting the stars, to the tracks of birds and quadrupeds on the ground (Chinese tradition would have it that the observation of these tracks suggested the invention of writing), to tattoo and even, for example, to the designs that decorate the turtle's shell ("The turtle is wise," and ancient text says—gifted with magico-religious powers—"for it carries designs on its back"). The term *wen* has designated, by extension, literature and social courtesy. Its antonyms are the words *wu* (warrior, military) and *zhi* (brute matter not yet polished or ornamented). (quoted in Derrida, 123–24)

Such a concept counters our narrow definition of "writing" marks of lines. In a fascinating series of lectures, "Aesthetics East and West," Philip Gould, an art historian and critic, further illuminated this aesthetic of the Chinese "line" in relation to "leaving things out." The "line," Gould explained, grows out of Chinese calligraphic interest, but as Gernet notes, it extends beyond this into "lines" in the veins of stones, the tracks of birds, the markings on a turtle's shell, the strokes connecting the stars, literature, and social courtesy. Though the British "line" lacks such natural and cosmic extensions, we begin to see the admiration for its economy and reticence, its withholding nature (han xu), in art and literature. The "line" in Chinese characters, the art of calligraphy and its extension into the visual art and design of China is what intrigued the modernists, always, about Chinese art. When Julian Bell visited the town of Han Yang Men, he noted that one of the most astonishing sights to a foreigner were the junks on the river. He observed:

> It is at first incredible that a boat with one square sail hung on a mast without any stays to support it should be so efficient. The whole thing is clearly preposterous to one's prejudices about seamanship. None the less, it works, and works admirably—I suppose by some sort of practical intuition like that of the painters and poets who astonish me *by all they dare to leave out.* [emphasis added] ("The Road to Wuchang")

Even in the construction of a boat, the British observer is struck by "all they dare to leave out," an elastic aesthetic principle that extends across the continents and ages to modernist painters and writers. This chapter advances then that the rhythmic "line" of the Chinese aesthetic is a muted partner or harbinger of the modernist movement.

"Rhythm" is expressed in the spirit of the line in calligraphy, painting, and by extension in this chapter, the line in literary modernism. Ling Shuhua in her "Introduction to Chinese Painting" explains the word "rhythm": "The rhythm of a painting comes from a knowledge of the subject. The technique of the brush brings it to life" (6). She reflects, "The spirit and rhythm are of chief importance in a Chinese painting. The exact portrayal of an object is of minor importance" (3). And the rhythm is expressed in the spirit of the line, and, to some degree, by the materials Chinese artists use. Since silk and untreated paper absorb paint instantly and cannot be erased or changed (as the oil paints used more frequently in the West), the signature "line" of the artist—as determined by the media, as well as the psychic state and experience of the "hand"—is more immediate. It is this perceptual and expressive "line" of Chinese art that interests Western artists then and now. Contemporary artists like Robert Motherwell have adopted these artistic materials—papers, silks, brushes—in order to explore the aesthetic practice of the East. Such explorations can be found in Motherwell's ink drawings, again a medium that the Chinese use frequently maintaining "that to express aesthetic emotion without the aid of colour was a far greater art than to express the feeling with its aid" ("Chinese Painting," 8). Similarly, given the attention to the white space and the material absorption of the paper, some of the watercolors of postimpressionists like Seurat and Signac seem like an extension of writing.

Roger Fry, confirming the importance of "line" in the West, also observes that European art started on a linear basis and sometimes returned to it. The emphasis on "line" in Blake enters into Aubrey Beardsley, and the flat, linear quality of Japanese and Chinese prints is reflected in Van Gogh and Manet, and continues into the contemporary experiments of Motherwell, Pollock, Klee, Matisse, and Picasso. Though not very well known, Matisse created vases with dancers in black outline (some of which were owned by the Steins), and some of Duncan Grant's murals and Tunisian earthenware vases show a similar preoccupation (Reed, ed., *Not at Home*, 153). This preoccupation with the "line" became a part of international modernism. Nevertheless, Fry also observed that Western knowledge and preoccupation with the representation of external appearances deriving from our scientific habits of observation, led the Western artist to focus more on the representation of the skeletal and muscular structure of the body, revealing more of what is inside the body rather than the "line" of the contour of the skin. Chinese artists of the Han period relied on the sculptural effects of the "line" as the painters relied on the "line" or the silhouette that they achieved without light sources that the West employed. Not under the same cultural and perhaps "scientific" pressure to represent things as they "are," Chinese artists, particularly of the Han, Tang, and Song Dynasties and later, created linear representations of people and nature that, nevertheless, evoked an emotional response from the viewer. Chinese art, according to Fry,

> never loses the evidence of the linear rhythm as the main method of expression. And this is only natural, the medium used being always some kind of water-colour, and the art of painting being always regarded as a part of the art of calligraphy. A painting was always conceived as the visible record of a rhythmic gesture. It was the graph of a dance executed by the hand. (*Transformations*, 73)

Again, painting is an extension, philosophically and pragmatically, of calligraphy or writing, China uniting the two arts in ways unarticulated in the West. Roger Fry promoted a way of seeing that broke down conventional distinctions of time, Europe and the East, and art and craft. Avatar of modernism, he sees "modernity" in Chinese Song landscapes. The "modernity," he says, consists of the "passionate and disinterested contemplation of nature," as well as the feelings of wonder, awe, romance, mystery inspired in the viewer. Song brush and ink paintings were often described as slender, graceful, and delicate, revealing "philosophical and mystical introspection" (Hunt, *The Genius of the Place*, 231). Similarly, Xiao Qian described Katherine Mansfield stories as Song portraits.

William Chambers and Roger Fry's vocabulary here could as easily apply to the "romantic" as the "modernist" period. The difference between the two is, importantly, in the kind of "contemplation" of nature in the romantic state as opposed to the modernist—what each would hear and see—and what each would include in writing of the moment of contemplation. The modernist, more self-conscious about the separation between the subject and the object— the painter and what he sees—would reflect on the psychology of the artist who is doing the seeing and how this shapes what is "seen." He would include more of the process of observing and writing and with a turn toward the scientific would move inward to examine the psychology of the artist and "seeing." Modernist metaphors emerge from the domain of science, electricity, energy, the lens, the microscope, the telescope, x-ray vision, and now the laser or sonar that enable them to sense and see "within." Though imagining the hidden, interior life is essentially a fictional act, the crucial metaphor of various technological devices comes into play to realize what remains an imaginative act. It is still the *artist's* vision that interests the modernists, not yet holding up the mirror to the viewers or audience, as the postmodernists will routinely do. The romantic view of nature, on the other hand, comes out of a philosophical tradition of contemplation and meditation, and words surface to express the fusion of subject and object: the harmony of the viewer and landscape that emerges from a mystical tradition or German romantic philosophy. In Chinese philosophy, the boundaries between the landscape and the artist— the "dao" of nature and the individual artist—are erased and this movement of spirit or energy enters into the "line" of the painting.

Fry views English nature paintings as "trivial" in their "conceptual" focus, and the Chinese landscapes, more "visual," their appearances clearer. These qualities appeal to Fry and contribute to developing modernist thinking that not only locates the value of "economy" in Chinese art but also transforms it into a literary value in modernism. It is the restraint and the economy in the landscapes that are "modern" according to contemporary definitions. In a recent exhibition of Chinese calligraphy from the collection of Christopher Luce at the China Institute, the reproductions of single characters are drawn from modernist vocabulary: rhythm, fluidity, geometrical design. Connections are made between fifteenth-century master calligraphers, Wu Kuan and Wen Zhengming, and the abstract expressionism of Robert Motherwell and Jackson Pollock.

In "Drawing or Design," Roger Fry reaffirms that "Chinese painting never ceases to be essentially an art of the drawn line, a perceptual and visionary line" rather than what he calls the "constructive" line of the West. The British modernists sought a new "linearity" (abstract, expressive, and suggestive); Chinese artists sought more articulation of the "subject" from the "object" in their representations, which traditionally contained the blurred boundaries, "flatness" and "linearity" for which the modernists yearned. In 1916, Fry writes from Paris, according to his granddaughter, that artists were more interested in the "line" of Seurat than Cezanne. "Line" was becoming an integral part of developing modernism observed also in Picasso and Matisse drawings as well as Beardsley. We can, for example, observe movement in the rhythmic line of Matisse's *The Dance* while *The Conversation* expresses a still moment, almost an Assyrian quality. Pamela Diamand, in describing Fry's interests, notes:

Interest in a tensile line and in volume was growing and thenceforward the contour ceased to be an integral part of the design, it had become skin enclosing something solid. (Diamand, REF, 9)

Fry notes in *Transformations* that "the contour is always the most important part of the form" (72) in Chinese art. Art must be alive, says Fry, and certain rhythms or lines suggest or evoke the spontaneous quality of life, unhampered by conceptualization. Line, of course, is an aesthetic quality that appears and disappears in European art also. Fry draws our attention to the contour drawings of Ambrogio Lorenzetti, the linear schemes of Ingres, and even goes so far as to proclaim Botticelli "an essentially Chinese artist" (*Tranformations*, 73). He points out Degas's understanding of a Chinese quality of placement of forms and Seurat's feeling for "intervals" or negative space, comparing him to the famous Wang Wei of the Tang period. Fry develops his ideas more fully in his Slade Lectures at Cambridge University in 1933–44. Urging his listeners to become "lovers" and not historians of art, he articulates further the concepts of "inner rhythm," "rhythmic line," "feng-shui," "genus loci." What is striking at this time — two years before the International Exhibition of Chinese Art comes to London when chinoiserie and Chinese fashion were the rage — is Cambridge's resistance to Fry's ideas. He notes in a 1934 letter to Charles Mauron that he still has "a mania" for doing research on the influences of Zhou bronzes and Neolithic pottery. Sadly, he observes:

> Not one of my colleagues at Cambridge of about my age has had the curiosity to come to my lectures, I don't say listen to me, but to see my slides, which are often of rare objects . . . they are charming and interesting people but so limited and set in their provincial rut and reflex conservatism that it shocks me. (*Letters*, ca. March–April 1934)

Roger Fry moves the discussion to the literary domain also. He advises that "writers should fling representation to the winds and follow suit" of painters (Reed, ed., *Not at Home*, 22), and Xu Zhimo urges Dickinson and Fry to come to China to "interpret to our serene elders as well as aspiring youngsters the true nature and charm of Western culture which they have been striving to understand and appreciate" (Letter to RF, 7 September 1922).

The "rhythm" of the stroke or line, as described by the Chinese, is elusive, but perhaps description of different aspects of this element will bring us closer. Florence Ayscough in her introduction to poems translated from the

Chinese with Amy Lowell alludes to the uniting of poetry, calligraphy, and visual art in the characters or ideographs of the Chinese language: the quality of Chinese thought and practice that fascinated Apollinaire, Pound, Fenellosa as well as the visual artists. The earliest writing was inscribed on bronzes (1500 B.C.), transformed into ancient pictorial script (800 B.C.), inscribed with the "knife pen." This was given up when the writing brush, called a "pencil" was adopted around 200 B.C. The image of "pencil," in fact, surfaces when, after intensive study, a student becomes a member of the Imperial Academy, an office in the Emperor's Palace, and becomes part of the "forest of pencils." The characters created "li," or "official script," is a simplified form of the earlier knife pen characters. Florence Ayscough describes in her book the "model hand," the "running hand," and the "grass hand," popular with poets and painters in this new style, which in its very vocabulary, "written pictures," breaks down our distinctions between handwriting and art. The genre of "written pictures," in Chinese poetry, is represented in the "hanging-on-the-wall poem" titled "Fishing Picture." The dissolving boundary is also captured in the poem "Calligraphy" by Liang Tongshu (ca. 18):

> The writing of Li Po-hai
> and the blue-green dragon.
> It drifts slowly as clouds drift;
> It has the wide swiftness of wind.
> Hidden within it lurk the dragon and the tiger.
>
> The writing of chia, the official,
> Is like the high hat of ceremonial.
> It flashes like flowers in the hair,
> and its music is the trailing of robes
> And the sweet tinkling of jade girdle-pendants.
> Because of his distinguished position,
> He never says anything not sanctioned by precedent.
> (quoted in Ayscough, *Fir Flower Tablets*, 154)

Roger Fry picks up on this quality of "rhythmic phrase" of the Chinese writer-painter. He states that it permeates the whole body and can only be achieved when the gesture becomes, after much observation, practice, and habit, to some extent, "unconscious." This rhythm happens "only when attention is liberated from actual forms which the hand is producing" ("English

Handwriting," 88). Fry would seem to be getting at another kind of knowledge here, what Foucault later labels the "positive unconscious" of knowledge: "a level that eludes the consciousness of the scientist [or artist] and yet is part of scientific [or aesthetic] discourse" (*The Order of Things*, xi). Trained as a scientist, turned artist and critic, often "ruthless" in his observations, according to Leonard Woolf, Fry perceives, nevertheless, science's inability to describe and explain the practiced yet "unconscious" phenomena of the artist's "line" or "stroke." He goes on to make an explicit connection between English handwriting and the East:

> Both the Persian writers of Arabia and the Chinese have grasped more clearly than Western scribes the two distinct aesthetic possibilities of script which we may call by analogy, "architectural" and "musical." ("English Handwriting," 89).

Fry, in a little-known letter to Robert Bridges, wrote that in copying something, as opposed to generating writing itself, "the rhythm [of writing] was somehow altered . . . it seems to depend on following the flow of ideas as they come into the mind as much as the rhythm of speech does" (18 December 1925). Different from Madame Blavatsky's automatic writing, a line of handwriting in Fry's view or a brushstroke from the Chinese perspective is not just a physical gesture but a "line" of "rhythmic vitality" that comes from deeper areas of the artist's consciousness and body. The whole body is involved in the stroke of the brush, thus reminding us of the American artist Jackson Pollock, who danced around his paintings as he executed the "stroke." The "dance" of the brush is expressive as the strokes and line reveal the psyche. Diane Gillespie notes that Virginia Woolf liked to write at a podium as a young woman in imitation of her sister, Vanessa Bell, at her easel. Both practice a "stroke," the musical and visual "line" of a sentence in a book or paint on a canvas that comes from the vitality of the body. Interestingly, Virginia Woolf, who believed that the pen moves in connection with the whole body, writes of the possibility of a "feminine sentence" in *A Room of One's Own*. Here she speaks in physical metaphors of the "pulse" and the "stride" of a man's mind compared to a woman's and how this rhythm enters the sentence and the book—through the hand. In another work, she speaks of the imagination being largely "a child of the flesh" (*Life as We Have Known It,* xxi). Observations of Woolf's handwriting (to be lost to future computer generations) and the rhythm of sentences in manuscripts reveal that the hand and the mind can take up a certain rhythm at different stages of revision. We can compare Woolf's holographs to the published versions of her novels, and perhaps note how different rhythms of sensation and consciousness enter her sentences. The words, sometimes, as she says, are "levitated" out of one and the beat of mind; pulse and language become a chord. This unity of being, subject and object in harmony, that Woolf and other modernists articulated about "rhythm" in writing was a synthesis practiced in traditional Chinese philosophy, art, and literary experience. Xiao Qian writes of an eleventh-century Chinese painter who, "in putting the leaves of an orchid on his silk paper, his first concern is to be the leaves he is painting" (*China but Not Cathay,* 9).

The rhythm of the object to be contained in the painting is visual, auditory, and tactile. Borrowing from the domain of music, Fry and the fifth-century Chinese critic Xian He have contributed much-needed words to describe evolving aesthetics—rhythmic line or vitality—and curiously, despite different cultural codings discussed earlier, they seem to be on the trail of the same concept. The "rhythmic line" that Fry values in the Chinese bronze animals described earlier can be related to the "rhythmic vitality" that was one of the most important canons of Chinese painting announced by the critic Xian He in "Record of the Classification of Painters," 490–500 A.D. In this first set of aesthetic principles and ranking of Chinese paintings, Xian He graded twenty-seven paintings, between 220–550 A.D., according to six canons, "Liufa," and these are considered to be the standard principles for evaluating art to this day. In his commentary and ranking system for paintings, Xian He considers the first canon to be the most important consolidation of all the others: "the expression of rhythmic vitality in the painting (qi yun sheng dong)." He states:

> In unrolling the scrolls, we share the experience of our predecessors, as well as our contemporaries, who expressed their strength and rhythmic vitality in their works within.

FLATNESS AND PLASTICITY

The Chinese also paid attention to another kind of "innerness." So much of what was "inside" figures in art—in the Western construction of "reality," the muscular and skeletal structure as a basis for a figure, as in Raphael's paintings—was "flattened" in human forms in Chinese painting. In looking at paintings like Monet's *Reflecting the Water Lily Pond at Giverny* (1920), the flatness of the surface and the view of the pond seen from both close up and above at the same time suggest Chinese multiple perspectives. There is a cosmic fluidity to the representation of the pond that blurs water and sky. Similarly Edouard Vuillard's *Morning in the Garden at Vaucressor* (1923), which pictures a woman in a flowered kimono standing in a garden of flowers, picks up the Japanese and Chinese inflection of flatness that Matisse also shares. Chinese figures, Roger Fry would say, had volume but they achieved it in another way (*Transformations*, 74). In looking at the wonderful Western Han tomb figures of a female dancer, about 2 B.C., we observe the line and flatness of the figure emerges rather than anything internal: the long sleeve of the dancer trails down:

>Their long sleeves
>Twirling and twisting fill the hall;
>Gauze-stocking feet
>Taking mincing steps
>Moving with slow and easy gait
>They hover about long and continuously
>As if stopped in mid–air;
>Dazed, one thinks they are about to fall.

The stillness of the pose inspires contemplation.

In an introduction to *Chinese Porcelain and Hand Stones* (1911), Fry writes admiringly of Song bowls and the Chinese respect for the "plastic values" of materials. He notes the "constant contemplation of the artist, and a more caring and tender intimacy" than the Western artist. He laments that the West has "too often supposed that material beauty lay in mere evenness, smoothness and completeness of texture combined with brilliance and transparency of color" in ceramics. The Chinese, on the other hand, "respect the life and quality of the material itself," an understanding that takes on imaginative and spiritual significance in their art. Fry admires "the purely plastic quality, the evidence of the most perfect control over matter" (*Letters*, introduction, 37) in this pottery. This quality emerges, according to Fry, in the "contemplation" of the Chinese artist as he becomes one with the materials. Xiao Qian reports an eleventh-century artist's advice: He who learns to paint flowers should take a stalk of the flower, place it in a deep hole in the ground and examine it from above (*China but Not Cathay,* 9). Instructing on the way "the real shape" of bamboo was to be painted, he wrote that bamboo should be placed in a bamboo stall in "clear moonlight so that its shadow fell on the white wall" (10). Again, the notion of the "line" or "silhouette" or "shadow" is salient. This line is of importance in the tradition of Chinese shadow puppetry still practiced today. Fry, in articulating the "plasticity" of Chinese sculpture demonstrates that the basic shape in Chinese art is the "egg," while the West operates with the form of a "cube" or "polyhedron." Architect William Chambers would assert that in Chinese architecture, the general form of almost every architectural composition is the pyramid (Preface, *Design*). English modernists admired the abstractions within.

Fry articulates then a progressive and more inclusive aesthetic stance for English art beginning around 1907, including not only French postimpressionism, but also what has been largely unacknowledged, the art of the East. In the Omega Workshop (1913–16), Fry, along with Vanessa Bell and Duncan Grant as co-directors, produced and sold all kinds of home furnishings: tables, chairs, carpets, pottery, dresses, printed books, woodcuts. Aside from the *Burlington Magazine,* this was Fry's only commercial venture and its demise probably had more to do with wartime economics than anything else. In this workshop—different from William Morris's Arts and Crafts movement in that it had no morally uplifting purpose—Fry encouraged the decorative talents and play of artists. His granddaughter, Pamela Diamand, recounts: "He was influenced by a profound desire to bring about a transformation in British taste; to provide for more cultured and progressive people, furnishings of all kinds which would bring the delights of color and intelligently organized form as well, he said, as fun into their homes at a price which they could afford" (REF, 4). She also observes that his Omega ceramics—Fry did most of the pottery—were influenced by Chinese ceramics of the early period, the Zhou, Qin, and Han periods as discussed in *Transformations* and the Slade Lectures. But it should be noted that the colors in Chinese ceramics were subdued and muted—the colors of the Chinese landscape—but this aspect did not influence Fry. Bright colors often dominate, and among Fry's caned chairs made for Omega there is one that is painted in red in imitation of Chinese laquer. Reacting against dark and drab Victorian interiors, the Omega artists painted bold colors. In insisting, however, that the Omega methods of reproduction "should preserve actual surface inequalities" of the materials (Diamand, REF,

3), Fry adopts a Chinese aesthetic value. One can observe this influence along with postimpressionist values in the Victoria and Albert collection of Omega ceramics.

THE LITERARY EFFECT OF VISUAL AESTHETICS

In China, poetry, painting, and calligraphy were known as the three perfections, and their integration, a "literary" art. The West observed boundaries between these arts until Fry and other modernists began articulating the desire to dissolve them. After reading Virginia Woolf's story "The Journey" in the *Nation* in 1923, Fry wrote:

> How lovely I think your "journey" is. You really needn't want to paint when you can do a landscape like that over the mountains. It's astonishing how much of a whole atmosphere you put into a few words. . . . There are landscapes in Proust which do certain things painting can't. I'm thinking most of the one of the Bois de Boulogne in autumn. (Letter to Virginia Woolf, 13 May 1923, King's College)

Woolf believed that they were all "under the domain of painting . . . [and] were all modern paintings to be destroyed . . . [we could] deduce from the works of Proust alone the existence of Matisse, Cezanne, Derain, Picasso" (*Moments of Being,* 140). Modernists like Gertrude Stein practiced the dissolution of the visual and the verbal, creating a new definition of "literary," or what we now label, "intertextuality." As cubism and abstract expressionism developed in Europe and America, artists erased the boundaries between painting, handwriting, poetry, and print as the Chinese had centuries earlier. Picasso and Braque incorporated words and print into their art during the cubist period, as did the dadaists; and American abstract expressionists like Franz Kline and Jackson Pollock became overtly engaged with Chinese calligraphy.

Calligraphy or writing is traditionally the foremost visual art in China, more than the pictorial. In fact, one learns to write by using the same eight strokes and dots that become the representation of bamboo. A bamboo painting is as close as you can get to writing. Consequently, a certain vocabulary has grown up about painting in China that relates to calligraphy as brushstroke, and poems expressed in calligraphy often share space with landscape on a Chinese scroll. The critic Liu Xie employed an argument to explain the origins of literature—and the closeness between characters and image—in explaining that the character "wen" means both "pattern" and "writing," as discussed earlier.

Chinese critics often speak of the "signature," a brushstroke that identifies the "handwriting" of an artist in which the verbal and the visual come together. It is said that the Emperor Qianlong's passion for calligraphy was so great that he collected and produced 42,000 poems. He wrote long inscriptions on paintings and directed artisans to incise texts into glazes of ceramic or carved into jade: "The addition of imperial writing was a high commendation for an object" (Freer Gallery commentary). Writing or calligraphy is so important in the culture that any time a word or a date or a signature painted with a brush or a seal, a colophon, is added to a painting or object, the value and art of the piece is enhanced. Strokes and lines are magical. The aesthetic "codes" of the West traditionally resisted this mixture of painting and writing. Condemning the addition of writing to a painting, a reviewer of the 1935–36 International Exhibition of Chinese Art in London, claimed that a painting by Huang Kung-wang "is terribly defaced by the admiring comments of the Emperor Qianlong" (Hobson, "The International Chinese Exhibition," 317). But the addition of appreciations, seals, and commentary of others incorporated onto the canvas of the artist is part of the tradition of painting in China, and suggests again diminishing boundaries between the artists, poets, and viewers of art—a distinction that most Western art upholds.

We also speak of "signature," but less often, sometimes in the brushstroke of a Matisse or a Rembrandt. Again as with the concepts of form and content, writing and image distinctions generally maintained in the West dissolve in Chinese cultural and aesthetic "codes" and practice. Ling Shuhua in a pamphlet on painting notes that poetry, calligraphy, and painting blur in the Chinese artist's experience: "the same ink and brush [is used] for poetry as for doing their writing" (*Painter's Choice*), and this is how poets started to paint. Focus on the "line" of a brushstroke also directs our attention to the execution of a work of art revealing the modernist interest in "process" demonstrating how things are made or constructed. Chinese art provides ample examples of the strokes, the "sketch" in the finished work of art dissolving the distinction (frozen into our language) between product and process. This erasure of the boundary between process and product, and the "showing" of the process, part of the modernist literary project, was incorporated into traditional Chinese art in an unself-conscious fashion. Brushes, always a treasured part of the artist's materials in the East along with the ink stone and ink, are quite varied in textures to enable the artist to achieve a variety of strokes and signatures. They have a range of suppleness and rigidity: some soft (made of rabbit's hair), some stiff, some long-handled to enable this.

Not content to separate the subject—the writer or artist or the reader—from the creation of the object—the work—modernists intertwined the two, questioning not only the nature of art but of perception and "reality" in general. It is this articulation of self-consciousness in modernism that distinguishes it from romanticism and Chinese art. Roger Fry, on the brink of modernism, breaks down the distinction between painting or drawing and handwriting. In the essay "Calligraphy," and another tract on "English Handwriting" (1926), he speaks of the "rhythmic idea" or "rhythmic phrase" in handwriting. He observes:

> Any artist as a result of constant drawing has formed rhythmic habits. Such a line tends to be as we say sensitive, its rhythm is so complex and so free that we cannot easily reduce it to any simple system of curvature. We feel it to be rhythmic but the rhythm eludes our analysis. (5)

This interest develops in correspondence with Robert Bridges, a member of the Society for Pure English, who writes to Fry requesting specimens of handwriting of famous people. He asks Fry to criticize the specimens from an aesthetic point of view: "Speak very plainly about the beauties and defects of the separate specimens. Detailed analysis of actual artistic qualities teaches better than anything else. . . . As for moral character and mental endowments or defects—this has a sound basis and is amusing and attractive to the reader" (10 January 1926).

The visual imagination of Chinese painters entered their poetry and fiction, and British modernism embraced this quality. Vanessa Bell wrote to Julian that painters are particularly struck by the ability of Chinese writers to picture what they see: "they see everything so clearly and one isn't left in doubt about colour which to me at least makes so much difference. One seems to live in a delicious world of silvery moving colours and lights and one is aware always that the writer is aware of the looks of everything" (5 June 1936).

Modernist writers also seemed to be preoccupied with the "line," the visual economy, to be found in Chinese painting, discussed earlier. This is sometimes reflected in the preoccupation with spare shape of "character" in modernist works. Virginia Woolf, for example, in shaping her novel *The Waves*, seeks, as she says in her *Diary*, to "give in a very few strokes the essentials of a person's character. It should be done boldly, almost as caricature" (*Diary*, 9 April 1930, 3:300). In fact, she says of this novel that "she means to have no characters." Rhoda walks across the room to the balcony where she sees the sky, the railings of the square and "two people without faces, leaning like statues against the sky" (*The Waves*, 106–7). This image of "people without faces" is a variation of "characters without features at all" that appears in Woolf's essay "Mr. Bennett and Mrs. Brown" and even Vanessa Bell's portrait of a reclining Virginia Woolf without facial features. The idea of the monumental and the statuesque, of getting her "statues" or "characters" against the universal sky without the details, is for Woolf the sign of great writing. Woolf is sketching characters with a modernist literary "line" that presents men and women not only in relation to one another but also in relation to time, space, the universe. For this reason, she often speaks admiringly of Thomas De Quincey who presents large visions.

This interest in the (out)lines of character—the forms, the shapes, the silhouettes, and the statues against the sky—reveals Woolf and other literary modernists' preoccupation with economy of description. In modernist writing we often see an aspect of a character or a physical gesture that reveals character, their bodies not fully represented. Woolf will often portray her characters in a few calligraphic lines or gestures: full descriptions of body or appearance are lacking. For example, Mrs. Dalloway is described in a stroke, "a narrow pea-stick figure; a ridiculous little face, beaked like a bird's" (*Mrs. Dalloway*, 14) or Miss Kilman in a flash of "a green mackintosh coat" that she wore year in, year out. We rarely get complete descriptions of physical appearance or bodies in Woolf, the modernist, but, rather, get the effect. Peter Walsh's vision ends the novel: "It is Clarissa, he said. For there she was." Woolf sketches nothing, but it fills us too with so much pleasure, though we only know Clarissa at that moment through the emotional response of Peter. Woolf portrays her characters from the "inside," blurring as modernists (and early Chinese painters) the line between inside and outside, the mind and the body. She resists the "storytelling" of British art, particularly of the Victorian period—putting in all the realist details of "getting on from lunch to dinner" or all the anatomical and physical details of realist description of characters to be found, for example, in the writing of John Galsworthy. She leaves things out and maps space, shape and silence into her narration, described more fully in my book, *The Reading of Silence: Virginia Woolf in the English Tradition* (1991).

Woolf's characters are often limned against time, as Mrs. Ramsay in *To the Lighthouse*, or space, as in *The Waves*. She harmoniously merges a backdrop of nature, time, the sound of birds, or the waves into a pattern or design in some of her novels. Like the artist she describes in "The Narrow Bridge of Art," we observe "the strange way in which things that have no apparent connection are associated in . . . [her] mind. Things which used to come single and separate do so no longer" (16) to capture the modern moment. She stands further back from life to catch its "rhythm" and gives "the outline rather than the detail" (18) and "molds blocks" (23). This same sense of the "outline" and the "shape" of character is captured in Woolf's essay "The Moment: Summer's Night," in which she explores the visual and sense impressions of what composes "the present moment." In the context of the heat of the day, tea caddies, snatches of conversation, mountains, meadow, moon, higgledy-piggledy, upside-down, human beings can only see themselves as "outlines, cadaverous, sculpturesque" ("The Leaning Tower," 7). The "cotton wool" of daily experience that blurs the lines recedes in her novels. When entering a house, Woolf says, "the square draws its lines round us . . . and thus we are boxed and housed" (8). It is the same with the houses of *To the Lighthouse*, *The Waves*, and *Between the Acts* until time, death, and nature enter and create the larger backdrop for the characters' lives. In the first section of *To the Lighthouse*, Woolf describes Mrs. Ramsay in retreat from "all the being and the doing" outlined against time as she marks the strokes of the lighthouse; later, in "Time Passes," she depicts the deteriorating Ramsay house silhouetted or (out)lined against the passage of time. In the last section of *The Waves*, we find Bernard summing up the lives of Jinny, Susan, Neville, Rhoda, Perceival, and Louis "boxed and housed" but silhouetted against time, the waves, and the sky. Bernard's challenge, as Woolf's is as the novelist, is to describe "a world seen without a self" (*The Waves*, 287). Perceival is a failed knight seen against the backdrop of India; Rhoda moves in a white space near a cliff; and Bernard, the novelist, enters into all of their lives diminishing lines of identity and ego. They could be figures in Winslow Homer's mysterious *A Summer Night* (1890).

Winslow Homer, like many nineteenth-century artists in the aesthetic movement, was drawn to the use of forms and silhouettes found also in Chinese art, which delights in moonlight scenes such as *Poet in Moonlight* and *Moon Viewing*. . . . Homer was drawn to the then popular "flat" Japanese style art derived from Chinese art. As this interest in "line" develops in modern art, it moves into the "mechanical line" of photography, film, collage, and cubism, as suggested by Rosalind Krauss in a lecture on "The Originality of the Avant Garde." It can be found in Picasso's sets for the Ballet Russe and Matisse's paintings, as well as in Chinese art, for example the dancing figures of the "Sagdian whirl," Persian religion, and a Tang Dynasty tomb or the simple sketch of a husband and wife parting on a tomb brick from the Wei Jin period, 220–317 A.D. (Asia Society exhibit, 2001). The "perceptual" line develops in modernist European art.

Leslie Hankins moved the "line" further into cinema in an inspiring lecture at the annual Virginia Woolf Society meeting in 2000, "Lotte Reininger's Silhouette Films, Science Fiction, Robots and Cartoons." Here she made the connection between Woolf's outline of characters and the techniques used by the filmmaker Lotte Reininger in the 1920s. In her essay "The Cinema," Woolf reflects after seeing the tadpole shapes in the early film *The Cabinet of Dr. Caligari:* "for a moment is seemed as if thought could be conveyed by shape more effectively than by words" (*Collected Essays,* 2:270). Perhaps a new film or production of the "play-poem" *The Waves* would visually embody Woolf's characters as silhouetted against the waves or sky of the universe: abstractions, lines. In this wonderful experimental novel, Woolf gives "the relation of the mind to general ideas and its soliloquy in solitude" (19). She adds to the traditional preoccupation of the novel, human relationships, that important dimension, the impersonal relationship of people not only to each other but to things in the universe: the sunrise, sunset, dreams, life, and death. The novel ends, "Against you I will fling myself, unvanquished and unyielding, O Death! *The waves broke on the shore*" (297).

Similarly, at the end of *Between the Acts,* Isa and Giles, the married couple, are silhouetted not against a domestic backdrop but "the great square of the open window [that] showed only sky now":

> Isa let her sewing drop. The great hooded chairs had become enormous. And Giles too. And Isa against the window. The window was all sky without colour. The house had lost its shelter. It was Night before roads were made or houses. It was the night that dwellers in caves had watched from some high place among rocks. Then the curtain rose. They spoke. (219)

They spoke against the backdrop of the theater of the universe.

Modernist Virginia Woolf notes also that "painting and writing have much to tell each other" in her observations on the "literary painter" Walter Sickert:

> The novelist after all wants to make us see. Gardens, rivers, skies, clouds changing, the colour of a woman's dress, landscapes that bask beneath lovers, twisted woods that people walk in when they quarrel—novels are full of pictures like these. The novelist is always saying to himself how can I bring the sun on to my page? How can I show the night and the moon rising? It must be done with one word or with one word in skilful contrast with another. (*Walker Sickert: A Conversation*, 32)

The blurring of boundaries between writing and visual image is a turn that will develop in modernism, as the "line" of writing becomes more important. Vanessa Bell, on the same tack, erases the boundaries between art and writing in the concept of a "stroke." She writes to Julian when he is in China, "It will be very impressive when you can talk and write Chinese. I wish we used a brush to write with. Do you by the way? It always seems to me it must be such a lovely way of writing" (2 January 1936).

In her essay "Modern Fiction," Woolf announces that the methods for representing mind, spirit, and character in the novel are no longer adequate:

> Let us hazard the opinion that for us at this moment the form of fiction most in vogue more often misses than secures the thing we seek. Whether we call it life or sprit, truth or reality, this, the essential thing, has moved off, or on, and refuses to be contained any longer in such ill-fitting vestments as we provide. (8)

Rejecting the "realism" of Galsworthy, Bennett, and Wells—"the getting on from lunch to dinner"—Woolf also sought new shapes for the novel. Saturated as she was with centuries of British representative art, she experimented with other kinds of language and form to represent character, movement, and states of mind and feeling, as suggested in the earlier discussion of "line." In its arts, China as well as other European art movements offered a challenge to the English modernists.

What the West learns then from the Chinese "codes" of perception and aesthetics is the dissolution of the boundary between the visual and the verbal and the subject and the object. The images and landscapes of China in poetry and painting circulated for centuries before the British articulated differences.

Unwittingly, British writers developed in tandem with the Chinese aesthetic principles discussed above—the expansion of consciousness, the dissolution of subject and object, the passion for line, the vitality of rhythm, the presentation of multiple views. Fry notes in his paper "Drawing or Design" that Chinese painting, "by saying very much less," makes it "possible to arrive at the expression of a great deal more." And the Chinese artist accomplishes this by taking the spectator into partnership "setting his imagination to work to complete the imagery" ("Drawing or Design," 4). The attentiveness to what is left out, the reticence discussed earlier in the "line," is part of the Chinese tradition that bears along with the color and patterns of French postimpressionists (Cezanne, Matisse, Derain, Braque, Vlaminck) on developing British modernism. Saying less is something that the English writers were also intent upon. This vocabulary may also describe a movement of the body, a sensation or feeling represented in a drawing by Picasso or a sentence by Woolf. "Line" may represent the inner life of an animal or of a character in a story. The aesthetic gesture, regardless of domain, is a self-conscious distillation of sensation, feeling, or experience.

For example, in the Beijing Opera, gestures, body postures, and hand movements as well as the use of theatrical objects, abstract in nature, shun the "representative" or the "realistic." Actors and objects achieve "rhythmic line" as the actors' movement of a common oar transforms into a boat; the holding of a whip by an actor becomes a man on a horse; four black flags, wind flags (feng qi) waved about by actors, become the blowing of a great wind; the movements of certain fingers of the hand or mincing steps dictated by theatrical conventions transform a male actor into a female.

This notion of gesture, the line of movement, the (out)lines of a character, is part of modern and postmodern discussion. James Joyce's sketches of his characters in *Dubliners* is an example. In "Araby," Mangan's sister is described in terms of shadows, light and lines: "We left our shadow and walked up to Mangan's steps resignedly. She was waiting for us, her figure, defined by the light from the half-opened door. . . . Her dress swung as she moved her body and the soft rope of her hair tossed from side to side" (30). Few details—such as dress swung, soft rope of hair tossed—create this character sketch, linear in its impulse—a gesture. Western painters, particularly of the romantic period, often created landscapes transmuted by sunrise, twilight, and moonlight: the kind of light that interests Chinese painters also. Moonlight produces silhouetted figures, and disregards the usual Western preoccupation of using light, shade, and details to render persons and objects. For example, the German romantic painter Caspar David Friedrich (1774–1880) created different versions of *Two Men Contemplating the Moon* at dawn and dusk. After Samuel Beckett saw a version of this work in Dresden with the setting moon, it is said that the silhouette inspired his setting for *Waiting for Godot*.

In his examination of Han relief pictures, silhouettes outlined or inscribed in stone, Fry notes the potency of "line." "See what an effect," he says, "is produced by the fluttering hands of the surprised lady on the right" (*Last Lectures*, 131). Similarly, one can observe in Han and Tang figures what Fry calls the "easy command of complicated gesture" (*Chinese Art*, 195) in the expression of the "lines." In Theatre Complicitie's recent production of "Street of Crocodiles," books become fluttering birds, large black umbrellas opening and closing transform into ominous birds, and billowing material represents waves of historical terror—magical staging techniques that, as the aging father in the play proclaims, are a "relief from content." Less is more.

In the manuscript version of Virginia Woolf's *Between the Acts*, Miss LaTrobe directs a local outdoor pageant. She observes, "Imagine what's left out. Often actors show us too much. The Chinese, I've been told, if they want to make us see—say a racecourse, just make a little boy do the horse with a clapper" (Leaska, *Pointz Hall*, 140). The clapper (ban) is the main instrument used in Beijing Opera for beating time. While musicians in the West "look" at time as the conductor waves a baton, Chinese musicians "listen" to time as kept by the clapper throughout a theatrical production. The clapper is made of three pieces of hard wood, two pieces fastened together while the third piece is tied with a cord to the others. The sound of the clapper creates the "line" of sound that creates the movement of a horse.

Similarly in the domain of literature, Virginia Woolf in "A Sketch of the Past," her most interesting autobiographical fragment, collects "floating incidents" (77) and desires to create characters in the modern novel who "could be made with three strokes of the pen" (73). Her expression contains traces not only of the strokes of calligraphy and writing, but also her aspiration as described in "Mr. Bennett and Mrs. Brown" to desert the conventions of Edwardian novels and catch the spirit and life—the line or gesture of character—in the legendary Mrs. Brown. Reluctant to show us too much, Woolf is no longer interested—as many modernist authors—in painting a character whole. Rhythmic line or gesture becomes a part of the art of a Beckett, Joyce, Brecht, or

Woolf character or the movements of Charlie Chaplin or the poetry of Ezra Pound or William Carlos Williams.

In *To the Lighthouse*, Lily struggles with the issue of where to place a "line" in a painting. She begins her painting in the first chapter in which we look at characters through "The Window"; she completes perhaps the same painting in the third chapter, "To the Lighthouse," when characters can no longer be perceived or seen as they travel to the lighthouse. Mrs. Ramsay is dead, and Cam, James, and Mr. Ramsay are far off abstractions or silhouettes in the distance, approaching the lighthouse in a boat. As Mr. Ramsay, James, and Cam reach the lighthouse, Lily, on shore, simultaneously turns to her canvas "with a sudden intensity, as if she saw it clear for a second, she drew *a line* there, in the centre. It was done; it was finished" (310). The relationships are suddenly clear in the placement of this line. Woolf's unwitting vocabulary of "rhythm," "line," "stroke," and "pause" to describe Lily's process and her own not only captures modernism but also Chinese traces: the lines and strokes of the calligraphic brush that creates a continuum from words to paintings. The modern reader—as the viewer of Chinese paintings, centuries ago and now—is brought into rhythmic partnership with the artist "to imagine what's left out."

Postscript

I have presented a constellation of personal, national, literary, and aesthetic conversations among Julian Bell, Vanessa Bell, Virginia Woolf, G. L. Dickinson, E. M. Forster, Ling Shuhua, Xu Zhimo, and Xiao Qian that illuminate the relation between two literary communities and cultures, Bloomsbury in England, and the Crescent Moon group in China. The backdrop for this conversation was the cultural and aesthetic movement of modernism. These relationships have been neglected in literary and cultural studies because of complicated cultural and sexual politics in England and China. Some of these figures were "elites" in their respective cultures, or were perceived as Anglophones, nationalists, traitors, or pacifists, and were regarded as anathema during a time of national crisis.

In creating a space for these figures to meet in this book, I mark an "open site" that, according to Foucault, is a space that is cultural, literary, and historical. It welcomes others. Jorge Luis Borges has written of the poet Ts'ui Pen who leaves "to various future times, but not to all, my garden of forking paths" (*Ficciones*, 97). The idea of knowledge as a labyrinth, where each point of departure leads to bifurcations, further pathways, divergences, and convergences, is developed in this study. At one time, Borges speculates that Ts'ui Pen might have said, "I am going into seclusion to write a book"; at another, "I am returning to construct a maze" (96), the book and the labyrinth being the same.

I experienced this maze when chance favored me and I found a sheaf of manuscripts at a literary auction that led me through a Chinese gate. This gate opened another, this time into reading about Chinese culture and Anglo-Chinese cultural and literary interaction that then forked into a conversation about modernism. Another path led to my trips to China during the writing of this book where I saw the landscapes I read about: Wuhan, where Julian Bell taught and met Ling Shuhua, Shanghai and Beijing, where Chinese intellectuals gathered, the breathtaking gorges of the Yangtze River, the garden city of Suzhou, the misty West Lake of the Chinese poets, the enormous buddhas of the Yungang Caves and the glorious Tang temples of the Wutaishan Mountains. In addition, I visited King's College, Cambridge University, where I walked the banks of the Cam as the Chinese writer Xiao Qian had seventy-five years earlier. All are part of the forking paths of this book. As I followed them—as a traveler, reader, and critic—I became dizzily aware of the problems that emerge as one works in past and parallel times in different cultural and literary epistemologies, periods, traditions (one in translation or in the second language of the Chinese authors), and places. I also discovered that regardless of what happens in politics, artists, writers, and scholars assemble their art, a "bricolage," as suggested by Levi-Strauss, from the cultural, political, and aesthetic fragments that emerge from cultural and economic contact. Criticism, literature, and art become dreamscapes, imaginative and aesthetic places that map where culture and politics may travel in the future. Without diminishing the human suffering that the imperialism of Europe, Japan, and America (after World War II) fostered, we now, at another point in time, move on to observe these political, literary, and aesthetic tracings on the surface of an international canvas of modernism.[1]

This book is founded upon the notion that communities can "condition" and "enrich" each other upon contact through actual travel or through imagination (arts, reading, and translation), as well as establish destructive patterns of economic and political relationship, as England has during certain periods of its relationship with China, beginning in the eighteenth century. I argue that there was aesthetic reciprocity between England and China beginning in the eighteenth century with the importation of Chinese ideas, aesthetics, and goods, and that the influence of the Chinese sensibility on England's literature and the visual arts developing in the nineteenth and twentieth centuries has sometimes been overlooked, largely because of Eurocentrism.

International modernism is not viewed only as a product of cultural imperialism. In encouraging a new cultural and aesthetic understanding and practice in a new geopolitical terrain, I bring into view the special role of British modernism in the Republican era when China was overwhelmed with Japanese and Russian political discourses, as well as nationalist and proletarian commitments inimical to modernism. I demonstrate that the artistic communities of Bloomsbury and the Crescent Moon group mutually influenced the avant-garde aspects of the other. This book, then, focuses on a modernism of China's own making, a movement begun in a precommunist period, and interrupted in its development.

Modernism is reconfigured here in the context of a nation with different social and political realities. Though the relation of modernity and modernism is often assumed—that is that a certain level of cultural and economic development precedes a "modernist" state of mind and literature—this study reveals something different. Modernist impulses sprang up in certain literary groups in China in the 1920s and 1930s, and yet the condition of modernity in the nation as a whole had not yet evolved. Such a view argues for the existence of multiple aesthetic, cultural, political, and economic discourses in a nation and against a monolithic notion of modernity or movement of modernism. In some cultural contexts as in China, the values of modernity are separated from the motivation toward modernism, and to argue that they must be in tandem is to return to an Anglo-Euro-American–centric view, consigning other patterns of development in other countries to the periphery.

There were cultural changes in China at the beginning of the century that prompted a shift in conciousness. First, a new sense of time emerged with the establishment and speed of new railways in the 1920s and 1930s. Then cultural tensions emerged in the movement away from the 3000-year tradition of using classical Mandarin as the literary language to the use of the colloquial language. This shift stimulated Chinese writers to invent a new language and to play with traditional forms of literature as part of the 1919 literary movement. In addition, the themes of literature began to change with stories about women's lives and dissatisfactions (Ding Ling and Ling Shuhua) and stories told from the point of view of the oppressed (Lu Xun). Perhaps these perceptions emerged more from abroad or from those Chinese who traveled than those at home, but there were, nevertheless, impulses toward both modernity and modernism in certain Chinese contexts.

Rejecting a unidirectional model of influence used by the inspiring yet traditional Asian scholar Bonnie McDougall in her early study of China's development of a literature based on a reaction to the "intrusions" of the West[2] or that view that the subjectivity of some of the authors in this study was contingent on "Western mediation" as advanced by Shi Shumei—this book moves toward a new discourse about China and England that might be described as a Moebius strip:

> The text is that Moebius strip in which the inner and outer sides, the signifying and the signified sides, the side of writing and the side of reading, ceaselessly turn and cross over, in which writing is constantly read, in which reading is constantly written and inscribed. The critic must also enter the interplay of this strange and reversible circuit and thus, like every good reader, become, as Proust says, "one's own reader." (Genette, *Figures of Literary Discourse*, 70)

Certainly, I entered this interplay of texts and places to question my cultural and critical assumptions at many turns. Distinguishing itself in its metaphors of "networks," "intertwinings," "interdependency," "dialogue," or "conversation," my study critically resists outworn models of Chinese and British essentialism or the polarities of East and West, and dramatizes differences and counterdiscourses within each category. Acknowledging earlier work on culture and imperialism, this book joins a critical current that moves to the next stage to represent incipient, resistant, and varied discourses in the "inner spaces" of nation, emerging from intellectual and artistic circles in both England and China. Given the thesis of the book—that there are multiple Chinas and Englands and discourses, including anti-imperialist and antinationalist counterdiscourses, as well as aesthetic discourses that ignored others—empirical British and Chinese intellectual and artistic communities presented here belie the stereotypes and generalizations. It does not trace "the origins of this" or "the decadence of that" or "the influence of this upon that" or the "mediation of this by that." I do not treat American and English literature as "models of imitation," as proposed, at times, by Qian Zhaoming, *Modernism and Orientalism*, in his examination of the effect of the "orient" on American poetry in the 1920s; nor is Chinese literary development viewed as a reaction to or embrace of the "intrusion" of the West. The conversations represented and analyzed here are an intertwining of cultures and empires, the product of a particular historical and cultural moment, modernism in England, 1910–41, and the Republican period of China, 1911–49. The East (particularly China, Japan, and India) was a major area of aesthetic adventure as well as commercial exploitation for the British; nevertheless, I explore the relation between the official discourses of war and nation and the "intimate spaces of community," as described by Partha Chatterjee, to be found in writing and the visual arts. I posit, as others before me, that there is always an aesthetic and imaginative space outside history while people live in it. This space is imagined, this space is literature, this space is art. Gerard Genette has described such a space:

> [Literature] breathes new life into the world, freeing it from the pressure of social meaning, which is named meaning, and therefore dead meaning, maintaining as long as possible that opening, that uncertainty of signs which allows one to breathe. (*Figures of Literary Discourse*, 41)

We may glance at a geographical map in which China is colored pink-red as a zone of British semicolonial activity in the late eighteenth or nineteenth century, or Japan in the 1930s and 1940s, or America after World War II, but such a map does not reveal the personal, cultural, and aesthetic spaces that exist alongside others and contribute to the development of a nation. The aesthetic map sketched in this book attempts to do this, even as politically driven periods, both past and present, as well as some postcolonial criticism, eclipse the aesthetic discourse. Virginia Woolf, working politics into her own language, observes that "art is the first thing to go in a time of [political] stress; the artist is the first of the workers to suffer" ("The Artist and Politics," 227). The experience of individuals in Bloomsbury and the Crescent Moon group exemplify this.

This book also addresses geographical and critical imbalances—perhaps the architecture of modernist, postcolonial, Bloomsbury, and Asian literary studies. Until recently, the role of China has been left out of the aesthetic matrix of a developing international modernism, perhaps because of Eurocentrism, but also because of lack of knowledge. Just as Chinese and American historians are bringing the West "back in" by presenting the foreigners in China as a part of modern Chinese history, this study introduces Chinese writers and aspects of the Chinese aesthetic into British modernism, and documents the participation of British writers in the developing Chinese modernism. Asian and British modernist studies linked in this book are moving in new directions and away from the xenophobic notion of the "alien" and "intruding" culture of the West. New studies now deconstruct the East-West polarity and fixed "namings" (East-West, Capitalism-Marxism) upon which "orientalism" and, sometimes, exclusionary Chinese identity, was built. This is a global critical movement that shifts interest away from the polarization that demonizes the West or that limits the experience of literature in juxtaposing literature for art's sake or literature for life's sake, intertwined as they are in all great art. Metaphors of "resistance," "interaction," "negotiation," "dialogue," "conversation," "translation," "translingual," and "transnationalism" appear in new studies suggesting new critical and cultural play—the unfixing of polarities. It suggests not only new metaphors but also forms of understanding to critically inaugurate a phase of cultural and literary description between England and China in the early twentieth century. In so doing, it opens up the study of comparative modernisms as well as an attempt to return the Chinese gaze toward England.

Chinese artists and intellectuals interested in the evolving "modernist" aesthetic—that is not solely British but an international, migratory movement—are a "resistant community." They develop their own vision informed by their experiences in cultural "diasporas," picking up bits and pieces of other languages, cultures, politics, and art, culturally matching or mismatching what is needed or what fits. As Roger Fry observed in a letter to Charles Vildrac: "As to art—there too we mustn't confuse the issue—no art useful to morals or politics. . . . It's as dangerous to do art politically as it is to do politics artistically" (17 February 1916). He argued for the internationalism of all that had to do with the intelligence and the spirit as did the writers in the Crescent Moon group and Bloomsbury. Though it may seem politically insensitive to ignore issues of culture and power, art often does. Picasso, when incorporating African sculptures into his modern art, did not think about Africa, but looked steadily at the sculptures that contain Africa.

As presented in this book, the British and Chinese landscape and relationship envisioned on Ling Shuhua's friendship scroll containing the inscriptions of both Bloomsbury and Crescent Moon figures in 1928—a mute historical and aesthetic document—eventually is realized in a cultural, literary, and aesthetic conversation that continues to this day. This book then is a double venture—within my cultural and linguistic limitations—to sketch a new complex cultural and literary space that is "between" China and England in the first half of the twentieth century. It presents China through the kaleidoscopic views of the literary group, Bloomsbury, as well as other English writers, and, to some degree, English writers from the Chinese perspective. It also presents my own personal changes as a critic as I learned to read, for example, Virginia Woolf or Katherine Mansfield, through "Chinese eyes." Yet as the Chinese poet and painter Ni Zan of the Yuan dynasty says of his bamboo paintings, I say of this book:

If people say that . . . [my paintings] don't look like bamboo, but more like water reed or hemp, I don't bother to object. They have every right to say that. Why should I mind what other people say? I can only paint the bamboo which has grown in my mind.

Appendix A

Index of Chinese and British Figures

For additional information on Chinese figures, consult Harold Boorman's *Men of Republican China;* on Bloomsbury, Alan & Veronica Palmer's *Who's Who in Bloomsbury,* S. P. Rosenbaum, ed. *The Bloomsbury Group.*

ACTON, HAROLD (1904–94) Writer, poet, translator, and collector of art. He wrote works on Chinese theater and poetry and spent time in Beijing in 1930s.

BA JIN (1904–) Inspired by the May Fourth 1919 movement, he established a literary supplement, *News of Current Events,* 1922, that included his free-verse poems written in *bai-hua.* After study at the Southeast China University and a year in France, 1927, he translated Russian novelists, and wrote *Destruction,* a short novel that portrays a young anarchist. His best-known novel is *Family* (1931), the first book in his trilogy, *Torrent,* that describes the deterioration of a feudal family after the May Fourth 1919 movement.

BELL, JULIAN (1908–37) Poet and activist, son of Vanessa and Clive Bell who studied at King's College, Cambridge University, and lived in Paris, 1927. He published collections of poems, *Winter Movement* (1930) and *Work for the Winter* (1936), but became increasingly interested in a more political life. While teaching at National Wuhan University, China, 1935–37, he had an affair with Ling Shuhua, the wife of Dean Chen Yuan of the same university. He died working for the Spanish Medical Aid as an ambulance driver in the Spanish Civil War, July, 1937.

BELL, VANESSA (1879–1961) Painter, eldest sister of Virginia Woolf. She had an unusually close relationship and weekly correspondence with her son, Julian, when he was teaching in China, 1935–37. Her career as a painter began when she exhibited at the New English Art Club, 1907–08, participated in Roger Fry's Omega Workshop, 1913, and developed as a painter while living with Duncan Grant.

BING XIN (1900–99) Stimulated by the May Fourth 1919 movement, she wrote short stories critical of the feudal system as well as stories that portrayed intellectuals. Inspired by Rabindranath Tagore, she wrote popular collections of poems, *Myriad Stars* and *Spring Water*. In 1923, she attend Wellesley College in the United States and is well known for her best seller, *Letters to My Little Readers,* for young people, and *Awakening,* essays about her experience abroad.

CHEN YUAN (also referred to as T. P., Tunpo; Hsi-Ying, courtesy name) Noted historian, cultural commentator, and literary critic, and husband of Ling Shuhua. He received his Ph.D. from the London School of Economics and worked with H. G. Wells when in England. He is best known for the founding of *The Contemporary Review* that published the writings of the Crescent Moon group.

DICKINSON, G. L. (1862–1932) Cambridge don, classicist, and political philosopher. Close friends with Roger Fry, Leonard Woolf, and Lytton Strachey, and tutor to Julian Bell. In 1914, Dickinson invented the phrase "a League of Nations," and worked with this organization toward international peace and reconciliation. He visited China in 1911, loved the country, inspired others to engage with China, and always welcomed Chinese students and intellectuals to King's College. He became friends with the visiting Chinese poet Xu Zhimo during his visit to Cambridge in the early 1920s.

DING LING (1904–86) Writer of international reputation who, together with her husband, Hu Yepin, joined the League of Left-Wing Writers headed by Lu Xun in 1930. After Hu's death, she joined the Communist Party, participated in propaganda work, and continued to write. After the establishment of People's Republic of China, she fell out of favor, was labeled a "rightist" in 1955, 1957, and 1966, during which periods she was imprisoned. Best known in the west for her 1927 novel, *Miss Sophie's Diary.*

ELMHIRST, LEONARD (1893–1974) Established Dartington Hall, Totnes, England, with his wife, Dorothy Straight Whitney, as a cultural haven for artists, particularly dancers. He welcomed Indian and Chinese writers and intellectuals into his community. Having studied agricultural sciences at Cornell University and worked as the secretary to Rabindranath Tagore, he worked with Tagore to establish a model agricultural community in India, as well as proposing one for China.

EMPSON, WILLIAM (1906–84) English poet and critic who took a special interest in the East, teaching English literature in Tokyo, 1937–39, and at Beijing, 1947–53. He is best known for his work *Seven Types of Ambiguity* (1930) and the introduction of "scientific" principles into literary criticism, along with his teacher, I. A. Richards, whom he met at Harvard University.

FORSTER, E. M. (1879–1970) Major English novelist. He was the biographer of his teacher, G. L. Dickinson (1934), and is best known for his novels *Howards End* (1910) and *A Passage to India* (1924). He was the friend and teacher of Xiao Qian, visiting Chinese journalist and writer at Cambridge University, 1941–43.

FRY, ROGER (1866–1934) Art critic and painter who influenced Bloomsbury and England's aesthetic tastes through his postimpressionist exhibitions in 1910 and 1912. He became interested in art of the East around 1906, an interest that developed over the years and blossomed in his Slade Lectures on Chinese Art at Oxford, 1933–34, just before his death.

GUO MORUO (1892–1978) Writer, historian, playwright, and translator who played a crucial role in the May 30th, 1925, movement, the activities sponsored by the Tokyo branch of the China League of Left-Wing Writers in 1930, and the founding of the People's Republic of China. He worked with Mao Dun and Zhou Yang. Best known for his translations of Goethe, Shelley, and Tolstoy and his poetic collections, *Ode to New China* (1949) and *The East Wind*.

HU SHI (1891–1962) Literary scholar turned politician and ambassador. He proposed reform of Chinese literature through the use of the vernacular (*bai-hua*) while studying at Cornell University, 1910–14. Proudest of his title "The Father of the Chinese Literary Renaissance," he studied with John Dewey at Columbia University from 1914–17. He returned to China to teach at Beijing University (1917–26), and became Chinese ambassador to the U.S. from 1937–39.

JIN DI Critic and translator of James Joyce's *Ulysses* into Chinese, 1994. He studied with William Empson at Beijing University from 1947–49; taught English literature for twenty-five years in Beijing and Tianjin; held lectureship and fellowships at University of Virginia.

KEYNES, J. M. (1883–1946) Economist, involved with official trade discussions on China, 1935. Best known for his book analyzing postwar Europe, *The Economic Consequences of the Peace*, 1919.

LAO SHE (1899–1966) Born into a poor family, his experience led to the writing of *Rickshaw Boy*, which portrays a corrupt regime inflicting misery on thousands of laborers. His *Four Generations under One Roof* written in the 1940s presents a vivid picture of China living under Japanese occupation during the Sino-Japanese War.

LING SHUHUA (or Ling Shu-hua, Chen Ling Shu-hua, Hsu Hua Chen, Mrs. Chen Yuang) (1900–90) Known as one of the best short-story writers in China, as well as a calligraphist and painter. Married noted historian and literary critic Chen Yuan in 1927, and published her first short stories in the magazine he founded, *Contemporary Review*. She also published successful short-story collections, *Flowers in the Temple*, *Little Brothers*, as well as her autobiography in English, *Ancient Melodies*. She had an affair with Julian Bell who was teaching at Wuhan University, 1935–37.

LU XUN (1881–1936) Began medical studies in Japan in 1904, but turned to writing in 1906 to nurture the morale of China. He founded the League of Left-Wing Writers in 1930, and became one of the most successful reformers and writers in China. Best known for "A Madman's Diary" (1918), *The True Story of Ah Q* (1920), and *Call to Arms* (1923).

MAO DUN (1896–1981) Initiated the Literary Research Society in 1920, and edited *Short Story Monthly*, which gave impetus to the drive for vernacular literature in China. Best known for his work *Midnight*, which depicts Chinese businessman, and society in general, in the 1930s.

MAO ZEDONG (or Mao Tse-tung) (1893–1976) Organizer of peasant associations in Hunan in 1925 during which time he drew away from Leninist analysis that described the urban proletariat as the leaders of the revolution. In 1945, with Communist Party membership at 1.2 million, Mao was the leader of a civil war (1946–49), which led to the establishment of the People's Republic of China. Movements such as the Great Leap Forward, 1958, in which communes were urged to produce "pig iron" in backyard furnaces, led to the disruption of agriculture and the starvation of thirty million people. The Cultural Revolution (1966–76) was also launched by Mao to combat elitism, revisionism, and the "bourgeois mentality" of the bureaucracy: millions died at the hands of the Red Guards, including many intellectuals and minorities.

QU QIUBAI (1899–1935) Emerged as one of the student leaders of the May Fourth 1919 movement, and published *New Society* magazine with Zheng Zhenduo. Central to the development of the theory of proletarian literature and art, he was one of the first leaders to systematically introduce Marxism to the Chinese. Both Qu and Lu Xun led a campaign against "nationalism in literature," as well as against the Crescent Moon group of which Chen Yuan and Ling Shuhua were a part. Allied with the Communist Party, he was captured and killed by Guomindong troops in 1935. Lu Xun collected Qu's numerous treatises and translations of the works of Gorky, Lunacharsky, etc., after his death.

RICHARDS, I. A. (1893–1979) English scholar and critic who initiated the study of literature according to scientific principles developing the method of "practical criticism." While a professor at Magdalene College, Cambridge University, he developed the idea of Basic English—a simplified way of teaching English to foreigners—with C. K. Ogden. He tried to introduce this method of teaching into China on his early visits in 1927, 1929–30, 1936–38. His last effort was foiled by the Sino-Japanese War and its disruptions. He always loved China and its landscapes. He is best known for his *Principles of Literary Criticism* (1924) and *Practical Criticism* (1929), as well as the publication of collections of poetry, *Goodby Earth and other Poems* (1958).

SACKVILLE-WEST, VITA (1892–1962) Novelist, travel writer, biographer, gardener, and aristocratic friend of Virginia Woolf. She is perhaps best known for Virginia Woolf's dedication of *Orlando* (1928) to her. She took an interest in Ling Shuhua and wrote the introduction to her autobiography, *Ancient Melodies,* in London, 1953.

SHEN CONGWEN (1902–88) Sympathizer with rural China, he established an influential literary supplement with Xiao Qian in 1933. During the Mao period, he withdrew from writing like many Chinese writers and researched Chinese apparel at the Museum of Chinese History. His early writing centers on western Hunan, its landscape and people: *The Cow* (1929), *The Autobiography of Shen Congwen* (1934), *Recollections of West Hunan* (1941).

TAGORE, RABINDRANATH (1861–1941) Leading Indian poet popular among Chinese intellectuals including Xu Zhimo, Lin Huiyin, and Xiao Qian. Xu Zhimo, the popular Chinese poet, traveled to India with him in 1924 during the time he was engaged in agricultural and literary projects in India with Leonard Elmhirst of Dartington Hall.

WALEY, ARTHUR (1889–1966) Translator and poet, appointed Assistant Keeper of Oriental Prints and Drawings at the British Museum in 1913. Though on the margins of Bloomsbury, he greatly influenced the group and England's images of China through his groundbreaking translations of poetry, most notably *A Hundred and Seventy Chinese Poems* (1918) and the Chinese novel *Monkey* (1946), for which Duncan Grant designed the jacket.

WEBB, BEATRICE (1858–1943) **AND SIDNEY** (1859–1947) Social reformers, Fabians, and economists. Sidney helped to found the Fabian Society (1884) and the London School of Economics and Political Science (1895). They were critical of China after their visit in 1911, as recorded in their letters and *China Travel Diary*, 1911–12.

WEN YIDUO (1899–1946) Participated in the May Fourth 1919 movement. Made efforts to formalize a new style of poetry, antifeudal and patriotic, in his collection *Dead Water* (1928), and wrote a number of books on the Chinese classics. Associated with the Communist Party, he publicly denounced the Guomindong for the death of Li Gongpu and was assassinated in 1946.

WOOLF, LEONARD (1880–1969) Statesman, writer, politician, publisher. Converted to socialism after his years as a colonial administrator in Ceylon (Sri Lanka) 1904–11; married Virginia Woolf in 1912; worked with the Women's Cooperative Movement and the Fabians beginning in 1913; founded the Hogarth Press with Virginia in 1917, establishing himself as a publisher and editor; and became an advisor to the Labor Party after World War I. He was a sharp political observer and wrote many political works including the antifascist *Quack, Quack!* (1931) and a popular five-volume autobiography.

WOOLF, VIRGINIA (1882–1941) Major modernist writer who created a method for capturing in writing "what people don't say" through experimental interior monologue and the representation of multiple points of view. She wrote *Three Guineas* (1938), a polemic about war, in "argument" with Julian Bell who had just died in the Spanish Civil War. She is best known for her novels, *Mrs. Dalloway* (1925), *To the Lighthouse* (1927), and her visionary, experimental writing in *The Waves* (1931).

XIAO QIAN (or Hsiao Ch'ien) (1910–99) Journalist, writer and translator who spent 1941–44 studying with E. M. Forster and Dadie Rylands at King's College, Cambridge University, as a sometime lecturer at the London School of Oriental and African Studies and as a war correspondent attached to the U.S. 7th Army for the journal *Tao Kung Po*. He published several collections of short stories and essays, *Chestnuts*, and *China but Not Cathay* being among the most popular. He turned to translation late in life, completing a translation of James Joyce's *Ulysses* with his wife, Wen Jieruo, in 1994.

XU ZHIMO (or Hsu Chih-mo, Tsu Chih-mo, Tsemon Tsu, Tseu Tcheung) (1897–1931) Studied history and banking at Clark University in Massachusetts, 1918, and political science at Columbia University, NYC, in 1920. He traveled to Cambridge University to study literature under the tutelage of G. L. Dickinson and Dadie Rylands. There he began to write poetry in 1921, modeling his poetry after the Romantics. After his return to China, he became an influential poet and personality. Founder of the Crescent Moon group, Crescent Bookstore, and a magazine, *Crescent Moon Monthly*, in 1928. He died a wildly popular poet at the age of thirty-four in an airplane accident.

YE JUNJIAN (or C. C. Yeh, Yeh Chun-chan) Leftist student of Julian Bell's and English translator for Agnes Smedley and W. H. Auden. He became a journalist and short-story writer, *The Ignorant and the Forgotten: Nine Stories* (1946).

YU DAFU (1896–1945) Entered Imperial University in Japan in 1919. When returning to China, he joined with Guo Moruo and Zhang Ziping in settling up the Creation Society, 1921, a literary society that advanced vernacular literature. Best known for a short story, "Sinking," which describes the depression suffered by Chinese students in Japan, enraged by foreign incursions in China. In 1932, he, Lu Xun, and Mao Dun created the "Shanghai Culture Circle's Proclamation to the World," a condemnation of the Japanese for their encroachment on Chinese soil.

YUAN, KEJIA (1921–) Researcher, Poet, Critic, Translator, Editor. He was among an influential group of poets in Southwest Associated University in 1946. Through the introduction of New Criticism into China, he demonstrated alternatives to dominant literary trends in China at the time. He also edited an important publication which re-introduced modernist literature into China, *Selected Works of Foreign Modernist Literature* (4 vols)., 1980–85.

Appendix B

*Selection from Ling Shuhua's Story
"Writing a Letter" with Julian Bell's Annotations*

WRITING a LETTERS

By Ling Hsu Hwa

On
It is Sunday morning, and Mrs Chang from the next door comes into
She brings with her two of her most precious possessions the
Miss Wu's study, bringing her child, and with a broad grin on her face.

"Good morning, Miss. Why, are you reading and writing on a
Do
Sunday ? Are you really wanting to take the imperial examination ?
I don't know how long I've been waiting for you to be free. When I
opened my eyes in bed this morning I heard the bells, and I said to
myself in a hurry " My goodness ! why, here's Sunday" . Ten days
ago I wanted to ask you to write a letter for me, but I see you go to
school everyday, and when you come back you're always reading and
say to myself
writing, so that I don't like to bother you. I think," I will answer him
later, but two letters have already come from him. . . . .
. . . . "Who ? Nobody. His father. You don't know what its like to
be blind with your eyes open (i.e. illiterate) How nice it must
being
be for you, to be able to write down everything you think of. I always
But
complain of my mother, not letting me go to school. She was afraid
that as soon as I started learning I should turn into one of these
My
modern girls and run away with some wild young man. My father was
other
dead keen on my going to school. Only the day before yesterday I com-
old lady
plained about it again to my xxxxxxxxxxxxxxx my Mrs. Chang, (her
mother) "You see, now I'm blind with my eyes open . That's all thanks
for
to you not letting me go to school. Look at that Miss Wu, how well
footnote she gets on, able to write as quick and clear as a book. (Literally,
" She can hold her brush for a thousand words) She's already quite a
still

3

lady (" a golden branch with jade leaves") and not at all a modern girl. Now the old lady is sorry and sends her granddaughter to school every day. ....

What do I want to say ? I have too many things to talk about. I often wonder how you can remember such thousands of words, and pick out the ones you want. As for me, when I'm working, I find it hard enough to chooose the right colours for my embroidery. Why, even when I'm thinking, we thought out in my mind, I cant get the right words out. I don't know how it is, but when I meet young ladies like you, as clear as crystal, I don't know what I'm saying. Once, when I was quarelling with his father, I said to him "Don't think I'll get stick on in your family for ever. Look here, tomorrow I'll find a job for myself: I don't care aloud lopsdy face like this. If I go and do the mending in Miss Wu's house, it'll be better than leading a dog's life with you. They dont shout at their servants. What do you know about the world ? You fly into a temper over next to nothing. I'm not your slave." You havn't seen his father yet ? He's got the temper of an ox, and his belly's full of grass (i.e. There's no sense in him) If he werent so foul-mouthed, he would be a major by now. Mrs Closs eldest son went into the army at the same time as he, and now he's a colonel. And I heard the other day that he's got the daughter of a rich familly for a second wife.

His father wore the uniform almost ten years. But he's unlucky, he's still only a lieutenant. He dosnt know when his money's coming, and he dosnt get any extras, it all goes on his food. Every month we wait for him to send us

something, but it never comes. If only he would send us the money regularly in time
he(pointing to the child) ought to have a proper suit. This dress his was made for
sister made for the fête last year, now its his turn for wearing it.
                                                                  it
You see I take good care of my money. And for all that, whenever his
                                                        savings
father comes back, he always grumbles that there's no money left for him
at home. I often say the grown-up people dont need to go dressing up about
                                                          object
(literally B are like withered flowers and bare trees) while a child
likes to look nice. (is like a flower) except for orphans; he ought
     to about
not to be dressed like a little beggar, he has a father. Don't you think
I'm right, Miss ? He's his father's pet. Every time he sends anything
                                                                   San
home, there's something for him, his sisters dont get a scrap. Sxx-Liu
is often cross, and goes away and cries. Sse-Liu is good, she dosnt mind
I say to them "there's long fingers and short fingers, and its no use
minding.")

.... I've had seven, there's three of
them alive now, the others were three boys and a girl. Each &
                    one of them
time died   their grandmother complained to Heaven and
Earth as if her heart was broken, and their father
quarrelled with me . You see what an odd man his father is;
I told him ' It all depends on Fate; if the God of Hell
                                                devils
hasn't got his name down in the book, then the ghosts won't
come to fetch him." He just answered me "its easy enough for
                                          harder
you to bear children, its much harder for me to feed them."
I didnt attend to him, I went away and cried. After all, its
part of my own flesh and blood being taken away from me,
                                                started
so its no wonder if I'm heartbroken. Ever since I had them

Selection from Ling Shuhua's Story "Writing a Letter"

I've never slept at night. As soon as I've closed my eyes, my second boy wants to go and piss, or that third girl starts crying with a stomach ache, or the baby screams because its hungry. Goodness knows how many times a night I had to get up to serve my lords and masters. Look, I'm only just over thirty, and already I've got grey hairs. ....

Dont touch the things on the table, my dear. Miss Wu will turn you out if you do touch ....

You're going to tell Grandma ? She won't listen to what you say, she'll take Miss Wu's word. Put it down, dont spoil it. You really are a spoilt child. Be good, my precious, put it down, and come and salute Miss Wu (with an imitation of a military salute) Be a good boy, do it again. Count your fingers. .... You see, there's no doubt about it, his father loves him best. No body's taught him all these tricks, he learned them by himself. He knows all right how to get round his father. Last time his father came back, he was so wrapped up in him, he went about calling "Daddy" the whole time. His sisters are diffferent, when they see their father they turn red and run away. His father gets angry and then he wont speak to them

I always say girls get bashfull; they havn't seen their father for more than a year. The two sisters are really cleverer than their brother, but a dog knows who to wag his tail for. Since no one takes any notice of them, there's nothing to show. His second sister is only eleven,

6

and she makes her brother's shoes. His third sister got a prize at
school, after the examinations, of an brass inkstand and four brushes.
Nowadays, theres not much difference between boys and girls. You
see, that Miss Hwang ? She works much better than a boy, earning a
hundred a month, not a copper for herself, for she just gives her
mother her pay-cheque without touching it. Old Mrs Hwang gets smarter
and smarter every day, with silks and satins, picking and choosing just
as she likes. Last time I went to a wedding, there she was
with yet another new dress - its a pity she can't paint over all
her wrinkles. His Grandma is five years older than Mrs Hwang, but
if she dresses up she looks a lot younger. Some time ago his
father sent back a satin dress length, without a word to say who
it was for. I said "its sure to be for his mother; a son always thinks
of his mother first. A mother has such a time bringing up a son,
it's only fair she should wear a nice dress." She wouldnt take
it. I got the tailor to come straight off and make it for her. She wore
it the day before yesterday to his aunts house, and everyone who
saw her said the older she gets, the finer she dresses, she's certainly
improved by age. (like the no Pai chiao grass, that turns red in autumn.) Do you believe that what one
eats and drinks depends on Fate ? You see that Miss Hwang ?
Whatever she wears, she looks like a sack of potatoes. While any dress
you choose to wear fits you like a glove. Thats the point of the
proverb " Dressed by her father, looks pretty, dressed by her husband,
looks lovely, dressed by herself, whats the good of it ?"

You're laughing at me. He never bothered to get me a dress,
and my hair almost grey ! You wouldnt have thought it, but since I
married him twelve years ago he never bought as much as a handkerchief

By permission of Hsiao-ying Chen.

Appendix C

Table of Contents, Selections of Modernist Literature from Abroad, *eds. Yuan Kejia, Dong Xengxun, Zheng Kelu, 1981*

前言	Preface by Yuan Kejia	袁可嘉			
後期象徵主義	**Post-symbolism**			意識流	**Stream of Consciousness**
維爾哈倫	Verhaeren *tr Ai Qing*	艾 青譯		普魯斯特	Proust *tr Gui Yufang*
瓦雷里	Valéry *tr Bian Zhilin*	卞之琳譯		伍爾夫	Woolf *tr Wen Meihui & Gou Xu*
里爾克	Rilke *tr Feng Zhi*	馮 至譯		喬伊斯	Joyce *tr Jin Di*
葉芝	Yeats *tr Yuan Kejia*	袁可嘉譯		福克納	Faulkner *tr Li Wenjun*
艾略特	Eliot *tr Zha Liangzheng (Mu Dan) & Zhao Luorui*	查良錚 趙蘿蕤譯		橫光利一	Yokomitsu Riichi *tr Ding Min & Dan Dong*
龐德	Pound *tr Du Yunxie*	杜運燮譯		超現實主義	**Surrealism**
勃洛克	Blok *tr Ge Baoquan*	戈寶權譯		布勒東	Breton *tr Jin Zhiping & Zhang Guanyao*
葉賽寧	Yesenin *tr Wang Shouren*	王守仁譯		艾呂雅	Eluard *tr Luo Dagang & Zhang Guanyao*
蒙塔萊	Montale *tr Lü Tongliu*	呂同六譯		阿拉貢	Aragon *tr Ye Rulian*
夸西莫多	Quasimodo *tr Xiao Mei & Li Guoqing*	曉 枚 李國慶譯		查良	Tzara *tr Fan Yuanhong*
洛爾伽	Lorca *tr Ye Junjian*	葉君健譯		狄蘭托馬斯	Dylan Thomas *tr Wu Ningkun*
梅特林克	Maeterlinck *tr Zheng Kelu*	鄭克魯譯		埃利蒂斯	Elytis *tr Li Yeguang & Yuan Kejia*
霍普特曼	Hauptmann *tr Xie Bingwen*	謝炳文譯		安德拉德	Mário de Andrade *tr Zhu Jingdong*
約翰·沁	Synge *tr Guo Moruo*	郭沫若譯		存在主義	**Existentialism**
表現主義	**Expressionism**			加繆	Camus *tr Meng An & Zheng Kelu*
斯特林堡	Strindberg *tr Fu Jiaqin*	符家欽譯		薩特	Sartre *tr Zheng Kelu & Jin Zhiping*
凱撒	Kaiser *tr Fu Weici*	傅惟慈譯		椎名麟三	Shiina Rinzō *tr Dan Dong*
托勒	Toller *tr Yang Yezhi & Sun Fengcheng*	楊業治 孫鳳城譯		安部公房	Abe Kōbō *tr Sun Lüheng & Sun Changling*
恰佩克	Capek *tr Yang Leyun & Jiang Chengjun*	楊樂雲 蔣承俊譯		瓦爾馬	Varma *tr Ni Peigong*
奧尼爾	O'Neill *tr Huang Wu*	荒 蕪譯		拉蓋什	Lakash *tr Ni Peigong*
卡夫卡	Kafka *tr Ye Tingfang & Li Wenjun*	葉廷芳 李文俊譯			

Shanghai, Shanghai Literature and Arts Press, 1981.

NOTES

INTRODUCTION

1. See, for example, the recent vivid account of Peter Hessler teaching in Fuling on the Yangtze River, *Rivertown* (2000), and Naomi Woronov teaching at Zhejiang University in Hangzhou, *China through My Window* (1988).

2. The Boxer Rebellion was an antiforeign, antimissionary movement begun in Shandong province in 1898. Christianity was being used by arrogant "foreigners" to "civilize" the Chinese, and when the Chinese rebelled, they were punished by the Germans and Russians who had more interest in North China than the English. Unrest spread throughout much of North China and included the murder and arson of thousands of foreign Christians, missionaries, and converts by the Boxers as well as damage to property. After the rebellion in 1901, the allies imposed a fine, $335 million, punishment upon the Chinese for the loss of foreign lives and property and created the Boxer Indemnity Fund. Part of these funds later supported Qinghua and Beijing Universities, which prepared Chinese students to study abroad as well as cultural projects and provided American and British intellectuals with travel to China to further cultural understanding and exchange.

3. Briefly, British imperialism beginning in the eighteenth century led to the British exposure to Chinese culture through consumer products such as porcelain, tea, silks, objets d'art, fashion, architecture, and garden design. Cultural contact between English and Chinese writers and scholars followed upon this trade route, particularly after the establishment of the Chinese Republic in 1911. Each culture had its windows open. "What happened"—the question of this book—is not only what happened among the figures presented here, but is the result of encounters in earlier periods of economic and cultural imperialism. This contact led to the creation of institutions such as the London University School of Oriental and African Studies, founded in 1909 upon what Lords Curzon and Cromer saw as the "fact" of England's great historical and imperial position (Said, *Culture and Imperialism*, 213*ff*). As a result of the study and renewed curiosity about China's archaeology, culture, and art, translations of Chinese

works began in earnest. Also, with the waning influence of the warlords and the growing stability of the republic, the British and Chinese began to travel more for study and pleasure in each other's countries.

4. There were a wide variety of literary groups and magazines vying during the May Fourth literary movement that persisted from 1919 through the early 1930s. In general, this movement was characterized by its humanist values, liberalism, interest in the West, and the use of vernacular instead of classical Chinese as the literary language. It was a period of cultural openness and probing. For more information, see Chow Tse-tsung, *The May Fourth Movement: Intellectual Revolution in Modern China* (1967); Lee Leo Ou-fan, *The Romantic Generation of May Fourth Writers* (1973); Merle Goldman, *Modern Chinese Literature in the May Fourth Era* (1977); Vera Schwarcz, *The Chinese Enlightenment: Intellectuals and the Legacy of the May Fourth Movement of 1919* (1986); and Ellen Widmer and David Der-wei Wang, eds., *From May Fourth to June Fourth: Fiction and Film in Twentieth-Century China*, (1993).

This is a small part of the puzzle of literary societies in China at the time; a more complete survey in the context of other literary groups such as the Creation Society and the Literary Association and modern fiction in China of the time, 1917–57, can be found in C. T. Hsia's *A History of Modern Chinese Fiction* and the above works.

5. For examples of Bloomsbury-bashing, and charges of snobbery and insularity, see the critics Roger Poole, *The Unknown Virginia Woolf*; John Carey, *The Intellectuals and the Masses*; and Tom Paulin's 1991 BBC production "J'Accuse." Paulin says of Woolf that "her books are nothing more than a highbrow version of the country diary of an Edwardian lady."

6. Edward Said illuminates the term, "orient," tinged as it is with British imperial light, making us aware through his reading of Foucault of the "archaeology" of the word in the British and French cultural enterprise. Given the history of Western imperialism and its cultural transformations, Said poses, then, a very important critical question: "How can one study other cultures and peoples from a libertarian, or a nonrepressive and nonmanipulative, perspective?" (*Orientalism*, 24). At this historical moment, we build upon this question.

7. Japanese critics have presented studies, such as Nairo Shiro *Yeats and Zen* (1984) and Masaru Sekine's *Yeats and the Noh* (1990); and Indian critic P. S. Sri wrote *T. S. Eliot, Vendanta and Buddhism* (1985). This study also relates to the new work evolving on "orientalism," beginning with Edward Said's *Orientalism* (1978) and *Culture and Imperialism* (1995), and extending to John M. MacKenzie's *Orientalism: History, Theory and the Arts* (1995); Matthew Bernstein and Gaylyn Studlar, editors of *Visions of the East: Orientalism in Film* (1997); and J. J. Clarke's *Oriental Enlightenment* (1997).

NOTES TO PAGES 39–79 / 413

ONE. JULIAN BELL PERFORMING "ENGLISHNESS"

1. Peter Stansky and William Abrahams write early and sensitively of Julian Bell's restlessness as he travels from China to the Spanish Civil War, *Journey to the Frontier: Two Roads to the Spanish Civil War* (1966).

2. Distinctions will be made between writings that appear in *The China Diary*, Julian's autograph, unpaginated notebook in King's College, Cambridge University, and *Julian Bell: Essays, Poems, and Letters*, known as the Memorial Volume, ed. Quentin Bell in 1938 after Julian's death.

3. Eddy Playfair is here referring to G. L. Dickinson's impersonation of a Chinese official in his satire *Letters from a Chinese Official* (1901).

4. Tape-recorded interview of Ye Junjian in Beijing, China, summer 1995.

5. Mr. Xu Zhengbang, curator of the Archives, Wuhan University, had conversations about Julian Bell with Professor Fang Zhong, dean of foreign languages, and friend of Bell's, 1935–37. Professor Fang died in 1999.

6. See Anthony Julius. *T. S. Eliot, Anti-Semitism and Literary Form* (Cambridge: Cambridge University Press, 1995).

7. Several letters between Julian and Vanessa in the early part of his travel by boat to China—which took three months—are preoccupied with the problem of Julian's venereal disease. Vanessa is particularly anxious about the quality of care he will get in China; Julian, anxious about the delay of his physical relationship with Ling Shuhua. See for example JB to VB, 22 November 1935.

8. I have located four of Ling Shuhua's letters to Julian Bell: 29 December 1936, written as Julian plans to leave China because of the scandal; 4 January 1936, written when she was visiting Beijing and planning to secretly meet Julian; 2 March 1937, and another undated, after Julian leaves Wuhan and they plan a rendezvous in Canton [Guanzhou] before he sails for England. Discretion or the chaos that sometimes engulfs life's papers has eclipsed Ling Shuhua's words.

9. Then, the New Life movement stressed the traditional virtues of moral conduct, propriety, righteousness, integrity, and the sense of shame. The movement, mounted by Chiang Kai-shek as a part of China's regeneration, used the branches of the YMCA in China as its organizing force during 1934–37. Young people like Ling Shuhua were subject to these repressive forces.

10. Ying Chinnery, the daughter of Chen Yuan and Ling Shuhua was about four or five years old at the time (though her official birth date is 1938). Eventually, she left China (1947), grew up in England, married John Chinnery, who established the Chinese Department at Edinburgh University, and founded, with her husband, the Scotland–China Association in 1965. Mrs. Chinnery has worked for the BBC World Service, and has been involved in international cultural exchange through the Scotland–China Association.

11. See recent discussions of collaborations between Sylvia Plath and Ted Hughes: Janet Malcolm's *The Silent Woman: Sylvia Plath and Ted Hughes* (1994); Lynda K. Bundtzen's *The Other Ariel*.

12. It is unusual that a woman, Miss Wu, is preparing for imperial examinations. These onerous exams, which required years of preparation, were usually reserved for men who then gained entrance to governmental posts based on performance. In some cases, as with Black Jade in Tsao Hsueh-Chin's *The Dream of the Red Chamber* (18th century), women were given such an education when a son had died: "Both Ju-hai and his wife loved their only daughter dearly and, after the death of their son, decided to give her the advantages of the kind of education usually reserved for boys" (Hsueh-Chin, 19). Miss Wu, however, is part of a new generation of twentieth-century women who initiated taking the preferment exams themselves.

13. Julian compares the compulsive chatter and self-preoccupation of Miss Bates to Mrs. Stephens, Julia Stephens's mother (Virginia Woolf's grandmother). Panthea Reid in *Art and Affection: A Life of Virginia Woolf* describes Mrs. Stephens as a demanding person unaware of other's needs. She wrote, according to Reid, hundreds of letters "appalling" in their preoccupation with Victorian values, bowel movements, and illness.

TWO. LITERARY COMMUNITIES IN ENGLAND AND CHINA: POLITICS AND ART

1. Tani Barlow (1991) writes of signs from the West that "accrue powers of their own" once they enter and circulate in the Chinese context; Xiaomei Chen (1992) similarly writes of the hybrid discourse that emerges from reciprocal constructions of East and West; Lydia Liu (1993), in the same vein, writes of "translingual practices" as one culture translates another, linguistically and aesthetically. Recently there also have been political discussions of the concept of the "third way": see, for example, Steven Lukes's review of Anthony Giddens's book *The Third Way, Times Literary Supplement* (25 September 1998), pp. 3–4. These contemporary stances reflect the thinking of the Crescent Moon literary group.

2. See, for example, the recent interest in the love life of Xu Zhimo reflected in Pang Natasha Chang's *Bound Feet and Western Dress* (1996), the story of the marriage of her great aunt, Zhang Youyi, to the well-known poet Xu Zhimo, and Hengwen Gao's *Xu Zhimo and the Women in his Life* published in China (2000). The growing interest in Ling Shuhua in China is revealed in Fu Guangming's 1992 translation of *Ancient Melodies*. In America, the growing interest in Chinese women writers, Ling Shuhua among them, is reflected in the translation of their stories, *Writing Women in Modern China*, ed. Amy D. Dooling and Kristina M. Torgeson (1998). In addition, we see the appearance of criticism about Ling Shuhua in articles by Janet Ng (1993) and Shi Shumei in *Lure of the Modern* (2001).

3. S. P. Rosenbaum, *The Bloomsbury Group, A Collection of Memoirs, Commentary and Criticism* (1975), is a useful compendium.

THREE. EAST-WEST LITERARY CONVERSATIONS

1. This concept is developed by Yip Wai-lim in *Diffusion of Distances: Dialogues between Chinese and Western Poetics* (1993).

2. See Sheldon Xiao-peng Lu, *From Historicity to Fictionality: The Chinese Poetics of Narrative*, which documents the Chinese preoccupation with "factual accuracy" in the production and reception of narrative texts. Lu writes that "narrative was history and fiction was considered defective history."

3. Ying Chinnery, Ling Shuhua's daughter, reports in a letter that Xu Zhimo "left a lot of letters and diaries with her [Ling Shuhua] when he went abroad.... I did see quite a few postcards by Xu in China when I was a child but obviously she didn't bring them abroad although she kept a lot of letters by others." (Letter to the author, 1 March 1998). In addition, Heng-wen Gao, has written a new book, *Xu Zhimo and the Women in His Life* (2000), an English summary of which reveals that a treasure chest of Xu's letters, some to Ling Shuhua, is missing.

4. Natasha Chang in *Bound Feet, Western Dress* credits Xu as a gifted calligrapher and poet, but reports the sadness of Zhang Youyi's marriage and her life as a woman in China: "Xu Zhimo never looked at me, only through me, as if I did not exist. All my life, I had lived with educated men like him" (90).

5. J. M. Keynes outlines the inequities in the German treaties in *Economic Consequences of the Peace* (1920).

6. See Voltaire's *Letters Concerning the English Nation;* Montesquieu's *The Persian Letters;* Oliver Goldsmith's *Citizen of the World.*

7. Personal communication by Xiao Qian, summer 1995. I did, by chance, find two of Xiao's letters to Forster in odd files in King's College Modern Archives, Cambridge University.

8. The Wolfenden Report which "decriminalized" homosexuality and prostitution was published in 1963; the Wolfenden Act, passed in the House of Commons, 1964.

9. Ye Junjian described Auden as "indiscreet" during his 1937 trip to Chinese frontier, and described Christopher Isherwood as "a gentleman." Interview by the author, August 1995, Beijing, China.

10. See Zhaoming Qian, *Modernism and Orientalism* (1995).

11. Jin Di was also the featured speaker at a 1996 James Joyce symposium held in Beijing and Tianjin, 5–9 July 1996.

FOUR. CHINESE LANDSCAPES THROUGH BRITISH EYES

1. See W. J. T. Mitchell, *Landscape and Power* (Chicago 1994) and *The Genius of the Place: The English Landscape Garden, 1620–1820*, ed. John Dixon Hunt and

Peter Willis (New York, 1975). The "positioning" of the West as "shutting out the view" can be found, for example, in the works of Edward Said, *Orientalism* (1978) and *Culture and Imperialism* (1995); Gayatri Spivak, "Can the Subaltern Speak?" in Nelson and Grossberg, eds. *Marxism and the Interpretation of Culture* (1988); V. G. Kiernan, *The Lords of Human Kind* (1986); and Benita Parry, *Conrad and Imperialism* (1983). David Bunn in an article about Thomas Pringle's African landscapes ("'Our Wattled Cot': Mercantile and Domestic Space in Thomas Pringle's African Landscapes," *Landscape and Power*, ed. W. J. T. Mitchell, 127–174) illustrates another critical turn in representing cultural "contradictions" and discourses of "resistance" despite imperialist activity.

2. Often in her letters, Vanessa apologizes for not being able to do enough for Shuhua but notes the difficulties of her life—helping Angelica with the babies, "the difficult roads and cold" of Charleston, the lack of fuel, and having only one servant to assist her with all the work. In addition, she is "anxious not to make difficulties between you and your husband" (Letter to LS, 7 March 1947). She, nevertheless, takes very seriously Julian's request (in a letter he had given to Eddy Playfair to be given to his mother in case of his death) that she take care of his friends. Vanessa aided Shuhua's daughter in getting into a school in 1947; recommended Marjorie Strachey as a teacher of English; asked David Garnett for help in publishing Shuhua's stories, though eventually Leonard Woolf published her autobiography in 1953; introduced her to Arthur Waley and Saxon Sydney-Turner; and encouraged her to attend Newnham College, though she could not help with admissions because "they keep strictly to the rules."

3. Shuhua, always enterprising, showed half of this collection of the Wen-ren-hua literary school of painters from Yuan and Qing dynasties at the Musée Cernuschi in Paris, 31 November 1962–25 February 1963. She had stored this collection in Sissinghurst Castle for four years when she traveled. The papers reviewed it, French television made it into an education program, and André Maurois wrote an introduction to the catalog. This collection was again shown in England in February–March 1967, in an exhibit titled "A Chinese Painter's Choice," Chinese painting from the fourteenth to the twentieth century, 23 February–25 March 1967, sponsored by the Arts Council of Great Britain. She would return for the opening from her teaching post at the University of Toronto, where she taught modern Chinese literature for a year.

4. Vanessa made an effort to get an art critic to review her exhibition at the Adam's Galleries in 1949, and encouraged Shuhua to ask Arthur Waley to open the exhibition but he and J. B. Priestley declined. She also told her to find someone to write an introduction to the show who would give an idea of her reputation in China (an issue in transnational artistic ventures as this book attests). Ling Shuhua also wrote an essay on landscape painting, "An Introduction to Chinese Painting," and it was circulated to the

New Statesman and the *Nation* by Hong Yin, but rejected by the editors because it "would require to be entirely rewritten," an issue of writing in a second language. In 1966, Quentin Bell wrote on behalf of Shuhua to the Victoria and Albert Museum to inquire if they were interested in holding an exhibition of Han rubbings from her collection. In 1967, Shuhua would write an article on Han cave rubbings for *Country Life*.

5. See Patricia O'Hara, "The Willow Pattern that We Knew: The Victorian Literature of Blue Willow," *Victorian Studies* (summer 1993), for excellent documentation of the popularity of the blue willow in literature in the nineteenth century.

6. As part of the historical practice of foot binding, women's toes were bent under, and the bone growth stunted so that the foot was like a crushed stump about two or three inches in length. A woman's walk had the motion of walking on stilts; they could not run. Foot binding came to an end in most places between the wars, but even in the 1940s, according to William Hinton, young girls could be found in the mountain counties of Shanxi with stunted feet (24).

7. See Homi Bhabha, "Signs Taken for Wonders," in *The Location of Culture*, 1994.

POSTSCRIPT

1. See Matei Calinescu, *Five Faces of Modernity* (1987); Michael Levensons' *A Genealogy of Modernism: A Study in English Literary Doctrine, 1908–22* (1984); Malcolm Bradbury and James W. McFarlane, *Modernism, 1890–1930* (1978); Stan Smith, *The Origins of Modernism*; Stephen Watt and Kevin Dettmar, *The Marketing of Modernism*; Bonnie Kime Scott, *The Gender of Modernism*; Ástrá dur Eysteinsson, *The Concept of Modernism*; Shari Benstock, *Women of the Left Bank*; Susan Stanford Friedman, *Mappings*.

2. See Bonnie McDougall, *The Introduction of Western Literary Theories into Modern China* (1970). Her early stance is best summed up in the first sentence: "The history of modern Chinese intellectual development can to a large extent be explained in terms of reaction to the intrusion of the West into China" (1). My work uses the concept of "network" to explain the cultural and aesthetic relationship between England and China. It attempts to understand what cultural needs and tensions are concealed in the mutual aesthetic receptivity of England and China in the early part of the twentieth century.

BIBLIOGRAPHY

Abrams, M. H. *The Mirror and the Lamp: Romantic Theory and Critical Tradition.* New York: Oxford University Press, 1953.

Acton, Harold. Letter to Julian Bell. Charleston Papers (hereafter referred to as CHAO), Modern Archives, King's College, Cambridge.

———. Letters to Ling Shuhua. Berg Collection (hereafter referred to as Berg), New York Public Library, New York.

Acton, Harold, and L. C. Arlington, trans. and ed. *Famous Chinese Plays.* Peking: Russell & Russell, 1937.

Acton Harold, and Chen Shih-Hsiang, trans. *Modern Chinese Poetry.* London: Duckworth, 1936.

Adams, Hazard, and Leroy Searle, ed. *Critical Theory since 1965.* Tallahassee: Florida State University, 1986.

Addison, Joseph. "Papers from *The Tatler* and *The Spectator* (1710–1712)" in *The Genius of the Place: The English Landscape Garden, 1620–1820,* edited by John Dixon Hunt and Peter Willis, 139–47. Cambridge: MIT Press, 1988.

Adorno, Theodor W. "Commitment." In *Aesthetic Theory.* Edited by Gretel Adorno and Rolf Tiedemann. Minneapolis: University of Minnesota Press, 1997.

Ahmad, Aijax. *In Theory: Classes, Nations, and Literatures.* London/New York: Verso, 1992.

Anderson, Benedict. *Imagined Communities: Reflections on the Origin and Spread of Nationalism.* London: Verso, 1983.

Anderson, Marston. *The Limits of Realism: Chinese Fiction in the Revolutionary Period.* Berkeley: University of California Press, 1990.

Anderson, William. *The Costume of China: Picturesque Representations of the Dress and Manners of the Chinese.* Singapore: Graham Brash, 1990.

Appadurai, Arjun. *Globalization.* Durham, N.C.: Duke University Press, 2001.

Ardener, Edwin. "Some Outstanding Problems in the Analysis of Events." In *Yearbook of Symbolic Anthropology,* vol. 1., edited by C. Schwimmer. London: C. Hurst, 1978.

Ardener, Shirley. *Women and Space: Gender Rules and Social Maps*. Oxford: Berg, 1993.
Ashcroft, Bill, Gareth Griffiths, and Helen Tiffin, eds. *The Empire Writes Back: Theory and Practice of Post-Colonial Literatures*. London, New York: Routledge, 1991.
Auden, W. H., and Christopher Isherwood. *Journey to a War*. London: Faber and Faber, 1973.
Ayscough, Florence, trans. *Fir Flower Tablets*, English versions by Amy Lowell. Conn: Hyperion Press, 1921.
Bachelard, Gaston. *The Poetics of Space*. Translated by Maria Jolas. New York: Orion Press, 1964.
Bakhtin, Mikhail. *The Dialogic Imagination*. Edited by Michael Holquist. Translated by Caryl Emerson and Michael Holquist. Austin: University of Texas Press, 1981.
——. *Problems in Dostoevsky's Poetics*. Edited by Caryl Emerson. Minneapolis: University of Minnesota Press, 1984.
Barlow, Tani. *Chinese Reflections: American Teaching in PRC*. New York: Praeger, 1985.
——. *Gender Politics in Modern China: Writing and Film*. Durham, N.C.: Duke University Press, 1993.
Barthes, Roland. *Empire of Signs*. Translated by Richard Howard. New York: Hill & Wang, 1981.
Baudrillard, Jean. *Simulacra and Simulation*. Translated by Sheila Faria Glaser. Ann Arbor: University of Michigan Press, 1994.
Bell, Julian Howard. "The Art of War." Julian Bell Papers (hereafter referred to as JHB) 1/1, Modern Archives, King's College, Cambridge.
——. *Chaffinches*. Songs for Sixpence, vol. 2. Cambridge: W. Heffner & Sons, 1929.
——. "China Diary, 1935–36." In *Julian Bell: Essays, Poems and Letters*, edited by Quentin Bell. London: Hogarth Press, 1938.
——. *China Diary and Notebook* [manuscript notes for a memoir]. JHB 3/2.
——. "Ecrasez L'Infame: Mr. Eliot's Gods." JHB/8.
——. "Hogarth Letter on Roger Fry." In *Essays, Poems and Letters*, edited by Quentin Bell. London: Hogarth Press, 1938.
——. *Julian Bell: Essays, Poems and Letters* (referred to as the Memorial Volume), edited by Quentin Bell. London: Hogarth Press, 1938.
——. Letters to Harold Barger. JHB 2/3.
——. Letters to Vanessa Bell. CHAO, 300 ALS, 1916–37.
——. Letter to Vanessa Bell [given to Eddy Playfair]. JHB 2/38.
——. Letters to John Lehmann, JHB 2/27, Fragments & Unidentified Papers.
——. Letters to Eddy Playfair. JHB 2/38.
——. Letters to Ling Shuhua. JHB 2.

———. Letters to Ling Shuhua. Berg.
———. Letters to Helen Morris nee Soutar, 1930–31, JHB 2/20.
———. Letters to Virginia Woolf. Monk's House Papers III (hereafter referred to as MHP). Correspondence, Sussex University, Brighton.
———. "A Naturalist's Point of View." JHB 7/8.
———. "Poetry as Pure Art." JHB 7/8.
———. "Politics and the Good Life." JHB 1/2.
———, ed. *Reminiscences of War Resisters in World War I, including We Did Not Fight, 1914–18 Experience of War Resisters*. New York: Garland Publishers, 1972.
———. "The Road to Wuchang [Wuhan]." In *The Fifth Graduation Album* (summer 1936) National Wuhan University, Wuhan, China.
———. "Romanticism." *Cambridge Review*, 7 March 1930.
———. *Still Life and Other Poems*. Woodside, Calif.: Occasional Works, 1987.
———. Testimonials in Support of Application to Wuhan University, by J. T. Sheppard and J. M. Keynes. JHB 3/1.
———. *Winter Movement and Other Poems*. London: Chatto & Windus, 1930.
———. *Work for the Winter*. London: Hogarth Press, 1936.
———. Wuhan University Archives. The course list 1935–36. "Advanced English Composition, Shakespeare, British and American Novels, Modern Literature and its Background."
Bell, Quentin. *Bloomsbury Recalled*. New York: Columbia University Press, 1995.
———. *Virginia Woolf: A Biography*. 2 vols. New York: Harcourt Brace Jovanovich, 1972.
———, ed. *Julian Bell: Essays, Poems and Letters*. London: Hogarth Press, 1938.
Bell, Vanessa. Diary 1937. CHAO/VB.
———. Letters to Julian Bell. Berg.
———. Letters to Julian Bell. CHAO 7/7.
———. Letters to Julian Bell in China, August 1935–July 1937. 82 Letters, #TGA 9311, Tate Gallery Archives, London. (3 originals and photocopies in CHAO, Box 11.)
———. Letters to Ling Shuhua. 5 December 1939–26, November 1955. Berg.
Bernal, Eileen. Letters to Julian Bell. JHB 2/7.
Bernstein, Matthew, and Gaylyn Studlam. *Visions of the East: The Orient in Film*. New Brunswick, N.J.: Rutgers University Press, 1997.
Berthoff, Ann, ed. *Richards on Rhetoric: I. A. Richards, Selected Essays, 1929–74*. New York: Oxford University Press, 1991.
Bhabha, Homi. *The Location of Culture*. London/New York: Routledge, 1994.
———. "The Other Question: Difference, Discrimination, and the Discourse of Colonialism." In *Out There: Marginalization and Contemporary Cultures*. Edited by Russell Ferguson. New York: New Museum of Contemporary Art, 1990.

———. "Signs Taken for Wonders: Questions of Ambivalence and Authority under a Tree outside Delhi, May 1817." In *"Race," Writing and Difference*, edited by Henry Louis Gates, Jr. Chicago: University of Chicago Press, 1986, 163–84.
———, ed. *Nation and Narration*. London/New York: Routledge, 1990.
Binyon, Laurence. *Chinese Art*. London: B. T. Batsford, 1935.
Blofeld, John. *The Chinese Art of Tea*. Boston: Shambhala, 1985.
Bloom, Edward A., and Lillian D. Bloom, eds. *Evelina*. Oxford: Oxford University Press, 1982.
Boorman, Howard L., and Richard Howard, eds. *Biographical Dictionary of Republican China*. 4 vols. New York: Columbia University Press, 1967–79.
Borges, Jorge Luis. *Ficciones*. Edited by Anthony Kerrigan. New York: Grove Press, 1962.
Bradbury, Malcolm, and James McFarlane. *Modernism, 1890–1930*. Hassocks: Harvester Press, 1978.
Brantlinger, Patrick. *Rule of Darkness: British Literature and Imperialism, 1830–1914*. Ithaca/London: Cornell University Press, 1998.
Bridges, Robert. Letter to Roger Fry. *Society for Pure English*, Tract 23, 10 January 1926.
BBC Advisory Committee on Spoken English (20 November 1933) Magdalen College Archives, I. A. Richards Collection, Cambridge University, Cambridge.
British Government, 1934 Report of the Board of Trustees for the Administration of the Boxer Indemnity Funds, King's College, Modern Archives, Cambridge.
Brower, Reuben, Helen Vendler, and John Hollander. *Essays in Honor of I. A. Richards*. New York: Oxford University Press, 1973.
Bryan, Derek. Interview by the author. Norwich, 27 January 1999.
Bryan, William Jennings. Introduction to *Letters from a Chinese Official, Being an Eastern View of Western Civilization*. New York: Phillips & Co., 1907.
Buck, Pearl. *Letter from Peking*. New York: Pocket Books, 1957.
Bunn, David. "'Our Wattled Cot': Mercantile and Domestic Space in Thomas Pringle's African Landscapes." In *Landscape and Power*, edited by W. J. T. Mitchell, 127–74. Chicago: University of Chicago Press, 1994.
Burgess, Anthony. Letter to Eddy Playfair. Eddy Playfair Papers, Modern Archives, King's College, Cambridge.
Butler, Judith. *Gender Trouble: Feminism and the Subversion of Identity*. New York/London: Routledge, 1990.
Calvino, Italo. *Six Memos for the Next Millennium*. Translated by Patrick Creagh. Cambridge: Harvard University Press, 1988.
Cao Xuequin. *Dream of the Red Chamber*. Translated by Chi-chen Wang. New York: Anchor, 1989.

Carey, John. *The Intellectuals and the Masses: Pride and Prejudice among the Literary Intelligentsia, 1880–1939.* London: Faber & Faber, 1992.
Carpenter, Edward. *Civilisation, Its Cause and Cure: and Other Essays.* London: Swan Sonnenschein & Co., 1908.
Caws, Mary Ann. *The Art of Interference: Stressed Reading in Verbal and Visual Texts.* Princeton: Princeton University Press, 1986.
———. "How She Matters Now: Personal Criticism and Virginia Woolf." *Massachusetts Review* (fall 1972).
———. *Robert Motherwell: What Art Holds.* New York: Columbia University Press, 1996.
———. *Women of Bloomsbury: Virginia, Vanessa and Carrington.* New York/London: Routledge, 1990.
———, and Sarah Bird Wright. *Bloomsbury and France.* Oxford: Oxford University Press, 1999.
Cawthorn, William. "Of Taste: An Essay Spoken at Anniversary Visitation of Tunbridge School, 1756." In *The Works of the English Poets.* Vol. 14. London: J. Johnson, 1810.
Chakrabarty, Dipesh. "Minority Histories, Subaltern Pasts," *Postcolonial Studies* 1, no. 1 (1998): 15–29.
Chambers, William. *Designs of Chinese Buildings, Furniture, Dresses, Machines, and Utensils.* New York: Benjamin Blom, 1968 [1757].
———. *A Dissertation on Oriental Gardening.* Farnborough: Gregg Press, 1972 [1772].
———. *Plans, Elevations, Sections, and Perspective Views of the Gardens and Buildings at Kew in Surrey.* Farnborough, Hants, England: Gregg Press, 1966 [1772].
Chang, Natasha Pang-Mei. *Bound Feet and Western Dress.* New York: Doubleday, 1996.
Chatterjee, Partha. *The Nation and Its Fragments: Colonial and Postcolonial Histories.* Princeton: Princeton University Press, 1993.
Chen Heng-zhe (also Sophia H. Chen Zen and Ch'en Heng-che). "My Childhood Pursuit of Education: In Memory of My Uncle, Mr. Chuang Szu-chien." Translated by Janet Ng. In *May Fourth Women Writers,* edited by Janet Ng and Janice Wickeri. Hong Kong: Renditions, 1996.
Chen Xiaomei. "Occidentalism as a Counterdiscourse." *Critical Inquiry* 18, no. 4 (summer 1992): 686–712.
———. *Occidentalism: A Theory of Counter-Discourse in Post-Mao China.* New York: Oxford University Press, 1995.
Chen Yuan (or Chen; T. P.; Tongbo; Hsi Ying; or Xiying, courtesy name). Letters to Julian Bell, 1937. CHAO.
Chinnery, Ying (Chen Xiying). Correspondence with the author. 1 February 1998.
———. Interview by the author. 26 January 1999. London, England.

Chow, Rey. "Violence in the Other Country: China as Crisis, Spectacle and Woman." In *Third World Women and the Politics of Feminism*, edited by Chandra Mohanty, Ann Russo, and Lourdes Torres, 81–100. Bloomington: Indiana University Press, 1991.

———. "Virtuous Transactions: A Reading of Three Stories by Ling Shuhua." *Modern Chinese Literature* 4 (1988): 71–85.

———. *Women and Chinese Modernity*. Minneapolis: University of Minnesota Press, 1991.

Chow, Tse Tsung. *The May Fourth Movement*. Cambridge: Harvard University Press, 1964.

Chu, Patricia. "Cultural Self-Inscription and the Anti-Romantic Plots of the Woman Warrior." *Diaspora* (1993).

Clarke, J. J. *Oriental Enlightenment: The Encounter between Eastern and Western Thought*. London/New York: Routledge, 1997.

Clarke, Suzanne. *Sentimental Modernism: Women Writers and the Revolution of the Word*. Bloomington: Indiana University Press, 1991.

Clifford, James. *Routes: Travel and Translation in the Late Twentieth Century*. Cambridge: Harvard University Press, 1997.

Coleridge, Samuel Taylor. *Selected Poetry and Prose of Coleridge*. Edited by Donald Stauffer. New York: Modern Library, 1951.

Conn, Peter. *Pearl Buck: A Cultural Biography*. Cambridge: Cambridge University Press, 1996.

Constable, John, ed. *Selected Letters of I. A. Richards*. Introduction by Richard Luckett. Oxford: Clarendon Press, 1990.

Cuddy-Keane, Melba and Kay Ki. "Passage to China: East and West and Woolf." *South Carolina Review* 29, no. 1 (fall 1996): 132–49.

Danforth, John, and John Fowler. *English Decoration in the Eighteenth Century*. Princeton: Pyne Press, 1974.

Denton, Kirk A., ed. *Modern Chinese Literary Thought: Writings on Literature, 1893–1945*. Stanford, Calif.: Stanford University Press, 1996.

Derrida, Jacques. *Grammatology*. Translated by Gayatri Spivak. Baltimore: Johns Hopkins University Press, 1976.

Dickinson, Goldsworthy Lowes. "Chinese Poetry," In *Inaugural Review of Chinese Students in Great Britain and Ireland, The Chinese Student* (1926), 6–8.

———. "Civis Brittanicus Sum." *Manchester Guardian*. Traveller's Tales. 18 February 1913, 18–19.

———. "The Greek View of Woman." In *The Woman Question*, edited by T. R. Smith, 1–11. New York: The Modern Library, 1918.

———. *The International Anarchy, 1904–14*. New York/London: The Century Co., 1926.

———. Introduction to *Points of View: A Series of Broadcast Addresses*. Freeport, N.Y.: Books for Libraries Press, 1930.

———. *Letters from a Chinese Official, Being an Eastern View of Western Civilization*. New York: McClure, Phillips & Co., 1903.

———. *Letters from John Chinaman*. London: R. Brimley Johnson, 1901.

———. Letters to Roger Fry. REF III, Modern Archives, King's College, Cambridge.

———. "A Malay Theatre." *Manchester Guardian*, 5 May 1913.

———. "Tale on Nanking [Nanjing]." *Manchester Guardian*, 8 April 1913.

Ding Ling. *I Myself am a Woman: Selected Writings of Ding Ling*. Boston: Beacon Press, 1989.

Dixon, John, and Peter Willis, eds. *The Genius of the Place: The English Landscape Garden, 1620–1820*. Cambridge: MIT Press, 1988.

Dooling, Amy D., and Kristina M. Torgeson, ed. *Writing Women in Modern China: An Anthology of Women's Literature from the Early Twentieth Century*. New York: Columbia University Press, 1998.

Dumas, Alexandre. *Camille*. New York: Modern Library, 1925.

Eagleton, Terry. *Literary Theory*. Minneapolis/London: University of Minnesota Press, 1983.

Eliot, George. *The Egoist* [1897]. Edited by Robert M. Adams. New York/London: W. W. Norton, 1979.

Eliot, T. S. *After Strange Gods: A Primer of Modern Heresy*. New York: Harcourt, Brace and Company, 1934.

Elmhirst, Leonard K. Elmhirst Papers, 37/5/1509, Carl A. Kroch Library, Cornell University, Ithaca, New York.

———. Letters to Ling Shuhua. LKE Overseas Collection, (hereafter referred to as LKE), Dartington Hall Archives, Totnes, England.

———. Letters to Xu Zhimo. LKE.

Eng, David. *Racial Castration: Managing Masculinity in Asian America*. Durham, N.C.: Duke University Press, 2001.

Eysteinsson, Ástráður. *The Concept of Modernism*. Ithaca: Cornell University Press, 1990.

Fairbank, Wilma. *Liang and Lin: Partners in Exploring China's Architectural Past*. With a foreword by Jonathan Spence. Philadelphia: University of Pennsylvania Press, 1994.

Felski, Rita. *The Gender of Modernity*. Cambridge: Harvard University Press, 1995.

Feuerwerker, Yi-tsi Mei. *Ding Ling's Fiction: Ideology and Narrative in Modern Chinese Literature*. Cambridge: Harvard University Press, 1982.

Fieldhouse, D. K. *The Colonial Empires: A Comparative Survey from the Eighteenth Century*. New York: Delacorte Press, 1965.

Forster, E. M. *Egypt: A Graeco-Alexandrian Encounter*. Edited by Hilda D. Spear and Abdel Moneim Aly. London: Cecil Woolf Publishers, 1987.

———. "The Feminine Note in Literature (1915)." Forster Papers, Kings College, Cambridge, Modern Archives (hereafter referred to as EMF).
———. *Friendship Gazette*. Vols. 1–4. A typed transcript made by Xiao Qian of 28 letters, 10 postcards, 1 telegram from E. M. Forster and 1 letter from Alice Forster, June 1941–July 1943. Additional comments by Xiao Qian on the letters and manuscript corrections by EMF. Forster Papers, Modern Archives, King's College, Cambridge.
———. *G. L. Dickinson and Related Writings*. London: Edward Arnold, 1973.
———. *G. L. Dickinson*. New York: Harcourt Brace Jovanovich, 1962 [1934].
———. Letters to Xiao Qian. 8 Letters, September 1943–February 1944. Transcribed by Xiao Qian. EMF.
———. *Locked Diary*, 1941. EMF.
———. *Maurice*. New York: Norton, 1971 [1914].
———. *A Passage to India*. New York: Harcourt, Brace & World, 1924.
———. *Two Cheers for Democracy*. New York: Harcourt Brace Jovanovich, 1951.
Foucault, Michel. *The Order of Things: An Archaeology of the Human Sciences*. New York: Random House, 1970.
Friedman, Susan Stanford. *Mappings: Feminism and the Cultural Geographies of Encounter*. Princeton: Princeton University Press, 1998.
———. "Uncommon Readings: Seeking the Geopolitical Woolf." *South Carolina Review* 29, no. 1 (fall 1996): 24–44.
Fry, Pamela Diamand. "Recollections of Roger Fry and the Omega Workshop." REF 3/2.
Fry, Roger. "Burlington House." REF 5/9.
———. "Calligraphy" (undated). REF 5/6.
———. "Chinese Porcelain and Hand Statues," REF 2/14a.
———. "The Double Nature of Painting." *Apollo* 89 (1933): 36–81.
———. Letters to Hsu Tsemon [Xu Zhimo], REF 3/90.
———. *Chinese Art*, vol. 8 of *Last Lectures*. Slade Professor of Fine Arts at University of Cambridge, 1933–34. With a introduction by Kenneth Clarke. New York/London: Macmillan & The University Press, 1939.
———. "Drawing or Design: Chinese Painting, Ma Lin, Han Dynasty." REF 6.
———. *Letters of Roger Fry*. Edited with an introduction by Denys Sutton. New York: Random House, 1972.
———. Letters to Gerald Brenan. REF 6.
———. Letters to Robert Bridges. REF 3/24.
———. Letters to Charles Vildrac. REF 11/40.
———. Letters to Virginia Woolf. REF 6.
———. "Oriental Art." *Living Age* (26 March 1910): 793–802.
———. *Transformations*. New York: Brentano's, 1928.

Fry, Roger, and E. A. Low. "English Handwriting." With 34 facsimile plates and artistic and paleographical criticism. *Society for Pure English*, Tract 23. London: Clarendon Press, 1926.
Galek, Marian. *The Genesis of Modern Chinese Literary Criticism, 1917–30*. London: Curzon Press, 1980.
Gamewell, Mary. *The Gateway to China: Pictures of Shanghai*. London: Fleming H. Revell, 1916.
Gao Heng-wen and Nong Sang. *Xu Zhimo and the Women in His Life* (in Chinese). Tianjin: People's Publishing Company, 2001.
Genette, Gerard. *Figures of Literary Discourse*. Translated by Alan Sheridan. New York: Columbia University Press, 1982.
Gibbs, Donald A., and Yun-chen Li. *A Bibliography of Studies and Translations of Modern Chinese Literature, 1918–1942*. Cambridge: Harvard University Press, 1975.
Giles, Herbert. *Gems of Chinese Literature*. New York: Paragon Book Reprint Co., 1965 [1898].
Gillespie, Diane, ed. *The Multiple Muses of Virginia Woolf*. Columbia: University of Missouri Press, 1993.
———. *The Sisters' Arts: The Writing and Painting of Virginia Woolf and Vanessa Bell*. Syracuse: Syracuse University Press, 1988.
———, ed. *Roger Fry*. Toronto: Oxford: Blackwell Publishers, 1995.
Goldman, Merle, ed. *Modern Chinese Literature and the May 4th Movement*. Cambridge: Harvard University Press, 1977.
Goldsmith, Oliver. *Citizen of the World; or, Letters of a Chinese Philosopher, Living in London, to His Friends in the East*. Edited by Austin Dobson. 2 vols. London: Dent, 1893 [1760].
Gould, Phillip. Lectures, "Aesthetics East and West." The China Institute, New York. 28 September–10 October 1995.
Grant, Duncan. Letter to Julian Bell. JHB 2/23.
———. Letters to Ling Shuhua. 3 letters. Berg.
———, illustrator. *Monkey [Xi You Ji]* by Wu Cheng'en. Translated by Arthur Waley. London: The Folio Society, 1968.
Gray, Basil. "The Chinese Exhibit, Poetry and Calligraphy." *Apollo* (December 1935): 313–17.
Grieder, Jerome B. *Hu Shi and the Chinese Renaissance: Liberalism in the Chinese Revolution, 1917–37*. Cambridge: Harvard University Press, 1970.
Ha Jin. *Waiting*. New York: Pantheon Books, 1999.
Hall, Stuart. *Essays and Dialogues*. New York: Routledge, 1995.
Han Minzhong. Correspondence with the author. Peking University, July 2001.

Hanley, Lynne. *Writing War: Fiction, Gender and Memory.* Amherst: University of Massachusetts Press, 1991.

Harris, David, ed. *Of Battle and Beauty: Felix Beato's Photographs of China.* Santa Barbara, Calif.: Santa Barbara Museum of Art, 1999.

He Li. "Modernism and China." Translated by Geremie Barmé. In *Modernism and Tradition: A Symposium. Renditions* 19 (spring 1983): 41–58.

Herdan, Innes Jackson. Interview by the author. Norwich, England, 27 January 1999.

———. *Liao Hongying [Hong Ying]-Fragments of a Life.* London: Larks Press, 1996.

Hinsch, Brett. *Passions of the Cut Sleeve: The Male Homosexual Tradition in China.* Berkeley: University of California Press, 1990.

Hinton, William. *Fanshen: A Documentary of Revolution in a Chinese Village.* New York: Random House, 1966.

Hobson, R. L. "The International Chinese Exhibition, 28th November, 1935, to 7th March, 1936." *Apollo* 22, no. 132 (December 1935): 311–12.

Hollington, Michael. "Richards and Empson in China." *Aumla Journal of Australasian Universities* 86 (November 1996): 81–92.

Holroyd, Michael. *Lytton Strachey.* London: Chatto & Windus, 1994.

Honig, Emily. *Sisters and Strangers: Women in the Shanghai Cotton Mills, 1919–49.* Stanford, Calif.: Stanford University Press, 1986.

Horton, Susan. *Difficult Women, Artful Lives.* Baltimore: Johns Hopkins University Press, 1995.

Hsia, Chih Tsing. *A History of Modern Chinese Fiction, 1917–57.* New Haven: Yale University Press, 1961.

———. Interview by the author, December 1997. New York.

Hunt, John Dixon, and Peter Willis. *The Genius of the Place: The English Landscape Garden, 1620–1820.* Boston: MIT Press, 1988.

Hu Shi, "Biography." Hu Shih Papers, Cornell University, Ithaca, New York.

———. "A Book of Experiments." Hu Shih Papers.

———. Letters to L. K. Elmhirst. LKE.

———. "A Lonely Literary Experimental Work and a Revolutionary Manifesto." in *Dr. Hu Shi's Personal Reminiscences.* Columbia University Oral History Project, part 1, no. 2. Interviewer, T. K. Tong

———. "New Culture Movement." Hu Shih Papers.

———. "One Thought." Hu Shih Papers.

———. "Tentative Thoughts on the Reform of Literature." Hu Shih Papers.

Hussey, Mark, ed. *Virginia Woolf A to Z: A Comprehensive Reference.* New York: Facts on File Inc., 1995.

Hutcheon, Linda. *Formalism and the Freudian Aesthetic: The Example of Charles Mauron.* Cambridge: Cambridge University Press, 1984.

———. *A Theory of Parody.* New York/London: Methuen, 1985.

Huyssen, Andreas. *After the Great Divide: Modernism, Mass Culture and Postmodernism.* Bloomington: Indiana University Press, 1986.

Jin Di. Interview by the author, 20 April 1995, New York City.

———. "Joycean Styles in Translation." Lecture, James Joyce Society, Gotham Book Mart, New York, 2 May 1995.

———. "The Odyssey of Ulysses into China." *James Joyce Quarterly* 27, no. 3 (spring 1990).

———. *Shamrocks and Chopsticks: James Joyce in China, A Tale of Two Encounters.* Hong Kong: City University of Hong Kong, 2001.

———. "Translating Ulysses, East and West." In *Joyce in Context*, edited by Vincent Cheng and Timothy Martin. Cambridge: Cambridge University Press, 1992.

———, trans. *Ulysses.* (in Chinese). Beijing: Peoples' Literature Publishing House, 1996.

Johnson, Barbara. "Rigorous Unreliability." *Critical Inquiry* 2 (1984): 278–85.

Joyce, James. *Dubliners.* New York: Viking, 1962 [1918].

Kai-yu Xu, ed. and trans. *Twentieth Century Chinese Poetry: An Anthology.* Ithaca: Cornell University Press, 1963.

Karatani, Kojin. *Origins of Modern Japanese Literature.* Translated and edited by Brett de Bary. Durham, N.C.: Duke University Press, 1993.

Kew History and Features. Kew Information Sheet, K5. London: Royal Botanic Gardens.

Keynes, J. M. *The Collected Writings of J. M. Keynes.* Edited by Donald Muggridge, vols. 6, 12. New York/Cambridge: Macmillan and Cambridge University Press for the Royal Economics Society, 1971–89.

———. Economic Advisory Council: Commission on China, 1930. John Maynard Keynes Papers, EA 1/2 Box 28, Modern Archives, King's College, Cambridge.

———. *The Economic Consequences of the Peace.* New York: Harcourt, Brace & Howe, 1920.

———. Foreword to *Julian Bell: Essays, Poems, and Letters*, edited by Quentin Bell. London: Hogarth Press, 1938.

Kinkley, Jeffrey C., *The Odyssey of Shen Congwen.* Stanford, Calif.: Stanford University Press, 1987.

———. ed. and trans. *Imperfect Paradise*, by Shen Congwen. Honolulu: University of Hawaii Press, 1995.

———. trans. *A Traveller without a Map*, by Xiao Qian. Stanford, Calif.: Stanford University Press, 1993.

Kipling, Rudyard. *Kim.* Edited with an introduction and notes by Edward Said. London: Penguin, 1989.

Ko, Dorothy. *Teachers of the Inner Chambers: Women and Culture in Seventeenth-Century China.* Stanford, Calif.: Stanford University Press, 1994.

Koestenbaum, Wayne. *The Queen's Throat: Opera, Homosexuality, and the Mystery of Desire*. New York: Poseidon Press, 1993.

Kuhn, Thomas. *The Structure of a Scientific Revolution*. Chicago: University of Chicago Press, 1980.

Lamb, Charles. "Old China." In *The Portable Charles Lamb*, edited with an introduction by John Mason Brown. New York: Viking, 1949.

Larson, Wendy. *Literary Authority and the Modern Chinese Writer*. Durham, N.C.: Duke University Press, 1991.

Lau, Joseph S. M., and Howard Goldblatt, eds. *The Columbia Anthology of Modern Chinese Literature*. New York: Columbia University Press, 1995.

Laurence, Patricia. "Beyond the Little Red Book: Contemporary Chinese Women Writers." *Nation* 4 (11 September 2000): 31–37.

———. "The China Letters: Julian Bell, Vanessa Bell and Ling Shuhua." *South Carolina Review* (spring 1997): 122–31.

———. "China's 'Yes' to Molly Bloom." Review. *English Literature in Transition* 45, no. 3 (2002): 363–66.

———. "The Facts and Fugue of War: From *Three Guineas* to *Between the Acts*." In *Virginia Woolf and War*, edited by Mark Hussey, 225–46. Syracuse: Syracuse University Press, 1991.

———. *The Reading of Silence: Virginia Woolf in the English Tradition*. Stanford, Calif.: Stanford University Press, 1991.

———. "Virginia Woolf and the East." Bloomsbury Heritage Series. London: Cecil Woolf Pub, 1995.

———. "Virginia Woolf in/on Translation." In *Virginia Woolf Miscellany*, edited with an introduction (fall 1999): 1–2.

Leask, Nigel. *British Romantic Writers and the East: Anxieties of Empire*. Cambridge: Cambridge University Press, 1992.

Leaska, Mitchell, ed. *Pointz Hall: The Earlier and Later Typescripts of between the Acts*. New York: University Publishers, 1983.

Lee, Hermione. *Virginia Woolf*. London: Chatto & Windus, 1996.

Lee, Leo Ou-fan. *The Romantic Generation of Modern Chinese Writers*. Cambridge: Harvard University Press, 1973.

———. *Shanghai Modern: The Flowering of a New Urban Culture in China, 1930–45*. Cambridge: Harvard University Press, 1999.

Lehmann, John. Letters to Julian Bell. CHAO.

———. *The Whispering Gallery, Autobiography*, vol. 1. London: Longman's, Green & Co., 1955.

Leung, Gaylord Kai Loh (Liang Hsi-hua). *A New Biography of Xu Zhimo*. 2d ed. Tapei: Lien Qing, 1994.

———. "Xu Zhimo and Bertrand Russell." *Renditions* 14 (autumn 1980): 27–36.
Lewis, Wyndham. "Men Without Art." In *Creatures of Habit and Creatures of Change: Essays on Art, Literature, and Society, 1914–56*. Santa Rosa: Black Sparrow Press, 1989.
Liao Hung Ying (Liao Hong Ying). Letters to Julian Bell, Vanessa Bell, Innes Jackson, JB, and Edith, November 1935–November 1937. JHB 16.
Liberty & Co. Catalogs, 1891–1936. Victoria and Albert Museum, The National Art Library, London: "Eastern Miscellaneous Bric-a-Brac, 1891; "Eastern Antiquities, 1897–1900"; "Fans, 1896"; "History of Feminine Costume, 1896"; "Liberty Bazaar: Chinese Blue and White Porcelain"; "A Permanent Exhibition of Most Characteristic Objects of the Far East, 1898."
Ling Shuhua (or Ling Shu hua, Ling Shu-hua, Chen Ling Shu-hua, Xu Hua Chen, Mrs. Chen Yuan, Sue Chen, Ling Jui-t'ang). *Ancient Melodies*. Introduction by Vita Sackville-West. New York: Universe Books, 1988.
———. *Ancient Melodies* (Chinese translation). Translated by Fu Guangming. China Overseas Chinese Press, 1994.
———. *Ancient Melodies*. Holographs. Berg.
———. "Childhood in China." *Spectator* (22 December 1950): 724.
———. *A Chinese Painter's Choice: Some Paintings from the 14th to the 20th Century, from the Collection of Ling Shuhua*. Catalog. London: Arts Council of Great Britain, 1967.
———. *A Collection of Short Stories* (in Chinese). Vols. 1–2. Tapei: Hongfan Bookstore, 1984.
———. "Embroidered Pillows" (from *Flowers in the Temple*). Translated by Marie Chan. *Renditions* no. 4 (spring 1975): 116ff.
———. Exhibition pamphlet. London. Ashmolean Museum, Oxford, 1983.
———. Exhibition pamphlet. Musée Cernuschi. Quai D'Orsay, Paris. Introduction by André Maurois. May 1964.
———. "The Gardener." *Country Life*, 1951.
———. "Han Cave Rubbings." *Country Life*. 1967.
———. "Intoxicated" (also titled "After Drinking"). In *Writing Women in Modern China*, edited by Amy D. Dooling and Kristina M. Torgeson, 175–96. New York: Columbia University Press, 1998.
———. "An Introduction to Chinese Painting." TS, Modern Archives King's College, Cambridge.
———. Letter to Julian Bell. Berg.
———. Letters to Julian Bell. CHAO.
———. Letter to Julian Bell. Tate Gallery Library, London.
———. Letters to L. K. Elmhirst. LKE.

———. Letter to Margery Fry. REF 8.
———. Letters to Vanessa Bell. Angelica Garnett Papers (hereafter referred to as AG) 1/12, Modern Archives, King's College, Cambridge.
———. Letters to Leonard Woolf. Berg.
———. Letters to Virginia Woolf. Berg.
———. Letters to Virginia Woolf. Monk's House Papers, Sussex University, Brighton.
———. "Memoir." Manuscript (5 pages). Berg.
———. "Mid–Autumn Eve." Translated by Marie Chan. *Renditions* no. 4 (spring 1975): 116–23.
———. "The Night of Midautumn Festival." Translated by Nathan K. Mao. In *The Columbia Anthology of Modern Chinese Literature,* edited by Joseph S. M. Lau and Howard Goldblatt, 111–19. New York: Columbia University Press, 1995.
———. "Once Upon a Time." In *Writing Women in Modern China,* edited and translated by Amy D. Dooling and Kristina M. Torgeson. New York: Columbia University Press, 1998.
———. "A Poet Goes Mad." Translated by Ling Shuhua and Julian Bell. *Tien Xia Monthly* 5 (1937): 401–21.
———. *Two Little Brothers.* Shanghai: Liangyou Bookstore, 1935.
———. "What's the Point of It?" (in English). *Tien Xia Monthly* 5 (1937).
———. *Women* (in Chinese). Shanghai: Commercial Press, 1938.
———. "Writing a Letter" (in English). *Tien Xia Monthly* 5 (1937): 508–13.
Link, Perry, Jr. *Mandarin Ducks and Butterflies: Popular Fiction in Twentieth Century Chinese Cities.* Berkeley: University of California Press, 1981.
———. *The Uses of Literature.* Princeton: Princeton University Press, 2000.
Liu, James J. Y., ed. *Language-Paradox-Poetics: a Chinese Perspective.* Princeton: Princeton University Press, 1988.
Liu, Lydia H. *Translingual Practice: Literature, National Culture, and Translated Modernity, China 1900–37.* Stanford: Stanford University Press, 1995.
Liu Shicong. Correspondence with the author, July 2001.
Location Register of Twentieth-Century English Literary Manuscripts and Letters: A Union List of Papers of Modern English, Irish, Scottish, and Welsh Authors in the British Isles. 2 vols. London: The British Library, 1988.
Lovejoy, A. O. *The Great Chain of Being: The History of an Idea.* Cambridge: Harvard University Press, 1936.
Lowe, Lisa. *Critical Terrains: French and British Orientalisms.* Ithaca: Cornell University Press, 1991.
———. "Des Chinoises: Orientalism, Psychoanalysis, and Feminine Writing." In *Ethics, Politics and Difference in Julia Kristeva's Writing.* New York, London: Routledge, 1993.

Lu, Sheldon Xiao-peng. *From Historicity to Fictionality: The Chinese Poetics of Narrative*. Stanford, Calif.: Stanford University Press, 1994.

Lu Jingquing. *Wanderings* (excerpts). Translated by Amy Dooling. In *May Fourth Women Writers*, edited by Janet Ng and Janice Wickieri. 73–94. Hong Kong: Renditions, 1996.

Lu Xun. *Selected Works*. Vol 1. Translated by Yang Xianyi and Gladys Yang. Beijing: Foreign Language Press, 1980.

Lukacs, Georg. "The Ideology of Modernism." In *Realism in Our Time: Literature and the Class Struggle*. New York: Harper and Row, 1971.

——. *Theory of the Novel: A Historic-Philosophical Essay on the Forms of Great Epic Literature*. Translated by Anna Bostock. Cambridge: MIT Press, 1996.

McDougall, Bonnie. *The Introduction of Western Literary Theories into Modern China, 1919–25*. Tokyo: Centre for East Asian Cultural Studies, 1970.

MacKinnon, Janice R., and Stephen R. MacKinnon. *Agnes Smedley: The Life and Times of an American Radical*. Berkeley: University of California Press, 1988.

Makiya, Kanan. *Cruelty and Silence: War, Tyranny, Uprisings, and the Arab World*. New York: Norton, 1993.

Mao Zedong. "Talks at the Yan'an Forum on Literature and Art, 1942." In *Mao Tse Tung on Literature and Art*. Beijing: Foreign Language Press, 1967.

Marcus, Jane. "Sapphistory: The Woolf and the Well." In *Lesbian Texts and Contexts: Radical Revisions*, edited by Karla Jay and Joanne Glasgow, 164–79. New York: New York University Press, 1990.

Marler, Regina, ed. *Selected Letters of Vanessa Bell*. New York: Random House, 1993.

Martin, Richard, and Harold Koda. *Orientalism: Visions of the East in Western Dress*. New York: Metropolitan Museum of Art, 1994.

Mason, William. "An Heroic Epistle to Sir William Chambers." In *The Genius of the Place: The English Landscape Garden, 1620–1820*, edited by John Dixon Hunt and Peter Willis. Boston: MIT Press, 1988.

Maurois, André. Letter to Ling Shuhua. Berg.

——. Introduction to Ling Shuhua Exhibition pamphlet, translated by Ilana Laurence. Quai D'Orsay, Paris, May 1964.

Meredith, George. *The Egoist*. Edited by Robert M. Adams. New York: Norton, 1979 [1879].

Miner, Earl. "Periods and Ideologies." In *Issues in World Literature*, edited by Caws, Laurence, Wright, 83–88. New York: Harper Collins, 1994.

Mitchell, W. J. T. *Landscapes and Power*. Chicago: University of Chicago Press, 1994.

Modern Chinese Literary Archive. *A Biographical Dictionary of Modern Chinese Writers*. Beijing: New World Press, 1994.

Mohanty, Chandra Talpade, Ann Russo, and Lourdes Torres. *Third World Women and the Politics of Feminism*. Bloomington: Indiana University Press, 1991.

Montesquieu, Charles de Secondat, baron de. trans. George C. Healy. *The Persian Letters*. Indianapolis: Hackett, 1999.

Moonan, Wendy. "Diverse Styles at the Birth of Porcelain." *New York Times*, 9 November 2001: E38.

Morley, David, and Kuan Hsing Chen. *Stuart Hall, Critical Dialogues in Cultural Studies*. London/New York: Routledge, 1996.

Morris, Helen, nee Soutar. Letter to Julian Bell. CHAO.

National Wuhan University Documents (unpublished library manuscripts)

———. Appointment of Professor Bell, Letter to Dean Chen, Wuhan, Document of Sino-British Cultural Association, no. 6965, 1935, #5. Letter of Appointment, National Wuhan University, Julian Bell, 1935, #5.

———. Board of Trustees of the Indemnity Fund, June 1937, no. 2097. Replacement for Julian Bell and Allocation of Indemnity Funds, #32.

———. Cables noting Julian Bell's delay of arrival in China, Aug.–Oct. 1935, #5.

———. Course Descriptions of Julian Bell, October 1935–July 1936.

———. List of Faculty, 1935, #8.

———. Replacement of Julian Bell by Lee Harvey, 1937–38.

———. Teaching Contract, Julian Bell, 1937, Document of Sino-British Cultural Association, no. 7071, #15.

Needham. Joseph. Letter to Ling Shuhua. Berg.

———. *Science and Civilization in China*. Vol. 1. Cambridge: Cambridge University Press, 1954.

Ng, Janet. "Writing in her Father's House: The Autobiography of Ling Shuhua." *Prose Studies: History, Theory, and Criticism* 16, no. 3 (December 1993): 235–50.

Ng, Janet, ed., and Janice Wickieri, trans. *May Fourth Women Writers: Memoirs*. Hong Kong: Renditions, 1996.

O'Hara, Patricia. "'The Willow Pattern That We Knew': The Victorian Literature of Blue Willow." *Victorian Studies* 36, no. 4 (summer 1993): 421–42.

O'Neill, Hugh B. *Companion to Chinese History*. New York/Oxford: Facts on File, 1987.

Orwell, George. "Why I Write." *A Collection of Essays*. New York: Doubleday, 1954.

Osborne, Harold, ed. *The Oxford Companion to Art*. Oxford: Oxford University Press, 1970.

Parsons, Trekkie. Letters to Ling Shuhua. Berg.

Paulin, Tom. "J'Accuse." British Channel 4 Television Program, 1991.

Pippett, Aileen. *The Moth and the Star: A Biography of Virginia Woolf*. Boston: Little Brown & Co., 1955.

Pirie, Antoinette (Toni). Letter to Julian Bell. JHB 2/37.
Plaks, Andrew H., ed. *Chinese Narrative: Critical and Theoretical Essays*. Princeton: Princeton University Press, 1977.
Playfair, Edward. Letters to Julian Bell, 1935– . 10 ALS (22 sheets), Playfair-Bell Correspondence, Misc. 82/5, Modern Archives, King's College, Cambridge University.
Poole, Roger. *The Unknown Virginia Woolf.* Cambridge/New York: Cambridge University Press, 1978.
Pound, Ezra. *Cantos.* New York: New Directions, 1965 [1917].
——. *Cathay: Poems after Li-Po* (from notes of Ernest Fenellosa). New York: Limited Edition Club, 1992.
Pratt, Mary Louise. *Imperial Eyes: Travel Writing and Transculturation.* London, New York: Routledge, 1992.
Prusek, Jaroslav. "Subjectivism and Individualism in Modern Chinese Literature." *Archiv Orientalni* 25 (1957): 261–86.
Pu Songling (P'ou Song Ling). *Strange Stories from a Chinese Studio.* Translated and annotated by Herbert A. Giles. New York: Boni and Liveright, 1925.
Qian, Xingcun (Qin Hongchun). "Examining Ling Shuhua's Work." Translated by Ming Chun-ho. *Sea Breeze Weekly Magazine* (12 December 1928): 259–64.
Qu Shijing. "Characterization, Theme and Structure of *Mrs. Dalloway.*" *Foreign Literature Studies* 31, no. 1 (1986): 105–109.
——. Interview by the author, 19–21 July 1995, Shanghai, China.
——. "Virginia Woolf in China." *Virginia Woolf Miscellany* (spring 1990, spring 1996).
——. "Woolf, Stream of Consciousness, Comprehensive Art." *Contemporary Literary Thought* 5 (1987): 132–44.
——, ed. *Critical Essays on Virginia Woolf* (in Chinese). Shanghai: Shanghai Press of Literature and Art, 1999.
——, ed. *Yi Shi Liu Xiao Shuo Li Lun* (*The Theory of Stream of Consciousness Novels: Joyce, James, Proust, Woolf*). Sichuan: Sichuan Literature and Art Publishing House, 1989.
Raine, Kathleen. *The Land Unknown.* New York: George Braziller, 1975.
Ramsay, Lettice. Letters to Julian Bell. JHB 2/42.
——. Letters to Vanessa Bell. Frank Ramsay Papers 4, Modern Archives, King's College, Cambridge.
——. Memoir. Frank Ramsay Papers 3/1.
Reed, Christopher, ed. *Not at Home: The Suppression of Domesticity in Modern Art and Architecture.* New York: Thames and Hudson, 1996.
Reid, Panthea. *Art and Affection: A Life of Virginia Woolf.* New York: Oxford University Press, 1996.

Richards, Dorothy. *Diary,* 1936. I. A. Richards Collection (hereafter referred to as IAR). Magdalene College Library, Cambridge University.

Richards, I. A. Correspondence concerning Advisory Committee of Spoken English, 1934–38. BBC Written Archives Center, Reading, England.

———. Magdalene College Richards' Collection, Boxes 7, 26, 27, 54–55, Cambridge University.

———. *Mencius on Mind: Experiments in Multiple Definitions.* London: K. Paul, Trench, Trubner, 1932.

———. *Practical Criticism.* New York: Harcourt Brace Jovanovich, 1929.

———. *Richards on Rhetoric.* Edited by Ann Berthoff. New York: Oxford University Press, 1991.

———. *So Much Nearer.* New York: Harcourt Brace Jovanovich, 1960.

Rose, Archibald. Biographical Summary. King's College Annual Report, November 1961, Modern Archives, King's College, Cambridge.

———. Economic Advisory Council: Commission on China, 1930. Keynes Papers, JMK/ EA 1/35, 1/39, 1/54 Box 28, Modern Archives, King's College, Cambridge.

———. Letters to J. M. Keynes. Keynes Papers, JMK/ EA 1/35, 1/39, 1/54 Box 28, Modern Archives, King's College, Cambridge.

———. Letter to Eddy Playfair. Rose Collection, Modern Archives, King's College Library, Cambridge.

Rosenbaum, S. P., ed. *The Bloomsbury Group: A Collection of Memoirs, Commentary, and Criticism.* London: Croom Helm, 1975.

Rushdie, Salman. *Midnight's Children.* New York: Avon, 1980.

Ruskin, John. "Modern Manufacture and Design." In *The Two Paths: Being Lectures on Art, and Its Application to Decoration and Manufacture, 1858–59.* New York: Wiley & Sons, 1883.

Russo, Paul, ed. *Complementarities: Uncollected Essays of I. A. Richards.* Cambridge: Harvard University Press, 1976.

Rutherford, Jessica M. F. *The Royal Pavilion: The Palace of George IV.* Brighton: Arts & Leisure Services (n.p., n.d.).

Rylands, Dadie. Letter to the author, 13 March 1996.

Said, Edward. *Culture and Imperialism.* New York: Knopf, 1993.

———. "Opponents, Audiences, Contituencies, and Community." *Critical Inquiry* 9, no. 1 (Sept. 1982): 1–26.

———. *Orientalism.* New York: Random House, 1979.

Saussure, Ferdinand de. *Course in General Linguistics.* Translated by Wade Baskin. New York: McGraw Hill, 1966.

Saussy, Haun. *The Problematics of Chinese Aesthetics.* Stanford, Calif.: Stanford University Press, 1993.

Schwarcz, Vera. *The Chinese Enlightenment: Intellectuals and the Legacy of the May Fourth Movement of 1919.* Berkeley: University of California Press, 1986.
Scott, Bonnie Kime. *The Gender of Modernism.* Bloomington: Indiana University Press, 1990.
Sen, Amartya. "A World Not Neatly Divided." *New York Times,* 23 November 2001: A39.
Shane, Sir Leslie. Review of *The Bloomsbury Group* edited by S. P. Rosenbaum. *The Month* (December 1954): 365–66.
Shen Congwen. *Recollections of West Hunan.* Translated by Gladys Yang. Beijing: Panda Books, 1992.
Shi Shumei. "Gender, Race, and Semicolonialism: Liu Na'ou's Urban Shanghai Landscape." *Journal of Asian Studies* 55, no. 4 (November 1996): 934–56.
———. *The Lure of the Modern: Writing Modernism in Semi-Colonial China, 1917–37.* Berkeley: University of California Press, 2001.
Sino-British Cultural Association. The Allocation of Funds for the University and the Board of Trustees of the Indemnity Fund, Lee Harvey replacement for Julian Bell after his resignation from Wuhan University, 1937.
———. Appointment Process of Julian Bell, 1935, to Dean Chen, Office of Education, Wuhan University, no. 6965.
———. Julian Bell's Wuhan University Teaching Contract, October, 1935–37, nos. 7071 and 1085.
Siu, Helen, and Zelda Stern, eds. *Mao's Harvest: Voices from China's New Generation.* New York: Oxford University Press, 1983.
Snodin, Michael, and Maurice Howard. *Ornament: A Social History.* New Haven: Yale University Press, 1996.
Sontag, Susan. *On Photography.* New York: Delta, 1977.
———. "Project for a Trip to China." *I, etcetera.* New York: Vintage, 1978.
Soutar, Helen. Letters to Julian Bell. JHB 2/50.
Spacks, Patricia. *Boredom: The Literary History of a State of Mind.* Chicago: Chicago University Press, 1995.
Spalding, Frances. *Duncan Grant: A Biography.* London: Chatto & Windus, 1997.
———. Letter to Ling Shuhua. Berg.
———. *Vanessa Bell.* New Haven/New York: Ticknor & Fields, 1983.
Spence, Jonathan. "Chinese Fictions in the 20th Century." In *Asia in Western Fiction,* edited by Robin W. Winks and James R. Rush. Honolulu: University of Hawaii Press, 1991.
———. *The Gate of Heavenly Peace: the Chinese and Their Revolution, 1895–1980.* New York: Viking, 1981.
Spivak, Gayatri Chakravorty. "Can the Subaltern Speak?" In *Marxism and the Inter-*

pretation of Culture, edited by Cary Nelson and Laurence Grossberg. Chicago: University of Illinois Press, 1988, 271–313.

———. *The Post-Colonial Critic.* Edited by Sarah Harasym. New York, London: Routledge, 1996.

Stansky, Peter. *On or about December 1910: Early Bloomsbury and Its Intimate World.* Cambridge: Harvard University Press, 1996.

———. "William Morris and Bloomsbury." Bloomsbury Heritage Series. London: Cecil Woolf, 1997.

———, and William Abrahams. *Journey to the Frontier: Two Roads to the Spanish Civil War.* Chicago: University of Chicago Press, 1966.

Stewart, Susan. *Crimes of Writing: Problems in the Containment of Representation.* New York: Oxford University Press, 1991.

Strachey, Lytton. *Eminent Victorians.* Harmondsworth: Penguin, 1948 [1918].

———. "A Son of Heaven." Manuscript in parts, British Museum, Strachey Papers, 6064A–D, 1913; integrated manuscript, courtesy Professor George Simson, Center for Biographical Research, University of Hawaii.

Su Xuelin. "Chen Xiying: Personal Anecdotes," Translated by Zhu Ying. *Luo Jia* 41 (1970): 1.

———. "In Memory of Ling Shuhua." Translated by Zhu Ying. *Luo Jia* 104 (July 1990).

———. Letter to Xiao Qian. Translated by Ming Ho. 20 May 1995.

Suleri, Sara. *The Rhetoric of English India.* Chicago: University of Chicago Press, 1992.

Sullivan, Michael. *Chinese Art: Art and Artists of Twentieth-Century China.* Berkeley: University of California Press, 1996.

———. "A Small Token of Friendship." *Oriental Art* 35, no. 2 (summer 1989): 76–85.

Tagore, Rabindranath. "Literary Debates in Modern China, 1918–37. "East Asian Cultural Studies Series, vol. 11. Center for East Asian Studies, Tokyo.

Talfourd, F., et al. *The Mandarin's Daughter, Being the Simple Story of the Willow Pattern Plate: A Chinese Tale.* London: T. H. Lacy, 185?.

Torgovnick, Marianna. *Gone Primitive: Savage Intellects, Modern Minds.* Chicago: University of Chicago Press, 1990.

Tremper, Ellen. *Who Lives at Alfoxton? Virginia Woolf and English Romanticism.* Lewisburg: Bucknell University Press, 1998.

Tsao-Hsueh-Chin. *The Dream of the Red Chamber.* Translated by Chi-Chen Wang. New York: Doubleday, 1958.

Tung, Constantine. "The Search for Order and Form: The Crescent Moon Society and the Literary Movements of Modern China, 1928–33." Ph.D. diss., Claremont Graduate School and University, California, 1971.

Tung, Timothy. Conversation with the author, spring 2001.

Tynyanov, Yuri. "On Literary Evolution." In *The Critical Tradition*, edited by David Richter, 727–34. Boston: Bedford Books, 1998.
Voltaire. *Letters Concerning the English Nation*. New York: B. Franklin Reprints, 1974.
Wang, David Der-Wei. *Fin-de-Siecle Splendor: Repressed Modernities of Late Qing Fiction, 1849–1911*. Stanford, Calif.: Stanford University Press, 1997.
———, and Ellen Widmer, eds. *From May Fourth to June Fourth: Fiction and Film in Twentieth-Century China*. Cambridge: Harvard University Press, 1993.
Wang, T. T. Letter to Leonard Elmhirst. 20 March 1964. LKE.
Wang Xin-di. Interview by the author. 20 July 1995, Shanghai, China.
Waley, Arthur. "Blake the Daoist." BBC Radio Transcription.
———. "Description of the Arthur D. Waley Papers 1912–1961." Manuscript Special Collections. Rutgers University Libraries, New Jersey.
———. *A Hundred and Seventy Chinese Poems*. London: Constable & Co., 1918.
———. *Three Ways of Thought in Ancient China*. Stanford: Stanford University Press, 1982. [1939].
———. *Translations from the Chinese*. Illustrated by Cyrus Le Roy Baldridge. New York: Knopf, 1919.
———, trans. *Monkey* [*Xi You Ji*], by Wu Cheng'en. Illustrated by Duncan Grant. London: The Folio Society, 1978.
Waley, Margaret (Mrs. Hubert Waley). "Arthur David Waley (1889–1966): A View from Within his Family." Manuscript, Arthur Waley Papers, Rutger's University Libraries, New Jersey.
Wang. Letter to L. K. Elmhirst. LKE.
Wang, Y. C. *Chinese Intellectuals in the West, 1872–1949*. Chapel Hill: University of North Carolina Press, 1966.
Webb, Beatrice and Sidney. *The Letters of Beatrice and Sidney Webb*. Vol. 3, 1892–1912. Edited by Norman Mackenzie. Cambridge: Cambridge University Press, 1978.
———. *The Webbs in Asia: 1911–12 Travel Diary*. Hampshire: Macmillan Press, 1992.
Welty, Eudora. "Place in Fiction." *Three Essays on Fiction*, 1962.
Wen Jieruo. Interview by the author. 20 March 2000. Beijing.
———. "Living Hell (from her memoirs)." Translated by Jeffrey Kinkley. In *The Columbia Anthology of Modern Chinese Literature*. Edited by Joseph S. M. Lau and Howard Goldblatt. New York: Columbia University Press, 1995.
———, trans. *Katherine Mansfield: The Collected Short Stories*. Harmondsworth, Middlesex: Penguin, 1981.
———, trans. *Maurice*, by E. M. Forster. Harmondsworth, Middlesex: Penguin, 1972.
———, trans., with Xiao Qian. *Ulysses*, by James Joyce.

Wen Yiduo. "The Laundry Song." *Twentieth Century Chinese Poetry.* Edited by Hsu Kai-yu. Garden City, N.J.: Doubleday, 1963.

Whistler, James McNeill, *Mr. Whistler's "Ten O'Clock": as Delivered in London, at Cambridge,* and at Oxford. Chicago: Alderbrink Press, 1907.

Widmer, Ellen, and David Der-Wei Wang, eds. *From May Fourth to June Fourth: Fiction and Film in Twentieth Century China.* Cambridge: Harvard University Press, 1993.

Williams, Patrick, ed. *Colonial Discourse and Post-Colonial Theory: A Reader.* Introduction by Laura Chrisman. New York: Columbia University Press, 1994.

Wilson, Jean Moorcroft. *Siegfried Sassoon: The Making of a War Poet, 1886–1918.* London: Duckworth, 1998.

Winks, Robin W., and James R. Rush, eds. *Asia in Western Fiction.* Honolulu: University of Hawaii Press, 1990.

Witke, Roxane, and Margery Wolf. *Women in Chinese Society.* Stanford, Calif.: Stanford University Press, 1975.

Witke, Roxane. *Comrade Chiang Ching.* Boston: Little Brown, 1977.

Wolfenden Report: Report of the Commission on Homosexual Offenses and Prostitution. Introduction by Karl Menninger. New York: Stein & Day Publishers, 1963.

Wong, Sau-ling Cynthia. "The Fable of Flush." *Virginia Woolf Miscellany* no. 75 (spring 1975): 7–8.

———. "A Study of Roger Fry and Virginia Woolf from a Chinese Perspective." Ph.D. diss., Stanford University, 1978.

Wong, Yanbo, and Ren Guang, eds. *A Selection of Chinese Classical Poems.* Beijing: China Esperanto Press, 1990.

Woolf, Virginia. "The Artist and Politics." *The Moment and other Essays.* New York: Harcourt Brace Jovanovich, 1948.

———. *Between the Acts.* New York: Harcourt Brace Jovanovich, 1941.

———. *Collected Essays.* 4 vols. New York: Harcourt Brace Jovanovich, 1967.

———. "Craftsmanship." *The Death of the Moth and Other Essays.* New York: Harcourt Brace Jovanovich, 1942.

———. *The Diary of Virginia Woolf.* Edited by Anne Olivier Bell. Introduction by Quentin Bell. 5 vols. New York: Harcourt Brace Jovanovich, 1977–84.

———. *Roger Fry: A Biography.* New York: Harcourt Brace Jovanovich, 1940.

———. *Kew Gardens.* London: Hogarth Press facsimile, 1927 [1919].

———. "The Leaning Tower." *The Moment and Other Essays.* New York: Harcourt Brace Jovanovich, 1948.

———. *The Letters of Virginia Woolf.* Edited by Nigel Nicolson and Joanne Trautmann. 5 vols. New York: Harcourt Brace Jovanovich, 1975.

———. Letters to Julian Bell. ALS, MHP.
———. Letters to Ling Shuhua. MHP.
———. *Life as We Have Known It*. By Co-Operative Working Woman with Introductory Letter by Virginia Woolf. New York: W. W. Norton, 1975 [1931].
———. "Modern Fiction." *The Common Reader*. New York: Harcourt Brace Jovanovich, 1925.
———. *Moments of Being*. Edited by Jeanne Schulkind. New York: Harcourt Brace Jovanovich, 1978.
———. "Mr. Bennett and Mrs. Brown." *Collected Essays*, vol. 1. New York: Harcourt Brace Jovanovich, 1967.
———. *Mrs. Dalloway*. New York: Harcourt Brace Jovanovich, 1925
———. "The Narrow Bridge of Art." *Granite and Rainbow*. New York: Harcourt Brace Jovanovich, 1958.
———. "On Not Knowing Greek." *The Common Reader*. New York: Harcourt Brace World, 1925.
———. *Orlando*. New York: Harcourt Brace Jovanovich, 1968 [1928].
———. Review of Pu Songling. "Chinese Stories." In *Collected Essays*, vol. 2, 7–9. New York: Harcourt Brace Jovanovich, 1967.
———. *A Room of One's Own*. New York: Harcourt Brace Jovanovich, 1957 [1929].
———. *Three Guineas*. New York: Harcourt Brace Jovanovich, 1938.
———. *To the Lighthouse*. New York: Harcourt Brace Jovanovich, 1927.
———. *Walter Sickert: A Conversation*. London: The Bloomsbury Workshop, 1992.
———. *The Waves*. New York: Harcourt Brace Jovanovich, 1931.
Wu Cheng'en. *Monkey* (Xi You Ji). Translated by Arthur Waley. Illustrated by Duncan Grant. London: The Folio Society, 1978.
Wu Pei-Yu. *The Confucian's Progress: Autobiographical Writings in Traditional China*. Princeton: Princeton University Press, 1990.
Xiao Qian (or Hsiao Ch'ien). *Chestnuts and Other Stories*. People's Republic of China: Panda, 1984.
———. *China but Not Cathay*. London: George Allen & Unwin, 1942.
———. *The Dragon Beards vs. Blueprints: Meditations on Post-War Culture*. London: Pilot Press, 1944.
———. *Etchings of a Tormented Age*. London: George Allen & Unwin, 1942.
———. *Friendship Gazette*, vols. 1–3 (1941–44). Modern Archives, King's College, Cambridge.
———. Interview by the author. 2 August 1995, Beijing, China.
———. Letters (ALS) from Xiao Qian to E. M. Forster. May and November 1943. EMF.
———. Letters to the author. 2 June 1994-15 September 1996.

———. Letters to W. J. Sprott, 1943–46. Sprott Papers, Modern Archives, King's College, Cambridge.

———. *Semolina and Others*. Hong Kong: Joint, 1984.

———. "Thinking of Old Friends for Fifty Years." *Yangching Wanbao (Canton Evening News)*. 7 December 1995.

———. *Traveller without a Map*. Translated by Jeffrey Kinkley. Stanford, Calif.: Stanford University Press, 1993.

———. "A Week in London" (manuscript). 12 TPS. Translated by Gladys Yang.

———, ed. *Harp with a Thousand Strings*. London: Pilot Press, 1944.

Xiao, Qian, and Wen Jieruo, trans. *Ulysses*, 3 vols. by James Joyce. Tianjing: Yilin Publishing House, 1994.

Xu, Zhengbang, curator of University Archives, Wuhan University, Wuhan China. Interview by the author. March 2000, Wuhan.

Xu, Zhimo (or Hsu Chih-mo or Tsu Chih-mo or Hsu Tsemou or Hsu Tse Mou or Tseu Tcheung, French transliteration). "Art and Life." Translated by Ming Ho. In *The Complete Works of Xu Zhimo*. Xianquang: Shang wu yin shu quan, 1983.

———. *The Complete Works of Xu Zhimo*.

———. Letters (3ALS, 3TLS) to Roger Fry, 1922–23. REF 3/90.

———. Letters to L. K. Elmhirst. LKE.

Yeats, William Butler. *The Collected Poems of W. B. Yeats*. New York: Macmillan, 1965.

Yeh, Wen-Hsin. *The Alienated Academy: Culture and Politics in Republican China, 1919–37*. Cambridge: Harvard University Press, 1990.

Ye Junjian (Yeh Chun Chan). Correspondence with Julian Bell, 1936–37. Modern Archives, King's College, Cambridge University.

———. *The Ignorant and the Forgotten: Nine Stories*. London: Sylvan Press, 1946.

———. Interview by the author. 3 August 1995, Beijing, China.

Yip Wai-lim. *Diffusion of Distances: Dialogues between Chinese and Western Poetics*. Berkeley: University of California Press, 1993.

———, ed. and trans. *Lyrics from Shelters, Modern Chinese Poetry, 1930–50*. New York: Garland Press, 1992.

Yu kuang-zhang. "The Sensuous Art of the Chinese Landscape Journal." *Renditions* 19–20 (spring–autumn 1983): 23–42.

Yuan Changying. "Southeast Flies the Peacock." In *Writing Women in Modern China*, edited by Amy Dooling and Kristina Torgeson. New York: Columbia University Press, 1998.

Yuan, Kejia. Interview by the author. Winter 1994, New York.

———. Poems in *Lyrics from Shelters, Modern Chinese Poetry 1930–50*. Edited and translated by Yip Wai-Lim. New York: Garland, 1992.

———. "The True Story about the Nine Leaves Poets" (typed manuscript). Talk given at Columbia University, 8 November 1993.

Yuan, Kejia, Dong Xengxun, and Zheng Kelu. *Selections of Modernist Literature from Abroad* (in Chinese). 8 vols. Shanghai: Shanghai Literature and Arts Press, 1980.

Zhang, Longxi. "The Challenge of East-West Comparative Literature." In *China in a Polycentric World: Essays in Chinese Comparative Literature,* edited by Yingjin Zhang. Stanford, Calif.: Stanford University Press, 1999.

Zhao, Luorin. Interview by the author. July 1995, Beijing, China.

Zhaoming, Qian. *Modernism and Orientalism.* Durham, N.C.: Duke University Press, 1995.

INDEX

Entries in bold refer to biographical sketches and other information in the appendices.

Abrahams, William, 2, 39, 234, 262
Abu-Lughod, Lila, 251
Achebe, Chinua, 346
Acton, Harold, **395**; and Bloomsbury group, 25, 120, 284, 288, 310; in China, 15, 25, 68–69, 186, 189–90
Adam's Galleries (London), 240–42, 324, 416n. 4
Adams pottery, 15, 334
Addison, Joseph, 315–16
Adorno, Theodor, 141–42, 343–44
Adventures of Three Kingdoms, The, 204
"Advisory Committee for Spoken English" (BBC; also known as Society for Pure English), 113–16, 380
aesthetic movement, 140, 141, 382
aesthetics (as a field of study), 362. *See also* art; hybridity; literary theory; modernism
"Aesthetics East and West" (Gould), 368
Africa, 10, 15, 128, 160, 242, 329, 346–47, 392
"After Getting Drunk" (Chinese poem), 187

"After Passing the Examinations" (Tang period poem), 258–59
Ahmad, Aijaz, 30–31
Ahmed, Leila, 251
"Album of Faded Photographs, An" (Xiao Qian), 199
Alexander, William, 223
"Alice in China" (Shen Congwen), 110
All Brothers Are Valiant, 204
Alton Towers (England), 321
American Board Mission School for Beggar Girls, 290
American Mercury, 152
Ancient History debate (China), 104
Ancient Melodies (Ling Shuhua's autobiography): autobiography as unfamiliar genre for Chinese women, 246, 261, 272, 281–85, 288; British publication of, 27, 84, 242, 284, 287–88; concubinage in, 255–62, 285; introduction to, 243, 284; Julian Bell's encouragement for, 84; Ling Shuhua's description of, 94–95; pedagogic approaches described in, 51; self-censorship in, 261–62, 285, 288–89; translation of, into Chinese,

Ancient Melodies (continued)
27–28, 219; Virginia Woolf's encouragement for, 83, 84, 243, 251, 263, 271–75, 282–84, 286–87; writing style in, 93–95, 256–62, 282, 285
Anderson, Benedict, 18, 31; on China's "antiquity," 127; on "cultural roots of nationalism," 10; on historical amnesias, 109; on imagined communities, 13, 101, 267; on "museumizing imagination," 336
Anderson, William, 33, 324
"Androgyny," 194. *See also* gender: male reversals of
Anemones and a Chinese Vase (Matisse), 303
anglo-chinois gardens, 33, 313–19, 324, 326, 334, 340
animals (in Chinese art), 363–64, 367, 375
Annam (Chinese territory), 160
anthropomorphism. *See* self
Apollinaire, Guillaume, 373
Appadurai, Arjun, 325
"Araby" (Joyce), 385
archaeology, 336
Ardener, Edward, 156
Arlington, L. C., 189
Arnold, Julian, 225
art: aesthetic space of, 391; animals in Chinese, 363–64, 367, 375; classification of Chinese, 375; consumerism's erasure of historical origins of, 341–46; as cross-cultural bridge, 246–54, 266–72, 391; and morality, 117; music likened to, 243, 338, 350; as part of author's critical form, 22; as representing the voice of an individual, 32, 247, 267, 280; in times of stress, 109, 113–18, 237, 239–40, 246–54, 263, 266–72, 286–87, 391. *See also* artists; calligraphy; ceramics; chinoiserie; fashion; gardens; paintings; porcelain; specific artists, movements, Chinese periods, and specific works of
"Art and Life" (Xu Zhimo), 141–45
art nouveau, 362
artists: Chinese conception of, 211–12; imperialist effects on, 227; in *To the Lighthouse*, 356–58. *See also* art; names of specific artists
Arts and Crafts movement (England), 118, 377
Asia Society, 239
Attiret, Jean-Denis, 326
Auden, W. H., 294; and Bloomsbury group, 120; in China, 25, 50, 61–62, 123, 186; as writer, 113, 189; and Ye Junjian, 48, 50
audiences: postmodernism's emphasis on, 371; shadow, 89, 282
Augusta (princess of Wales), 319, 320
Austen, Jane, 94, 209, 255, 283, 314, 323
authoritarianism (fascism), 52–54, 160, 170; suppression under, 21, 55, 58, 129, 140, 142–45, 158, 183–85, 188–89, 196–98, 206, 285. *See also* nation and nationalism; propaganda; Spanish Civil War; World War II
autobiography: cross-cultural discussions of genre of, 33, 83, 84, 246, 251, 271–75, 285; as literary sources, 11, 20, 21; self-censorship in, 261–62, 285, 288–89; as unfamiliar genre for women in China, 246, 261, 272, 281–85, 288; Virginia

Woolf's, 386; Xiao Qian's, 197, 199, 202, 219. See also *Ancient Melodies* (Ling Shuhua's autobiography); self
Ayscough, Florence, 373

Ba Jin, 293, 359, **395**
Babbitt, Irving, 137
Babylon, 170
bai-hua language (vernacular Chinese), 283, 291, 294
Bakhtin, Mikhail M., 18, 20–22, 31, 57, 206, 265
Bali, 309
Balieon H., 136
Ballet Russe, 190, 383
Balzac, Honoré de, 209
Banting, John, 190
barbarians: Bloomsbury's reversal of views of, 156, 165, 167, 225, 364; and blue and white willow patterned porcelain, 298, 301–2; Chinese conception of non-Chinese as, 79–80, 199, 200; Chinese elements in Kew Gardens as product of, 321; imperialism depicted as practice of, 167, 225. See also "civilization"; primitivism
Barger, Harold, 69–70, 137
Barlow, Tani, 103, 139
Barme, Geremie, 111
Barthes, Roland, 29
Basho, 356
Basic English, 116, 117, 124
Baudelaire, Charles, 292, 294
Baudrillard, Jean, 323, 341, 343
BBC (British Broadcasting Corporation): Advisory Committee for Spoken English for, 113–16, 380; Arthur Waley's talk on, 312;

Dickinson's talk on, 171; Forster and Xiao Qian's letters on, 178; Leonard Woolf's talk on, 286; Ling Shuhua's plays for, 288; Virginia Woolf's talk on, 113
Beardsley, Aubrey, 369, 371
Beato, Felix, 33, 224, 324
Beckett, Samuel, 270, 366, 367, 386, 387
Beijing (China), 58, 59, 389; Acton on, 190; Alexander's sketches of, 223; attempts to save old, 153; Boxer Indemnity Fund effects on, 46; Boxer Rebellion in, 166, 171–75; destruction of, after Second Opium War, 33, 224–25; Dickinson on, 135; gardens in, 317; Julian Bell on, 72–74, 78; Ling Shuhua's father as mayor of, 1, 76, 247, 255–62, 285; 2008 Olympics in, 35. See also Beijing Opera; Beijing University
Beijing Academy of Social Sciences, 218
Beijing Normal University (China), 103
Beijing Opera: men playing women in, 173, 186, 190, 192, 193, 302; non-representational aspects of, 385, 386
Beijing University (China), 58, 100, 103, 106, 110, 123, 203, 218; Beida branch of, 290; and Boxer Indemnity Funds, 412n. 3; Crescent Moon members at, 100, 103–4, 106, 107, 110; Empson at, 215; Japanese takeover of, 124; Literature Institute of, 134
Beixin Book Company, 199
Bell, Angelica, 120, 228, 269, 288; Julian and Vanessa on, 22, 69, 89, 227

Bell, Anne Olivier, 287
Bell, Clive, 72, 119, 120, 288, 309, 349; on "civilization," 161; as conscientious objector, 39
Bell, Julian, **395**; Bloomsbury heritage of, 2–3, 37–40, 120, 182; as Cambridge graduate, 37, 41, 53, 54, 64, 89, 229; on China, 33, 41, 44, 128, 181, 222, 227–34, 237; correspondence of, with Ling Shuhua, 60, 76–82, 230, 232–33, 413n. 8; death of, in Spanish Civil War, 1, 38, 62, 83, 234–35, 242, 247, 249; diary of, 32, 39–40, 47, 53, 63, 64; as English professor at Wuhan University, 1, 5, 7, 15, 17, 25, 32, 37, 39, 41–82, 88, 116, 124, 137, 221, 227, 263, 389; hobbies of, 5, 9, 38–40, 48, 62, 229–33; Ling Shuhua's romance with, 1, 7–8, 32, 41, 44, 63–82, 100, 227–28, 235, 246, 262, 263, 274–75, 389; Ling Shuhua's romance with, secrecy concerning, 2, 8, 63, 238, 261, 262–63; on Ling Shuhua's writing, 248, 256, 271, 278, 282–84; Ling Shuhua's writing collaboration with, 5, 7–8, 82–99, 248, **403–7**; location of letters of, 23, 39; memorial volume of writing of, 238; photograph album of, 1, 5–6, 18, 79; political outlook of, 60, 312–13; racism of, 56, 66–68, 181; return of, to England after China, 234; and Roger Fry, 54, 120, 240, 349; sexism of, 56–57, 68, 72, 74, 77, 80–81; sexuality of, 63–65, 73, 75–77, 82, 89; Tibetan travels of, 6, 9, 48, 59; Vanessa's Chinese gifts from, 18, 336–39; Vanessa's relationship and correspondence with, 22, 37–38, 44, 48, 56–57, 60–61, 65, 69–70, 72–74, 77, 79, 82, 89, 94, 96, 136, 181, 189, 227–29, 232–34, 335, 349, 350, 380, 384, 416n. 2; venereal disease of, 64–65, 70, 72; as Virginia Woolf's nephew, 1, 2, 68; as writer, 3, 84, 95, 189–90, 228–29; Wuhan University termination by, 44
Bell, Quentin, 65, 69, 120, 235, 238, 349; on Julian's politics, 60; and Ling Shuhua, 243, 288, 354, 417n. 4
Bell, Vanessa, **395–96**; biographies of, 2, 263; as Bloomsbury group member, 25, 119; on China, 33, 35, 223; and French art, 241–42; Julian's Chinese gifts to, 18, 336–39; and Julian's death, 234–35, 237, 238; and Ling Shuhua, 1, 84, 188, 234–42, 246, 248, 260–61, 263, 269–74, 284, 286, 308, 324–25, 337; location of letters of, 23; and Omega Workshops, 377; as a painter, 1–2, 112–13, 237, 269, 374, 381; political outlook of, 312, 313; relationship and correspondence of, with Julian, 22, 37–38, 44, 48, 56–57, 60–61, 65, 69–70, 72–74, 77, 79, 82, 89, 94, 96, 136, 181, 189, 227–29, 232–34, 335, 349, 350, 380, 384, 416n. 2. *See also* Charleston House
Benjamin Altman Collection of Chinese Porcelains, 4
Bennett, Arnold, 384
Bentham, Jeremy, 52, 116
Berg Collection (New York Public Library), 2, 3
Berthoff, Ann, 115
Between the Acts (Woolf), 247, 268, 382–84, 386
Bhabha, Homi, 12, 31, 34, 202, 325

Bian Zhilin, 15, 123, 208, 294
"Big Rug, The" (Xiao Qian), 199
Bing Xin, 7, 26, 51, 264, 278, 284, **396**
Binyon, Laurence, 129, 223–24, 309, 348, 350, 360
biography (as literary source), 11, 22. *See also* autobiography; journals; letters; self; specific biographies
Birth of Landscape Painting in China, The (Sullivan), 313
Blake, William, 219, 312, 369
"Blake the Daoist" (Waley), 312
Blavatsky, Madame, 374
Bloomingdale's department store (New York City), 329
Bloomsbury and France (Caws and Wright), 241–42, 347
Bloomsbury group: Chinese influences on, 29, 178, 180–82, 358–87; Chinese links of, 5–9, 11, 29, 32, 33, 37–99, 149, 150, 152, 246, 262–63, 286, 312; conversation in, 263; Crescent Moon group's similarities to, 19–20, 28, 33, 91, 99, 100, 107, 112, 118; cross-dressing in, 172, 173; description of, 2–3, 11, 118–25; fluctuating reputation of, 28; Ling Shuhua's relations with, 1, 63–99, 241–43, 246–54, 266–79, 284–88; members of, 25; rejection of usual hierarchy of civilization by, 156, 165, 167, 225, 364; and sexuality, 88–89, 187; tenets of, 118–25. *See also* Cambridge University; letters; literary theory; modernism; names of specific members of
Bloomsbury Recalled (Q. Bell), 60
Bloy, Leon, 365
blue and white willow patterns (on porcelain), 15, 33, 254, 298–308, 326; British mass production of, 334–35; in British tea rooms, 333, 334; Lamb on, 186, 324; in *New Yorker*, 267; story associated with picture on, 298, 300–302, 305, 343; substituting the sign for the real in, 342–43. *See also* chinoiserie; porcelain
Blunt, Anthony, 89, 242, 288
Bo Zhuyi, 34
boarding schools (England). *See* Leighton School; Owens School
Borges, Jorge Luis, 388
Bose, Nanalal, 146
Boston Museum of Fine Arts, 240, 243, 244, 364
Boswell, James, 246
Bottega di un Antiquario, La (Frans Francken Il Giovane), 345
Botticelli, Sandro, 372
Bound Feet and Modern Dress (Chang), 142
Bowen, Elizabeth, 266
Boxer Indemnity Funds, 164; Bertrand Russell as administrator of, 46, 152; British scholars' visits to China paid for by, 16–17, 41; and Chinese railway development, 226; Chinese scholars' visits to West paid for by, 42, 75, 131–32, 140; effects of, 46; as English looting of China, 167; origins of, 411n. 3; purposes of, 41; and Wuhan University, 62
Boxer Rebellion, 129, 164, 165, 200, 266; Dickinson on, 15, 44, 136, 164–71, 175, 181, 316, 340; explanation of, 166–68, 411n. 3; fallout from, 14–15; Strachey on, 15, 166, 171–76. *See also* Boxer Indemnity Funds

Braque, Georges, 378, 385
Brecht, Bertolt, 190, 387
Brenan, Gerald, 172
Bridges, Robert, 114, 374, 380
Bridgman, Eliza, 290
Brighton (England), 254, 319, 322–24, 327
Brighton Workers' Education Association, 254
Briscoe, Lily. *See* "Chinese eyes"; *To the Lighthouse* (Woolf)
British East India Company, 300, 332, 334, 336, 341
British Economic Advisory Council, 225–26
British Museum, 213, 223–24, 305, 308–9, 336
Brittain, Vera, 113
Brontë, Charlotte, 293
Brontë, Emily, 93
Brooks, Cleanth, 219
Brown, Felicia, 233
Browning, Elizabeth Barrett, 110, 143
Browning, Oscar, 180
brushstrokes. *See* "line"
Bryan, Derek, 48, 230
Bryan, William Jennings, 169–70
Buck, Pearl, 84, 153–54, 274
Buddhism, 139–40, 142, 161, 169, 199
Burgess, Anthony, 65
Burlington House (London): International Chinese Art Exhibition at, 15, 229, 242, 335, 337–39, 372, 379
Burlington Magazine, 377
Burma, 82, 160
Bussy, Simon, 348
Butler, Judith, 60, 126, 173, 174, 198
Butterfly literature (in China), 54, 55, 205

Byatt, A. S., 2
Bynner, Witter, 294
Byron, Lord, 141, 143, 145, 341

Cabinet of Dr. Caligari, The (film), 383
"Cactus Flower" (Xiao Qian), 199
"Call to Arms" (Lu Xun), 211–12
calligraphy, 4, 368; Chinese valuing of, 338; Innes Jackson Herdan's, 75; Ling Shuhua's, 3; Ling Shuhua's father's, 255; painting and writing linked in, 34, 97, 243, 297–98, 353–54, 370, 373, 378–87; similarities between modernist paintings and, 371, 378; by Western artists, 378. *See also* "line"
"Calligraphy" (Fry), 380
"Calligraphy" (Liang Tongshu), 373
Calvino, Italo, 366, 367
Cambridge (Mass.), 265
Cambridge (Phillips), 346
Cambridge Review, The, 52, 54, 55
Cambridge University (England): admission policies at, 168; Fry's Slade Lectures on Chinese Art at, 15, 125, 351, 363, 372, 377; homosexuality at, 180, 196; Julian Bell as graduate of, 37, 41, 53, 54, 64, 89, 229; Virginia Woolf's influence at, 209; Xaio Qian at, 176, 182, 208, 216, 389; Xu Zhimo's attendance at, 6, 9, 12, 25, 50, 123, 126, 129–33, 139, 146–47, 152–53, 347. *See also* King's College (Cambridge); names of professors and students at
Can Xue, 359–60
Canada, 288
Canton (China). *See* Guanzhou
Cao Baohua, 123

Cao Ming, 207
Cao Yu, 26
Cao Yulin, 290
Carey, John, 119
Caribbean postcolonialism, 346–47
Carpenter, Edward, 143, 156, 183–85, 196
Carrington, Dora, 25, 153, 172, 309
Castle, The (Kafka), 210
Cathay (Pound), 34, 309
"Cathay landscape," 302
"Catherine" (Shaw), 172
Catholicism, 296, 299, 338. *See also* Christianity
Caws, Mary Ann, 241–42, 347
Cawthorn, William, 314–15
ceramics (Chinese): influence of, on British, 15, 125, 348, 377–78; sent to Vanessa by Julian, 336–37, 339; shapes of, 253. *See also* blue and white willow patterns; chinoiserie; porcelain; specific brands of British pottery
Ceylon, 15, 161, 181, 309, 348
Cezanne, Paul, 347, 371, 378, 385
Chambers, William, 300, 313–17, 319–23, 340, 342, 351, 361, 364, 370, 377
Chang, Natasha Pang-Mei, 142, 152
Chaos in China (Giles), 164, 286, 294
Chaplin, Charlie, 190, 387
Charleston House (England), 81, 112, 237, 269, 270; Chinese art in, 18, 336–37, 339
Chatterjee, Partha, 31, 34, 202; on autobiography, 281–82; on community as a sphere of the intimate, 11, 18, 21, 101, 391; on discourses within fields of power, 252
Chekhov, Anton, 84, 283
Chen, Amy Ling ("Mei"; Ling Shuhua's sister), 261, 288, 290
Chen, K. K., 261
Chen, Su Hua Ling (or Chen, Shu-Hua Ling). *See* Ling Shuhua
Chen, Xiaomei, 103, 139
Chen Duxiu, 289, 292
Chen Ling Shuhua. *See* Ling Shuhua
Chen Tongbo. *See* Chen Yuan
Chen Xuezhao, 193
Chen Yuan (Chen Tongbo; Xiying) (Ling Shuhua's husband), **396**; Bloomsbury links of, 40–42; as Crescent Moon group member, 3–4, 17, 101, 103–4, 106, 107, 109, 110, 144; discovery of Julian Bell's affair with Ling Shuhua by, 74–75, 78–79, 275; editing of Ling Shuhua's work by, 95, 284; fluctuating reputation of, 27, 109; house of, 5; in Julian Bell's photograph album, 6; Ling Shuhua as wife of, 3, 8, 44, 63, 64, 72, 76, 82, 109–10, 264; as "losing face" through scandal, 65, 74, 78, 238, 261; and Margery Fry, 17, 64; as May Fourth movement member, 26, 100; personal characteristics of, 78–79; social background of, 108; as UNESCO delegate, 238, 262, 286; and the West, 12, 40–41, 103, 104, 286; at Wuhan University, 17, 44, 46, 58, 103, 227, 263, 264; and Xu Zhimo, 71, 262
Chengdu (China), 48
Chesham House, 327, 328
Chesterton, G. K., 53

Chetwynd Society, 136
Ch'i Pai shi (China), 189
Chiang Kai-shek, 60, 107, 109, 110, 413n. 9. See also nationalists
Chiang Kai-shek (Madame), 42
Chiang Yee, 325
"Childhood in China" (Ling Shuhua), 259, 271–72
children (as naive narrators), 262, 271–72, 282, 285
Children (Ling Shuhua), 284
Chin, Y. C., 152
China: author's trips to, 3–5, 8, 12, 28, 231, 319, 336, 338, 388–89; British perceptions of, as antique, stable, and civilized, 4, 18, 127–29, 135–37, 156, 158–75, 222–34, 267, 274, 298–325, 334; British travelers to, 25, 49, 123, 135–37, 194; effects of upheavals of, on literary record, 23, 116, 147, 178–80, 182, 221, 287; England's trade with, 13, 33, 168–70, 175, 182, 222–24, 299–300, 305–6, 316, 331–32, 336, 341, 350, 411n. 2; famine in, 159, 166, 201; "floating population" in, 151–52; length of trips between England and, 15, 222, 227; Ling Shuhua's return to post–Cultural Revolution, 246; National Art Exhibition in, 150; omission of, from critical examinations of international modernism, 189, 391–92; Republican period in, 4, 10, 13, 26–27, 266, 389, 391; student uprisings in, 110, 289–90; subjugation of, by foreign powers, 160, 166, 168–69, 171, 175, 182, 194–95; tea from, 332, 333; as "weak man of Asia," 110, 143, 152, 155, 160,

194–95, 289–91; Western interests of intellectuals in, during Republican period, 10, 12, 13, 25–26, 57–58, 100, 104, 106–12, 129–34, 139, 277–78, 288–93, 412n. 4. *See also* Boxer Rebellion; civil war; Crescent Moon group; cross-cultural perspectives; Cultural Revolution; East; foraging (cultural); Hong Kong; landscapes; May Fourth movement; modernism; nation and nationalism; People's Republic of China; Sino-Japanese War; Taiwan
China Campaign Committee, 42
China Diary (J. Bell), 32, 39–40, 47, 53, 63, 64
China Diary (S. and B. Webb), 162
China Institute, 368, 371
China's Position in International Finance (L. Woolf), 164, 286
Chinese Art (Binyon), 348
"Chinese Chippendale" furniture, 323
"Chinese eyes" (as metaphor for "other" ways of seeing), 9–10, 24, 33, 34, 178, 182–83, 210, 240–42, 324–41, 346–52, 393
Chinese language: author's study of, 4; rebellion against classical, 289–91, 293–94; vernacular, 283, 291, 294. *See also* translations
Chinese League of Left-Wing Writers, 106, 111, 112. *See also* Society of Literary Studies
Chinese people: Dickinson on, 195; Eurocentric labels for, 104, 130–31, 153, 204; Julian Bell's stereotypes concerning, 56, 66–68. *See also* specific Chinese intellectuals and politicians

Chinese Porcelain and Hand Stones (Fry), 376
"Chinese Written Character as a Medium for Poetry, The" (Fenellosa), 205
Chinese-English Dictionary, A (Giles), 294
Chinnery, John, 413n. 10
Chinnery, Ying (Ling Shuhua's daughter), 78–80, 250, 269–70, 272; biographical sketch of, 413n. 10; birth of, 284–85; in England, 286, 416n. 2; in Julian Bell's photograph album, 6, 79; on Ling Shuhua, 70–71, 415n. 3; on Ling Shuhua's sister, 261; on Xu Xuelin, 264
chinoiserie: British and Chinese elements fused in, 34, 323, 334, 342–43; as British domestic art, 15, 171, 327, 334–39, 345–46, 362; conflicting views of, 343–44; definition of, 224, 323. *See also* ceramics; porcelain
Chin-shi hsiang, 190
Chitty, J. R., 164, 286
Chow, Rey, 21–22, 31, 280–81
Christianity, 161, 166, 168, 169–70, 200, 296, 365, 411n. 2. *See also* Catholicism; missionaries
Chuang Tzu, 159, 312
Chungking (China), 4
"Cinema, The" (Woolf), 383
Citizen of the World, The (Goldsmith), 170–71
civil war (China), 182; as background of Julian Bell's Chinese visit, 39, 59–60; Chinese modernists writing during, 26, 109, 159; destruction associated with, 14, 18–20, 23, 127, 178–80, 221; and Ling Shuhua, 237, 266, 271, 286; and Xiao Qian, 182, 210, 221; and Xu Zhimo, 147–52. *See also* communists (Chinese); nationalists
"civilization," 33; Bloomsbury's rejection of usual hierarchy of, 156, 165, 167, 225, 364; and blue and white willow patterned porcelain, 298, 301–2; Chinese as embodying, 135, 137, 160, 165–71, 180–81, 225, 322, 338, 361; Christian missionaries as bringing, to China, 166, 411n. 2; as crumbling during modernist era, 101, 160, 161, 175; Eliot on, 40; foraging "primitive" nations for, 329–31, 337; Julian Bell on, 77; non-imperialist British search for new definition of, 184–85, 312–13. *See also* barbarians; primitivism
"Civilization: Its Cause and Cure" (Carpenter), 156
Cixi (empress of China), 15, 166, 171–75
Clark, Kenneth, 15
Clark University (Massachusetts), 130, 132
Clarke, Suzanne, 143
class (social): Dickinson on, 168; "elite," in literary communities, 101, 107–10, 129, 247, 250, 254–65, 279–80; in England, 292; Forster on, 182, 183–84; in Lawrence's work, 209; in Ling Shuhua's work, 90, 277, 279; personal relationships across, 183–84; Woolf on, 117–18, 185–86; World War I effects on, 185–86; Xu Zhimo on, 150; Yu Dafu on, 291

"Class Structures in Literature" (Yu Dafu), 291
Clifford, James, 12, 31, 32, 37, 44
"Climbing the Ling Ying Terrace and Looking North" (trans. Waley), 305
Coleridge, William Taylor, 341
Collected Essays (Woolf), 218
colonialism. *See* imperialism; postcolonialism
Columbia Anthology of Chinese Women Writers (Dooling and Torgeson), 109
Columbia University (New York City), 130, 132, 220, 224
"Commentaries" (Eliot), 52
communists (American), 219
communists (Chinese): literary control by, 92, 93, 219–20; polemics of, 19, 20; and Ye Junjian, 49–51. *See also* Chinese League of Left-Wing Writers; civil war; Mao Zedong; Marxism; People's Republic of China; propaganda
communists (English), 60–61
communists (Soviet), 163, 164
community(-ies) (conversation; dialogue; friendship): Chinese associations with, 156; Eliot's view of ideal, 53; "imagined," 18–19, 101; literary and cultural issues within, 24; multiple voices as emerging from, 21–22; negotiations of meaning between, 21–22, 29–30, 389; refuge offered by transnational, 150. *See also* Bloomsbury group; Crescent Moon group; family; Friendship scroll; intimate spheres; letters; translations; travel
Conan Doyle, Arthur, 293

concubinage, 65, 254–62, 285
Confessions (Cao Ming), 207
Confucius and Confucianism, 137; in Chinese translations of Western works, 293; religion associated with, 169–70; and repression of the self, 141, 142, 144–45, 158–59, 192, 206; on responsibility to others, 91, 138, 207, 281; writings of, 306
Conn, Peter, 153, 274
Conrad and Imperialism (Parry), 21
Consciousness. *See* Self; Stream-of-consciousness style
consumerism (and art), 341–46
contemplation (and Chinese painting), 351–55, 358
Contemporary Review (British publication), 101, 108
Contemporary Review (Chen Yuan's publication), 101, 103, 104, 106–9, 264
"contrapuntal perspectives" (and imperialism), 8, 10, 19, 21, 31–32, 223, 340–41, 360, 391. *See also* cross-cultural perspectives
"conversation." *See* community(-ies)
Conversation, The (Matisse), 371
"Conversion" (Xiao Qian), 200
Cornell University (Ithaca, New York), 132, 145, 147, 289
Cornford, John, 2
Country Life, 272
Course in General Linguistics (Saussure), 29
Courtauld Art Museum, 242
Cowper, William, 283
Cozens, Alexander, 357
"Craftsmanship" (Woolf), 113–18
Crantson, Catherine, 333

Creation Society, 106, 111, 144, 412n. 4
Crescent Moon group: Bloomsbury group's links to, 5–9, 11, 149, 246, 262–63, 312; Bloomsbury Group's similarities to, 19–20, 28, 33, 91, 99, 100, 107, 112, 118; British influences on, 29, 57–58, 123; changing Chinese views of, 19, 20, 28, 106–9, 219, 264, 277–78; Chen Yuan as member of, 3–4, 17, 101, 103–4, 106, 107, 109, 110; description of, 3, 11, 100–112; Ling Shuhua as member of, 3–4, 17, 277; name of, 103, 144; as part of May Fourth movement, 10; purposes of, 103; tenets of, 20, 33, 104, 107–8, 140–41; Xu Zhimo as founder of, 17, 101, 104, 106–7, 110, 123, 127, 144, 157–58. *See also* letters; specific members of
Crescent Moon Monthly, 103, 107, 108, 110, 112, 144
"Cricket, The" (Xu Zhimo), 140
Criterion, 52
Critical Essays (Woolf), 218
Critical Terrains (Lowe), 251
Crook, Steve, 2
cross-cultural perspectives, 246; on British modernist writers, 202–15; of Chinese people working in Japan, 49; of contemporary postcolonial literature, 346–47; Dickinson's and Xu Zhimo's, 33, 126–76; Forster's, 176–98; on individualism and self-expression, 137–60, 281–82, 295; Julian Bell's, 37–99; on landscape gardening, 313–19; misunderstandings in, 247–49, 265; of modernism, 358–67; Richards' experiments in, 122–23; of studying Crescent Moon and Bloomsbury groups, 24–34, 360–67, 388–93; on translation, 295. *See also* community(-ies); "contrapuntal perspectives"; East; foraging (cultural); "global criticism"; hybridity; imagining each other; nation and nationalism; pluralism; translations; travel; West

Cuddy-Keane, Melba, 218
Cultural Revolution, 216; Ling Shuhua's visit to China during, 244, 246; as responsible for gap in literary record, 23, 178–80, 182, 221; search for self-expression after, 158; treatment of intellectuals during, 150, 182, 264, 292; in Wang Anyi's story, 206–7; Western interests considered transgressive during, 134, 179–80, 218, 282. *See also* Red Guards
culture. *See* cross-cultural perspectives; foraging (cultural); identity; nation and nationalism
Culture and Imperialism (Said), 30
cummings, e. e., 134
Cunard, Nancy, 190
"Curios," 345–46
"cut sleeve," 187

Dai Hongzhen, 218
Dalcroze, Emile, 309
Dame Aux Camelias, La (Dumas), 204
Dance, The (Matisse), 371
Daoism, 159, 169, 170, 312, 352, 355; and the self, 138, 139–42, 355
Dartington House (Totnes, England), 3, 145, 150, 309
Darwinism. *See* Social Darwinism

Daughter of Confucius (Wang Suling), 274
Daughters of the American Revolution (Wood), 303
Davenport pottery, 15, 334
Davidson, Angus, 172
Day Lewis, C., 284
De Quincey, Thomas, 341, 381
De Zoete, Beryl, 309, 310
decorum. *See* restraint
Degas, Edgar, 372
Delacroix, Eugene, 196
Delftware, 334
"Demoiselles d'Avignon, Les" (Picasso), 356
Deng Xiaoping era, 246
department stores. *See* Liberty & Co.
Derain, André, 378, 385
Derby pottery, 343
Derrida, Jacques, 115, 116
Des Chinoises (Kristeva), 167–68
Descartes, Rene, 138, 158
Designs of Chinese Buildings, Furniture, Dresses, Machines, and Utensils (Chambers), 321–22. *See also* Chambers, William
Dewey, John, 120
Diaghalev, Sergei, 172
"dialogue." *See* community(-ies)
Diamand, Pamela, 348, 371–72, 377
diaries. *See* journals; titles beginning with "diary"
Diary (D. Richards), 74–75
Diary (J. Bell), 32, 39–40, 47, 53, 63, 64
Diary (V. Bell), 39, 234–35
Diary (V. Woolf), 38, 115, 218, 267, 367, 381
diaspora. *See* travel

Dickens, Charles, 201, 293
Dickinson, Goldsworthy L., 152, 332, **396**; as Bloomsbury group member, 25, 119, 120, 182, 241; on the Boxer Rebellion, 14–15, 44, 164–72, 175, 316, 340; and Chen Yuan, 8, 40; in China, 15, 25, 35, 135–37; on China, 127–29, 156, 158–60, 162–71, 180–81, 228, 233; and Forster, 137, 178, 180–81, 195; homosexuality of, 183–86, 188, 196; mysticism of, 135–37; papers of, 137; political views of, 168; and Waley, 306, 309, 312; and Xu Zhimo, 9, 33, 55, 127, 132–33, 139, 147, 149, 154, 347, 362, 372
Dictionary of National Biography, 247
Diffusion of Distances (Yip Wai-lim), 35
Dinesen, Isak, 250
Ding Ling, **396**; changing reputation of, 19, 264; lover of, 101; as modernist writer, 26, 206, 278; on women, 92–93
Ding Yi, 107, 110, 156
displacement. *See* travel
Dissertation on Oriental Gardening, A (Chambers), 313–17, 319, 321–22
Doll & Richard Gallery (Boston), 240
Dollfuss, Engelbert, 53
Doll's House, A (Ibsen), 80
Dong Hu (Wuhan University lake), 231–32
Donne, John, 219, 346
Dooling, Amy D., 109, 264
Dostoevsky, Fyodor, 20, 57, 200
"Dostoevsky's Polyphonic Novel" (Bakhtin), 20, 206
"Double Nature of Painting, The" (Fry), 241

"Drawing or Design" (Fry), 371, 385
Dream of the Red Chamber, The (Tsao Hsueh-Chin), 74, 187, 192, 204, 414n. 12
dress. *See* fashion
Dubliners (Joyce), 385
Duckworth, George, 59
Duckworth, Stella, 59
Dumas, Alexander, 204, 293
Duthuit, George, 350

Eagleton, Terry, 122
East: Bloomsbury group's interest in, 178, 180–82, 253–54; breaking down polarity between West and, 103, 139, 155–60, 390–93, 414n. 1; "decadence" of, 196, 341; Dickinson's "performance of," 126, 136; Fry and Richards's admiration for, 124–25; as geographical place and place of the mind, 253; tropes of, in West, 298–324, 340; Westernizing of, 163; West's "peaceful penetration" of, 160. *See also* China; Japan
East India House, 327, 328
East Lake (near Wuhan University), 5, 58
"Eastern Antiquities, 1897–1900" (Liberty catalog), 329
economy of style. *See* restraint
Edinburgh University, 264, 413n. 10
Edwardian literature and politics, 19–20, 118, 386. *See also* verisimilitude
ego. *See* self
Egoist, The (Meredith), 296, 305
Egypt, 181
Elgin, James Bruce, 225
Elgin, Thomas Bruce, 225

Eliot, T. S., 34, 40, 123, 219, 294, 309; on China, 137; Julian Bell on, 52–53; as modernist writer, 141, 143, 208, 367
elites. *See* class
Elmhirst, Dorothy, 309
Elmhirst, Leonard, **397**; and Ling Shuhua, 244, 246; and Waley, 309; and Xu Zhimo, 107, 144–52, 244, 262
"Embroidered Handkerchief, An" (Ling Shuhua), 192–93
"Embroidered Pillows" (Ling Shuhua), 280–81
emotions. *See* self; sentimentalism; sexuality
Empson, William, 120, 219, **397**; in China, 25, 46, 116, 123, 155, 215, 221
Eng, David, 185
England: autobiography in, 281–82; Chinese intellectuals in, 6, 9, 12, 25, 41, 42, 50, 75, 100, 103, 104, 106, 107, 123, 126–27, 129–33, 139, 146–47, 176, 182, 206, 286, 362; Chinese territories given to, 160, 182, 195; Chinese translations of literature of, 15, 44, 46, 123, 143, 210, 212, 214–16, 218–19, 221, 225, 293–96; gardens in, 313–19; homosexuality as illegal in, 183–86, 196, 197, 217; imperialism as issue in, 11, 15–16, 18, 33, 60, 67–68, 129, 137, 152, 160–61, 164–69, 175, 181, 182, 209; Julian's return to, after China, 234; length of trips between China and, 15, 222, 227; Ling Shuhua in, 147, 238–39, 264, 284, 286–87; Ling Shuhua's exhibits in,

England (continued)
241–44; postcolonial rewritings of literature of, 346–47; trade with China by, 13, 33, 168–70, 175, 182, 222–24, 299–300, 305–6, 316, 331–32, 336, 341, 350, 411n. 2; travelers from, to China, 25, 49, 123, 135–37, 194. *See also* Bloomsbury group; Boxer Rebellion; Cambridge University; cross-cultural perspectives; English language; foraging (cultural); imperialism; literary theory; modernism; Opium Wars; romanticism; rentimentalism; West; World War I; World War II

"English Friends" (Leung), 129
"English Handwriting" (Fry), 380
English language (British concerns about), 113–18; Ling Shuhua's writings in, 247–50, 263, 272–73, 282, 284, 287, 288, 417n. 4
English Review, 152
English-Chinese gardens, 33, 313–19, 324, 326, 334, 340
Ernst, Max, 4
"Escrasez L'Infame" (J. Bell), 52, 53
"Essay on Aesthetics" (Fry), 348
Etchings of a Tormented Age (Xiao Qian), 202
ethnology, 336
Eurocentrism: allegations about Woolf's, 247, 249–50; in overlooking of China's influence on England, 389, 391; of some Chinese people's nicknames, 104, 130–31, 153, 204
Evangelical movement (England), 119
existentialism, 111
expressionism, 378
Eysteinsson, Astradur, 326–27

Fabians, 162–65, 168, 196. *See also* socialism
Fairbank, Wilma, 106, 153
Falling Leaves, The (Xu Zhimo), 143
family: Chinese conceptions of, 122–23, 156, 159, 195, 206, 207, 259, 272; cross-cultural misreadings of depictions of, 265. *See also* children; Confucius and Confucianism; Yuan Changying
famine. *See* poverty and famine
Fang Zhong, 2, 44
fans, 305
Far Away and Long Ago (Hudson), 84
Farewell My Concubine (film), 192
fascism. *See* authoritarianism; nation and nationalism; propaganda; Spanish Civil War; World War II
fashion, 335; Dickinson's "Eastern," 126, 136; Liberty catalog on female, 328–29, 331; Xu Zhimo's "Western," 126, 129
Faulkner, William, 218, 220
Fay, Eliza, 181
feelings. *See* self; sentimentalism; sexuality
Felski, Rita, 344
feminism: Ling Shuhua's, 255–62, 275–81; Virginia Woolf's, 20, 90, 175, 218–19. *See also* sexism
Fenellosa, Ernest, 205, 373
Fenichell, Jill Weitzman, 342
fiction (novel; short stories): author's examination of, for cross-cultural purposes, 24, 181–84; Chinese term for, 204; Chinese views of, as "defective history," 132, 204, 362; as literary source, 11; poetry as part of Chinese, 205; poverty depicted in,

200–201, 203, 207; suppression of homosexuality in, 183–85, 196–98; transnational, 181–98, 209; as valued genre in Republican China, 204–5; Woolf on, 204, 217. *See also* modernism; proverbs; short story genre; socialist realism; stream-of-consciousness style; translations; verisimilitude; specific titles and authors

Fielding, Henry, 254

First International Chinese Art Exhibition (Burlington House, London), 15, 229, 242, 335, 337–39, 372, 379

First Opium War. *See* Opium Wars

"Flatness" (in British and Chinese art), 34, 239, 364, 369, 371, 375–78, 383

Flaubert, Gustav, 277

Fleming, Peter, 62

Flowers in a Chinese Vase (Redon), 303

Flowers in the Mirror (Li Ju-Chen), 167

Flowers in the Temple (Ling Shuhua), 192, 275

Flush (Woolf), 46

foot binding, 302, 417n. 6

foraging (cultural): of China by English, 18, 35, 66–68, 72, 124–25, 127–29, 135–41, 156, 158–76, 181, 186–98, 222–34, 239, 267, 274, 298–327, 329–31, 334, 336, 340–41, 360; of England by Chinese, 18, 19, 33, 46, 108–9, 123, 126, 128, 129, 134, 137–45, 152–56, 198, 203–5, 246, 249, 326, 358–60. *See also* Bloomsbury group; Crescent Moon group; cross-cultural perspectives; literary theory; pluralism; romanticism; sentimentalism

Formosa. *See* Taiwan

Forster, E. M., **397**; and Beatrice Webb, 163, 164; as Bloomsbury group member, 25, 119, 152, 241; Chinese translations of works by, 208; and Dickinson, 137, 178, 180–81, 195; homosexuality of, 183–85, 188–89, 196; postcolonial consciousness of, 20, 177–85, 209–10; travels of, 347; and Xiao Qian, 33, 58, 176–80, 182, 183, 187, 188, 196–98, 200–201, 208–9, 212–13, 216, 217, 221, 295; on Ye Junjian, 48. *See also* titles of works by

Foucault, Michel, 31, 138, 252, 365, 366, 374, 388

Foundation of Aesthetics, The (Ogden, Wood, and Richards), 121, 123

France: Africa's influence on, 10, 128; Chinese students in, 132; Chinese territories given to, 160, 182, 195; and Forster, 178; as influence on English gardens, 314, 316, 317; Julian Bell in, 37, 41; Ling Shuhua and Chen Yuan in, 238, 286; Ling Shuhua's exhibits in, 241–43; and Opium Wars, 68; postdecolonized peoples in, 168; Vanessa Bell's interest in art of, 241–42; Xu Zhimo in, 147. *See also* postimpressionist exhibits; versailles; specific artists from

Frankfurt School, 343–44

Frans Francken Il Giovane, 345

Frederick (prince of Wales), 319

Frederick the Great, 321

Freer Collection of Art (Washington, D.C.), 303

Freud, Sigmund, 138, 140, 158, 161
Friedman, Susan Stanford, 12, 31
Friedrich, Caspar David, 386
Friendship scroll (Ling Shuhua's), 5–7, 13, 17, 18, 146–47, 238, 262, 392–93. *See also* Bloomsbury group; community(-ies); Crescent Moon group; intimate spheres; specific individuals
Friendship Gazette, 178
Frost, Robert, 218
Fry, Margery, 75; and Bloomsbury group, 120–21, 124–25; as Bloomsbury link to China, 16–17, 25; in China, 7, 41–42, 64, 65; and Ling Shuhua, 262
Fry, Roger, **397**; on art and politics, 113, 392; on art as consumer item, 344; art work of, 15, 42, 146–47, 347; as Bloomsbury group member, 25, 119, 120, 152, 241; on China, 35, 333; on Chinese art, 15, 125, 239, 240, 292–93, 298, 321, 322, 332, 350, 355, 361, 363–64, 369–78, 380, 385, 386; and Dickinson, 135, 137, 170, 188; and Julian Bell, 54, 120, 240, 349; on "line," 369–75, 386; and Margery Fry, 7; on new ways of seeing foreign art, 347–51, 363; on "plasticity," 376–78; and postimpressionist exhibits, 15, 347, 348, 350; on science as antidote to ego, 365–66; on Vanessa Bell, 234; and Waley, 309, 312; Woolf's biography of, 240; and Xu Zhimo, 129, 132, 154–55, 347, 362, 372. *See also* Omega Workshop
Fu Guangming, 219
Fu-jen University (China), 103

Furencarral (Spain), 234
furniture, 323. *See also* Omega Workshop
Fussell, Paul, 185

Gabler, Hans, 296
Gai Qi, 356
Galleries Lafayette (Paris), 329
Galsworthy, John, 381, 384
Gao, Heng-wen Gao, 71
gardens (*anglo-chinois*), 33, 313–19, 324, 326, 334, 340. *See also* Sackville-West, Vita
Gardiner, Rolf, 132
Garnett, Angelica Bell. *See* Bell, Angelica
Garnett, David ("Bunny"), 39, 132; and Ling Shuhua, 82, 90, 271, 416n. 2; on Virginia Woolf, 349
Garnett, Henrietta, 18, 284
Gaskell, Mrs., 283
Gate of Heavenly Peace, 110
Gems of Chinese Literature (Giles), 294
gender: analysis of, 280–81, 343–45; male reversals of, in Beijing Opera, 173, 186, 190, 192, 193–94, 302; performance of, 173, 174; Strachey's play with, 171–75. *See also* men; women
Genette, Gerard, 390, 391
"gentleman" (as term for elite), 129
"geopolitical thinking," 12
George III (king of England), 320
George IV (king of England), 320
Germany: ambassador to China from, 163, 166; Chinese territories given to, 160, 182, 195; Mei Lanfang's influence in, 190
Gernet, J., 367–68

Gerome, J. L., 196
gesture. See "line"
Giddens, Anthony, 414n. 1
Gilbert, William, 141, 172
Giles, Herbert A., 164, 205, 286, 294, 306
Gillespie, Diane, 286, 374
Gilman, Charlotte Perkins, 95
Gissing, George, 201
Glasgow (Scotland), 333–34
Glasgow and Willow Tea Rooms (Edinburgh), 333
"global criticism," 9, 10, 29, 392
Goethe, Johann Wolfgang von, 136–37
Gogol, Nikolay, 283
Goldsmith, Oliver, 165, 167, 170–71
Gone Primitive (Torgovnick), 24, 56
Good Earth, The (Buck), 274
Gothic elements (in Chinese gardens), 317
Gothic Revival movement (England), 118
Gould, Philip, 368
Grant, Duncan: as Bloomsbury group member, 25, 119; and blue and white willow pattern, 303, 305; on China, 35; as conscientious objector, 39; on Ling Shuhua's art, 241, 244; and Omega Workshops, 377; as a painter, 2, 112–13, 172, 238, 269, 369; as Waley's illustrator, 15, 310. *See also* Charleston House
Gray, Basil, 338
Great Britain. *See* England
Greece (ancient), 168, 196, 323, 361, 366
Greek View of Life, A (Dickinson), 196
Gu Cheng, 157
Gu Gong, 157

Gu Zhegang, 104
Guandong (Chinese territory), 160, 315
Guang Xi (China), 334
Guanzhou (China), 78, 321; British trade with, 224, 342; porcelain from, 334; upheaval in, 23, 62, 268
Guernica (Picasso), 40
Guo Moruo, 26, 133, **397**
Guomindang. *See* nationalists

H. D. (Hilda Doolittle), 143
Ha Jin, 195, 207
Haggard, Rider, 293
"ha-ha" (garden feature), 314
Hall, Stuart, 4, 35–36, 40, 325
Hamilton, Alexander, 130, 131
Hampson, John, 201
Han Minzhong, 218
Han period: art and literature of, 4, 125, 204, 243, 288, 308, 312, 336–38, 348, 360, 363, 364, 369–70, 376, 377, 386; cross-cultural networks in, 28; plays set in, 265
Han Yang Men (China), 231, 368
handkerchief symbolism, 192–93
Hangzhou (China), 246, 317, 333
Hankins, Leslie, 383
Hankou (China), 1, 59, 62, 73, 268, 294
Hankow (China). *See* Hankou
Hanlin Academy (Beijing), 259
Hardy, Thomas, 110, 122–23, 134, 143
Harvard University, 137, 219
Harvey, Leo, 50
"Hat Given to the Poet by Li Chien, The" (Chinese poem), 187
He Fu, 219
He Li, 53–54, 111
Hebei Province (China), 76
Hegel, G. W. F., 158

Herdan, Innes. *See* Jackson, Innes
Heretics Club (England), 123
Hero (film), 166
"Heroic Epistle to Sir William Chambers" (Mason), 314, 340
Hessler, Peter, 411n. 1
"heteroglossia," 20–22. *See also* pluralism
Hevia, James C., 332
Hills, Jack, 59
Hinduism, 161
Hinsch, Brett, 187, 192, 193–94
Hinton, William, 201
history: fiction as "defective," 132, 204, 362; official vs. personal, 11–16, 21
"History of Feminine Costume" (catalog), 328–29, 331
History of Modern Chinese Literature (Hsia), 218, 220
Hitler, Adolf, 52, 145, 161, 267, 270, 309
Hobson, R. L., 337–38
Hogarth Press, 54, 84, 120, 172, 242, 270, 284
Holland, Henry, 323
Holtby, Winifred, 113
Homer, Winslow, 382–83
Homeros (Walcott), 346
homosexuality, 33; Auden's, 50, 186; British taboos on, 183–86, 196, 197, 217; at Cambridge University, 180, 196; Carpenter's, 183–85, 196; in China, 162, 174, 183, 186–98, 217; Dickinson's, 183–86, 188, 196; Forster's, 183–85, 188–89, 196; and Julian Bell, 68–69, 89; transnational, as literary theme, 184–86. *See also* lesbianism
Hong Kong, 10, 160, 218, 224, 359

Hong Ying, 262–63
Hooker, Joseph, 320
Horton, Sue, 250
Housman, A. E., 56
"How Words Fail" (Woolf), 113
Howard Journal, 42
Howard League, 41
Howard's End (Forster), 179, 180, 182, 200
Hsia, C. T., 26, 100, 206, 218, 219–20
Hu Qiuyuan, 291
Hu Shi, 220, **397**; at Beijing University, 106, 146; on Chinese modernism, 292; and Crescent Moon group, 144; on cross-cultural benefits, 246; fluctuating reputation of, 27; as May Fourth movement member, 26, 27, 55, 110; and the West, 12, 26, 27, 60, 289, 290, 293; and Xu Zhimo, 71, 148
Hu Shizhi, 104
Hu Yepin, 92–93, 101
Huang Kung-wang, 379
Hudson, William Henry, 84
Hugo, Victor, 293
humanism. *See* romanticism; sentimentalism
Huntington, Samuel, 176
hybridity: author's use of, 12; of Chinese and English aesthetics, 313–25, 334, 338; Fry's interest in, 241. *See also* chinoiserie; cross-cultural perspectives; pluralism
Hypatia, 7
"hyperreal," 342–43

Ibsen, Henrik, 80
identity: as formed through travel, 37, 49, 51; lack of fixity in, 35, 249, 343,

347, 359; pluralism of, as best hope for the world, 176
imagining each other: author's role in, 23–24, 388–89; China and England's, 13–16, 28, 253–54, 274, 359, 388–93; Woolf's and Ling Shuhua's, 267
imagism, 205, 361
imperialism: British, in China, 13, 223–27, 361, 389, 411n. 2; centrality of, in the West, 21; as displacing sense of community, 11; as issue in England, 11, 15–16, 18, 33, 60, 67–68, 129, 137, 152, 160–61, 164–69, 175, 181, 182, 209; "new imperialism" in England, 137, 165, 175–76, 182, 312–13; as producing "contrapuntal perspectives," 8, 10, 21, 31–32, 223, 340–41, 360; waning of British, 336. *See also* Boxer Rebellion; "civilization"; missionaries; postcolonialism; trade
"In a Station of the Metro" (Pound), 205
"In Time of War" (Auden), 294
India: aesthetics of, 315, 323, 361; as alternative to East-West polarity, 103; art of, 15, 348; British influence on, 242; dance in, 309; Dickinson on, 168, 195; and Forster, 178, 180–84, 198; Mutiny in, 336; postcolonial views of England from, 346–47; tea from, 332, 333; as "uncivilized" from British standpoint, 66, 67, 160, 181–82; Xu Zhimo's visit to, 107, 139, 148–51
Indian mutiny, 336
Indianapolis, Ind., 240
indifference (of the universe), 366–67, 370

individualism. *See* self
Indochina (Chinese territory), 160
Ingres, Jean, 196, 372
interiority. *See* "flatness"; "line"; "plasticity"; psychology; "rhythm"; self; stream-of-consciousness style
Intermediate Sex, The (Carpenter), 196
International Anarchy (Keynes), 160
International Chinese Art Exhibition (Burlington House), 15, 229, 242, 335, 337–39, 372, 379
"intertextuality," 378
intimate spheres (friendship; personal relations): Chatterjee on, 11, 18, 21, 101, 391; in collaborating on translations, 90; cultural differences relating to, 63, 64; Forster on transnational possibilities of, 176, 182, 183–98; and handkerchief metaphor, 192–93; literary genres associated with, 13, 29, 204; Xiao Qian on, 202. *See also* community(-ies); letters; sexuality
Introduction of Western Literary Theories into Modern China, 1919–1925, The (McDougall), 108
"Introduction to Chinese Painting" (Ling Shuhua), 369, 416n. 4
Irvine, Magnus, 42
Irving, Washington, 293
Isherwood, Christopher, 120; in China, 25, 50, 61–62, 123, 186; and Ye Junjian, 48, 50, 186–87
Ishiguro, Kazuo, 346–47
Islam (Moorish influences), 161, 319, 323
Italy, 178, 182, 239, 314

Jackson, Innes (later, Innes Jackson
    Herdan), 25, 41, 63, 73–75, 77,
    231–32
James, Henry, 158, 208
Jameson, Fredric, 12, 194
Jane Eyre (Brontë), 123, 210
Japan: art from, 331–32, 348, 355–56;
    British views of, 66, 162; China's
    subjugation by, 160, 182, 195, 289,
    290; Chinese visitors in, 132,
    194–95; invasion of China by, during Republican period, 12, 23,
    59–60, 110, 124, 148, 149, 151, 221;
    Ling Shuhua in, 269, 284–85; literary journals in, 293; poetry of, 205;
    socialist circles in, 57; translations of
    British works published in, 214,
    293, 295; on Western realism, 298;
    Ye Jungian in, 49. *See also* Sino-Japanese War
jardin anglo-chinois, Le, 33, 313–19,
    324, 326, 334, 340
Java, 15, 348
Jen, Gish, 273
Jesuit missionaries, 299, 338
Jiang Jieshi. *See* Chiang Kai-shek
Jiangsu (China), 150
Jin Di, 26, 215, 295, **396**
Johnson, R. B., 166
Joos Dance Company, 145
journalism (Xiao Qian's), 202, 210
journals: landscape, 228; as literary
    sources, 11, 13, 20, 21; missing,
    70–71. *See also* self; titles beginning
    with "Diary"
"Journey, The" (Woolf), 378
Journey Not the Arrival Matters, The
    (L. Woolf), 286
Journey to the Frontier (Stansky and
    Abrahams), 2, 39, 262

Joyce, James, 57, 82, 134, 158, 218,
    295, 385, 387; Xiao Qian on, 202,
    208, 212–15
Jung, Carl, 158

"K." *See* Ling Shuhua
K (Hong Ying), 262–63
Kafka, Franz, 210
Kaiding (Chengdu, China), 230
Kalles, F. H., 62
Karatani, Kojin, 355–56, 358
Kavanagh, Patrick, 296
Kenyon College, 219
Kermode, Frank, 52
Kew Gardens (London), 319–24, 327
"Kew Gardens" (Woolf), 320
Keynes, John Maynard, 190, 349, **398**;
    on authoritarianism, 160; as
    Bloomsbury group member, 25,
    119, 152, 241; Chinese railway project of, 33, 131–32, 164, 225–26,
    313, 324; on Julian Bell, 40; marriage of, 76
Ki, Kay, 218
Kiernans, V. G., 21
King's College (Cambridge University,
    England), 136; archives of, 3, 23, 39,
    137, 178; Arthur Waley at, 308, 312;
    author's visit to, 389; Chinese writers at, 28, 50–51, 126–27, 129–33,
    176, 182, 389; Dickinson at, 137;
    Julian Bell's thesis at, 54
King's College Discussion Society, 136
Kingston, Gertrude, 172
Kinkley, Jeffrey, 109, 199, 202
Kipling, Rudyard, 60
Kirby, William C., 224
Klee, Paul, 369
Kline, Franz, 378
Koestler, Arthur, 178

Kong Xiaojong, 218
Korea, 160
Krauss, Rosalind, 383
Kristeva, Julia, 167–68, 253
Kryptoff, Igor, 299
Kubla Khan, 299
"Kubla Khan" (Coleridge), 341
Kuhn, Thomas, 366
Kuling (Jiangxi, China), 230
Kwantung (Chinese territory), 160

labyrinths, 388
Lamb, Charles, 186, 283, 296, 302–3, 324, 364
Lambourne, Lionel, 341
landscape painting (Chinese), 16, 17, 243–44, 338, 351; differences between European and, 357; as influence on British culture, 222–325; lack of human subjects in, 55, 138, 351, 355–56, 362–67; of Song Dynasty, 158, 159, 334, 338, 351, 356, 370
landscape painting (European), 240–42, 324–25
landscapes (actual Chinese): Julian Bell's love of, 9, 41, 228–33, 237, 324; in Julian Bell's photograph album, 6; Ling Shuhua's descriptions of, 95–97, 99; Richardses' love of, 9, 125; and "self" in China, 139–40, 158. *See also* blue and white willow patterns; landscape painting (Chinese); landscape painting (European); specific places
Lang Shihning (Castiglione), 338
language. *See* Chinese language; English language; translations
Lao She, 26, 293, **398**
Lao Tzu, 159

Laurence, Patricia: on Chinese art, 239, 253, 336, 338; critical form used by, 22; travels of, to China, 3–5, 8, 12, 28, 231, 319, 336, 338, 388–89; as Woolf scholar, 2, 4, 382
Lawrence, D. H., 53, 141, 198, 265; Xiao Qian on, 202, 209, 210
Lawrence, T. E., 178
League of Left-Wing Writers, 106, 111, 112
League of Nations, 15, 128, 164, 171, 175
"Leaning Tower, The" (Woolf), 38, 113, 254–55, 295
"leaving things out." *See* restraint
Leavis, F. R., 117, 219
Lee, Leo Ou-fan, 19, 26, 31, 130, 152
Left-Wing Writers, 106, 111, 112
Legge, James, 294, 360
Lehmann, John, 68, 69, 187, 228
Leighton School (England), 37, 68
lesbianism, 192–93
Leshan (Sichuan province, China), 268–69, 272, 275
Lessing, Doris, 218
Letter, The (film), 341
Letter from Peking (Buck), 154
letters: cross-cultural, between artists, 266–75; as expressing personal voice, 51, 90, 93; between Forster and Xiao Qian, 176–80; gaps in, 23, 70–71, 147, 178–80, 182, 264, 415n. 3; as literary sources, 11, 13, 20–27, 263; previously unpublished, between Crescent Moon and Bloomsbury group, 1, 22–27, 388; quality of Julian Bell's, 233; quarrels between Ling Shuhua and Julian Bell through, 76–82; and short story

letters (continued)
  genre, 92–93. See also self; voice; specific correspondents
"Letters from a Chinaman" (Dickinson), 15
Letters from a Chinese Official. See Letters from John Chinaman
Letters from John Chinaman (Dickinson), 15, 44, 136, 164–71, 175, 181, 316, 340
Letters to a Chinese Official (Bryan), 169–70
Letters to an English Nation (Voltaire), 171
Leung, Gaylord, 129, 132–33, 184
Lévi-Strauss, Claude, 389
Lewis, Percy Wyndham, 53, 365
Leyland, Frederick R., 303
Li Bo, 34
Li Ju-chen, 167
Li Po, 297
Li Po-hai, 373
Lianda (China), 123
Liang and Lin (Fairbank), 153
Liang Qichao, 107, 130, 293
Liang Shicheng, 106, 153
Liang Shiqui, 144
Liang Tongshu, 373
Liao Hong Ying, 17, 41, 42, 73, 74–75
Liberty, Arthur Lasenby, 327, 328
Liberty & Co. (London), 327–34, 336; as mini-museum, 15, 327–28, 336, 341; porcelain sold by, 299, 345
"Liberty Bazaar, The" (catalog), 328
Life as We Have Known It (Llewelyn Davies), 90
Life of Charlotte Bronte (Gaskell), 283
Light in August (Faulkner), 220
Lin Changmin, 71, 152–53

Lin Huiyin, 71–72, 106, 152–53
Lin Shu, 293–94
Lin Yutang, **398**
"line" (gesture; outlines; shadows; silhouettes; strokes): in British and Chinese art, 34, 239, 347, 381; in British gardens, 314–16, 322; calligraphic, 351, 378–87; exposure of, in Chinese art, 353, 362, 369, 379–80; as "leaving things out," 367–75; Lily Briscoe's, 352, 387; Ling Shuhua's references to, 353, 369; literary application of concept of, 378–87; rhythmic, 348, 364, 368–75, 380, 385, 387. See also calligraphy; verisimilitude
Ling Shuhua ("Sue"), **398**; and Acton, 189, 190; as art collector, 3, 243, 244, 288, 416n. 3, 417n. 4; as autobiographer, 27–28, 83, 84, 93–95, 243, 247, 251, 255–63, 271–75, 282–85, 288–89; Bloomsbury links of, 32, 33, 40–42, 63–100, 227–89; on British modernists, 210; as calligrapher, 3, 63, 243; as children's story writer, 51, 247, 262, 284; on Chinese painting, 362, 369, 379; as Crescent Moon member, 101, 109–10; and Elmhirst, 145, 146; in England, 147, 238–39, 264, 284, 286–87; feminism of, 255–62, 275–81; fluctuating reputation of, 19, 27, 91, 99, 109, 193, 246, 263, 264, 279–80; friendship scroll of, 5, 6–7, 13, 17, 18, 146–47, 238, 262, 392–93; gifts given by, 68, 238–39; house of, 5; Julian Bell's correspondence with, 60, 76–82, 230, 232–33, 413n. 8; Julian Bell's romance with,

1, 7–8, 32, 41, 44, 63–82, 100, 227–28, 235, 246, 262, 263, 274–75, 389; Julian Bell's romance with, secrecy concerning, 2, 8, 63, 238, 261, 262–63; Julian Bell's writing collaboration with, 5, 7–8, 82–99, 248, **403–7**; as "K," 2, 262–63; leaves China before PRC, 250, 266, 286; lost writings of, 23, 147, 264, 287; and Margery Fry, 17, 64; marriage of, 1, 3, 63, 72, 109–10, 249; as May Fourth movement member, 26, 289; as one of the "three talents of Luo Jia," 6, 263–65, 289; as painter, 1, 3, 8, 63, 82, 223, 237, 239–40, 243, 247, 261, 264, 273, 275, 285; as part of Crescent Moon group, 2–3, 32; self-censorship by, 261–62, 285, 288–89; social background of, 1, 8, 76, 108, 247, 254–62; sources used for study of, 23; suicide threats by, 74, 77–79, 88, 95, 268; translations by, 247–49, 288; and Vanessa Bell, 1, 84, 188, 234–42, 246, 248, 260–61, 263, 269–74, 284, 286, 308, 324–25, 337; and Virginia Woolf, 1, 33, 46, 83, 84, 94–95, 113, 201, 210, 246–54, 266–79; Western art shows of, 240–41, 243, 244, 324, 416n. 4; Western travels of, 12, 23, 25, 238, 286, 288; as writer, 1, 3, 8, 63, 82–99, 192–93, 204, 223, 243, 256–62, 264, 272–81; writing style of, 93–95, 256–62, 275–80, 282, 285; and Xu Zhimo, 70–72, 146–47, 415n. 3. *See also* Chen Yuan; Chinnery, Ying

Link, Perry, 12, 20

"liquidation of reference" (of objects), 341–46

Listener, The, 178

literary criticism. *See* literary theory

Literary Studies Society, 110, 111, 144

literary theory (literary criticism): author's conception of, 22; Bell's teaching of, in China, 46, 52, 53, 362; Bloomsbury's contribution to Chinese, 206; Marxist, 210–11, 218, 362; Richards,' 120–25, 155; undeveloped, in PRC, 220. *See also* aesthetics; "global criticism"; propaganda; specific literary critics and movements

literature. *See* art; fiction; letters; literary theory; poetry; short story genre; translations; specific works, authors, literary communities, and movements

Literature Institute of Peking University, 134

"Little Zhu," 145–46, 150

Liu, James, 355

Liu, Lydia, 31, 35, 103, 202, 295, 355

Liu Bingshan, 218

Liu Na'ou, 91

Liu Shicong, 218

Liu Xie, 378–79

Liverpool (England), 300, 303

Llewelyn Davies, Margaret, 90

Lloyd Jones, Richard, 114

Locked Diary (Forster), 178

London, Jack, 293

London (England): Chen Yuan in, 103, 286; Kew Gardens pagoda in, 319–24, 327; Ling Shuhua in, 147, 238–39, 264, 284, 286–87

London Mercury, 90, 249, 271

London School of Economics, 103, 131, 132, 162, 286
London Society for Women's Service, 171
London University School of Oriental and African Studies, 132, 147, 200, 288, 310, 411n. 2
Long-Winded Remarks from a Red-Haired Barbarian (Xiao Qian), 165–66
Lopokova, Lydia, 76, 190, 306, 349
Lords of Human Kind, The (Kiernans), 21
Lorenzetti, Ambrogio, 372
Louis IV (king of France), 321
Louisa Ulrika (queen of Sweden), 320–21
Love in a Small Town (Wang Anyi), 206–7
"Love Song of J. Alfred Prufrock, The" (Eliot), 141, 208
Lowe, Hansen, 48, 230
Lowe, Lisa, 13–14, 167–68, 251
Lowell, Amy, 373
Lu Jingquing, 92
Lu Xiaoman, 71, 148
Lu Xun, **398**; and Agnes Smedley, 154; career of, 101, 211–12; and Chen Yuan, 103, 104, 106; fluctuating reputation of, 27; as May Fourth movement member, 26; on photos of Mei Lanfang, 193; and the West, 12; and Ye Junjian, 49
Lu Yin, 193
Lucas, Peter, 84
Luce, Christopher, 371
Lukes, Steven, 414n. 1
Luo Jia, 264

Luojia Hill (near Wuhan University), 5, 264. *See also* "three talents of Luo Jia"

Macartney, Lord, 33, 222–24, 226, 305, 319, 341
Madame Bovary (Flaubert), 277
Madame George Charpentier and Her Children (Renoir), 303
"Madly Singing in the Mountains" (trans. Waley), 306
"Malay Theatre, A" (Dickinson), 163
Malaysia, 181
Mallarmé, Stéphane, 294
Man Who Died, The (Lawrence), 210
Manchester (England), 308
Manchester Guardian, 170
Manchuria (Chinese territory), 160
Manet, Edouard, 369
Mann, Thomas, 158
Mansfield, Katherine, 57, 143, 210, 253, 283; Ling Shuhua likened to, 97, 204; Xiao Qian on, 202–4, 213, 370
Mao Dun, 263, 293, **398**
Mao Zedong, **398–99**; and class barriers, 291; on Crescent Moon group, 20; and Ling Shuhua's writing, 19, 99; on literature, 19, 54, 55, 57, 92, 116, 157–59, 220, 221; on nation as a blank paper, 202; poems by, 231; and Ye Junjian, 19. *See also* Cultural Revolution
Mappings (Friedman), 12
Marco Polo, 299
"Mark on the Wall, The" (Woolf), 221
Martin, Kingsley, 42, 288
Marvell, Andrew, 314

Marx, Karl, 158
Marxism: criticism of Ling Shuhua work's under, 19, 91, 99; and cross-cultural literary analysis, 210–12, 219–20; and hunger, 200; as influence on Ye Junjian, 49–51; on Joyce, 134; on modernism, 27, 53–54, 57, 111–12, 218, 359; resistance to literary, in China, 123, 141, 156–58, 219–21; and self, 142, 156–58; of Terry Eagleton, 122. *See also* communists; Mao Zedong; socialist realism
Marxist Literary Research Society, 57
Mason, William, 314, 321, 340
Masood, Syed Ross, 178, 184
Matisse, Henri, 239, 303, 347, 350, 369, 371, 376, 378, 379, 383, 385
Matthieson, Francis, 219
Maurice (Forster), 184, 185, 188–89, 196–98, 216–17
Maurois, André, 241, 243–44, 288
Mauron, Charles, 38, 372
Mauron, Marie, 8, 46, 65
Max Emanuel (elector), 321
May Fourth 1919 movement: on Beijing Opera practices, 192; and Chinese modernism, 216, 291–92; Chinese persons associated with, 26, 289; and self-expression, 11–12, 55, 57–58, 137–41, 143, 157, 158, 193, 202, 261–62, 283–84; tenets of, 291–92, 412N. 4; Western influence on, 10, 19–20, 46, 100, 101, 126–27, 264; and women, 80, 90, 92–93. *See also* Crescent Moon group; names of members of
McDougall, Bonnie, 108, 292, 390

McIntosh, Charles Rennie, 333
Mei (Ling Shuhua's sister: Amy Ling Chen), 261, 288, 290
Mei Lanfang, 190, 193, 194
Memoir (Ling Shuhua), 252–53, 284, 285, 287
men (in China): abusive, as writing topic, 92; China seen as "weak man of Asia," 110, 143, 152, 155, 160, 194–95, 289–91; as feminine, 162, 174, 186–98; friendships between, 187–88; relations between women and, 187–88. *See also* gender; specific men
Mencius, 306, 348, 352, 364–65
Mencius on Mind (Richards), 125, 306, 348, 364–65
Mendiant Ingrat (Bloy), 365
Meredith, George, 296, 305, 324
Meredith, Hugh Owen, 184
Metropolitan Museum of Art, 4, 329, 333–34, 348
Mi Fu, 96–97
Mi Youren, 96–97
Miao Su-Yun, 244
Michaelis, Mary, 16, 41, 120
"Mid-Autumn Festival, The" (Ling Shuhua), 280
Middle School (Cambridge), 71
Midnight's Children (Rushdie), 346
"Mikado" (Gilbert and Sullivan), 172
Milton, John, 314
Milton (Blake), 312
Miner, Earl, 137
Ming Dynasty: art of, 337, 362; fiction in, 204, 292; porcelain of, 300
Minton, Thomas, 334
mise en abime, 128, 222, 298, 303

missionaries: as "barbarians," 200; and blue and white willow patterned porcelain, 299; as "civilizing" Chinese, 166, 224; foreign, in China, 14–15, 17, 166, 167, 169–71, 175, 177, 188; schools run by, 199, 290. *See also* Boxer Rebellion; Christianity

Mitchell, W. J. T., 222, 313

Mocatta, Rebecca, 308

"Modern Fiction" (Woolf), 101, 290, 384

modernism: "aesthetic voyaging" associated with, 10, 300, 326; Bloomsbury's contributions to, 3, 20, 25, 57, 352; Chinese contributions to British, 94, 96, 109, 111, 129, 144, 205, 222, 286, 297–325, 327–36, 353, 358, 361–75; Chinese intellectuals' incipient, 13, 26, 93, 123, 129, 134, 155–60, 205–6, 292, 389–90; Chinese views of British, 202–15; comparative, 392; creating a map of, 29–30; Crescent Moon group's involvement with, 4, 20, 93, 109, 123; economy of style in, 205, 207, 228, 244, 348, 360, 368, 371, 380–83, 385, 386–87; evolving international, 20, 21, 32–36, 82–99, 109, 111, 123, 143–44, 149, 155, 186, 216, 241, 309, 326–27, 346–52, 358–67, 369, 391–93; focus on process as characteristic of, 353–54, 368–69, 379; and indifference of the universe, 366–67, 370; as influenced by visual aesthetics, 378–87; "interrupted," 101, 210, 214, 216–21, 291, 359; and Julian Bell in China, 44, 52–55, 82–99; lack of verisimilitude associated with, 350–51, 355, 357–67, 369–75, 384; movements related to, 360–61; pluralism in, 11, 20, 117–18, 216–17, 356, 385; 1980s Chinese debates about, 27, 53–54, 111–12, 218, 359; and sentimentalism, 143. *See also* cross-cultural perspectives; foraging (cultural); postmodernism; psychology; self; stream-of-consciousness style

"Modernism and China" (He Li), 53–54, 111

Modernism and Orientalism (Qian Zhaoming), 390

Mohanty, Chandra, 202, 250, 251

"Moment: Summer's Night, The" (Woolf), 382

Monet, Claude, 376

Mongols, 199

Monkey (Wu Cheng'en), 14, 310

Monk's House (England), 18, 242, 262, 287, 337

Montesquieu, Baron, 167, 171

Moore, G. E., 53, 119, 121, 312

Moore, George, 283

Moorish elements (in British gardens), 319, 323

More Translations from the Chinese (Waley), 306

Morning in the Garden at Vaucressor (Vuillard), 376

Morris, William, 377

Motherwell, Robert, 369, 371

Mozambique, 329

"Mr. Bennett and Mrs. Brown" (Woolf), 96, 185, 381, 386–87

Mrs. Dalloway (Woolf), 159–60, 218, 220, 276, 278, 279, 344, 346, 381

"Mrs. Dalloway in Bond Street"
(Woolf), 341–45
multiplicity. *See* pluralism
Murasaki, Lady, 254, 308
Murry, John Middleton, 203
Musée Cernuschi (Paris), 241–43
museums: Chinese experience of, 339; department stores compared to, 15, 327–28, 336, 341. *See also* archaeology; specific museums and exhibits
music, 163, 361; art likened to, 243, 338, 350. *See also* "rhythm"
Mussolini, Benito, 52, 161

Nage, Kalidas, 146
Naipaul, V. S., 13
Nanjing (China), 58, 153; Japanese rape of, 49; nationalists in, 109, 124; porcelain from, 299, 300, 334
Nankai University (China), 123
"Narrow Bridge of Art, The" (Woolf), 246–54, 382
Nash, John, 323
Nation, 378
nation and nationalism, 4; art as made by self rather than by, 32, 247, 267, 280; autobiography as inscription of, 282; Chinese allegories regarding, 194–95, 285; friendship as possible basis for relations between, 182–98; and "imagined communities," 18–19; as issue for May Fourth writers, 11–13, 49, 57, 129, 279; as issue in China, 21, 156, 157, 265; lack of fixity in, 343, 359; Mao's metaphor for, 202; pluralism and ambivalence in discourses of, 10–11, 20–21, 24, 390; propaganda as literature to serve, 19, 108, 116, 140–41, 156–59, 220, 282, 291; suppression of self by, 21, 55, 58, 129, 140, 142–45, 158, 183–85, 188–89, 196–98, 206, 285. *See also* authoritarianism; imperialism; propaganda; transnationalism; specific countries, leaders, and wars
National Art Exhibition (China), 150
National Wuhan University (China). *See* Wuhan University
nationalists (Guomindang): Chen Yuan and Ling Shuhua's association with, 27; against the communists, 148, 149; Crescent Moon group seen as sympathetic to, 107, 109; in Ding Ling's story, 206; literary censorship by, 92; migration of, to Taiwan, 23. *See also* Chiang Kai-shek; civil war; Taiwan
naturalist (Julian Bell's definition of), 229–30. *See also* nature
nature. *See* indifference; landscapes (actual Chinese); romanticism; landscapes
Needham, Joseph, 288
"negroes," 56
New Criticism, 121, 123, 219, 221
New Culture movement (China), 104, 106
New Fiction, 293
new imperialism (in England), 137, 165, 175–76, 182, 312–13
New Leaves Anthology, 220
New Life movement, 73, 413n. 9
New York Public Library, 2, 3
New Yorker, 267
Ng, Janet, 261
Ngũgĩ wa Thiong'o, 13
Ni Zan, 393

Nicolson, Ben, 242
Nicolson, Harold, 270
Nicolson, Nigel, 287
Nieh, Fujian, 48
Night in Florence, A (Xu Zhimo), 144
No Longer at Ease (Achebe), 346
Nottingham (England), 209
novels. *See* fiction; specific titles

"Oaths of Friendship" (Chinese poem), 187
Oberlin College, 219
O'Brien, Edna, 287
Observer, 284
Odyssey (Homer), 346
"Of Taste" (Cawthorn), 314–15
Ogden, C. K., 116, 117, 123
"Old China" (Lamb), 302–3
Old Summer Palace (Wanshoushan, China), 33, 68, 224–25
Omega Workshop, 125, 327, 365, 377–78
"On Being Ill" (Woolf), 184
"On Finding a Painting of Buddha on the Wall of His Prison Cell" (poem), 42
On or about 1910 (Stansky), 289
"On Photography" (Lu Xun), 193–94
"Once upon a Time" (Ling Shuhua), 192–93
170 Chinese Poems (trans. Waley), 305, 306, 348
Opium Wars, 33, 68, 160, 164, 165, 182, 223–25, 324, 341
Orientalism (Said), 30
"Orientalism" (style), 316
Orientalism and Modernism (Zhaoming), 34

"Original Chinese Extravaganza entitled The Willow Pattern Plate, An" (drama), 300
Original Letters from India, 1779–1815 (Fay), 181
"Originality of the Avant Garde, The" (Krauss), 383
Orwell, George, 55, 113–15
Othello (Shakespeare), 192
"other": Lily Briscoe as, 346; Lowe on, 167–68; Said on, 30–31, 360, 412n. 6; Torgovnick on, 14. *See also* "Chinese eyes"; racism; sexism
outlines. *See* "line"
Owens School (England), 37, 39, 68
Oxford movement (England), 118
Oxford University, 41, 42, 75, 132

pacifism, 20, 39, 112–13, 131
pagodas (as garden elements), 33, 313–23, 327
"Painter's Choice, A" (Ling Shuhua's exhibit), 244
painting (Chinese): calligraphy's link between writing and, 34, 97, 243, 297–98, 353–54, 370, 373, 378–87; Chinese valuing of, 338; and contemplation, 351–55, 358; lines and strokes revealed in, 353, 362, 369, 379–80. *See also* calligraphy; landscape painting (Chinese); landscapes (actual Chinese); specific paintings and artists
Painting of the Far East (Binyon), 350
paintings (Chinese): Ling Shuhua's landscape, 243–44
Parry, Benita, 21
Parsons, Trekkie, 288

Partridge, Ralph, 172
Passage to India (Forster), 67, 181–84, 209
Pater, Clara, 305
Pater, Walter, 140
Patience (Gilbert and Sullivan), 141
Paulin, Tom, 119, 412n. 5
"Peach Blossom Fan, The," 190
Peacock Room, 303
Pearsall Smith, Logan, 114
Pei Ju-Lian, 46. *See also* Bell, Julian
Peking. *See* Beijing
PEN Conference, 178
People's Daily, The, 53, 111
People's Liberation Army (PRC), 202
People's Literature Press (Beijing), 123
People's Republic of China (PRC), 26, 182, 219, 238, 264, 266. *See also* China; Cultural Revolution; Mao Zedong; People's Liberation Army
Persia, 299–300
Persian Letters (Montesquieu), 171
"Personal Impressions of H. G. Wells, Edward Carpenter, and Katherine Mansfield" (Xu Zhimo), 143
personal relations. *See* intimate spheres
"personalism." *See* sentimentalism
personality. *See* self
Phillips, Caryl, 346
photograph albums, 1, 5–6, 18, 79
Picasso, Pablo, 40, 347, 356, 369, 371, 378, 383, 385, 392
"picturesque," 315
Picturesque Representations of the Dress and Manners of the Chinese (Alexander), 223
Pinter, Harold, 366
Pippett, Aileen, 119, 262
Piri, Toni, 73
"place," 4–5. *See also* travel; specific places
"plasticity" (in British and Chinese art), 34, 348, 364, 375–78
Plato, 137
Playfair, Eddy (Julian Bell's correspondence with): on civil war, 60; on Forster, 183; on India and China, 181; as intermediary between Vanessa and Julian, 416n. 2; on Julian Bell's literary collaboration with Ling Shuhua, 83, 84, 86, 88; on Julian's Chinese name, 46; on Julian's duties at Wuhan University, 44, 48, 50; on Julian's romance with Ling Shuhua, 63–66, 68, 69, 72, 73, 76–78
playfulness (in Chinese art), 363–64
"Plumage Bill, The" (Woolf), 253
pluralism (multiplicity): of author's sources, 22; in Chinese paintings, 376; among Forster's characters, 182; of identity as best hope for the world, 176; Ling Shuhua's observation of, 255, 278; in modernism, 11, 20, 117–18, 216–17, 356, 385; in notions of nation, 10–11, 20–21, 390; postmodernism's association with, 10, 20–22, 24, 26–27, 217, 240–42; of scenes in Chinese gardens, 317, 319; of textual readings, 29–30. *See also* "Chinese eyes"; cross-cultural perspectives; hybridity
Poems of Chih-mo, The (Xu Zhimo), 144
"Poet Goes Mad, A" (Ling Shuhua), 89, 95–99, 353–55, 357, 358

poetry: calligraphy's combining of painting and, 97, 243, 378–79; as part of Chinese fiction, 205; translation of Chinese, into English, 4, 15, 187–88, 199, 205, 223, 227, 258–59, 294, 296–98, 305–6, 308–12, 324, 348, 360, 373; translation of European, into Chinese, 294. *See also* translations; names of specific poets, anthologies, and poems

politeness. *See* restraint

"Politics and the English Language" (Orwell), 113–15

"Politics and the Good Life" (J. Bell), 52

Pollock, Jackson, 369, 371, 374, 378

polygamy (Julian Bell's tendency toward), 63–65, 73, 75–77, 82. *See also* concubinage

Poole, Roger, 119

Pope, Alexander, 53, 54, 174

porcelain: British importation of Chinese, 334; British production of, 15, 299, 334, 342–43; China's invention of, 299–300; friendships between men depicted on, 187–88; in Metropolitan Museum of Art, 4. *See also* blue and white willow patterns; ceramics; chinoiserie

Possession (Byatt), 2

postcolonialism: assumptions about West in, 247, 249–51; author on, 4, 128, 216; concerns of scholars in, 21, 111, 167–68, 202, 261; literature written under, 346–47; universalist emphasis of, 10, 13, 30–31. *See also* imperialism

Post-Impressionist Exhibits, 14, 347, 348, 350

postmodernism: audience emphasis of, 371; Bloomsbury and Crescent Moon groups' foreshadowing of, 20; in China, 216; cliches of, 4, 101; pluralism associated with, 10, 20–22, 26–27, 217, 240–42; and postcolonial rewritings of English literature, 346–47

Potter, Sally, 221

Pound, Ezra, 34, 143, 205, 209, 214, 309, 373, 387

poverty and famine, 159, 166, 199–203, 207

Power, Eileen, 152

Practical Criticism (Richards), 121, 123

PRC. *See* People's Republic of China

pre-Raphaelite movement (England), 118

Pride and Prejudice (Austen), 94

Priestley, J. B., 288, 416n. 4

primitivism: as American term, 156, 165; Bloomsbury's reversal of views of, 156, 165, 167, 225, 364; and blue and white willow patterned porcelain, 298, 301–2; Europeans' foraging of developing nations for examples of, 329–31, 337; sentimentalism as associated with, 56, 57; Torgovnick on, 24, 56; used to bolster sense of superiority, 329–30. *See also* barbarians; "civilization"

Princes of Wales Theater (Liverpool), 300

Princess from the Land of Porcelain, The (Whistler), 303

Principia Ethica (Moore), 53

Principles of Literary Criticism (Richards), 52

Proctor, Dennis, 181

propaganda: Crescent Moon group's opposition to, 144; and "imagined communities," 19; as literature to serve a nation, 19, 108, 116, 140–41, 156–59, 220, 282, 291; as stifling self-expression, 140, 149, 150, 156–57, 282; as univocal, 157; Woolf on, 113–18; Xiao Qian's work on Mao's, 202. *See also* socialist realism

prostitutes: and handkerchief symbolism, 192–93; male, in China, 162, 188, 197

Proust, Marcel, 57, 158, 208–9, 218, 378

proverbs (in Ling Shuhua's writing), 93–95, 98

psychology (interiority): Bakhtin on, 57; in Chinese writing, 98–99, 110, 175–79, 206, 285, 289; in Western modernism, 112, 182–83, 203–4, 207–9. *See also* self; sentimentalism; stream-of-consciousness style

Pu Songling, 254, 306

Pu Yi ("the last Chinese emperor"), 1

Puccini, Giacomo, 172

Qian Zhaoming, 390

Qian, Xingcun, 91, 97, 279, 280

Qianlong (emperor of China), 166, 379

Qin Dynasty art, 125, 363, 377

Qin Hongchun, 193, 279–80

Qin Shi Xiang, 189

Qing Dynasty, 192, 266, 281, 292, 300

Qing Hua School (Shanghai), 106

Qing Ting-piao, 338

Qingdao (Chinese territory), 160

Qinghua University (Shanghai), 106, 123, 140, 144, 411n. 3

Qu (Chinese emperor), 166, 171–75

Qu Qiubai, 57, 106, **399**

Qu Shijing, 26, 218, 221

Quack, Quack! (L. Woolf), 170

Queen Victoria (Strachey), 15

Queer Diaspora (Eng), 185

racism: British, 56, 66–68, 161–62, 166, 181, 200, 301, 302, 329–30, 341; Chinese, 199; toward India, 181. *See also* barbarians; primitivism

railroads (Chinese), 33, 131–32, 164, 225–27, 313, 324

Raine, Kathleen, 38, 40, 41, 53, 89

Raise the Red Lantern (film), 259

Ramsay, Lettice, 25, 120

Ranelagh (England), 319

Ranson, John Crowe, 219

Rao Mengkan, 106, 144

Rape of the Lock (Pope), 174

Raphael, 375

rationality (Julian's), 51–57, 94. *See also* science

"Reading in the Studio Douqiu" (Gai Qi), 356

Reading of Silence: Virginia Woolf in the English Tradition, The (Laurence), 4, 382

realism. *See* socialist realism; verisimilitude

"Record of the Classification of Painters" (Xian He), 375

Red Guards, 23, 150, 179–80, 336. *See also* Cultural Revolution

Redon, Odilon, 303

Reed, Christopher, 344, 345

Reflecting the Water Lily Pond at Giverny (Monet), 376

Reid, Panthea, 414n. 13

Reininger, Lotte, 383

Remains of the Day, The (Ishiguro), 346–47
Rembrandt, 379
Ren Jisheng, 123
Renoir, Jean, 303
representational art. *See* Edwardian literature and politics; socialist realism; verisimilitude
restraint (decorum; leaving things out; politeness; reticence; sedateness; simplicity; understatement; withholding): as Chinese characteristic, 286, 358, 361–75; modernism's economy of style as form of, 205, 207, 228, 244, 348, 360, 368, 371, 380–83, 385, 386–87; self-censorship as form of, 261–62, 285, 288–89. *See also* imagism; modernism; voice: suppression of
reticence. *See* restraint
"rhythm": in British and Chinese art, 34, 242–43, 347, 361, 382, 385; of Lily Briscoe's stroke, 352; of a line, 348, 364, 368–75, 380, 385, 387. *See also* music
Ricci, Matteo, 188, 224
Richards, Dorothy, 9, 74–75, 125, 233
Richards, I. A., **399**; on art and politics in Cambridge, 113–17; Bell's use of works of, 52, 53; and Bloomsbury group, 120, 152; in China, 15, 25, 46, 74–75, 122–25, 155, 221; and Chinese landscapes, 9, 233; on comparative studies, 36, 295; on Mencius, 125, 306, 348, 352, 364–65; on sentimentalism, 55–56; on translation, 364–65; translations by, 306, 348
Richards on Rhetoric (Berthoff), 115
Richardson, Dorothy, 213–14
Richardson, Samuel, 51, 254
Rilke, Rainer Maria, 294
Roaming in the Clouds (Xu Zhimo), 144
Rob Roy (Scott), 283
Roger Fry: A Biography (Woolf), 240
romanticism: Chinese interest in Western, 18, 19, 33, 46, 108–9, 123, 126, 128, 129, 134, 140–45, 152–56, 203–5, 358–59; Dickinson's, 136; Julian Bell on, 52, 54; in Ling Shuhua's autobiography, 84; and modernism, 370–71
Room of One's Own, A (Woolf), 252–53, 255, 275, 278, 351; on androgyny, 194; Chinese translations of, 46; on "feminine sentence," 374; on women's education, 258, 259
Room with a View, A (Forster), 182
Rose, Archibald, 8–9, 25, 46, 152, 190; and Chinese railway project, 131–32, 164, 225–26, 312–13
Ross, Denman Waldo, 348
Rossetti, Dante Gabriel, 143
Royal Brighton Pavilian (England), 319, 322–24, 327
Ru Chen, 157
Rushdie, Salman, 202, 346
Ruskin, John, 344
Russell, Alys, 196
Russell, Bertrand, 367; as Bloomsbury group member, 25, 119, 120, 152, 309; and Boxer Indemnity Fund, 46, 152; divorces of, 130–31, 196; and Xu Zhimo, 129, 130–31, 153, 158–59
Russell, Dora, 7, 42
Russia (Soviet Union): China's subjugation by, 160, 182, 195; Chinese

students in, 132; as influence on British gardens, 319, 323; literature of, 204, 256, 257, 283–84; Mei Lanfang's influence in, 190; socialist realism in, 57; translations from language of, 84; Webbs' support for, 163, 164; and Xu Zhimo, 107, 149; and Ye Junjian, 49, 50. *See also* specific writers from
Rylands, George ("Dadie"), 50, 120, 127, 129, 172, 208, 306

Sackville-West, Vita, 1, 25, 84, 241–43, 284–86, 288, **399**
Sadler's Wells Ballet, 145
Said, Edward, 34, 202, 313; on "contrapuntal perspectives," 8, 10, 19, 21, 340; on orientalism, 339–40; on the "other," 30–31; on representation of other cultures, 360, 412n. 6
St. James Park (London), 321
Santiniketan (India), 148–50
Sanyu, 366
Sassoon, Siegfried, 183, 184, 196
Saturday Review, 15, 166–67
Saussure, Ferdinand de, 24, 29–31, 155, 156, 295
Saussy, Haun, 31, 35, 202, 253
Schloss, Sigismund, 308
Schorer, Mark, 219
Schreiner, Olive, 250
science: as antidote to ego, 365–66; and Bloomsbury group, 120–21, 171; inadequacies of, 374; and verisimilitude, 370; and Western metaphors of seeing, 363, 370–71
Scotland-China Association, 413n. 10
Scott, Bonnie Kime, 25
Scott, Walter, 283, 293

Scott-James, R. A., 90, 249, 271
scrolls: Chinese handling of, 339; Chinese landscape, 305, 306, 356; Ling Shuhua's friendship, 5, 6–7, 13, 17, 18, 146–47, 238, 262, 392–93
Second Opium War. *See* Opium Wars
sedateness. *See* Restraint
seeing, 223; as bond between Bells and Ling Shuhua, 237, 242; bricolage created by, 313, 342, 389; with "Chinese eyes," 9–10, 24, 33, 34, 178, 182–83, 210, 240–42, 324–41, 346–52, 393; Western metaphors connected with, 363, 370–71. *See also* psychology; specific art exhibits and works
Selections of Modernist Literature from Abroad (Yuan Kejia), 134, 218, 220, **409–10**
self (anthropomorphism; individualism; subject; subjectivity): art as made by, rather than by nation, 32, 247, 267, 280; Chinese conceptions of, 159, 271, 281–82; and Chinese landscapes, 297, 362–67, 371; in Chinese modernism, 155–60, 205, 362–65, 380, 381, 384–85; Confucianism's repression of, 141, 142, 144–45, 158–59, 192, 206; Crescent Moon group's interest in, 19, 20, 55, 57–58, 126, 128, 129, 137–41, 202–4; Ling Shuhua's treatment of, 275–80; literary genres dealing with, 283–85; May Fourth writers' interest in, 11–12, 55, 57–58, 137–41, 143, 157, 158, 193, 202, 261–62, 283–84; science as antidote to, 365–66; suppression of, by nations, 21, 55, 58, 129, 140, 142–45, 158,

self (*continued*)
  183–85, 188–89, 196–98, 206, 285; Woolf's expression of, 159–60, 357–58. *See also* autobiography; intimate spheres; journals; letters; modernism; psychology; romanticism; sentimentalism; sexuality; stream-of-consciousness style; travel; voice
Semaine Bonte, La (Ernst), 4
Sen, Amartya, 176
Sen, Rabintiti Mohan, 146
Sense of an Ending, The (Kermode), 52
sensibility. *See* sentimentalism
"Sensuous Art of the Chinese Landscape Journal, The" (Yu Kuangzhong), 228
Sentimental Modernism (Clarke), 143
sentimentalism ("personalism"; sensibility): in Chinese literature, 205–7, 285; Chinese use of term, 207; deadening of, 159; Dickinson's, 137; as influence on Chinese intellectuals, 33, 55, 57–58, 110, 142–43, 154–55, 171, 203, 206; in Ling Shuhua's autobiography, 84; Mansfield's, 203–4; Western views of, 51–57, 94, 155, 199, 207. *See also* romanticism; self
Seurat, George, 369, 371, 372
sexism: Bunny Garnett's, 349; Dickinson's, 168; Julian Bell's, 56–57, 68, 72, 74, 77, 80–81. *See also* feminism; women
sexuality: Julian Bell's, 63–65, 73, 75–77, 82, 89; as writing topic, 88–89, 91–92, 128, 140–42, 153, 168, 182, 184–85, 206–7, 256, 261–62, 280. *See also* concubinage; homosexuality; lesbianism

shadow audiences, 89, 282
shadow language, 156
shadow puppetry, 377
shadows. *See* "line"
Shamrocks and Chopsticks (Jin Di), 215, 295
Shandong (Chinese territory), 160, 289, 290
Shane, Leslie, 119
Shanghai (China), 4, 106, 127, 130, 150, 182, 200, 389; Boxer Indemnity Fund effects on, 46; British trade with, 224; gardens in, 317; male prostitution in, 197; Pearl Buck in, 153
Shanghai Academy of Social Science, 218, 221
Shanghai Museum (China), 4, 338, 364
Shanghai Public Library (China), 225
Shanghai Translation Publishing House, 219
Shanghai Triangle (film), 341
Shao, Penjian, 48
Shaw, George Bernard, 114, 172
Shelley, Percy Bysshe, 55, 131, 136–37, 143, 145, 153, 341
Shen Congwen, **400**; *Contemporary Review* publications of, 101; as Crescent Moon member, 107, 110, 144; fluctuating reputation of, 19, 109; as modernist writer, 26; and the West, 12, 110
Shen Ming-chen, 297
Shi Shumei, 35, 91, 103, 216, 278, 390; on Virginia Woolf and Ling Shuhua, 247, 249, 250
Shi Ying, 43
short story genre, 92, 204–5, 275–79, 283–84. *See also* specific stories and authors
Short Story Monthly, 203, 283

Shou Kuo Yi-I, 243
Sichuan (China), 58, 59, 225, 250, 267, 268–70, 272
Sickert, Walter, 241, 384
Signac, Paul, 369
Silent Traveller books (Chiang Yee), 325
silhouettes. *See* "line"
Silk Road, 28, 239
simplicity. *See* restraint
Sims, John, 60
"Sinking" (Yu Dafu), 194–95
Sino-British Cultural Association, 42, 43
Sino-Japanese War: and Agnes Smedley, 154; Chinese modernists writing during, 26; and Crescent Moon group, 33, 109; and Julian Bell's Chinese visit, 39, 49, 50, 59–62, 81; and Ling Shuhua, 33, 201, 237, 247, 249–53, 266, 267–71, 275, 286, 287; as national crisis for China, 12, 14, 18–20, 124, 127; railroad destruction during, 227; as reducing East-West openness, 13; and Xiao Qian, 182
Sissinghurst Castle (England), 241, 242, 284, 285, 288, 416n. 3
Sitwell family, 189
"Sketch of the Past, A" (Woolf), 386
Slade Lectures on Chinese Art (Roger Fry), 15, 125, 351, 363, 372, 377
Smedley, Agnes, 50, 153, 154
Smyth, Ethel, 183
So Much Nearer (Richards), 122
social Darwinism, 52, 156, 329
socialism (Fabianism), 162–64, 183–84; and self, 138, 141–42. *See also* Fabians; socialist realism
socialist realism, 13, 54, 57–58, 92, 104, 106, 108, 143, 156–57. *See also* propaganda

society. *See* nation and nationalism
Society for Pure English (BBC's Advisory Committee on Spoken English), 113–18, 380
Society of Literary Studies, 110, 111, 144. *See also* Chinese League of Left-Wing Writers
Sofia (queen of Sweden), 321
"Some Truth about Opium" (Giles), 294
Somerville College (Oxford University), 75
"Son of Heaven, A" (Strachey), 15, 171–76
Song Binghui, 218
Song Dynasty, 292, 308, 337, 348, 360, 376; landscape painting of, 158, 159, 334, 338, 351, 356, 370
Sotheby's auction (London), 1–2, 388
sources (author's), 11, 13, 20–27, 34
Soutar, Helen, 64, 121
Southeast Flies the Peacock (Yuan Changying), 259, 264–65
Southey, Robert, 341
South-West Associated University (China), 123
Soviet Union. *See* Russia
Spalding, Frances, 2, 263
Spanish Civil War: Julian Bell's death in, 1, 38, 62, 83, 234–35, 242, 247, 249; Julian Bell's decision to participate in, 77, 82, 233–35; Julian Bell's service in, 37–40, 50, 234; Woolf on, 268
Spartans, 168
Spectator, 260, 271
Spence, Jonathan, 360
Spivak, Gayatri, 31, 249, 251
Spode-Staffordshire pottery, 15, 299, 334, 343

Sprott, W. J. H., 179, 180, 209
Staffordshire pottery. *See* Spode-Staffordshire pottery
Stanislavski, Konstantin, 190
Stansky, Peter, 2, 39, 234, 262, 289
Steffans, Lincoln, 283
Stein, Gertrude, 160, 369, 378
Stein, Leo, 369
Stephen, Adrian, 39
Stephen, Julia Duckworth (Virginia Woolf's mother), 59, 414n. 13
Stephen, Leslie (Virginia Woolf's father), 22, 59, 247
Stephen, Thoby, 59
Stevens, Wallace, 34, 205
Story of the Stone, The. See Dream of the Red Chamber, The
Stowe, Harriet Beecher, 293
Strachey, Julia, 172
Strachey, Lytton, 153, 198; as Bloomsbury group member, 25, 120, 185, 241; on the Boxer Rebellion, 15, 166, 171–76; on Old Summer Palace, 224–25
Strachey, Marjorie, 284, 288, 416n. 2
Strachey, Pippa, 171
Straight, Dorothy Whitney, 145, 147, 149
Strange Stories (Pu Song-Ling), 254
stream-of-consciousness style, 54, 57, 159–60, 214, 216, 218, 359–60. *See also* psychology; specific works using
"Street of Crocodiles" (drama), 386
Strindberg, August, 93
Strokes (brushstrokes). *See* "line"
"Stronger, The" (Strindberg), 93
student massacres (in China), 110, 289–90
Studies on Virginia Woolf by American and European Critics (Qu Shijing), 221

Su Xuelin: on Beijing University, 100, 103; on Chen Yuan, 78, 104, 110; on *Contemporary Review*, 103; on Ling Shuhua, 63, 264, 275; as May Fourth writer, 289; as one of the "three talents of Luo Jia," 6, 263–65, 289; on Wuhan University, 58, 268–70
subject. *See* self
subjectivity. *See* self
"Suburb" (as code word), 185, 197
"Sue." *See* Ling Shuhua
suicide: Ling Shuhua's threats of, 74, 77–79, 88, 95, 268; Virginia Woolf's, 211, 238, 268, 285, 287
Suleri, Sara, 202, 325
Sullivan, Arthur, 141, 172
Sullivan, Michael, 5, 6–7, 313
Summer Night, A (Homer), 382–83
superpowers, 175–76, 181
surrealism, 208, 359–60
"Survey of Stream of Consciousness Fiction in Britain and America" (Yuan Kejia), 134
Suzhou (China), 317, 333, 389
Sweden, 320–21
Swedish East India Company, 321
"Swimming" (Mao Zedong), 231
Swinburne, Algernon Charles, 143
Sydney-Turner, Saxon, 416n. 2
Sykes, Romola, 84
Szechuan province (China). *See* Sichuan (China)

Ta Kung Pao (Shanghai newspaper), 200, 210, 294
Tagore, Rabindranath, 400; on Chen Yuan, 104; in China, 146, 153, 244; on Crescent Moon group, 108; and Crescent Moon group's name, 103, 144; and Elmhirst, 145, 146, 244;

and Forster, 178; and Ling Shuhua, 7; and Xu Zhimo, 107
Taiwan (Formosa), 10, 23, 160, 219, 220, 329, 359
Tale of the Genji (Murasaki), 254, 308
Tang Dynasty, 137; art of, 18, 239, 327, 337, 348, 360, 370, 386; poetry of, 158, 159, 205, 258–59, 308, 348; porcelain of, 299; tea in, 332; temples of, 389
Tao Kai-yu, 297
Ta Kung Pao, 294
Taoist Book (Chuang-Tzu), 312
Tate, William, 219
Tate Gallery Archives (London), 3, 23
tea drinking, 332–34
Temperance movement, 333
"Ten O'Clock" lecture (Whistler), 300
Tess of the D'Urbervilles (Hardy), 122–23
Tey-Heat, Josephine, 84
theater (Chinese), 163. *See also* Beijing Opera
Theatre Complicitie, 386
Things Seen in China (Chitty), 164, 286
Third Way, The (Giddens), 414n. 1
Three Guineas (Woolf), 112, 116, 175, 235, 247, 252, 255
"three talents of Luo Jia," 6, 260, 263–65, 289. *See also* Ling Shuhua; Su Xuelin; Yuan Changying
Tian Xia Monthly, 49, 88, 95
Tiananmen Square (Beijing), 110
Tianjin (China), 46, 197
Tianjin Daily, 291
Tibet, 6, 9, 48, 59, 199
Tiger, The (Xu Zhimo), 144
Times (London), 181
Times Literary Supplement, 284
"To Tan Ch'iu" (Chinese poem), 187

To the Lighthouse (Woolf): Chinese references in, 9–10, 326; Julian Bell's teaching of, in China, 44, 54; Lily Briscoe's line in, 352, 387; modernist characteristics of, 29, 352, 382; translation of, 221; and Victorian shibboleths, 91; woman artist in, 356–58. *See also* "Chinese eyes"
Tolstoy, Leo, 7, 84, 209, 293
Tomlin, Stephen, 172
Torgeson, Kristina M., 109
Torgovnick, Marianna, 14, 15, 24, 56
Tractarian movement (England), 118
trade (between England and China), 13, 33, 168–70, 175, 182, 222–24, 299–300, 305–6, 316, 331–32, 336, 341, 350, 411n. 2. *See also* imperialism
"Tradition and the Individual Talent" (Eliot), 123, 208
"Tragedy of a Literary Friendship" (T. Tung), 179
Transformations (Fry), 372, 377
Transition, 214
translations: Acton's, 189, 190; of Bengali poems into English, 144; of British literature into Chinese, 44, 46, 123, 143, 208, 210, 212, 214–16, 218–19, 221, 293–96; of Chinese literature into English, 4, 15, 187–88, 199, 205, 223, 227, 254, 258–59, 294, 296–98, 305–6, 308–12, 324, 348, 360, 373; concepts lost in, 93–96, 364–65; of Crescent Moon group's writings into English, 82–99, 108, 247–49; and cultural predispositions to certain styles of expression, 57–59; as form of cross-cultural networking, 28; Herbert Giles's, 164, 205, 306; of Ibsen into Chinese, 80;

Translations: *(continued)*
  ideological tampering with, 293–94; of Joyce into Chinese, 212, 214, 215, 295–96; by Ling Shuhua, 288; of Ling Shuhua's autobiography into Chinese, 27, 219; of Ling Shuhua's stories into English, 82–99, 247–49; Pound's, 34, 205; by Richards, 306, 348; of Virginia Woolf's works into Chinese, 44, 46, 218–19, 221; the Woolfs' involvement with, 84; Woolf's views of, 254; of Xiao Qian's book, 199; by Xu Zhimo, 203; Ye Junjian's skills in, 49, 50; by Yuan Changying, 264. *See also* travel; specific translators

Translations of English Poetry, 294

Translingual Practices (Liu), 295

transnationalism. *See* cross-cultural perspectives; fiction: transnational; nation and nationalism; pluralism; translations; travel

travel: author's, 3–5, 8, 12, 28, 231, 319, 336, 338, 388–89; of Chinese intellectuals to the West, 12, 25, 28, 41, 42, 50–51; "domestication of the foreign" through, 231; of English intellectuals to China, 15–16, 25, 28, 227–34; erotic possibilities associated with, 182–98; fashions bought during, 126–27; Forster's, 347; as freeing people of their cultural and political constrictions, 89, 326, 359; Julian Bell's, 6, 9, 48, 59, 227–34; postcolonial, 346–47. *See also* cross-cultural perspectives; seeing; translations; specific places and travelers

Traveller without a Map (Xiao Qian), 197, 199, 202, 219

"Travellers' Tales" (Dickinson), 170

Travels of Fa-hsien, The (trans. Giles), 164, 294

"Treasures from the National Palace Museum, Taipei" (Metropolitan Museum of Art), 329

Trevelyan, Bob, 201

Trilling, Lionel, 219

Tristram Shandy (Sterne), 346

True Story of Ah Q, The (Lu Xun), 104

Ts'ui Pen, 388

Tu Fu, 297

tuberculosis, 203, 204

Tung, Constantine, 108

Tung, Timothy, 179

"Turandot" (Puccini), 172

Turkey, 329

Turner, J. M. W., 357

Twain, Mark, 283

Two Cheers for Democracy (Forster), 209

Two Little Brothers (Ling Shuhua), 275

Two Men Contemplating the Moon (Friedrich), 386

Tynyanov, Yuri, 26, 28

Ulysses (Joyce), 82, 134, 220; Chinese translations of, 212, 214, 215, 295–96

"Under the Fence of Others" (Xiao Qian), 199

understatement. *See* restraint

United Nations, 151–52, 238, 262, 286

United States: attempts to publish *Ancient Melodies* in, 261, 288–89; Chen Yuan in, 286; Chinese students in, 132, 146, 195, 219, 289; imagism in, 205; individualism in,

138; involvement of, with China, 182, 225; *Letters of John Chinaman*'s reception in, 167, 169–70; Ling Shuhua's emigration to, 23; Ling Shuhua's exhibits in, 240, 243, 244; Ling Shuhua's sister in, 261, 288; Mei Lanfang's influence in, 190; Xu Zhimo in, 130, 131. *See also* primitivism; specific places and museums in

Universal Magazine, 320
universalism, 10, 13, 30–31, 183
Universities China Mission, 16, 41
University of California–Berkeley, 219
University of South Asia, 264
University of Toronto (Canada), 147
University of Virginia, 295
Uses of Literature, The (Link), 20
utilitarianism, 52, 57, 116, 117

Valéry, Paul, 294
Van Gogh, Vincent, 369
Van Vechten, Carl, 190
Vauxhall (England), 319
Veiled Sentiments (Abu-Lughod), 251
Venice, 299
verisimilitude (representation): lack of, in modernism, 350–51, 355, 357–67, 369–75, 384. *See also* Edwardian literature and politics; socialist realism
Versailles (France), 289, 290, 321
Victoria (queen of England), 15, 171, 173, 174
Victoria and Albert Museum (London), 328, 378, 417n. 4
"View of the Family from Within, A" (M. H. Waley), 309
Vildrac, Charles, 234, 392

Vildrac, Rose, 312
Village in the Jungle, The (L. Woolf), 181
Virginia Woolf (O'Brien), 287
Virginia Woolf and her Art of Fiction (Qu Shijing), 221
Virginia Woolf Miscellany, 263
Virginia Woolf Society, 383
vision. *See* seeing
visual metaphors, 93–96
Vlaminck, Maurice de, 385
Vogue, 254, 308
voice: art—not nation—as representing an individual's, 32, 247, 267, 280; in letters, 51, 90, 93; "loudspeaker," 291; multiplicity of, 20–22; propaganda as projecting only single, 157; of the "subaltern," 251; suppression of, by nations, 21, 55, 58, 129, 140, 142–45, 158, 183–85, 188–89, 196–98, 206, 285. *See also* letters; self; sexuality: as writing topic
Voltaire, 165, 167, 171
vorticists, 312, 360, 365
Voyage Out, The (Woolf), 253
Vuillard, Edouard, 376

Waiting (Ha Jin), 195, 207
Waiting for Godot (Beckett), 386
Walcott, Derek, 346
Waley, Arthur, 152, 239, **400**, 416nn. 2, 4; author's interest in, 4; background of, 308–12; as Bloomsbury group member, 25, 120, 241, 288, 306, 308; and British Museum, 223–24; on China, 159, 228; as never having visited China, 306; translations of Chinese literature by, 4, 15, 187–88, 199, 205, 227, 254, 258–59, 294,

Waley, Arthur (*continued*)
  296–98, 305–6, 308–12, 324, 348, 360; and Xu Zhimo, 129, 149
Waley, Hubert, 309
Waley, Margaret H., 309, 312
Walpole, Horace, 283, 313, 321
Walter Sickert (Woolf), 241, 384
Walton, William, 172
Wanderings (Lu Jingquing), 92
Wang, David Der-wei, 220, 292
Wang, S. K., 42, 43
Wang, T. T., 133, 262
Wang Anyi, 206–7
Wang Shijie, 58
Wang Suling, 274
Wang Wei, 34, 96–97, 372
Wanshoushan (China), 33, 68, 224–25
War and Peace (Tolstoy), 84
wars: looting of art objects following, 329, 332, 336; trying to create art during, 109, 113–18, 237, 239–40, 246–54, 263, 266–72, 286–87, 391. *See also* pacifism; specific wars
Washington State University, 286
"Waste Land, The" (Eliot), 53
Waves, The (Woolf), 98, 218, 234, 252–53, 367, 381–83
Webb, Beatrice, **400**; and Bloomsbury group, 120, 152, 196; in China, 15, 25, 35; on Chinese "barbarism," 162–65, 188; and Forster, 177; and romantic love, 141–42
Webb, Sidney, 15, 25, 35, 120, 141–42, 152, 162–65, 188
Wedgwood pottery, 15, 334
Week in London, A (BBC talks), 178, 213
Wei, S. T., 293
Weihaiwei (Chinese territory), 160

Weinstein, John, 265
Wells, H. G., 104, 129, 143, 283, 384
Welty, Eudora, 4, 5, 247, 255, 297–98
"wen" (Chinese concept of), 367–68, 379
Wen Jieruo, 212, 214–16, 295–96
"Wen Ren Hua" (painting style), 243, 288, 416n. 3
Wen Yiduo, 7, 12, 106, 110, **400**; and Crescent Moon group, 144, 202; as modernist writer, 26, 133
Wen Zhengming, 371
West: breaking down polarity between East and, 103, 139, 155–60, 390–93, 414n. 1; centrality of imperialism in, 21; China's intellectuals' interest in, during Republican period, 10, 12, 13, 25–26, 57–58, 100, 104, 106–12, 129–34, 139, 277–78, 288–93, 412n. 4; Chinese intellectuals' interest in, during Cultural Revolution, 179–80, 218, 282; "decadence" of East contrasted with, 196, 341; essentializing of, 30–31; idealization of China in, 267; notions of "self" in, 139, 363; nudity in, 142, 366; postcolonial assumptions about, 247; and sentimentalism, 51–57, 94, 155, 199, 207; Xu Zhimo's "performance" of, 126, 129. *See also* Bloomsbury group; England; Eurocentrism; imperialism; romanticism; science; self
West Lake (China), 389
Western Hills (China), 229, 240, 354
"What's the Point of It" (Ling Shuhua), 89, 99, 275–78
"When I Was in Xia Village" (Ding Ling), 206

Where Angels Fear to Tread (Forster), 182
Whistler, James McNeill, 300, 303
Whitman, Walt, 183, 218
Wilde, Oscar, 196
Williams, William Carlos, 34, 143, 205, 387
willow pattern plates. *See* blue and white willow patterns
Wilson, Jean Moorcroft, 184, 196
Wilson, Woodrow, 175
withholding. *See* restraint
Wolfenden Report, 186
"Woman Like Me, A" (Xi Xi), 206
Woman Question, The, 168
women: on being artists, 356–58; in concubinage, 65, 254–62, 285; as consumers, 344–46; and Crescent Moon group, 109; cross-cultural views of literary, 122–23, 246–65; education for, 254–55, 258–59; Ling Shuhua's depiction of, 90–99, 255–62, 275–81; May Fourth movement on, 80, 90, 92–93; postcolonial analyses of, 250–51; as sentimental, 56, 57; sexuality not a topic written about by Chinese, 88–89, 256, 261–62, 280; short stories written by Chinese, 206–7; universities' admission of, 140, 168; Western association of sentimentalism with, 56–57, 155; during World War I, 186. *See also* feminism; sexism; names of specific women
Women (Ling Shuhua), 275
Women and Gender in Islam (Ahmed), 251
Women's Normal University (China), 103

Wood, Grant, 303
Wood, James, 123
Woodman, Dorothy, 42, 242, 288
Woodman, Helen, 120
Woolf, Bella, 164
Woolf, Leonard, **400**; as Bloomsbury group member, 25, 241; Chinese art in home of, 18, 262, 337; on Dickinson, 137; effects of World War II on, 270; as exempt from military service, 39; and Forster, 178, 181, 183; and Julian Bell, 349; and Ling Shuhua, 1, 84, 94–95, 263, 274, 285–88, 416n. 2; political writings and activities of, 20, 119, 120, 161, 164, 170, 171, 175, 181, 286, 294; on Roger Fry, 349, 374; and translations, 44, 46, 84, 218, 309; and Xiao Qian, 211. *See also* Hogarth Press; Monk's House; specific works by Woolf, Virginia, **401**; on art in wartime, 109, 113–18, 246–54, 266–72, 286–87; as Bloomsbury group member, 25, 119, 161, 241; on blue and white willow pattern, 305; on Dickinson, 136–37; on expression of the self, 157, 176, 184; feminism of, 20, 90, 175, 218–19; on fiction, 204, 217; Forster's lecture on, 209; on Julian and Vanessa, 228, 234–35; Julian's correspondence with, 44, 46, 54, 58–59, 63, 69, 70, 82, 112–13, 181, 229, 252–53, 349; and Ling Shuhua, 1, 33, 46, 83, 84, 94–95, 113, 201, 210, 246–54, 266–79; mental health of, 39, 95, 227, 238; as modernist writer, 20, 93, 98, 158, 159–60, 366, 367, 381–84, 386–87; on Pu Songling, 306; "strokes" an

Woolf, Virginia (*continued*)
"lines" of, 374–75; suicide of, 211, 238, 268, 285, 287; and translations, 84, 218–19, 221; on Waley, 308; works of, taught by Julian Bell in China, 44, 54, 221; on World War II, 38, 40, 112, 113, 150, 171, 247, 249–51, 267, 270–71, 282; Xiao Qian on, 202, 209–11, 213. *See also* Monk's House; titles of works by

Worcester pottery, 343

words. *See* translations

Wordsworth, William, 143

Work for the Winter (J. Bell), 189–90

World Literature, 295

World Trade Organization, 35

World War I: effects of, on China, 289, 290; effects of, on England, 14, 127, 129, 160, 161, 185–86; pacifism during, 20, 39, 112–13, 131

World War II: and Bloomsbury group, 33, 109, 160, 161, 178; Kew Gardens pagoda during, 320; and Ling Shuhua, 33, 287; as national crisis for England, 12, 14, 33, 81, 127, 149; Waley's translation work in, 309–10; Woolf on, 38, 40, 112, 113, 150, 171, 247, 249–52, 267, 270–71, 282

Woronov, Naomi, 411n. 1

Wright, Adrian, 187

Wright, Frank Lloyd, 356

Wright, Sarah Bird, 241–42, 347

Writer's Life, A (Woolf), 219

"Writing a Letter" (Ling Shuhua), 89, 90–95, 99

Writing Women in Modern China (Dooling), 264–65

Wu Bin, 47

Wu Cheng-en, 15, 310

Wu Houkai, 219

Wu Junxie, 218

Wu Kuan, 371

Wu Pei-Yi, 281

Wuchange (China), 231–32

Wuhan University: archives of, 3; Auden and Isherwood's visit to, 60–61; and Boxer Indemnity Funds, 41, 46; Chen Yuan's position at, 17, 44, 46, 58, 103, 227, 263, 264; Julian Bell as English professor at, 1, 5, 7, 15, 17, 25, 32, 37, 39, 41–82, 88, 116, 124, 137, 221, 227, 263, 389; Julian Bell's contract with, 42–44; Julian Bell's students at, 46–51; Julian Bell's termination by, 44; Ling Shuhua not a teacher at, 264; Ling Shuhua's departure from, 250; links of, with West, 6, 58; photographs of, 6, 239; Richards at, 124; Roger Fry's art presented to, 42, 347; Sino-Japanese War's effects on, 62, 268–70; Yuan Changying's play produced at, 265. *See also* Dong Hu (lake); East Lake; Luojia Hill; "three talents of Luo Jia"; specific persons associated with

Wutaishan Mountains (China), 389

Wyler, William, 341

Xi Xi, 206

Xia Yan, 359

Xi'an (China), 60, 166

Xian He, 375

Xianying. *See* Chen Yuan

Xiao Qian, **401**; and Acton, 190; on Bloomsbury and Crescent Moon groups, 19, 107; on British modernist writers, 202–15, 370; on China, 165–66, 179–80, 192; on Chinese painting, 375, 376–77; in England, 25, 176, 182, 184, 200, 208, 213, 216, 286, 389; and Forster, 33, 58, 176–80, 182, 183, 187, 188, 196–98, 200–201, 208–9, 212–13, 216, 217, 221, 295; journalism of, 202, 210; on Julian Bell and Ling Shuhua, 2, 66; on Margery Fry, 7; as modernist writer, 26, 198–202; poverty of, 198–202; on Richards, 221; translations by, 212, 214, 215, 295–96; and the West, 12, 132, 134, 178–80

"Xiying's Small Talk" (Chen Yuan), 103

Xu Beihong, 7

Xu Shenru, 130

Xu Zhengbang, 2, 49, 58, 60, 78–79, 264, 270

Xu Zhimo, **401**; at Beijing University, 106, 146; British modernists preferred by, 213; at Cambridge University, 6, 9, 12, 25, 50, 123, 126–27, 129–33, 139, 146–47, 152–53, 347; and Chen Yuan, 71, 262; as Crescent Moon founder, 17, 101, 104, 106–7, 110, 123, 127, 144, 157–58; and Dartington Hall, 145, 309; death of, 112, 155; and Dickinson, 9, 33, 55, 127, 132–33, 139, 147, 149, 154, 347, 362, 372; fluctuating reputation of, 27, 57–58, 109, 129, 144, 145; and Ling Shuhua, 70–72, 146–47, 415n. 3; as link between Crescent Moon and Bloomsbury groups, 6, 17, 40, 123, 129–34, 203, 262, 312; lost letters of, 23, 147, 415n. 3; as May Fourth movement member, 26, 127; personal characteristics of, 137, 152–55; as poet, 6, 140, 144; romanticism of, 110, 126, 128, 129, 134, 137–56, 199, 202, 203, 206; social background of, 108; translations by, 203; wives of, 71, 142, 148, 150, 152–53, 414n. 2

Xu Zhimo and the Women in His Life (Gao), 71

Yale University, 62, 219, 295

Yan'an (China): Mao's talk on literature at, 19, 55, 57, 157, 159

Yangtze River: author's experiences at, 4–5, 389; Julian Bell's journey to, 84, 230; rapids on, as trade barrier, 225; Wuhan University near, 58, 59

Yangzhou (China), 333

Yanjing University, 124, 290

Ye Junjian (C. C. Yeh), **401**; and Auden, 48, 50, 186–87; on Chen Yuan, 104, 263; on Crescent Moon group, 109; on Julian Bell and Ling Shuhua, 2, 66; as Julian's student, 48–51; on Ling Shuhua, 110, 263, 284; as modernist writer, 26; travels of, with Julian Bell, 6, 9, 48, 59, 230; on Waley's translations, 312; and the West, 132

Ye Shengtao, 293

Years, The (Woolf), 252

Yeats, William Butler, 34, 219, 294, 309, 364

Yeh, C. C. *See* Ye Junjian

Yellow Book, 108

"Yellow Wallpaper, The" (Gilman), 95

Yi Ling Publishers, 296

Yiming Ren, 218
Ying Chinnery. *See* Chinnery, Ying
Yip Wai-lim, 31, 36, 111, 249, 334
Yong Zhimou, 166
"Young Girl, The" (Mansfield), 203
Yu Dafu, 26, 194–95, 291, **401–2**
Yu Kuang-zhong, 228
Yuan, E. K., 47
Yuan Changying, 6, 260, 263–65, 289
Yuan Dynasty, 292, 337, 393
Yuan Kejia, 26, 123, 134, 218, 220–21, **409–10**
Yungang Caves (Shanxi Province), 336, 389

Zhang, Carsun, 150
Zhang, P. C., 145, 150
Zhang Ai Lang, 26
Zhang En-Shou, 47
Zhang Ko-Yu, 290–91
Zhang Longxi, 139
Zhang Yimou, 259, 341
Zhang Youyi, 150, 152–53
Zhao Luorin, 208, 218
Zhaoming Qian, 34
Zhejiang (China), 150
Zhong, C. C., 47
Zhou En-lai, Mrs., 246
Zhou Libo, 134
Zhou period art, 4, 308, 338, 361, 363, 364, 372, 377
Zhou Shihmei, 48
Zhu, S. Y., 145–46, 150
Zhu Naizhang, 221
Zwemmer Gallery (London), 240

www.ingramcontent.com/pod-product-compliance
Lightning Source LLC
Chambersburg PA
CBHW030514230426
43665CB00010B/606